W. W. GREG

COLLECTED PAPERS

W. W. GREG

COLLECTED PAPERS

EDITED BY J. C. MAXWELL

OXFORD
AT THE CLARENDON PRESS
1966

Oxford University Press, Ely House, London W. 1
GLASGOW NEW YORK TORONTO MELBOURNE WELLINGTON
CAPE TOWN SALISBURY IBADAN NAIROBI LUSAKA ADDIS ABABA
BOMBAY CALCUTTA MADRAS KARACHI LAHORE DACCA
KUALA LUMPUR HONG KONG TOKYO

PRINTED IN GREAT BRITAIN

PREFACE

IN 1958 Sir Walter Greg chose a substantial number of his writings to be published as *Collected Papers*, and thoroughly revised a number of them. After his death on 4 March 1959, the list and materials passed into the hands of Professor F. P. Wilson, but his many commitments prevented him from seeing the collection through the press, as he would have been uniquely qualified to do.[1] On Professor Wilson's death the task fell to me.

The list drawn up in 1958 contains thirty-seven items, twenty-seven of which appear in this volume. The other ten have been excluded for various reasons, but it is worth while putting on record what Greg himself intended to publish. In chronological order (with the exception of item 8) the omissions are:

1. 'A Dramatic Fragment' (*Modern Language Quarterly*, vii [1904], 148–55).

This is an account, with transcription and reconstructed text, of article 22 in B.M. Egerton MS. 2623. Greg proposed, in the reprint, to prefix the title 'Oswald', from the principal character in the play. Professor Wilson had marked this for exclusion, noting that a facsimile would be required, and querying whether it might appear in a volume of the *Malone Society Collections*. It is to be hoped that this will prove possible.

2. 'The Authorship of the Songs in Lyly's Plays' (*Modern Language Review*, i [1905], 43–52).

After some hesitation, I have decided to omit this, because I do not think Greg would have maintained his position if he had lived to read the discussion of the problem by Professor G. K. Hunter in the Appendix to his *John Lyly* (1962). If files of the *Modern Language Review* were as scarce as those of the *Modern Language Quarterly*, I might have acted otherwise, but Greg would have been the last to wish a

[1] I have found only a single sheet of notes in his hand containing corrections and annotations, which I have added, with his initials, where they seemed relevant.

superseded view to be given further currency on grounds of sentimental piety. He corrected the text fairly extensively in 1958, but the changes are almost all stylistic. The initial footnote is worth quoting: 'This was my contribution to the first number of *The Modern Language Review*. I imagined that I had failed to infect anyone with my scepticism, and might have hesitated to reprint the article, till to my surprise I found Professor C. S. Lewis writing: "If, as most scholars think, [Lyly] did not write the admirable songs which appeared in the 1632 collection of *Six Court Comedies*, he certainly wrote plays exactly fitted to contain these songs" (*English Literature in the Sixteenth Century* [1954], p. 317).' This note indicates that Greg had not, in the interval, interested himself much in the problem. He did not, in 1958, refer to the article by J. R. Moore, *P.M.L.A.* xlii (1927), 623–40, which must have been one of the grounds for Lewis's statement about the general belief of scholars, though when R. W. Bond published his rejoinder (*Review of English Studies*, vi [1930], 295–9), he had referred Bond to it: see the latter's Addendum (*R.E.S.* vii [1931], 442). These two notes by Bond were not mentioned by Greg in 1958. He did, however, in a 1958 footnote, recognize that his argument about 'prick-song' was 'over ingenious', and that the word is in fact, as Hunter notes (p. 369), 'conventionally and generally used of the nightingale'. All in all, I am fairly sure that Greg would have approved of the omission of this essay.

3. 'Prince Henry's Players' (*Gentleman's Magazine*, ccc [1906], 67–68).

This is a very brief note, in the form of a letter to the editor, reproducing a list of players from B.M. Harley MS. 252. The substance is readily available in E. K. Chambers, *The Elizabethan Stage* (1923), ii. 188, with acknowledgement to Greg.

4. '"I Sing of a Maiden that is Makeless"' (*Modern Philology*, vii [1909], 165–7).

This prints, along with the lyric that gives it its title, a previously unpublished thirteenth-century version from Trinity College, Cambridge, MS. B. 14. 39. As this is now available in Carleton Brown's *English Lyrics of the XIIIth Century* (1932), no. 31, there is no point in reprinting it. Greg added a footnote, referring to comment he had received from several correspondents. The self-evident correction 'hu' for þu' in l. 15 (made by Carleton Brown without comment) was sent to Greg by G. C. Moore Smith, R. B. McKerrow, and G. L. Kittredge, the last two of whom cited the Vulgate original (Luke i. 34), 'quomodo fiet istud'.

5. 'A Ballad of Twelfth Day' (*Modern Language Review*, viii [1913], 64–67).

This is likewise a first printing, with brief introduction and notes, of a thirteenth-century poem from the same Trinity College MS. It is no. 26 in Carleton Brown's collection. Greg's revisions were merely stylistic.

6, 7, and 8. 'Hamlet's Hallucination' (*Modern Language Review*, xii [1917], 393–421); 'Re-Enter Ghost' (ibid. xiv [1919], 353–69); 'The Mouse-Trap—A Post-script' (ibid. xxxv [1940], 8–10).

The first of these was, of course, an historic article, as all readers of the 'epistle dedicatory' to J. Dover Wilson's *What Happens in Hamlet* (1935) will recall. But the interest of all three is very much bound up with the whole controversy of which they form a part, and I am not convinced that they are really worth republishing on their own. Greg himself was ready to drop them and had made no annotations on them; otherwise I would have hesitated to make an omission which might be interpreted as clipping the wings of his most daringly speculative venture.

9. 'A Collier Mystification' (*Review of English Studies*, i [1925], 452–4).

10. 'Alteration in Act I of "Titus Andronicus"' (*Modern Language Review*, xlviii [1953], 439–40).

Both these are slight and specialized pieces, which do not seem to me quite in keeping with the nature of this collection. Greg had made no revisions in the first, and only stylistic ones in the second: he proposed to prefix 'The Alleged' to the title.

The omission of these ten pieces has made it possible to add three more substantial articles, nos. 11, 18, and 21. Though the first two are not in the 1958 list, Greg must have intended to include them: he revised them thoroughly and prepared them for publication in the normal way.

No. 18 is one of Greg's most notable writings. In his memoir (*Proceedings of the British Academy*, xlv [1959], 321), F. P. Wilson quoted what Pollard wrote to Greg: 'I think that for weight of argument, conciseness, and the pleasure with which it can be read the lecture is your masterpiece', and Professor Wilson himself described it as containing 'perhaps the finest statement of his views on the relations of bibliography and textual criticism'.

No. 21, which I have added on my own authority, is an interpretative piece, related to Greg's textual work on *Lear* somewhat as 'The Damnation of Faustus' (23) is related to the edition of that play. It strengthens the representation of a side of Greg's work that is otherwise rather neglected in this collection.

The papers have been reproduced exactly as Greg left them, with occasional additions, such as dates not accessible to Greg at the time of revision, and corrections of obvious slips arising in the process of revision—such as an alteration which has given 'less . . . as' instead of 'less . . . than'. Very occasionally I have silently corrected a minor error that had escaped Greg, and once I have (in an unrevised paper) deleted an otiose 'as to': a locution to which Greg's revisions show him to have grown very sensitive.

The amount of revision is very variable. It is most extensive in 1, where there are scores of stylistic changes, as well as some deletions and additions, the latter duly dated by Greg.[1] 2 also has a good many alterations, especially in the Notes. 3 has few changes apart from the new footnote.

[1] In this paper, Greg made some attempt to distinguish between the historical Francesco Peretti and Francesco de'Medici on the one hand, and Webster's Francisco on the other, as F. L. Lucas later did in his edition of Webster, but he was not at all consistent. I have attempted to observe this distinction throughout. Strictly speaking, this ought to have been accompanied by a distinction between the historical Bracciano and Webster's Brachiano, but as Greg used Webster's spelling throughout, I have let it stand.

4 is heavily corrected and annotated. For 5, the copy prepared by Greg is, exceptionally, not the printed version but a corrected and annotated typescript. 6 is almost unaltered, apart from the additional note. 7 is lightly revised, and the transcriptions corrected in a few places. 8 and 9 are lightly corrected with a deletion (noted in a footnote) in the former. The alterations in 10 are indicated in Greg's initial footnote. 11 is extensively revised. 12 is lightly corrected, apart from the new footnotes. 13 is carefully corrected, principally for the purpose indicated by Greg in his initial footnote. 14 is lightly revised, as are 15, 16, and 17 (with an important footnote). 18 has some revisions and a couple of brief additions. There are no revisions of substance in 19 and 20. 21, as already noted, was not proposed for reprinting by Greg, and is reproduced without change. In 22, which, as stated in Greg's initial footnote, reproduces only part (about a third) of the article from which it is taken, there are hardly any revisions except in the first paragraph. 23 has few revisions, apart from the insertion of references to the 1950 text of the play, and 24 none of substance except for added footnotes. 25 has two trifling revisions and an added footnote. 26, 27, and 28 are lightly revised; 29 and 30 rather more extensively.

This is not the place to write at large on Greg's life and work—admirable accounts have been published by F. P. Wilson in *Proceedings of the British Academy*, xlv (1959), 307–34, and by various writers in *The Library*, 5 Ser. xiv (1959), 151–74—but perhaps I may mention that a study of the bound volumes and miscellaneous papers put at my disposal has been rewarding in ways not directly related to the production of this volume. The firmness and self-assurance of Greg's very early work in the *Modern Language Quarterly* (1899–1904) is exhilarating. It is delightful to see how, at the age of twenty-five, in reviewing the first volume of George Saintsbury's *History of Criticism*, he feels no need to conceal his justified sense of intellectual superiority. The review begins: 'We must confess to a keen sense of disappointment . . .' (iv [1901], 7) and continues in the same vein, though doing justice also to the genuine learning of Saintsbury's book. In a review of December 1901 (iv. 193), my eye is caught by the query: 'When, in the name of sanity, may we ask, are we to have done with this childish raking together of irrelevant rubbish, which an average schoolboy would be ashamed to show up to an indulgent form-master?' And in July 1902 (v. 81), a review of an early work by a scholar even more long-lived than Greg himself, if somewhat less distinguished, contains the sentence, 'We may give Herr Schücking credit for the conscientious labour he has devoted to the collecting of the materials for his essay, but it is impossible to have the least respect for his judgment or literary sense'.

Many years later, Greg was sufficiently interested in the fact that the editor of *The Library*, with what seems remarkable prudery for 1926, had refused to publish part of his review of Miss Seaton's edition of *Venus and Anchises* (New Ser. vii. 329–32), to transcribe the offending paragraphs, the final sentence running, 'one need only put [Fletcher's poems] beside such a work as Carew's *Rapture* to see the gulf that separates what is at worst gorgeous rhetoric from mere piddling in the service of God Priapus'.

I am indebted to Professor Arthur Brown of University College, London, for checking Greg's readings of a number of manuscripts in the British Museum, notably that of *The Escapes of Jupiter*, and for other valuable comments. On the Massinger articles, I have received help from Dr. J. G. McManaway of the Folger Shakespeare Library, and from Professor Philip Edwards of Trinity College, Dublin.

CONTENTS

PREFACE *page* v

LIST OF PLATES xiii

COLLECTED PAPERS

Reference is made in the Preface to the author's own selection of 37. The original numbers of these are given in parentheses.

1 (1) Webster's *White Devil*: An Essay in Formal Criticism 1

2 (2) Fairfax's Eighth Eclogue 29

3 (6) Theatrical Repertories of 1662 44

4 (8) The Bakings of Betsy 48

5 (9) What is Bibliography? 75

6 (14) John of Basing's 'Greek' Numerals 89

7 (15) An Elizabethan Printer and His Copy 95

8 (16) Massinger's Autograph Corrections in *The Duke of Milan* 110

9 (17) More Massinger Corrections 120

10 (18) *The Spanish Tragedy*—a Leading Case? 149

11 *The Escapes of Jupiter* 156

12 (20) The Riddle of Jonson's Chronology 184

13 (21) Shakespeare's Hand Once More 192

14 (22) A Question of Plus or Minus 201

15 (23) The Present Position of Bibliography 207

16 (24) Three Manuscript Notes by Sir George Buc 226

17 (25) Bibliography—An Apologia 239

18 The Function of Bibliography in Literary Criticism Illustrated in a Study of the Text of *King Lear* 267

19 (26) A Formulary of Collation 298

20 (27) Was There a 1612 Quarto of *Epicene*? 314

21 Time, Place, and Politics in *King Lear* 322

22 (28) Entrance in the Stationers' Register: Some Statistics 341
23 (29) The Damnation of Faustus 349
24 (30) Old Style—New Style 366
25 (31) The Rationale of Copy-Text 374
26 (32) The Printing of Shakespeare's *Troilus and Cressida* in the First Folio 392
27 (33) Was the First Edition of *Pierce Penniless* a Piracy? 402
28 (35) *Ad Imprimendum Solum* 406
29 (36) Richard Robinson and the Stationers' Register 413
30 (37) Samuel Harsnett and Hayward's *Henry IV* 424

INDEX 437

LIST OF PLATES

I. Page of Harington's translation of *Orlando Furioso* (B.M., MS. Add. 18920) — *facing p.* 108

II. Page of *The Duke of Milan*, 1623, with Massinger's autograph corrections (Folger Library) — " 112

III. Page of *The Roman Actor*, 1629, with Massinger's autograph corrections (Folger Library) — " 128

IV. Title-page of *George a Green*, 1599 (Folger Library)

V. Title-page of *Locrine*, 1595 (Martin Bodmer)

VI. Letter from Buc to Dudley Norton, 1 July 1611 (S. P. Dom. James I, vol. 65, art. 2)

VII. Letter from Buc to Robert Cotton, 10 Mar. 1620/1 (MS. Cotton, Jul. C. III, fol. 49)

VIII. Inscription in Buc's *Δάφνις Πολυστέφανος*, 1605 (Huntington Library)

IX. Dedication of Buc's *History of Richard III* dated 1619 (MS. Cotton, Tiber. E. X, fol. 1 *a*)

X*a*. Marginal note made by Buc as censor on a passage in *Sir John Barnavelt* (B.M., MS. Add. 18653, fol. 5 *b*)

b. Fragment of a draft memorandum by Buc concerning the Revels Office (MS. Cotton, Tiber. E. X, fol. 190 *b*)

c. Censor's licence appended by Buc to *The Second Maiden's Tragedy* (MS. Lansd. 807, fol. 56 *a*)

(IV–X*c*) *between pp.* 232 *and* 233

I. Webster's *White Devil*

An Essay in Formal Criticism[1]

I. Comparison of Sources

Although the actual authority that Webster used in writing his play on the story of Vittoria Accoramboni is not known, we may safely assume that it was in the main a faithful relation of the facts of the case, in so far as they would lie within the cognizance of some contemporary annalist or pamphleteer. Several such accounts have survived in manuscript; some have at various times found their way into print. The earliest known version of the story is a pamphlet entitled *Il miserabile e compassionevole caso della morte dell' illustrissima Signora Vittoria Accoramboni*, which appeared at Brescia in 1586. The same place and year saw the publication of Giovanni Baptista Brendola's *Sonetto et Canzone fatti nella morte dell' illustrissima Signora Vittoria Corambona*. Both these appeared within a year of Vittoria's death. Next we find the story given in bald outline by Cesare Campana in his annals of universal history entitled *Historie del Mondo dall' Anno 1580 fino al 1596*, published at Venice in the latter year. A French version appeared at Lyons in

[1] [1900, December. *The Modern Language Quarterly*, iii. 112. When writing this essay I was clearly much influenced by J. A. Symonds's study of Vittoria Accoramboni, printed in his *Italian Byways* (1883). The historical events involved have since been more fully treated by F. L. Lucas in his edition of Webster's Works (1927, i. 70–90), without, however, being able to establish the dramatist's immediate source. The general view has been that Webster drew on accounts reaching England in news-letters and the like. This is confirmed by the latest critic to investigate the matter, Gunnar Boklund, who claims to have identified both the main and two subsidiary sources used in the writing of the play (see *The Modern Language Review*, October 1958, liii. 564–6). In fact the critical outlook has changed appreciably in the last sixty years. Nevertheless this early study seems to me to retain enough interest to excuse reprinting, especially in its analysis of dramatic structure. The theory of scenic alternation was at the time popular, and as advanced by some in an unduly rigid form, came in for a good deal of justifiable criticism; but I think that in the looser form here advocated it contains at least a measure of truth; and I am confident that what I term 'dramatic *enjambement*' (perhaps a less pedantic description would be 'theatrical run-over')—here first, I believe, formally recognized—was a frequent device of Elizabethan stage-craft that played a part in several plays by Shakespeare and his followers.—1958.]

1621. Henri Beyle included a translation from a manuscript account in his *Chroniques et Nouvelles*; and what seems to be the most authentic account, the work of an unknown writer, commonly referred to as the 'anonimo del Campidoglio', was printed by Professor F. Odorici in the *Archivo Storico* for 1862. The story is likewise told in the lives of Sixtus V by Casimiro Tempesti and J. A. von Hübner; the former, however, suffers from the ecclesiastical bias unavoidable in an 'authorized' work, and the latter is decidedly superficial. The fullest and most recent treatment the subject has received is in the monograph by Professor D. Gnoli, which appeared at Florence in 1870. The only accounts that Webster could have seen are those contained in the Brescia tract and Campana's history. The former of these is not in the British Museum, and I am unable to say whether or not it may have supplied him with his material, while he certainly consulted a fuller account than that of Campana.

The probability is that Webster used some manuscript account obtained either directly or indirectly from Italy. We are at first tempted to imagine that this differed considerably from the received history of the events, since there are a number of points in the play for which it is difficult to account. Thus in the stage direction to Act II, sc. i,[1] we find a mention of 'little Jaques the Moor', of whom we hear nothing further; in the dumb shows in II. ii two characters, Christophero and Guid-Antonio, are casually introduced, though they are not mentioned in the play; in Act V Lodovico and Gasparo in disguise are frequently referred to in stage directions etc. as Pedro and Carlo, though these names do not occur in the text; finally, in the stage direction in v. i where Francisco enters, one Farnese appears among his followers, of whom we hear no more, and whose presence, considering the rivalry between the Medici and Farnesi families, seems unlikely. These facts are, however, capable of another explanation, for Webster may have made a sketch or rough version of the play of an elaboration from which he was afterwards forced, probably by the exigencies of stage and cast, to depart, but which left traces in the stage-

[1] I refer throughout to my own arrangement of scenes. A table of correspondences with that found in the quarto of 1672, and in Hazlitt, is given on p. 28.

manager's copy. There are, indeed, other suggestions of undeveloped motives in the play, the most striking of which perhaps occurs in the 'Arraignment' scene, where Monticelso, addressing Vittoria, says:

> You were born in Venice, honourably descended
> From the Vittelli.

So far as I am aware there was no connexion between the Accoramboni who came from Gubbio and the Vitelli who belonged to Città del Castello. It was, however, for the murder of one Vincenzo Vitelli that Lodovico Orsini was outlawed and obliged to fly from Rome. It is possible therefore that Webster intended to work a connexion here and make Lodovico the murderer of some kinsman of Vittoria's, which would account for Brachiano's suit against him, and also give point to his remark about Vittoria being in a position to get his pardon from the duke.

Thus we shall, I think, be safe in assuming that Webster knew the story very much as we read it in the history of *cinquecento* Rome, and that, where his tragedy differs from the received account, the divergence is deliberate. It must be remembered that in the case of Webster, as of Jonson, we are dealing with a conscious and careful artist, whose work is the outcome of leisure and thoughtful consideration, very different from the promiscuous botching of Henslowe's hacks. As regards his actual source, the name of the heroine would seem to point to a popular narrative, since Corambona and Corimbona are the forms most commonly found in the floating literature of the day. Very likely it is lurking among the manuscript collections of our public or private libraries, very likely it has perished. Its absence is probably of less consequence than that of the source of any other of our great romantic plays would be.

The history of this extraordinary romance, as well as Webster's particular attitude towards it and towards Italian life in general, has been discussed by J. A. Symonds in a more than usually brilliant essay. It is therefore unnecessary to give more than the barest outline of the story. Vittoria was born at Gubbio in 1557, and the chroniclers represent her as early endowed with every grace of body and of mind. At the age of sixteen she was married to Francesco Peretti,[1] nephew of the Cardinal of Montalto, who later succeeded Gregory XIII in the papacy under the name of Sixtus V. It was not a wealthy match, and her extravagance soon involved her husband in debt; gossip also seems to have made light of her name. In the meantime Marcello, the second of her six brothers, a desperate and ambitious *bravo*, had become the dependant and confidant of Paolo Giordano Orsini, the powerful Duke of Brachiano, and conceived the idea of raising the fallen fortunes of his house by trading on his sister's beauty and his patron's lust. In this plan he was ably seconded by his mother Tarquinia. Brachiano had, in 1553, married Isabella, daughter of the Grand Duke Cosimo and sister to Francesco and the Cardinal de' Medici, and in 1576 had, with the concurrence of her brothers, caused her to be put to death on a probably well-founded suspicion of infidelity. She left an only son, Virginio, who subsequently succeeded to his father's titles. Having now fired the duke's imagination and ascertained his readiness to make Vittoria his duchess, Marcello turned his attention to the removal of his brother-in-law. One night in April 1581 Peretti was sent for from his house on urgent business. Next morning his body was found on Monte Cavallo. The murder was planned by Tarquinia and Marcello; there is no evidence that Vittoria was cognizant of the plot. Suspicion, however, was at once aroused, and the young widow, together with her mother, sought refuge in a villa of the duke's, where she was shortly afterwards privately married to him. As soon as news of this marriage lent colour to the public gossip of Rome, Gregory declared it void. The duke made a show of submission, and Vittoria returned to her father's house. Thence she was removed by the Pope's orders, and finally committed to the fortress of S. Angelo, where she remained for more than a year. She was tried for the murder of her husband, but nothing could be proved, and she was finally released on condition of retiring to Gubbio. Soon afterwards she again went through the form of marriage with the duke, and the pair actually had the audacity to come openly to Rome. The

[1] His real name was Francesco Mignucci; he assumed that of his uncle, Felice Peretti, but is commonly known to history as Francesco Peretti.

marriage was again declared null, but before any further steps could be taken, Gregory died. The duke took the opportunity of celebrating his marriage a third time, openly and in Rome. In April 1585 Montalto was elected to the papacy, and the Duke and Duchess of Brachiano found it prudent to retire from Rome. They sought asylum in Venetian territory and finally settled at Salò, on the Lago di Garda, where the duke died suddenly in the following November. A contemporary writer speaks of his succumbing to a trifling fever, but there was also suspicion of poison. Vittoria removed with her household to Padua, where disputes soon arose between her and Prince Lodovico Orsini, the duke's executor, who had always shown a marked hostility towards her. One night a band of armed men broke into the house. Marcello was absent, but they found Vittoria's youngest brother, Flamineo, in the hall. He fled wounded to his sister's apartment. The murderers followed him into the room and stabbed Vittoria as she knelt at prayer. They then dispatched Flamineo. A few days later, Lodovico and his followers were apprehended by the Venetian authorities. The prince was strangled in prison by order of the Republic; seventeen of his followers were executed, while others were condemned to prison or the galleys.

It remains to see what use Webster has made of this material. The point in which he has departed most widely from history is the character and role of Isabella. The real Isabella, as we have seen, was put to death five years before the murder of Vittoria's husband, whereas the dramatist makes both alike the victims of Brachiano's passion, and furthermore, for the sake of dramatic contrast, represents Isabella as a faithful and loving wife. This device supplies a stronger motive for the hostility shown by the Medici towards Vittoria than is to be found in history. There is, of course, a contrast, though it is more implied than expressed, between her and Vittoria. Indeed, it almost seems as though Webster intentionally avoided bringing the two characters into opposition. He may have feared for Vittoria the contrast with the gentler, loving, and more amiable character of the wife; whereas Isabella's weakness, and her almost criminal renunciation of her rights as a wife, a mother, and a Medici, must have become all too evident. We should be made to accept her unreservedly as a type of unselfishness fully to appreciate the scene of her 'supposèd jealousy'. Isabella as it is wins our pity, but can claim neither our respect nor admiration; Vittoria commands our admiration, while she scorns our pity and is careless of our respect.

The part played in history by Isabella's son, Virginio, is a doubtful and at most a minor one. The character of Giovanni is Webster's own creation. In actuality he was probably at least as old as Vittoria, and it is perhaps worth mentioning that he married Flavia, niece of Francesco Peretti. He seems, as in the play, to have frequented the Medicean court, but so far from executing justice on Lodovico, was accused by him, in an intercepted letter written after arrest, of being accessory to the plot. In the last scene he appears in the conventional character of the virtuous young prince, and, as the text now stands, as an intolerable prig: but the last speech of the play should undoubtedly be given to the English ambassador.

The dramatic connexion between Lodovico and Isabella is Webster's creation. In history he only comes to the fore after Brachiano's death, but it was, of course, necessary for the purposes of the stage to make the instrument of Vittoria's murder a much more important personage throughout the play. To this end, and with a view to supplying a more adequate motive for his animosity towards Vittoria, the dramatist conceived the device of making him the silent lover of the duchess. For the same reason he suppressed his surname, placed him among Francisco's followers, and made his banishment the result of Brachiano's suit.[1] In reality Prince Lodovico Orsini was, of course, of Brachiano's household, and his outlawry and flight from Rome happened at the same time as his patron's. To my mind the changes are admirably suited to produce the required effect.[2]

[1] He was, of course, banished by the Pope, but it must have been at Brachiano's instigation, else how could Vittoria have obtained his pardon 'for one kiss to the duke'?

[2] On this point I find myself in disagreement with Symonds, who writes: 'He has ascribed different motives from the real ones to Lodovico in order to bring this personage into rank with the chief actors, though this has been achieved with only moderate success.' I think, however, that Webster has given him all the importance he intended and that it is sufficient.

In depicting Vittoria's husband, Isabella's fellow-victim, Webster had to draw chiefly on his imagination. In history his character is altogether shadowy, but the little we learn of him suggests that he was far from the long-eared coxcomb of the play. The one thing we know regarding the actual Francesco Peretti is his devotion to Vittoria, and the fatal friendship he was led to extend to her kinsmen, which made him fall an easy prey to their villainy. Since the name he bears in history might have led to confusion with the Duke of Florence, Webster has transferred to him the name of his mother Camilla, who does not figure in the play.

A more important part is played by his uncle the Cardinal. In his case, too, the dramatist has drawn but scantily upon his sources. Not only is the name Monticelso substituted for that of Montalto,[1] and the title Paul IV for Sixtus V, but the character has undergone a considerable change. In outward position Monticelso combines the characters of Montalto and the Cardinal de' Medici, Francisco's brother, which gives him a closer, if rather an ill-defined, connexion with the family of the Grand Duke.[2] The historical Cardinal was noted for his 'politic' character, which drew from Gregory, when he begged him not to proceed in the matter of his nephew's murder, the often-quoted phrase, 'Veramente costui è un gran frate'. When, however, this conciliatory attitude had won for him the papacy, he showed himself an active and relentless enemy to the lawless factions of the Roman states. In the play, on the other hand, he is represented as the bitter arraigner of Vittoria and enemy of the duke, although he is unlikely to have felt much personal sorrow at the death of his nephew; though, indeed, his resentment for the most part wastes itself in smoke, and he becomes useless as an agent in the deep-laid plots of Francisco, who says of him:

Monticelso,
I will not trust thee, but in all my plots

[1] Can it be that Webster misread Montalto as Montcelto in the manuscript accounts and euphonized it into Monticelso?

[2] His position is certainly not that of Francisco's brother nor of Giovanni's uncle, and yet he in one place speaks of 'our sister duchess'. This must be the fossil remnant of an earlier draft, unless indeed we regard it as an instance of the not uncommon misprint 'our' for 'your'.

I'll rest as jealous as a town besieg'd.
Thou canst not reach what I intend to act.
Your flax soon kindles, soon is out again,
But gold slow heats, and long will hot remain.

Even the episode of the excommunication pronounced by him against Vittoria and the duke, which, though not historical, seems at first sight to suggest the character of Sixtus, really bears out this contention, for nothing more is heard of it: it is a mere theatrical squib beside the studied revenge of Francisco. It is a mistake to use Jove's thunder to no purpose unless you wish to make it ridiculous. Webster may not have wished to go as far as this, and possibly thought the Pope's action would make Francisco's plot more possible, in the same manner as his supposed concurrence determines Lodovico; but the whole scene is superfluous, and retards the action at a critical point.

The part played by the Duke of Florence, a character who is never mentioned in connexion with Vittoria's tragedy by the historians, deserves attention. It would seem that Webster was not satisfied with the merely outward unity of action which characterizes this story above most others, and sought to weld the plot yet more firmly together by supplying a motive and directing force which should regulate the course of events and work its will with the slow persistence of destiny. To this end he created the part of Francisco de Medicis, who, though he is not often prominent on the stage, makes his influence felt throughout. It is he who, after a seeming reconciliation with Brachiano, secures the removal of Camillo, in order to give free rein for the duke to run 'into notorious scandal'; it is he who, with the same object, says to Monticelso, when the unlooked-for presence and open defiance of the duke make the condemnation of Vittoria impossible:

My lord, there's great suspicion of the murder,
But no sound proof who did it . . .
The act of blood let pass; only descend
To matter of incontinence;

to which Vittoria's quick wit replies:

I discern poison
Under your gilded pills.

It is he again who suggests to Brachiano's mind the possibility of carrying off Vittoria from the house of convertites, and by thus openly defying the papal authority, placing himself within reach of his revenge; lastly, it is he who dogs their steps to Padua, and through the ready instrument of the desperate Lodovico finally accomplishes his end. The device by which he and his confederates gain the freedom of the Duke of Brachiano's court becomes less fantastic than at first appears when we remember that disguise of some sort was necessary. The Moor commander of one of the Venetian territories—in this case Corfu—of course suggests Othello, but it should be remembered that it is the very post for which Lodovico was about to start at the time of his final arrest. The fiction of the Capuchins enabled Webster to contrive a death-bed horror after his own heart.

In passing to Francisco's dependent, Marcello, we approach some of the most intricate problems of dramatic construction that the play presents. The parts played by the two brothers are reversed. In the case of the elder this merely amounts to a change of name; the case of the younger, the Marcello of the play, is more complicated. Still a boy when murdered together with his sister, he is represented by Webster as a young soldier in the retinue of the Duke of Florence, thus borrowing features from his brother Camillo, who fought under Filibert of Savoy and eventually died in France, and is also endowed with the outspoken rectitude of another brother, Ottavio, Bishop of Fessombrone. A striking dramatic contrast is thus obtained between the brothers, but this involved further changes in the plot. In the historical account, as we have seen, the elder brother escaped the hands of Lodovico (he was subsequently surrendered by the Venetian Republic into the power of Sixtus and executed) whereas the younger shared Vittoria's fate. This form of the 'catastrophy' is proper to the tragedy of 'pity' that history offers us, but Webster chose to represent a tragedy of 'terror', in which it was necessary that Vittoria and her elder brother should die together. He consequently had the unused material of his Marcello's death left ready to hand. He might, of course, have discarded it;[1] but the extravagant

[1] Symonds remarks that Webster introduced the fratricide 'without any adequate object beyond that of completing the study of a type he loved'.

villainy of the quarrel and murder appropriately mark the turn of fortune, the beginning of the débâcle, and the consequent madness of Cornelia and her winding of her son's corpse lend to the final scenes a touch of fantastic pathos such as Webster delighted in, and which, it must be allowed, he treated with the hand of a master. All this is, of course, entirely the dramatist's invention. So too is the extravagant scene, which would be melodramatic were it not so instinct with passion, between Flamineo and Vittoria; in connexion with which it may be observed that the 'anonimo del Campidoglio' records that, after Brachiano's death, Vittoria, seeing herself left unprotected amid her enemies, endeavoured to shoot herself, but was prevented by the historical Flamineo.[1]

Of all the characters in the play it is perhaps Flamineo that is most closely studied from the original, at least in so far as his personality is concerned. The details of his various crimes and the manner of his death are, of course, unhistorical, but with these we have already been concerned. A comparison with Bosola, his companion picture in *The Duchess of Malfi*, is tempting, and is skilfully treated in Symonds's essay.

> As in this world there are degrees of evil,
> So in this world there are degrees of devil;

and not degrees only but every variety and gradation. The wickedness of Flamineo is as distinct from that of Bosola as Vittoria's is from either.

The historical Marcello, I have already remarked, found an able confederate in his mother, Tarquinia. The name is an ominous one in the light of subsequent history, and when altering the character, Webster naturally altered the name. The one he chose has likewise its associations. The part of Cornelia is one that may be called decorative; she exercises no influence on the plot, and like Queen Margaret in *Richard III*, stands apart from the dramatic *personae* and outside the action of the piece, producing, especially in the early part of the play, the effect of a Greek chorus, as where she breaks in on amorous dialogue with the cry:

> Woe to light hearts, they still forerun our fall![2]

[1] She is also said to have attempted suicide in the castle of S. Angelo; this may, however, be another version of the same story.

[2] Symonds compares her to a Cassandra and an Ate.

Later on, in the 'winding' scene, Webster has put into her mouth several reminiscences of the mad Ophelia, which make it rather difficult to appreciate the scene on its own merits. It is all the more puzzling as the finest points in the scene are original, namely the dirge and Flamineo's exclamation, 'I would I were from hence!'

Of the minor characters, the most important is Zanche, a Moorish waiting-woman of Cornelia's, who combines, as Symonds pointed out, the roles of Caterina, a Bolognese in the service of Vittoria, and a mysterious Greek sorceress somehow connected with Marcello, together with whom she was executed at Ancona. I am not, however, satisfied of the actual existence of this latter, but incline to regard her as a double of Caterina, who was herself later accused of witchcraft; and though I am not aware that she was ever executed, she was certainly arrested, and Sixtus refused a petition on her behalf by his sister Camilla. The use made of Zanche in the last act, where the dull and lascivious farce takes place in the very presence of the dead, deserves notice. It is certainly not justified for the purpose of giving Francisco details of the murders, but seems to be introduced for a reason unlike that of most comic interludes, which serve to relieve tension, namely by the ghastly contrast to heighten the effect of the tragedy.

Lastly, we come to the central figures of the play, Vittoria and her lover Duke Brachiano. In their case Webster has been prodigal of his subtlest characterization, and it is only after repeated readings and careful study that we appreciate the full complexity and minute painting of the portraits. The duke is drawn throughout in reference to Vittoria; he seems to have no existence except in relation to her. He is, however, no mere effect or reflection of her power, for his dramatic character undergoes a visible and rational growth within the narrow compass of the play. In the first act he is merely fascinated by her wonderful and audacious charm, enchanted by her beauty, seduced by purely physical attractions. Abandoned as he is to the pleasures of sense and ready to sacrifice no matter what to the satisfaction of his desire, less perhaps from the mastery of his passion than from a cynical disregard of all other considerations, he listens, half in amusement, to Vittoria's suggestion of murder. The cross to his purpose in his discovery by Cornelia only makes him more determined. If he cannot attain his end by the easy means of hoodwinking Camillo he will adopt other and more violent measures. His mind is soon made up:

> Send Doctor Julio to me presently.
> Uncharitable woman! thy rash tongue
> Hath rais'd a fearful and prodigious storm:
> Be thou the cause of all ensuing harm.

In the second act he appears in a particularly revolting light. His attitude towards Isabella is truly fiendish, and it is only his complete absorption in his passion for Vittoria that makes his acting with his wife humanly conceivable. In the fourth act he reappears with Vittoria in what is the most subtle scene in the play. Goaded by jealousy into a fit of ungovernable rage, it is only when she turns and lashes him with her own shame and the ruin of her house that the full power of her witchery first works upon him. He wakes as from a dream:

> I have drunk Lethe.
> Vittoria! my dearest happiness, Vittoria!

His passion is no mere vulgar lust, but a deep imperative need of companionship and possession. However criminal it may be, it is in his love for the White Devil only that, in the course of his wild life, he is touched to a finer issue. The only other occasion on which the two come into dramatic relation is the death-bed scene in Act V, and it is here that Brachiano's devotion appears most intense, though revealed only in a few exclamations among the terrors of the death agony and the horrors of delirium. The sting of death is parting from the world that holds her:

> O thou strong heart!
> There 's such a covenant 'tween the world and it,
> They're loath to break. . . .
> Where 's this good woman? Had I infinite words
> They were too little for thee. Must I leave thee?

Tortured beyond endurance by the masquerading Capuchins, he breaks out in one last despairing cry: 'Vittoria!' We see the powerful villain run to earth, cornered at last; and as he slips from this life, taunted with damnation in the life to come, it is not on his court or his guards that he calls for protection against the fantastic murderers that dance amid the shadows of his fevered brain; it is not to the church that he appeals for grace in the hereafter: it is to the woman whom he has seduced, dragged through the depths of public disgrace and private infamy and now leaves defenceless among her enemies, that he turns with the simple confidence of a child turning to its mother.[1]

Who was the woman who could inspire such trust and devotion in a man like Brachiano? Surely not either a light wanton or an ambitious profligate. The character of Webster's heroine develops amid the scenes of horror through which she passes. Her attitude towards her lover changes as, with the progress of the action, his love for her changes and grows. She first appears as an ambitious schemer, a 'politic' wanton, arrogantly vicious in the knowledge of her beauty and her power. She is less a violator of the moral order than one for whom moral considerations have no meaning. In this respect, in her simple passionless 'atheism', she remains consistent throughout, in contrast to Flamineo, who, in spite of his superb outward show of villainy, is in ceaseless conflict with his conscience. We next see her, proud and defiant, before her judges. So far from possessing the 'innocence-resembling boldness' Lamb speaks of, it would almost be an insult to suppose she is other than guilty. And yet it is not so much that she brazens out her guilt as that she is not conscious of it. It is possible that Webster has indulged in a peculiar touch of dramatic irony, which may account for the singular diversity of opinions among critics regarding her attitude at the trial. Is she actually guilty of the charges brought against her? She hinted at the removal of Camillo and Isabella; but was she actually consenting to their deaths? She helped to befool her husband that she might the more securely meet her lover; but is she in act a faithless wife? For the solution of these questions we lack evidence as completely as her accusers at

[1] Webster, while blackening the duke's character, has made him physically less repulsive. In history he is represented as monstrously corpulent and as suffering from some loathsome disease. In representing him as an accomplished soldier, he has, however, not departed from history. In the following account of Vittoria, I again find myself in disagreement with Symonds, who regards ambition as her dominant characteristic. The analysis of her character, with which the third section of his essay opens, deserves, however, careful attention.

the trial.[1] Undaunted as she is by her moral guilt—for to herself her own will is sufficient justification—no wonder that she presents a bold front to her judges if she is technically innocent of the crimes whereof they accuse her. The question, however, little affects the reading of her character; for this, the moral guilt is sufficient, and, innocent or guilty, we may assume that her bearing would have been much the same. It only makes the difference of regarding her appeal to the ambassadors—

Humbly thus,
Thus low, to the most worthy and respected
Lieger ambassadors, my modesty
And womanhood I tender—

in the one case as the spontaneous impulse of a woman believing herself wronged, in the other as a daring card in her game. Throughout her arraignment she shows complete confidence in her cause. She is not even careful to defend herself, but seizes every opportunity of striking back at her accusers, her replies to Monticelso in particular revealing the spiteful joy she might have felt at lashing a snarling cur. Her sentence appears to take her by surprise, and her rage breaks out:

Francisco. You must have patience.
Vittoria. I must first have vengeance!

The scene in which Vittoria and the duke quarrel divides with the 'arraignment' the honours of the play. In it we find the subtlest and most complex delineation of character to be met with in Webster, or probably in any of the dramatists except Shakespeare. Brachiano, on her appearance, taunts her with a sarcastic insult. She meets him with dignified astonishment, which, when she understands the source of his jealousy, turns to protestation and entreaty. At last he stings her with a reference to Isabella:

Brachiano. I was bewitched;
For all the world speaks ill of thee.

[1] Since the scene in Act I seems to be her first interview with the duke, and he is as yet doubtful of his success—cf. his words 'Quite lost, Flamineo!'—it would seem that she was innocent, unless it was on the very evening of the murders that Brachiano attained to the end of his 'long suit'.

Vittoria. No matter;
I'll live so now, I'll make that world recant,
And change her speeches. You did name your duchess.
Brachiano. Whose death God pardon!

and she breaks out in words that recall those in the trial scene:

Whose death God revenge
On thee, most godless duke! . . .
What have I gained by thee but infamy?
Thou hast stained the spotless honour of my house,
And frighted thence noble society.
. . . What do you call this house?
Is this your palace? . . .
Who hath the honour to advance Vittoria
To this incontinent college? Is't not you?
Is't not your high preferment?

So through a long tirade she lashes him and brings him to her feet and spurns him:

O thou fool,
Whose greatness hath by much o'ergrown thy wit!
What dar'st thou do, that I not dare to suffer,
Excepting to be still thy whore?

Her brother interposes—she is going too far—and she turns upon him like a wild-cat: 'Hence, you pander!' Gradually, her end attained, she grows milder and adopts a tone of self-pity:

Am I not low enough? . . .
Your dog or hawk should be rewarded better
Than I have been. I'll not speak one word more.

And to the end of the scene, in Symonds's phrase, we feel her melting humour in the air. The dramatic situation closes with Brachiano's words 'Think on a duchess' title'.

The manner in which she works on the duke is the result of consummate art, for Webster has depicted in her not only a glorious woman, but a supreme actress. And yet it is not the outcome of cold calculation; her pride, her fury, her despair, are alike genuine. Nor are they merely the passions of an ambitious creature who sees her dream of advancement shattered; she remains a woman throughout. She feels her womanly pride outraged, her victorious beauty challenged, and the bitterness of her resentment is the measure of her love for the duke, for to her his person and his honours are essentially one. It is not that her affections are less keen than those of other women, but that in her they are controlled by calculating ambition and the lust for power; actions and words that in others would be inconsistent are in her but glimpses of different sides of a complex character.

We see her next at her husband's death-bed. She presses to his side:

O, my loved lord! poison'd!

She soothes him and humours his delirium; he taunts her with the frailties of womankind, and she winces. The hair of her young head is already streaked with grey through much living; in his fever the duke gibes at it, but she keeps her place by right at his side. The words she utters are few, but she is always ready at the first call of the dying man. When he is dead she leaves the scene with the cry, 'O me! this place is hell!' Uttered as it is at the moment when the call upon her wifely ministrations finally ceases and her thoughts are free to face her own situation, it is natural enough. Francisco is not her friend, but he recognizes the genuineness of her grief: 'How heavily she takes it!' It is not merely that at a stroke the prize for which she has risked all escapes her, nor that she sees herself helpless and surrounded by ruthless enemies—her self-possession could have steeled her against these—but that she sees done to death before her the only man who in force of will and spirit was her equal, who was bound to her by community of glorious desires and unscrupulous purpose, and in whose want her life must thenceforth be void and incomplete. Thus although it is not the impulse of any light love, nor primarily a deep sensuous desire, that is the mainspring of Vittoria's character, it is likewise possible to assign too important a place to mere worldly ambition, and Webster may have intended to depict in her a more natural and kindly passion than his critics have been apt to recognize, for when her moments are already numbered he puts into her mouth the words:

O, my greatest sin lay in my blood,
And now my blood pays for't.[1]

[1] Had Webster intended to stress Vittoria's ambition, he could have shown his duke as the unprepossessing lover that history depicts. The fact of his departing from

In the remaining scene of the play Vittoria plays the part of a caged wild-cat. Terrible and fascinating in the consistency of character in which no moral misgiving has place, she fights ruthlessly, desperately against fate. It is not easy to die in the height of youth and beauty; her desires in this world are unfulfilled, and to her pagan spirit what lies beyond is little compensation:

> My soul, like to a ship in a black storm,
> Is driven I know not whither.

Yet, brought face to face with death, she regains her proud scornful assurance in face of her judges. Her last words sum up the pathos of a life that opened with such fair promise:

> O, happy they that never saw the court,
> Nor ever knew great men but by report!

The historical Vittoria, kneeling in her silken night-rail, died with forgiveness upon her lips. Her dignity and sweetness were not without their effect on her murderers. 'Ohimè!' exclaimed Count Paganello, one of the ruffian crew, 'Ohimè! che havemo fatto? Havemo uccisa una santa.' There is something theatrical in either version of her end, which helps little towards understanding her character.

Such, it seems to me, is Webster's reading of Vittoria's tragedy, and at least it offers no greater difficulties than any other.[1] The action in the play has naturally been much condensed throughout. The arraignment follows immediately upon the murder, Vittoria's first marriage with the duke, its annulling, and her long confinement being omitted. Her flight with Brachiano to Padua follows at once upon her escape (or release), the story thus jumping from November 1582 to the

his model as regards Brachiano at the same time as he drew such a woeful coxcomb in Camillo bears out the view put forward above.

[1] Against the supposition of wantonness is the evidence of the repulsive physical taint in the duke; against the idea of the ambitious adventuress, the testimony of her amiable character as a girl, her gentle and forgiving death, and the respect always shown towards her by Montalto; against the suggestion of constraint, the fact that she could easily have obtained protection from him or from the Pope; lastly, against the possibility of her having been a weak woman who allowed herself to be led into criminal acts against her will, what scanty evidence we possess regarding her character, especially her firm behaviour in the castle of S. Angelo. A singularly unsuccessful and ill-judged attempt to whitewash Vittoria was made in an article in the *Nineteenth Century* for January 1899.

election of the new Pope in April 1585 and omitting her second marriage and her residence with the duke at Brachiano. Her final marriage takes place at Padua instead of Rome, and Brachiano's death and her own end follow immediately upon it. Actually the duke did not die till 10 November, nor did her murder take place till 23 December.

II. Division into Scenes

The play was printed four times in quarto. The text in the first two editions, those of 1612 and 1631, is not divided; that of 1665 introduced the division into acts; that of 1672 the further division into scenes. These divisions, introduced many years after the writing and original staging of the play, though accepted in the main by the modern editors, cannot be regarded as possessing the least authority. They stand equally condemned on internal evidence. Fresh scenes are frequently marked in spite of characters remaining on the stage, as at the entrance of Brachiano immediately after the trial scene; and on the other hand no new scene is marked where the stage remains empty, as at the beginning of the scene between Vittoria and Flamineo in Act v. The division into acts is equally unsatisfactory, the break during which Vittoria and Brachiano travel from Rome to Padua coming in the middle of an act; and a fresh one is made to begin after the 'Barriers', though the action is perfectly continuous. The case is different with the stage-directions, which, dating from 1612, are of greater value, and probably derive from a prompt copy.

It must be borne in mind that our stage early rejected the continental habit of marking a new scene wherever there was a change in the actors on the stage, which is merely a theatrical technicality unrelated to dramatic construction. The English habit of marking a new scene only when the stage was left empty came much nearer rendering its true dramatic value as a significant subdivision of the act. It sacrificed, however, the clear simplicity of the foreign method, and may at times, as in the present play, give rise to perplexity.

This perplexity is due to the conventional construction of the Elizabethan stage, a clear idea of which should be borne in mind. The typical form may be taken as consisting of a wide shallow platform, without curtain, but with entrances towards the sides, and in the centre a 'traverse' or curtain which when drawn aside revealed a kind of inner stage. On this any furniture required could be arranged while the traverse was closed, and it consequently represented, when displayed, a definite locality until the traverse was again closed. Above it was a balcony, which was used whenever an actor was required to appear at a window or on a tower or the like. The outer stage could never have any furniture, and was consequently in no way localized in the minds either of players or audience, which accounts for the perplexing confusions of scene that frequently arise. Since a play was acted continuously without break, no change of scene could take place on the inner stage without an intervening scene on the outer; and although it is possible that consecutive scenes, involving a change of dramatic locality, may have been acted on the outer stage alone, the change being left to the imagination of the audience, the natural course would be alternate outer- and inner-stage scenes.[1] This alternation is, in the main, what we find in the present play. For instance, the procession to the judgement-hall would be on the outer stage; the 'arraignment' necessarily on the inner; Flamineo's feigned madness on the outer; Francisco's plot, necessitating a table, on the inner; the quarrel between Flamineo and Brachiano on the outer; the great scene with Vittoria, necessitating a bed, on the inner. But this simple arrangement is complicated in two ways. The first is the carrying over characters from one scene to another—a kind of *enjambement*. Of this the play affords three examples. The first is in connexion with the trial scene. It is preceded by a scene on the outer stage in which various characters pass on their way to the judgement-hall. The stage is at moments empty, but since the characters all form a part of a procession, as it were, the whole may be treated as forming one scene. At the direction 'exeunt', Flamineo, Marcello, their guards, the lawyer, and the French, English, and Spanish ambassadors, are left on the stage. We should, of course, suppose that they all go off, but in the stage-direction

[1] [Naturally when the inner stage was in use the action spilt over onto the outer stage as well, so that it is more accurate to speak of outer-stage and whole-stage scenes.—1958.]

to the 'arraignment' (which, by the way, has never been marked as a new scene) only the ambassadors are mentioned as re-entering, though, of course, all reappear on the stage. The explanation is simple enough: the ambassadors alone 'exeunt', and pass behind to take their places on the bench; then the traverse is drawn aside, and the brothers, with the guard and the lawyer, merely join in the scene without leaving the stage. It may be noticed also that Flamineo must necessarily be near the front of the stage as he is the only character who has an 'aside' in the course of the scene.[1] The next instance is in the house of convertites. When Vittoria appears the quartos have the stage-direction 'Enter Vittoria to Brachiano and Flamineo', and no new scene is marked in that of 1672. Hazlitt marked a fresh scene and altered the direction to 'Enter to Vittoria, Brachiano and Flamineo', but strangely enough forgot to supply their previous exit. But there is no reason to suppose the original direction wrong if we remember that, in the language of the old stage, 'enter' as often as not means 'is discovered', as is plain from such directions as 'Enter Faustus in his Study' (*Doctor Faustus*, 1604, scene i). The matron probably leaves the stage when Flamineo takes the letter from her early in the scene, so that at the close he and the duke are alone. Vittoria cannot merely enter to them in the ordinary sense, for a change of scene is necessary, and, moreover, the inner stage is required for the bed; but the traverse would be drawn apart and Vittoria would enter, that is, be discovered, Brachiano and Flamineo passing into the new scene without exit. The third case occurs in the last act. The quartos have the direction: 'Enter Brachiano, presented in bed, Vittoria and others.' Now, there are cases in which a bed is actually thrust onto the stage from behind a curtain, with a person lying in it (e.g. in Heywood's *Maidenhead Well Lost*); but we can hardly suppose that Webster would have tolerated such a clumsy expedient in his play. The natural manner in which to overcome the difficulty would be to draw back the traverse and discover the duke and others. I have no doubt that this is what was intended. There is an unexpected complication, however, in Francisco's

[1] It is possible that the opposite of this happens at the end of the scene, some characters remaining on the stage after the traverse has been drawn.

words: 'See, here he comes'; perhaps we are to imagine that Brachiano is just being led to his bed as the scene opens.

But beyond these definite cases there are others in which the traverse could conveniently be used. When Francisco tells Flamineo of Cornelia's madness, he replies:

> I will see them;
> They are behind the *traverse*; I'll *discover*
> Their superstitious howling.[1]

Here then there can be no doubt how the scene was managed. When the ladies withdrew, the corpse would remain on the stage to enhance the effect of Brachiano's apparition. Then the traverse closed, and the following scene proceeded on the outer stage only.[2] We have now reached an alternate use of the outer and inner stages, except in one instance, namely where the second, third, and fourth scenes of the play all apparently need the inner stage. The first two of these are far too important to be merely outer-stage scenes, scene iii especially calling for a large stage to accommodate various groups, and scene iv requiring furniture since Brachiano is invited to sit down. The dumb-shows would probably be managed by the curtain over the back entrance. Some device must therefore have been used to clear the inner stage, and the most natural would be to close the traverse in scene ii upon the duke's exit and let Flamineo and Cornelia continue the scene on the outer stage, to open the inner stage again for scene iii, as far as the point where Monticelso and the rest come forward on Brachiano's exit, and again for the whole of scene iv. We thus obtain perfect alternation throughout.

From the point of view of editing, it is often in these cases difficult to know whether or not a new scene should be marked. In any case, the editor has nothing to do with the technicalities of the ancient stage, and either a new scene with proper exits and entrances should be given, or no notice should be taken.

[1] Even the direction here reads: 'Cornelia . . . *discovered* winding Marcello's corse.' I dare say there are others, but it is the only instance I remember at the moment where the word occurs in an old stage-direction. [*The Tempest*, F 1623, v. i. 171. 'Here Prospero discouers Ferdinand and Miranda, playing at Chesse.'—1958.]

[2] [Here I have omitted a suggestion that the inner stage was used for the scene of the papal election, based on the false assumption that the balcony formed part of the inner stage.—1958.]

I think, however, that on closer examination the difficulty largely disappears, for it will be seen that two clearly differentiated cases exist. In the one case there is a clear change of scene, the more or less vague locality of the outer stage merging into the more definite one of the inner. Thus the gallery leading to the judgement-hall merges into the hall itself; the anteroom in the house of the convertites merges into Vittoria's apartment; the gallery in the duke's palace merges into the death-chamber. In these cases a new scene is clearly necessary. On the other hand, in the cases where the traverse is merely resorted to as a device to enlarge the stage temporarily and for some particular object, to introduce onto it characters or properties which it would be awkward to move onto the outer portion, or to gain time for and indicate a subsequent change of scene, no notice need be taken by literary editors, since the use is theatrical and not dramatic, and on stages differently arranged other methods would be employed.

I now propose to take the scenes in order and discuss their relation as regards time and place.

1. Scene—Rome, where the action continues till the end of scene 11. Possibly a gallery or anteroom to a judgement-hall, not, however, the same as scene 5, since Lodovico is banished by the Pope, not Francisco, as appears from the Pope signing his pardon. More probably, however, a street, since at the opening of the play the quartos read 'Banished?' (query, not exclamation), as if Lodovico had not heard his own sentence, but had just received the news from his friends. Time—not specified, but shortly before the death of Gregory XIII. Webster, however, makes Monticelso's election follow immediately upon that event, whereas there seems in fact to have been a considerable interval. Montalto was elected on 24 April 1585.
2. Scene—Camillo's house or grounds. Symonds suggests the garden, which is likely enough, for a carpet and cushions are brought onto the stage. Flamineo tells his sister that 'my lord attends you in the banqueting-house', but there is no change of scene, and the duke talks of darkness hiding Vittoria's blushes. Time—not specified.

Properly an interval must be supposed, since in scene 3 on the following day it is already reported that Lodovico has turned pirate. In any case it is night.

3. Scene—a room in Francisco's palace. Time—probably the following day, for we learn in scene 2 that Isabella is in Rome and the meeting could hardly have been postponed.
4. Scene—a room in Camillo's house. Time—the same evening, since in the preceding scene Flamineo announced Camillo's murder for 'to-night'.
5. Scene—a gallery leading to the judgement-hall in Francisco's palace. Time—probably the following day, since news of Isabella's death arrives after the trial.
6. Scene—the hall in Francisco's house. Francisco had, of course, no jurisdiction in Rome; but the present case had been entrusted to him and Monticelso by the Pope. The incident of the stool shows that Francisco is in the position of host. Time—continuous with the preceding. I may mention that all the quartos, except that of 1672, mention Isabella among the characters that 'enter'! No doubt Zanche was intended, one actor playing the two parts and the direction finding its way in from a stage copy.
7. Scene—probably the same as scene 5. Time—continuous with the preceding. I think it is quite necessary to mark a new scene here, not only because the inner stage is wanted again for the next scene, but that in the quarto Francisco, Monticelso, and Giovanni are left on the stage, whereas they are certainly not present during what follows. Hazlitt has supplied an exit for Giovanni for other reasons. Thus we may assume that the traverse was closed again at this point, leaving the stage the same as in scene 5. The only question is whether Lodovico and Marcello remain on the stage all the time, or whether they re-enter with the ambassadors. The former is the more probable.
8. Scene—a room in Francisco's palace. Time—possibly the same day; but it would be better to suppose an interval of at least one night, since in the following scene the duke is represented as having frequent 'recourse' to

Vittoria in her confinement. No long interval can elapse, since the Pope is all the while 'on his death-bed'.

9. Scene—an anteroom in the house of convertites. Time—the same day.
10. Scene—the same, Vittoria's apartment. Time—continuous with the preceding.
11. Scene—a street or square in front of a church where the conclave is held; that is, the piazza before St. Peter's, the conclave being held in the Vatican. Time—the following day, since news of Vittoria's flight arrives during the course of the scene.
12. Scene—Padua, where the remainder of the action takes place. A room in Brachiano's palace, namely, either the palace of the Foscari in the Arena, or a house called De' Cavalli, both of which he had hired. Time—after an undefined interval occupied by the journey from Rome to Padua; in reality about six months later.
13. Scene—probably a gallery in the same. Time—immediately after the preceding.

Dumb-show. Scene—the courtyard of the palace; perhaps the Arena. Time—continuous with the preceding.

14. Scene—probably the same as scene 13. Time—continuous with the preceding.
15. Scene—a room in the palace. Time—continuous with the preceding.
16. Scene—probably the same as scene 14. Time—probably immediately after the preceding.
17. Scene—probably the same. Time—probably immediately after the preceding.
18. Scene—Vittoria's apartment. Time—immediately after the preceding.

Thus we see that the scene lies between Rome (scenes 1–11) and Padua (scenes 12–18), while the time may be arranged as follows:

Day I, Scene 1. Interval.
Day II, Scene 2.
Day III, Scenes 3 and 4.
Day IV, Scenes 5 to 7.
Day V, Scenes 8 to 10.

Day VI, Scene 11. Interval.
Day VII, Scenes 12 to 18.

Since the journey from Rome to Padua is made by sea—

We may attire her in a page's suit,
Lay her post-horse, take shipping, and amain
For Padua—

the total duration of the action could not be less than about three weeks, even omitting the first scene, which is more or less introductory. The above analysis is of no more value than such tables usually are, for the reason that, in common with most of the dramatists of his day, Webster is indifferent to the details of time and place.

III. General Construction

As regards the grouping of scenes into acts it is well to remember that, as far as the English drama is concerned, these divisions are largely academic. The action was continuous, one scene succeeding another without interval.[1] The convention of the five acts was an inheritance from the Senecan drama and from its Italian offspring. Nevertheless it must be admitted that many of our old plays seem to fall naturally into five divisions. Aristotle divided a tragedy into three parts and placed the turn of fortune in the middle. It may be questioned how far his view is borne out by the practice of the Greek tragedians: such plays as the *Electra* hardly support it. At all events it is probably more in accordance with the spirit of the romantic drama to postpone the climax and concentrate the catastrophe.

It will be well in the first place to locate the climax and the turn of fortune in the present play. The climax, the point of culmination of the plot, round which it revolves and on which it hinges, should obviously possess a dramatic value corresponding to its architectonic importance. This might at first sight lead one to the conclusion that the 'arraignment' is the climax of the play. One consideration, however, should at once suggest that this is unlikely, namely, that this scene comes early in the third act, whereas, in the Elizabethan

[1] [This applies to the 'public' theatres: in the 'private' houses there were often intervals of music.—1958.]

drama, the climax is usually found in the fourth.[1] On closer inspection it will, I think, be evident that it is on the scene in the house of convertites rather than on the trial that the plot turns. It is not till the offer of the title of duchess that Vittoria has gained her end or Brachiano really won her. Again, the 'arraignment' does not stand alone. The two scenes resemble one another in having each an introductory scene leading up to it, but the trial itself is followed by the news of Isabella's death—the most admirable scene in the play—and Flamineo's feigned madness, which is closely related to it. The interest which has been wrought up to a high pitch of intensity is allowed to dissipate again; it is eminently a scene of evolution, not of climax. The scene of Brachiano's jealousy, on the other hand, leads up to the culminating point of the play, in which Vittoria attains momentarily to the height of her ambition. This point is likewise the turn of fortune, for by the very move by which the pair think to triumph they step into the net woven for them by Francisco. Brachiano's words, 'Think on a duchess' title', are instinct with a dramatic irony which suggests a parallel to those with which a later dramatist closed his greatest work, 'Dem Fürsten Piccolomini'.

There can be no doubt that the climax and the turn of fortune are intended in the present play to lie at the same point, but it may well be questioned whether the second is sufficiently emphasized. The touch of irony is a subtle one, not easily perceived except in the light of subsequent events. It is not till the second scene of the last act that the murder of Marcello strikes the keynote of a losing game; there intervenes before that a great deal of uninteresting and rather irrelevant business, which retards the action and weakens the dramatic effect. Both the climax and the turn of fortune require greater concentration, an effect which Webster has endeavoured to attain, as far as the former is concerned, through giving greater prominence to the duke's offer to Vittoria by omitting the actual marriage.

Having now settled the main point, we can turn to the division of the play into acts. It seems to me that if we clear our mind of the absurd arrangement of the late quarto, we can at once distinguish five distinct groups of scenes into which

[1] See B. Worsfold's *Principles of Criticism*, 1897, p. 211.

the play falls. The first of these, including scenes 1 and 2, introduces the tragic motive, here the lawless love of Vittoria and Brachiano, which is the mainspring of the action. It is introduced after the accepted model of the romantic stage, a short expository introduction, which is here also an integral part of the action, preparing for an important scene setting forth the initial dramatic situation. Scenes 2 and 3 constitute the second group, the function of which is to set forth the tragic fault, the murder of Camillo and Isabella, which supplies the matter of the tragedy. These two acts together form a sort of introduction, and may be regarded as equivalent to Aristotle's δέσις or 'complication'. The plot is now before the spectator and the action under way. Similarly the next two acts contain the evolution. Act III, which consists of scenes 5–7, depicts the obstacles encountered by the guilty pair; they are not defeated, but neither do they triumph. Vittoria is arrested, but the charge of murder has to be abandoned, the charge of incontinence remains unproven, and though she is detained in a reformatory this does not prevent her meetings with her lover. Act IV, including scenes 8–11, contains the seeming triumph, leading up to the climax, a point at which, by a stroke of irony, the very move that appears to secure their safety leads them into the meshes of Francisco's plot. Lastly Act V, namely scenes 12–18, which is inordinately long, owing to the detail with which Webster loves to elaborate his scenes of horror, but which is nevertheless continuous throughout, contains the retribution and forms the catastrophe.

I append a tabular analysis giving the correspondences between the various divisions into act and scene and a few other details. In the column headed 'Staging', inner and outer refer, of course, to the two methods of mounting a scene, on the whole stage or on the forescene only, as described above; an arrow indicates *enjambement* by means of the traverse.[1]

[1] [Martin W. Sampson in his edition in 'The Belles-Lettres Series' (Boston, Heath, 1902) and F. L. Lucas in his edition of Webster's Works (London, Chatto & Windus, 1927, vol. i) agree in the main with my proposed division: Lucas, however, follows 1672 in making the scene in the house of convertites continuous, whereas Sampson follows Hazlitt in dividing it into two (IV. ii, iii); both make the dumb-show of the Barriers part of the following scene (V. iii) and make this include Brachiano's death (V. iv).—1958.]

Sc. No.	4° 1672 Act	4° 1672 Sc.	Hazlitt Act	Hazlitt Sc.	Proposed Division Act	Proposed Division Sc.	Action	Staging	Locality	Time	Description of Act	Analysis
									ROME			
1	I	i	I	i	I	i	Lodovico's banishment	outer . .	A street . .	Day I	The tragic motive.	Introduction
2		ii (iii)		ii		ii	Camillo hoodwinked. SEDUCTION OF VITTORIA	inner, outer	Camillo's house, the garden.	Interval. Day II		
3	II	i	II	i	II	i	BRACHIANO REJECTS ISABELLA. Camillo's mission	inner, outer	Francisco's palace, a room.	Day III	The tragic fault.	
4	III	i	III	i		ii	Murder of Isabella and Camillo . . .	inner . .	Camillo's house, a room.	Do.		
5		ii		ii	III	i	Procession to the judgement-hall. . .	outer .	Francisco's palace, a gallery.	Day IV	The fight for victory.	Evolution.
6						ii	ARRAIGNMENT OF VITTORIA. News of Isabella's death	inner . ↓ .	Do. a hall .	Do.		
7		(iii)				iii	Flamineo's feigned madness	outer . ↓ .	Do. a gallery .	Do.		
8		iv		iii	IV	i	Francisco's plot	inner . .	Do. a room .	Day V	The seeming triumph.	[Climax.]
9	IV	i	IV	i		ii	Brachiano's jealousy. Quarrel with Flamineo	outer .	House of convertites, a gallery.	Do.		
10				ii		iii	BRACHIANO PROMISES VITTORIA THE DUCHESS'S TITLE	inner ↓ .	Do. a room .	Do.		
11		ii (iii)		iii		iv	Excommunication. Lodovico vows vengeance	outer . .	A street . .	Day VI		
										Interval.		
									PADUA.			
12		iv (v)		iv	V	i	The revels. Flamineo and Marcello quarrel .	inner . .	Brachiano's palace, a room .	Day VII	The retribution.	Catastrophy.
13		vi		v		ii	Flamineo murders Marcello	outer . .	Do. a gallery .	Do.		
							Dumb-show of the Barriers	inner . .	Do. courtyard.	Do.		
14	V	i	V	i		iii	Brachiano poisoned	outer .	Do. a gallery .	Do.		
15		(ii)				iv	BRACHIANO'S DEATH	inner ↓ .	Do. a room .	Do.		
16		iii (iv)				v	Cornelia's dirge for Marcello	outer, inner	Do. a gallery .	Do.		
17		v				vi	Lodovico's plot overheard	outer . .	Do. do. .	Do.		
18				ii		vii	DEATH OF VITTORIA AND FLAMINEO . .	inner . .	Do. a room .	Do.		

2. Fairfax's Eighth Eclogue[1]

EDWARD FAIRFAX, well known for his translation of Tasso's *Gerusalemme Liberata*, which appeared in 1600, was likewise the author of twelve eclogues, as we learn from a letter written by his great-nephew, Brian Fairfax, to Bishop Atterbury on 12 March 1704/5. This letter, no. XCII of the 'Atterbury Correspondence' (iii. 255), contains the following particulars:

He [Fairfax] wrote other ingenious eclogues [*i.e.* wrote eclogues as well as *Godfrey of Boulogne*], and presented them to the Duke of Richmond and Lenox, of which his son William (1636) gives this account, in his annotations upon them; viz. 'These bucolics were written in the first year of the reign of King James, and, from their finishing, they lay neglected ten years in my father's study, until Ludowic, the late noble Duke of Richmond and Lenox desired a sight of them, which made the author to transcribe them for his Grace's use. That copy was seen and approved by many learned men; and that reverend divine Dr. Field, now bishop of Hereford, wrote verses upon it; and these following were written by Wilson Scotobritannicus:

Et Phœbum, castasque doces, Fairfaxe, sorores
  Salsa verecundo verba lepore loqui,
Ulla nec in toto prurit lascivia libro,
  Pagina non minus est quam tibi vita proba.

Chaste is thy muse as is a vestal nun,
And thy Apollo spotless as the sun;
No wanton thought betray'd by word or look,
As blameless is thy life as is thy book.

But the book itself and the Bishop's encomium perished in the fire, when the Banqueting-house at Whitehall was burnt, and with it part of the Duke's lodgings where the book was; but with my father's help, I recovered them out of his loose papers, &c.'

The original manuscript, containing annotations by William Fairfax, was still preserved among the family papers

[1] [1901. July. *The Modern Language Quarterly*, iv. 85. Further annotations were contributed in August 1903 (vi. 73) by R. B. McKerrow: these are here printed along with the others or are if necessary substituted for my original conjectures, and are distinguished by brackets and initials.—1958.]

in 1737, when Mrs. Elizabeth Cooper printed one of the eclogues, the fourth, in her *Muses Library* of that year. Since then the manuscript seems to have disappeared, but another eclogue, the number of which is not given, has been discovered in a Bodleian manuscript in the hand of Thomas, third Lord Fairfax, and was printed by W. Grainge in his edition of the author's *Daemonologia* (1882); while one, evidently the same, is said to have appeared in *Philobiblon Miscellanies*, vol. xii (*see* Hazlitt, *C. and N.*, ii. 212). Furthermore, Mr. A. H. Bullen, writing the notice of Fairfax in the *Dictionary of National Biography*, calls attention to an eclogue in B.M. Addit. MS. 11743 (misprinted 11473) as being probably one of the same series. Since the style resembles that of the other two, and the heading is similar to that in the Bodleian manuscript (Mrs. Cooper gave no 'Argument'), and as the manuscript in which it is found contains 'a large Collection of Poetical Pieces written by or relating to Members of the Fairfax Family', the probability approaches as near certainty as is possible in such cases, and I offer the present reprint in the confident belief that the poem is a fragment of the lost series.[1]

The author's reputation as a poet has declined from its zenith. Mrs. Cooper could speak of him as 'the only Writer down to D'Avenant, that needs no Apology to be made for him, on account of the Age he lived in'. Of the matter of the eclogues the same amiable critic wrote:

> the Learning they contain, is so various, and extensive, that according to the Evidence of his Son, (who has written large Annotations on each) No Man's Reading, beside his own, was sufficient to explain his References effectually.

Of the probable truth of this statement the reader may in the case of the present poem judge for himself.

The manuscript of the eclogue is unfortunately imperfect at the end, two leaves only being preserved, which form folios 5 and 6 of the collection in which they are found. They are written in a very neat hand of the early seventeenth century, chiefly of an Italian character but with occasional English

[1] The 'Argument' and five stanzas have already appeared in K. Windscheid's *Englische Hirtendichtung von 1579–1625* (Halle, 1895).

forms. The whole has been revised and punctuated by the same hand, though in a blacker ink. These corrections have been silently introduced into the present text. The original spelling has been retained, together with the use of capitals; the punctuation, on the other hand, has been modernized, the original being in many cases more than usually clumsy.

The manuscript is evidently a careful transcript of the original, but is not the work of a very educated man. Thus although *u* and *n* and the like are usually clearly differentiated, they appear hopelessly confused in proper names, having doubtless been indistinguishable in the original. Thus in ll. 47 and 48, 'Pithius' and 'Nonius' appear as 'Pithins' and 'Nomins', in l. 112 we have 'Mutezmnas' for 'Mutezumas', in l. 158 'Arzimas' for 'Arzinas', and in l. 138 'Orphens' for 'Orpheus'. The only case of confusion, except in these names, is in l. 134 where we find 'sponts' for 'spouts': the transcriber probably had no notion what was meant, and the apparently meaningless 'lions' in the same line may equally be his blunder.

The few other corrections that appeared necessary are enclosed in square brackets. I may add that there is a bad stain at the head of the leaves which has rendered two words in the top line on fol. 5^{b} almost illegible. (See note on l. 37.)

My very best thanks are due to Dr. Henry Jackson and Mr. F. M. Cornford, of Trinity, and to the University Reader in Geography, Mr. H. Yule Oldham, of King's College, Cambridge, without whose generous help I could never have attempted to elucidate the author's allusions.

[fol. 5^{a}]

Ecloga Octava

Ida and Opilio

The Argument

Opilio skornes the dayes of ould
And boasts the wealth of præsent times,
Rekons what sailors brought home gould
Or found new trades in unknowne Climes.

Opil: Bright may this riseing beame on Ida shine!
Crowne thy blith forhead with this wreath of beach
And bless the morning with some himne divine.
Hear'st not how Philomele her babe doth teach?
How sweet shee chirps? but sing the best shee can,
There is noe Musicke like the voice of man.

Ida There dull conceit, who cut Terpanders string,
And his gross eare, who caus'd the Lords of Rome
To force the morning birds leave of to sing,
Could of my Musick giue a fitter dome
Then thy deepe cunning; let my reed be still,
Except Pans iudge sitt yet on Tmolus hill.

But if thou deigne to tune thy seavenfould pipe,
Sitt in this shade or that vnpollisht caue,
Where the wild vine with clusters never ripe
Orefrets the vault, and where the yong Nimphs haue
There dancing schoole, but thrust the Ladies out,
Or be their Orpheus while they friske about.

Opil: Nor is thy rubeck out of tune soe farre;
But this the fault of skilful singers is,
To be most squemish when most prai'd they arre,
Though vnbesought they never cease; such blis,
Such comfort, in your selves you poets find;
But that the com̃on fault is of mankind.

But, Ida, let vs sing or Rufus death,
Or Monforts treasons, or great Warwicks fraies,
Or to what dittie els thou list giue breath;
Praise if thou wilt the sheephards of our dayes,
That find each yeare new lands, new seas, new starrs.
And thence bring pearls in ropes and gold in barrs.

How is this age with wealth and wisdome blest!
How poore and simple were the elder times!
That wanted all the gould found in the west
And thought the world not wonned in three climes;
And he that of Antipodes durst tell
Was tearm'd an Heretick and damn'd to hell.

[fol. 5b] They had noe house with goulden [tiles which] shone,
They lackt the ransome of the Peruan king,
Pedrarias pearle and Moralis stone
And pretious trees that did in Puna spring,

With other blessing which those countreys yeild,
Divine Tobacco and rich Cucheneild.

Ida Stay, sheephard! stay, for thou condemnest those
Thou kennest not; perdie the times of ould
Were not soe rude or poore as you suppose;
They wanted neither Iewels, stones, nor gould,
Let Cleopatras pearle, Pithius his vine,
Nonius his Opall match those Iemmes of thine.

The Persian Darichs who can number them,
Talents of Greece and Sesterties of Rome?
Who weighes the Shekels of Hierusalem,
That did from Ophir and from sheba come?
Doubtless our saylors noe such riches find
In Lunaches, and Cacoas of Inde.

Opil: Yea but there wealth to them was nothing worth,
Their ignorance knew not to vse their good,
They only tooke what until'd earth brought forth
When caves were howses, leaves clothes, Akornes food;
The earths rich parts, that silke, spice, vnguents send,
They kn[e]w not, Finister was ther worlds end.

Ida Perchance thou hast some curious feaster seene
That serves his wildfoule with ther feathers on,
And wraps up Antick-like his napkins cleene,
Or know'st that Lord of France with pearle and ston
That sawceth all his meate, or hast hard tell
In how rich towres Dorados Ingas dwell.

If soe, yet did those dayes our times surpass
In costly buildings, vtensils and [cheare];
Let Ciprus house that earth[s] seaventh wonder was,
Let Æsops platter, Celers barball deare,
Let Plotins fatall perfumes witnesse bee,
They were as rich, as wise, as mad as wee.

Nor did there knowledge with cape vincent end:
Plato can tell thee of Atlantis land;
The place where Salomon for gould did send
Is by the Parian gulfe; Eudoxus fand
The point Speranza; and those men of Inde
Metellus saw, the Norwest streit did find.

[fol. 6a] And if that navy, which the stormes sterne blast
In the third Henries dayes to England brought,
King Fucusur vpon this Island cast,
When from his owne expel'd new lands he sought
In ships five masted, built of Chinas mould,
Then was the Northeast passage sail'd of ould.

Opil: The land of nusquam where king Nemo dwels,
Vtopia, and Lucians realme of lights,
Fronter Atlantis, whereof Plato tels,
And he that to the west his voiage dights
To seeke for Ophir, may teach Salomon
To saile from Ioppa, not from Ezion.

Noe, noe, that earths back side, that nether land,
Where like deepe fretworke in some heighroof'd hall,
The mountains hang and towres reversed stand,
If they wist whether, ready still to fall,
To our forefathers ever was vnkend;
They thought the earth had bounder side and end.

But wise Columbus wist the world was round,
That night was but earths shade, that the sun beame
His midnight light bestowed on some ground
Not all on waues and fishes in the streame,
And of the globe hee knew the sea possest
But the seaventh part, firme land was all the rest.

Thereby [hee] gathered many people dwelt
Twixt Spaine and China, and what god they feard,
What wealth they had, what heat or could they fealt
He longed to discrie, and that way steard,
Where a new world he found, yet on the same
Americk entred, and it beares his name.

I will not praise the Ruffian that first found
The calme Southsea, nor yet the man who past
The Ocean[s] stormy mouth, nor him to ground
That Mutezumas spatious pallace cast,
Nor the bould swinheard to his friend vntrew
Who kil'd the ransom'd king of rich Perù.

But listen while I praise in rurall songe
Such hardie groomes as this faire Isle sent forth
To grope their way in darke nights halfeyears long,
To feele the Iuly winter of the North,

To sweat at Christmas with the lines whot aire
Or droope in six months showres by springs of Zaire.

[fol. 6b] The cheife of these and all the rest biside
Is he that on this ball of sea and land
Did three long years in ioyfull tryvmph ride
And the vast round girt in a golden band,
Grand pilot of the world, who learn'd this feat
Of the wise stearman of Noyes carrak great.

Great Amurath did to his picture bend
And at his name Rome did an earthquake feele,
Spaines Iennet proud he did to stable send,
Which stampt to powder with his brazen heele
The worlds halfe conquer'd globe, but now surpriz'd,
The stall houlds him whom scant the world suffiz'd.

Noe thunders rage, noe Tuffons furious rore,
Noe lions strange which rise, no spouts that fall
Dismai'd his courage, but from Albion's shore,
From Tarenat, from Helens garden smal
To London safe he brought his Argo backe;
And yet this Iason doth his Orpheus lack.

His fellow rivall of his honour sought
For mines of gould on Metas vnknowne side,
England admir'd the savages he brought,
But when his oare was in the furnace tride
It proued Marcasite, the shining rocks
Beguile his eyes, soe fortune vertue mocks.

Oft he neigh perish't in the frozen piles
Of swimeing Ice, while longe he sought in vaine
A passage that way to Moluccas Iles.
Nor he that three times saild that cowrse againe
Had better happ, but with bare hope came home;
The time for that discovery is not come.

And hee the shores and creekes of newfound Land
Who lett to farme and fished all the banke,
Lost his delight vpon an vnknowne sand,
And lost himselfe when his light frigot sanke;
And yet some say that from the Ocean maine
He will returne when Arthur comes againe.

Of those that with the Russ our trade began
The first were turned by Arzinas frost
To images of Ice, and some that ran
To vaigats and Petzora there were lost,
Soe merciless, alas, is waue and winde;
U[n]happy [P]akin, thou art hard to find!

. . . . .

NOTES

7 *There* i.e. their. This spelling recurs in ll. 17, 55, and 73, and in the form *ther* in ll. 60 and 62, beside the usual form as in l. 56. In l. 18 an *i* was inserted in an original *ther*.

Terpander A Greek musician and lyric poet of the seventh century B.C. [This line seems to be due to imperfect recollection of a passage in Plutarch's *Moralia* (*Antiqua Instituta Laconica*), which, in P. Holland's translation of 1603, appears as follows: 'But if any man passed one point beyond this ancient musike, they would not endure him, insomuch as the *Ephori* set a fine upon the head of Terpander . . . [and] hung up his harp upon a stake or post, onely because he had set to it one string more than ordinarie . . . and when *Timotheus* at the feast *Carneia* plaied upon the harpe for to winne the prize, one of the *Ephori* taking a skeine or knife in his hand, asked him, on whether side, either above or beneath, he would rather have him to cut a two the strings which were more than seven' (p. 477, ll. 8–17). It will be noticed that it was not Terpander's string which was cut. There must be indeed some confusion in the original story, for Terpander is generally supposed to have added three strings to the lyre, not one.—McK.]

8 *And his gross eare, who caus'd the Lords of Rome To force the morning birds leave of to sing* [The reference is, I think, to a story told by Pliny, *H.N.*, xxxv. 38. Lepidus, during the Triumvirate, being entertained by the magistrates of a certain place, was lodged in a house surrounded by trees. Next day he complained of having been kept awake by the singing of the birds. Accordingly they had a dragon painted on long strips of parchment and surrounded the grove with it, which so terrified the birds that they at once became silent. Compare also Nashe's *Summer's Last Will and Testament*, 'At a solemne feast of the *Triumuiri* in Rome, it was seene and obserued, that the birds ceased to sing, and sate solitarie on the house tops, by reason of the sight of a paynted serpēt set openly to view'.—Sig. B 1^{v}.—McK.]

10 *dome* That is, 'doom', here used in the sense of 'judgment'.

12 The reference is to the story told in Ovid's *Metamorphoses*, XI. Pan challenged Apollo to a musical contest, pipe against lyre. The judge, Tmolus, the god of the mountain of that name, decided in favour of Apollo, and his judgment was approved by all the others, except Midas, who was consequently graced with asses' ears by the slighted god. 'Pan's judge' is the judge who

gave his voice in favour of Pan. The meaning of the passage therefore is: 'Do not bid me sing unless it be before such an uncritical judge as Midas.'

19 *rubeck* Apparently for 'rebeck', a kind of fiddle.

21 ff. So Horace:

> Omnibus hoc uitium est cantoribus, inter amicos
> ut nunquam inducant animum cantare rogati,
> iniussi nunquam desistant.—*Satires*, I. iii. 1.

26 *Warwick* Richard Neville, Earl of Warwick and Salisbury (1428–1471), the famous 'king-maker' of the Wars of the Roses.

30 *pearls* The scribe first wrote *ropes* and altered it *currente calamo*.

34 *wonned* i.e. inhabited. However, though in O.E. *wunian* is sometimes found with an accusative, the word never seems to have possessed a passive.

35 ff. 'Many of the Ancients denyed the Antipodes, and some unto the penalty of contrary affirmations' says Sir Thomas Browne (whatever exactly that may mean) in the *Vulgar Errors*, I. vi. (ed. 1646, p. 24), and again, 'I have often pitied the miserable Bishop that suffered in the cause of Antipodes; yet cannot but accuse him of as much madness, for exposing his life on such a trifle, as those of ignorance and folly, that condemned him' (*Religio Medici*, i. 26; *Temp. Clas.*, p. 40). The Bishop referred to is Virgilius, Bishop of Salzburg, said to have been burnt in the eighth century for heretically maintaining the existence of the antipodes.

37 [*tiles which*] The reading here is open to question, there being a bad ink stain at the head of the leaves, which has partly covered this line. All can, however, be deciphered with ease, except these two words. The second, moreover, may be taken as certain in spite of the rather unusual shape of the *w*, and about the last three letters of the first there can also be no doubt. The second letter may be either an *a* or an *i*, while the first is certainly a tall letter. If the second is an *a*, the first is probably a *b*, and the word 'bales', which was the view of G. F. Warner and A. W. Pollard of the British Museum, who kindly examined the passage for me. In this case it would refer to Atahuallpa's ransom (see next line), for which bundles of golden ornaments etc. were brought by carriers (see Prescott). After, however, examining the line under a powerful glass, I am convinced that the letter is a *t*, and the word consequently 'tiles'. I believe that I can also distinguish the dot of the *i*. In this case the reference is to some building with a golden roof. The author probably intended the golden city of Manoa, called on that account 'El Dorado' (cf. l. 66), or he might possibly be thinking of the golden roofs of the temples of Japan described by Marco Polo, which proved a great incentive to Columbus and his followers. As, however, all the other allusions in the stanza are to America, the former would appear the more likely explanation. [Compare also Saris's account of Edo (Tokyo) and of the houses with their 'ridge-tiles and corner tiles richly gilded', *The Voyage of Captain John Saris to Japan*, 1613. . . . *Hakluyt Soc.* 1900, p. 133.—McK.]

38 *Peruan king* (the *u* has been altered from *n*) Atahuallpa. The amount of his ransom actually collected amounted to 1,326,539 *pesos de oro* (equivalent to about £3,500,000) besides silver estimated at 51,610 marks (see W. H. Prescott's *Conquest of Peru*, Bk. III. ch. vii).

39 *Pedrarias pearle* Pedrarias Davila (Pedr' Arias d'Avila) after murdering Balboa (l. 109) succeeded him as governor of Darien. [This pearl is described in 'The Decades of the newe worlde or west India. . . . Wrytten in the Latine tounge by Peter Martyr of Angleria, and translated into Englysshe by Richarde Eden, 1555'. It was bought 'euen in *Dariena* for a thousande and two hundreth Castelans of golde . . . and came at the length to the handes of *Petrus Arias* the gouernoure', who gave it to his wife. Decade III. bk. x. folio 141.—McK.]

pearle The word is here a disyllable.

Moralis stone Andreas Moralis, or Morales, a pilot of good repute at the time of the early Spanish discoveries in America—like Juan de la Cosa—obtained a famous diamond from a native on the north coast of South America. See Eden, *The first three English Books on America*, ed. Arber, p. 156. [It may be worth noting that the description of this referred to is from the same work, Dec. III. bk. iv. folio 112. Moralis bought it from a native 'for fyue of our coũterfect stones made of glasse of dyuers colours, wherwith the ignorant younge man was greatly delyted'.—McK.]

40 *Puna* The island of Puná is situated in the Gulf of Guayaquil, separating Ecuador from Peru. Possibly the author had in mind the passage in Montaigne: 'The wonderful, or as I may call it, amazement-breeding magnificence of the never-like seene cities of Cusco and Mexico, and amongst infinite such-like things, the admirable Garden of that King, where all the Trees, the fruits, the Hearbes and Plants, according to the order and greatness they have in a Garden, were most artificially framed in gold' (Florio's *Montaigne*, III. vi; *Temp. Clas.*, vol. v. p. 207). Montaigne likewise alludes to Atahuallpa's ransom (*Temp. Clas.*, p. 213), the whole essay being very much on the same subject as the present eclogue. In this passage, however, a more probable source is perhaps the account of the trees of gold in Sir Walter Ralegh's *Discovery of Guiana*.

42 *Divine Tobacco* This eclogue was evidently not written to please the new sovereign.

Cucheneild, i.e. Cochineal. The form is unknown to *O.E.D.*

47 *Cleopatras pearle* A reference to the well-known story of Cleopatra dissolving a pearl in a cup of wine.

Pithius (written *Pithins*) properly 'Pythius', a Lydian who gave Darius a golden plane and a golden vine (see Herodotus, vii. 27). [Fairfax perhaps took these allusions, as he did that to Nonius in the next line, from Pliny, *H.N.*, ix. 58, and xxxiii. 47.—McK.]

48 *Nonius* The manuscript reads 'Nomius', or rather 'Nomins', or 'Nonims' (the six minims are indistinguishable) no doubt through an error of the transcriber. Nonius was a Roman senator proscribed by M. Antonius on account of his possessing an opal of great value (see Pliny, *Nat. Hist.*, XXXVII. vi. 21, and C. W. King, *Antique Gems* (1860), p. 65).

49 *Darich* A Persian coin, both gold and silver, said to derive its name from Darius.

54 *Lunaches and Cacoas of Inde* [Two forms of currency. For the first read 'lumaches', shells used as money in Congo. See *A Report of the Kingdome of*

Congo ... Drawen out of the writinges and discourses of Odoardo Lopez a Portingall, by Philippo Pigafetta. Translated out of Italian by Abraham Hartwell ... 1597. Book I. ch. iv. p. 22. Reprinted in Purchas's *Pilgrimes.*

Cacoas were used in the empire of Montezuma. 'I haue heeretefore said that their currant money is of the fruits of certaine trees, like our almonds, which they call *Cachoas.*'—*The Historie of the West-Indies,* 1626 (?). (An enlarged edition of *The Decades of the Newe Worlde,* 1555.) Decade v. ch. iv. folio 195.—McK.]

60 *kn*[*e*]*w* The manuscript reads 'know'.

Finister, i.e. Cape Finisterre (*finis terrae*) the NW. point of Spain.

65 *hard* For 'heard'; a northern form still surviving in Scotland.

66 *Dorado* For 'El Dorado'.

Ingas Incas, princes of Peru. The spelling is that used by Ralegh.

68 [*cheare*] I am indebted to Dr. Jackson for this emendation. The manuscript reads 'theare', and this was certainly what the transcriber intended to write, for he has carefully inked it over when revising the poem. He evidently misread the original; *t* and *c* are often indistinguishable in the secretary hand.

69 *Ciprus house* There was no such 'wonder'. It may be a mistake for 'Cypris' house', i.e. some temple to Venus, but the only temples reckoned among the seven wonders were those of Artemis at Ephesus and Zeus at Olympia. [We should surely read 'Cyrus' house', which was indeed reckoned among the wonders of the world.—McK.]

earth[*s*] The scribe omitted the *s*.

70 *Æsops platter* Aesopus was a Roman actor who acquired great wealth. The expensive 'platter' was a dish of singing and talking birds (*cantu aliquo aut humano sermone vocales*) which cost 100,000 sestertii (see Pliny, *Nat. Hist.*, x. 72).

Celers barball deare. [This must be the fish 'mullus', bought by Asinius Celer at Rome during the reign of Caligula for eight thousand sesterces. See Pliny, *H.N.*, ix. 31. The names 'mullet' and 'barbell' are used by Cotgrave as almost synonymous.—McK.]

71 *Plotins fatall perfumes* ['Plotins' should certainly be 'Plotius'. L. Plautius Plancus, being proscribed by the Triumvirs, was betrayed in his place of concealment at Salernum by the smell of unguents. See Pliny, *H.N.*, xiii. 5. Hence his perfumes would be rightly termed 'fatall'. The form of the name is probably due to Pliny's words, 'L. Plotium, L. Planci . . . fratrem, proscriptum . . .' —McK.]

76 *Parian gulfe* Paria was an early name for that part of S. America now occupied by Venezuela. The Gulf of Paria is still used for the large gulf opposite Trinidad. Fairfax is alluding to the tradition that grew up after the wealth of S. America became known, that that was Solomon's Ophir. Ida maintains that far from a Spanish headland being the *finis terrae* of the ancients, they had crossed the Atlantic westward to America and southwards to the Cape of Good Hope.

Eudoxus Eudoxus of Cyzicus, who according to Strabo attempted to circumnavigate Africa. He lived about 130 B.C. (Strabo, ii. 98–100).

fand i.e. found. Like 'hard' (l. 65) it is a northern form and is now obsolete, being replaced in Scotland by 'fan'.

77 *The point Speranza* The Cape of Good Hope, named 'Cabo de boa esperança' by King John II of Portugal.

78 'Plinie affirmeth out of Cornelius Nepos (who wrote 57 yeeres before Christ) that there were certain Indians driven by tempest upon the coast of Germanie, which were presented by the King of Suevia unto Quintus Metellus Celer, the Proconsull of France.' See Sir H. Gilbert's 'Discourse to prove a passage by the North-west to Cathaia', chap. iv. § 2, printed in Hakluyt (1599–1600), vol. iii. p. 16. Pomponius Mela (iii. 5), quoting from the same lost work of Cornelius Nepos, makes the gift come from the King of the Baeti. See Pliny, *Hist. Nat.*, ii. 67. [I cannot fully explain this stanza, but there is almost certainly reference to the following incident related by Holinshed (from Matthew Paris) as having occurred in the year 1254 (Hen. III. 38). 'About this season (8th Feb. according to Mat. Par.) were certeine ships driuen by force of wind and weather into certeine hauens on the north coasts of England towards Barwike, which ships were of a verie strange forme and fashion, but mightie and strong. The men that were aboord the same ships were of some farre countrie, for their language was vnknowne, and not vnderstandable to any man that could be brought to talke with them. The fraught and balast of the ships was armour and weapon, as habergeons, helmets, speares, bowes, arrowes, crosbowes, and darts, with great store of vittels. There laie also without the hauens on the coast diuerse other ships of like forme, mold, and fashion. Those that were driuen into the hauens were staied for a time by the bailiffes of the ports. But finallie, when it could not be knowne what they were, nor from whence they came, they were licenced to depart without losse or harme in bodie or goods.'—McK.]

81 *King Fucusur* No such legend appears to be recorded. Certain 'Indians' stranded at Lübeck in the days of Barbarossa (1152–1190) are mentioned both by Aeneas Sylvius Piccolomini (afterwards Pius II) in his *Cosmographia* and by Gomara in his *Historia general de las Indias*; but King Fucusur seems equally unknown to chroniclers such as Holinshed, to Hakluyt, to Nordenskiöld, whose *Voyage of the Vega* contains an elaborate history of the North-East Passage, and even to Schiern, whose paper *Om en ethnologisk Gaade fra Oldtiden* in the *Aarböger for nordisk Oldkyndighed og Historie* for 1880 is specially devoted to similar legends. [Who King Fucusur was I cannot say, but would suggest that he *may* have been the person called by Marco Polo Facfur, king of Manzi (South China), who was driven from his kingdom and fled to the islands of the Ocean Sea in 1268 (Marco Polo, ed. Yule, ii. 108), though as will be noticed the dates do not correspond. Facfur is called by others Fanfur. Considerable search has failed to show that the connexion had previously been suggested. Fairfax indeed only puts it forward as a hypothesis.—McK.]

86 *Lucians realme of lights* Possibly the Islands of the Blest described in Book II of the *Vera Historia*, where there was no night, but a certain kind of light always filled the land resembling the twilight just before dawn.

87 The reading of the manuscript appears at first sight to be 'Front sr', which I supposed to be a blunder for 'Front on', until Mr. Oldham suggested

as an emendation 'Frontier'. Reference to the manuscript then proved that what I had taken for an *s* was really a badly formed *e*, the word being 'Fronter'. The verb 'to frontier' is not uncommon in writers of the time in the sense of to border upon or, as we say, to march with. Thus the actual form 'fronter' was used in 1586 by Ferne—'that part of the country a frontering the sea' (*Blaz. Gent.* ii. 32, quoted in *O.E.D.*). Opilio's argument runs: 'No, your instances prove nothing; Plato's Atlantis is a myth, a worthy neighbour of No-man's-land, Utopia, and Lucian's fanciful realms; moreover, if you are going to place Ophir on the east coast of America, you will have to suppose that Solomon's ships sailed from some Mediterranean port such as Joppa (i.e. Jaffa) and not from the traditional Red Sea port.'

90 *Ezion* i.e. Ezion-geber, 'on the shore of the Red Sea, in the land of Edom', 1 Kings ix. 26.

94 *whether* i.e. whither.

96 *bounder* a boundary; 'prob. a corruption of BOUNDURE (cf. *border*), taken as *bounder*, "that which bounds"' (*O.E.D.*).

102 *seaventh part* The reference here is to 2 Esdras vi. 50 ff. (English version, not in Vulgate or Douay), where the portion of the earth covered by water is given as one-seventh. Columbus, however, though relying largely on ecclesiastical arguments, based his views on the so-called Ptolemaic system, which, while exaggerating the proportion of land to sea, did not go so far as Esdras. Geography books inform us that the sea covers some three-quarters of the surface of the globe.

103 [*hee*] The reading has been altered and is uncertain.

106 *that* First written *what*.

108 *Americk* Amerigo Vespucci (Americus Vespucius), the famous Florentine explorer, who first realised that the land to which Columbus had shown the way, was not a part of Asia, but a New World. The name America was given to it in his honour by Martin Waldseemüller of St. Dié in 1507.

109 The first to discover the Pacific was Vasco Núñez de Balboa, who saw it from the summit of the Sierra de Quarequa in the Isthmus of Panama, on 25 September 1513.

110 Magellan, who entered the Pacific through the straits that still bear his name, on 27 November 1520.

111 *Ocean*[*s*] The scribe omitted the *s*. Hernando Cortés.

112 *Mutezumas* [apparently written *Mutezmnas*] i.e. Montezuma II, the last Aztec emperor of Mexico. Perhaps the spelling of the eclogue is to be preferred in this instance: Cortés in his letters writes the name 'Muteczuma'.

113 Francisco Pizarro, an illegitimate son of Gonzalo Pizarro and Francisca Gonzales, is said to have been deserted by his parents, and to have spent his youth as a swineherd. Atahuallpa had shown him and his Spaniards the greatest kindness and courtesy, in return for which he was treacherously seized, and after being made to pay an enormous ransom (cf. l. 38) was sentenced and executed on a fictitious charge of treason.

119 *line* The equator, a common expression then as now.

whot Hot, a form occasionally found in fifteenth and sixteenth centuries.

120 *showres* The word has been inserted afterwards in the same ink as the punctuation and the other corrections, and being in the same hand as the text, makes it possible to ascribe the corrections to the original scribe.

Zaire, the old name for the Congo.

121 Sir Francis Drake, whose voyage of circumnavigation lasted from 13 December 1577 till 26 September 1580.

126 *Noyes carrak* i.e. Noah's ark. Magellan was similarly compared to Noah.

127 *Amurath* The Sultan, more usually known as Morad III, whose reign, rendered remarkable by his weakness and cruelty, lasted from 1574 to 1595.

129 *Spaines Iennet* i.e. Philip II.

Iennet or 'genet', a breed of small Spanish horses.

133 *Tuffon* for typhon, whirlwind; Greek *τυφῶν* or *τυφώς*. Etymologically distinct from 'typhoon', a modern loanword from the Chinese *ta fung*, 'great wind'. Perhaps an allusion to the terrific storm, lasting fifty-two days, that Drake encountered after passing through the Straits of Magellan. In this storm the *Marigold* sank and the *Elizabeth* became separated from the flagship and returned home, leaving Drake to complete the voyage. The flagship, originally named the *Pelican*, was rechristened the *Golden Hind* on entering the Straits.

135 *Albion's shore* 'Nova Albion' was the name given by Drake to the country round San Francisco Bay, a name which continued in use for more than two centuries.

136 *Tarenat* Ternate no doubt is meant, where Drake arrived in November 1579. It is one of the Moluccas. [The form 'Tarenate' is used by Stow, *Annals*, 1615, p. 904^b, l. 20.—McK.]

Helens garden This can only refer to the Island of St. Helena—but Drake did not call there.

138 *Orpheus* He was one of the Argonauts who accompanied Jason and recorded his deeds.

139 *fellow rivall* Sir Martin Frobisher (1535?–1594) who in 1576 made a voyage in search of the North-West Passage. He returned with some 'savages' (Esquemos) and some ore, which, contrary to the opinion of the London goldsmiths, was declared auriferous by the Italian alchemist Agnello. The voyages of 1577 and 1578 were for the express purpose of collecting this ore, which, however, proved rubbish. Subsequently Frobisher commanded the *Triumph* at the time of the Armada.

140 *Meta* i.e. Meta Incognita, the name given by Queen Elizabeth to what was at the time supposed to be the shores of a northern strait leading to the Pacific, similar to Magellan's in the south, but which later proved to be only a bay in Baffin Land.

143 *Marcasite* The term was formerly applied to the black pyrite, which was what Frobisher collected. It is now used for the 'white iron pyrites', or iron disulphide.

147 *Moluccas Iles* The Moluccas or Spice Islands are a small group in the Malay Archipelago. They were of great value, and consequently a bone of contention, as the only home of two of the most valued spices, the clove and the nutmeg.

148 John Davys or Davis (1550?–1605) who made three voyages to the North-West in 1585, 1586, and 1587.

151 Sir Humphrey Gilbert (1539?–1583) who planted in Newfoundland the first English colony in North America, and returning home in the *Squirrel*, a boat of only ten tons, perished off the Azores on 9 September 1583.

153 *delight* [Sir Humphrey Gilbert's largest vessel, the *Delight*, was wrecked on 29 August 1583, between Cape Breton Island and Newfoundland. Sir Humphrey himself perished a week later in the *Squirrel*, a vessel of only ten tons burden.—McK.]

154 *frigot* i.e. frigate; the form is uncommon, but is occasionally found in the sixteenth and seventeenth centuries.

157 The earliest expedition was that of 1553 and consisted of three ships under Sir Hugh Willoughby commissioned to search for the North-East Passage to Cathay and India by a 'Mystery and Company of Merchant Adventurers for the discovery of regions . . . unknown' founded in 1552. In this expedition the crews of two ships were frozen to death at Arzina (or Warsina), an inlet 'near to Kegor, where Norwegian Lapland marches with Russian' (*D.N.B.*). The third ship succeeded in reaching the White Sea and the commander, Richard Chancelor, was allowed to proceed to Moscow, where he obtained letters patent from the emperor. Armed with these, he returned to England in 1554 and the following year the 'Company of Merchant Adventurers' became the 'Muscovy Company'. A letter from George Killingworth, their first agent, 'touching their entertainment in their second voyage', dated 27 November 1555, was printed by Hakluyt together with the Company's charters from Queen Mary and John Vasilivich, the emperor of Russia, dated the same year.

158 *Arzinas* The manuscript reads 'Arzimas', no doubt through an error of the transcriber.

160 *vaigats* or Waigatz, an island in the Arctic Ocean off the north coast of Russia, between it and Novaya Zemlya. The reference is to the voyage of Arthur Pet and Charles Jackman in 1580, in which Jackman lost his life.

Petzora, or Petchora, a river in the north of Russia, flowing into the Arctic Ocean.

162 *U[n]happy* The word is miswritten 'Uphappy' in the manuscript.

[P]akin The manuscript reads 'Takin', presumably by mistake for 'Pakin', i.e. Pekin. Bacon in his *New Atlantis* uses the form 'Paguin'.

3. Theatrical Repertories of 1662[1]

I do not think the following lists of plays acted in some of the London and provincial houses shortly after the Restoration have ever been printed in full, though one occasionally finds references to them. They occur in the (British Museum) MS. Sloane 1900, described as 'Sir Edw. Browne's Memorandum Book, 1662', where they occupy fols. 63^{b}–60^{b} in the reversed volume. It is uncertain by whom they were written, and it is evident that the entries were not all made at one time. I take it that they represent the plays which the writer himself saw, and that the sums of money entered are what he paid for seats for himself and friends. The repertories at this date probably consisted very largely of old plays, since the newer generation of playwrights had not yet had much time in which to stock the stage. At the New Theatre we have the *Surprisal* and the *Committee* by Sir Robert Howard and *Cornelia* by Sir W. Bartley. This last was never printed, but is said to have been acted in Gibbon's Tennis Court, Vere Street, Clare Market, on 1 June 1662. At Covent Garden we have the *Surprisal* again; at Cambridge the *Rump*, a topical play by John Tatham; and at the Middlesex house *Love à la Mode*, a piece supposed to have been written by T. Southland. But the most up-to-date, naturally enough, was Sir William Davenant's own house (entered as distinct from the New Theatre) at which the Duke of York's men performed. Here we find record of three pieces by Sir William himself, the *Siege of Rhodes*, the *Playhouse to Let*, and *Law against Lovers*, a *rifacimento* of *Measure for Measure* and *Much Ado*; also the *Villain* by T. Porter and the *Slighted Maid* and the *Stepmother* by Sir Robert Stapylton. All the other pieces recorded date from before the Civil Wars. *Love in a Maze* is Shirley's *Changes*; the *Girl worth Gold* is Heywood's *Fair Maid of the West*; the *Little Thief* is Beaumont and Fletcher's *Night Walker*, the *Tamer Tamed* their *Woman's Prize*; the *Moor of Venice* is, of course, *Othello*. That many of the old plays continued to be popular is natural enough;

[1] [1906, July. *The Gentleman's Magazine*, ccci. 69.—1958.]

Beaumont and Fletcher, Jonson, Shakespeare, Shirley, always held Restoration audiences. Massinger and Middleton were not unpopular, and even Brome one would expect to find represented. But the occurrence of some of the plays is certainly surprising. Several seem to have lived on in the provinces. *Greene's Tu Quoque* by John Cooke was first published in 1614. *Ignoramus* was a Latin comedy of about the same date, but no doubt the version here mentioned was the translation by Robert Codrington printed in 1662. *George a Greene or the Pinner of Wakefield* dates back to the sixteenth century, but had perhaps been revised at some subsequent date. *Mulleasses the Turk*, a tragedy by John Mason, had appeared in 1610. The *Merry Milkmaids*, written by one I.C., was originally printed in 1620, but a new edition had appeared in 1661. It is strange that any of these old pieces should still have held the stage. Nor should we quite have expected to find Chapman's *Bussy D'Ambois*, although it was several times reprinted, or Ford's powerful but crude tragedy. Marlowe's *Dr. Faustus*, of course, was 'Printed with New Additions as it is now Acted' in 1663. It is interesting to find the old spelling 'Fostus' surviving. I imagine that the explanation of there being no sum entered opposite the *Virgin Martyr* (another play one would hardly have expected to hold the stage, but which was reprinted as late as 1661) is that 'Mr. Weld'[1] stood the entertainment.[2]

MS. Sloane 1900

fol. 63b At the New Theatre in Lincolnes Inne fields.

Beggars bush	1 – 0	Kings players
Alchymist	2 – 6	K. P.
Renegado	2 – 6	

[1] [Professor Arthur Brown reads this name as 'Wild'.—J.C.M.]

[2] [It matters little, but a few of the sums are uncertain. That paid for *Ignoramus* at Norwich looks like '7–6', but the horizontal stroke may be accidental, and that for *Mulleasses* looks like '9–0', an original '0' having been altered to '1'. The sum paid for *The Elder Brother* at the Cockpit appears to be '15–0', and so I originally printed it, but I now think that what I took for a '1' is more likely an accidental mark. The sum for *The Villain* at Davenant's house was first written '2–6' and later altered. The sum for *The Surprisal* at Covent Garden again looks like '7–6'. The note opposite *Doctor Faustus* at the Cockpit is obscure: I originally printed the first word as 'Quens (?)', but doubt now whether this is possible: the word is perhaps 'Licens:' i.e. licensed.—1958.] [Allardyce Nicoll, *History of English Drama, 1660–1900*, i (1952), 310 n. 4, writes that the word is 'undoubtedly' 'Licens:'—J.C.M.]

Ioviall Crew		1 – 6
Widdow		1 – 0
Humorous Lievtenant		1 – 0
Love in amaze		1 – 0
Bartholomew faire		1 – 6
Surprisall		1 – 6
Maids tragedy		3 – 0
Cornelia		1 – 6
Virgin Martir	Mr Weld	0 – 0
The Fox		2 – 6
The Committee		1 – 6
Imposture		1 – 6

fol. 63a At the Kings Armes Norwich.

Tu quoque	1 – 6
Ignoramus	1 – 6
Pinner of Wakefield	1 – 6
Muliasses	1 – 0
Girle worth Gold	1 – 6
Tis pity shee is a whore	1 – 6
The little thiefe	1 – 6
A new way to pay old debts	1 – 6
The fair quarrell	2 – 6

fol. 62b At the Cock Pit in Drewry Lane.

	s d	
Silent woman	2 – 0	K. P.
Elder Brother	5 – 0	
D'Ambois	2 – 0	
More of Venice	1 – 0	
Chances	2 – 0	
Tamer Tamed	2 – 0	
Wit without money	2 – 0	
The opportunity	2 – 0	
Dr Fostus	1 – 0	Licens: Players

fol. 62a At Salisbury or Dorset Court.

Maid in the Mill	2 – 6
Spanish curate	1 – 0
Bondman	5 – 0

fol. 61b At Sr Will Davenants theatre in Lincolnes Inne fields.

2 part of the Siege of Rhodes	1 – 6
Gratefull Servant	1 – 6
Villaine	3 – 0
Hamlet Prince of Denmarke	1 – 6
The Slighted maid	2 – 6
Law against lovers	2 – 6
The Stepmother	2 – 6
Playhouse to bee let	2 – 6

fol. 61a At the King Playhouse in Covent Garden.

Rollo Duke of Normandy	1 – 6
The Surprisal	1 – 6
Loyal Subiect	2 – 6

fol. 60b At the Cardinalls cap in Cambridge.

Philaster	1 – 6
Changeling	1 – 6
Rump	1 – 0
Wit without mony	1 – 0

Red Bull.

Merry Milkmaids	1 – 6
a Mad world my masters	1 – 6

Middlesex house. Love all a mode.

These lists are immediately followed in the manuscript by an itinerary in the same handwriting dated 1662. It may not be too daring, perhaps, to hazard the suggestion that the houses at Norwich and Cambridge were not regular theatres, but some inn or hostelry. The wandering troupes very likely still haunted, if not the inn-yard as of old, at least some hall or room which could be cleared for performance.

4. The Bakings of Betsy[1]

THERE is, among the Lansdowne manuscripts at the British Museum, a folio volume of no great bulk, which, if we believe the story it tells, is perhaps the most pitiful of all monuments to the vanity of antiquarian endeavour. For it embraces, or at least purports to embrace, the entire remains of that extensive collection of the unprinted drama of the earlier seventeenth century brought together, or supposed to have been brought together, about a hundred years later by John Warburton, Somerset Herald, prefaced by a long list of the treasures alleged to have perished. The story of that disaster is one of the best known of literary anecdotes: how the zealous antiquary laboriously gathered together this unique collection of pieces by Shakespeare and others; how he handed it over for safe custody to his cook, who made use of the precious leaves for some obscure process connected with her trade,[2] and how the owner made no further inquiry on the subject till he had devoured all but three and a half out of a total of some fifty or sixty plays. The story has been told over and over again with every kind of facetious adornment, till no history of literature is complete without it, and our national biography has to take serious account of the eccentric herald and his cook Elizabeth B.

I wish someone would tell me who invented Elizabeth B. I write of her in this perhaps unduly familiar manner because I have to confess that I do not know her name. The earliest authority on the subject that I have been able to discover is a certain Cuthbert Clutterbuck, who, in a letter dated Kennaquhair, 1 April 1822, tells how the 'Author of

[1] [1911, July. *The Library*, ii. 225–59.]

[2] [The use of waste paper to put under pies in the baking appears, however, to have been customary. C. R. Baskervill, writing in *Modern Philology* (May 1915, xiii. 52) under the heading 'A Forerunner of Warburton's Cook', quotes from *Naps upon Parnassus*, 1658, the account given by the unknown editor of how he rescued these poems from destruction by the keeper of an ale-house, where the author in his cups had inadvertently left them: 'Much adoe I had to recover Them out of the good Womans hands, who left the bottoms of her Pies (that baking) in very great jeopardy, for want of them: yet at last I did get them, as many as you see there are of them.']

Waverley' found the privacy of his bedchamber invaded by a distressed female, who introduced herself as 'the spirit of . . . that unhappy Elizabeth or Betty Barnes, long cook-maid to Mr. Warburton, the painful collector, but ah! the too careless custodian, of the largest collection of ancient plays ever known'. The curious reader will find this letter printed at the beginning of Scott's *Fortunes of Nigel*, but I fear he will find no further indication of the source of the story thus circumstantially given. The only other credible witness I have been able to discover is the *Dictionary of National Biography*, and there in the article on John Warburton,[1] the name of his servant is given, not as Betty Barnes, but as Betsy Baker. Unfortunately again no authority is quoted, and I have diligently searched all the general references given at the end of the article without being able to obtain any light on the subject whatever. It only remains to point out that if the name Betsy Baker is correct, this play-burning cook was called by what has been almost a generic name from the days of Langland to our own, and chose her parents with curiously prophetic insight.

Apart from this matter of the name the original source of the story seems to be Warburton's own memorandum appended to the list of the lost plays. Warburton was, perhaps not without cause, one of the most unpopular of men, and any joke at his expense was sure to be readily believed and widely circulated. One must be prepared for exaggerations: and, indeed, in 1891 a contributor to *Notes and Queries* (Ser. 7, xii. 15), signing himself A. Hall, went so far as to ridicule the whole story. That any statement of the Somerset Herald should command implicit belief can, it is true, hardly be maintained; but in the present instance the information he gives is so little to his credit as an antiquary that there is at least a strong presumption that he is telling the truth.

It will be well to give Warburton's list exactly as it stands, more particularly as none of the copies at present available are quite satisfactory. It was first printed, at a time when the manuscript was still in the possession of the first Marquis of Lansdowne, by Reed in his 'Variorum' Shakespeare of 1803 (ii. 371–2). The whole of his account, however, is very careless

[1] [By W. P. Courtney.]

and several titles are altogether omitted from the list. A much more accurate copy was contributed over the initials of J. Haslewood to Brydges's *Censura Literaria* in 1807 (v. 273). After censuring both Reed and 'the second part of the Catalogue of the Lansdowne MSS.' for errors, he adds some interesting observations of his own. 'The writing', he says of the list, 'is in a very different hand from his [Warburton's], and did not the "many years collecting" imply their being obtained at various times, I should have supposed had been an index to them, made sixty years or more before his memorandum was written. The orthography is certainly of an earlier period than the strange diction of Warburton, which is not that of old spelling, but of false spelling.' He further appends extracts from the catalogue of Warburton's sale in November 1759,[1] including, besides the Lansdowne volume, *The Tyrant, a Tragedy.* 4to, which appears in the list, and *Demetrius and Marina, or the Imperial Imposter and Unhappy Heroine, a Tragedy.* Fol., which does not.

The Lansdowne catalogue mentioned by Haslewood is the sale catalogue of April 1807,[2] and when he speaks of 'the Lansdowne MSS. No. 849', he is referring to the number of the lot. This has caused some confusion, since of course by 'the second part of the Catalogue of the Lansdowne MSS.' one now understands the second volume of the Catalogue made after the collection had found a home in the British Museum, and published in 1819, in which the manuscript is numbered 807. The sale catalogue prints Warburton's list entire, and far more accurately than Reed. Haslewood indeed corrects some further errors (though in the particular point which he cites as evidence of inaccuracy in the Catalogue he is wrong) but he follows both his predecessors in the serious mistake of printing Warburton's memorandum at the end of the whole list, instead of at the end of the first page only.

In September 1815 Frederick Thornhill reprinted Reed's list in the *Gentleman's Magazine* (lxxxv. 217–22 and 424) with comments of his own and corrections from a private

[1] I have been unable to find a copy of this.

[2] The sale, of course, never took place, the nation acquiring the collection *en bloc* for £4,925. I presume that the sale was first postponed pending negotiations, for the money was not paid till the October following.

transcript with which he had been favoured; but though this correspondent of the great Silvanus Urban had 'been informed' that the original document was now safely lodged at the British Museum, he apparently did not see the desirability of consulting it himself, and so robbed his communication of much of the value it might otherwise have possessed. In 1819 appeared the second part of the big British Museum Catalogue of Lansdowne Manuscripts, in which the list is printed with commendable though not quite consistent care, but in which Warburton's note is again misplaced. The list given by Fleay in his *Life of Shakespeare* (1888) is less accurate than a comparison of accessible copies might have made it even without recourse to the original.[1]

The volume, as I have said, is now numbered 807 of the Lansdowne Manuscripts. It is a thin foolscap folio bound in russia. The end papers are modern. An original flyleaf is preserved, but not numbered; then comes a leaf with the Warburton and Shelburne[2] book-plates on the verso, then Warburton's list, mounted and reckoned as folio 1. The plays follow: *The Queen of Corsica* occupying folios 2–28, *The Second Maiden's Tragedy* folios 29–56, *The Bugbears* folios 57–77. At the end is an imperfect play in quarto occupying folios 78–88. It is a fragment of *The Benefice* by R. Wild containing III. iv. to the end. That completes the collection as now extant. Here is the description of it as it is alleged to have once existed:

Manuscripts [*recto*

The Hon^{r}. Loves by Will. Rowley[3]
Henry ye 1st. by Will. Shakespear & Rob. Davenport

1 Gifford, in the introduction to his edition of *Massinger* in 1805, recounts the usual tale and ends by giving the titles of the three survivors as mentioned by Reed. He adds: 'These, it is said, are now in the library of the marquis of Lansdowne, where they will, probably, remain in safety till moths, or damps, or fires mingle their "forgotten dust" with that of their late companions.' For this piece of impertinence he was not undeservedly rebuked by his reviewers, to whom he retorted in the preface to his second edition in 1813 with more spirit than discretion. Nevertheless in that edition the offending passage still stands, despite the fact that the manuscripts in question had in the interval passed into public custody.

2 [William Petty succeeded as Baron Wycombe and Earl of Shelburne in 1761 and was created Marquis of Lansdowne in 1784.]

3 The second word has been variously read as 'Hon^{r}.', i.e. honourable, or 'Hon^{d}.', i.e. honoured. The superior letter resembles a 'd', but a comparison with other cases shows that 'r' is certainly intended.

The fair favourit
Minervas Sacrifise Phill. Masenger
Duke Humphery Will. Shakespear
Citty Shuffler
Sr. Jon. Sucklings Workes
Nothing Imposeble to love T.C. Sr Rob. le Green
The forc'd Lady A T. Phill. Massinger
The Governer T. Sr. Corñ. Fermido
The Lovers of Loodgate
The Flying Voice by Ra. Wood
The Mayden Holaday by Chriš. Marlowe
The Fatal Love
The Puritan Maid ye. Modest Wife & ye. Wanton Widow
by Tho. Middleton
The London Marchat[1] [*sic*] A Com̃. by Jon[2] Ford.
The King of Swedland
Love hath found out his Eyes by Tho. Jorden
Antonio & Vallia by Phill. Massinger
The Dutches of Fernandina T. Hen. Glapthorn
Jocondo & Astolfo C. Thõ. Decker
St. Geõ. for England by Will. Smithe
The Parliamt of Love by Wm. Rowley
The Widows Prise C. Wm Sampson
The Inconstant Lady Wm. [*sic*] Wilson
The Womans Plott Phill. Massinger
The [Marchants Sarifice [*sic*]] Crafty Marchat [*sic*] C Shack.
Marmio⟨n[3]
An Interlude by Ra. Wood worth Nothing
The Tyrant A Tragedy by Phill. Massenger
[The Yorkshire Gentlewoman & her Son T.][4]
The None Such A C. Wm. Rowley
The Royal Combate A C. by Jon. Forde.
Philenzo & Hipolito A C. by Phill. Massenger
Beauty in A Trance Mr.[5] Jon. Forde.
The Judge A C. by Phill. Massenger.
A good beginning may have A good end by Jon. Ford
Fast and Welcome C.[6] by Phill. Massinger

[1] [The second 'a' may have been altered from 'n'.]
[2] [The superior letter is doubtful.]
[3] The title first written has been crossed out: the name is crowded in and the end is no longer visible.
[4] This entry is crossed out.
[5] [Greg read 'A C.': Professor Arthur Brown writes that this is certainly wrong, but that 'Mr.' is not certain.—J.C.M.]
[6] The 'C.', standing for Comedy, is interlined.

Belive as yo^u. list C. by Phill. Massinger
His^t. of Jobe by Rob. Green
The Vestall A Tragedy by H. Glapthorn
The Noble Tryall. T. H. Glapthorn

After I had been many years Collecting
these MSS Playes, through my own
carlesness [*sic*] and the Ignorace [*sic*] of my S⟨er[1]
in whose hands I had lodgd them they
was unluckely burnd or put under
⟨Pye bottoms, excepting ye three which followes.
J. W.⟩

Manuscripts [*verso*

Yorkshire Gentlewoman and her Son T
The Hon^r. of Women A. C. by P. Massinger
Alexias or ye chast Glallant [*sic*] T. P Massinger
The Vestal A Tragedy H. Glapthorn[2]
The Noble choise T.C. P. Massinger
A Mask R. Govell
2t. p^t. Maidens Trag̃. Geo. Chapman
The Great Man T.
The Spanish Purchas C.
The Queen of Corsica T. by F. Jaques
The Trag^d. of Jobe Good
The Nobleman T.C. Cyrill Turñuer
A Play by Will Shakespear
Bugbear C. Jo^n. Geffrey[3]
Orpheus C.
Tis Good Sleeping in A Whole Skin W. Wager
Farry [*sic*] Queen[4]

There was a time when I entertained serious doubts respecting the genuineness of a material part of Warburton's alleged memorandum, for I could not find it in the manuscript itself. The volume in question has been repaired at some comparatively recent day, and the list of plays mounted on a

[1] The catalogue gives the letters 'Ser', but only the first is now clearly legible. The edge is frayed, but there can never have been room for the full word.

[2] The 'H.' has been altered.

[3] [A 'J' appears to have been altered to 'G'.]

[4] The second 'r' of 'Farry' has been altered, but there does not seem any doubt of the reading.

guard. Now if the slip on which the list of supposed manuscripts is written be carefully examined, it will be observed that the end of the memorandum as printed above is wanting, and there are indications that suggest, what is indeed the case, that the slip can never have contained more writing than now appears. It was, therefore, very difficult to account for the entry in the catalogue. One day, however, I observed that at some period the slip had been fastened down to the original flyleaf by means of wafers. This fact, which I might indeed have learned from the Catalogue or from Haslewood, gave the clue to the mystery. For on a closer inspection I discovered that Warburton's writing had run off the slip on to the leaf to which it was attached, and there the end of the memorandum, though very faint, may still be traced. A careless binder had almost destroyed the evidence of the nefarious Betsy's crime.

So far then the document bears examination. I should add that after comparing several letters of Warburton's written between 1750 and 1760 preserved in the British Museum, I see no reason to question the authenticity of the note, nor, in spite of obvious differences in the writing, to deny that the list itself may likewise be in his handwriting. To the point raised by Haslewood concerning the archaic spelling of the list there is an obvious reply—namely that the titles are of course copies; and I would call attention to one small point in favour of their having been written by Warburton. For in the note he has accidentally left out the second 'n' in 'Ignorance', while in the list we twice find 'Marchat' for 'Marchant', There remain, however, plenty of difficulties in connexion with this list. It is written on the two sides of a long narrow slip of paper. At the head of each page is the word 'Manuscripts', but the list fills neither page. On the recto, however, the titles came down to within a few inches of the foot, leaving only a small space in which the note has been subsequently inserted. On the verso they fill less than half the page. The presence of the note has been taken to imply that the list must have been written out from memory. This may, I think, be at once dismissed as improbable. A man so little careful of his manuscripts as to leave them long unsought in the care of his servant, could never have sat down and written out a list of fifty or sixty titles and authors from memory. Moreover, the note is written in a different style and ink from the list, even supposing the hand to be the same. We shall, therefore, be justified in assuming that the list was among the papers rescued, and that it consequently dates from many years before the note. It may, in that case, have been compiled from the actual manuscripts enumerated, though there is nothing to prove that it was. It should be noticed that it is not quite clear whether the memorandum is intended to apply to the plays on both sides of the paper, or only to the list at the foot of which it stands. Nor does it appear what the relation of the two lists is. Is that on the verso a mere continuation of the other? If so, why was the verso used when there was still room on the recto? Moreover, *The Vestal* appears in both lists, and so does *The Yorkshire Gentlewoman*, though this was struck out again on the recto. *The History* and *The Tragedy of Job* are also very likely the same. Are these mere oversights? After it had lain hid for many years did Warburton himself remember accurately the significance of the list? That he owned some of the plays in it we know, that others perished seems likely, but was there really the wholesale destruction that the collector in his disappointment would have us believe? This is a question that probably can never be answered for certain, but it may be that a closer examination will at least suggest a possible solution. The investigation will take us rather far afield, but I hope that it may repay us for our wanderings by the light incidentally thrown on the bibliography of the seventeenth-century drama in general.

The dislocation of our knowledge of the English book trade that occurs about the year 1640 is eloquent of the debt we owe to Professor Arber for his transcript of the Stationers' Register, but is not in itself a good thing, and it is with keen anticipation that many students look forward to the now promised continuation of that great work.[1] Our present ignorance is rather specially unfortunate in the case of the drama, since not only do the entries of individual plays continue, but there also occur from time to time entries of whole batches of plays, mostly old ones, evidently made with a view to extensive publishing ventures consequent upon the

[1] [1640–1708, edited by G. E. Briscoe Eyre, 3 vols. 1913–14.]

closing of the theatres during the Civil War and under the Commonwealth. These entries, though neglected by recent critics, were utilized by some of the earlier biographers of the English stage, and many references will be found in the *Biographia Dramatica* of 1812. From these scattered notes Fleay reconstructed the entries of 1653 and 1660 in his *Life of Shakespeare* (1880), and these lists, though inaccurate, have up to the present been by far the best at the disposal of students. They possess additional value through being printed in parallel columns with that of Warburton's alleged collection.

I propose in this place to print in full some of the chief play-entries from the later volumes of the Stationers' Register. Of these the above-mentioned entries of 1653 and 1660 form perhaps the most important, for the reason that they were largely inoperative, and therefore preserve for us the titles of many plays which are not now discoverable. The real nature of the entry belonging to 1646 does not seem to have been previously recorded, and I have on my conscience a statement to the effect that the publishers of the Beaumont and Fletcher folio of the following year dispensed with the formality of entry. This is now seen to be incorrect. Fleay, however, only mentions four plays under this date, and it was a remark by the anonymous editor of Wilson's *Inconstant Lady* printed in 1814, to the effect that the entry contained forty-eight plays, that first suggested further search. By a lucky chance my friend Mr. Plomer happened at the time to be consulting the later Registers for other purposes, and he kindly undertook to transcribe for me the entries now printed here.[1]

A

Liber E p. 53.

4°. Sept'. [1646] . . .

Mr Robinson. & Mr Mozeley

Entred for their Copies vnder the hands of mr Langley & mr whitaker warden these Seu'all Tragedies & Comedies here vnder mencõned (vizt.) [(Saluo iure cuiuscumqꝫ)][2]

[1] In the 1646 entry there are certain additions in a different hand. These are distinguished by an asterisk prefixed. [I have since had the opportunity of correcting the entries myself and have made a few trifling corrections.]

[2] These words in brackets are deleted in the original.

xxiiij^s^.

*Mad Lover. Wild goose chase. Litle french Lawyer Loyall Subiect Spanish Curate. Custome of ye Country. Double Marriage wife for a Month. Island Princes Pilgrime. *The Lawes of Candy. Womans prize or the Tamer tam'd Knights of Malta The Captaine The Noble Enemie or the humerous Leiftenant. *The Woemen pleased. Bonduca or Boadicia [Mounsieur Perrollis][1] *mistaken Chaunces. *The Sea Voyage Maid of the Mill. Queene of Corinth. Coxecombe. Noble gentleman. Beggars Bush Honest mans fortune Martiall Maid. The Emperor Valentinian. The Prophetesse. The Lovers pilgrimage. The Lovers progresse.	by m^r^ Beamont & m^r^ Flesher.

B

Loue & honor. Distresses Fair Favourite	by S^r^ W^m^. Davenant.	By S^r^. W^m^. Davenant
Newes from Plymouth		

Country Captaine Varieties	by my Lord of Newcastle.	p. 54. Mr Robinson & Mr Mozeley.

[1] These words in brackets are deleted in the original.

Doubtfull heire
Imposture.
Brothers
Cardinall
The Sisters
} by M[r] Shirley

Maior of Quinborough.
The passionate Louer } *1st. & 2[d]. parts.
Spartan Ladies } by M[r] Carlile
Switzer
The Corporal } by M[r] Wilson.

---

*The princes. by M[r] Killegrew
*The fatall friendship. by m[r] Burroughes.

A few notes may serve to make the bearing of these entries clear. The first thirty plays will at once be recognized as constituting the entry for the folio of 'Comedies and Tragedies written by Francis Beaumont and Iohn Fletcher Gentlemen. Never printed before, and now published by the Authours Originall Copies' printed for Robinson and Moseley in 1647. That volume, however, if we include in it *The Wild Goose Chase*, published as a supplement in 1652 and standing second in the above list, contained thirty-six pieces, none of which had been previously entered or printed. The omission of six plays does not appear to have been discovered at the time, but, as will be seen from a subsequent list (C), the missing titles were duly entered to the same stationers on 29 June 1660, perhaps in anticipation of the new and enlarged edition, which, however, did not appear till 1679, and was then published by Martyn, Herringman and Marriot.[1] The alternative title of *The Humorous Lieutenant* looks as though there had been more than one manuscript, for no trace of the 'Noble Enemy' is found in the folio text. I am unable to guess what 'Mounsieur Perrollis' can be.

Of Davenant's plays, *Love and Honour* was printed in 1649, while the other three first appeared in the folio published by Herringman in 1673. The five plays by Shirley were published, together with *The Court Secret*, in the *Six New Plays* of 1653. *The Mayor of Queenborough* first appeared,

[1] [An assignment of Robinson's share in the Beaumont and Fletcher plays was made to Martyn and Herringman on 20 January 1672/3.]

published by Herringman, in 1661, with a title-page ascribing it to Middleton. The two parts of Carlell's *Passionate Lovers* were printed in 1655, but *The Spartan Ladies* is not known, though it was advertised by Moseley along with *The Discrete Lover* and *Osman* among 'Books I do purpose to Print very speedtly [*sic*]' in a catalogue found at the end of some copies of Middleton's *Two New Plays* of 1657.[1] Wilson's *Switzer* is extant in manuscript (BM. MS. Add. 36759), and has been edited by Professor Feuillerat; while of *The Corporal* unfortunately nothing but a list of dramatis personae remains (Bodl. MS. Rawl. Poet. 9). *The Princess* by Thomas Killigrew was included in the collected folio of his plays published by Herringman in 1664. Neither of *The Fatal Friendship* nor of Mr. Burroughes does anything further appear to be known. A tragedy bearing the same title was later written by Catherine Trotter and printed in 1698.[2]

B

September. y^{e}. 9th: 1653. . . . Liber E p. 285. m^{r}. Mosely

Entred also for his Copies the severall Playes following.

xx[j]^{s}. vj^{d}.[3]

The Widdowes Prize. by M^{r}. W^{m}. Samson
Witt in Madnesse } Rich: Brome.
The Louesick Maid, or the honour of Young Ladies. by } Rich: Brome.

[1] As pointed out by Baker (*Companion to the Playhouse*, 1764). The only copy that I have seen which has the catalogue is that at Trinity College, Cambridge. The catalogue is in two quires, a^{8} b^{2}. Later the two leaves of b were cancelled, and a full sheet, B^{8}, appended to the remaining copies of a. I have a copy of the catalogue in this form at the end of Massinger's *Three New Plays* of 1655. In this among the 'Books lately Printed' appear Carlell's *Discrete Lover* and *Osmond*. *The Spartan Ladies* has vanished, but its place is taken by *The Deserving Favourite*. This was an old play printed as early as 1629, of which Moseley issued an edition in 1659. I suspect that *The Spartan Ladies* was the title borne by another manuscript of this play. The name would be appropriate enough to the ladies who resolve to die with their lover and brother, while there are points which would even make Sparta not unsuitable as the scene of the action. [This suggestion is rejected by G. E. Bentley (*The Jacobean and Caroline Stage*, i. 117[1]), who points out that Sir Humphrey Mildmay describes 'the Spartan Lady' as 'a Newe play' when he saw it on 1 May 1634.]

[2] [This may, of course, have been based on the earlier piece.]

[3] It should be noticed that the sum has been altered from 21*s*. 6*d*. to 20*s*. 6*d*. This brings it right for forty-one plays. 'Henry I & Henry II' is counted as one piece.

The Discreet Louer, or the Foole
would bee a Fauourite. by } Lod: Carlel.
Osman, the Great Turke, or
The Noble seruant. both by
The Countrey man
The Siege. by W^{m}: Dauenant.
The Iew of Venice, by Tho: Decker.
The Woman's mistaken. by. Drew, & Dauenport.
The History of Cardenio, by M^{r}. Fletcher. & Shakespeare.
The Gouernour. by S^{r}. Cornelius Formido.
The Kings Mistresse
Beauty in a Trance. by M^{r}. In^{o}. Ford.
More Dissemblers besides Women.
A right Woman, or Women
beware of Women. } M^{r}. Tho:
No Witt, no helpe like a Woman Middleton.
The Puritan Maid, modest Wife
& Wanton Widdow. by.

p. 286. more to M^{r}. Mosely

The Noble Choice, or the Orato^{r}
The Wandring Louers, or ye Painter
The Italian Night peece, or
The Vnfortunate, Piety
Alexius the Chast Gallant or.
The Bashfull Louer. } by Phill:
A Very Woman, or ye Womans Plot. Massinger.
The Iudge, or Beleiue, as yo^{u} list
The Prisoner, or ye Faire Anchoress
The Citie honest man, or ye Guardian.
The Spanish ViceRoy, or ye Hono^{r}: of Women.
Minerva's Sacrifice, or ye Forc'd Lady
The Maid's Tragedie. 2^{d}. part
The Crafty Merchant. or the
Souldred Citizen } by Shakerly Marmion.
The Politique Bankrupt, or
which is y^{e}. Best Girle.
The Foole without Booke. } by W^{m}:
A Knaue in Print, or One for another Rowley.
The Polititian, by Iames Shirley.
The spãnish Duke of Lerma.
The Duke of Guize } by Henry Shirley.
The Dumbe Bawde &
Giraldo, ye Constant Lover
The merry Deuill of Edmonton. by W^{m}: Shakespeare.

Henry y^{e}. first, & Hen: ye 2^{d}. by Shakespeare, & Dauenport.
The Nobleman, or Great man. by Cyrill Tourneur.
The Inconstant Lady by M^{r}. Arth. Wilson.

C

29 Iune 1660.

Liber F p. 193. Mr Hum: Robinson & Mr Hum: Moseley.

Entred for their Copies (vnder the hand of Mr Thrale Warden) the severall Plays following. vizt

The false one.
The Nice Valour or the passionate Madman.
Witt at severall Weapons.
The Faire Maid of the Inne.
A Maske of the Gentlemen of Graies Inne and the Inner Temple at ye Marriage of the Prince and Princesse Palatine of the Rhene.
Foure Plays or morall Representations in one.
all Six Copies written by Fra: Beamont & Iohn Fletcher.
} iij s

D

The 29th of Iune 1660.

Liber F p. 196. Mr Hum: Moseley.

Entred for his Copies (vnder the hand of Mr Thrale Warden) the severall Plays following. That is to say

The Faithfull Friend. a Comedy
A right Woman a Comedy.
} by Francis Beamont & Iohn Fletcher
The History of Madon King of Brittain by F: Beamont.
The Womans Plott. a Comedy.
The Prisoners. a TragiComedy.
The Honour of Women. a Comedy.
Believe as you list. a Tragedy.
The forced Lady. a Tragedy.
The Tyrant. a Tragedy.
The Bashfull Lovers.
The Gardian
Philenzo & Hypollita. a TragiComedy
Antonio & Vallia. a Comedy.
Fast & Welcome. a Comedy.
} by Philip Massinger.
The History of King Stephen.
Duke Humphrey. a Tragedy.
Iphis & Iantha, Or a marriage without a man. a Comedy.
} by Will: Shakespeare.

The Vestall. a Tragedy.
The noble Triall. a TragiComedy. } by Hen: Glapthorne.
The Dutchesse of Fernandina a Tragedy.

The Sodered Citizen. a Comedy by Shakerley Marmion.

The Fatall Love. a French Tragedy. } by Geo: Chapman.
A Tragedy of a Yorkshire Gentlewoman and her Sonne

The Royall Combate. a Comedy.
An ill beginning has a good end, & a bad begining may have a good end. a Comedy } by Iohn Forde.
The London Merchant. a Comedy.

[This page is bracketed and summed 'xiij s.']

p. 197. The 29th of Iune 1660.

Mr Hum: Moseley. Entred for his Copies (vnder ye hand of Mr Thrale Warden) the severall Plays following. That is to say

The None such. a Comedy.
The booke of ye 4. hon^{ble}. Loves. a Comedy. } by Wiłłm Rowley.
The Parliament of Love.

Gustavus King of Swethland. } by Tho: Decker.
The Tale of Ioconda and Astolso. a Comedy.

The fatall Brothers. a Tragedy. } by Robt. Davenport
The Politick Queen. Or murther wil out.

Nothing impossible to Love. a TragiComedy by Sr Robt. Le Greece

The Prodigall Scholar. a Comedy. by Tho: Randall.

The Christmas Ordinary. a Comedy by Trinity Coł. Oxford

Love hath found his Eyes. by Thomas Iordan.

[This page is bracketed and summed 'v^{s}. vj^{d}.']

It will, of course, be noticed that there are a number of titles common to the lists of 1653 and 1660, and we cannot do better than, with the full copies of Moseley's entries and Warburton's catalogue before us, to reconstruct the parallel table given by Fleay. The entry of the six plays by Beaumont and Fletcher (C) has already been discussed, and need not occupy us further.

Nine plays are common to the two entries (B, D) and of these six occur in Warburton's list:

1653		1660		Warburton	
1. Alexis the Chaste Gallant, or the Bashful Lover.	Massinger.	The Bashful Lover.	Massinger.	Alexias or the Chaste Gallant.	Massinger.
2. A Very Woman, or the Woman's Plot.	Massinger.	The Woman's Plot. C.	Massinger.	The Woman's Plot.	Massinger.
3. The Judge, or Believe as you list.	Massinger.	Believe as you list. T.	Massinger.	Believe as you list. C. The Judge. C.	Massinger. Massinger.
4. The Spanish Viceroy, or the Honour of Women.	Massinger.	The Honour of Women. C.	Massinger.	The Honour of Women. C.	Massinger.
5. Minerva's Sacrifice, or the Forced Lady.	Massinger.	The Forced Lady. T.	Massinger.	Minerva's Sacrifice. The Forced Lady. T.	Massinger. Massinger.
6. The Crafty Merchant, or the Soldered Citizen.	Marmion.	The Sodered Citizen. C.	Marmion.	The Crafty Merchant.	Marmion.
7. A right Woman, or Women beware Women.	Middleton.	A right Woman. C.	B. & F.		
8. The Prisoner, or the Fair Anchoress.	Massinger.	The Prisoners. T-C.	Massinger.		
9. The City Honest Man, or the Guardian.	Massinger.	The Guardian.	Massinger.		

Nine titles are common to the 1653 entry (B) and Warburton's list:

	1653		Warburton	
10.	The Widow's Prize.	Samson.	The Widow's Prize. C.	Sampson.
11.	The Governor.	Formido.	The Governor. T.	Formido.
12.	Beauty in a Trance.	Ford.	Beauty in a Trance.	Ford.
13.	The Puritan Maid, Modest Wife and Wanton Widow.	Middleton.	The Puritan Maid, the Modest Wife, and the Wanton Widow.	Middleton.
14.	The Noble Choice, or the Orator.	Massinger.	The Noble Choice. T-C.	Massinger.
15.	The Maid's Tragedy, 2nd Part.		Second Part Maiden's Tragedy.	Chapman.
16.	Henry I and Henry II.	Shakespeare & Davenport.	Henry I.	Shakespeare & Davenport.
17.	The Inconstant Lady.	A. Wilson.	The Inconstant Lady.	W. Wilson.
18.	The Nobleman, or Great Man.	Tourneur.	The Nobleman. T-C. The Great Man. T.	Tourneur.

Twenty titles are common to the 1660 entry (D) and Warburton's list:

	1660		Warburton	
19.	The Tyrant. T.	Massinger.	The Tyrant. T.	Massinger.
20.	Philenzo and Hypollita. T-C.	Massinger.	Philenzo and Hippolito. C.	Massinger.
21.	Antonio and Vallia. C.	Massinger.	Antonio and Vallia.	Massinger.
22.	Fast and Welcome. C.	Massinger.	Fast and Welcome. C.	Massinger.
23.	Duke Humphrey. T.	Shakespeare.	Duke Humphrey. T.	Shakespeare.
24.	The Vestal. T.	Glapthorne.	The Vestal. T.	Glapthorne.
25.	The Noble Trial. T-C.	Glapthorne.	The Noble Trial. T.	Glapthorne.
26.	The Duchess of Fernandina. T.	Glapthorne.	The Duchess of Fernandina. T.	Glapthorne.
27.	The Fatal Love. T.	Chapman.	The Fatal Love.	
28.	A Yorkshire Gentlewoman & her Son. T.	Chapman.	Yorkshire Gentlewoman & her Son. (T.)	

29. The Royal Combat. C.	Ford.	The Royal Combat. C.	Ford.
30. An ill beginning has a good end, & a bad beginning may have a good end. C.	Ford.	A good beginning may have a good end.	Ford.
31. The London Merchant. C.	Ford.	The London Merchant. C.	Ford.
32. The Nonesuch. C.	Rowley.	The Nonesuch. C.	Rowley.
33. The Four Honourable Loves. C.	Rowley.	The Honourable Loves.	Rowley.
34. The Parliament of Love.	Rowley.	The Parliament of Love.	Rowley.
35. Gustavus, King of Swethland.	Dekker.	The King of Swedland.	
36. Joconda & Astolso. C.	Dekker.	Jocondo & Astolfo. C.	Dekker.
37. Nothing impossible to Love. T-C.	Le Greece.	Nothing impossible to Love. T-C.	le Green.
38. Love hath found his Eyes.	Jordan.	Love hath found out his Eyes.	Jordan.

Twenty-three titles occur in the 1653 entry (B) only:

39. Wit in Madness.	Brome.
40. Love-sick Maid, or the honour of Young Ladies.	Brome.
41. The Discreet Lover, or the Fool would be a Favourite.	Carlell.
42. Osman the Great Turk, or the Noble Servant.	Carlell.
43. The Country Man.	
44. The Siege.	Davenant.
45. The Jew of Venice.	Dekker.
46. The Woman's Mistaken.	Drue & Davenport.
47. The History of Cardenio.	Fletcher & Shakespeare.
48. The King's Mistress.	
49. More Dissemblers besides Women.	Middleton.
50. No Wit, no Help like a Woman.	Middleton.
51. The Wandering Lovers, or the Painter.	Massinger.
52. The Italian Night Piece, or the Unfortunate Piety.	Massinger.
53. The Politic Bankrupt, or Which is the best Girl.	
54. The Fool without Book.	Rowley.
55. A Knave in Print, or One for Another.	Rowley.
56. The Politian.	J. Shirley.
57. The Spanish Duke of Lerma.	H. Shirley.
58. The Duke of Guise.	H. Shirley.
59. The Dumb Bawd.	H. Shirley.
60. Giraldo, the Constant Lover.	H. Shirley.
61. The Merry Devil of Edmonton.	Shakespeare.

Eight titles occur in the 1660 entry (D) only:

62. The Faithful Friend. C.	Beaumont & Fletcher.
63. The History of Madan, King of Britain.	Beaumont.
64. The History of King Stephen.	Shakespeare.
65. Iphis & Iantha, or a Marriage without a Man.	Shakespeare.
66. The Fatal Brothers. T.	Davenport.
67. The Politic Queen, or Murder will out.	Davenport.
68. The Prodigal Scholar. C.	Randall.
69. The Christmas Ordinary. C.	Trin. Coll Oxon.

Lastly, there are eighteen items which appear only in Warburton's list:

70. The Bugbears. C.	J. Geffrey.
71. A mask.	R. Govell.
72. The History of Job.	R. Green.
73. Tragedy of Job.	
74. The Queen of Corsica. T.	F. Jacques.
75. The Maiden's Holiday.	Marlowe.
76. A play.	Shakespeare.
77. St. George for England.	Wil. Smith.
78. Works.	Suckling.
79. 'Tis good sleeping in a whole skin.	W. Wager.
80. An interlude.	R. Wood.
81. The Flying Voice.	R. Wood.
82. The City Shuffler.	
83. The Fair Favourite.	
84. The Fairy Queen.	
85. The Lovers of Ludgate.	
86. Orpheus. C.	
87. The Spanish Purchase.	

Many of these pieces are not otherwise known: this is the case with nos. 12, 13, 22–29, 32, 35–38, 43, 46, 48, 53–55, 57–60, 63–67, 77, 79, 80–81, 85, 87.[1] Concerning the rest brief notes may be desirable. I have mainly followed the references given by Fleay.

1. *The Bashful Lover* was licensed by Herbert 9 May 1636, and printed in 1655 together with nos. 2 and 9. *Alexius, or the Chaste Lover*, was licensed by Herbert 25 September 1639. There is extant in the Bodleian (MS. Douce 171, fol. 48^b) a fragment of an English comedy on the loves of Alice and Alexis. It is described as the author's draft, extending as far as III. i, but with an argument of the whole, and as belonging to the early seventeenth century. Alexis was, of course, a very common name in fiction.

2. *A Very Woman* was licensed 6 June 1634, and printed as above. *The Woman's Plot* was acted at court in 1621 [Inner Temple MS 515. no. 7, printed by J. T. Murray, *English Dramatic Companies*, ii. 192].

3. *The Judge* was licensed 6 June 1627. *Believe as you List* was licensed 7 May 1631, apparently as reformed from an earlier piece to which licence had on political grounds been refused on 11 January, and the manuscript is preserved (BM. Egerton 2828).

4. *The Honour of Women* was licensed 6 May 1628. *The Spanish Viceroy* was admitted by the King's players, 20 December 1624, to have been performed by them without licence ['Variorum' Shakespeare, 1821, iii. 209].

5. *Minerva's Sacrifice* was licensed 3 November 1629.

6. *The Crafty Merchant, or Come to my Country House*, by William Bonen, was licensed 12 September 1623.

7. Printed with Middleton's name in 1657 together with no. 49.

8. *The Fair Anchoress of Pausilippo* was licensed 26 January 1640. *The Prisoners* was properly the title of a play by T. Killigrew printed in 1664.

9. *The Guardian* was licensed 31 October 1633, and printed with nos. 1 and 2 as above.

10. [*The Widow's Prize* was licensed by Herbert on 25 January 1625 on condition that his reformations of abusive matter were observed: Chalmers, *Supplemental Apology*, pp. 219–20.]

11. Extant in the British Museum (MS. Add. 10419). The manuscript, dated 1656, was purchased at the Heber sale, and bears the inscription, 'This Play formerly belonged to John Warburton, Somerset Herald'.

14. *The Orator* was licensed 10 January 1635.

[1] [But G. E. Bentley, *The Jacobean and Caroline Stage*, adds a little on 12, 38 and 59.—J.C.M.]

15. One of the plays preserved from Warburton's collection. It bears Buc's licence dated 31 October 1611.

16. *The History of Henry the First* was licensed as by 'Damport', 10 April 1624.

17. By Arthur Wilson: preserved in a manuscript in the Bodleian (Rawl. Poet. 9A).[1]

18. *The Nobleman*, by Tourneur, was entered in the Stationers' Register 15 February 1612, and acted at court 23 February following, and again in 1612–13.

19. A manuscript in quarto of *The Tyrant* was in Warburton's sale in November 1759.

20. A 'Philipo and Hippolito' was a new play of the Admiral's men 9 July 1594, and a 'Julio and Hyppolita' is in the German collection of 1620. A manuscript is said by Collier (*Henslowe*, p. xxxi) to be among the Conway papers.

21. 'Antony and Valia' was a play of the Admiral's men in 1595. A manuscript (of the second half of the seventeenth century) with Antonio of Ragusa as a character is in the Bodleian (Rawl. Poet. 93), but the chief characters are said to be Octavio and Alessandra.

30. *A bad Beginning Makes a good Ending* was acted at court by the King's men in 1612–13.

31. This is the name of the play disturbed by the Citizen in *The Knight of the Burning Pestle*.

33. 'Die 4 bestendigen Liebhabers' was a play of English origin current in Germany (Mecklenburg) *c.* 1660 (Herz p. 68).

34. *The Parliament of Love* was licensed as Massinger's, 3 November 1624: the manuscript (imperfect) is preserved (Dyce MS. 39).

39. *Wit in a Madness* had been previously entered, together with *The Sparagus Garden* and *The Antipodes*, 19 March 1640.

40. Licensed 9 February 1629 and acted at court as *The Lovesick Maid* 6 April following.

41–42. Printed together in 1657.

44. Printed in the folio of 1673.

45. There is extant in manuscript a German play, *Josephus, Jude von Venedig*, which may be in some way related.

47. 'Cardenna' was acted at court 8 June 1613, 'Cardenno' in 1612–13. [For the attribution see Chambers, *Shakespeare*, ii. 539–42.]

49. Printed in 1657 with no. 7.

50. Printed in 1657.

51. *The Wandring Lovers* was licensed as Fletcher's, 6 December 1623.

[1] [And in two other manuscripts: see R. C. Bald, *Library*, 4 Ser. xviii (1937–8), 287–313.—J.C.M.]

52. *The Unfortunate Piety* was licensed 13 June 1631.

56. Printed in 1655.

61. *The Merry Devil of Edmonton* was entered 22 October 1607 and printed four times before Moseley's entry, and even the edition of 1655 was not issued by him but by W. Gilbertson.

62. *The Faithful Friends* is preserved in manuscript (Dyce MS. 10).

68. Presumably Thomas Randolph is the author intended. [The piece may possibly be *The Drinking Academy*, preserved in a manuscript in the Huntington Library, and attributed on internal evidence to Randolph.]

69. *The Christmas Ordinary* was printed, as by 'W. R. Master of Arts', in 1682. ['W. R.' was William Richards, Fellow of Trinity College, Oxford; the piece was not acted in college, but doubtless at Helmdon, Northants, where Richards was rector.]

70. *The Bugbears* is one of the rescued manuscripts. At the end is the inscription, 'Iohannus [*sic*] Jeffere scribebat hoc', but he may have been only the scribe, or one of them, for the manuscript is in several hands.

71. There seems to be no other mention of this writer.[1]

72–73. These are presumably the same. The play was not entered in 1594 as stated by Stephen Jones (*Biographia Dramatica*, 1812) so that Warburton remains our sole authority. Therefore 'Rob. Green' is very likely the same as 'S^{r}. Rob. le Green', i.e. Le Grys (cf. no. 37). There was a piece called *Job's Afflictions*, written by R. Radcliffe in the first half of the sixteenth century.

74. One of the rescued plays.

75. *The Maiden's Holiday* was entered as by Marlowe and Day, 8 April 1654.

76. Most likely one of the plays mentioned in the other lists: either 47, 64, or 65.

78. Suckling's *Fragmenta Aurea* had been several times printed, but other matter was left in manuscript till *The Last Remains* of 1659. After that there was more than one complete edition.

82. *The City Shuffler* was acted at Salisbury Court and temporarily stayed by Herbert in October 1633 ('Variorum' Shakespeare, 1821, iii. 172).

83. By Davenant, licensed 17 November 1638, and printed in the folio of 1673.

[1] [J. Q. Adams in his edition of *The Dramatic Records of Sir Henry Herbert* (1917), p. 30, n. 3, suggested that this was identical with *The Masque*, licensed by Herbert on 3 November 1624, and was the work of Richard Gunnell, author of *The Hungarian Lion* (1623). See G. E. Bentley, *The Jacobean and Caroline Stage*, iv. 518–19.—J.C.M.]

84. [An opera called *The Fairy Queen*, based on *A Midsummer Night's Dream*, was performed at the Queen's Theatre and printed in 1692.]

86. A fragment is said by Reed (*Biographia Dramatica*, 1782) to be in the British Museum, but I have been unable to find it.

Now anyone who studies the above lists with care will find ample food for reflection. For my own part I feel it extremely difficult to make up my mind whether Moseley was a knave or Warburton a liar. Each is intrinsically probable, yet there seems hardly evidence enough to substantiate both charges. Could we call general evidence of character, it might not indeed be hard to do so, but we had better stick to the case before us.

It is chiefly the alternative titles in Moseley's 1653 entry that excite suspicion against him, for in several cases there is independent evidence which suggests that the alternative titles really belonged to different plays. The implication, of course, would be that Moseley was trying to smuggle through two plays for a single fee. In three cases Warburton enters, as belonging to separate plays, titles given by Moseley as alternative. This, as we shall see when we come to cross-examine Warburton, is not very serious, but there is better evidence to follow. The first four plays of 1653 (i.e. nos. 1–4) bear double titles, and in each case each title appeared separately in Herbert's Office Book. Moreover, in the case of several plays still extant there is nothing to suggest the alternative title at all. *The Very Woman* contains no woman's plot; *Believe as you List* contains no judge; *The Guardian* deals with the court and not the city. *The Great Man* seems a foolish second-title for *The Nobleman*.[1] It might be suggested that Moseley meant each as an alternative entry, leaving himself the option of publishing either play. This, however, seems very unlikely, and there is no evidence that the Stationers' Company would ever have sanctioned such a proceeding.

[1] [*The Soddered Citizen*, now fortunately recovered, has among its characters 'A wealthy Citizen' whose name 'Vndermyne' might certainly suggest the title *The Crafty Merchant*. But *The Crafty Merchant* is ascribed on Herbert's excellent authority to William Bonen, whereas *The Soddered Citizen* is almost certainly by the literary highwayman John Clavell, and the extant manuscript has probably been corrected in his hand.]

Moreover *Henry I and Henry II* is clearly entered as one play, though such a title seems incredible. In no less than nine cases plays entered under double titles in 1653 were re-entered under one only in 1660. This almost forces us to the belief that not nine but eighteen plays were really involved, whether we suppose that Moseley discovered his mistake and rectified it of his own accord, or that the Company discovered it and forced him to do so.

There is something to be said in Moseley's favour. The fraud supposed would have been a dangerous one to practise, for had the Company discovered it, it is unlikely that they would have been satisfied with mere re-entry. Moreover in two cases (1 and 9) the title re-entered in 1660 is that under which Moseley had himself published the play in the interval. This looks like mere blundering. A solution is perhaps suggested by the case of *The Spanish Viceroy* (no. 4), for there is nothing to prevent our supposing that the play acted without licence in 1624 was subsequently revised and licensed under another title in 1628. However disinclined we may be to follow Fleay in all his hazardous identifications, it remains probable that some revision and re-writing did take place in the Massinger plays, and it is conceivable that this may account in part at least for the difficulties noticed. Even in the case of *Believe as you List* (no. 3) it may be submitted that the political events upon which the plot was based were not recent, that a play presumably founded upon them is recorded by Henslowe as early as 1601, and that it is not inconceivable that Herbert licensed in 1627 a play substantially the same as another which he refused in January 1631, when the peace with Spain was a tender sapling of a few months' growth. It is possible, therefore, that divergent versions of certain plays existed under different titles. If then it be supposed that the manuscripts in Moseley's hands bore both titles, or that he was aware of the double nature of the plays he hoped to secure, and also that the duplicate entries of 1660 may be explained as mere oversights, it may not be impossible to account for the puzzles of the entries in the Registers. That grave difficulties remain, in view of the apparent irreconcilability of the alleged duplicate titles of extant pieces, must, however, be admitted: I content myself with suggesting possibilities in a case in which I have admittedly no satisfactory theory to offer.

Should it have chanced that Moseley acted honestly in the matter, and that his entries are correct, it follows, of course, that the authenticity of Warburton's list must go by the board. For the close agreement between that list and the entries has been generally and necessarily held to indicate that Moseley's collection must have formed the bulk of Warburton's, and probably came into his hands *en bloc*. If then Moseley's alternative titles are genuine, how comes it that in three cases Warburton has made separate plays of them? We are at once confronted with the question: Is Warburton's list what it purports to be, a genuine catalogue of a collection of manuscript plays, or is it a fabrication from various sources? And it becomes at this point important to know whether Warburton was acquainted with the Stationers' Registers or not. There is definite evidence that he was. For one of his plays which has survived is headed the 'The Second Maydens Tragedy'. The heading is late, and has been borrowed from Buc's licence of 31 October 1611, at the end: 'This second Maydens tragedy (for it hath no name inscribed) may wth the reformations bee acted publikely.' This must be the play entered as 'The Maid's Tragedie. 2^{d}. part', in 1653, and there surely can be no doubt that Warburton had this entry as well as the manuscript before him when he entered the play in his own list as '2^{d}. p^{t}. Maidens Trag̃.'. Warburton thus knew a source which would account for perhaps three-quarters of his own list. We must therefore scrutinize his evidence somewhat closer. If this complete collection came originally from Moseley, it could hardly be, as he represents it, the result of many years' collecting; it must have come *en bloc*. There is, however, the possibility that he added to it from other sources, so that this point should not be pressed. The entries of 1653 and 1660 account for thirty-eight out of a total of fifty-six items in the list, so that only eighteen remain. Two are entered under other dates. One, 'A Play by Will Shakespear', is also probably one of those entered. One is known from Herbert's licences. Suckling's Works imply no special knowledge. The two 'Jobs' are most likely identical. There remain twelve which we can only account for as representing actual manuscripts. Two of these manuscripts actually exist in the Lansdowne volume. As regards the ten others, it must be borne in mind that Warburton may have had a better knowledge of the Registers from 1640 onwards than we as yet can boast, and the same may even possibly apply to the licences of the Masters of the Revels.[1] We are therefore by no means bound to assume that they all represent actual manuscripts. And there are certain suspicious points about the list. Of the twelve plays just mentioned, nine occur in the shorter list on the verso of the leaf, and these nine include the two out of three plays rescued complete which are not otherwise recorded: moreover, the last few entries on this side are somewhat irregular, and many have been added later. Of the last ten titles, the only one previously recorded is Tourneur's *Nobleman*, whereas in the list on the recto of the leaf there are only nine items not in Moseley's entries, and of these four are known from other sources. The fragmentary play of Wild's rescued is not entered in the list at all; nor is *Demetrius and Marina*, which appeared at Warburton's sale; but these may have been acquired later. On the other hand, *The Tyrant*, which is represented as having been destroyed, was also in the sale, and is presumably still extant somewhere. So again with Formido's *Governor*, which survives in the British Museum (MS. Add. 10419). It may be a different manuscript, of course, but it bears a note, possibly in Heber's own hand-writing, stating that it is the same. Again Massinger's *Believe as you List*, entered both in 1653 and 1660, is in Warburton's list of victims, yet the autograph manuscript is now safe in the British Museum (Egerton 2828). Here again we may suppose two manuscripts, but it will be well to remember that Moseley's collection must have consisted mostly of official playhouse copies bearing the Master's licence, that we know that this was the case with one early play preserved—*The Second Maiden's Tragedy*—and that it is just the official licensed copy of *Believe as you List* that has survived. There is also a slight difficulty that arises if we suppose Moseley's alternative titles to be genuine, and Warburton to

[1] [In fact the full text of the later Registers now available throws no further light on Warburton's list. The suggestion that he knew Herbert's Office Book may, I think, be rejected.]

have inherited his collection. For some of the plays had been printed, and if Moseley had sent a play to the press, it is most unlikely that he would have ever seen the copy again, still more unlikely that he would have replaced it among his unprinted stock. There is one point on which Warburton clearly had some authority independent of the Register. In the 1653 list we find 'Alexius the Chast Gallant', in Warburton's 'Alexias or ye chast Glallant'. Now Herbert's licence has 'Lover' for 'Gallant'. If Herbert is correct, we have another instance in which Warburton followed the Register and not the manuscript. If Herbert was right! We cannot tell; but as Moseley added a second title, *The Bashful Lover*, he would have had a motive for altering 'Lover' to 'Gallant', while Herbert would have no reason for a change.

This, I think, concludes the evidence I have been able to extract from the lists. That it amounts to a disproof of Warburton's extraordinary claim I do not pretend. But taken all together, I think that it does throw considerable doubt upon the story. My own idea of what happened is somewhat as follows. Warburton in the course of his antiquarian researches came across a few manuscript plays and grew interested in the subject. He collected notes, probably from various sources, but chiefly from Moseley's entries, and compiled a list of the titles of such pieces as he thought it might be possible to recover in addition to those of the plays he already possessed.[1] Some he actually did succeed in finding and a few further manuscripts coming into his hands were added at the end of the list. The collection and list were then laid aside, a few manuscripts finding their way among the rest of the collector's archaeological litter, the bulk, however, within reach of the parsimonious fingers of Betsy the baker of pies. Long afterwards her master discovered his loss, and no longer in the least remembering either the extent of his collection or the nature of his list, added in a fit of natural vexation the famous memorandum. If this be so, we have undoubtedly to lament the loss of a few pieces, perhaps of considerable interest, but not the dramatic holocaust that has made famous the name of the 'pie-eating Somerset Herald'.

[1] [We should have to assume that the titles of the two classes got mixed in compiling the list, and it is not altogether easy to see how this occurred.]

5. What is Bibliography?[1]

IT is a commonplace among those who have written on the subject, that bibliography has grown from being an art into being a science, and if we are content not to press the terms too closely, the remark may be accepted as indicating a certain truth. There was a time not so long ago when the typical occupation of bibliographers was the writing of elegant essays on individual points of archaeological or artistic interest, more or less closely, and more or less accidentally, connected with books. It is no reproach to a generation of book-lovers, many of whom are fortunately still active in our midst, that this should have been so. If bibliography is to-day a science by which we co-ordinate facts and trace the operation of constant causes, if we are gradually evolving a rigorous method for the investigation and interpretation of fresh evidence, if we are able, within the sphere of our work, in any way adequately to reconstruct the past out of the indications of the present, it is in a large measure due to the patient accumulation and recording of facts achieved by those bibliographical pioneers. As has happened over and over again in the history of science, these workers pursued the subject for its own interest and their individual amusement, and in doing so evolved a powerful instrument of investigation, of the practical applications of which they never dreamed. All this we have inherited, and our debt is great. Nevertheless the difference is not merely one of knowledge, but of outlook as well. Reading through that remarkable series of papers in which our founders sought to determine the true position of bibliography in its various branches, I cannot help thinking that a sense of dissatisfaction with the artistic method, a perception, perhaps dim as yet, of the scientific developments of which the subject was capable, present in the minds of those pioneers, is among the chief causes of our being assembled here this evening. And although in this paper I am not concerned with individual

[1] [1914. A paper read before the Bibliographical Society, 19 February 1912. Printed in the *Transactions* of the Society (1914), xii. 39–53.]

bibliographers or books, I cannot refrain from remarking on the prominence accorded to one name, that of Henry Bradshaw. He is mentioned by Mr. Wheatley as the one man in whose hands bibliography had become an exact science, and I was more particularly struck by the instance of his work cited in support of this opinion, namely, his investigation into the order of the *Canterbury Tales*. I fancy that this is hardly the point which most critics would have chosen as an instance of bibliographical research, but it will be the chief object of my paper to-night to argue that the question is nevertheless of the very essence of the subject.

But if bibliography is a science, it can hardly as yet be called a satisfactory science. I am inclined to think that it suffers from its name, and I half regret that 'bibliology' is past praying for. When 'bibliography' does not mean the writing of books, it must mean the description of books. This limitation of sense seems to me unfortunate, for though the description of books may form an important branch of bibliography it is certainly not synonymous with it. It will perhaps be contended that bibliography has been, probably that it must be, a descriptive science. In a sense this is true. In a sense every science is descriptive. But in so far as a science is merely descriptive it is sterile. You may dissect and you may describe, but until your anatomy becomes comparative you will never arrive at the principle of evolution. You may name and classify the colours of your sweet peas and produce nothing but a florist's catalogue; it is only when you begin grouping them according to their genetic origin that you will arrive at Mendel's formula. It is the same everywhere. Facts are observed and catalogued by the systematizers, and then suddenly, as if by chance, an idea is born that introduces order and logic into what was chaos, and we are in possession of a guiding principle, of an instrument of thought and investigation, that may transform the whole of our relation to knowledge or alter the face of the physical globe. Perhaps no discoveries that we make in bibliography are likely to have such far-reaching results as these, but they are quite capable of revolutionizing the subject itself and the methods by which it is pursued. That is why any tendency to confine the scope of bibliography within descriptive limits seems to me deplorable. And its name encourages—I believe has encouraged—the belief that bibliography consists in the compilation of bibliographies. You might as well say that geography means map-making, or bacteriology the breeding of disease. Moreover, the objections to restraining the scope of bibliography are not merely the theoretical ones I have mentioned. They are of serious practical importance as well. For the wider applications of bibliography, of critical bibliography, are no mere playthings. They are essential to the advance of knowledge. Therefore they will be made—they are being made. All that is done by restricting the official cognizance, so to speak, of bibliographers, is to exclude from the field of these new developments the only men who by training are qualified to carry them to a successful issue.

Before I pass to a consideration of the meaning and methods of bibliography a word must be said regarding its scope. The view has been, and I believe still is, maintained by many able practitioners that bibliography is properly confined to the study of printed books. Manuscripts, they hold, belong to another department. Now, I do not wish to waste words over a matter of verbal definition. But when I read the accounts of bibliographical descriptions given by these same writers I observe that a large part of their method is just as applicable to manuscripts as to printed books. And as it happens to be in the methods of the science that I am at present interested, I regard the distinction between written and printed books as irrelevant. What I am concerned with is a system of investigation and a method of description, and if, with minor modifications, it can be made to apply to clay cylinders and rolls of papyrus as well as to codices of vellum or paper, so much the better. It is the method itself, not the object to which that method is applied, that gives unity to a science. You may state the laws of motion in a form more suitable to the movements of the planets, as did Newton, or in one more suitable to those of an electron, as is the modern tendency; but that does not affect the principles of rational dynamics. Thus it may be called bibliography, or it may be called by any other name you please, but what I want understood is that the characteristics of the science about which I am speaking cut far deeper than the distinction between writing and printing and apply to the transmission of all symbolic representation of speech or other ordered sound or even of logical thought. This will, I hope, obviate useless discussion. But I confess for my part that the view which would confine the term 'bibliography' to the study of printed books seems to me a very foolish one. When I read in a German cyclopaedia that there is one science of *Bücherkunde* and another of *Handschriftskunde*, I begin to wonder whether there is one science of geometry and another of selenometry. And if we are to pay any regard to names at all, it seems perverse to confine to printed books a science of which the name was in use, and the principal methods of which had been invented, centuries before printed books existed. We shall next be told that Richard de Bury was no bibliophile!

Now let us consider for a moment what bibliography really is. Before we can describe or classify any book we must be able to find out about it. Descriptive, or as I shall call it, systematic bibliography presupposes an acquaintance with the elements of the science. I call them elements in Euclid's sense. They are elementary not because they are easy but because they are fundamental: they are the prerequisites of all further study. But I do not think these elements have as a whole received the attention they deserve. Too often they are brought in incidentally in the course of instructions for describing books, and as though they had no significance in themselves and no application outside the pages of a catalogue. Take a single instance. The elaborate and highly important rules for ascertaining the format of a book are commonly given as though their sole object was to guide the describer in his choice of what particular symbol to put at the end of a title. If that were so, I confess it would seem to me simpler to toss up. I believe that many people would be puzzled to say exactly wherein lies the importance of putting such symbols at all. It is regarded as part of the game, just as in arithmetic children are taught to play certain tricks with a row of figures and extract something called a square root, though as to how the result is obtained, or what it really means, nothing is said. In reality, of course, the rules of format have nothing to do with description. We require them to discover how a sheet of paper has been folded. And we require to know how the sheet has been folded, not in order to put a particular symbol in a catalogue, but because it is an important bibliographical fact. Its importance, by the way, only partly arises from its being a salient factor in the history of the book. It is mainly due to considerations lying beyond the field of what is usually called bibliography. For it is only a knowledge of the format that enables us to say in the case of a printed book (for a manuscript has no true format) that if variants occur on such and such a page they may be expected also on such and such other pages. Thus a matter which is really of very small importance to the cataloguer, becomes of great significance to the textual critic —though, indeed, he is only just beginning to wake up to the fact. So again with the much-debated question of U and V. This is almost always discussed in the form of rules for transcription. Yet what rules a cataloguer follows is really a matter of mere academic interest. What is important is the practice of the old printers and the gradual advance of philological awareness that it reveals. My complaint is that, all through, bibliography is studied and taught—so far as it is taught—too much from the point of view of the cataloguer or descriptive bibliographer, not enough for the interest of the principles involved, and that as a consequence those wider applications of the subject that lie beyond the cataloguer's horizon suffer. The printed book or the manuscript itself is an object of intense interest, and the booklover must wish to find out everything he can about it, irrespective of any actual description. And it is the elements of bibliography that supply him with a method and a set of logical tools as it were for the prosecution of his search. Any description he may find it convenient to make is merely a means of communicating to others, or of recording for his own subsequent information, the results at which he has arrived, and, however useful, is of purely secondary concern.

Thus the elements of bibliography are what every bibliographer will have more or less to master. He will probably not cover the whole field, for it is a large one, but he will require an intimate knowledge of certain parts and some familiarity with the paths that lead from one part to another, if he is to do any good in his subject. The expert in typography is unlikely to be also a skilled palaeographer, but he will require some knowledge of the handwritings upon which various types are based. Both alike will need some familiarity with the history of paper-making, though they will probably leave the closer investigation of water-marks to a specialist. What is important is that every serious bibliographer should have some general plan of the subject in his mind that will, so to speak, enable him to find his way about, and to understand the advances made in other fields and the possible light they may throw upon his own immediate studies.

Those who have followed me so far will not be surprised that I call the field a wide one. It includes the study of book-making and of the manufacture of the materials of which books are made, it includes a knowledge of the conditions of transcription and reproduction, of the methods of printing and binding, of the practices of publication and bookselling —it includes the whole of typography and the whole of palaeography. Naturally enough the subject tends to shade off into others that are not bibliographical. Bookbinding is certainly a province of bibliography, yet it almost merges into a fine art, as do even more clearly book-illustration and illumination. Bibliography has to take cognizance of these subjects, but it can never make them altogether its own. Book-plates have a purely superficial connexion with books: their study is but a bastard branch of the subject. Another useful limitation lies in this, that bibliography only concerns itself with processes that leave their mark on the character of the finished book. Printing it is very largely concerned with, but it does not study the mechanism of the modern steam press. Pens it is certainly interested in, but hardly in their growth or manufacture. It attends to the preparation of vellum, though indifferent to the breeding of calves.

That typography is a branch of bibliography will probably be allowed by all except the adherents of the narrowest 'descriptive' school. It is, indeed, the most progressive branch of all, the one in which bibliographers have won their greatest successes of recent years, and if it shows any signs of severing itself from the parent stock, it is in the direction of becoming a graft upon biology. But it has not done so yet. It has only illustrated, like almost every other science, the value of the comparative method and the general significance of the evolutionary idea. Far less unanimity will attend the inclusion of palaeography. Yet, obviously, this stands in exactly the same relation to manuscripts as typography does to printed books. If, therefore, bibliography is to take cognizance of manuscripts we must necessarily include palaeography in its field. To my mind a bibliography which should exclude either manuscripts or printed books from its purview would be robbed of more than half its interest and significance.

Descriptive, or to use the wider term, systematic bibliography, the classification of individual books according to some guiding principle, seems to be regarded by most writers on the subject as bibliography *par excellence*. It is this part of my subject therefore that has been the most exposed to the onslaughts of previous writers, and I shall not say very much about it. A few remarks will, however, be relevant, and may conceivably be useful. It is sometimes said that a bibliographer should distinguish the relative merit and importance of the books enumerated, and that the ideal bibliographer will read and judge as well as record and describe. The ideal bibliographer will not waste his time over what is no concern of his. His subject is books, not universal knowledge; and the relevant sense of the word 'book' is that in which the Ellesmere *Canterbury Tales* is a book, not that in which Chaucer's *Book of the Duchess* is a book. To the bibliographer the literary contents of a book is irrelevant. This does not mean that special bibliographies should not be compiled, or that the merits of the works included, or somebody's opinion thereon, should not be recorded. It means that this is not the task of the bibliographer. The criticism of a work on hydrocarbons is the business of a scientific chemist, that of a novel is the business, so it seems, of a cash chemist.[1] It is not that of a bibliographer. The only bibliography which is really the business of a bibliographer is a bibliography of bibliography. This we may call bibliography raised to the second power, all other bibliographies are the product of bibliography and some other subject. Thus the compilation of bibliographies is in truth but a mixed and subsidiary art. The mere bibliographer who criticizes the works he catalogues is guilty of

[1] [Boots's circulating library had recently banned a novel.]

impertinence: at best he is only the systematizer of the other men's knowledge.

If anyone thinks that I am unduly limiting the functions of the bibliographer in this direction and depriving him of a part of his hereditary domain, I will endeavour to make up for it by what I believe to be a logical and necessary extension of his activities elsewhere. For I have at length come to the real subject of this paper, namely, to what I shall call critical bibliography.

After what I have said it should I think be clear that I regard bibliography as an important subject. It is one which may quite legitimately be pursued for its own sake and it is by those who so pursue it that it is likely to be most advanced. Possibly every subject that is worth cultivating possesses some intrinsic value apart from practical applications. But I do not think that bibliography is one of the great sciences, of which pure mathematics is the type, whose interest would hardly be diminished by entire dissociation from the actual world. At any rate I freely confess that my own interest in bibliography is by no means purely bibliographical. It is literary. I stumbled into bibliography by accident. Finding it impossible to obtain the information I required about a certain class of literature, I set to work to collect it. It was the results of bibliography that I wanted, but my search led me to the far greater discovery of the importance of the subject itself. Any value my literary work may have will be chiefly owing to that discovery. For, if I may be allowed a violent metaphor which is always coming to my mind, it is only by the application of a rigorous bibliographical method that the last drop of information can be squeezed out of a literary document. Thus in spite of my interest in bibliography it is as the handmaid of literature that I still regard it, and it is this side of my theme that I wish to develop to-night.

There is a remark in Dr. Copinger's inaugural address before this Society that recently caught my attention. 'Bibliography', he said, 'has been called the grammar of literary investigation.' It is an extraordinarily penetrating remark, but one which seems to me to have been strangely misunderstood. Bibliography has hardly ever attempted to be the grammar of literary investigation; it has tried to be a dictionary. It has chronicled and described, sometimes it has even criticized, the books needed for the study of literature, and it has rendered valuable service in this line; but seldom if ever has it concerned itself with the methods of that study. By this, of course, I do not mean either the canons of criticism—if there are any—or the methods of literary history; I mean what is antecedent to both, namely the investigation of texts. Strictly bibliographical investigation forms three-quarters of textual criticism, and therefore of the work of the scientific editor. For editing should be none the less scientific because it must at the same time be literary. No editor, however sure his taste, ever did valuable work without technical skill in handling textual evidence: just as no editor, however scientific, is worth his salt without taste. And apart from taste he requires much knowledge that has nothing to do with bibliography. He requires a thorough knowledge of linguistics and a thorough knowledge of antiquities. But these are presupposed in the subject and differ with the accidents of the subject. What is constant as a requirement, what every editor, what every textual investigator needs, what may therefore be truly called the grammar of literary investigation, is critical bibliography. Critical bibliography is the science of the material transmission of literary texts, the investigation of the textual tradition as it is called, in so far as that investigation is possible without extraneous aids. It aims at the construction of a calculus for the determination of textual problems.

This, of course, is no new science: editors have been forced to solve the problems as they went along, and in doing so they have necessarily evolved a method of their own. It is strange, however, when one inquires into the subject, how little and often how unsatisfactory is the writing of a general nature in this connexion. I say this advisedly in spite of full knowledge of, and sincerest respect for, the profound observations for instance of Westcott and Hort in connexion with the manuscripts of the Greek Testament. Everywhere the editor suffers from not being a bibliographer; he gives himself all sorts of unnecessary trouble and arrives at all sorts of impossible results. In the current number of one of the chief critical journals a writer goes hopelessly wrong over the order of two issues of a printed book, simply because he does not know how to distinguish an original leaf from a cancel.[1] It is pathetic to find editors discussing the order of undated editions on a basis of vague probabilities, when often the erroneous retention of a catchword or some similar bibliographical trifle puts the matter beyond dispute. It is not that bibliographers ought to rush into the task of editing, but that editors ought to give themselves a thorough bibliographical training. For a large part of their work is bibliography, critical bibliography, and this can only be properly carried out when the elements of the subject have been mastered. For anyone without a competent knowledge of bibliography to endeavour to deal with textual evidence is mere impertinence. It is the task of bibliographers at present to systematize the knowledge acquired in this department and to perfect the method, in order that it may be acquired with the least possible trouble and applied with the greatest possible certainty.[2] There is much to be done in this line. Too often far-reaching deductions are drawn from wholly inadequate premises, tables of textual relationship too often invite the sneer that they resemble figures of Euclid in which a bomb has exploded,[3] too often sources of error are overlooked, too often consequences ignored. A classical scholar who enjoys the reputation of being one of the ablest as well as one of the severest textual critics in this country is content to speak of a single manuscript preserving the original reading in a case where the variants are of the α type (a : bcd) and the genetic relation of the texts of the β (ab : cd).[4] But I am here inventing technical terms for a science which has not yet been reduced to rule.

As I have said, no attempt has yet been made to systematize critical bibliography, and I confess that I am by no means clear in my own mind what we shall finally agree to include

[1] [I have forgotten the particular instance I had in mind.]

[2] [R. B. McKerrow performed an invaluable service in his *Introduction to Bibliography for Literary Students*, but that epoch-making work did not appear till 1927, fifteen years after the present paper was written.]

[3] [The phrase was, I think, Saintsbury's.]

[4] [The allusion is to A. E. Housman. Of course the reading of the single manuscript may be what the author wrote, but only if there has been either conjectural emendation or coincident error in the course of transmission.]

under the name, always supposing that we recognize such a subject at all. To begin with it will embrace all that an editor requires in the way of knowledge and method, apart from linguistics and *realien*. But how much more it may be expedient to include I will not venture to guess.

It will by now have become evident why I said that I regarded the determination of the order of the *Canterbury Tales* as a typical bibliographical problem. It is, of course, true that in considering it we require to take into account local and temporal allusions in the text itself, which have nothing to do with bibliography. Yet the problem is essentially one of textual transmission. For if we can account for the actual order of the tales in the various extant manuscripts, we shall have solved the problem of the original order provided that there ever was one. Similarly all questions of textual transmission are questions of critical bibliography.

Bibliography is a wide subject and the field of critical bibliography is no less extensive. But it may not unreasonably be suggested that the more immediate concern of this Society is with the bibliography of English literature. And now, with your permission, I will spend what remains of my allotted hour in describing a dream of my own. It is of a course of lectures on English bibliography which may one day be delivered at one of our so-called seats of learning, neither this year nor next year, but perhaps some day. And I will tell you what, as I dream, the lecturer will tell his class. He will begin with the general principles of textual transmission, which are for the most part obvious enough, how a number of steps often intervene between the work as it formed itself in the author's mind and as it reaches modern readers. He will pass on to describe the conditions under which manuscripts were written and copied, the kinds of mistake that scribes habitually made, and the manner in which bibliographical investigation may reveal them, the extent of the corruption to be expected and the degree to which it is reasonable to rely on the textual tradition. He will consider the influences to which manuscripts have been subjected, the injury they have suffered, the degree to which this can be repaired, the reagents that may be used with safety, the way vellum should be treated, and the way it should not.[1] He will then deal with the principles of textual criticism, the grouping of manuscripts according to their genetic relations, the manner in which those relations are to be determined, and the way in which they affect the choice of readings: in what cases a reading in the archetype can be postulated with certainty, in what cases it is only a matter of probability: what evidence forces us to suppose conflation, what latitude should be allowed for coincidence: when conflation is due to the scribe, when to a reviser: how archetypal foliation may be inferred and what is its importance. He will then proceed to take individual monuments of literature and describe the manuscripts in which they are preserved and the relation of those manuscripts. He will also consider the contents of various manuscripts and the light which they may throw upon the works contained. He will not neglect external evidence as regards the authors and their works, but will direct attention to the main contemporary authorities and records to be studied. Further, he will consider the appeal of the manuscripts; the learned English manuscripts of Anglo-Saxon times, the popular manuscripts of the centuries following the Conquest. *Pari passu* he will investigate the changes in the methods of book-making and the gradual changes in handwriting. He will indicate the evolution from the half-uncial of the earliest charters to the final dissolution of Saxon writing about 1200, and from the adoption and adaptation of the Carolingian minuscule to the book and current hands of the fifteenth century: he will also trace the elaboration and decay of the system of contractions borrowed from Latin writing. Naturally he will not be able to deal fully with all the extant manuscripts of all surviving works, but he will consider all the more important monuments, and will in particular devote attention to those that present problems of a typical nature. He will discuss the so-called three texts of the *Vision of Piers Plowman*, for if bibliography is not concerned with the question whether they are the work of one author or of three, it is concerned with the determination and differentiation of

[1] [Malice reported that the authorities at the British Museum once boiled a Caxton indulgence on vellum by way of cleaning it, and were surprised to find that it had shrivelled to half its size.]

the three types, a question the investigation of which has been as yet only begun, but which when answered will go far towards answering the other. Similarly he will discuss the already mentioned problem of the order of the *Canterbury Tales*, so far as this depends for its solution on the arrangement in the manuscripts.

He will next pass to the introduction of printing, and indicate the differences which that event made in the transmission of texts. He will discuss the relation of editions and their grouping, and also the minor differences which copies of the same edition present, and he will indicate how the change from manuscripts to printed books affects the problems of textual criticism. He will call attention to the particular errors which are likely to happen in composition and imposition, as he previously did to those peculiar to copying. He will describe the differences of type and their value in dating books, and also the particular literal confusions to which each is liable. He will consider methods of detecting false imprints and misleading dates. He will then proceed to deal with individual works, and beginning with the great compilation known as the *Morte Darthur*,[1] will trace the fortunes of English literature as they depend on the printed page. He will call attention to the difference between various ages in the extent to which we may presume an author to have exercised control over the first edition of his work, or over the first and subsequent editions as well. He will enumerate the many small points, the corrections, the cancels, the withdrawals, that bear witness to editorial supervision, and will discuss the relations of the author, the publisher, and the printer, the control that one had over the other, and that those in authority had over them all. He will expound the conditions of copyright and estimate the effect they had on literary production. Following in the footsteps of our Honorary Secretary he will reconstruct the history of the first folio of Shakespeare's plays from the evidence of exceptional copies and other bibliographical peculiarities, and he will explain the variants in the different issues of *Paradise Lost*. He will account for the duplicate setting of Erasmus's

[1] [The paper was of course written long before any manuscript of Malory's work came to light.]

Paraphrase, and estimate the force of trades-unionism in the sixteenth century. Nor will he forget the manuscripts of a later date. He will give help in the deciphering and dating of Tudor and Stuart hands, and will discuss the most satisfactory way of printing works written in them. This is an important matter, and he will devote considerable attention throughout to various styles of editing. For there is no one method which is correct to the exclusion of others; it is a question which is best adapted to peculiar needs. And it is largely the business of the bibliographer to see that, whatever method is adopted, it is carried out consistently and made to yield the very best results of which it is capable.

It is no light task that I have sketched, and we may well wonder how many men there are to-day who would be capable of undertaking it with any chance of success. But the way to success lies through failure, and until someone has been found bold enough to make the venture there is no knowing what may or may not be possible. Anyhow that is my dream, and it is to the preliminary task of asking the necessary questions, of defining the problems, and systematizing the method, that I invite the Bibliographical Society this evening.

6. John of Basing's 'Greek' Numerals[1]

MR. ROBERT STEELE, in his learned little book on early Arithmetics lately issued by the Early English Text Society,[2] touches incidentally on a matter about which I have long felt curious, and which would perhaps repay further study than, so far as I know, it has yet received. After remarking (p. xvi) that most probably the forms of 'our present numerals are derived from Greek sources through the so-called Boethian "apices", which are first found in late tenth century manuscripts', he proceeds: 'Another Greek form existed, which was introduced into [western] Europe by John of Basingstoke in the thirteenth century, and is figured by Matthew Paris; but this form had no success.' I hope to show in a moment that John's innovation did not fall quite so flat as Mr. Steele seems to imply, but a few words must first be said about Matthew's account of it. The passage in the *Chronica Maiora*, which relates the remarkable achievements of John of Basing or Basingstoke under the date 1252, is well known, but the description is not free from difficulty, and the whole account is so interesting from various points of view that I venture to give it at length as it appears in Archbishop Parker's manuscript, which is believed to be partly autograph (C.C.C.C. no. 16; ed. Luard, 1880, v. 284–5):

Diebus insuper sub eisdem, ne mala veniant inconcomitata, magister Johannes de Basingestokes, archidiaconus Legrecestriæ, vir quidem in trivio et quadrivio experientissimus, Græcis ac Latinis literis ad plenum eruditus, viam universæ carnis ingressus, gemitus et lacrimas multiplicavit comitis [Simonis] memorati. Hic magister J[ohannes] intimaverat episcopo Lincolniensi Roberto, quod, quando studuit Athenis, viderat et audierat ab peritis Græcorum doctoribus quædam Latinis incognita. Inter quæ reperit duodecim patriarcharum, filiorum videlicet Jacob, testamenta; quæ constat esse de substantia Bibliothecæ, sed per invidiam Judæorum dudum fuisse abscondita, propter manifestas, quæ in eisdem patent, de Christo prophetias. Unde idem episcopus

[1] [1923, June. *The Library*, iv. 53–55.]
[2] [*The Craft of Nombrynge*, ed. R. Steele, E.E.T.S., E.S. 118, 1922 for 1916.]

misit in Græciam, et cum ea habuisset, transtulit de Græco in Latinum, et quædam alia. Hic insuper magister J[ohannes] figuras Græcorum numerales et earum notitiam et significationes in Angliam portavit, et familiaribus suis declaravit, per quas figuras etiam literæ repræsentantur. De quibus figuris hoc maxime admirandum, quod unica figura quilibet numerus repræsentatur, quod non est in Latino, vel Algorismo, quas huic paginæ duximus protrahendas. Fiat stipes, et in eodem lineas exeuntes, ut quælibet angulum rectum, acutum, vel obtusum faciat, protrahas, hoc modo [and so forth, adding figures and some mystical interpretations: see the table on p. 93].

It will be noticed that two apparently contradictory statements are here made about John's numerals: first that they also represent letters, which is, of course, true of ordinary Greek numerals but not of those figured; and secondly that by them any number (presumably up to some limit) can be expressed by a single (complex) sign, which is true of the numerals figured but not of ordinary Greek. At first sight it looks as though Matthew had confused two different notations, but further examination shows that the statement as to representing letters is really meant to apply to the numerals figured, for later on after reproducing an elaborate symbol (which has no proper significance) Matthew adds: 'Hæc autem figura omnes numerales secundum Græcos figuras complectitur, et omnibus litteris est aptabilis.' This being so, the only meaning I can attach to the statement is that the symbols may equally be used to express letters in some sort of cipher-writing. Since, the alphabetic order once fixed, any numerals can, of course, be used to express letters, just as any letters can be used to express numerals, this statement seems at first futile; it should, however, be observed that the fact that in John's notation any number (up to 99) is expressed by a single sign does give it a cryptographic convenience greater than either the Roman, 'Arabic', or true Greek system can boast. The origin of these numerals is another matter: whether it is to be sought in ogham writing I do not know; it seems remotely possible, but can hardly have been known to Matthew.

The system of numeration whose introduction Paris ascribes to John of Basing is one that must have been fairly well known, and was even occasionally used, throughout the later Middle Ages. There seems no reason to doubt Matthew's account of its having been brought to England from Greece; but though he definitely speaks of it as Greek ('Figuræ numerales secundum Græcos'), men like John of Basing and Robert Grosseteste must, of course, have known that it was not the ordinary Greek notation, and they may very likely have believed it to be of eastern origin. Such, we may fairly suppose, was the view taken early in the sixteenth century by Cornelius Agrippa in his second book *De occulta philosophia* (1533), chapter xix. Here, after mentioning the systems of number current among the Hebrews, Egyptians, Aethiopians, Chaldeans, and Arabians, he continues (trans. J. F., 1651, p. 233): 'Moreover I found in two most ancient books of Astrologers, and Magicians, certain most elegant marks of number, which I thought good to set down in this place', and then proceeds to describe what is essentially the same system extended for use up to 9999. This notation, however, was not always reserved for occult purposes, and signs agreeing exactly with those given by Agrippa are used to number the openings of a German fifteenth-century manuscript in my possession, *Liber dialogorum sancti Gregorii, &c.*[1]

The passage in Matthew's *Chronica Maiora* may perhaps afford the clue to a puzzle in another manuscript belonging to his own century and to his own abbey of St. Albans. This is Royal MS. 14 C. VII in the British Museum, a volume really consisting of three distinct works, namely: *A*, the *Chronica Minora* or *Historia Anglorum*, Matthew's own abridgement of his larger work, extending from 1070 to 1253; *B*, 'tertium volumen' of the *Chronica Maiora*, 1254 to 1259, really the conclusion of the Parker manuscript; and *C*, an anonymous St. Albans continuation, 1260 to 1272, in a late fourteenth-century hand. Like the Parker manuscript of the *Chronica Maiora*, the present *Historia Anglorum* is believed to be partly autograph: it contains a bare record of John of Basing's death in 1252. The recent Catalogue of the Royal Manu-

[1] The same notation is given by Joannes Noviomagus in his first book *De numeris*, chap. xv, Paris (and Cologne?), 1539. He calls the numerals astrological or Chaldean and cites Rodolphus Paludanus Noviomagus as his authority. From this work they are reproduced by Matthaeus Hostus or Hostius, *De numeratione emendata*, chap. ix, Antwerp, 1582 (and 1572?), who calls them astronomical numbers.

scripts duly notes that the gatherings are 'numbered at the end, with catch-words, and marked with peculiar figures on the second page of the first five or six leaves'. It does not, however, mention that what I may call the authoritative numbering at the foot of the last page of each quire (I^9–XIII^9) extends to the end of *A* only, whereas the 'peculiar figures', which constitute a regular if cryptic set of signatures at the foot of the first verso of each sheet (*arcus*) of the quire, run through both *A* and *B*. They were, therefore, added later than the authoritative numbering in *A*, but before the accession of *C* to the collection. These 'peculiar figures', some of which are red and some black, so far as I can discover are perfectly arbitrary signs, and some of them are repeated at irregular intervals. Now, it seems possible that certain of these signs are derived from the numerals described in the *Chronica Maiora*. Thus we twice have a cross (which does not stand for ten) and twice an arrow. These two signs (with the respective values of 55 and 33) are specially selected by Matthew for mystical interpretation, 'quasi ab æterno provisa'. And if it be objected that Matthew's cross is upright (+) while that of the signatures is saltire (×), I must point out that Matthew particularly remarks of this 'most worthy' sign that 'qualiter volvitur idem signat'. Again the sign which is written like 'f' may well be derived from that for thirty; while another, a circle with a tail to it, which occurs with modifications no less than four times, closely resembles the sign which in the later developments of the system stood for ninety-nine. This suggests that from the first more than one variety of the notation may have been recognized, and that at least some confused remembrance of these mystical 'Greek' numerals may have lingered among the monks of Matthew's own abbey in the generations after his death.

In order that readers may judge for themselves of the likelihood of these speculations I reproduce herewith the various notations involved. I need only add that the symbols given in Parker's manuscript are obviously incorrect: in the sign for nine the line should make an obtuse angle with the stem (*stipes*), while in that for seventy it should make an acute angle. Agrippa writes the signs upright like Paris; otherwise his symbols only differ from those here shown in having a

MATTHEW PARIS: MS. C.C.C.C. 16

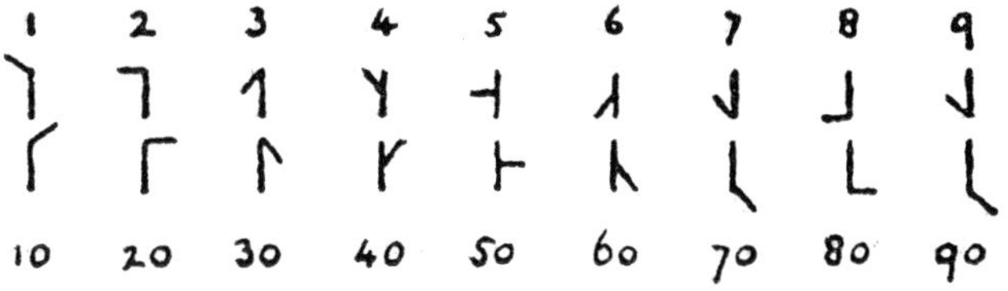

GERMAN XV CENT. (& CORNELIUS AGRIPPA)

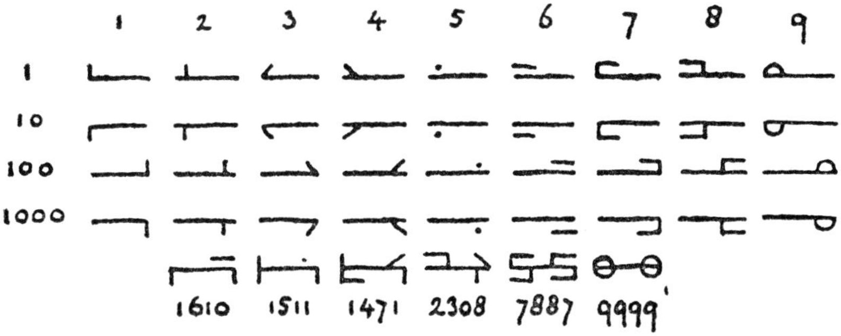

SIGNATURES IN MS. ROYAL, 14 C. VII

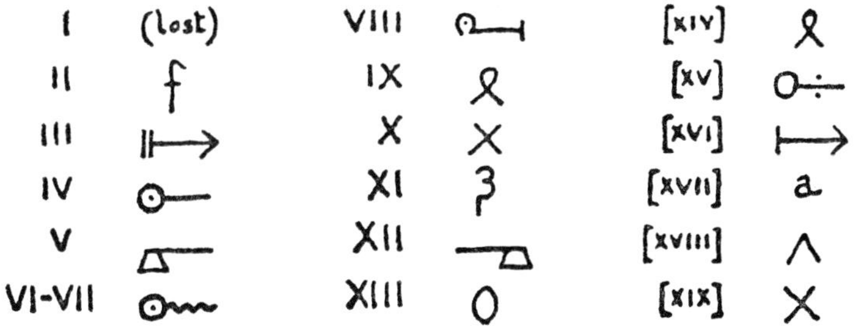

short line instead of a dot for 5, &c., and a square instead of a semicircle, for 9, &c., variations which suggest that he followed a slightly more archaic tradition. If the first quire of the Royal manuscript was ever signed all trace of the signature has disappeared; the seventh evidently never was signed, it is an irregular gathering of three leaves only.[1]

[1] [The Provost of Eton wrote: 'Apropos of your paper on Basing's numerical signs, you may care to know that there is a copy of them in the XIIIth cent. Graeco-Latin psalter from Ramsey Abbey, no 468 at Corpus Chr. Camb. I have copied it in my catalogue in loc. [ii. 399]. I *think* I have seen it utilized in MSS. to mark the references to marginal notes, but I am not sure.' Dr. M. R. James no doubt had in mind another Matthew Paris manuscript at C.C.C.C. (MS. xvi) in which at least one of the signs from MS. Royal 14 C. vii is used for the purpose of reference, as was pointed out to me by the librarian, Geoffrey Butler.]

7. An Elizabethan Printer and his Copy[1]

THE British Museum possesses a manuscript, classed as Additional 18920, which is thus described in the official catalogue: 'cantos XIV.–XLVI. of Ariosto's "Orlando Furioso," translated into English stanzas of *ottava rima* by Sir John Harington; with notes, *etc.* The copy, in Sir John's own handwriting, used for the original edition of the work by Richard Field, in 1591. It has numerous corrections and alterations of passages, with instructions to the printer. Paper; end of XVIth cent. Quarto.' A few details may be added. The manuscript is imperfect both at the beginning and the end: not only are the first thirteen cantos missing, but the Argument to canto XIV is likewise absent; and though the poem itself is complete at the end, the text breaks off in the middle of the Allegory. The volume has also suffered severely at the hands of the binder, the margins being cropt in such a way as greatly to injure all prose portions (notes, commentary, &c.) and likewise marginal additions, though the original verse text is untouched. The leaves now measure about 8¾ by 6½ inches. Though itself evidently a fair copy, the manuscript has been extensively revised, in some cases additional stanzas being written in the margin, in others substitutions being pasted over the original text, while minor alterations are frequent. At the foot of the first page preserved are the initials 'E. H.' in another hand: we may fairly suppose them to be those of some later Harington, the family having been much addicted to the preservation of old papers. A note at the beginning, added when the manuscript came to the Museum, states that it was 'Purchased of Messrs. Boone. 24 Apr. 1852. (from Sale at Sotheby's)'.

The fact that we possess copy which has actually passed through the hands of an Elizabethan printer does not appear to be generally known to bibliographers. In spite of Harington's manuscript having been for over seventy years in the British Museum, almost the only allusion to it I have seen is in a short

[1] [1923, September. *The Library*, iv. 102–18.]

contribution to *Notes and Queries* in 1910.[1] Yet it is hardly necessary to insist on the importance of the information to be derived from such a source. Like other autograph copies of literary works, it tells us much that is curious of the manner in which the composition took shape: its outstanding interest, however, is the opportunity it affords us of watching an Elizabethan compositor at work and noting some of the technicalities of his craft.

With the literary interest of the manuscript I am not at present concerned, but I should like, before passing on, to give a single sample of the alterations introduced by the translator in the course of revision. In Ariosto the first two stanzas of canto XXXIII run as follows (in ed. Venice, 1584:)

1

Timagora, Parraſio, Polignoto,
  Protògene, Timante, Apollodoro,
  Apelle, più di tutti queſti noto,
  E Zeuſi, e gli altri, ch'a quei tempi foro,
  De' quai la fama (mal grado di Cloto,
  Che ſpenſe i corpi, e dipoi l' opre loro)
  Sempre ſtarà, fin che ſi legga, e ſcriua,
  Mercè de gli ſcrittori, al mondo viua.

2

E quei, che furo à nostri dì, ò ſon ora,
  Leonardo, Andrea Mãtegna, Gian Bellino,
  Duo Doſſi, e quel, ch'à par ſculpe, e colora
  Michel, più che mortal, Angel diuino,
  Baſtiano, Rafael, Titian, ch'onora
  Nõ mẽ Cador, che quei Venetia, e Vrbino,
  E gli altri di cui tal'opra ſi uede,
  Qual de la priſca età ſi legge, e crede . . .

This is rendered by Harington, according to the edition of 1591:

1

Tymagoras, *Parrhaſius*, *Polignote*,
  Timant, *Protogenes*, *Apollodore*,

[1] See, however, a note by H. F. B. Brett-Smith in Sidney Lee's *Life of Shakespeare*, 1916, p. 42.

Zewces, a man for skill of ſpeciall note:
Apelles eke, plaſt all the reſt before:
Whoſe skill in drawing, all the world doth note
And talke of ſtill (to writers thanks therefore)
Whoſe works and bodies, time & death did waſt,
Yet ſpite of time and death their fames doth laſt.

2

With others that in theſe our later dayes
Haue liu'd, as *Leonard* and *Iohn Belline*,
And he that carues and drawes with equall praiſe,
Michell more then a man, Angell diuine,
And *Flores*, whom the Flemmings greatly praiſe,
And *Raphael* and *Titian* paſſing fine:
With diuerſe others that by due deſart,
Do merit in this praiſe to haue a part.

On turning to the manuscript, however, we find that the last couplet underwent alteration; it originally ran, not as the printer found it, but thus:

Allſo owr Englyſhe Hillyard by deſart
that meryts in this prayſe to have his part./

The curious may speculate on the reason for the change. Free as habitually Harington's version of Ariosto is, it may have occurred to him that he had here taken a rather unusual liberty. The alteration certainly marked no failing of his regard for the English miniaturist, for having removed his name from the text Harington wrote in his notes on the passage:

Yet I may ſay thus much without parciallitie, for the honour of my country, as myne authour hath done for the honour of his: that we haue with vs at this day, one that for limming (which I take to be the verie perfection of that art) is comparable with any of any other country. And for the prayſe that I told you of *Parrhaſius*, for taking the true lynes of the face, I thinke our countryman (I meane *M*r *Hilliard*) is inferiour to none that liues at this day: as among other things of his doing, my ſelfe haue ſeen him, in white and blacke in foure lynes only, ſet downe the feature of the Queenes Maieſties countenaunce; that it was euẽ thereby to be knowne; and he is ſo perfect therein (as I haue heard others tell) that he cã ſet it downe by the Idea he hath, without any paterne; which (for all *Apelles* priuiledge) was more (I beleeue) then he could haue done for *Alexander*.

In these same notes Harington apologizes for having ousted Mantegna: 'Alſo there was *Andrew Mantinea* (whom I forgot [!] to put in, by ouerſight in his dew place, but I will make him amends here)'. This is interesting since it shows that the secondary Italian artists were more to him than mere names, and that he rated Mantegna above the Dossi and Sebastiano del Piombo, whom he likewise excludes for the sake of introducing Frans Floris (de Vriendt). I hope that this sample of Harington's work in revision may encourage others to examine his manuscript further from the literary point of view.

Meanwhile I pass to bibliography. That the manuscript has actually been through the printer's hands is evident from the fact that he has placed in the margins a series of symbols indicating the points at which the several pages of the printed text begin. To take a sample at random, we find the following signs occurring in cantos XVII–XVIII:

M.p̃r'.	m·2·	m 3·	m 4	m·6·	m 7
·131·	132	133·	134	136	137·

m·8·	m·9·	m·10	m·11·	m·12·
138	139	140	141	142

These are, of course, signatures and numeration, and it will be observed that the signature 'm·5·' and the number '135' are absent. Turning to the printed text we find that the page in question begins with some of Harington's notes in prose. In the earlier portion of the poem these notes must have been supplied to the printer separately, for they are absent from the manuscript; the earliest notes there preserved are those to canto XXVI.

The remarkable thing, however, about these symbols is the system upon which the signatures are rendered. The numbers 131–42 refer to pages, not folios, and the quire 'M' is a regular ternion of six leaves. Thus the signs 'M.p̃r'.', 'm·2.', . . . 'm·12·' likewise refer to pages, and not to leaves; so that 'm 3·' corresponds to the page bearing the signature 'M 2' in the printed book, 'm 7' to 'M 4', and so on. This eccentric method must have been very inconvenient, but it seems to have been traditional, and may date from the cradle-days of printing. It can at least be traced to Venice and the early years of the sixteenth century. 'Galeni librorum pars quinta', a folio printed by Aldus in 1525, contains the *editio princeps* of Galen's commentary on a tract of Hippocrates, the copy for which is still extant in the Vatican library. A page of this manuscript has been reproduced by Dr. Johann Mewaldt ('Die Editio princeps von Galenos In Hippocratis de natura hominis', *Sitzungsberichte der königlich preussischen Akademie der Wissenschaften*, 1912, pp. 892–903, tafel viii) and it shows the printer's sign '13/Aa' at the point at which Aa 7 recto begins in the printed text.

Harington not only subjected his manuscript to elaborate revision, but prepared it for press with care. It contains several interesting directions to the printer. Thus after canto xxiii he wrote: 'Between the xxiijth booke and the xxiiijth I would have a ſpare leafe . . .' (the rest of the note is shorn off). The printer marked in the margin 'Q 8 | R.p$^{\text{r.}}$ | R 2 |', and further at the head of canto xxiv 'R 3' (replacing 'Aa 3' deleted). In the printed volume we in fact find Q 4 verso blank, R 1 recto blank, R 1 verso occupied by an engraved plate, and the text resuming on R 2 recto (= 'R 3' of the printer's notation). Harington asked for a blank leaf, Field gave him a blank opening. Presumably it served equally well its purpose, which seems to have been to mark a break in the text. It will be observed that the printer's original intention was to begin a fresh alphabet in the signatures ('Aa' &c.): he did in fact begin a fresh quire, leaving Q with four leaves only in place of the normal six, though six are allowed for in the pagination (Q 4 recto = p. 185, R 2 recto = p. 193).

Below the notes to canto xxix is a not very clear direction apparently concerned with the manner in which a quotation from Ovid '*De fastis*' should be printed; and below those to canto xxxiii: 'Yow muſt quote the numbers by the ſydes, as I have donne in the ſtory', that is, the page-references must be made to suit the printed text. But the most important of these directions occurs where 'ends the notes of the xlvjth and laſt canto', and runs: 'M^{r} ffeeld I dowt this will not come in in the laſt page, and thearfore I wowld have [yow ?] immedyatly in the next page after the fynyſhinge of this laſt booke, with some prety knotte. to ſet down the tytle, and a peece of the Allegory as followeth in this next page./ I would have the allegory (as allſo the appollygy and all the proſe that ys to come except the table [)] in the ſame printe that Putnams book ys./' It was this direction that formed the subject of a communication to *Notes and Queries* (May 1910, p. 404), in which Mr. C. Hughes pointed out that it affords important confirmation of *a* Puttenham's alleged authorship of the famous *Art of English Poesy*, which was printed by Field two years before *Orlando*, and is in fact in the same type as the 'allegory'. It should perhaps be mentioned that the word 'Putnams' in the direction has been gone over with the pen, but it does not seem to have been altered. I confess that to me Harington's instructions regarding typographical arrangement are not very clear, and I may observe that by 'the appollygy' he appears to refer to a section at the beginning, not at the end, of the printed volume. Whether Field interpreted his wishes correctly I do not know: what he did was to place a 'prety knotte', in the shape of a printer's ornament, below the notes to canto XLVI, and continue immediately with the heading and text of the Allegory. The position of the 'knotte' he indicated by inscribing in the manuscript a symbol, now rather obliterated but apparently

51

no doubt the number which the ornament bore in his stock. The signs added by the printer are all written, not in chalk or pencil, but in ink.

Incidentally it may be observed that on the whole the manuscript is remarkably clean and shows little material sign of having passed through the printer's hands. There is no reason to suppose that all printers would handle their copy with equal care, but it is clear that the present manuscript at least was treated with respect and perhaps returned to the author; and it may have been too readily assumed that any copy sent to an Elizabethan printer would in the nature of things be destroyed. After all, at a time when circulation in manuscript was still common and manifolding unknown, and when a carefully written copy of a work was more esteemed than one printed (as can, I think, be demonstrated), a printer must often have been called upon to deal with copy which the owner valued and would expect to receive again in good condition.

It may be thought that so far I have been dealing with points of mere antiquarian curiosity. Certainly if this were all we could learn from the manuscript, it could hardly claim the singular importance I have ascribed to it. Its real value, however, for bibliographical criticism, lies in the opportunity it affords for observing how far an Elizabethan compositor followed his copy in the matter of spelling, punctuation, and the like. While it is of course dangerous to generalize dogmatically from a single instance, such an actual example is evidently of the greatest use in checking or corroborating *a priori* speculation on the point. I propose, therefore, to print on opposite pages the opening stanzas of canto XXIX as they stand in the manuscript and in the print of 1591, and subject their peculiarities to a close analysis. But before doing so there is one passage of particular orthographic interest to which I should like to call attention. This is the final couplet of stanza 79 in canto XXXIV, which stands thus at the foot of fol. 202[a] of the manuscript:

> this was that guyft (beet ſayd withowt offence)
> that Conſtantyn gave Sylveſter long ſens.

Here the author seems to have felt that 'beet' was perhaps not altogether a satisfactory spelling, for in the margin below he added the alternatives 'b'it be't', whether as a direction to the printer or merely by way of trial it is impossible to say. Field chose the second alternative, and printed:

> This was that gift (be't ſaid without offence)
> That *Conſtantin* gaue *Silueſter* long ſince.

It will be seen that there is here but one slight deviation from modern spelling, and that so insistent is the printer's desire for uniformity in this respect that he has actually substituted 'ſince' for 'ſens' to the detriment of the rime. One rather wonders whether Harington read his proofs.

MS. Addit. 18920, fol. 140ᵃ.

The contents of yᵉ. xxix. book.

fayr Jsabel, to loose her hed is gladd,
To ſave her chastitie, from Pagans might,
to pacifye her ghoſt, the Pagan sad,
maketh a bridg, at which falls many a knight:
Orlando cometh thither, being madd,
Jnto the water both together light.
from thence, the madman onward stil proceeds,
and by the way, doth ſtraung, and monſtrous deeds./

1

Oh myndes of men, vnconſtant, and vnſtable,
as ſubiect vnto chawnge, as weſtern wynde,
In all deſygnmentẹ fond, and varyable,
but cheefly thoſe, that love breeds in the mynde:
Loe hee that late devyſd, all hee was able,
to ſlawnder and defaſe, all women kynde,
yet now with them whome hee ſo ſore revylde,
evn of the ſudden hee ys reconcylde./

2

Certes, moſt noble dames I ame ſo wrothe,
with this vyle turke, for this his wycked ſinne,
for ſpeaking ſo great ſlawnder, & vntroth,
of that ſweet ſex, whoſe grace I fayn would win:
that till ſoch tyme, hee ſhall confeſſe the troth,
and what a damned error, he was in,
I ſhall him make be ſo in conſcyence ſtownge,
as hee ſhall tear his fleſhe, and byte his townge./

3

But with what folly, hee was then poſſeſſed,
the ſequell of the matter playn doth ſhow,
for hee that yeſterday him ſelfe profeſſed,
to all the kynd a ſworn and open foe:
now to a ſtrawnger, on in ſtate diſtreſſed,
whoſe byrth, whoſe kin, whoſe name, he doth not know,
with one ſmall glawnce, and ſober caſt of ey,
was ſo enthralld hee woos her by and by./

Field's Edition, 1591, p. 234.

THE ARGVMENT.

Faire Iſabell, to looſe her head is glad,
To ſaue her chaſtitie from Pagans might:
To pacifie her ghoſt, the Pagan ſad,
Maketh a bridge, at which falls many a knight:
Orlando commeth thither, being mad,
Into the water both together light.
From thence the madman onward ſtill proceeds,
And by the way doth ſtraunge and monſtrous deeds.

1

Oh mynds of men, vnconſtant and vnſtable,
As ſubiect vnto chaunge, as Weſterne wynde,
In all deſignments fond, & variable,
But chiefly thoſe, that loue breeds in the mynd:
Lo he that late deuiſd all he was able,
To ſlaunder and deface all women kynd,
Yet now with them whom he ſo ſore reuild,
Eu'n on the ſudden, he is reconcild.

2

Certes (moſt noble Dames) I am ſo wroth,
With this vile Turke, for this his wicked ſin,
For ſpeaking ſo great ſclander and vntroth,
Of that ſweet ſex, whoſe grace I fayn would win,
That till ſuch time, he ſhall confeſſ the troth,
And what a damned error he was in:
I ſhall him make be ſo in conſcience ſtoung,
As he ſhall teare his fleſh, and byte his toung

3

But with what folly, he was then poſſeſſed,
The ſequell of the matter playn doth ſhow;
For he that yeſterday him ſelfe profeſſed,
To all the kynd, a ſworne and open foe:
Now to a ſtraunger, one in ſtate diſtreſſed,
Whoſe birth, whoſe kin, whoſe name he doth not
With one ſmall glañce, & ſober caſt of ey, (know,
Was ſo enthralld, he woos her by and by.

4

And as new fanſy doth his hart enflame,
ſo to new ſpeach yt doth his towng dyrect,
a new diſcowrce new reaſons hee doth frame,
with great pſwacions but to ſmall effect:
for ſtill the godly fryre refutes the ſame,
exhorting her ſoch ſpeeches to neglect,
and faſt to hold her purpoſe good and holly,
of ſarving god, and leaving wordly folly./

5

Sent· Saying the way of death, ys large, and ſpacyous,
but that to lyfe, ys ſtrayt, and full of payn,
Rodomownt ſeeing him, ſtill ſo awdacious,
In ſpyte of him this doctryn to mayntayn:
ſtepps to him, and wth hand & towng vngracious,
ffyrſt bidds him get him, to his ſell agayne,
Then his long beard, grown on his aged chin,
all at one pull, hee pylleth from the ſkin./

6

And ſo far foorth his wrath and fury grew,
Simile hee wryngs his necke as pincers wryng a nayle,
and twyſe, or thryſe, abowt his hed him threw,
Simile as huſbandmen, that threſhe do toſſe a flayle:
Dyvers reports, doe afterward enſew,
but which be trew, and which of truth do fayle,
Is hard to ſay: ſome ſay hee was ſo battered,
that all his lymms, abowt a rocke wear ſkattered/

7

Som ſay that to the ſea hee hurled him
thowghe dyvers furlongs diſtant from the place,
and that hee dyde, becawſe hee cowld not ſwim,
others report, ſom ſaynt did him that grace:
to ſave his lyfe, and heale each broken lim,
and to the ſhore, to bring him in ſhort ſpace.
the lykelyhood heerof, who lyſt may way,
for now of him I have no more to ſay./

4

And as new fanſie doth his heart enflame,
So to new ſpeach it doth his toung direct,
A new diſcourſe, new reaſons he doth frame,
With great perſwaſions, but to ſmall effect:
For ſtill the godly Frire refutes the ſame,
Exhorting her ſuch ſpeeches to neglect,
And faſt to hold her purpoſe good and holly
Of ſeruing God, and leauing wordly folly,

5

Saying the way of death is large and ſpacious, *Sentence.*
But that to life, is ſtraight and full of paine.
Rodomont ſeeing him ſtill ſo audacious,
In ſpite of him, this doctrine to maintaine:
Steps to him, and with hand and toung vngracious
Firſt bids him get him to his cell againe,
Then his long beard, growne on his aged chin,
All at one pull, he pilleth from the skin.

6 *Simile.*

And ſo farre foorth his wrath and furie grew,
He wrings his necke, as pincers wring a naile,
And twiſe or thriſe about his head him threw,
As husbandmen that threſh, do toſſe a flaile: *Simile.*
Diuerſe reports do afterwards enſew,
But which be true, and which of truth do faile,
Is hard to ſay: ſome ſay he was ſo battered,
That all his limbs about a rocke were ſcattered.

7

Some ſay that to the ſea he hurled him,
Though diuerſe furlongs diſtant from the place,
And that he dide, becauſe he could not ſwim:
Others report, ſome ſaint did him that grace,
To ſaue his life, and heale each broken lim,
And to the ſhore did bring him in ſhort ſpace.
The likelyhood hereof, who liſt may way,
For now of him, I haue no more to ſay.

The contrast between these texts is apparent to the most cursory inspection. Harington's spelling is at least as archaic and irregular as that of the average educated writer at the end of Elizabeth's reign. By comparison Field's is regular and modern; it is, indeed, more consistently modern than that of most printers of the time. Of course this is only generally, though it is very generally, true. Here and there Harington may chance to have the modern and Field the archaic spelling. For instance, Harington twice has the word 'ſlawnder' (1^6, 2^3) in which the diphthong was normal in his day and the 'w' is a personal idiosyncrasy: Field once prints 'ſlaunder' and once 'ſclander', the latter being an etymological spelling which modern usage has discarded. Again Harington (in 5^2) has 'ſtrayt' for narrow, where Field prints 'ſtraight'; but the forms were not distinguished in Elizabethan English. Lastly, Field prints in a single line (6^1) the forms 'farre' and 'furie' where Harington happened to write 'far' and 'fury'.

Sometimes, though rarely, Field made alterations in the text that cannot be brought within the bounds of orthography. On the border is that (in 6^5) whereby 'afterward' becomes 'afterwards', which seems to show that the modern form was already becoming prevalent. In another place (7^6) he actually alters a sentence by substituting 'did bring' for 'to bring': Harington's construction is quite correct, but Field's is rather easier to follow. It may, of course, be an author's correction in proof.

The same remarks apply to punctuation. Harington's is curiously mechanical. In every stanza of the extract there is a colon at the end of the fourth and a full stop at the end of the eighth line, quite regardless of the sense (see particularly the colon after 7^4). All the other lines end with a comma, except one which is accidentally unpointed, and two which are allowed full stops. Within the line there is usually at least one comma marking a pause, which may or may not be grammatically required. Field evidently had no intention of following his copy in this respect any more than in its old-fashioned spelling. In two stanzas out of the eight he discards the central colon, in one he alters the final stop to a comma (and in one accidentally omits it). Heavier stops are used at the end of other lines where demanded by the sense.

The internal commas largely disappear, and there is a distinct, though by no means consistent, tendency to confine them to grammatical positions, as may be seen in the last line of the Argument and the first of stanza 5. But again there is no uniformity: in the very last line Field has introduced a purely rhetorical comma which is not in the manuscript.

The exceptions, however, hardly affect the general rule. In spelling, and to a less extent in punctuation, the tendency of the printed text towards modernization is sufficiently uniform to render any departures from standard usage noticeable. And when we find that such anomalies as occur reproduce with few exceptions the peculiarities of the copy, we can hardly doubt that it is the influence of that copy upon the eye of the compositor that is responsible for his lapses from the norm.

Evidence of the influence of the copy on punctuation is restricted but clear. Field, as we have seen, held himself in no way bound to place a colon after the fourth line, and consequently when he does so in spite of the sense, as in stanzas 3 and 5, we may fairly put it down to the influence of the copy. And once this influence is established it may plausibly be traced in a number of cases in which ungrammatical commas are retained as in the first line of the Argument, the third of stanza 1, and notably in the second of stanza 5.

The most obvious copy-spelling is the queer word 'Frire', where the manuscript has 'fryre' (4^{5}). The spelling 'friar' was well established at the end of the sixteenth century, and the present variant almost raises a suspicion that the compositor may have been uncertain of the author's meaning. Another clear instance is 'wordly' for 'worldly' (4^{8}), a form that was quite archaic. A curious case is the anomalous 'confeſſ' (2^{5}), where the compositor decided, in pursuance of his general custom, to discard the final 'e', but was yet led by his copy to retain the 'ſſ': a strange lapse for a skilled workman. Two rather striking examples occur in the rimes of the last stanza, where we find 'lim' for 'limb' (cf. 'limbs' in 6^{8}) and 'way' for 'weigh'. It may be that here the compositor wished to retain the eye-rimes, though we have seen that he showed no such solicitude elsewhere. Similar cases are the rimes 'holly' for 'holy' (4^{7}) and 'ey' for 'eye' (3^{7}), though it will be noticed that the line in which the latter occurs is a little crowded and that the spelling 'glañce, &' has been introduced (for ms. 'glawnce, and') to make room for a word turned over from the line before. There are also some other spellings that are worth record, though not individually of much evidential value. Thus we find 'looſe' for 'lose' (A^{1}), 'ſequell' (3^{2}), 'enthralld' (3^{8}), 'fanſie' (4^{1}, ms. 'fanſy'; cf. 1^{6} 'deface', ms. 'defaſe', and 4^{3} 'diſcourſe', ms. 'diſcowrce'), 'foorth' (6^{1}), 'twiſe or thriſe' (6^{3}, ms. 'twyſe, or thryſe,'), and 'dide' for 'died' (7^{3}, ms. 'dyde'). Finally, in view of Field's general habit of modernizing medial 'y' to 'i', the half-dozen cases in which he failed to do so (conspicuously in the rimes of stanza 1) may reasonably be set down to the influence of the copy. I should add that 'pilleth' (5^{8}, ms. 'pylleth') is not a copy-spelling but the normal Elizabethan form.

The conclusion to which the evidence leads is then as follows. In such a printing house as Field's, which was as good as any to be found in London at the time, it is evident that the compositors had a recognized standard of their own in the matter of spelling and to a lesser extent in punctuation, and that they adhered to this standard with very fair consistency. Their work was certainly more uniform and more modern than that of any save a very few of the most punctilious writers of their day. This standard they followed without conscious regard for the idiosyncrasies of the author: nevertheless, when they were puzzled by a word in the manuscript, or whenever their attention relaxed, the peculiarities of spelling and punctuation present in the copy tended to be transferred to the printed text. We must be careful how we generalize from the practice obtaining in an office like Field's, and it is reasonable to suppose that inferior craftsmen would have a less rigorous standard, and that while they would make more errors and themselves introduce more anomalies they would also be more influenced by the manuscript before them and transfer more copy-spellings to the printed text.

This conclusion, arrived at from the analysis of an actual instance in which we can watch the compositor at work, agrees I think, sufficiently closely with that to which more general considerations have already led critics of the bibliographical

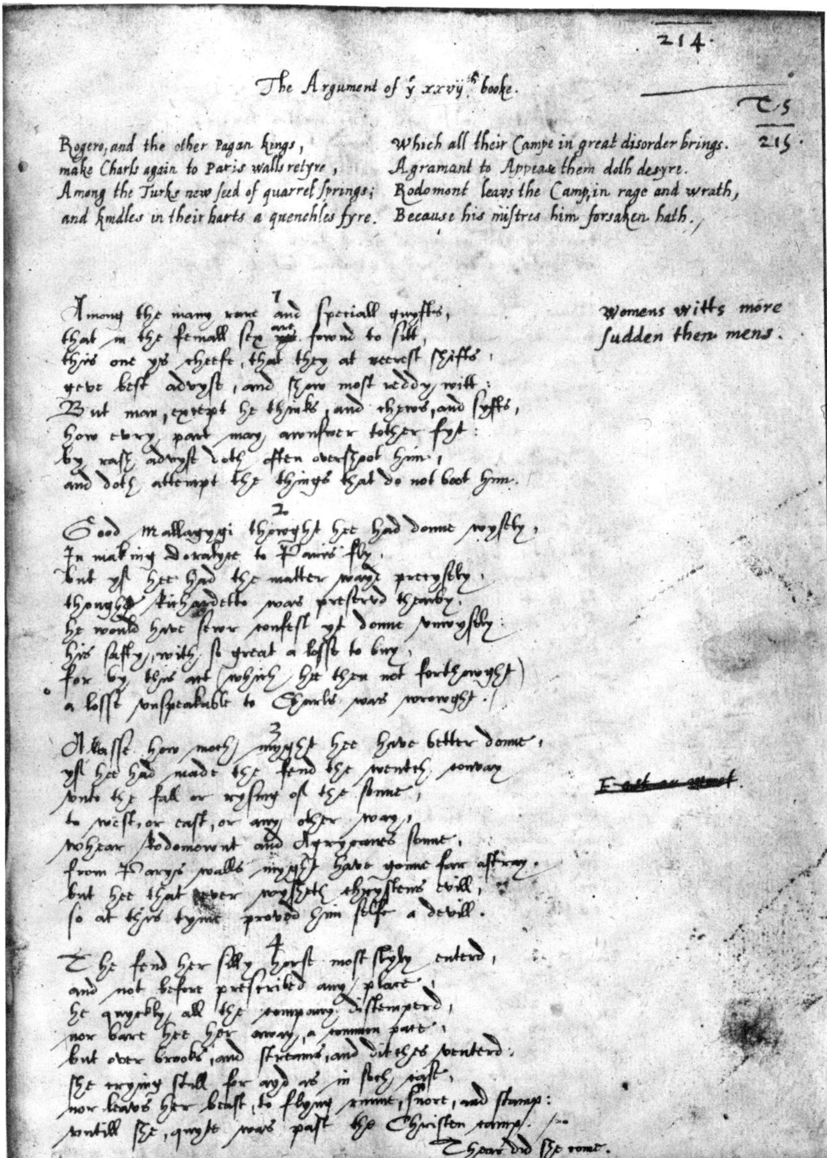

214.

215.

The Argument of ye xxvijth booke.

Rogero, and the other Pagan kings,
make Charls again to Paris walls retyre,
Among the Turks new seed of quarrel springs;
and kindles in their harts a quenchles fyre.
Which all their Campe in great disorder brings.
Agramant to Appease them doth desyre.
Rodomont leavs the Camp, in rage and wrath,
Because his mistres him forsaken hath.

1

Among the many rare and speciall gyfts,
that in the female sex are found to sitt,
this one ys cheefe, that they at neerest shifts
geve best advyse, and shew most reddy witt:
But man, except he thinks, and throws, and syfts,
how every part may answer to her fyt:
by rash advyse doth often overshoot him,
and doth attempt the things that do not boot him.

Womens witts more sudden then mens.

2

Good Malagigi thought he had done wysely,
In making Doralyce to Paris fly,
but yf he had the matter wayd precisely,
though Richardetto was preserved therby,
he would have ever confest yt done unwysely
his safty, with so great a losse to buy,
for by this act (which he then not forethought)
a losse unspeakable to Charls was wrought.

3

Alasse how much might he have better donne,
yf he had made the fend the wenche convay
unto the fal or rysing of the sonne,
to west, or east, or any other way,
whear Rodomont and Agramants sonne,
from Parys walls might have gone farr astray.
but he that ever worketh christians evill,
so at this tyme proved him selfe a devill.

~~[illegible]~~

4

The fend her silly horse most slyly entred,
and not before prescribed any place;
he quickly all the company distempred,
nor bare he her away a common pace:
but over brooks, and streams, and ditches ventred,
the urging still for ayd as in such case,
nor leavs her beast, to flyng, runne, snort, and stamp:
untill she quyte was past the Christen campe.

Thear did she come.

I

school. And if these critics claim that Harington's manuscript confirms their belief that a number of Shakespeare's actual spellings are preserved in the printed editions of his plays, and consequently that unusual spellings there found may legitimately be used to support his authorship of other writing in which they occur, I think they must be allowed to be within their rights.

The accompanying facsimile reproduces, in the same size as the original, fol. 119[a] of Harington's autograph manuscript, and gives an idea of one of the more tidy and less corrected passages. The arguments are not usually written in double columns and not always in Italian script: sometimes they appear to have been added later. The printer's symbol

$$\frac{\text{T·5}}{\text{215·}}$$

is seen in the margin opposite the 'Argument'. Above it is the number '214·', and probably a 'T·4' has been shorn off at the top. This upper symbol indicates the page occupied in the printed edition by the engraved plate to canto XXVII.

8. Massinger's Autograph Corrections in *The Duke of Milan*, 1623[1]

It does not often happen that we are able to obtain the opinion of an old author upon his critics and ascertain how far their textual conjectures correspond with his intention. But one book printed just three hundred years ago does afford us this rare opportunity.

When Gifford published the second edition of his *Massinger* in 1813 he was able to announce a discovery of great interest, to wit a presentation copy of the first quarto of *The Duke of Milan* with an inscription and corrections in the author's own hand. This, we learn, had once been in the possession of a Mr. Gell, of Hopton, Derbyshire (presumably Philip Gell, father of Sir William, the classical archaeologist), who gave it to Mr. Blore (evidently Thomas Blore, the topographer, who married Philip Gell's widow), who gave it to Octavius Gilchrist, who lent it to his friend Gifford. It subsequently appeared in the sale of Gilchrist's books in January 1824 (No. 877), was bought by Thorpe for £11. 11*s*., and passed to the Bibliotheca Heberiana. At the Heber Sale in June 1834 (ii. 3807) it was bought by Rudd for £3. 3*s*. It is now in the Dyce Collection at South Kensington.

This copy was presented by Massinger to his 'Honorable Freinde Sr Francis Foliambe Knight and Baronet' and to it he prefixed an epistle in verse. It is merely a presentation inscription, the play being dedicated to Lady Stanhope, but nearly ten years later Massinger did dedicate a play to this patron, namely *The Maid of Honour* in 1632. The verses, which are not themselves of any interest, were printed by Gifford at the end of his second edition (iv. 593) where he also supplied a hand-traced facsimile. A better photographic reproduction has since been published in the official *Handbook of the Dyce and Forster Collections* (1880). Gifford thought that this undoubted specimen of Massinger's autograph 'proves, beyond a doubt, that the MS. of the *Parliament of Love*, is

[1] [1923, December. *The Library*, iv. 207–18.]

from his own hand', an opinion for which there is not the slightest ground.[1] Curiously enough neither T. C. Croker, who edited Massinger's *Believe as you List* for the Percy Society in 1849, nor Samuel Beltz, the former owner of that manuscript, appears to have been aware that any authenticated writing of the poet was in existence. Both believed that the title of their play, written on the vellum wrapper, was autograph and consequently that the play was not. The reason for this is evident, for the title is in the hand that supplied the scene headings and directions throughout, and they assumed that the manuscript must have been prepared for the stage by the author. We now know of course that the exact opposite is true; the text of the play is in the poet's autograph, while the title (which incidentally spells his name 'Massenger') and the directions are (as we have learned to expect) in the hand of a theatrical reviser.[2] I may add that though *The Parliament of Love*, which likewise belonged to Dyce, cannot be regarded as autograph, the collection does contain another interesting Massinger relic. This is a copy of Phineas Fletcher's *Sicelides*, 1631, bearing on the title the inscription 'Philip Massinger his Booke'. I see no reason to differ from Dyce's opinion that this rather faint signature is both genuine and autograph.[3]

Though the dedication shows that the play was printed with the author's approval, it is clear that he did not himself revise the proofs, since in two places the printer has left a blank where he was unable to read his copy. Indeed it seems likely that it was these blanks that directed the author's attention to the need for correction when sending a presentation copy to his friend. It follows that, beyond their immediate importance for the restoration of the text, these corrections have a bibliographical interest as showing, in one instance at least, the degree of accuracy which an unaided compositor was able

[1] Unless I am greatly mistaken *The Parliament of Love* is in the same hand as *The Welsh Embassador*, a Cardiff manuscript printed by the Malone Society two or three years ago. Moreover it seems likely that the two plays remained together for some time, since they have suffered from damp in a very similar manner.

[2] [Namely Edward Knight, book-keeper of the King's company.]

[3] [I here omit a paragraph that was based on the mistaken assumption that the preliminaries formed a single sheet (A^4), whereas they in fact form two half-sheets ($A^2\chi^2$) printed separately.]

to attain in the opinion of the author whose work he was setting up. Moreover, I think that an analysis of the corrections will throw a good deal of light upon the sources of error and the proper methods of emendation. I will first give a list of the manuscript corrections in the text.

	References			*Text of Q1 1623*	*Text as corrected in MS.*	*Text of Q2 1638*
	Act & Sc.	*1623*	*1813, vol. i*			
1	I. i	B 2, l. 22	p. 242	hauing	hatinge	having
2	I. iii	B 4, l. 20	p. 246*	: and	one	: and
3		C 4, l. 3	p. 256	such,	[*deleted*]	such,
4		D 1^{v}, l. 35	p. 260*	his [*or* her]	her	his
5	II. i	D 2^{v}, l. 35	p. 262	ttue	trewe	true
6		D 3^{v}, l. 2	p. 263	successe	accesse	successe
7		E 2, l. 15	p. 271	touc'd	touchde	touch'd
8	III. i	F 3^{v}, l. 1	p. 284	And what	And on what	And what
9	III. ii	G 2^{v}, l. 32	p. 292*	Secretarie	Sectarie	Secretary
10		G 3, l. 3		trussed	t[. . . . .]	trussed
11	III. iii	H 1^{v}, l. 5	p. 299*	Might	[m]ust	Might
12			*	Faile not / to kill her } [*in the margin*]	[*transferred to text*]	[*in the margin*]
13		l. 7	*	seale	soule	seale
14		l. 17	p. 300	With	w^{ch}	With
15		l. 30		false [*like* falle]	false	false
16		H 2, l. 31	p. 302	glaze	glasse	glase
17		H 3, l. 22	p. 303	it	yet	it
18		l. 30	p. 304*	deadly	deadly hatred	deadly
19	IV. iii	I 2^{v}, l. 24	p. 312	pleasure,	pleasures	pleasures,
20		I 4, l. 27	p. 316*	winning	joyning	winning
21		I 4^{v}, l. 3	p. 317*	[*blank*]	phisicꝗ	[*blank*]
22		l. 11		Dion	Dian	Dian
23		l. 28	p. 318*	limbe	lumpe	limb
24		K 1, l. 9		posterie	posteritie	posterity
25		K 1^{v}, l. 19	p. 320*	[*blank*] cracke	iimmecracke	[*blank*] crack
26	V. ii	L 4^{v}, l. 8	p. 336*	earthy	earthly	earthy
27		M 1, l. 24	p. 337	make	wake	wake
28		l. 33	p. 338	art	acte	act
29		M 1^{v}, l. 10		looke	tooke	took
30		M 3, l. 4	p. 341*	honour	owner	honour
31		M 3^{v}, l. 31	p. 344*	with	w^{ch}	with
32			*	last	lust	last
33		M 4, l. 3		breath	breach	breach

This table needs a few words of explanation. The numbering of the acts and scenes follows Gifford's division. In referring to Gifford's second edition I have starred those passages which he annotated; the other corrections were made silently as having already been introduced in earlier editions. One of the corrections (4) is of an error found in some copies only, the text having been corrected in this

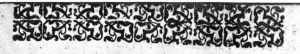

THE DVKE OF MILLAINE.

Act. Prima. Scæ. Pri.

Graccho, Iouio, Giouanni, with Flagons.

Gra. TAke euery man his flagon: giue the oath
To al you meet: I am this day, the state drun-
(I am sure against my will) And if you finde (kard;
A man at ten, that's sober, hee's a Traitor,
And in my name arrest him.
Io. Very good Sir:
But say hee be a Sexton?
Gra If the bells,
Ring out of tune, as if the street were burning,
And he cry 'tis rare Musicke: bid him sleepe,
'Tis a signe he has tooke his liquour; And if you meet
An officer preaching of sobriety,
Vnlesse he read it in *Geneua* print,
Lay him by the heeles.
Io. But thinke you tis a fault
To be found sober?
Gra. It is Capitall Treason,
Or if you Mittigate it, Let such pay
Fortie Crownes to the poore; But giue a pention
To all the magistrates, you find singing catches,
Or their Wiues dauncing; For the Courtiers reeling,
And the *Duke* himselfe, (I dare not say distemperd,
But kind, and in his tottering chaire carousing)
They doe the countrie seruice. If you meet,
One that eates bread, a child of Ignorance,
And bred vp in the darkenesse of no drinking,

against his will you may initiate him

instance in the course of printing. Another (15) is of a defective letter ('ſ' was broken so as to resemble 'l'), another (5) of a mere 'literal': these corrections indicate that the author went through the text with considerable care. Two others (21, 25) consist of the filling in of blanks, and a third (12) of the transference to the text of certain words printed as a stage-direction. Two corrections (10, 11) have been cropt by the binder, the first so badly as to be now unintelligible, while two others (14, 20) are also slightly damaged. The addition of the readings of the second quarto (1638) shows which of the errors were obvious to a subsequent compositor who clearly had nothing but his own wits to guide him.

The loss of one of the corrections (10) is unfortunate. The line, which is spoken by a beadle of a sectary, runs:

> When I had worm'd [i.e. pierced] his tongue, and trussed
> his hanches,

and the intention is clear enough, while it seems not inconceivable that *trussed* should mean 'whipt'. However, such a sense is not recorded, and it is possible that the word substituted by Massinger was *trounced*, most likely spelt *trounsed* (since there seems to be a trace of a long letter).

The first question that suggests itself is whether the corrections are all of misprints or whether any indicate a change of intention on the part of the author. I can see no reason why the printer, if he had *earthly* before him, should have substituted the less usual *earthy* (26),[1] though it is easy to suppose that the author, recurring to the passage, might be displeased with the associations of the latter. But with this possible exception it would seem that all the altered readings are misprints. In one other case Gifford apparently found evidence of a change of intention, for noting the alteration of *winning* to *joyning* (20) he added: 'This material improvement we owe to Massinger's revision.' But a little consideration will show how easily *ioyning* might be misread *wyning*, and I may add that the confusion would be rather particularly easy in Massinger's hand. As to the graphic origin of many of the errors there can be no question. The confusion of *and*

[1] [Greg here seems to have underrated the probability of sheer carelessness. The corruption of *earthly* to *earthy* occurs in the Folio text of *Richard II*, I. iii. 69, set up from printed copy.—J.C.M.]

and *one* (2) is of course easy in English hands, and it should be noticed that in Massinger's pseudo-Italian script an English final *e* sometimes occurs in place of the usual ε, which would make it all the more likely. The punctuation, however, must have been careless. *Dion* for *Dian* (22) is probably due to a similar confusion. The error *successe* (6) for *accesse* can only be explained by assuming some accidental mark before the *a*, most likely an exaggerated descender from the line above. These are rare in Massinger's writing, but he occasionally brought down the straight tail of his *y* in such a way as possibly to suggest an *ſ*, and the words *my fortunes* occur immediately above. That *a* and *u* were easily confused is shown by the misprints *seale* for *soule* (13) and *last* for *lust* (32). The error *with* for *which*, occurring twice (14, 31), shows that contractions were used, and Massinger actually uses them in making his corrections. In *Believe as you List* he appears to write *with* in full (probably with the object of avoiding confusion) but his *w*ᶜ*h* often resembles *w*ᵗ*h*, and I should not be surprised to find this misprint frequent in his plays. Probably *glaze* for (vb.) *glasse* (16) is due to the copy having *glase* and the printer misunderstanding it; *it* for *yet* (17) suggests a misreading *yt* which would be unlikely in Massinger's writing unless for some reason it was cramped. I do not know that he ever used the spelling *yt*, but he did use *yf*. The error *limbe* for *lumpe* (23) is less easily explained, but it may be a minim error combined with a compositor's emendation. Again *make* for *wake* (27), *art* for *act* (25), *looke* for *tooke* (29) are all of familiar types, and it may be observed that Massinger's Italian *r* is of a form peculiarly liable to be confused with *c*. There remains *breath* for *breach* (33), and again it must be remarked that Massinger's *ch* and *th* are usually of the English form and are very easily mistaken. If therefore we assume that the manuscript from which *The Duke of Milan* was set up was in parts cramped through alteration, there is no difficulty in the way of supposing it autograph, and some reason to believe that it was.

That the copy was here and there obscure through the introduction of alterations and imperfect deletion there is clear evidence. The appearance at one point as a stage-direction of the words *Faile not to kill her* (12), which quite clearly belong to the text and are restored to it by the author's correction, can only be accounted for on the supposition of marginal revision. This is borne out by another correction in the same line whereby *must* is substituted for *Might* (11). There should be no confusion between these words, and we may reasonably assume that *Might* was the original reading of the copy, obscurely corrected. We see the same in the redundant *such* (3), which appears at the end of one line in anticipation of the next. It was not an uncommon error for a writer to forget where to begin a fresh line of verse, and he sometimes omitted to delete the repeated word adequately. That the copy was obscure in other places, possibly also through alteration, is shown by those passages where the compositor was unable to read a word. Twice he left a blank, once for *phisicꝭ* (21), once for *iimme* (25), both words which might easily puzzle him unless quite clearly written. A like difficulty probably accounts for the omission of the word *hatred* (18), though here the compositor left no blank as he did later on.

The error *honour* for *owner* (30) is evidently of the oral type. This does not mean that the copy was necessarily read out to the printer; apparent errors of hearing often occur through a compositor or transcriber trying to carry too many words in his head at once. The same tendency may account for *Secretarie* in place of *Sectarie* (9), unless indeed the printer was unfamiliar with the word. The remaining errors may be classed as errors of carelessness for which no particular reason can be assigned. They include a broken letter (15), a 'foul case' (5), slight omissions (7, 8, 19, 24), and slight substitutions, *hauing* for *hating* (1), *his* for *her* (4).

To sum up, the 33 errors corrected by Massinger may be classed as follows: one unknown (10, possibly a careless slip), one possibly correct (26, author's revision), two probable mishearings (9, 30), six due to confused or illegible copy (3, 11, 12, 18, 21, 25), fifteen to graphic confusion (2, 6, 13, 14, 16, 17, 20, 22, 23, 27, 28, 29, 31, 32, 33), while eight are mere careless slips of one sort or another (1, 4, 5, 7, 8, 15, 19, 24).

It is, I think, distinctly encouraging to find that over two thirds of the printer's errors (on the author's own showing were due to causes readily discernible by the critical eye, and almost half to well-recognized graphic confusions, some of which can be definitely connected with known peculiarities of the author's hand; and of the remainder all but three or four are obvious even to a casual inspection. If modern bibliographical and palaeographical methods of analysis in textual criticism stood in any need of further support, I think they would find it in ample measure in Massinger's corrections.

If we wish to ascertain the real degree of accuracy with which the compositor worked we shall have to inquire whether the author's revision was really exhaustive. Massinger corrected 33 errors, but of these only 22 were serious enough to mislead the compositor of the second edition (1638), while a number of others were at once corrected in the first collection of Massinger's plays (1759). The severest critic could hardly maintain that more than 18 errors of any consequence received the author's castigation. The other 15 I shall disregard, partly because they do not matter, partly because it is very probable that there are other similar slips which the author himself overlooked and his editors have not thought worth recording. Now, there are four other passages in the play that Gifford in his first edition (before he had seen Massinger's corrections) declared to be corrupt. In III. ii he supposed that 'A hemistich, or more, is lost' from the line (G 4^{v}, l. 6; 1805, i. 295; 1813, i. 297):

He is trayn'd vp for his Masters ease.

There is no sufficient reason to believe the passage corrupt, and the suggestion was dropt in the following edition. Similarly in I. iii (C 3, l. 23; 1805, i. 251; 1813, i. 254) he originally emended (unsatisfactorily) a passage which he was later content to mark as defective 'as it escaped the notice of the author'. The 'metre is complete', but so far as I can see the text as it stands cannot be correct, and I am bound therefore to agree that Massinger must have overlooked it. The possibility of this is clearly shown in another passage in III. ii (G 4, l. 24; 1805, i. 294; 1813, i. 296) where the margin contains as a direction the words *This will tempt me*, which clearly belong to the text (as in the case of correction

12 above). Gifford rejected them as 'an addition of the prompter, or an unnecessary interpolation of the copyist'. Such an explanation cannot for a moment be entertained, but it is true that the previous editors' attempt to work them into the text was awkward, and the most likely explanation is that they were an alternative reading imperfectly deleted when the passage was altered, for the text is quite satisfactory without them. I conjecture that had Massinger noticed them in the quarto he would have crossed them out. Lastly there is a passage in IV. ii which reads in the original (I 1^{v}, l. 26; 1805, i. 308; 1813, i. 310);

> Nay spare your labour, Lady, we know our exit,
> And quit the roome.

The earlier editors altered *exit* to *Duty*, and this was retained by Gifford even when, in his second edition, he remarked: 'Massinger has made no alteration here, so that exit is perhaps the genuine reading.' In this case Gifford failed lamentably to learn his lesson. Although the special sense is not recorded in the *Oxford English Dictionary* there is no doubt that *our exit* means 'our cue for going', and one can only wonder that any one should wish to alter it. The explanation seems to be that the first editor followed the second quarto, where the word is unfortunately printed in italic, thus suggesting the possibility of its being a stage-direction.[1]

It would seem, therefore, that there are certainly two errors of importance which were overlooked by the author when making the corrections in his presentation copy. These bring the total of more or less serious mistakes of the press up to 20. The text of the play fills 87 pages and runs to some 3,000 lines. There is therefore one textual problem in every $4\frac{1}{3}$ pages or 150 lines. This is not a bad record for the much-abused compositor faced with what evidently was a far from perfect copy. There is no reason to suppose that his performance was in any way exceptional.

[1] Printing from the second quarto the earlier editors found eleven of the errors of the first already corrected. Ten further errors they set right themselves. The most ingenious of their emendations (25) Gifford rather grudgingly accepted. Two (4, 12) he originally rejected. He had perhaps some excuse in either case, but a better critic would have accepted them, and an honester man would have modified his description of his predecessors' conjectures as 'void alike of ingenuity and probability'.

We may sympathize with Gifford when he wrote: 'It is impossible to pass over these corrections without a sigh for the fallacy of criticism. Alas! alas! who knows whether much of the ingenious toil to explain nonsense, in the Variorum edition of Shakspeare, is not absolutely wasted upon mere errors of the press!' It requires no great divination to tell that the amount of such devoted labour has been great, but it is an error to suppose it wasted. Explanation is safer and less heady work than conjecture, and even when perverse it has served both to define the possibilities of interpretation and to help the formation of a severer code of emendation. Only through the discipline of endless trial and failure can be won the sure sense of where explanation becomes impossible and alteration of the text necessary. It is the fine flower of criticism and few attain it. Elsewhere Gifford writes: 'No sagacity in another could have furnished this most happy emendation, which now appears so necessary, and so obvious. I have been tempted to smile in the course of this revision at the surprising gravity with which we sometimes labour to explain the unintelligible blunders of a careless compositor.' The smile is a little too complacent. If, in the passage in question—

> Obserue and honor her as if the seale
> Of womans goodnesse only dwelt in hers—

any one but the author had proposed the emendation *soule* (13), I think an editor excusably might, and I believe that in fact Gifford would, have argued that the emendation was neither 'necessary' nor 'obvious'. But I would go further and maintain that, were emendation once proved unavoidable, so far from the correct conjecture being beyond the 'sagacity' of any but the author, it should have been easily within the power of modern critical method. At least I cannot imagine Mr. Dover Wilson, for example, being even particularly elated over such an editorial feat. And perhaps we may see herein a measure of the advance made by textual criticism in one direction since Gifford's day. There are others in which it has been even greater.

Postscript.—A further and more minute examination of the original has revealed several further slight alterations made by the author, together with one of greater consequence which the binder has done his best to obliterate. They are of interest as revealing the care Massinger bestowed on his revision, and especially his concern for spelling, but, beyond adding to the list of small errors of carelessness to the compositor's discredit, they do not materially affect the conclusions previously reached.

I do not think that Gifford noticed any of these corrections. Where Q2 corrected the text, he of course follows it; where it did not, he only adopted the correction in one instance (viii) and here he took over the conjectural alteration of his predecessors. The error (in ix) of *Franc.* for *Forza* (i.e. *Sforza*) may be considered as adding one to the serious mistakes overlooked by the author in revision, but it was not beyond the capacity of the compositor of Q2 to correct.

I hope the list is now complete, but some of the corrections are so obscure that it is difficult to be certain.

	Reference	*1623*	*Correction*	*1638*
i	D2, l. 18	conceal'd:	conceal'd,	conceal'd:
ii	D3, ll. 12–13	As . . . passions:	(As . . . passions)	As . . . passions:
iii	D4, l. 1	discents	descents	descents
iv	G1^v, l. 21	fouor	fauor	favour
v	H3, l. 9	routed	rooted	rooted
vi	l. 16	bake	backe	back
vii	l. 17	discliame	disclaime	disclaim
viii	K4^v, l. 13	And assurance	And [a]n assurance	And assurance

ix M1^v to M4. In 1623 *Forza* appears ten times among the speakers' names, and once in a stage-direction, for *Sforza* (presumably through confusion in the manuscript). In ten places an *S* has been prefixed by Massinger, one he overlooked. All are corrected in Q2. Once, M3^v, l. 5, *Franc.* has been printed by mistake for *Forza*. This was overlooked, but is corrected in Q2.

9. More Massinger Corrections[1]

WHILE he was at Oxford John Addington Symonds bought from a local bookseller a fat quarto volume in an old worn calf binding containing eight plays of Massinger's. The volume, which is said to have come from the Harbord Library at Gunton in Norfolk and to have been sold on the death of the fourth Lord Suffield in 1853, had in it a large number of early manuscript corrections which tradition ascribed to the author himself. When, in 1877, Symonds was obliged to break up his home at Clifton and go into exile in the Alps, he gave the volume to Mr. Edmund Gosse, who has since preserved it among his dramatic treasures, though he 'unfortunately' took it to pieces and had the contents separately bound.

I take these particulars from a note contributed by Mr. Gosse to Professor A. H. Cruickshank's monograph on *Philip Massinger* (Oxford, 1920, p. 222). The fact that the fly-leaf of the original volume is preserved with several interesting inscriptions makes it possible to add a few details. One pencil note gives five guineas as, I suppose, the price at which the volume was purchased. Another is: 'Edmund Gosse from J. A. Symonds June 1877'. This suggests that the gift was made just before the final collapse of Symonds's health early that month, which prostrated him for several weeks and made life in England clearly impossible. He reached Davos, accidentally, early in August, but the Clifton house was not finally abandoned till three years later. The most important inscription, however, is in ink, and, though the initials are not easy to decipher, it apparently runs: 'J A S from J A S March 7/64'. This date is after Symonds had left Oxford; it is, indeed, about that at which he settled in London at the end of a foreign tour. If he bought the volume while still in residence the inscription must mean that he gave

[1] [1924, June. *The Library*, v. 59–91. Modesty shall not debar me from quoting what A. W. Pollard wrote to me about it: 'I don't think this will arouse much enthusiasm in the average reader of The Library, but it is jolly good, and all editors of 'Elizabethan' plays ought to be obliged to pass an examination in it.']

it to his father (whose initials were the same as his own) when he left the paternal roof. It would, of course, have come into his possession again on Dr. Symonds's death in 1871.

Although the 'tradition' that the corrections were by Massinger himself was confirmed on internal grounds by Swinburne, who examined them in 1882–3, no one seems to have ventured to publish any confident opinion on the point. I am glad to be able to say that all the more extensive corrections in the plays are unquestionably autograph and that I see no reason to doubt that the smaller alterations (with possibly a few trifling exceptions) are in the same hand as the rest. Thanks to the kindness and hospitality of Mr. Gosse I have been able to make a minute examination of the quartos in question, and it is with his sanction and encouragement that I now put forward the results of the pleasant afternoons spent in his study.[1]

There are one or two peculiarities about the collection that formed the old calf-bound volume that deserve attention. On the fly-leaf already mentioned (which is really the blank A1 of *The Bondman*) there stands a list of contents written in a contemporary hand, not Massinger's. It is as follows (I add in brackets the dates of the editions):

1. The Bondman. [1624]
2. The Renegadoe. [1630]
3. The Emperour of the East. [1632]
4. The Roman Actor. [1629]
5. The Picture. [1630]
6. The Fatall Dowrye. [1632]
7. The Maid of Honour. [1632]
8. The Duke of Millaine [1623]

These are all first editions and form a collection of Massinger's plays printed down to 1632 complete save for the omission of *The Virgin Martyr*. The earliest play not included

[1] My attention was first called to the corrections through the list printed by Prof. Cruickshank as an appendix to his book already mentioned. Since, however, his list only contains about half the alterations found, and is otherwise not wholly reliable, it seemed worth while undertaking a more detailed investigation. [Gosse's collection of plays was sold at Sotheby's in April 1929, the eight Massinger items going to Spencer for £1,150. In 1936 they were bought from Spencer's estate 'at a reasonable price' by the Folger Shakespeare Library.]

is the *New Way to Pay Old Debts* of 1633. The obvious inference is that we here have a collection of his works made by Massinger, presumably for some friend or patron, in 1632–3. The exclusion of *The Virgin Martyr* cannot have been due to copies not being available, for though originally printed in 1622 a second edition had appeared in 1631; nor can it have been due to the play being partly Dekker's, since *The Fatal Dowry*, written in collaboration with Field, is included. I can only conclude that Massinger took no great pride in his share of this work.

The corrections, which are found throughout the first four plays, cease in the second act of *The Picture*. The next two pieces have no corrections, and though a few are found in *The Duke of Milan* they are of a rather different nature from the rest. The most important in this play are two restorations of single lines cut away by the binder, while the final pages contain the imperfect correction of a recurrent error of which the author must have been previously aware: otherwise the only alterations found are trifling typographical restorations of doubtful significance, which may of course not be Massinger's at all, and are even possibly accidental. There is no reason to suppose that *The Duke of Milan* was read through with a view to correction as some earlier plays of the volume must have been. We are perhaps justified in concluding that the collection was corrected as far as the second act of *The Picture* before being sent for binding, and that it was only when, on its return, it was discovered that *The Duke of Milan* had been cropt in the process (as nearly always happened, by the way) that the corrections in that play were added.[1]

A word should be said regarding the manner in which the corrections have been made. A very large number which consist of changes of punctuation and the restoration of defective letters involve no more than small pen-marks in the text itself and are often difficult to detect. It is more than likely that in spite of my endeavours I have missed a few. In most cases, however, in which a change of reading or even of

[1] The treatment of the *Duke of Milan* is peculiar in two other respects. While the plays are not arranged in strict chronological order, it is rather strange to find *The Duke*, which is the earliest in date, placed last, and it will be noticed in the list that it is marked off from the rest by rules. At present I am not clear how these peculiarities are connected with that mentioned in the text.

spelling was involved, the whole word has been struck out and re-written in the margin. This accounts for the number of small and apparently irrelevant differences of spelling that mark the corrections. On the other hand, where the correction consists in the addition of a final letter, this is often crowded in at the end of the word on the top of any punctuation there may be. In these cases it is not possible to say whether the letter was intended to be merely added or to replace the point. I have felt constrained to assume the latter in my list (e.g. 16), since the omission of the point sometimes seems desirable (e.g. 294), but it is by no means certain that this was the author's intention. That considerable care and labour have been bestowed on the work of correction is evident: at the same time it has been in some respects hastily and superficially performed. A few of the alterations appear to be themselves certainly incorrect. Many evident errors have been overlooked. For instance, in *The Roman Actor*, IV. ii, 'ɥad' (230) is corrected, but in the previous line 'iuʇɟice' still stands, and other more serious misprints in the same play and in the later acts of *The Picture* might be quoted.

It should be added that not a few of the faults corrected occur only in some copies of the originals. This is, of course, true of most of the letters or words damaged through accidents of the press, though a few seem fairly persistent. It is not always quite easy to distinguish these cases from those where definite corrections have been made while the sheets were going through the press. But in examining the copies at the British Museum I have observed a number of undoubted cases of correction, and further search would probably reveal a few more.[1] The list is as follows (I add the exact form of the correction where this differs from Massinger's): in *The Bondman*, 8 (Sicilie), 12, 14, 15 (no), 18, 19, 35, 36 [no comma], 49 (where); in *The Renegado*, 69, 77 (mande),

[1] I should mention that the number of copies possessed by the Museum are, of *The Bondman*, 1624, three; *The Renegado*, 1630, three; *The Emperor of the East*, 1632, four; *The Roman Actor*, 1629, two; *The Picture*, 1630, two; *The Duke of Milan*, 1623, three. Not all the copies have all the corrections; indeed it is evident that in some instances the error and in others the correction is the commoner reading. In one case there are three variations: in another one copy preserves what is apparently an altogether earlier form of the text. The copy of *The Bondman* from which the second edition (1638) was printed contained some uncorrected readings.

78–79 [variant text in one copy], 83 [but erroneously substituted for the prefix to the previous line]; in *The Emperor of the East*, 94, 95, 151 (If euer *but also* If feuer); in *The Roman Actor*, 158, 159, 160, 163, 166 (I would), 169 (Par.), 170 (Monarchs), 172, 216, 217, 218 (be), 219 (you *only*), 220 (tremble,) 221, 223 (moderation. Take), 224 (thee. Haue), 228 and 232, 229 (could), 230, 244 (Pinion'd).[1]

I will now give the list of three hundred corrections I have detected in six plays. These I have numbered consecutively for reference. Under each play the first column gives the act and scene according to the modern division, the second the page and line of the original quarto, the third the volume and page of Gifford's second edition. In this column an asterisk marks those corrections which are either not of a nature to affect a modernized text, or which were in substance adopted by Gifford. The fact that he often introduced a practically equivalent correction makes it impossible to distinguish satisfactorily between the two categories. The remaining columns give the original reading of the quarto as printed in the copy in question, and the reading as corrected in manuscript. In giving these readings I have not thought it desirable to retain the use of italic type, since Massinger made no attempt at distinction.

1. The Bondman, 1624

	A. & S.	*1624*	*1813*	*Reading*	*Correction*
1	I. i	B 1, l. 4	ii. 5*	Timagorus	Timagoras
2		l. 10	*	Timagorus	Timagoras
3		B 1^v, l. 17	6	loue,	liue,
4	I. ii	B 2, l. 25	8	with	this
5		l. 28	*	me,	me?
6	I. iii	B 3^v, l. 30	13	meat	meats
7		B 4, l. 10	14*	Firmenty	Fermenty
8		l. 34	16*	surely	Sicelie
9		B 4^v, l. 36	18*	giuen	giuen,
10		C 1^v, l. 12	20*	Churle [rle *defective*]	Churle
11		l. 15	21	I	[*deleted*]
12		C 2, l. 1	*	Achon	action
13		l. 2	*	counsels [els *defective*]	counsailes,

[1] In 222 both the Museum copies have the variant spelling 'Hyppollitus'. [Greg later noted that the Princeton copy has the corrected readings in 158, 159, and 170.—J.C.M.]

	A. & S.	*1624*	*1813*	*Reading*	*Correction*
14		l. 3	22*	Hand	Heard
15		l. 31	*	nor	noe
16		C 2v, l. 35	24*	Steward,	Stewards
17		C 3, l. 4	*	Amber:	Amber,
18		C 3v, l. 18	25*	scale?	scale,
19		l. 19	*	beame.	beame?
20		C 4, l. 13	26*	of	our
21	II. i	D 2v, l. 18	36*	fam'd	fann'd
22		l. 37	37*	vayle	vale
23		D 3, l. 2		For so	For, so
24		l. 3	*	selfe;	selfe,
25		D 3v, l. 11	38*	honour,	honour;
26		l. 28	39*	Loose	Looseth
27			*	sent	scent
28		l. 38		owe	awe
29	II. ii	D 4v, l. 22	41*	Sir,	Sir?
30		E 1, l. 1	42	yet	for
31		E 1v, l. 14	44	cunning	com̃inge
32		l. 19	*	Cleora.	Cleora?
33		E 2, l. 33	45*	wept;	wept,
34	II. iii	E 3v, l. 37	50*	Chyrurgion	Chyrurgions
35	III. ii	F 2v, l. 21	58*	selfe,	selfe?
36		l. 36	*	vnderstanding, parts	vnderstanding parts,
37	III. iii	G 1, l. 2	64*	now,	now (
38		l. 3	*	pride.	pride)
39		l. 18	65	worme,	wormes
40		G 1v, l. 1	*	foundation	foundation,
41		l. 8	*	too too	too
42		l. 9	*	iudgement;	iudgement,
43		G 2, l. 25	67	Leaue her off,	Staue her of.
44		G 2v, l. 24	69*	during	daringe
45	III. iv	G 3v, l. 8	71*	Timandra.	Timago:
46		l. 30		eares	feares
47	IV. i	G 4v, l. 18	74	still	yow
48				on	on,[1]
49	IV. ii	H 3, l. 30	81*	when	where,[2]
50		H 3v, l. 8	82	[*short line*]	[*adds*] pray you leaue mee.
51	IV. iii	I 1v, l. 30	88*	tempter	temper
52	V. i	I 4v, l. 2	95*	Cleor.	Cleora.
53		K 2, l. 26	100	recouer'd.	recouer'd?
54	V. ii	K 4, l. 32	105*	Beyound	Beyond
55	V. iii	K 4v, l. 23	106*	not be	not to be
56		L 1, l. 22	108*	the	thy
57		L 2, l. 18	110	gods, and	gods His
58		L 3v, l. 7	113*	deuices,	deuices)
59		L 4, l. 36	116*	[*no prefix*]	Gra. [*prefixed*]

2. The Renegado, 1630

	A. & S.	*1630*	*1813*	*Reading*	*Correction*
60	I. i	B 1, l. 20	ii. 126	nose	lippe
61	I. ii	C 1, l. 20	136*	you [?, u *defective*]	yow
62	I. iii	C 2, l. 13	139*	loue:	loue,[3]
63		l. 14		My	in My
64		l. 25	*	such;	such,
65		C 3v, l. 3	142*	looke,	looke?
66		C 4v, l. 20	146	least	least the[4]
67	II. iv	D 3v, l. 1	152*	passions sute,	passions, sute
68		D 4v, l. 4	155*	owne:	owne)
69		l. 9	156*	greatnesse?	greatnesse,
70		l. 10	*	selfe.	selfe?[5]
71	II. v	E 2, l. 35	160*	breach [?, h *defective*]	breache
72	III. iii	F 4v, l. 25	177*	T'will [T *defective*]	t'will
73		G 2, l. 24	180	Gennet to her Stallion	mare to her prowd Stallion
74	III. iv	G 2v, l. 20	181*	passe	passe.
75		G 3, l. 30	183	easie.	easie?
76	III. v	G 3v, l. 24	184*	imaculate	im̃aculate
77		H 1v, l. 14	188*	made	mam'd[6]
78	IV. i	H 3v, l. 16	193	of	[*deleted*]
79				my	my good
80	IV. ii	I 1, l. 12	197*	safet,	safetie
81	IV. iii	K 1v, l. 26	209*	tells [*indistinct*]	tells
82	V. ii	K 4v, l. 2	215*	[*no prefix*]	franci: [*prefixed*]
83	V. iii	L 2v, l. 9	221*	[*no prefix*]	Vitelli: [*prefixed*]
84	V. viii	M 2v, l. 12	232*	fore-gale	fore-right gale

3. The Emperor of the East, 1632

	A. & S.	*1632*	*1813*	*Reading*	*Correction*
85	I. i	B 2, l. 21	iii. 249*	piety,	pittye
86		l. 32		musicke?	musicke Sr?
87	I. ii	C 1, l. 2	256*	off	off,
88		l. 3	*	by	by,
89		C 1v, l. 10	258*	demeaner	demeanour
90		C 2v, l. 3	260*	too	to
91		l. 13		Constantinople?	Courte?
92		l. 30	261*	stamp'd [m *defective*]	stamp'd
93		C 3v, l. 1	262*	ventem	vent'em
94		l. 13	*	them	their
95		C 4, l. 32	264*	care	feare
96		C 4v, l. 33	266*	Nimph.	vmph.
97		D 1, l. 24	267*	wooned	woone
98	II. i	D 2, l. 18	iii. 269*	fixed	fix'd
99		l. 35	270*	It	Is
100		D 3v, l. 2	272*	folish	foolish

	A. & S.	*1632*	*1813*	*Reading*	*Correction*
101		l. 16	*	in	in the
102		E 3, l. 19	282*	garded	guarded
103		E 3ᵛ, l. 3	*	I [*defective*]	I[7]
104		E 4ᵛ, l. 4	284*	You [Y *defective*]	You
105	III. ii	F 2ᵛ, l. 27	290*	yong	yong,
106		l. 33	*	wisdome,	wisdome (
107		l. 34	*	height,	height)
108		F 3, l. 30	291	to you	[*deleted*]
109		F 3ᵛ, l. 12	292	kinde	kinde of
110		F 4, l. 6	*	I [*defective*]	I
111		G 1, l. 21	296*	ransone	ransome
112	III. iii	G 1ᵛ, l. 17	297*	garded	guarded [8]
113	III. iv	G 2ᵛ, l. 11	299*	sister:	sister!
114		l. 28	300*	str	Stirre
115		G 3, l. 14	*	beg	beg a
116		l. 24	301*	Sufficient	Sufficient,
117		l. 33	*	pity	pitty
118		G 3ᵛ, l. 2		thy	the
119		l. 19	302*	counsell,	counsell?
120		G 4ᵛ, l. 10	304*	vse	vse,
121		l. 11		obserue	handle
122			*	Eudoxa	Eudoxia
123		l. 24	*	I [*defective*]	I
124		H 1, l. 5	305*	Athen.	Athenais.
125		l. 11	*	I [*defective*]	I
126	IV. i	H 1ᵛ, l. 23	306*	I [*defective*]	I
127		l. 24		Princesse	Empresse
128		H 2, l. 20	307	swing	swinge
129		H 2ᵛ, l. 5	308*	Ath.	Athenais.
130	IV. iv	I 1, l. 14	315*	bounties;	bounties
131		l. 20	*	sicke	sicke,
132			*	heate	heate,
133		I 1ᵛ, l. 6	316*	Kings	Kings,
134		l. 13	*	Impossible,	Impossible!
135		l. 17		They	Hee
136		l. 24	317	fraide	defray'd
137		l. 33	*	I [*defective*]	I
138		I 2, l. 2	*	certainely:	certainely [9]
139		l. 5	318*	camer	cancer
140		l. 25	*	hearbes	hearbes,
141		I 3, l. 9	320	this admiration	thie admiration
142	IV. v	l. 27	321*	Pulch.	Pulcheria
143		K 1ᵛ, l. 13	327*	white	white,
144			*	red	red,
145		l. 24	328*	neuer:	neuer
146			*	equall'd	equall'd.
147		K 2, l. 9	329*	pray	prey
148		l. 17	*	fee [f *defective*]	fee
149	V. iii	L 4, l. 32	343	flights	flight
150		M 1, l. 8	345	niggle	iuggle
151		M 1ᵛ, l. 3	346*	I feuer	yf ever
152		M 2ᵛ, l. 33	349	My grace on all.	[*deleted*]

4. The Roman Actor, 1629

	A. & S.	*1629*	*1813*	*Reading*	*Correction*
153	ep. ded.	A 2, l. 10	ii. 329*	me,	me (
154		l. 11	*	power	power)
155	I. i	B 1, l. 12	331*	stocke	socc.
156		B 1^{v}, l. 3	333*	vice.	vice)
157		l. 18	*	gald	galld [10]
158		l. 26	*	Catta	Catti
159			*	Dacie	Daci
160		l. 29	334*	vs.	vs?
161		B 2, l. 1	*	Sceane	Scæne
162		l. 6	*	sorrow	sorrow,
163		l. 34	335*	eb	bee
164		B 3, l. 1	337*	grieue	gieue
165	I. ii	l. 9	338*	[*stage-direction*]	[*adds*] with a letter
166		B 3^{v}, l. 11	339*	for to	I woulde
167		l. 23		his	its
168		B 4, l. 13	340*	pattent.	pattent?
169		l. 36	341*	[*no prefix*]	pa: [*prefixed*]
170			*	New workes	monarkes
171		l. 38	*	Parth.	[*deleted*]
172			*	dispute.	dispute?
173	I. iii	C 1, l. 9	343*	Marcellus,	Marcellus (
174		l. 10	*	Rome.	Rome)
175		l. 25	344*	Deprau'd	Deprau'd,
176		C 1^{v}, l. 9	345*	libell	libell,
177		l. 18	*	Cæsar,	Cæsar (
178		l. 19	*	compehended	comprehended)
179		l. 32	*	Condemne	Condemnd
180		C 2, l. 6	346*	which	with
181		l. 14	*	Cancillus	Camillus
182		C 2^{v}, l. 16	347*	Arithmatique	Arithmetique
183	I. iv	C 3^{v}, l. 4	349	and	[*deleted*]
184	II. i	C 4^{v}, l. 26	352*	yours.	yours;
185		l. 27	353*	yeeres,	yeeres;
186		D 1, l. 12	*	Purple,	Purple!
187		l. 13	*	heyre,	heyre?
188		l. 34	354*	it,	it.
189		D 2, l. 15	355*	off	off,
190		D 2^{v}, l. 8	357*	intelligence	intelligence:
191		l. 10	*	Ælius, Lamia	Ælius Lamia
192		D 3^{v}, l. 9	359*	we	(we
193		l. 10	*	courtesie,	courtesie)
194		l. 16	*	doe,	doe.
195		D 4, l. 12	360*	promped	prompted
196		E 2^{v}, l. 1	367*	me, [e, *defective*]	mee
197		l. 5	*	sonne,	sonne (
198			*	liuing,	liuing)
199		l. 26	368*	redeeme [*second* e *defective*]	redeeme
200		E 3, l. 16	369*	hauə	haue

this page follows the letter

Heauie on you? away with 'em, stop their mouthes
I will heare no reply, O *Paris*. *Paris* — *Exeunt Guard Aretinus, Iulia, Canis, Domitilla.*
How shall I argue with thee? how begin,
To make thee vnderstand before I kill thee,
With what griefe and vnwillingnes 'tis forc'd from me?
Yet in respect I haue fauourd thee. I will heere
What thou canst speake to qualefie, or excuse
Thy readinesse to serue this womans lust.
And wish thou couldst giue me such satisfaction
As I might burie the remembrance of it;
Looke vp. We stand attentiue;

Par. O dread *Cæsar*,
To hope for life, or pleade in the defence
Of my ingratitude were againe to wrong you.
I know I haue deseru'd death. And my suit is
That you would hasten it, yet that your highnes
When I am dead (as sure I will not liue)
May pardon me I'll onely vrge my frailtie,
Her will, and the temptation of that beautie
Which you could not resist. How would poore I then — coulde
Fly that which followd me, and *Cæsar* sude for?
This is all. And now your sentence.

Cæs. Which I know not
How to pronounce, O that thy fault had bin
But such as I might pardon; if thou hadst
In wantonnesse (like *Nero*) fir'd proud *Rome*
Betraide an armie, butcherd the whole Senate,
Committed sacriledge, or any crime
The iustice of our *Roman* lawes cals death,
I had preuented any intercession — had
And freely sign'd thy pardon.

Par. But for this
Alas you cannot, nay you must not Sir
Nor let it to posteritie be recorded
That *Cæsar* vnreueng'd, sufferd a wrong,
Which if a priuate man should sit downe with it — yt
Cowards would baffull him.

Cæs.

	A. & S.	*1629*	*1813*	*Reading*	*Correction*
201	II. i	E 3^{v}, l. 16	370*	him.	him,
202		l. 17	*	me,	me.
203	III. i	E 4, l. 21	371*	words	swordes
204			*	command	command,
205		l. 22	*	you	you,
206			*	remoue.	remoue
207		E 4^{v}, l. 8	372*	retch	reach
208		l. 15	*	mortall	im̃ortall
209		l. 36	373*	tyrannie	tyrann
210	III. ii	F 2^{v}, l. 27	378*	you. [*point defective*]	you.
211		F 4, l. 2	381*	circumstance,	circumstance.
212		l. 18	382*	steepie	steep
213		F 4^{v}, l. 25	384*	has	has!
214	IV. i	G 2^{v}, l. 13	389	not	[*deleted*]
215		l. 14		respects	respects not
216		G 4, l. 4	392*	compliant	complaint
217		H 1, l. 6	394*	both	both?
218	IV. ii	H 2, l. 1	396*	pe	bee
219		l. 2		yuu command to me	ever you com̃and mee
220		l. 14	397*	tremele	tremble.
221		l. 20	*	geete	great
222		H 2^{v}, l. 9	398*	Hypollitus	Hypolitus
223		l. 22	*	moderation take	moderation, take
224		H 3, l. 32	400*	thee, haue	thee. haue
225		l. 35	*	before	(before[11]
226			*	thee)	thee
227		l. 36	*	bosome,	bosome)
228		H 3	*	[*page transposed*]	[*note*] this page followes the later
229		H 3^{v}, l. 20	ii. 403*	would	could
230		l. 30	*	ɥad	had
231		l. 36	*	if	yf
232		H 4	402*	[*page transposed*]	[*note*] this page misplacd
233		l. 15	401*	soule	soule!
234		H 4^{v}, l. 18	404*	This	(This[12]
235		I 1, l. 5		act	are
236		l. 9		nor	or
237		l. 22	405	grim	[*deleted*]
238		I 2, l. 1	407*	thee?	thee,
239		l. 6	*	however	(however
240		l. 7	*	it:	it)
241	V.	I 4, l. 13	412*	assure	as sure
242		I 4^{v}, l. 4	413*	still'd	stil'd
243		l. 12	*	me	me,
244		K 1^{v}, l. 35	417*	Pinn'd	pinion'd
245		K 2, l. 7	*	passage	passage,
246		l. 11	*	follow'd	follow'd,
247		l. 32	418*	man	man,
248	V. ii	K 3, l. 31	421*	iumpe	impe

4. The Roman Actor, 1629—*cont.*

	A. & S.	*1629*	*1813*	*Reading*	*Correction*
249	V. ii	K 3, l. 35	*	I [*defective*]	I
250		K 3ᵛ, l. 2	*	danger	danger,
251		l. 8	*	health	health,
252		l. 14	*	hard	heard
253		l. 25	422*	neglected	neglected ?
254		K 4, l. 5	*	[*text and s.d. too close*]	[*division marked*]
255		l. 15	423*	Domitia	Domitia,
256		l. 33	424	this	'tis
257		K 4ᵛ, l. 5	*	to	to her

5. The Picture, 1630
(corrections in the first two acts only).

	A. & S.	*1630*	*1813*	*Reading*	*Correction*
258	com. v.	A 4ᵛ, l. 9	i. clx*	or [*indistinct*]	or
259		l. 10	*	write	writt
260		l. 12	*	admir'd	admire
261	I. i	B 1ᵛ, l. 15	iii. 118*	satisfie	Satietie
262		l. 26	*	if	(if
263		l. 27	*	vndertakings;	vndertakings)
264		B 2, l. 4	119	or	Sʳ.
265		B 2ᵛ, l. 8	120*	mistersse	mistrisse
266		B 3, l. 8	122*	wone	woone
267		l. 10	iii. 122*	followes	[*mark added perhaps equivalent to a dash*]
268		B 3ᵛ, l. 12	124*	wracke	racke
269		B 4, l. 16	125	fight	fights
270	I. ii	B 4ᵛ, l. 13	126*	brauely,	brauelye[13]
271		C 1, l. 5	127*	time.	time,
272		C 1ᵛ, l. 9	128*	bxt	but
273		C 3, l. 35	133*	example [le *defective*]	example
274	II. i	D 3, l. 30	142*	A Post.	[*deleted*]
275		l. 32	*	horne	horne aside. A post
276		D 3ᵛ, l. 23	144*	more	more,
277		D 4, l. 3	*	deere	deere,
278	II. ii	E 1ᵛ, l. 25	149*	ranke	ranke,
279			*	file	file,
280		E 2ᵛ, l. 28	151*	In one hue.	[*deleted*]
281		l. 33	152*	Resolue	Resolues
282				her, like	acres
283		E 3, l. 32	154*	I should	should I
284		l. 34	*	manner	manners
285		E 4, l. 7	155*	enuirond	enuirond,
286		l. 8	*	arme	arme,
287		l. 9	*	fled	fled,
288		l. 11	*	dame	damne[14]

	A. & S.	1630	1813	Reading	Correction
289	II. ii	E 4v, l. 26	157*	I	I,
290		F 1, l. 13	158*	must	must haue
291		l. 19		double	doubld.
292		l. 22	*	mony:	mony,
293		F 1v, l. 2	159*	Idol	Idol,
294		l. 8		soulder,	souldier
295		l. 13	160	tosses	trifles

6. The Fatal Dowry, 1632 (no corrections).

7. The Maid of Honour, 1632 (no corrections).

8. The Duke of Milan, 1623 (corrections of a different character).

	A. & S.	1623	1813	Reading	Correction
296	I. i	B 1, l. 31	i. 239*	[*cropt in binding*]	[*repeated in margin*] against his will you may initiate hym
297		B 1v, l. 37	241*	[*cropt in binding*]	[*repeated in margin*] His guards are stronge, and sure, His coffers full
298	I. iii	C 4v, l. 14	257*	your [u *defective?*]	your
299		l. 24	*	Ruffian [R *defective?*]	Ruffian
300	V. ii	M 1v–M4	338–45*	[*In eight cases an* S *has been prefixed to the incorrect* Forza *where this appears as a speaker's name.*]	

Notes to the List

1 (48) The correction appears to be erroneous.
2 (49) The comma is an error.
3 (62) It was perhaps intended to delete the stop altogether.
4 (66) Error for *the least*.
5 (70) The query stands for a mark of exclamation.
6 (77) Either *man'd* or *mann'd* is intended.
7 (103) In this and similar instances the correction takes the form of '*J*'.
8 (112) Strictly the *u* appears to have been inserted after the *a*.
9 (138) Possibly a comma is intended.
10 (157) Probably *galld* is intended, though it looks rather like *galed*.
11 (225) The parenthesis before *that* in the same line was left standing in error.
12 (234) The parenthesis at the beginning of the next line should have been deleted.
13 (270) The *y* being defective has been touched up, and an *e* added after the comma: some stop is certainly required.
14 (288) Presumably *damme* is intended.

On a rough analysis the three hundred alterations in the list are seen to fall into the following classes: (i) the reparation of accidents of the press and binding, twenty-eight; (ii) changes of intention on the part of the author, fourteen; (iii) alterations made apparently in error, five; (iv) corrections of punctuation, one hundred and eight; (v) corrections of spelling, twenty-two; (vi) corrections of small miscellaneous errors, thirty-three; (vii) corrections of more substantial errors of carelessness, twenty-four; (viii) corrections of errors due to confused copy, seven; and (ix) corrections of graphic errors, forty-nine.[1] These nine classes must be considered in detail.

(i) We may first dispose of the unimportant group of cases in which some accidental damage has been remedied, including the restoration of two lines cut off by the binder. I should perhaps say 'real or fancied damage', for it is not always clear that the text stood in need of any attention (see in particular 298, 299). Massinger seems at times to have written his *J* over *I* whenever he thought the latter at all indistinct, and I suppose it must have been some fancied imperfection that led him in one place (231) to strike out *if* in the text and substitute *yf* in the margin. The twenty-eight alterations assigned to this class are 10, 13, 61, 71, 72, 81, 92, 103, 104, 110, 123, 125, 126, 137, 148, 196, 199, 210, 231, 249, 254, 258, 270, 273, 296, 297, 298, 299.

(ii) When considering the Foljambe copy of *The Duke of Milan*[2] we found very little to suggest any change of intention on Massinger's part. Here the case appears rather different, for while it is not of course possible to be certain in every instance, some clear cases of such alteration do occur. In one place (50) Massinger adds a phrase which fills out a half line to full dimensions, while in another (152) he strikes out a phrase and leaves a half line standing. In either case we may

[1] The numbers in the classes do not add up to three hundred because two alterations often constitute but a single correction, while some are composite in nature and appear in more than one class. It will, of course, be understood that in some instances the division between classes is in a measure arbitrary, and the assignment of particular alterations to one class or another is often conjectural. The classes themselves are determined by convenience rather than logic.

[2] In the text the letters *DM* followed by a numeral refer to the corrections recorded in my former article.

be dealing with a confusion in the copy (such as no doubt underlies 280) and the same may also be true of two instances where Massinger reduces a redundant line to due proportion by a small deletion (108, 237). But there can be no question that he elsewhere (73) altered a rather coarse line on realizing that the word 'jennet' did not imply a female. Revision thus established is also naturally seen in the cases already mentioned and again where we find 'To vvitnesse my good change' for 'To vvitnesse of my change' (78–79),[1] 'I thinke That she respects not' for 'I thinke not That she respects' (214–15), 'what ever you comãnd mee' for 'what you command to me' (219), and even in 236, *or* for *nor*, all apparently stylistic alterations, and further in such verbal changes as *steep* for the more fanciful *steepie* (212, cf. *DM* 26), and *defray'd* for the rare aphetic form *fraide* (136), for which the present is, I venture to think, the only clear instance quoted in the *O.E.D.* Two stage-directions are altered, one (165) by the addition of a warning that a letter is needed, the other (183) in a manner not readily intelligible.

But by far the most interesting of these alterations occurs at the beginning of *The Renegado* (60), where some one is said to be

An Austrian Princesse by her Roman nose.

This line is quoted by the *O.E.D.* as the earliest instance of the phrase in question, but to say you know the Habsburgs by their Roman nose is, of course, nonsense; you know them by their 'German lip'. Now *lippe* is actually given in Massinger's correction, and that he allowed *Roman* to stand may be no more than an oversight. It is just conceivable that the compositor misread *German* as *Roman* and, having done so, automatically changed *lippe* to *nose*.[2] I fancy, however, that there may be more than this behind the apparently innocent alteration. *The Renegado* was licensed for the stage by Sir Henry Herbert on 17 April 1624, but was not printed till

1 The original reading seems to have been 'To prooue that I haue power', found in some copies of the quarto and apparently altered in the later impressions of the sheet. If so, the manuscript alteration represents a further tinkering by the author.

2 Supposing the phrase to have been already current, which is not certain. The second instance quoted in the *O.E.D.* is dated 1650. It is explanatory, and certainly implies that the phrase was in use though not necessarily familiar.

1630, being registered under his hand on 22 March. Now, on 11 January 1631 Herbert refused on political grounds to license an unnamed play of Massinger's, alleging that it contained 'dangerous matter . . . ther being a peace sworen twixte the kings of England and Spayne'. This was the piece re-submitted after alteration and duly licensed on 6 or 7 May under the ambiguous title of *Believe as you List*. The exact extent of the alterations is unknown—they involved the preparation of a fresh manuscript—but in one place the author inadvertently reproduced a phrase of the original version: 'His nose! his German lippe!' This apparently did not escape the eye of the censor, for in the extant manuscript the word *German* is struck out and *very* substituted in a hand which is not Massinger's. It is difficult to avoid the suspicion that the official who objected to the 'German lippe' of *Believe as you List* was also responsible for the absurd 'Roman nose' of *The Renegado*. It is true that the treaty with Spain was not signed till 5 November 1630, but the previous negotiations lasted some considerable time.

(iii) That Massinger should have made mistakes in his alterations may seem curious, but the fact hardly admits of doubt.[1] He evidently worked rapidly and without very close attention, as is shown by the many errors he overlooked. One may recall that lists of errata, both ancient and modern, are perhaps more liable to misprints than any other compositions. Anyhow in 23 the comma should have been inserted after and not before *so*, while in 48 and 49 no comma can be tolerated at all. In 47 the sense is not greatly affected by the alteration of *still* to *yow*, and I think that in making it Massinger must have overlooked the *you* in the next line. The passage, however, is not free from difficulty, and though *yow* is hardly satisfactory it is possible that some other correction is needed. Perhaps *though* would give the required sense. One last case is of greater interest. In *The Emperor of the East*, IV. i, Chrysapius says:

> Howere I run the hazard of my head fort
> Should it arriue at the knowledge of the Princesse . . .

[1] Besides the errors here considered there are two clear slips, *least the* for *the least* (66) and *gaurded* for *guarded* (112), due to a misplaced caret-mark, two minim-errors (77, 288), and one seeming confusion (270).

and we find *Princesse* altered to *Empresse* (127). But, as Professor Cruickshank points out, this cannot be correct since the words are addressed to the empress herself. I can only imagine that Massinger wrote *Empresse* by mistake for *Emperour*.

(iv) Punctuation is responsible for the largest group of corrections, one hundred and eight, over a third of the total. There is no need to give the list in detail. The alterations vary from the most trivial to others seriously affecting the sense (e.g. 36, 267), among the most important being the correction (howbeit imperfect) of the parentheses in 225–7 and the removal of a comma in the name *Ælius Lamia* (191). The punctuation introduced by Massinger is often distinctly heavy, as in 'soone fading white, and red,' (143–4) and 'march'd in ranke, and file,' (278–9) and there is a noticeable partiality for parentheses where the printer (like the modern editors) was content with commas. This vast amount of punctual correction suggests either that the copy was in general lightly pointed, or that the compositor paid scant regard to it. Probably the former, for we find that *Believe as you List* varies considerably in this respect. Where Massinger is writing carefully, as in the opening passage, the punctuation is pretty full, though even here there is a tendency to leave lines unstopped at the end; but in other portions of the manuscript, where the writing shows a more current style, the pointing is at times very defective. Punctilious in principle, in practice Massinger seems to have been a loose writer.

(v) His interest in spelling, already observed in connexion with *The Duke of Milan* (iii, v), is evidenced in no less than twenty-two corrections. A dozen, perhaps, are such as one might expect from a careful press-reader of the time, and the quarto readings might have been included among small errors of carelessness (7, 22, 27, 54, 89, 90, 100, 157, 182, 242, 268, 288). But we also find *im̃aculate* for *imaculate* (76), *fix'd* for *fixed* (98), *guarded* for *garded* twice (102, 112), *pitty* for *pity* (117: also *pittye* as a correction of *piety*, 85), *prey* for *pray* according to the modern distinction (147), *Scæne* for *Sceane* (161), *Hypolitus* for *Hypollitus* (222), and finally *woone* for *wone* meaning 'won' (266). This last was a peculiarity of Massinger's spelling (as earlier of Munday's) and it appears to have effectually concealed his meaning from the compositor, who could hardly otherwise have misread *woone* as *woond* (97). The most interesting of these alterations, however, is that of *swing* to *swinge* (128) in the line:

Her absolute sway, and swing ore the whole state.

Here, according to the *O.E.D.*, the form *swinge* is etymologically correct, but *swing* is recognized as a popular variant, for which the present passage among others is cited.

(vi) The thirty-three corrections of miscellaneous small errors include, of course, a variety of kinds. In four instances Massinger expands a name abbreviated in the quarto (52, 124, 129, 142). Turned letters, literals, and the like, including an error of imposition, account for nine more (163, 200, 218, 219, 220, 228 and 232, 230, 272, 294). Lastly, there are twenty small misprints due, so far as one can see, to mere carelessness (51, 56, 80, 99, 111, 114, 141, 149, 158, 159, 167, 195, 207, 216, 221, 229, 259, 265, 283, 300).

(vii) The more substantial errors for which carelessness seems responsible are twenty-four. In some cases it is not hard to see how the mistake arose. It was no doubt a gap in the classical education of the compositor that was responsible for 'the buskind scæne and humble stocke' (155). Massinger corrected the last word to *socc*, with the Latin *soccus* in mind, but we may safely assume that he wrote *socke* in the copy. If, in 164, we suppose Massinger to have written *gieue* for *give* it is hardly surprising that the compositor should have printed *grieue*. That he did write *gieue* is practically certain, for that is what he has written in the margin by way of correction, and the same queer spelling is found both in the Foljambe verses and in *Believe as you List*. We find the word *heard* misprinted *Hand* in one place (14) and *hard* in another (252) which may point to a copy-spelling *hard*, but I do not think that this can be shown to be personal. No less than twelve errors consist of the omission of a small word (55, 63, 66, 84, 86, 101, 109, 115, 257, 290) or part of a word (208, 244), the most notable of the former being *fore-gale* for *fore-right gale* (84) and of the latter *Pinn'd* for *Pinion'd* (244). The reverse tendency is illustrated by two instances, the duplication of *I* in 11 and of *too* in 41. All these are as likely to be errors of the copy as of the press. The six remaining cases are substitutions. For three mere carelessness seems responsible: *with* for *this* (4), *yet* for *for* (30), and *and* for *his* (57). But in the case of *obserue* for *handle* (121), *for to* for *I woulde* (166), and *her*, *like* for *acres* (282), it is difficult not to suspect some definite cause. Graphic confusion seems out of the question, and I can only fall back on the conjecture of some imperfect or obscure alteration in the copy.

(viii) Of such confusions in the copy we found ample evidence in *The Duke of Milan*. The chief indications afforded by our present list are the erroneous attribution of certain speeches. The most instructive is 83, where a long speech by Vitelli is interrupted by a half line spoken by Asambeg. To this the prefix *Asam*. is correctly given, but none appears where Vitelli's speech is resumed. The natural inference is that the words of Asambeg were added in the margin to complete an originally short line. (The error was observed in the course of printing, and the printer was directed to insert the speaker's name, *Vitelli*. But instead of adding it in the right place he substituted it for the prefix *Asam*. Consequently in the later pulls the passage shows a double error.) In another passage (169 and 171) the speaker's prefix *Parth*. originally stood in the quarto two lines too late. That these two lines were a marginal addition is borne out by the fact that they contain the extraordinary misprint of *New workes* for *monarkes*, which could hardly have occurred unless the writing had been so crowded as to be illegible. (Here again a partial correction was made in the course of printing: the prefix *Par*. was inserted in its right place, and *Monarchs* duly supplied, but the incorrect *Parth*. was left standing.) In two other cases (59, 82) the omission of the speaker's name may be a mere oversight, and in 45 we may suppose that the copy had *Tima*., which the compositor expanded as *Timandra* instead of *Timagoras*. But the necessary rearrangement of 274–5 shows that the words *A post*, which belong to the text, have got tacked on to a stage-direction, which in the quarto stands two lines above, but was most likely written in the margin of the copy. Finally, a detached and unmeaning half line, which now stands in the middle of a long speech (280), is perhaps attributable to an obscure alteration by the author himself rather than to a careless cut by the prompter as

Gifford supposed. Seven corrections have been considered under this head.

(ix) At last we come to the important class of graphic confusions, to which forty-nine errors may be plausibly assigned. A curious group of seven consists of the erroneous omission of a final *s* (6, 16, 34, 39, 269, 281, 284), and to them may also probably be added the *Loose* which Massinger corrects to *Looseth* (26), but which we may suspect to have been *Looses* in the copy. (A solitary instance of the erroneous insertion of final *s*, in 149, is less likely to be a reflex error[1] than a mere slip.) The omissions are indeed confined to two plays, The *Bondman* and *The Picture*, but as these were printed by different firms at a distance of six years, we must look less to the compositor than to the author for an explanation. And I think we shall find it in a particular irregularity of his writing. Massinger's hand is, of course, of a very mixed type, but he usually makes a bold English final *s* which no compositor could mistake. Occasionally, however, he uses a final *s* of the small Italian type, which, since it occurs but rarely, might, if carelessly formed, be easily mistaken for a comma or even overlooked. Another peculiarity, for which it is less easy to account, but which must presumably have a graphic origin, is the omission of an initial *s* or *f*, as in *words* for *swordes* (203), *eares* for *feares* (46), and *care* for *feare* (95). It would seem that in these cases, in which the error is the reverse of one previously observed (*DM* 6), the compositor must have mistaken the long initial letter for a descender from the line above.

Most of the other confusions are of recognized types. A number are minim errors, as *m* for *nn* in 21 and *nn* for *m* in 31. We find *them* for *their* in 94, and a glance at the first page of *Believe as you List* will show how close the resemblance is. In *Cancillus* (181) we have *nc* for *m* and in *camer* (139) the reverse. Here Massinger writes his correction *cancer* in the margin, and I think that apart from the sense anyone would read it as *camer*. In 248, where the quarto has *iumpe* for *impe*, the minim error was probably helped by the compositor's

[1] [If a particular type of error is of frequent occurrence in the copy, a compositor may be led to assume its presence where in fact the copy is correct. This is what I term a 'reflex' error.]

ignorance of field sports. A very simple one is *niggle* for *iuggle* (150) in the passage:

> Take heed daughter,
> You niggle not with your conscience,

but it elicited a pseudo-learned note from Gifford, and has become the authority for a sense 'to trifle (†*with* a thing)' in the *O.E.D.*, which must be rejected. That Massinger was prone to these minim errors is shown by his very corrections, for to replace *dame* (288) he writes *damne*, apparently by mistake for *damme*, and to replace *made* (77) he writes *mam'd*, certainly by mistake for either *man'd* or *mann'd*. This last quarto error is difficult to explain, but possibly *made* (which offers a certain sense) arose through a *mãde* in the manuscript (it is corrected to *mande* in some copies of the original). Minim confusions can also be traced in other more complicated cases. If, in 209, Massinger wrote *tyrann* (i.e. 'tyrant'), the compositor (perhaps unfamiliar with the form) may have misread the second *n* as *ie* when he printed *tyrannie*. So too *where* was misread *when* in 49. The misprint *surely* for *Sicelie* (8) is partly a minim error; the confusion of *r* and *c* being another recognized possibility of Massinger's hand (*DM* 28), which reappears in *act* for *are* (235). Here we also get *t* for *e*, and when our author writes an English *e* rather large, as he often does, the resemblance with *t* is sometimes striking, so much so that we apparently even get the reflex error of *e* for *t*, as in *piety* for *pittye* (85) and *Leaue* for *Staue* (43, the confusion of Italian *S* and *L* being common).

Massinger's *e*'s are responsible for a good deal of trouble. If he writes an English *e* it is liable to confusion, not only with *t*, but of course with *d* as well (97, 260: though in the former case the error could hardly have arisen but for the eccentric spelling). Similarly his *d* is mistaken for *e* (179, 291). If, on the other hand, he writes a Greek ϵ (he seldom uses the Italian form) it may either be mistaken for *r* (15) or for *y* (118: the reverse error in 56 is apparently a slip), and a study of his manuscript shows that the printer is hardly to blame. This partly accounts for the appearance of *They* in place of *Hee* (135). *Hee* is what Massinger has written in the margin, and it is, including the capital, his usual spelling. But as our author is otherwise sparing of capital letters, it was not difficult for the compositor to mistake his print-like *H* for a badly formed Italian *th*. Massinger's *a* is misread as *u* (1, 2, 44) and as *o* (28); his *i* and *o* get confused (3) and possibly his *o* and *u* likewise (31). In *action* the *ti* has been misread as an Italian *h* (an easy error) and the word consequently printed in italic as *Achon* (12). The substitution of *which* for *with* (180) seems to show that the latter was sometimes contracted (cf. *DM* 31). The use of the contraction *o*ʳ is presumably responsible for *of* appearing by mistake for *our* (20), and some further confusion may explain our finding *or* in place of *S*ʳ. (264), for it will be observed that Massinger sometimes writes *s*ʳ with so small an *s* as to resemble *o*ʳ. Confusions presumably graphic, but which do not appear to be traceable to any personal peculiarity, are *this* for *'tis*, perhaps written *t'is* (256), *satisfie* for *Satietie* (261), and *tosses* for *trifles* (295: see below, p. 144). The error *assure* for *as sure* (241) is most likely a misreading of the manuscript, since only there could there be any doubt whether an *s* was final or not. Massinger sometimes uses a short Italian *s* both at the beginning and end of words. We may, therefore, perhaps suppose the other error of division, *I feuer* corrected to *yf ever* (151), to be likewise a misreading.[1] As a general rule Massinger's word-division is very clear.

Three curious errors require further discussion. In 96 we get the astonishing *Nimph* corrected to *vmph*. I do not know what form Massinger's capital *V*, if he ever used such a letter, took, but I see no reason to suppose that it resembled *N*.[2] But we may perhaps conjecture that in the copy the word was written *Humph*. Massinger's print-like *H* might, I think, be mistaken for *N*, but I should add that the confusion possibly occurred in English hands as well (see *Love's Labour's Lost*, ed. J. D. Wilson, 1923, pp. 110–11). In

1 Possibly, however, *If euer* became *I feuer* through an accident of the press, and this was miscorrected to *If feuer*. All three readings are found in various copies, and the order is uncertain.

2 Of course, a small *v* might, and in Massinger's hand sometimes does, resemble a certain form of capital *N* (that made like a small letter with an exaggerated first minim), but I am not clear that this form was sufficiently common at the time to make confusion possible. I do not think that Massinger's *v* could be mistaken for a small *n*.

170 *New workes* is corrected to *monarkes*. The writing must, one would suppose, have been rather obscure to allow of *mon* being turned into *new w*, and we have already found independent evidence that the passage was a marginal addition. We have also seen that *a* and *o* were capable of confusion (28, above). But it is possible that the error here was rather more complicated. It should be noticed that in writing his correction in the margin Massinger made an *a* of the well-recognized form in which the minim is detached from the circle, and which is therefore liable to be misread as *or* (see A. W. Pollard, *Shakespeare's Hand in 'Sir Thomas More'*, 1923, pp. 82, 120). When we remember that Massinger's *r* is also liable to confusion with *c*, it seems possible that the compositor misread *ark* as *orck* though he printed *ork*. It is, of course, clear that the copy had the spelling *monarkes* like the correction: when, in the course of printing, the error was corrected the word was spelt *Monarchs*. Lastly, in 91, *Constantinople* is corrected to *Courte*. Since the court is at Constantinople the sense in the quarto is quite satisfactory, but the metre clearly shows that *Courte* must be the original reading. How then did the error arise? I can only conjecture that the compositor misread *Courte* as *Conple* and took this to be a contraction for *Constantinople*. A small accidental mark might easily turn Massinger's *r* into *p*, while another (possibly part of the same offset) may have supplied a contraction mark above.

It is time to consider what light the corrections throw on the work of Massinger's editors.[1] A good many of the errors corrected occur, as we saw, in certain copies only of the originals, and these (so far as they have been ascertained) were finally purged from the text by Gifford, to whose credit be it said that he was not always content to rely upon a single copy of an early print. A number of other corrections of spelling and punctuation are not of a sort to affect a text in which these details were modernized. Further, there are many small corrections that would be made by any competent editor as a matter of course. Among these we may perhaps reckon as of some interest eighteen, all of which reached Gifford from his predecessors (viz. 16, 45, 56, already found in the second edition of *The Bondman*, 1638; 21, 55, 97, 155, 164, 179,

[1] [Namely T. Coxeter, 1759, J. M. Mason, 1779, W. Gifford, 1805 and 1813.]

181, 241, 260, 281, made by Coxeter; 34, 252, 259, 283, 284, added by Mason). The number of more important corrections which are found in Gifford's text number twenty-nine, of which perhaps four (84, 96, 274–5, 280) deserve special commendation. Out of the twenty-nine corrections, fourteen are due to Coxeter (41, 59, 82, 83, 85, 139, 208, 209, 242, 248, 261, 267, 274–5, 290: the very creditable arrangement in 274–5 being proposed in a note and silently appropriated by Gifford), seven to Mason (26, 44, 51, 171, 180, 203, 280: the second in a note), and eight to Gifford (20, 84, 96, 101, 115, 212, 225–7, 217).[1] It should, however, be remarked that although, according to Gifford, 'Mr. M. Mason tried to reform [225–7], but failed', his proposed arrangement only needs a comma after *Bosom* to be perfectly correct; and that in 84 Mason got as near the truth as *right Fore-gale*, Gifford restoring *fore-right gale* by comparison with *The Bondman*, III. iii (1624, G1^{v}, l. 10). A few other points should also be noticed. In 44, where Gifford merely printed *daring*, Mason retained *during* in the text with the note, '*Daring*, unless *during* shall mean *enduring*', which at least showed proper caution. In 169–71 Coxeter had the misfortune to print from a copy of the original containing the corruption. Mason left the text as he found it, but in a note he actually arrived by conjecture at the correct readings (except that he needlessly altered *that* to *who*). Gifford blamed Mason, perhaps justly, for not consulting the original, but showed no appreciation of the considerable critical feat he had achieved. In 209 Coxeter, of course, altered *tyrannie* to *tyrant* instead of Massinger's *tyrann*. Gifford, retaining *tyrant*, remarked: 'I have not removed Coxeter's emendation from the text; though it seems, by no means, necessary.' The meaningless half line of 280 was rightly removed from the text by Mason. He made no mention of the fact, but this is the only justification I can find for Gifford's statement that he 'gave the passage unfaithfully'. Gifford, of course, omitted it likewise, noting that 'There is both an imperfection and a

[1] The correction 212 does not appear to be necessary, and the alteration was probably made by Massinger on stylistic grounds. If so, Gifford's taste agreed with his author's, though that hardly justifies his editorial method. It may, of course, occur in some copies of the original.

redundancy in this speech, as it stands in the old edition'. What imperfection he found I do not know. Gifford deserves credit for his ingenious restoration of *Umph* for *Nimph* in 96, where Coxeter and Mason had been content with a makeshift *Ha!* In 165 he recognized, like Massinger, the necessity for the letter, though he introduced it in a separate direction some lines below.

The other side of the picture is even more interesting. There are some fifty passages in which Gifford's text does not incorporate even approximately the alterations made by Massinger. These include six out of the seven in which the author may be taken to have altered his original intention, and the four or five in which the alteration he made appears to be wrong. There remain just forty. In fourteen there is on the face of it no particular reason to suspect error, and Gifford cannot be blamed for leaving apparent well alone (see 6, 53, 66, 109, 118, 128, 136, 149, 150, 167, 183, 235, 236, 291).[1] In thirteen others he left the text as it stood, although in some cases it was manifest nonsense, and in all there were indications which should, I think, have aroused an editor's suspicions. In nine instances he saw clearly that the text was wrong, but failed to hit the right alteration. Lastly, in four (curiously enough all in *The Bondman*) he rejected correct emendations introduced by his predecessors. The last three groups require attention.

In several passages Gifford was at pains to defend the erroneous readings of the quartos. In 11, where the line in the original runs:

> Ile saue my lips, I rest on it.—He thinkes women . . .

instead of omitting the *I*, as sense and metre demand, Gifford explained the phrase as equivalent to 'I am fixed, determined, on it; a metaphor taken from play, where the highest stake the parties were disposed to venture, was called *the rest*'. But there is no evidence that in this sense the word was ever used verbally, and it seems very doubtful whether the phrase could bear the supposed meaning. Again, in 57 the quarto has:

> Next to the Generall, and the gods, and fautors . . .

[1] I give him the benefit of 150, though only a very elementary palaeographical knowledge is required for the detection of the error. He actually annotated the passage.

'which, in the language of the author, means the *favouring* gods', says Gifford confidently. But the author apparently did not agree, for he corrected it to 'the gods His fautors'. 'Alas, for Massinger!' as his editor remarks. And in 295 Honoria, dispensing bounty, is made to say: 'for other tosses take A hundred thousand crownes,' 'Meaning, perhaps,' says Gifford, '*for trash to fling away*', a suggestion for which there appears no warrant. The *O.E.D.*, quoting the passage, suggests doubtfully 'a payment'. Indeed, the true correction *trifles* is not very obvious.

In most instances, however, Gifford passes over the difficulty without comment. In 31 the quarto reads:

> your true Courtier knowes not
> His Neece, or Sister from another woman,
> If she be apt and cunning.

This is superficially so plausible that it would certainly require closer attention than Gifford was in the habit of bestowing to perceive that *cunning* does not really fit the context. Once this is realized, however, emendation should not be difficult, for the use of *coming* in the sense of 'forward' is well recognized from the beginning of the seventeenth century.[1] In 294 the sense is hardly in question: Gifford, of course, corrected the slight misspelling of the quarto, but instead of removing the unnecessary comma, as Massinger appears to have done, he actually replaced it by a semicolon, which no system of punctuation could approve. In two passages false grammar (39, 135) and in one false metre (91) should have warned an editor that something was amiss, but, whereas in the former two the correction was sufficiently obvious, no one could be expected to guess that *Constantinople* was a misprint for *Courte*. In 141 the awkwardness of the repetition in 'cease this admiration at this obiect' might have suggested that the first *this* should be *thie*.

[1] [Cf. *Troilus and Cressida*, III. ii. 139–41 (Globe), where the quarto (1609) reads:

> see see your sylence
> Comming in dumbnesse, from my weaknese drawes
> My very soule of councell.

'Comming' is also the folio reading, but Pope was perhaps right to read 'Cunning'. If so, the error was the reverse of that in Massinger.]

Four cases remain that are all pretty evident nonsense. Gifford seems quite unperturbed by the Austrian princess with a Roman nose (60). When the quarto makes Theodosius say that he has delivered Eudoxia 'into your handes, to vse And obserue, as you please,' he does not attempt to explain the sense or accent of *obserue*, for which Massinger substitutes *handle* (121). If he found any meaning in the lines (264):

> If I am so rich or
> In your opinion, why should you borrow
> Additions for me?

he kept it to himself: the simple substitution of *S*r. for *or* makes the passage clear. Finally, in 282 (where the context is too long to quote), how he can have thought that *her, like* made any possible sense is hard to guess, though one may well doubt whether the most ingenious of editors would have divined that the proper emendation was *acres*.

Against these may be set the nine cases in which Gifford seems to have perceived that the quarto reading could not stand, but accepted a wrong emendation into his text. As a matter of fact, in some instances he has silently taken over an alteration made by one of his predecessors, and I question whether his boasted consultation of the old copies had been sufficiently minute to warn him that he was departing from the original reading. In any case, three of these false emendations are due to Coxeter, namely: *your gadding* instead of *this gadding*, where the quarto reads 'I cannot brooke with gadding' (4); *Lead* instead of *Staue*, where the quarto has 'Leaue her off' (43); and *fight begin* instead of *fights begun* (i.e. *fight 's begun*), where the quarto has 'yet ere the fight begun' (269). In three other instances Gifford silently introduced false emendations of his own where his predecessors had been content to reproduce the faulty readings of the quartos. Thus in 108 he omitted *madam* instead of *to you* from the line:

> Auert it heauen.—Heauen is most gratious to you, madam;

in 237 he omitted *with* instead of *grim* from the line:

> And stood grim death now within my view and his . . .

and in 256 (where the context is lengthy) he got round the impossibility of the reading 'and in you this murther' by supposing the sense broken (printing 'murder,—') instead of changing *this* to *'tis*. The three remaining cases were the subject of annotation. In 63, where the quarto reads:

> I must expresse my loue:
> My aduise, and counsell. You are young
> And may be tempted . . .

he correctly replaced the colon by a comma, but in the next line, which is obviously defective, he added at the end the name *Vitelli*, 'which seems to have dropt out at the press', instead of prefixing *in* at the beginning, though even apart from authority this is clearly the preferable emendation. In 75 the quarto ends a speech with the line:

> And what are your employments? neat and easie.

Gifford observed that 'The old copy has no mark of interrogation after *easy*, which seems to prove that the [last three] words originally belonged to' the next speech, to which he therefore transferred them. The emendation was creditable; but, after all, it is much simpler to supply the query. Lastly, in 86, the quarto prints the defective line:

> What meanes this solemne musicke?—It vshers . . .

in which Gifford supplied the word *Sir*, 'the most innocent one that occurred to me', and which has the merit of being correct; but he inserted it at the beginning of the second speech instead of at the end of the first. This was sheer bad luck.

We have seen that in thirteen cases Gifford either tacitly accepted or actively defended the quarto text where it was more or less obviously in error. The four passages in *The Bondman* in which he returned to the original reading, rejecting the correct emendations of his predecessors, deserve close attention. In 30 the text runs in the quarto:

> Remember too, I charge you
> To teach my Horse good manners; yet this morning,
> As I rode to take the ayre, th'untutor'd Iade
> Threw me, and kic'kd [*sic*] me.

In this Coxeter made the simple and correct substitution of *for* in place of *yet*. Gifford silently restored *yet*, placing it, however, before instead of after the semicolon. It may be questioned whether this is really a less violent alteration, and it gives at best but a strained sense. It would have been better to have left the punctuation as it was and have interpreted *yet* in the obsolete sense of 'yet again'. Indeed, it is just possible, though not I think likely, that this was the author's original intention. Again, at the very beginning of the play, the quarto gives Leosthenes the awkward, though perhaps not impossible speech: 'In that trust I loue' (3). Gifford, following it in the reading *loue*, remarked that 'In the modern editions it is unnecessarily altered to *live*'. In point of fact, it is *live* in Mason's text alone, and the alteration, which is correct, certainly improves the sense. In the course of II. i, Leosthenes, warning Cleora of the dangers of the court, says in the quarto (28):

> when nor Father
> Is here to owe you; Brother to aduise you;
> Nor your poore seruant by . . .

Gifford following this remarked: '*Owe* (i.e. own) . . . is evidently right. The *property* of Cleora was in the father: this is distinguished from the only right the brother had;—*to advise*. The modern editors, not comprehending this, sophisticate the text, and print—*here to* awe *you!*' Apparently Massinger, too, failed to comprehend this fine distinction, for *awe* is his own correction. Last of all, at the end of Act III, the quarto has a particularly absurd misprint, representing Cleora's anger as 'Rising from your too amorous eares' (46). Coxeter was evidently asleep, for he printed *ears*, which Mason 'corrected at random' (according to Gifford) to *Fears*. Gifford himself chose to print *cares*, remarking that Mason's 'correction was not amiss; but the genuine word is undoubtedly that which I have given'. Oh irony! *feares* not *cares* was what the author meant.[1]

[1] Though not strictly relevant I am tempted to mention one other trap into which Gifford fell. It will be remembered that in a passage in *The Renegado* Massinger altered 'To vvitnesse of my change' to 'To vvitnesse my good change' (78–79). Gifford, of course, knew nothing of this and followed the quarto reading. He appended, however, the following note: 'The reader must be convinced, long ere this, that the modern editions of Massinger offer a very inadequate representation of his works. Numerous as the errors pointed out are, a still greater number have been

Perhaps there are lessons for all of us in the tricks which fate has played on the editors of Massinger. For my own part I confess that after many years' devotion to ultra-conservatism in the textual field, the close study of independent sources—not in Massinger alone, but in earlier dramatists as well—has bred some suspicion of the assumed looseness of Elizabethan thought, syntax, and vocabulary, and consequently a deeper sense of the necessity of emendation, though perhaps seldom greater tolerance of individual emendations. To be critically acceptable an emendation must satisfy two criteria: it must afford an absolutely satisfactory text, and it must explain the corruption. Such evidence as we are able to bring to bear—for instance, these corrections of Massinger's—does, I think, tend to show that true emendations generally fulfil these tests, and it is encouraging that this should be so. But emendation remains, notwithstanding, a difficult and a hazardous business, and there are two limitations to what I have just said that require to be borne in mind. For one thing the authentic text of even the best writer is by no means always absolutely satisfactory in the first instance; for another corruptions do occur, the causes of which seem beyond discovery. In either of these cases it is evident that, even should a correct emendation suggest itself, it must fail to satisfy one or other criterion, and can never prove wholly acceptable.[1]

corrected in silence: of these the source is generally obvious; here, however, is one for which no motive can be assigned; it is a gratuitous and wanton deviation from the original, that no degree of folly can justify, no excess of negligence account for:—In Coxeter and Mr. M. Mason the passage stands thus—"To prove that I have power"!' Neither folly nor negligence is needed to justify (if it ever could) or account for this reading, which is that of certain copies of the original. It was, I think, subsequently altered by the author, but is not on the face of it wrong. That 'the modern editions of Massinger offer a very inadequate representation of his works' is unhappily still true.

[1] [In 'Still More Massinger Corrections', *The Library*, 5 ser. v, Sept. 1950, 132–9, J. E. Gray listed forty-eight more alterations made by Massinger, all but one of which he thought were genuine corrections. Dr. J. G. McManaway has furnished me with another, which should precede Greg's 1: *The Bondman*, B 1, l.3. At the first occurrence of the name '*Timagorus*', Massinger inserted a mark which makes it seem to read 'Timagorŭs'. This must have been an attempt to convert the 'u' to an 'a'. Since no one before Dr. McManaway noticed it, Massinger was clearly right to switch to a clearer form of correction. I have also, thanks to Dr. McManaway, been able to delete three erroneous full-stops from Greg's 1 and 2.—J.C.M.]

10. *The Spanish Tragedy*—a Leading Case?[1]

It is well known that Kyd's famous play has come down to us in two different forms, one the shorter version as originally performed, the other containing certain additions, commonly, but almost certainly erroneously, ascribed to Ben Jonson. The enlarged text was first printed in the quarto of 1602, and since previous to 1909, when the British Museum acquired a remarkably fine copy, this edition was only known to editors from the imperfect copy in Malone's collection, the standard modern editions of the play (by J. Schick and F. S. Boas) rely for a part of the additions upon reprints of later date. A proposal that the Malone Society should include the quarto of 1602 among its publications for the current year led to some investigations into the bibliographical history of the play, and the results proved so unexpectedly interesting that no apology is needed for presenting a brief summary to readers of *The Library*. Two remarks only are needed by way of preface. One is that none of the evidence detailed below is new: but it is only the great strides that have been made in our familiarity with the habits of Elizabethan printers and publishers in the course of the last twenty years that has made a clearer and more comprehensive interpretation possible. The other, which is really part of the same, is that while this interpretation is here advanced with considerable confidence, it is fully recognized that the results are indeed matter of inference, however legitimate and plausible, and should not be confused with ascertained fact.

It is perhaps not so well known as it should be that there are portions of the Registers of the Stationers' Company

[1] [1925, June. *The Library*, vi. 47–53. The thesis here argued I think makes this article worth reprinting in spite of the evidence having been more fully presented in the introductions to the Malone Society reprints of the enlarged and original texts of *The Spanish Tragedy* that appeared in 1925 and 1949 respectively. I have omitted the end of the article, dealing with the later history of the play. The rest I have reprinted practically unaltered, but have added notes where further information or further consideration suggests modification of the views originally expressed. —1958.]

which, for some reason that it is difficult to understand, Arber was not allowed to include in his *Transcript*. At the end of his second volume (ii. 879) will be found a significant note to the effect that folios 427–86 of Register B are filled with decrees and ordinances, of which he was only permitted to make a few meagre extracts. 'These Ordinances are chiefly the decisions or arbitrations of the Executive of the Company upon complaints of or disputes between individual Stationers.' They appear to be distinct from the Court Book of 1576 to 1603,[1] which is lost, but whose successors, containing the minutes of the Court of Assistants, are preserved though unprinted. It will be abundantly evident that until the Company of Stationers allows these important records to be fully examined and published our knowledge of the early book-trade, and with it our knowledge of the literary conditions of the time, must rest on a very precarious basis.[2]

But by a stroke of good fortune the history of *The Spanish Tragedy* is one of the few matters concerning which a corner of the veil has been lifted, for certain extracts were made from the forbidden pages by William Herbert in his edition of Ames's *Typographical Antiquities* in 1785–90 (see p. 1160 in vol. ii). From these extracts and from Arber I take the following external facts bearing on the original publication of Kyd's play. In July 1592 Abel Jeffes, printer, was in trouble with the authorities for printing a book 'without authority' (Herbert). The date is fixed as about the 22nd, when John Wolf went 'to the Court to Croyden', where Archbishop Whitgift had a palace, 'about Ieffes disorder' (Arber, i. 560). Jeffes made matters worse by resisting search and refusing to deliver 'the barre of his presse', as a guarantee against further printing, or to have his stock 'brought to the hall', and on 7 August it was 'ordered, by a full court, that for his said offence he shall be committed to ward'. We hear no more of the matter till 18 December following, when 'according to the direction of the lord Archbishop of Canterbury his grace'

[1] [This opinion of Arber's is certainly mistaken.]

[2] [With the generous sanction of the Court of the Stationers' Company, the Bibliographical Society has now been able to remedy the defect by printing editions of the Court minutes from 1576 to 1602 contained in Register B, prepared by Miss Eleanor Boswell and myself, in 1930, and of Court Book C down to the end of 1640, prepared by William A. Jackson, in 1957–8.]

Jeffes again appeared 'In full court' and made his humble submission. The inference is that for over four months the delinquent languished in the Company's private lock-up,[1] and though it is perhaps unlikely that during these months, when London was first experiencing the full effects of one of the worst outbreaks of plague, his incarceration was strictly enforced, we may feel assured that, even if he regained personal liberty pending his formal act of submission, he was not allowed actively to pursue his profession until that act had been duly performed.[2] It is worth noting his entries of copy during this period. He registered a ballad on 15 July, and on 7 August (the very day of his committal) a book, actually with the Archbishop's licence, though presumably this had been obtained some time before. Then on 6 October he entered three items,[3] after which his name does not appear till 18 March following. That his submission on 18 December was an important affair necessitating some preparation, appears from the fact that on the 13th and 14th of the month some officers of the Company, together with John Wolf, waited on the Archbishop at Lambeth 'about Ieffes disorder' (Arber, i. 561).

Now one of the three works entered as Jeffes's copy on 6 October was *The Spanish Tragedy*. For this, it should be incidentally remarked, the registration fee of 6*d*. remained unpaid, but no one seems to have questioned the validity of the entry on this ground. In any case Jeffes's first act on making his peace with the authorities was to complain that another stationer, Edward White, had pirated this particular book. White retorted that Jeffes had previously pirated his, White's, *Arden of Feversham*. The Court of Assistants considered the case at their session on 18 December, and decreed 'that all the books of each impression shalbe confiscated &

1 [This is pure fiction. The Company had no prison of its own: it had, however, authority to commit offending members to one of the public jails.]

2 [Another mistake. He printed at least one edition of Nashe's *Pierce Penniless* during this period.] [See below, p. 405.—J.C.M.]

3 [One of these was Chaucer's Works, to be printed for the Company. This was charity on the Company's part, a permit to print one of its copies for his own benefit. He was, indeed, in no position to undertake the printing of such a work himself, but he was able to assign his rights to Adam Islip on 20 December 1591, no doubt for a consideration, and this enabled Islip to obtain from George Bishop the contract for the printing of Speight's Chaucer, which appeared in 1598.]

forfayted . . . to thuse of the poore of the company[1] . . . that either of them shall pay for a fine—10s a pece . . . And as touching their imprisonment for the said offence, yt is referred ouer to some other conuenient tyme'. White paid his fine in the following May. There is no record of Jeffes having ever done so: in December 1595 he was again in trouble, his press and type were seized, brought to Stationers' Hall, and broken up. I may add that White's entry of *Arden* is dated 3 April 1592, and that so far as I am aware no trace of Jeffes's pirated edition of this play has ever been found. Since we can hardly suppose that Jeffes, even if personally at liberty, was suffered to work his press between 7 August and 18 December 1592, his piracy must have been printed before the first of these dates, and of course after 3 April.[2]

I now turn to the internal evidence. Of the unexpanded text of *The Spanish Tragedy* three editions are known, each in a single copy only. Two bear the dates 1594 and 1599 respectively, one is undated. There is now no question that the unique copy without date in the British Museum is the earliest: this has been proved at needless length but with complete cogency by Schick. It bears the imprint, 'At London Printed by Edward Allde, for Edward White', and is unquestionably a copy of White's confiscated edition.[3] The edition of 1594, a copy of which is preserved at Göttingen, bears the words, 'London, Printed by Abell Ieffes, and are to be sold by Edward White', implying that Jeffes was the printer and publisher and White merely the bookseller. Before the next edition appeared Jeffes had, by an entry dated 13 August 1599, assigned his interest in the play to William White, who was no connexion of Edward. The third extant

[1] [It looks as though White and Jeffes had been allowed to redeem their confiscated stocks for a money payment. At the end of the Warden's accounts for 1592–3 Richard Collins, the Clerk, added the following note (Arber, i. 563): 'Memorandum that there should be put into the receiptes of this accoumpt iij^{li}x^{s}. Receaved of Edward White and Abel Jeffes for confiscated bookes. The which by mistakinge were put into the poore accoumpt And nowe by a Court are brought hither . . . Teste R/C.' Since the books were confiscated 'to thuse of the poore of the company', one would have supposed that the money had been properly credited to the poor account.]

[2] [This, of course, is again mistaken.]

[3] The suggestion that, since, as we shall see in a moment, it cannot have been the first edition, it may have been a reprint issued by White through a friendly arrangement with Jeffes, may be safely rejected. In such a case Jeffes's name would certainly have appeared.

edition, the Bridgewater copy of which is now in the Huntington Library, California, must therefore be later than 13 August this year, since it has the imprint: 'At London Printed by William White, dwelling in Cow-lane'—a case in which the functions of printer, publisher, and bookseller were combined in one person.

But the undated print, though the earliest that survives—or to speak more cautiously, the earliest known—was certainly not the first to be printed, for it bears on its title-page a statement (repeated by its successors) to the effect that it was 'Newly corrected and amended of such grosse faults as passed in the first impression'. This not only proves that an earlier edition had appeared, but implies that its text was seriously defective. It may, of course, be no more than a publisher's puff announcing the supersession of a carelessly printed edition by one more typographically accurate, but it at least raises suspicion, and should on the face of it, and I think by analogy, mean a good deal more. 'Newly corrected, augmented, and amended' and 'Newly imprinted and enlarged' are the formulas used in substituting the 'good' for the 'bad' quartos of *Romeo and Juliet* and *Hamlet* respectively: 'Newly corrected and augmented' that which appears in the probably similar case of *Love's Labour 's Lost.* And if this point can be brought into relation with the very remarkable imprint of the 1594 edition, which calls aloud for explanation, a considerable step will have been taken towards unravelling the history of this curious affair.

Having now presented, I hope with impartiality, the evidence, I will proceed to offer my interpretation of it. In the spring or early summer of 1592 Abel Jeffes printed an edition of *The Spanish Tragedy*. It is unlikely to have been earlier, since 1591 was a year of very slight activity in the field of dramatic publication. His edition contained what we have learned to call a 'bad' text, one seriously corrupted from the genuine playhouse version, and presumably obtained by more or less shady means. Perhaps on this account he forbore to enter the play in the Register of the Company. In the latter part of July he got into trouble with the authorities—in effect the ecclesiastical authorities apparently—and on 7 August he was committed to ward. For nineteen weeks he either remained actually in prison or at least debarred from exercising his craft,[1] but during this time he got wind of an intention on the part of Edward White (whose rights he had himself invaded) to publish another edition of the popular tragedy, and resolved to protect his own interest therein by getting it formally entered as his copy. This he did on 6 October. But White, who had obtained what is certainly an excellent text, presumably with the consent of the actors and with the express purpose of replacing Jeffes's debased version, reckoned that in view of his rival's precarious position it would be safe to ignore him, and proceeded with his publication. However we may sympathize with and approve of White's action, there can be no doubt that he was flying in the face of the regulations of the Company. And, as it proved, he had miscalculated. Jeffes in December made his peace with the authorities, and at the same time lodged a complaint against White, the result of which we have already seen. This left Jeffes in possession of the field, but strictly what he owned was the copyright of his own bad text, not of White's good one. White's claim may have been indefinite, and one would give a good deal to have heard it argued before the Court of Assistants, but it would appear to have been not wholly negligible. Any way, like reasonable men, Jeffes and White came to terms, and the next edition, containing White's text, was printed by Jeffes, while the distribution was entrusted to White.

I am sensible that there is a possible objection to one point at least in my proposed reconstruction. I do not know of any instance of what we now technically call a 'bad' quarto as early as 1592, and the fact that criticism tends to regard this type as a product of the plague of 1592–4 may be thought somewhat to invalidate my postulate. On the other hand, the words on the undated title-page, which were repeated in 1594 and 1599, are strong; and there must have been some specific inducement that caused Jeffes in 1594 to take his quondam rival into some sort of partnership. These considerations together leave very little doubt in my mind that Jeffes's lost text was seriously defective, but I think that it may very well happen that, as our bibliographical knowledge of this difficult

[1] [Not so.]

field grows more definite, we may have to recognize that the first edition of *The Spanish Tragedy* can hardly have been quite of the same type as the first of *Hamlet*. After all, it was one of my theses in writing on *Two Elizabethan Stage Abridgements* (1923), that not all 'bad' quartos are of one kind, 'and that we should look with suspicion on any theory that claims to be universally applicable'.

I do not think I am claiming too much if I call this episode in the history of *The Spanish Tragedy* a 'leading case' in dramatic bibliography. Unless my interpretation of the evidence is at fault, and it is, of course, admittedly conjectural, we have here an instance of a stationer printing a bad and surreptitiously obtained version of a popular play, and, by a belated entry in the Stationers' Register, defeating the owner of a good authorized text in his purpose of publishing the same, while we see him at the same time debarred from appropriating to his own use the good text obtained by his rival, and thus forced in the end to come to an understanding with him. To bibliographical students of the text of Shakespeare the importance of these facts—if facts they are—will not need stressing.[1]

[1] [The argument of this article is supported by a curious story preserved in the State Papers Domestic for 1631 and told in the collection of essays published in honour of Professor F. P. Wilson in 1959.] [Greg here refers to the second of his 'Two Notes', 'Copyright in Unauthorized Texts', in *Elizabethan and Jacobean Studies Presented to Frank Percy Wilson* (1959), pp. 62–64. On this whole subject, Greg's chief opponent was the late Professor Leo Kirschbaum, in 'Is *The Spanish Tragedy* a Leading Case?', *J.E.G.P.* xxxvii (1938), 501–12 and *Shakespeare and the Stationers* (1955). For a brief account, see the *Revels* edition of *The Spanish Tragedy* by Philip Edwards (1959), who agrees in the main with Greg, while rejecting the contention (p. 154) that 'strictly what [Jeffes] owned was the copyright of his own bad text, not of White's good one': 'copyright . . inhered in the work, and not in good or bad versions of it' (p. xxx, n. 2).—J.C.M.]

II. *The Escapes of Jupiter*[1]

THE well-known collection of manuscript plays, mostly theatrical copies from the first half of the seventeenth century, bought at the sale of Lord Charlemont's library in 1865, is now classed as MS. Egerton 1994 in the British Museum. Two of its articles are thus described in the official catalogue:

3. Play in five acts, without title, in which the characters are Raphael, Treadway, Ashburne, Lord and Lady Averne, an abbot, *etc.* Apparently *autograph*; with corrections and passages marked for omission. f. 52.

4. "The escapes of Jupiter," or the stories of Calisto, Danae, Semele, and Alcmena; in five acts. In the same hand as the preceding. f. 74.

The first to make use of this interesting volume was A. H. Bullen, who in 1883 printed a critical account of its contents as an appendix to the second volume of his *Collection of Old English Plays*, and also included editions of four of its items in that and the subsequent volumes of his work. It was in the fourth volume, issued in 1885, that he gave a text of the titleless play of which the description has been already quoted, and succeeded in identifying it with a recorded piece by Thomas Heywood. He began his Introduction as follows:

In Sir Henry Herbert's MS. Office-Book, under date Sept. 3rd, 1624, is the entry:—"for the Cock-pit Company a new play called the Captive [*sic*] or the Lost Recovered, written by Hayward," *i.e.* Heywood. The lost recovered! Lost for two centuries and a half was this comedy of dear Tom Heywood, until I recovered it from Egerton MS. 1994 . . .

The play is without title or author's name in the MS. After reading the first page I judged that the author was Heywood, and this impression was soon confirmed beyond all doubt. In the MS. the present play is immediately followed by a piece called *Calisto*, which consists of scenes from Heywood's *Golden Age* and *Silver Age* . . . *Calisto* and *The Captives* are written in the same desperately difficult handwriting,—peculiar to these two plays, and not found in any other part of the

[1] [1925. 'Anglica', Brandl-Festschrift: *Palaestra*, nos. 147–8, ii. 211–43.]

volume. There can be no doubt that whoever transcribed *Calisto* transcribed also *The Captives*. But from internal evidence alone—putting aside the testimony afforded by the handwriting, and ignoring the entry in Sir Henry Herbert's Office-Book—any competent reader could plainly perceive that the play is Heywood's.

It would be unwise to attach very much importance to Bullen's enthusiastic confidence, since he was equally certain in his ascription to Shirley of the Duke of Newcastle's *Captain Underwit*,[1] but in view of the converging evidence of the style, the association with the *Ages*, and appropriateness (in spite of the minor divergence) of the title recorded by Herbert, no one, I believe, has ventured to question the correctness of the identification.[2]

Bullen does not appear to have claimed the play as being written in Heywood's own hand.[3] Nevertheless there is ample evidence to support the cautious statement of the catalogue that it is 'apparently autograph'. The fact of two manuscript plays by the same author being found in the same handwriting

[1] 'No other playwright of that day could have given us such exquisite poetry as we find in *Captain Underwit*.' A. W. Ward, writing in the *Dictionary of National Biography* (s.v. James Shirley), states that Bullen made the ascription 'somewhat doubtfully', but this is quite incorrect. His actual words are: 'I have little doubt, or rather no doubt at all, that *Captain Underwit* is one of' the plays left in manuscript by Shirley; and elsewhere: 'it is absolutely certain . . . that *Captain Underwit* is a comedy of Shirley's.' Perhaps, after all, he was not so far astray, for tradition assigns to Shirley some share in His Grace's labours. Anyhow this over-confidence does not detract from the credit due to Bullen for having identified *The Captives* and for being the first to decipher, if somewhat imperfectly, the very difficult writing.

[2] It is fully endorsed by A. C. Judson, who produced a new edition of the play for the Elizabethan Club of Yale University in 1921. This 'semi-popular edition', while correcting a number of Bullen's mistakes, is still far from accurate, and is indeed of little value for critical purposes. I am not here concerned with *The Captives*, but there is one point to which I should like to call attention, if only as a warning to dramatic historians. At IV. i. 350 (Judson's numbering) we learn that 1530 was the year of the heroine's birth. Such an antiquated date is unusual in a comedy of this sort, and in fact the date was first written 1600, then altered to 1630 and finally to 1530. But it is natural to suppose that the first date was not put down without intent. The lady then was really born in 1600. We are also told (I. iii. 104) that she is not yet twenty years of age. Lastly we read (V. iii. 69): "t must bee in leap-yeare then, Not now'. Many plays have been dated upon no surer evidence than we here have for 1619 as the year of composition. And yet we know that the piece was licensed in 1624, which *was* a leap-year! Was Heywood, therefore, revising earlier work? It may be.

[3] Bullen also tentatively ascribed to Heywood another piece which immediately precedes *The Captives* in the manuscript, namely *Dick of Devonshire*. This is written in a neat and rather beautiful hand, but the character of the corrections proves it to be unmistakably that of a scribe.

itself affords some presumption that they are autograph, and when we consider that no sane person would have employed a scribe who wrote such an atrocious hand, the presumption is considerably strengthened. Still, where we have no accredited writing of the author in question,[1] the only proof that can be given that a document is autograph is that derived from the nature of the corrections made therein, and it was doubtless upon such evidence that the cataloguer relied. Happily it is abundant; and though there will probably always be people prepared to argue that any correction may be scribal, it is of a sort to which palaeographers are rightly accustomed to attach weight. I will content myself with two instances from the second play, in which correction is much less frequent than in *The Captives*. They occur close together in the first act (fols. 75*b*, 76*a*). The first passage reads:

why did you off a douughter take the name
but to bee stild a mother, and to bee.
as prowd hearafter off a bewteous Child
as shee was att [thy] *your* byrthe, natur hath stinnted y[u]
off nothinnge wch shee hadd nor shall your Issue
[ffayle] *want* off your known perfection, should all wom⟨en
bee off your strict [per] [strict] [perversnes] *and peevish abstinence*
posterity shoold ffayle and mankinnd Cease

Here the words within brackets have been crossed out,[2] mostly it would seem while the ink was still wet, and those printed in italic have been interlined. It is a pretty exercise to determine the exact order in which the alterations have been made, but any reasonable person who applies his mind to it will, I think, remain convinced that we have here to do with an author composing as he wrote and making corrections *currente calamo*. The second example is perhaps even clearer:

shee is the dowghter off an antient kinnge
that swayde the Attick scepter, who sollicited
by many suitors. fyrst beegan the order
off profest [virgins]. [who ffyrst]*Maydes and* drewe to her society
Douughters off kinnges and princes, all devoted
To abandon men and Chuse virginity

[1] [We do, in fact, possess at least a couple of signatures of Heywood's, and although the script is different from that of the plays, the manner of writing is consonant.]

[2] Each pair of brackets indicates a separate deletion.

Here it is evident that the italicized words are no mere substitution, since without them the line is not metrical, and it is hardly possible to doubt that when the writer set down the words 'of profest virgins. who ffyrst drewe'[1] he had in mind a continuation other than that we now find. But at this point he perceived that in 'who ffyrst' he was repeating words already used in the two previous lines and altered his intention. When, however, he substituted 'and drewe to her society' he left in the middle of the line a redundant syllable which he then removed by changing 'virgins' to 'Maydes'.[2]

But while it is upon such alterations as these that the proof of autography must ultimately rest, it is in the present instance possible to reinforce it by two interesting demonstrations. One of these concerns a very rare spelling which occurs in several of the early editions of Heywood's plays, the other a graphic peculiarity which clearly explains a repeated and extraordinary misprint found in a particular quarto.

The asseveration which in modern English we write *ay* appears normally as *I* in the work of scribes and printers of the late sixteenth and early seventeenth centuries.[3] In several of the first editions of Heywood's plays, however, we find a more or less consistent use of the unusual spelling *ey*. The same spelling occurs, I believe exclusively, in the two manuscript plays under consideration. In *The Captives* there are fifteen instances, more than half of which occur in a single short passage in IV. i (fol. 67*a*). I have not troubled to decipher the whole of the second play, but there are at least four instances of *ey* (only one of which coincides with the printed text), while I have observed none of the spelling *I*.

1 The colour of the ink shows that 'drewe' was written immediately after 'ffyrst': the pen was redipped before the next word was written.

2 Both quotations are from passages of the manuscript which differ widely from the printed text and represent practically free composition. Judson quotes some very convincing instances from *The Captives* in the introduction to his edition.

3 According to the *Oxford English Dictionary* the word, of 'origin unknown', appeared 'suddenly about 1575', soon became 'exceedingly common', and 'was at first always written *I*'. It gives the spelling *ey* as current from the seventeenth to the nineteenth centuries, but the only instances quoted are from Heywood and Byron. The spelling *aye* first appears (in the parliamentary sense) in 1669. [I have ventured to alter Greg's *aye* in the text to *ay*. The *O.E.D.* head-word is 'Aye, ay', but this does not conform to present-day usage. The 1669 quotation in fact has the plural *ayes*, so is no evidence for the singular *aye*, for which the earliest quotation given is 1857.—J.C.M.]

A good deal of attention has recently been paid to the survival of so-called 'copy-spellings' in the early editions of Elizabethan plays, and it may, therefore, be worth going somewhat fully into the evidence in the present case. A cursory examination of Pearson's 1874 reprint of Heywood's plays (which was, however, not always made from the earliest editions) yielded results which may be summarized as follows.

In the *Brazen Age* and 2 *Iron Age* no instance of the word in question seems to occur.[1]

In 1 and 2 *Edward IV*,[2] 1 and 2 *If you know not me*, *The Fair Maid of the Exchange*, *A Woman Killed with Kindness*, *The Four Prentices*, 1 and 2 *Fair Maid of the West*, *The Silver Age*, *The English Traveller*, *The Late Lancashire Witches*, *A Challenge for Beauty*, *Love's Mistress*, *The Rape of Lucrece*, *Fortune by Land and Sea*, and the *Dialogues and Dramas*, the only spelling is *I*.

In 1 *Iron Age* and *The Wise Woman of Hogsden* both *I* and *ey* appear, but whereas the former play affords but rare instances of either, the latter yields only a single *I* to about nine examples of *ey*.

Lastly, in *The Golden Age*, *A Maidenhead Well Lost*, and *The Royal King and Loyal Subject*, I have found the spelling *ey* only.

There is little doubt that an experienced compositor, if he were paying attention to the sense, would alter the copy-spelling *ey* to *I*. But an inferior craftsman would be likely to retain it, and the attention of even the adept is liable to wander at times. It may not be without significance that both in *A Maidenhead Well Lost* and in *The Wise Woman of Hogsden* the first time the word occurs it is spelled not *ey* but *eye*, being apparently mistaken for the ordinary word *eye*, a fact which points to the compositor being unfamiliar with the spelling *ey* for *I*. Where then the spelling *ey* occurs we can feel pretty certain that the copy had that form, though we cannot infer from the spelling *I* that the copy did not have *ey*. At the same

[1] [In fact *Ey* occurs once in 2 *Iron Age*, Pearson, p. 365.] [For other instances, see Arthur Brown's note in *Modern Language Review*, l (1955), 497–8. Professor Brown tells me that the spelling occurs, outside Heywood, in Rowley's *A Shoemaker a Gentleman*, and in Richard Johnson's *Seven Champions of Christendom*.—J.C.M.]

[2] Of doubtful authorship. In part 1 Pearson gives one instance of the spelling *Ay*, *ay*, but this is a misprint.

time the two spellings are separated in the Heywood quartos much more consistently than on general grounds we should expect, and it is difficult to avoid the suspicion that the quartos may fall into two distinct groups, the one of four or five printed from autograph copy, the other printed from transcripts of various kinds.[1]

It would of course be rash to assume that no one but Heywood ever used the spelling *ey*, though it is unquestionably rare, and with one exception I have certainly never noticed it outside the plays already mentioned. The first to remark on the peculiarity was, I believe, F. G. Fleay, who as long ago as 1890 assigned *Nobody and Somebody* (licensed 1606) to Heywood on the strength of the spelling *ey*, 'which is, as far as my knowlege extends, peculiar to him'.[2] He did not, however, give any details.[3]

So much for the evidence of the spelling, now for the misprint.

The Wise Woman of Hogsden first appeared in 1638, and the quarto exhibits some extraordinary errors in the numbering of the acts.[4] We find namely at the beginning of the fourth the heading 'Actus 46. Scena prima', and at the beginning and end of the fifth 'Actus 56. Scena prima' and 'Explicat [*sic*] Actus 56'. It is, of course, pretty evident that the errors arose through the misreading of some form of contraction, but it is not till one examines the manuscript that what exactly happened becomes clear. Either of the plays will serve: I take the second. This is headed quite normally 'Actus primus scena prima', and all goes well as far as the end of the second act.

[1] Heywood gives us to understand that all his plays before *The Rape of Lucrece*, that is 1 and 2 *Edward IV*(?), 1 and 2 *If you know not me*, *The Fair Maid of the Exchange*, and *A Woman Killed with Kindness*, were surreptitiously printed from copies obtained by shorthand. None of these exhibit the *ey* spelling.

[2] In the quarto, which is undated, I find three instances of *ey*, but *I* occurs as well. The attempt of some Shakespearian editors to interpret 'Loues eye' in Sonnet 148. 8 as 'Love's ay' is certainly wrong.

[3] I suspected at one time that his attention had been drawn to the peculiarity by the remarkable passage in IV. i of *The Captives*, and that he might be generalizing from it. But this cannot have been the case, for I am quite sure that he never consulted the manuscript, and Bullen misprinted the word as *ay*, in every instance. Heywood's hand is far from clear, and once or twice it would be quite reasonable to read *ay*, but of the general intention there can be no doubt.

[4] It should be observed that it is one of those in which the spelling *ey* is most frequent.

Here, however, the writer gets impatient. He no longer writes 'secundus' in full, nor does he adopt either of the correct and normal contractions, '2us' or '2^{s}'. Instead, what he writes is: 'Explicit Actus 2s.' and below: 'Actus 3s scena prima.' Moreover in '2s' and '3s' he writes an ordinary English (or 'Secretary') final 's', which, in a careless hand such as his, is indistinguishable from a '6' made, as it is often is, with the loop first. There is little doubt that anyone ignorant of the sense would read these symbols as '26' and '36', and so, even more certainly, '56' at the end of the play.

This graphic peculiarity, then, like the unusual spelling already noted, affords an additional presumption in favour of the manuscript in which it is found being in Heywood's own hand. Proof it cannot be called, since, if the work could otherwise be regarded as that of a scribe, it might be argued that the same scribe had been employed to copy out other of Heywood's plays. Taken, however, in connexion with previous considerations, the nature of the corrections and the character of the hand, I think that this corroborative evidence should remove any possible doubt of the two plays in the Egerton manuscript being holograph pieces by Heywood.

I now pass to the consideration of the second of the two plays, and more particularly of its relation to the printed texts of *The Golden* and *Silver Ages*. It is headed at the top of the first page 'Calisto', but since the adventures of that young lady occupy only the first of the five acts, it is impossible to take this as the title of the whole play. However, on the otherwise blank verso of the last leaf (fol. 95*b*) there is written in a different, though perhaps contemporary, hand, 'The Escapes of Iupiter',[1] and no more suitable title for the play could be imagined.

That the piece consists of scenes from Heywood's *Golden Age* and *Silver Age* was pointed out by Bullen, who added that the text presented 'many variations from the printed copy'.

[1] That is, the love-lapses. The word occurs in *The Golden Age* (v. i, sig. I4, p. 72), where Neptune, enumerating Jupiter's amours, adds: 'Such scapes may breed iust feares', and the whole phrase is employed by Lodge in his *Margaret of America* (1596): 'The escapes of Jupiter, the wanton delights of Venus, and the amorous deceits of Cupid.' [Also *The Two Noble Ladies*, l. 1740 (Malone Society Reprint): 'Sing in her eares the scapes of Iupiter.']

He also transcribed, from fol. 82*a*, the song evidently called for by Danae with the words:

> Command our Eunuch's with their pleasing'st tunes
> To charme our eyes to rest,

but which is missing from the printed text (*Golden Age*, IV, sig. I 1ᵛ, p. 67); and again the one on fol. 76*a*, remarking quite justly that 'Of the charming song "Haile beauteous Dian, Queene of Shades" the MS. gives a far inferior version' (see *Golden Age*, II, sig. D3ᵛ, 4, pp. 27–28). Two problems will engage our attention: Which of the two versions, print or manuscript, is the earlier? and: Of what character was the revision that turned one into the other?

The Golden Age and *The Silver Age*, first printed in 1611 and 1613 respectively, are plays dealing with the early history of the world, as represented in classical mythology, from the days of Uranus to those of Hercules. In this, naturally, the loves of Jupiter play a conspicuous part, and the stories are not unskilfully interwoven, especially in the earlier piece, with other, perhaps weightier, themes. Let us first see exactly how the scenes of the manuscript correspond with those of the printed plays.[1]

The first act of *The Escapes* tells the story of Calisto. It corresponds to the second act of *The Golden Age*, except that it omits the initial chorus by Homer, beginning with the entry of Lycaon and Jupiter (fol. 74*a*; *G.A.*, C4ᵛ, p. 20), and has a different hymn to Diana (fol. 76*a*; *G.A.*, D3ᵛ, p. 27) consisting of two stanzas instead of three. After Jupiter has carried off the struggling Calisto in his arms, Heywood wrote 'Explicit Actus primus', but crossed it out again and added a twelve-line speech by Homer, after which he repeated the explicit (fol. 78*b*). The first four lines of this speech form the opening of the chorus at the beginning of Act III of the printed version (*G.A.*, E3, p. 35), while the last six correspond to those at the end of the chorus beginning Act IV (*G.A.*, G3ᵛ, p. 53).

1 Manuscript and prints are alike divided into acts only, though changes of scene are sometimes implied. I refer to the former by folios, of which the play occupies nos. 74 to 95 of the whole manuscript. The two printed plays I cite as *G.A.* and *S.A.*, adding the signature of the original edition and the page of Pearson's reprint in vol. iii of Heywood's Dramatic Works (1874). [Quotations are from the original quartos.]

The second act is devoted to Danae and corresponds to the latter part of Act IV of the printed play. It begins (fol. 79*a*) with the entry of the Beldams (*G.A.*, H1, p. 57), and, with the insertion of the song already noticed, continues till Jupiter's departure (*G.A.*, I3^{v}, p. 71). Then follows immediately another speech by Homer (fol. 83*a*) the first four lines of which form the opening of the chorus at the end of the last act of the printed version (*G.A.*, K2, p. 77), and the remaining eight are parallel to lines 5–12 of the chorus that opens Act IV of *The Silver Age* (unmarked, H4^{v}, p. 146).

The third act belongs to Semele. It opens with a scene (occupying fol. 84*a*) to which there is nothing corresponding in print, but with the conversation between Juno and Iris (fol. 84*b*) agreement begins with the fourth act of *The Silver Age* (I1, p. 147), and continues to the end of Jupiter's lament over Semele (*S.A.*, K1, p. 155). Again Homer closes the act with a speech, this time of fourteen lines (fols. 86*b*, 87*a*), corresponding to the middle portion (ll. 21–34) of the opening chorus of Act II (*S.A.*, C2^{v}, p. 97).

The last two acts deal with Alcmena. The fourth again opens with a scene (fol. 87*a*, *b*) which is only represented in print by the dumb show that follows the chorus just mentioned. Then on the entry of Jupiter with thunder and lightning (fol. 87*b*) agreement begins with Act II of the printed play (*S.A.*, C3, p. 98), and continues to the parting of Jupiter and Alcmena (*S.A.*, D3, p. 107). Six lines by Homer, which have no printed counterpart, conclude the act (fol. 90*b*). The fifth continues from the same point in the printed text, and agreement is carried on to Jupiter's theophany which closes Act II of the printed version (*S.A.*, F2, p. 122), after which a final ten-line speech of Homer, which has no close parallel in the printed version, concludes *The Escapes of Jupiter*.

In considering the priority of these versions there is one important point to be borne in mind. There does not appear to be any difference in style between the handwriting of the two plays, and the date of *The Captives* is fixed by Herbert's licence as 1624, which is thirteen years later than one and eleven years later than the other of the printed quartos. This fact raises a presumption in favour of the priority of the *Ages* which it would take strong evidence to rebut.

In point of fact it is not difficult to show, both from general and particular considerations, that in *The Escapes* we have a purely derivative text. One peculiarity must immediately strike the attention, namely that though the play contains five acts it deals with only four episodes. But in a piece of this type, if the composition were original, we should certainly expect to find 'every act a play'. There is no lack of material. Ceres, Europa, Leda, all cry out to have their stories told; most of all Io, who is mentioned more than once in the course of the play. But if *The Escapes* is a *réchauffé* of *The Ages* all is simple enough. For those plays are both constructed on the same model (though the first much better than the second), namely three acts of general history alternating with others devoted to Jupiter's love affairs. There was therefore room for no more than four of these out of many equally tempting, and hence in rewriting Heywood was constrained to 'cut an innocent *wife* in the middle to serve *her* in twice'.

There is another peculiarity that points in the same direction. If the jealousy of Juno was to be a theme in the play, one would expect it to appear throughout. Instead Juno is abruptly introduced in the course of the third act with the dialogue (fol. 84*b*):

Iuno Hast' fownd him Iris.
Iris madam I have
Iuno wheare
Iris In the [Court] *feilds* off Cadmus Coortinnge theire
The ffayrest off her lyne yonnge semele.

On turning, however, to the *Ages* this apparent anomaly is at once explained, partly by the fact that it is not till the third act of *The Golden Age* that Juno becomes her brother's spouse, and partly by the fact that various references to her jealousy are found in those portions of the text that have no counterpart in *The Escapes* (*G.A.*, IV, G4, p. 55; V, I3^{v}, p. 72). In the same way *The Escapes* retains Jupiter's promise to rescue Danae (fol. 82*b*):

Danae Alas my Lord I never lov'd till nowe
and will you leeve mee?

Iupiter ffayrest queene I must.
but to returne wth a most potent Army
Despight off Arges, Darraine, or Acrisius
To ffree you ffrom this durance,

but offers no explanation of its non-fulfilment as does the printed version (see *G.A.*, v, I4, p. 73).

Once again, at the end of the third act Homer's speech or chorus begins with the lines (fol. 86*b*):

off Iupiter thus deified, and made
supreame off all the gods wee still proceede . . .

As they stand in *The Escapes* these are quite unintelligible, since we have not been told of Jupiter's apotheosis, which, however, forms the fitting conclusion of *The Golden Age*.

These more general considerations find ample confirmation when we examine the details of the revision. In Act II of *The Silver Age* Jupiter, planning the deception of Alcmena, delivers the following speech (C3, 3^v^, p. 98):

Three nights I haue put in one to take our fill
Of daliance with this beauteous *Theban* dame.
A powerfull charme is cast or'e Phœbus eies:
Who sleepes this night within the euxine sea,
And till the third day shall forget his charge
To mount the golden chariot of the Sunne,
The Antipodes to vs, shall haue a day
Of three daies length. Now at this houre is fought
By *Iosua* Duke vnto the Hebrew Nation,
(Who are indeede the Antipodes to vs)
His famous battle 'gainst the *Cananites*,
And at his orison the Sunne stands still,
That he may haue there slaughter . . .

This is reproduced in *The Escapes* with but minor (though rather puzzling) alterations, but after it was written the passage corresponding to the last five and a half lines as given above was scored through. It is easy to conceive a motive for the deletion, and it is more natural to suppose that the lines were cancelled after being transcribed than to believe that, once cancelled, they were on revision restored.[1]

[1] To suggest that the sun, on this famous occasion, really stood still, not in reply to Joshua's prayer to Jehovah, but in furtherance of the adulterous intrigues of Jove,

Further evidence of the same kind is afforded by passages in which the reading of the printed text has been written down in the manuscript and immediately cancelled in favour of another. One such occurs at the very end of *The Escapes*. Here the quarto reads (*S.A.*, II, F2, p. 122):

> *Ioue* is our patron, and his power our awe,
> His maiesty our wonder: will, our law

whereas the first of these lines stands in the manuscript thus (fol. 95*a*):

> Iove is our patron, [and] his great power our Awe.

But a more striking example is one that occurs a little earlier, namely where Alcmena says (*S.A.*, II, E2v, p. 115):

> Giue me my dower and Il'e be gone away:

for in the manuscript (fol. 93*a*) Heywood actually wrote 'giue mee my dower' and then struck out the first two words and interlined above them the more explicit 'returne'.

While there is, therefore, no doubt that in many parts, and I think in general, the printed text represents the original and the manuscript a revised version, there are yet a few points that at least suggest the possibility that the text which was before the author when he made his revision differed in some respects from the quartos. At the same time, the interpretation of the evidence is not very clear, and I am not myself inclined to attach much importance to it. One point concerns the stage directions, which would seem to have been to some extent edited before printing. Thus in Diana's hunting (*G.A.*, II, E1v, 2, pp. 31–32) the text speaks (twice) of 'Bugles' while the directions (thrice) calls them 'Hornes'. In *The Escapes* (fol. 77*b*) we find 'Bugles' throughout, but it is difficult to suppose that the change was made out of a desire for consistency since the word has disappeared altogether from the first text passage, so that the correction would have had to be made in the first and second direction in anticipation of the later occurrences of the word in the text. It looks more as if

might well be regarded as blasphemous, and it is perhaps rather strange that the passage should have apparently passed without comment in 1613, especially in a play acted at court before the punctilious James.

Heywood were following an exemplar in which text and directions were consistent.

The other point is a most curious one. In *The Silver Age* the text at the end of Act IV and beginning of Act V (of which the heading is missing) runs thus (K1, p. 155—Jupiter is lamenting the fatal rashness of Semele and holding in his arms the infant Bacchus that he has rescued from the flames):

> This all that's left
> Of *Semele*, vnto the heauens Il'e beare,
> Whose death this *Motto* to all mortals lends:
> He by the Gods dyes, that 'boue man contends.
>
> HOMER.
>
> *Let none the secrets of the Gods inquire,*
> *Lest they (like her) be strooke with heauenly fire.*
> *But we againe to* Hercules *returne,*
> *Now on his iourney to the vaults below . . .*

Corresponding to this in *The Escapes* (fol. 86*b*) we read:

> But In the Interim this even all thats left
> off Semele, vnto the heavens I'l beare.
> off whose death lett Tymes future make this vse
> let none [lyk] the secrets off the gods Inquire
> least they lyke her by hevenly flames Expire/
> Hee ascendinnge in the throne and then
> Homer Enters: and speakes

the following chorus being altogether different. Here, in respect of the printed version, it is to be observed (1) that Homer usually speaks in six-line stanzas, so that a couplet at the beginning of a chorus is anomalous, (2) that the use of 'her' with antecedent understood is curious after the necessary break and change of speaker, and (3) that in the manuscript the couplet forms the end of Jupiter's speech not the opening of Homer's. These facts are neatly explained bibliographically if we assume that the couplet 'Let none . . .' is really an alternative to the couplet 'Whose death . . .', but that the latter was imperfectly deleted, and the former written either in the margin or else below the line marking the end of the act, so that the printer was misled into supposing that it formed part of the chorus. Further, if the text was obscured by alterations at this point, it would account for the omission of the heading to Act v. Thus it seems possible that when revising Heywood had before him a manuscript in which the alteration had been correctly made, though of course he may quite well have himself perceived and corrected the error in the printed text. But I am bound to admit that the explanation does not altogether satisfy me. For one thing a couplet at the beginning of a chorus, though anomalous, does occur elsewhere (viz. *S.A.*, II, C2, p. 96, and end of v, L1^v, p. 164); for another the heading to Act IV is likewise missing; while if the explanation should be correct the printed text has certainly been altered in conformity with the error, as the 'But' in the next line shows.

The foregoing discussion bears out the presumption afforded by the handwriting, and we may conclude that *The Escapes of Jupiter* belongs to a date at least ten years later than the plays on which it was founded. Of the circumstances of the revision we know nothing. That it was made with representation in view is clear from such a direction as that in Diana's hunting (fol. 77*a*), 'A songe Iff you will', but there are no indications whatever, such as we find in *The Captives*,[1] that the manuscript was prepared for the stage. Our ignorance is tantalizing: we should have liked to know what inducement Heywood had to rewrite and revise the text throughout, when it would have been so easy to take the required portions of the printed copies and supply in them the alterations necessitated by the different scope of the new play.

One great and obvious alteration that was made in revision requires explanation: Why was the order of the Alcmena and Semele stories reversed? The reasons are, I think, pretty clear, though perhaps no one alone was decisive. For one thing, the rather elaborate theophany with which the Alcmena ends

[1] Namely the stage-manager's notes. *The Captives* was, of course, licensed by Herbert, but no inscription of his appears in the extant copy, though the last page is blank. Neither is any licence found in *The Escapes*, though again there is ample room: but in this case there is no record of its having been licensed. A small bibliographical peculiarity is worth mentioning. On every alternate recto is a number which may quite likely be in the same hand as the text. This shows that the play was written on loose *sheets* each of four pages, these being numbered as written. The play fills eleven sheets, two pages (5_4, 11_4 = fols. 83*b*, 95*b*) being blank. *The Captives* is numbered in the same way. Again there are eleven sheets and the last page (11_4 = fol. 73*b*) is blank.

made a more effective climax than the mere firework display that disposed of Semele. For another, it was the Alcmena that most naturally fell into two acts, and it was probably sound theatre to place the most elaborate episode last. But the most important consideration, I think, was afforded by the nature of the various episodes. The Calisto, the Danae, and the Semele are all romantic stories with a more or less tragic event. The Alcmena is an avowed farce,[1] to which one might apply Thomas Southerne's title of *The Innocent Adultery*; for once the intentions of the divine ravisher proceed according to plan and all ends in laughter. By placing this last Heywood not only sent his audience away happy, but in fact reproduced in miniature the construction of the classical trilogy with its satyric appendage.

Neither *The Golden Age* nor *The Silver Age* has any claim to be considered great drama, though, to speak from personal predilection merely, the first seems to me much superior to the second.[2] No attempt was made to recast in any way the

[1] It is, of course, from Plautus, a favourite of Heywood's.

[2] I also have a distinct impression that the text of the first is appreciably sounder than that of the second. This, together with the fact that *G.A.* has the spelling *ey* and *S.A.* the spelling *I*, tempts me to conjecture that the former was printed from Heywood's autograph and the second from a transcript, also that the compositor was a good deal more successful in coping with Heywood's hand than was the scribe. An attentive reader will doubtless make many textual conjectures in both plays. I append a few which may throw some light on the handwriting of the copy: *G.A.*, B1ᵛ, p. 6, 'either power or *steele* must arbitrate', ? *skele* = skill (k is a very obscure letter in Heywood's hand); C1ᵛ, p. 14, 'let me first *reward* the Oracle', ? *reword* = re-word, repeat; C3, p. 17, 'this place is . . . onely *for free* women', ? *free for* (*for* and *fre* would be hardly distinguishable); D2ᵛ, p. 25, 'without *men*', the rime requires *man* (often indistinguishable); E4, p. 37, 'Set on *them*', ? *then* (the words would look the same); F2, p. 41, how *Gigantomachia* came to be printed *Gigomantichia* I would not pretend to say: *S.A.*, B4, p. 92, 'That I may glaze my *harpe* in the bloud / Of Tyrant Pretus', ? [*s*]*harpe* [*sword*] (perhaps an omission due to illegible copy) [Greg is quite wrong here: Perseus is the speaker, and *harpe* is the word for his sickle-shaped sword (Ovid, *Met.* V. 69, 176).—J.C.M.]; C3, p. 98, 'Let her bee like a Bachinall *in rage*', read *inragd* (MS. *Inradgd*, clearly the original reading); F2ᵛ, p. 124, 'some *friend* remoue her', ? *fiend* (*fiend* and *frend* could be easily mistaken); G1, p. 129, 'This is a sport—/Aboue th'Olimpiads' (the incomplete line eked out with a rule probably indicates illegible copy). Copies of *G.A.* vary to some extent in their readings. A startling difference appears on the title-page where some copies (e.g. B.M., King's) read 'the *defining* of the Heathen Gods', corrected in others (e.g. B.M., Garrick) to *deifying*. Another is on H4, p. 64, 'Madam you haue not seene a *cleere* stone' (King's) sometimes corrected to *cleerer* (Garrick). It is possible that other instances occur, since there are a number of readings in Pearson's reprint unsupported by either copy at the British Museum.

substance of the scenes extracted for *The Escapes*, but the language was very considerably modified, and while one would hardly deny that on the whole it has been considerably improved, it would be at least as difficult to maintain that the final result is at all commensurate with the labour involved. I have not compared the texts throughout, as the labour of deciphering the manuscript is considerable, but I have received the impression that, though the extent of the revision varies considerably from scene to scene, the general tendency as the work proceeded was to make less alteration on purely literary grounds. I will endeavour by a few examples to indicate the character of the revision.

One rather marked tendency is the removal of riming lines. It is true that couplets are often retained at the end of scenes even where the text is altered. In the original Juno thus sums up the success of her plot to destroy Jove's latest paramour (*S.A.*, IV, K1, p. 155):

> Ha, ha, ha.
> Fair *Semele's* consum'd , 'twas acted well:
> Come, next wee'l follow *Hercules* to hell.

Since the latter story has no place in *The Escapes* the passage had to be altered, but the substituted lines run (III, fol. 86*b*):

> Ha ha ha
> shee's vanisht Into nothinnge, Iris see,
> As shee is nowe, such all off them shall bee.

Similarly before Diana's hunting the lines (*G.A.*, II, E1v, p. 31):

> Satyres and fawnes ring out your pleasing quire,
> This done, our Bugles shall to heauen aspire

are, in the manuscript, for no very obvious reason, replaced by (I, fol. 77*b*):

> satyres and ffawnes attend vs in the Chace,
> whats this daye doone is, virgins ffor your grace.

But in all other positions, at the end, and still more in the middle, of speeches, where couplets frequently appear in the printed version, the rimes habitually disappear in the manuscript. This is sometimes achieved with only slight change, as where Jupiter, having disposed of the guardian beldams, seeks the bed of Danae (*G.A.*, IV, I2^{v}, p. 69):

> *Iup.* They are deafe in rest, then gentle sweet ly further,
> If you should call, I thus your voyce would murther,
> And strangle with my kisses.
> *Dan.* Kisses, tush.
> I'le sinke into my sheetes, for I shall blush.
> I'le diue into my bed.

Here the manuscript (II, fol. 82*b*) merely transposes *murder* and *strangle* (incidentally changing *deafe* to *dead*) and reduces the lady's speech to the words 'To hyde my blushes | I'l synke mee in my shetes'. This is certainly an improvement. So, I think, is the revision of Semele's boast (*S.A.*, IV, I1^{v}, 2, p. 148):

> *Hebe* shall be my hand-mayd, and my wine
> The hand of *Ioues* owne cup-bearer shall fill,
> Il'e begge of him the Troian *Ganimed*
> To be my page; and when I please to ride,
> Borrow his Eagle through the ayre to glide

the last lines of which become in the manuscript (III, fol. 84*b*):

> I'l begg off him the Troian Catamite
> to bee my page, and when I please to take
> The pleasure, off the Ayre borrowe his Eagle
> Mownted vpon whose wings Il Cutt the Clowdes.

But at other times the revision is more extensive. Here is a characteristic passage from the cozening of Calisto—Jupiter is disguised as a nymph (*G.A.*, II, E2, 2^{v}, p. 33):

> [*Iup.*] Sweet will you sit, or on the verdure lye?
> *Cal.* Rather then leaue you, I will loose the sport
> *Iup.* I'le finde you pastime, feare not, Oh my Angell,
> Whether wilt thou transport me, grant me measure.
> Of ioy before, I surfet on this pleasure.
> *Cal.* Come shal's lye downe a little?
> *Iup.* Sooth I will.
> I thirst in seas and cannot quaffe my fill,
> Behold before mee a rich Table spread.
> And yet poore I am forc'd to starue for bread:
> We be alone, the Ladyes farre in chace,
> And may I dye an Eunuch by my vowe,
> If bright *Calisto* you escape me now.
> Sweet bed-fellow your hand, what haue I felt,
> Vnlesse blancht snow, of substance not to melt?

Cal. You gripe too hard.
Iup. Good sooth I shall not rest
Vntill my head be pillowed on thy breast.

The manuscript reads (I, fols. 77*b*, 78*a*):

[Iupiter] hear then repose our selves.
⟨Ca⟩listo and leave the sport:
Iupiter I'l find you pastime fer't not: opportunity
whether wilt thou transport mee?
Calisto com, sitt then
Iupiter Close to your syde, nay nearer might it bee
I thyrst monngst sprinngs and Canott quaff my ffill
Heares a Tantalian ffeast beeffore mee plact
wch starves my stomake though it glutts mine ey
wee are alone, they ffar ffrom sight or Eare,
And may I dy an evenuch Iff I loose
so sweet advantage.
Calisto whats that you whisper
thus to your selff.
Iupiter only my love to thee
ffayre bedffellowe thyne hand
Calisto There
Iupiter what have I ffelt
vnlesse blanc't snowe off substance not to melt
Temperd wth lyvely warmth
Calisto you gripe too hard.
Iupiter howe sweetely could I rest
Iff my faint head [wh] weare pillowed on your brest.

From these last lines it will be seen that even in the revision Heywood did not eschew rime altogether.

As a rule the work of revision, if hasty, is competently done and shows adequate knowledge of the needs of the situation and the text of the original. There are, however, occasional oversights. I have already pointed out the meaningless allusion to the deification of Jupiter that survives from the earlier version. A verbal peculiarity may be added. It would seem from the revision that with the lapse of years the author's taste, or else that of his audience, had grown slightly more fastidious in the matter of erotic description. Where in the Calisto scene we read in the original (*G.A.*, II, E2^{v}, p. 33):

Thy bosome lend.
And by thy soft paps let my hand descend

the revised text has (I, fol. 78*a*):

lett mee gloue my hand
[In your] beetwixt your Ivory bressts.

But this fanciful expression had already served in the original text where Semele says to her lover (*S.A.* IV, I3^v, p. 151):

In my warme bosome I will gloue thy hand,

and this was retained when the revision reached this later point (III, fol. 85*b*).

Further to illustrate Heywood's methods as a reviser I have given at the end of this article a longer passage from the two texts, arranging them in parallel columns. For the purpose the opening scene of *The Escapes* (fol. 74*a*, *b* = *G.A.*, II, C4^v, pp. 20 ff.) may serve as well as another, and we can here watch Heywood beginning with sparing alterations, then gradually getting into his stride, till, by the foot of the page, he is practically writing a new text. But revision was not everywhere so extensive. With this opening scene we may for instance compare that between Juno and Iris near the end (V, fol. 94*b* = *S.A.*, II, F1, 1^v, p. 121), where in a speech of 23 lines there are only some half dozen variants. It may also be well to transcribe in this place one of the new scenes added in writing *The Escapes*. I have preferred Jupiter's courting of Semele to Amphitrio's victory over the Teleboans, and I give it just as it stands in the manuscript, only replacing some rules by leads (fol. 84*a*).

Actus 3s scena prima.

An Arbor discovered shephards and shephardesses discoverd. Iupiter lyke a woodman wth semele /

A songe.
Com Lett the Musick off the spheres
free semele from future feares.
Most woorthy off the state shee beares.
so Ihoue dooth vowe it
The Charites, the graces all
The Muses nine in generall
That wthin vneven nombers fall
shall all allowe it.

for when Olimpick Iove commands
who hath the Trisulk in his hands
There is no power on Earthe wth stands
nor is it woonder
Then all you rurall gods that dwell
on Mowntaine vayle on Hill in Cell
ffrom her all Clowdy dowbts expell
or dye by thonder

Iupiter What Earthe or Ayer the water or the ffyere
Aboue, beelowe, or weare more regions
vnder the moone. wch might participate,
off greater power then the' elements can yeilde
all rarityes the thoughts can apprehend
are in thy power devinest semele.
semele som thinngs theire bee, wch doo so far transcend
the weak Conceptions off mortality
wee canott giue them name. they are Indeede
beyond all rapture. such are those I finde
In my Congression wth great Iupiter
Iupiter Tasted thou hast as yet but Terrhen sweetes
able to relishe comon appetite.
And breede a Casuall surffett even to death
but Iff ffayre semele Continewe mine
wth nectar and Nepenthe thou shalt ffeast
And then, those glorious lights vpon the Earth
shall shinne to thee as darknes. thou beeinge made
a zodiack starr to light the lower woorld.
Semele Can I bee less? th' hast made mee Iupiter
so' ambitious in thy love. that I beegin
all ready halff to skorne. mortality
Then (Iff I am ([unl] vnlesse you flatter mee)
the prime and Cheyfest bewty vpon Earth
when as you say youl rayse mee to the spheares
giue mee a double fulgence
Iupiter semele,
The Morninnge starr, not bright Artophilax
nor vesper wch my doughter Venus Claimes.
shall in theire greatest splendor dare wth thee
To enter Into least comparison.
Thou shalt bee what I promisse, ffare thee well
hee that hath all the Chardge ore gods and men
Though ffor a seasoñ hee retyre him selff
yet must not bee lonnge absent

Semele I Intreate you
spare mee your leasurd howers
Iupiter This kisse hath seald them thynne.

Hee goes one way shee departs sadd wth the shephard

What bearing, one is tempted to ask, have the above results, such as they are, upon the wider problems of dramatic history? *The Escapes of Jupiter* adds one more to the indubitable instances of revision to be taken into account by those who seek to minimize the practice. Further it illustrates how revision is apt to introduce broken lines and other textual irregularities. On the other hand the instance is one which lends no support to the hypothesis of 'continuous copy'. If such revision was habitual with Heywood it certainly helps us to understand his extraordinary claim to have had a whole hand or at least a main finger in over two hundred plays, and it helps to legitimize the search which has been made for traces of revision in Heywood's other pieces. It has, of course, been suggested that the *Ages* themselves represent the rehandling of earlier material, and I have not been altogether guiltless myself of advancing theories on the subject. Indeed, from a controversial point of view, I should have been pleased to find that *The Escapes* contained the original version of scenes refashioned in the *Ages*. That, however, is out of the question, and re-reading *The Golden Age* and its sequel, I cannot honestly say that I find any striking traces of revision —far less than those which mark *The Escapes* as derivative. If I here, by way of conclusion, draw attention to one or two points that seem to need explanation, it is rather because, to the detective mind, it is pleasant to ponder over bibliographical and literary puzzles, than because I seriously desire to defend the speculations of which Fleay was so prolific a father.

There is, near the end of *The Golden Age* (v, I3^{v}, 4, p. 72) a passage that is certainly curious. When Pluto refers to the jealous suspicions of 'my sister *Iuno*', Neptune replies:

And blame her not, the faire *Europaes* rape,
Brought from *Ægenor*, and the *Cadmian* rape,
Io the daughter of old *Inachus*,
Deflour'd by him; the louely *Semele*,

Faire *Læda* daughter to King *Tyndarus*
With many more, may breed a iust suspect,
Nor hath hee spar'd faire *Ceres* Queene of Graine,
Who bare to him the bright *Proserpina*.

Here the second line is obviously wrong: it makes no sense, and such a repetition is impossible with Heywood. Moreover, Agenor was the grandfather of Semele, who is elsewhere called the Cadmian Queen; and Semele is separately mentioned below. There is here without doubt some disturbance of the text, though it may be no more than a confused alteration in the author's manuscript: with the possible exception of a couplet in a chorus previously mentioned, it is the only instance of textual dislocation I have observed. But there is another point: we are here in the last act of *The Golden Age* and Jupiter's affair with Semele does not occur till the fourth of *The Silver Age*. To which it may, of course, be replied that Heywood writing the first of his *Ages* had probably not decided what particular divine amours should enliven the second, if it should ever come to birth.

My other point is of a wider and a vaguer character. In general we may say that the bulk of *The Golden* and *Silver Ages* is not markedly inconsistent in style with the date of publication, and the existence of *The Escapes* seems to imply that this sort of confection had not altogether lost its savour even for a later audience. But can we say this of all passages? Consider the following lines (*G.A.*, III, G1, p. 48):

Æge[*on*]. Arme royall *Titan*, Arme *Enceladus*,
A pale of brandisht steele hath girt thy land.
From the earths Cauernes breake infernall fires,
To make thy villages and hamlets burne.
Tempestuous ruin in the shape of warre
Clowds all thy populous kingdome, At my heeles
Confusion dogges me, and the voyce of death
Still thunders in mine eares.
Tyt[*an*]. Ist possible? Beare *Saturne* first to prison
Wee'l after parly them.
Ence[*ladus*]. Come Angels arm'd, or Diuels clad in flames,
Our fury shall repell them. Come they girt
With power celestiall, or infernall rage,
Wee'l stand their fierce opposure.

This recalls the impostumed style with which in the years following the Armada the imitators of Tamburlaine astounded the ears of the groundlings—high-hearted days that Heywood certainly remembered, but five years or more before he is known to have put pen to paper—while if the last lines recall some well-known words of Hamlet's, it does not follow that they are dependent on the extant text.

But these are speculations upon which I have no business to be entering here.

A passage from the two texts, arranged in parallel columns, follows.

The Golden Age. . . C4

Actus secundi, Scœna prima. . . .

Enter Lycaon *with his Lords*, Iupiter *with other Lords of* Epyre. C4v

Lycaon. After long warre, and tedious differences,
Betwixt King *Melliseus* and our selfe,
What craue the Epyre Lords?
Iupiter. This King *Lycaon*,
Since truce and hostage hath tane vp these broiles,
And ended them in peacefull amity,
Since all the damadge by the Epyrians done,
Is on our part aboundantly made good:
We come *Lycaon* to demand the like
Of thee and of thy Kingdome, and for proofe,
That all our malice is extinct and dead,
We bring thy hostage backe, demanding ours.
Lycaon. Receiue him Lords, a Banquet instantly,
You shall this day braue Epyre feast with vs,
And to your boord your hostage shall be brought,
There to receiue him freely, meane time sit,
And taste the royall welcomes of our Court.
Iup. *Lycaon's* iust in keeping these conditions
So strictly with a reconciled foe.
Lyc. But faire prince, tell me whence you are deriu'd,
I neuer heard King *Melliseus* had
A Prince of your perfections?
Iupiter. This demand
Startles my bloud, being borne I know not where, D1
Yet that I am of gentry at the least,

Calisto, fol. 74a

Actus primus scena prima.

Enter Kinnge Lycaon, wth his Lords, And Iupiter wth other Lords off Epyre Ec'

Lycaon After Lonnge warr and much effuse off bloodd
beetwixt kinnge Mellisæus and our selff
what Crave you Epyre lords?
Iupiter This kinnge Lycaon.
synce Truice on boath-sydes hath tane vpp these broyl⟨s⟩
and ended them in peacffull amitye
since all the damadge by th' epyrians dooñ
Is on our part abowndantly made goodd
wee com Lycaon to demande the lyke
off thee and off thy nation, and to proove
In vs all mallyce is extinct and dead
wee brinnge thy hostadge back: demandinge ours
Lycaon Receive him Lords; A Banquet Instantly
you shall this daye brave Epyre feast wth vs.
And to the boord your hostadge, shall bee brought.
theire to receive him ffreely, meane tyme sitt
and tast the royall welcoms off our Coort.
Iupiter pelagia's kinnge in this is honorable

Lycaon say princly yonnge man whence are you deriu'd?
wee never hear'd that the' great Epyres king
was blest wth a male-Issue.
Iupiter your Demand
startles my bloodd as beeinnge Ignorant
whence, or ffrom whome, It may claime Iust discent,
yet that I am a gentleman at least
ey and perhapps to nobler Titles heyre

My Spirrt prompts me, and my noble thoughts
Giue me approued warrant, being an infant
Two beauteous Ladyes found me in a caue,
Where from their voluntary charity,
Bees fed me with their hony, for that cause
The two bright Ladies cal'd me *Iupiter*,
And to their Father *Melliseus* brought me,
My Foster-father, who hath train'd my youth,
In feats of Armes, and military prowesse,
And as an instance of his deerest loue,
Hath honor'd me with this late Embassy.

A banquet brought in, with the limbes of a Man in the seruice.

Lyca. We are satisfi'd: Princes sit round and feast,
You are this day *Lycaons* welcom'st guest.
Iup. This meat distasts me, doth *Lycaon* feast vs
Like Caniballes? feed vs with humane flesh?
Whence is this portent?
Lycan. Feede Epyrians, eate,
Lycaon feasts you with no common meate.

Iup. But wher's the Epyre Lord we left as hostage?
Lyca. Behold him here, hee's at the table with you,

This is the Epyres head, and these his limbes,

Thinkes *Melliseus* that *Lycaon* can
(Discended of the valiant *Tytanoys*)
Bury his hatred, and intoombe his spleene
Without reuenge? bloud in these warres was shed,
And for that bloud your hostage lost his head.
Iup. Beare wrong that list, & those can brooke it best,
I was not borne to suffrance: thoughts mount hye,
A King hath wrong'd me, and a King shall dye.
Lycaon. Treason, treason.
Iup. Downe with the tyrant, and that hatefull crue,
And in their murdrous breasts your blades imbrue.
Lycaon. Our guard. *A confused fray, an alarme.* D1v.

my genius prompts mee. and my storyes thus.
Beeinnge fortunes outcast: In myne Infancy,
too princly damsells ffownde mee in a cave
where ffrom theire voluntary Charity
Bees ffedd mee wth there hony, ffor wch Cawse,
they boathe Agreede to Call mee Iupiter
Then brouught mee to theire father Epyres kinnge
who gave mee breedinnge answeringe to a spir⟨it⟩
that aymes all ready att a diadem.
and should hee whose adopted soon I am
Chuse elc-where to succeede him in his throne
this swoord that gave mee knight hoodd from his hand
shall never rest in []peace vpon my thigh
Till wth it I have [wandred] traveld through the woorld
And purchast mee a scepter/

Lycaon A brave spiritt
I see you are the fyrst in Embasye
then take your place next vs.

Iupiter This ffeast offends mee.
Thinnks kinnge Lycaon wee are Canniballs
To ffeede on humaine ffleshe?

Lycaon no better stomacks? fol. 74[b]
you see wee ffeede you wth no Comoñ Cates

Iupiter Theire sight is woorse then surffett: speak Lycaon
where is the Epyre Lord wee left wth you?

Lycaon beehould him heare.

Iupiter where?

Lycaon At the Table wth you/
This is *his* head and these his martyr'd limbs
Cook't ffor your tast. stand you a mazd at this?
Thinnks Mellisæus that Lycaon Can
discended ffrom the valiant Tytanoys/
ffor all the bloodd in fformer battayles shedd
bee Calm'd by woords wth out a Iust revendge
no; had thy soveraigne's selff bin then in place.
Lyke ffate hee had Indurd:

Iupiter Tyrant; my kinnge?
beare wronges who list, and those can brooke them best
I was not borne to servyle sufferance.

ffyrst shall my sword in more bitts parcell thee
then thou this Epire Lord.

Lycaon Treason: a guard.

Iupiter *and the Epyriens beat off* Lycaon *and his followers.*

Iup. Lycaon's fled, make good the pallace gates,
And to th'amazed Citie beare these limbs,
So basely by the tyrant massacred.
Happly his subiects by our words prepar'd
May shake their bondage off, and make this warre,
The happy meanes to rid a tyrant thence.
Beare in your left hands these dis-membred limbes,
And in your right your swords, with which make way,
Courage braue Epyres, and a glorious day, *Exeunt.*

A Confused ffray Lycaoñ: beaten off, Enter Iupiter

Iupiter The Tyrants ffledd, make good the pallace gates.
And to distract the Citty beare these limbes
so basely manngled throuugh the populous streetes,
The horriddnesse off wch sadd spectacle.
May stampe in them such deepe Impression
off hate, to the Author off the blooddy Act
that Itt may breede revolt such Inhumanity
beeinge boath distastfful and detestable
And may avayle vs mch: Attend vs Lords.
slippe not this fayre advantadge

12. The Riddle of Jonson's Chronology[1]

HAD Ben Jonson any fixed practice in dating?—that is the fundamental question which the historical student of his works needs to ask. Did he adopt the date of the incoming year on 1 January, or did he cling to the old date up to and including 24 March? The latter practice, which reckoned the year from Lady Day, I shall call the Legal dating, since it was used in official documents; the former I shall call the Calendar dating, since it was followed in almanacks and the like: New Year's Day never meant anything but 1 January. It seems curious that we should know so little about the literary practice with respect to this important point in England[2] in the early seventeenth century, and particularly the practice of so careful a writer as Jonson; but although some reasonable inquiries, beside many irresponsible assertions, have been made, it is clear that the problem is still far from solution. To recapitulate opinion would be tedious, and perhaps invidious; we are here concerned with the evidence alone.

Jonson was a bad man who seldom dated his letters. There are, however, one or two interesting exceptions. The quarto of *Volpone* has an epistle dated 11 February 1607. The play was not entered in the Stationers' Register, but the date on the title-page is 1607, and this is very probably, though not necessarily, a Calendar date. Jonson is said to have sent Drummond a copy of his poem on 'My Picture left in Scotland' with the date 19 January 1619, which again would be probably a Calendar date.[3] A later letter is dated 4 February

[1] [1926, March. *The Library*, vi. 340.] [An important article, confirming Greg's later statement, *Some Aspects and Problems of London Publishing between 1550 and 1650* (1956), p. 83, that 'almost all books were dated according to the calendar year', is W. L. Edgerton's 'The Calendar Year in Sixteenth-Century Printing', *J.E.G.P.* lix (1960), 439–49.—J.C.M.]

[2] In Scotland New Style, that is the Gregorian calendar, was introduced in 1600, and at the same time was made the independent change to the Legal use of the Calendar year. In England, on the other hand, however the year might be reckoned, all dates are Old Style down to 1752. It took the Bolshevist revolution to introduce reason into Russia.

[3] [Jonson had left Hawthornden by 17 January, but lingered at Edinburgh or Leith, whence the letter appears to have been written, till the 25th.]

1631, but there seems nothing in the contents to show which year is intended. In the manuscript in which it is preserved it precedes copies of other letters of 1631, but I do not suppose that any reliance can be placed on the order. We are thus reduced to an examination of the dates attached by Jonson to many of his plays and masques as those of performance, and to collation of these with evidence otherwise available. Our discussion will, of course, fall into two parts: a consideration of those cases in which external evidence affords reasonably certain ground for dating, and the application of the results so attained to those cases in which no such certainty is obtainable.

The separate editions of plays yield little to our purpose. However, *The New Inn* was printed in 1631 as having been performed in 1629, and since it was licensed by Herbert on 19 January that year, the probability is that it was acted before Lady Day. If so, the date is reckoned by the Calendar. With the separate editions may conveniently be classed the three folio plays passed through the press by Jonson in 1631 but not published till 1640. Among them is *The Staple of News*, which is dated 1625. But at the end of III. ii occurs a passage (ll. 299 ff.):

> All the countrey
> Expected from the city most braue speeches,
> Now, at the Coronation. . . . . . . yet
> If *May-Day* come, and the *Sunne* shine, perhaps,
> They'll sing like *Memnons* Statue, and be vocall.

This can only have been written between 2 February and 1 May 1626. The lines might, of course, be a later insertion, but this is the less likely in that a date early in the year is also suggested by the Induction which seems to assume a Shrovetide performance. Presumably, therefore, the '1625' on the title is a Legal date.

The masques and entertainments are naturally more helpful. The *Coronation Entertainment*, which included the *Panegyre* on the opening of Parliament, was entered in the Stationers' Register on 19 March 1603/4, the very day of the latter function, and I should imagine published immediately. It is remarkable that the date in the imprint is 1604. Nevertheless the *Entertainment* is dated 15 March 1603, and the *Panegyre* 19 March 1603; both Legal dates. In the *Masque of*

Blackness the date 6 January 1605, in the *Masque of Beauty* 10 January 1608, and in the *Haddington Masque* 9 February 1608, are all Calendar dates. These three pieces were published together in an undated quarto in the spring of 1608 (entered 21 April). The *Masque of Queens* was printed in a quarto of 1609 (entered 22 February 1608/9) with the Calendar date 2 February 1609. No other masques appeared in print before the folio of 1616. *Lovers made Men* was printed in 1617 (without entry and without imprint) and bore the Calendar date 22 February 1617. Next we have a group of three quartos, undated and without either entry or imprint, containing the *Masque of Augurs*, 6 January 1621; *Neptune's Triumph*, 6 January 1623; and *The Fortunate Isles*, 6 January 1624. These are all Legal dates. It should be observed, however, that only the first masque was actually performed on the date given: *Neptune's Triumph* was postponed and finally abandoned; *The Fortunate Isles* was put off from the 6th to the 9th. There can be no doubt that these three quartos, like that of *Lovers made Men*, are privately printed libretti, prepared in anticipation of the performance to serve as souvenirs for the guests. Lastly, *Love's Triumph* was performed on 9 January 1631, so that the quarto, which gives 1630 as the date alike of performance and of printing, has two Legal dates; and the undated quarto of *Chloridia* also has the Legal date Shrovetide 1630, the masque having been given on 22 February 1631.

Before proceeding I will just summarize without comment the evidence we have obtained so far. We find Legal dates used for the two official functions of the Coronation and the opening of Parliament in 1603/4. After that we meet with no Legal date till we come to the three privately printed texts of 1622–5, two published masques of 1630/1, and one play of 1625/6 printed in 1631. On the other hand, we have Calendar dates in four published masques in 1605–9 and one private text of 1617, as well as apparently in one play of 1629 published in 1631.

We turn to the folio of 1616, which Jonson is supposed to have passed through the press with some care, and in whose pages if anywhere we may expect to find authoritative evidence of the author's usage. The data are as follows. *Volpone* is assigned to 1605, but allusions in the text have been supposed to necessitate a date about February 1606. This has, however, also been doubted, and the case must be regarded as one of the problems of Jonson's chronology, not as a basis of argument. *Epicene* is dated 1609. It has been contended, but on no valid ground, that this must mean 1609/10.[1] There is no objection to the date December 1609. No date appears for the *Coronation Entertainment*, but the *Panegyre* retains its Legal date, 19 March 1603. The four masques of 1605–9 all retain their Calendar dates from the quartos. *The Golden Age Restored* bears the date 1615; this has been claimed as the masque performed on 1 and 6 January 1616, but the identification cannot be regarded as certain.

Comparing the evidence of the folio with that already collected, we are at once struck by the fact that, with two exceptions, there is no certain instance of a Legal date before 1620. The exceptions are the official occasions of James's Coronation and the opening of his first Parliament. Moreover, it is noteworthy that in the folio the former of these dates has been removed, so that we cannot but suspect that the second may remain by oversight. That would point to a definite intention to use Calendar dates throughout the authorized collection of the author's works. After 1620 all Jonson's own dates follow the Legal reckoning, with one probable, but by no means certain, exception in *The New Inn*.

What then of the two disputable dates in the folio? The volume closes with a series of seven masques or entertainments none of which had been previously printed and of which the final one alone is dated. The last two are *Mercury Vindicated from the Alchemists* and *The Golden Age Restored*, the latter bearing the date 1615. There seems no reasonable doubt that these two are the masques performed at Court, one on 6 and 8 January 1615, the other on 1 and 6 January 1616; but the question is which is which. There is also no doubt

[1] [On the ground, presumably, that the Children of her Majesty's Revels, who presented the play, did not receive their new charter till 4 Jan. 1609/10. But they had been acting for some time at Whitefriars, and as the Children of Whitefriars they gave five performances at court during the Christmas season of 1609–10, which presumably included *Epicene*. By the time the play came to be printed it would inevitably be attributed to the Children of her Majesty's Revels.]

that, although it cannot be checked throughout, the arrangement of the folio is generally chronological. If it is so in this instance, then the date 1615 is a Legal one, contrary to the apparent practice of the collection. Brotanek concluded that this must be so because he found allusion in the *Golden Age* to the Overbury scandal. But the opening lines, to which I suppose that he refers, need not have any specific application, and it is indeed, on general grounds, very improbable that they should. Chambers, on the other hand, points out, pertinently, I think, that the 'device' of the 1615 masque was reported as not 'extraordinary', and that this applies better to the *Golden Age* than to *Mercury Vindicated*. I certainly myself incline to this opinion, and I would suggest that Jonson intentionally placed *The Golden Age Restored* last, as supplying an appropriate ending for the collection, and that he added the date in this instance just because he was departing from the chronological order. I therefore regard this as confirming the Calendar dating of the folio.

There remains *Volpone*, '1605'. The crucial passages are:

> Were there three porcpisces seene, aboue the bridge,
> As they giue out? . . .
> There was a whale discouer'd, in the riuer,
> As high as *Woolwich* . . . (II. i. 40–41, 46–47)

Howes[1] records in 1605/6: 'The 19. of Ian. a great Porpus was taken aliue at Westham, in a small creeke a mile, & a halfe within the land . . . & within few dayes after, a very great Whale came vp within 8. mile of Lon.' Now, although this entry is incorrectly described by the poet's latest editors as being 'in terms almost identical with Jonson's' (for West Ham, far from being above London Bridge, is barely above Woolwich), there is a good deal of weight in the contention that dramatist and annalist are alluding to the same events. Conclusive, however, it is not, while other allusions, so far as they can be checked, fit somewhat better with an earlier date. A confident decision either way would be unwise, but, in view of the double possibility of interpolation and coincidence, I cannot regard the evidence as sufficiently certain to negative the presumption of a Calendar date.

[1] [In his continuation of Stow's Chronicle, 1618, p. 880.]

Completely consistent Jonson's practice certainly was not. But the survey we have taken I think does point to a definite change at a particular date. If we assume that about 1620 Jonson abandoned his former habit of using Calendar dates and adopted the Legal reckoning, we shall find in the earlier period only two certain exceptions, which may be accounted for without much violence, and in the later period one, which may not be an exception at all. The change would synchronize with his visit to Scotland, though the connexion is not obvious.

It has, of course, no bearing on Jonson's own usage, but for completeness it may be as well to see what happened in the posthumous collection of 1640–1, the so-called 'third volume' of his Works. The practice here is undeniably inconsistent, and the question is complicated by the appearance of several dates that cannot be correct on any reckoning. *Pleasure Reconciled to Virtue* seems certainly to have been performed on 6 January 1617/18: the folio dates it 1619. The so-called *Masque of Owls* is known to have been given at Kenilworth on 19 August 1624: the folio dates it 1626. *Pan's Anniversary* is supposed to have been designed for James's birthday, 19 June: if so, the folio date 1625 cannot be correct, for he died on 27 March.[1]

The most significant point connected with the dating of the collection is that while the Calendar date of *Lovers made Men* in 1617 is retained from the quarto, and the Calendar date, 6 January 1623, added for the hitherto unprinted *Time Vindicated*,[2] the Legal dates, 1621 and 1623, given in the quartos of the *Masque of Augurs* and *Neptune's Triumph* are replaced by the Calendar dates, 1622 and 1624. Presumably the same was intended in the case of *The Fortunate Isles*, but instead of altering the Legal date of the quarto, 6 January 1624, to 1625, it was incorrectly given as 1626. This seems clearly to indicate an intention of adhering to Calendar dates in this collection, and consequently when, among the earlier masques, we find *News from the New World Discovered in the*

1 [The folio date being obviously wrong, Brotanek's date of 19 Jun. 1620 is now generally accepted (Simpson, *Jonson*, x. 604).]

2 [Since this was written a quarto has come to light and is in the Pforzheimer Library. It is undated but gives the date of performance on Twelfth-night 1622. This Legal date was therefore altered in reprinting.]

Moon of 6 January 1621,[1] dated by the year alone 1620, we may conjecture that this is not a Legal date but merely an error. And when at the end we find *Love's Triumph* and *Chloridia* retaining from the quartos their Legal dates, 1630, I again suspect that the reason is either ignorance or carelessness.

There remain two questionable dates in this, as in the earlier, volume. *Christmas his Masque*, which begins the series, is dated 1616 merely, and *The Vision of Delight* is said to have been presented 'in Christmas, 1617'. Neither can be certainly dated from internal evidence or by external record. I should take 'in Christmas' to mean not Christmas-day but Christmas-tide, and the most probable occasion is always Twelfth-night. The presumption in favour of a Calendar date would therefore point to 6 January 1617. This is the conclusion reached by Brotanek and Reyher, who identify it with the masque performed on 6 and 19 January that year. If so, it is earlier than *Lovers made Men*, 22 February 1617, which precedes it in the volume, but it is obvious that the order of printing was determined merely by the dates on the copy, not by any knowledge of the actual order of production, and the editor apparently jumped to the conclusion that in any year Christmas must follow Shrovetide. There seems then no proper place for *Christmas his Masque*, nor has any one suggested an exact date for it. But it seems to be designed to introduce rather than to conclude the Christmas festivities, the unusual occasion giving point to the title, and I conjecture that it was at any rate designed for St. Stephen's night, which I take to be the first of the 'twelve days'. The date 1616 would therefore place it correctly on a Calendar reckoning. But there is no trace of such a performance.

Thus it would seem that while, after publishing the first volume of his Works, Jonson altered his customary dating from the Calendar to the Legal use, after his death his first editor, Sir Kenelm Digby, reverted, errors and ignorance apart, to the more rational and more popular method.

NOTE.—In cases where the evidence for the date of performance seems certain I have not thought it necessary to discuss it above. The data for the

[1] [This, long the accepted date, is an error. The masque was actually performed on 17 Jan. and 29 Feb. 1619/20 (Simpson, *Jonson*, x. 596).]

masques are admirably collected and discussed in Rudolf Brotanek, *Die englischen Maskenspiele*, Vienna, 1902, and Paul Reyher, *Les masques anglais*, Paris, 1909, while the whole subject is covered down to 1616 in E. K. Chambers, *The Elizabethan Stage*, Oxford, 1923. We now have also C. H. Herford and Percy Simpson, *Ben Jonson*, vols. i and ii, Oxford, 1925 [vols. iii–xi, 1927–52].

13. Shakespeare's Hand Once More[1]

It is now eleven years since Sir Edward Maunde Thompson completed the memorable investigation of 'Shakespeare's Handwriting' in which he sought to prove, from an examination of the six accepted signatures, that the poet wrote the three pages added to the British Museum MS. Harley 7368 by the hand known as D. It is four or five years since he expounded his view afresh, with some additional details and with some modification, in one of the papers collected by A. W. Pollard under the title of 'Shakespeare's Hand in the Play of Sir Thomas More'. We may reasonably suppose that his case is before us in as complete and convincing a form as it is likely to assume, and there has been ample time for his palaeographical arguments to be considered by all who are interested in the subject.

I cannot help feeling that if Sir Edward's case has sometimes received less than its due recognition, the fault lies partly with the manner of its presentation. There is a wide-spread suspicion that claims have been advanced which cannot be fully substantiated; and those who believe in the Shakespearian authorship of the three pages have found themselves handicapped by being supposed to endorse and build upon views which they feel to be in some details at least open to doubt. It is possible, therefore, that some good purpose may be served by a statement of how, after a decade, the palaeographical case appears to a moderate believer in the Shakespearian authorship, and how much of the detail of that case can be taken as established. I only wish to add that, while I make no claim to any such minute familiarity with the documents as led Sir Edward to his confident ascription, the conclusions I express below are the result of my own study,

[1] 1927, *The Times Literary Supplement*, 24 Nov. and 1 Dec. [The editor insisted that this should be tacked onto a notice of certain works that had recently appeared. I now print it in the form originally intended as a considered summing-up of the purely palaeographical evidence in favour of the Shakespearian authorship of the famous three pages in 'The Booke of Sir Thomas Moore'.—1958.] [For a recent discussion see Harold Jenkins, *Malone Society Collections*, vol. VI (1962 for 1961), 179–92.—J.C.M.]

and have been reached independently of any criticism by others. My acquaintance with hand D is based on long and repeated examination of the original, as well, of course, as facsimiles: the signatures I know mainly in facsimile only.

For simplicity I shall speak of the six signatures as constituting a single document of comparison, and shall refer to them or their hand as S, while our other document, the *More* edition, or its hand, I shall refer to as D.

I will begin with one or two general observations. The scribes of both S and D write substantially the ordinary English ('secretary') hand of the time, as distinct from the more modern Italian. But English hands in Shakespeare's day differed among themselves as much as our modern hands do. And within the broad distinction I think there is some general similarity of style between S and D. Among the dramatists of the time, Chettle, Heywood, Kyd, Munday, Samuel Rowley, to mention only a few, wrote English hands; but I do not think that any of their writing could plausibly be ascribed to the hand that wrote the signatures. And although the hand C of the *More* manuscript (probably that of a playhouse reviser) bears a general resemblance to D, and has even been confused with it, I agree with Sir Edward that it is with D rather than C that S shows affinity. There are, of course, differences as well as likenesses between S and D, both in general effect and in detail; and I think that, if Sir Edward had emphasized this rather more, he might have avoided some misapprehension. But the differences are hardly of a kind that cannot be explained by the lapse of the ten, fifteen, or twenty years that separate the documents; and although it is idle to pretend that the necessity of accounting for differences does not *pro tanto* weaken the case for identity it appears to me that the opposite attempts to demonstrate the diversity of the hands fail signally.

There are eleven minuscule letters common to S and D, and it is mainly upon a comparison of these as they appear in the two documents that the case for identification must rest. Sir Edward has analysed the forms in detail, and indicated their points of likeness. They are, in general, the forms normally found in the English hand, and no very striking individualities are, therefore, to be expected. Still, not all hands use normal forms, and even among normal forms minor variations occur. It follows that, even if only a single common type of each letter were found in each document, the agreement of these forms would not be without some cumulative weight. But the case is much stronger than that. For five out of the eleven letters assume two or three distinct forms, and these forms appear both in S and D. Such multiple agreement acquires considerable significance, even though the individual forms may be common. Of 'e', 'h', and 'p' two clearly marked varieties occur in S and the same occur in D, while of 'a' and 'k' three concurrent varieties can be distinguished. Taken altogether these agreements must be allowed to establish a case of some *prima facie* strength.

It is possible that in presenting the evidence Sir Edward may have occasionally overstressed a likeness or represented a peculiarity as more uncommon than in fact it is. But, if any deductions have to be made on this score, it may well happen that they will be more than balanced by the discovery of other points of resemblance which eluded even Sir Edward's scrutiny. For example, I fancy I can detect in the Record Office signature an inclination to complete the 'a' after the German fashion, in which it might be mistaken for 'oi'. This form is, of course, well recognized in D, and its combination with the overhead curl, as in this signature, also occurs there (ll. 92, 93), and it must be remembered that the strength of the case for identification increases in geometrical proportion with every fresh point of resemblance.

Beyond the similarity in the formation of individual letters there is at least one graphic trick or habit that S and D have in common. This is the addition of a long fine upstroke to certain initial letters. Such a peculiarity is not uncommon in the hands of the time; but it is far from being general, and in addition to the resemblances already noted its appearance must materially strengthen the case. Moreover, this initial stroke is made in exactly the same way, as appears from its having once in each document formed an 'elongated needle-eye' loop, through the pen touching the paper in descent before the upstroke was begun. The resemblance here is very striking, and must be allowed due weight, though it would be an exaggeration to regard it as constituting by itself a proof of identity.

Hitherto I have been concerned to show how a case of some cogency was built up for supposing the hand of the Shakespeare signatures to be the same as that of the *More* addition; but if it stopped here it would have been difficult to claim it as compelling. Anyhow Sir Edward sought to clinch it by pointing out four peculiarities present in S on the one hand and in D on the other that may be considered as individual characteristics. These are:

(i) The occurrence, as the only non-English letter, of an Italian long 'ſ' in four out of the six signatures, and the occasional appearance of the same as the only non-English letter in D;

(ii) the occurrence in both documents of an exaggeratedly 'spurred' 'a' which is alleged to be practically unique;

(iii) the occurrence, among other varieties found in both documents, of an altogether anomalous form of 'k';

(iv) Similarly, the occurrence, among other varieties, of an unusual form of 'p'.

As Sir Edward has developed his case, and as I have summarized it above, the evidence appears remarkably strong. If it could stand it would, I think, come as near proof as the conditions of the case allow, and I for one should feel it difficult to escape the conclusion drawn. Unfortunately I am persuaded that considerable deductions must be made before the claims advanced can be accepted as correct.

(i) It is with respect to the occurrence of the Italian long 'ſ' in D that my view differs most sharply from Sir Edward's. In his original statement of the case he found three instances. One of these (in l. 102) he later abandoned in deference to the opinion of 'some of my friends, experts in palaeography'. A second, I am convinced, must also go. According to Sir Edward there is in l. 113 a word 'warre', which (before being crossed out in favour of 'hurly') was altered to 'warres' by the addition above the line and 'in minute size' of an Italian long 'ſ'. The addition of a long 's' of any sort at the end of a word would, of course, be anomalous: it is not a final form of the letter. Moreover, there could, at the time, have been no reason for inserting it above instead of on the line. But I am confident that the word is not, and never was, 'warre': it was from the start 'warrs'. The appearance of an 'e' is merely due to a deletion stroke having traversed the loop of the 's'; and what Sir Edward took for super-script Italian long '*ʃ*' is nothing but the upward curl (deformed by a slight flick of the pen) which normally terminates the English final letter. The third instance of an Italian long '*ʃ*' in D is in the word 'seriant' at l. 17. As to this there can be no manner of doubt, and its significance as almost the only non-English letter used by the scribe cannot be disputed. It has on the other hand been suggested that the word was not written by D at all but by C (and it has been pointed out, acutely enough, that the word also contains an Italian '*r*'); but repeated examination of the original has convinced me that this is quite out of the question. All C (the playhouse scribe) did was to prefix the direction 'Enter' to the speaker's name, previously written by D.

(ii) The 'spurred' 'a' is found in the Record Office signature, and in it the normal point at the foot of the first minim of the so-called 'open' 'a' is abnormally carried round to the left into a horizontal spur. A similar form unquestionably occurs in D. Originally Sir Edward specified eight instances. This led to a good deal of misapprehension, for these eight examples differ considerably among themselves, and only one offers a really remarkable parallel to that of S. This was later recognized, and in revising his case, Sir Edward confined his attention to the word 'that' in l. 105. Of this he wrote:

> I have kept a constant watch for the occurrence of this spur in the numerous documents of the period that have passed under my eyes, but I have never yet observed it in any, except [S and D]. I have also had the benefit of the valuable assistance of my old colleague Mr. J. P. Gilson . . . who has kindly examined many collections of MSS. on my behalf.

The weight of this evidence is considerable, but in estimating it we are bound to remember that very few documents have been subjected to so close a scrutiny as D. Let us consider wherein exactly the resemblance lies. As I have said, the point at the foot of the first minim is normal and quite common, and attention has been directed to a number of hands in which this point assumes a more or less exaggerated form.

The hands of John Knox, Francis Bacon, and others have been cited, but in none of these is there any close parallel to the 'a' of S and D. I could adduce better instances myself, but they would not be really relevant. Much the closest that has been found so far is that pointed out (in a communication of 27 August 1925) by R. W. Chambers in the hand of George Chapman. But even this parallel, though striking, is not perfect. What distinguishes the 'a' of the Record Office signature and of D's 'that' is that the pen, descending in a deep curve from the overhead arch, is carried to the left into the horizontal spur and then to the right *horizontally* till it ascends to form the second minim. In Chapman's 'a' (as in many of D's) the spur hardly becomes truly horizontal, and the pen after making it travels back some way up the curve before descending again to complete the first minim, then re-ascending immediately for the second. This is a much more formal formation. I think, therefore, that in its full peculiarity the resemblance between S and D in this instance remains unchallenged and unparalleled. At the same time the distinction between these particular 'a's and the more normal type is slight, and their occurrence should perhaps be regarded less as a personal trait than as an accident—an accident that clearly *might* have happened to Chapman. Although, therefore, I fully admit the remarkable nature of the coincidence, I am unable to allow it quite the same weight as Sir Edward.

(iii) One of the varieties of 'k' is described as being formed thus:

> The stem is rounded at the base like a modern cursive *l*, and the pen is carried upwards to the level of the middle of the stem, and then, without being lifted, forms the cross-bar by moving horizontally to the left and then travelling back on the same line to the right, a heavy dot or comma being afterwards added above the cross-bar to represent the central loop of the normal letter.

This most eccentric form Sir Edward found in the second Will signature and in the word 'knees' at l. 110 of D. The letter might be formed in the manner described, and I should be content to think that it was. But after a careful examination of the word in D it seems to me probable that the 'k' was formed in the normal manner (namely, by bringing up the stroke from the foot and forming a small loop to the right before carrying the pen left for the cross-stroke) and that the only reason why it appears peculiar is that in the left-hand portion of the loop the pen was lifted and so failed to mark. Of course the failure to establish a parallel in this abnormal form of 'k' (if failure it is) in no way detracts from the surely remarkable coincidence that the *three* normal formations of the letter found in D all reappear in S.

(iv) Besides the normal form of 'p' Sir Edward described one made up of a downstroke, a cross-stroke, and a curve joining the head of the former to the end of the latter. This he found in the Museum signature and in the words 'peace peace' at l. 50 of D. It is a perfectly possible form of 'p', being, indeed, the normal formation of the capital, and also apparently that given in the Beau Chesne-Baildon 'secretarie Alphabet' (which, by the way, is often far from normal); but it is certainly unusual. The formation in D, however, appears to be uncertain. In spite of the appearance they present to a superficial inspection, it seems possible that the two 'p's were formed in the normal manner; and so long as this is possible, we have, I conceive, no right to assume that they were written differently from, say, the initial of the third 'peace' in the same line. Indeed, after examining the original through a strong glass I am inclined to think that the two 'p's were actually formed after the normal model, though it is impossible to speak with certainty on the point.

I have assumed above that Sir Edward is correct in his analysis of the formation of the 'k' and 'p' of the signatures. I can express no reasoned opinion myself; for I have not had the opportunity of subjecting the original signatures to any minute examination, and I am quite unable to subscribe to the convenient belief sometimes expressed that 'properly prepared photographic facsimiles are every bit as good as—and from several view-points even better than—the original writings'.[1] At the same time, lest I should be thought to take an unsporting line, I will add that, so far as it is possible to judge from facsimiles, I am inclined to believe that Sir

[1] [It is of course true that a photograph will sometimes reveal details, such as differences of ink, that cannot be detected by the eye in the original.]

Edward is right regarding the formation of the 'p' in the Museum signature (written on greasy vellum), but not regarding that of the 'k' in the second Will signature. This appears to be an imperfect letter formed by shaky fingers. I think that the stroke from the foot has been carried up rather high and the pen then lifted to form a single cross-stroke, which has intersected the upstroke. The general intention is that of the normal letter, but the formation has been simplified to suit the capacity of a failing hand.

The result, then, of this discussion is to suggest that of the four points that were to put the Shakespearian authorship of the *More* addition beyond question, two must be abandoned as doubtful, while the other two are somewhat reduced in force, though by no means disposed of.

It appears to me that the palaeographical case for the identity of S and D falls into two parts. We may suppose that Sir Edward, in the course of his minute and patient comparison of the documents, became convinced by numerous hardly definable traits of resemblance that the two hands were in fact the same. To this conviction on the part of an experienced palaeographer at the end of an exhaustive investigation I cannot but attach great weight. But nothing is more difficult than to convey to others the grounds, however valid, upon which such a conviction is based. When, therefore, he came to the task of exposition Sir Edward was naturally led to seek for concrete points by which to bring his case clearly home to the reader. He was fortunate in finding several such, but, unless my view is mistaken, he failed to submit them to a sufficiently severe and detached criticism, and was thus led to make somewhat larger claims than the facts actually warrant. In so doing he exposed his case to rather damaging attack; and of this his critics have taken eager, though not on the whole very able, advantage. Since Sir Edward's conclusions supplied the inspiration that prompted research on other lines, doubt regarding the security of his foundations has been felt to leave the argument somewhat in the air. It is with the object of avoiding this inconvenience that I have ventured, perhaps rashly, on a restatement of the palaeographical case.

I do not pretend that, thus restated, the case, though of considerable weight, approaches complete proof; and I doubt whether the available data are extensive enough to make complete proof possible. If we are to believe that Shakespeare wrote the three-page addition to *More*, it must, I think, be on the ground of the convergence of a number of independent lines of argument—palaeographic, orthographic, linguistic, stylistic, psychological—and not on any one alone. But in the more limited field I should feel inclined to advance the following propositions:

(1) The palaeographical case for the hands of S and D being the same is stronger than any that can be made out for their being different.

(2) The hand of S is more nearly paralleled in D than in any other dramatic document known to us.

(3) Setting S aside, it can be shown that D was not written by any dramatist of whose hand we have adequate knowledge.

If these propositions can be established, I think that together they incline the balance of probability in favour of identification. More than this I would not claim. I feel tempted, however, to add one more proposition of a somewhat challenging nature, namely:

(4) On purely palaeographical grounds there is less reason to suppose that all six signatures were written by the same hand than there is, granting this identity, to suppose that the hand of the signatures also wrote the addition to *More*.

14. A Question of Plus or Minus[1]

PROFESSOR Dover Wilson, in the course of his discussion of the copy for the first quarto of *Hamlet* that appeared in *The Library* some twelve years ago,[2] invented the term 'repetition-bracket' for a peculiar phenomenon of that version. It consists in the repetition of a line or phrase within a scene, and points, according to his view, to the intervening lines being an addition to the original text. He quoted in particular the following instance from I. ii (1603, B4–B4v):[3]

> *Ham.* I am very glad to see you, good euen sirs:
> * But what is your affaire in *Elsenoure?*
> Weele teach you to drinke deepe ere you depart.
> *Hor.* A trowant disposition, my good Lord.
> *Ham.* Nor shall you make mee truster
> Of your owne report against your selfe:
> Sir, I know you are no trowant:
> * But what is your affaire in *Elsenoure?*
> *Hor.* My good Lord, I came to see your fathers funerall.

This is the first and perhaps the most striking example. The others cited are: I. v (1603, C4) '. . . briefe let me be. [14 lines] . . . briefe let me be'; II. i (1603, D2–D2v) 'And bid him ply his learning good *Montano*. [26 lines.] *Cor.* And bid him ply his musicke'; III. ii (1603, F3) '*Ofel.* What meanes this my Lord? [1 line]. *Ofel.* What doth this meane my lord?'; v. i (1603, H4), 'Goe fetch me a stope of drinke, . . . [12 lines] . . . Fetch me a stope of beere, goe.'

It is not necessary for my present purpose to inquire the precise nature of mechanism of the supposed insertions. Nor do I propose to raise the question whether Dover Wilson is right in seeing in these 'repetition-brackets' evidence of insertion at all. It seems possible to regard them as quite likely results of memorial reconstruction. But whatever their

[1] [1930, Jul. *The Review of English Studies*, vi. 300–4.]

[2] 'The Copy for *Hamlet*, 1603', Jul. 1918, ix. 153 ff.

[3] In this and other quotations I have marked with a star the lines containing the 'bracketing' phrases.

significance in the 1603 *Hamlet* may be, there are undoubtedly certain texts, derived from playhouse copies, in which similar phenomena might very plausibly be regarded as evidence of insertion. The usual method of making an addition to the text of a manuscript play was to place some mark at the point at which the insertion was to stand and then to write in the margin or on a separate slip the additional lines, concluding with the following line of the original text. Here is an example from *The Second Maiden's Tragedy* (B.M. MS. Lansdowne 807, fol. 32^{a}):

Hel. mass so it does
let a man thinck on't twice, yor grace hath hapned
vpon a straung waie, yet it proues the neerest:
o———
I do beseech yor ma^{tie}, looke cheerfull
yo^{u} shall not want content, . . .

A separate slip supplies the addition:

Ty. nay more to vex his sowle giue comaund straite
they be deuided into seuerall Roomes
wher he may only haue a sight of her
to his myndes torment, but his armes and lips
lockt vp like fellons, from her
Helu. now yo^{u} win me
I like that crueltie passing well my lord
Ty. giue order wth all speed
Hel. Thoe I be ould
I need no spurr my l: *Honor* prickes me
I do beseech yor grace look cheerfullie &c.

Now it is evident that if a compositor, with this manuscript before him, were to follow his copy exactly, he would get two consecutive lines nearly identical, and he might be trusted to use his intelligence to omit one of them. In that he would be following the author's or reviser's intention, and his text would preserve no bibliographical evidence of the addition. If, however, the intended position of the extra lines were at all ambiguous—and that position is by no means always so clearly marked as in the example just cited—a very different condition might result. Suppose, for example, that in this case the compositor were to insert the addition a line too low, it is obvious that he would produce a text substantially similar to the one Mr. Dover Wilson quotes from *Hamlet*, and one in which the 'repetition-bracket' would be genuine evidence that the 'bracketed' lines were an insertion. The question arises whether this principle can in practice be put to critical use.

I wish to direct attention to two passages of *The Honest Man's Fortune* as printed in the Beaumont and Fletcher folio of 1647, which present features similar to those we have been discussing. They occur close together in the first scene, and indeed on the same page of the folio (p. 151, sig. 5T2). The first is as follows—Montague is awaiting news of the issue of a law-suit in which his fortune is at stake:[1]

Enter Longueville.

Mont. Longueville thou bringst a cheerfull promise in thy face.
There stands no pale report upon thy cheeke,
To give me feare or knowledge of my losse, tis red and lively.
* How proceeds my suit?
Long. That's with labour sir, a labour that to those of *Hercules*
May adde another; or (at least) be cald
[An] imitation of [his] burning shirt:
For twas a paine of that unmercifull
Perplexity, to shulder through the throng
Of people that attended your successe:
My sweaty linnen fixt upon my skin,
Still as they puld me, tooke that with it; 'twas
A feare I should have left my flesh among 'em:
Yet I was patient, for (me thought) the toyle
Might be an emblem of the difficult
And weary passage to get out of Law.
And to make up the deare similitude,
When I was forth seeking my handkircher
To wipe my sweat off, I did finde a cause
To make me sweat more, for my Purse was lost
Among their [fingers].
Dub. There twas rather found.
Long. By them.
Dub. I mean so.
Mont. Well, I will restore
* Thy dammage to thee: how proceeds my suit?
[*Long.*] Like one at Brokers; I thinke forfeited.

[1] Certain corrections of the folio text are made in square brackets; they are derived from the manuscript to be mentioned later.

The second instance occurs when, the cause lost, the lawyers pass over the stage and refuse so much as to notice their now destitute client:

Long. Let me see I pray sir,
Never stood you upon the pillory?
1 Law. The Pillory?
Long. O now I know you did not.
Y'ave eares, I thought ye had lost 'em; pray observe,
Here's one that once was gracious in [your] eyes.
* *1 Law.* O my Lord, have an eye upon him.
Long. But ha' you nere a Counsell to redeeme
His Land yet from the judgement?
2 Law. None but this, a writ of errour to remove the cause.
Long. No more of errour, we have been in that too much already.
2 Law. If you will reverse the judgement, you must trust to that delay.
Long. Delay? Indeed he's like to trust to that,
With you has any dealing.
2 Law. Ere the Law proceeds to an *habere facias possessionem.*
Dub. That's a language sir, I understand not.
Long. Th'art a very strange unthankfull fellow to have taken Fees of such a liberall measure, and then give a man hard words for's money.
[*Mont.* So, tis gone.]
1 Law. If men will hazzard their salvations,
What should I say? I've other businesse. [*Exit Law.*]
Mont. Y'are ith' right;
That's it you should say now prosperity has left me.

Enter two Creditors.

* *1 Cred.* Have an eye upon him; if
We lose him now, he's gone for ever; stay
And dog him: Ile goe fetch the officers.

In the first of these passages we get a repetition of the phrase 'How proceeds my suit?' and it is pretty evident that the first time it occurs it is a mistake. For one thing, when we have divided the lines properly it is seen to be metrically redundant; and, what is more important, Longueville replies, not to this important question, but to Montague's previous reference to his flushed face. It would seem, therefore, quite plausible to suggest that the 'bracketed' lines are actually an addition that has been worked into the text half a line too late, even though the objection might be raised that it is curious to draw attention to Longueville's lively colour if no explanation is to follow.

In the second passage the words 'have an eye upon him' seem to possess on their first occurrence no meaning whatever, in spite of the superficially specious echo of the previous line, which is in fact mere coincidence. The only possible criticism of the insertion theory in this case is that the presence of a stage-direction and speaker's name immediately before the second occurrence slightly complicates the mechanism.

In spite of the slight objections I have indicated, I think that, had any one drawn my attention to these two passages, I should have accepted the explanation of them as additions made in the copy without much hesitation, and I fancy that in doing so I should not have stood alone.

It happens, however, that for *The Honest Man's Fortune* we are lucky enough to possess a second text in a manuscript (no. 9) in the Dyce collection. This was prepared for relicence by Herbert, 8 February 1624/5, at a time when the 'Originall' of 1613 was 'Lost'. This is not the place to discuss the relation of the manuscript and the printed text, nor am I at present prepared to pronounce upon it.[1] Suffice it to say that, in spite of certain specific differences of the text, the relation must be a very close one, as appears from the numerous passages of incorrect lining common to the two; that each in many instances corrects the other; and that the manuscript has a particular bearing upon the problem in hand.

In the first place, the conclusion we have already come to that the repetitions are the result of accident is confirmed by the manuscript, which omits in each case the first occurrence of the words. But what I think is of more particular significance is that in the first of the two passages the 'bracketed' lines ('*Long*. That's with labour sir, . . . Thy dammage to thee:') are marked for omission. There are a number of passages so marked in the manuscript, and in each case the folio prints the full text, in spite of the fact that it seems to be derived from another playhouse manuscript which was probably similarly scored, though perhaps not always at the

[1] [The play has since been edited and the relation of the texts discussed at length by Johan Gerritsen (Groningen, 1952).]

same points. In view of these omissions I think that the minor objections to the insertion theory that we noted above acquire fresh weight. I suggest, in fact, that we have to do, not with additions at all, but with excisions. It would seem that whoever worked on the manuscript subsequently used as copy for the folio, when he made the cuts in question, cancelled, either by accident or design, the words immediately following the cut, and then repeated them in the margin at the head of the cut to serve as a link. It would be natural enough to do so, since where a passage was cancelled it was often necessary to supply such a link; indeed, the Dyce manuscript affords an excellent instance of this very practice.[1] And such an accident would exactly account for the text as we find it printed in the folio. It is true that in the second passage quoted the manuscript does not indicate any omission, but it is difficult to suppose that the confusion had not the same origin in both instances, and I have little doubt that the cause was a cut in the prompt copy.

It would appear, therefore, that the 'repetition-bracket' may be brought about in two diametrically opposite ways, and may point either to addition or to subtraction. And when we recall that the insertion theory always requires us to suppose that the printer mistook by a line or so the place of the insertion, we may wonder whether the omission theory has not at least equal claim to consideration. I am not saying which explanation, if either, applies to the instances in the 'bad' first quarto of *Hamlet*, but I hope that before any critic yields to the temptation of extending to more reputable texts Dover Wilson's conclusions regarding 'bracketed' additions, he will consider rather carefully the possibilities of the case and whatever evidence may be available.

[1] Fol. 20*b*, where the words 'but I may spare my labour. heer's my lady' have been written in between the lines at the head of a long passage marked for omission.

15. The Present Position of Bibliography[1]

It is an undesigned coincidence that my predecessor in this chair closed his term of office with an address on the history of bibliography[2] and I am opening mine with one on its present position. But it is, perhaps, not without significance, for it is time that bibliography took stock of the situation. Unless I am mistaken a certain change of outlook is taking place among bibliographers, and a certain change is also observable in the way in which bibliography is looked on from the outside. No doubt the two are related: let us hope as an outward and visible sign of inward and spiritual grace.

The outward sign is at any rate the more manifest and the easier to evaluate. It is now nearly twenty years ago that, with what many may have thought at the time, and what looking back I cannot but confess, was the temerity, not to say the arrogance, of youth, I ventured to address you on the question 'What is Bibliography?'[3] At the end of my paper on that occasion I indulged in the dream of a course of bibliography to be delivered in one of our English universities. I did not venture to make it a professorial course, and I do not think I much expected to see my hope fulfilled. It is true that the course I dreamed of has not yet been delivered, but it will be some day. For, as you all know, there has now been a bibliographical chair in the University of London for over ten years. To that chair the University appointed the only fitting person, Alfred Pollard. Both foundation and appointment were, I think, important for the University, and there can be no doubt of their importance for bibliography. There is, indeed, one point upon which criticism might fasten. The chair is, I understand, one of English Bibliography. It is possible that such a title may encourage the idea that bibliography is a descriptive matter, whose function is the more or less detailed enumeration of books dealing with some specified subject.

[1] [1930, Dec. *The Library*, xi. 241–62.] Presidential address given before the Bibliographical Society on 20 Oct. 1930.

[2] ['Bibliographical Societies and Bibliography', by G. F. Barwick, read 17 Mar. 1930: *The Library*, Sept. 1930, xi. 151–9.]

[3] 19 Feb. 1912 [see p. 75].

In fact, to suppose that bibliography can be parcelled out into linguistic, literary, or regional departments is to harbour a dangerous fallacy. At the same time there is no objection to linking bibliographical training with the teaching of English or any other literature, in the study of which it is so necessary an instrument; and as long as the training is in the hands of a teacher of Mr. Pollard's stamp and on the lines on which he has started it, we may rest assured that, far from the chair becoming a stronghold of antiquated modes of thought, it will continue to be a centre of the new light.

The teaching of bibliography seems to me at the moment a matter of some consequence, for upon it depends not only the position which the study itself may be expected to hold in the future, but also the progress likely to be made in certain other studies, and even the lines upon which those studies will probably develop. It is gratifying, therefore, to find that a good deal of attention is being given in various quarters to bibliographical instruction. London not only boasts a professorship, but has also, at University College, a lectureship, which for several years had been held with distinction by Mr. Esdaile. Its subject, however, is what I should describe as librarianship rather than bibliography—at least the very useful little book which is, I understand, the outcome of one course delivered, is mainly concerned with such help in finding one's way about among books as a librarian might be expected to supply for his readers. Some more informal instruction is also given to students of literature both at University College and at King's.

Looking beyond London I am handicapped by a very extensive ignorance of academic curricula, and I must not be supposed to be wilfully ignoring either the aspirations or performance of the younger universities if I confine my few remarks to Oxford and Cambridge, those kind mothers in whose families I feel myself most at home. One other university, I know, recently did a bibliographer a very high honour indeed.[1]

Academically speaking, Cambridge, with a tradition in bibliography going back to Henry Bradshaw, might lay some claim to be regarded as the particular home of that study

1 [I have not been able to identify Greg's reference here.—J.C.M.]

in England, and it was of course by many years the earliest to have a formal and endowed readership in our subject. Among the many courses of lectures that have been delivered on the Sandars foundation, there are several important contributions to various branches of the study—have not all three who occupy this platform today in turn held the post?—but the discontinuity involved in annual appointment has of necessity forbidden any systematic teaching, and characteristically Cambridge has tended in the past rather to foster individual bibliographical talent than to found anything of the nature of a school. But the need for definite instruction is making itself felt even here, and some individual help for students is available, though as yet the subject has found no favour in the eyes of authority.

Much more promising are the prospects of bibliography at the sister university—Oxford, the home, let us hope, not of lost causes alone. The distinction between two attitudes, no less than between the older and the modern approach, is pointed by a comparison of the work done by the Baskerville Club at Cambridge and the Oxford Bibliographical Society. And here we find that bibliography is a subject for regular instruction in the B.Litt. course of the English school. From among the scholars who have been and are connected with that school it is perhaps invidious to select any for special mention, but one may suspect that bibliography owes its position in the course mainly to the initiative of Mr. Percy Simpson. His realization of its importance in literary studies is testified by a number of striking essays, starting with his valuable, if unfortunately named, *Shakespearian Punctuation* in 1911. In this he was assisted, as he has also been in the teaching of bibliography, by Mr. R. W. Chapman, a scholar whose enthusiasm embraces alike cancel leaves and silver spoons—both worthy objects. Mr. Chapman's connexion with books is of course professional, and indeed the recognition of the value of bibliographical study at Oxford is, I believe, primarily due to the University Press, and even so perhaps to a fortunate accident. There was a time when the belief prevailed there that anyone with a good classical education on the broad lines of the Oxford tradition was sufficiently equipped to undertake the editing of any English author. Of course, this simple faith was bound sooner or later to lead to disaster, and one day a book appeared that was a real disgrace, and which received well-merited castigation. The Secretary to the Delegates at the time was a gentleman who combined a valuable capacity for learning by experience with a useful gift of forcible language. He at once saw the need for an English scholar on whose help and judgement the Press could rely. What he said is irrelevant, but since then Mr. Simpson has been at hand to furnish expert advice.[1]

The academic recognition of bibliography is one manifest sign of its altered position in the world. Another might be found in the fact that in 1920 a bibliographer was invited to give evidence before a government committee on the teaching of English. On that occasion I had the honour of putting my views before an authoritative body, which in its elaborate report found room for the following paragraphs:[2]

We also wish, in relation to research work, to draw attention to the importance of training advanced students of English language and literature in Bibliography. . . . The wide scope of bibliographical investigation . . . was made clear in the evidence of [the witness]:

'It is not, as often supposed, confined to the invention of printing and the classification of the products of the early presses: rather it covers the whole study of the material transmission of literature in its widest sense. Since practically all extant literature has at some time passed through a stage of material, as opposed to oral or memorial, transmission, and since the fundamental task of criticism is the establishment of the text, bibliography has been well styled the "grammar of literature".

[1] [The editor of *The Library* refused to let me print the story as I gave it in my address. What Charles Cannan said was, 'My God, we've got to get in a bloody expert!' 'And I', added Percy Simpson, 'am the bloody expert.'

Through some unaccountable lapse, I omitted to mention the leading part played by Strickland Gibson in the teaching of bibliography at Oxford. I now have before me the syllabus of an exhaustive course of fourteen lectures covering the technical and practical aspects of the subject, delivered by him in the Hilary Term of 1931. Gibson was not only a teacher but a collector, and his bibliographical collections are now housed in what is called the Bibliography Room in the New Bodleian, which is presided over by Herbert Davis, Reader in Textual Criticism with the title of Professor—welcome evidence, to me, of the recognition of the kinship of the two studies.—1958.]

[2] *The Teaching of English in England.* Report of the Departmental Committee on the Position of English in the Educational System of England. 1921 (§ 223, pp. 241–2).

'Thus bibliography may be defined as the systematic study of the transmission of the written word whether through manuscript or print, and it aims at the evolution of a critical organon by which the utmost possible results may be extracted from the available evidence. It forms the greater and most essential part of the duty of the editor, but its value in criticism is by no means confined to the editor. It will be found of service in every field of investigation, and cannot be neglected even by the "aesthetic" critic without loss.

'It frequently happens that the close examination of an old print or manuscript, the actual arrangement of the words on the page or the material condition of the leaves, still more frequently the comparison of different editions or different manuscripts, suggests to the bibliographical eye the solution of problems towards which literary critics have been long and blindly groping.' . . .

We are convinced that in every University where research work in English is undertaken provision should be made for instruction in bibliography.

It was gratifying to find my personal confession of faith thus accepted by the committee, and the practical corollary from it so unequivocally endorsed. It was also a little surprising, and it may have required some guidance to lead the committee to its conclusion, for the effect of my evidence at the time seemed to be a little confused. I remember the chairman[1] recalling how he first came to realize that the canon and text of the New Testament were not something given in the form in which they are familiar to us today, but that this form was the result of the patient labours of generations of scholars upon ancient and often obscure originals; and how this realization had let in a flood of new light on his mind. The same applied, of course, to the canon and text of Shakespeare, or any other author. Some other members of the committee thought how nice it would be if, when Shakespeare was being read in schools, the children could be shown a copy of the First Folio, that they might realize in what guise his plays appeared to his earliest readers. Perhaps it would—the late Mr. Folger might have been asked to loan out some of his superfluous copies for the purpose—but personally the prospect does not appeal to me. I think the chairman, unlike some members of the committee—who had probably not read my memorandum—had grasped the

[1] [Sir Henry Newbolt.]

meaning of bibliography sufficiently to realize that it is a subject which, though its function in literary scholarship may be usefully indicated in the school curriculum and the ordinary university course, should, so far as method is concerned, be reserved for postgraduate study by those who are actually called upon to use it. But that a government committee on teaching should actually desire to hear about bibliography, and should include in their report a sympathetic reference to its importance, is, it seems to me, a remarkable acknowledgement of its claim to be regarded as a serious study.

Thus in the last quarter of a century, and largely in the last ten years, bibliography has come to be recognized as something of account in literary scholarship, and we may well ask to what this revolution is due. To what change, if any, does it correspond in its own outlook? Briefly I should say that bibliography has become self-conscious: it is beginning to discover its own significance. The amateur and the dilettante are giving place to the expert and the scholar. I know that this sounds abominably priggish, but I assure you most earnestly that it is not priggishly meant. We are all of us, at least if we are worth our salt, amateurs and dilettanti of the subjects to which we devote our study. And the scholar, the specialist, may be an exceedingly dusty person. For the amateurs and dilettanti I have a profound respect; not only because they are the very founders and builders of our craft, and because they loved it in the right, the only, way, but no less for the vast and precious knowledge they garnered for our use. How often we, who call ourselves scholars, are but the gleaners that come after!—'But have you not—how say you?—what we call *Gelehrte*?' a foreign visitor once asked Henry Sidgwick. 'Oh, yes,' Sidgwick replied, making the most of his inimitable stammer, 'but here we call them p-p-prigs!'—But when we have humbly admitted the truth of this, there remains, I think, a difference of approach, that may be rightly held—for I would not appear too modest—in some measure to redress the balance. The amateur studies the things he loves for their own sake, usually as individuals or as examples of some more or less restricted class. He notes and describes. Others do the like. Gradually from the accumulated stores of many individual searchers emerge resemblances and contrasts, general lines of cleavage or of development: in short the facts become co-ordinated and therefore significant. Every fact a scholar uses may have been recorded before; it is in his appreciation of its relation to other facts, of its application to other problems, that he distinguishes himself from the amateur. I have heard it said of a Cambridge philosopher[1] that he would talk with any man on his own subject, and that at the end of half an hour he would know more about that subject than the man himself. What he possessed was a power of seeing the significance of facts, the power of scientific combination. And this sense of significance and relation, if it does not make the scholar superior to the amateur, at least enables him to give immeasurably greater vitality to their study. He no longer contents himself with observation and record—important as these must always remain—beyond the outward facts he seeks the latent meaning, the hidden cause. In his hands the subject ceases to be descriptive and static, it becomes dynamic and historical.

But it may still be questioned whether my claim that in bibliographical studies the scholar has succeeded the amateur is in fact true. Granted the validity of the distinction I have in mind, I think it is. I need not enlarge on the scholarly *expertise* of those who are active in the field today—I shall have a word to say about some of them later. Still, amateur or dilettante seems a curious term to apply, with any sense of limitation, to such a man as Henry Bradshaw, and I can fancy Mr. Pollard's eyebrows lifting. Bradshaw is rightly regarded as the founder, or one of the founders, of the modern study of typography, perhaps the most 'scientific' branch of bibliography, and many notable advances in other departments are equally connected with his name. I might plead that no single instance, not even several instances, need invalidate my main conclusion. But I do not know that I need do so. I think the reader of Bradshaw's collected papers, while he will wonder at the range of their subjects and the grasp of the treatment, will find little hint of any synthesis, or conscious attempt to bring the various threads into such a relation as to weave a significant pattern. In this respect his work belongs to the elder school, and it is by his sadly fragmentary published

[1] [G. E. Moore.]

work that we are condemned to form a judgement. It may be that if we read between the lines, or turn from his papers to his life, we sometimes get a hint that the wider significance of his investigations and their possible interrelations may not have been altogether absent as a background to his thought. I have sometimes wondered whether, if one could have looked into that wonderfully stored mind, one would not have discovered that he was in truth the first of the moderns, and whether it was not mainly a scholar's modesty that forbade his claiming a wider generality for his studies than he did. I fancy we get an occasional glimpse of something of the sort, particularly in his work on Cornish-Breton glosses. Of course it is implicit likewise in his Chaucerian studies. True, his printed paper, 'The Skeleton of Chaucer's Canterbury Tales' (Memorandum 4), really begins where bibliography leaves off. But that Bradshaw himself recognized the subject as bibliographical appears from a letter he wrote to Furnivall (7 August 1868) in which he says: 'My only point is my method, which I always insist on in everything in bibliography—arrange your facts rigorously and get them plainly before you, and let them *speak for themselves*, which they will always do.'[1]

But this is a digression. However it has come about, and whoever may have helped in the process, I think there can be no doubt of the general trend of development from the accumulation of particular knowledge to a realization of its significance, or that in becoming aware of the process bibliography is at the present moment entering on a new phase of its career. The change of outlook is one fraught with possibilities. There is a brilliant little book on mathematics in the Home University Library, that in my Cambridge days we used to know as 'Whitehead's shilling shocker'—it now costs half a crown. Among many other wise things, it contains the remark that usually the last thing to be discovered concerning any science is what it is about. If we can answer that question with respect to bibliography, then it may at least be supposed to have attained to maturity as a serious study. Can we?

[1] *Memoir*, p. 349. Prothero prints 'vigorously', but 'rigorously' must be what Bradshaw intended. Curiously enough Bradshaw regarded typography as 'a contribution to the history of art' (letter to G. I. F. Tupper, 6 May 1870, facing p. 360).

Probably the answer must still be tentative, and there will be little unanimity respecting its precise form. But if bibliography has become self-conscious it will at least be recognized that the question is a pertinent one, and that a good deal may depend on getting the right answer. I will give you my own, but I do not ask you to accept it, for I have no leisure this afternoon to develop my thesis as I should like. If you will grant me so much indulgence I shall hope to do so upon some future occasion.

Very briefly I would put it thus. I take it for granted that bibliography is the study of books as material objects. But what are books? and why should we study them? Now, although bibliography is not directly concerned with the contents of books, it is ultimately the contents that are of value, and books are of importance only as the vehicle by which those contents reach us. Books are our main link with the thought and action of the past, the bibliographical facts are important as they relate to the way in which books fulfil their function. I should therefore give my answer as follows: Bibliography is the study of the material transmission of literary and other documents; its ultimate aim is to solve the problems of origin, history, and text, in so far as this can be achieved through minute investigation of the material means of transmission. The answer may be unexpected, but I think it is strictly logical. I have sought to give it such a form as to bring out what seems to me the real significance of bibliography: incidentally it has the merit of discountenancing the descriptive heresy, and also of avoiding any ambiguity that may lurk in the word 'book' itself.

I do not suppose that all, or perhaps any, of those to whose labours bibliography owes the interest now taken in it in the wider world of literary studies, would agree with my answer as it stands. But at least, if true, it accounts for that interest, and I think that it, or some similar conception, will be found underlying and inspiring the work of many to whom we chiefly owe the introduction of the new spirit into bibliography, and who are likely to be chiefly instrumental in directing its development. They are well known to you all, and perhaps to mention names may be a delicate matter. But I am in a privileged position this afternoon: I am speaking to you from the chair, and there is no one to call me to order. For once I can give you my candid opinion of those with whom I have been to some extent associated in what will perhaps one day be recognized as a significant critical movement, and has certainly been an exhilarating adventure.

In the first place there is Alfred Pollard, he who has so long and so ably guided the destinies of this Society, and under whose benign dictatorship it is now my proud privilege and satisfaction to occupy the strictly constitutional chair. Mr. Pollard got his training and won his bibliographical spurs in the old school, and affection and conservatism alike make him sometimes cling to its ways. But no one is younger of mind than he, and neither affection nor conservatism has blinded him to the significance of new ideas or stood in his way as an apostle of the new learning. Much of the advance has been directly due to him, more still to his encouragement and inspiration. In breadth of view and imaginative grasp of the significance of new discoveries he has often been ahead of those by whom the discoveries were made. And where he has not himself been our leader in new fields of exploration he has been content to follow the tracks of younger and less experienced men with the generosity of the true scholar. I cannot remember who it was said to me not long ago that Mr. Pollard was a remarkable instance of a man who had produced his best work when he had passed the age of fifty. I do not know whether that is true or whether it is really unusual, but I am certain that in the last twenty years his work has grown less encumbered by traditional modes of thought. We are all familiar with the core of conservative prejudice often found in the professed radical and iconoclast. Mr. Pollard's conservatism is something far more innocent than that: a conservatism of the heart that the mind knows and can at need strip off. I see him, as it were, still fondly huddling some rags of weathered garment round the stark limbs of the athlete that should be his chiefest glory.

Next to Mr. Pollard I see his henchman in our government, R. B. McKerrow. I believe that few realize the full debt which bibliography, as well as this Society, owes to his patient and extraordinarily unassuming labours. Unless I am much mistaken, his pamphlet bearing the characteristically modest and uninviting title of 'Notes on Bibliographical Evidence for Literary Students and Editors of English Works of the Sixteenth and Seventeenth Centuries', reprinted from our *Transactions* for 1911–13, was one of the most important influences in awakening literary students to the need for a bibliographical equipment. He has now recast and enlarged it, and I have no doubt whatever that future scholars will reckon as one of the principal landmarks in the history of the subject his curiously named *Introduction to Bibliography*. I rather disapprove of the title: for one thing I wanted it myself; for another his book is a pretty thorough survey of the particular field he has chosen. Dr. McKerrow is the realist, for ever questioning, for ever probing after new facts or after the interpretation of old ones, and he has, I believe, the greatest technical knowledge and skill of any bibliographer, in this country at least. When a problem baffles us we all take it to him, and seldom, if ever, in vain. I am persuaded that, had he stood on Sinai when Moses received the graven tables, he would have there and then sat down to hunt the tell-tale flaw that would reveal the method of production—and he would have found it.

Then there is John Dover Wilson. He is of imagination all compact. And imagination, I would remind you, is the highest gift in scientific investigation, even if it may be at times the deepest pitfall. Whether his conclusions stand or not—and I am sure that he himself would be the last to claim finality for them—he has at least introduced a new spirit and a new outlook into the secular task of editing Shakespeare, and it will never be the same again. And whether we agree with his arguments or whether we do not, to follow him in his attack on age-old problems or down new vistas of unsuspected possibilities is always an exhilaration and a delight. Reading him I am constantly reminded of a story in the papers a few years ago. A company of French soldiers were tethering a captive balloon in a high wind, when the monster got out of hand. The men were swept off their feet. Some let go and were dashed to the ground, others held on and were carried away. Even so, under the fascination of Professor Wilson's ingenuity, I am ever in doubt whether to let go and risk a nasty fall, or to cling desperately and be borne I know not whither.

I must not continue this catalogue of personalities, though it were easy and is tempting to do so. But there is one other I should like to mention, though he was never, I regret to say, a member of this Society, and was indeed rather a lone wolf, belonging consciously to no school or movement. I mean the late Henry Bradley. I am convinced that no keener mind was ever bent upon bibliographical problems, but so many-sided were his intellectual interests and activities, that perhaps few bibliographers realize the brilliance of the contributions he made to their own studies. And it was, to me at least, a great disappointment that not one of his essays that touched on bibliography was included in the memorial volume published by the Oxford University Press. The reason was, I believe, that they were accessible elsewhere; some in the proceedings of the British Academy, of which he was for many years a Fellow. But those familiar with his papers on the numbered sections of Anglo-Saxon poetry[1] and on Abbo of Fleury will not be surprised at my mentioning him here.

Bradley, as I have said, was never a member of this Society, and I cannot help feeling that it points to some failure on our part that we did not reckon him one of us. I once heard Mr. Pollard say that if the Bibliographical Society really fulfilled its mission every professor of English in the country who understood his job would find it necessary to belong to it. I think he was right; though perhaps the blame does not rest with the Society alone. Teachers of English are sometimes a little afraid of the technical side of books, and I won't blame them. I was once talking bibliographical shop with R. W. Chapman in the presence of a professor of English. It was at Oxford, somewhere about the gate of the Parks: the time near midnight. We had dined well and were in a confidential mood. After a while the professor said wistfully: 'You fellows are making literature a very difficult subject. I think I should have done better to go on the Stock Exchange.'

But if it might in any case have been a hard task to make the

[1] [I have been told by those with a right to speak that this paper contains more ingenuity than substance. But I think it shows the right sort of bibliographical imagination. (See p. 261.)]

professorial horse drink at the cold springs of bibliography, I hardly think that the Society has done all it might to lead him thereto. While the significance of bibliography for literature has gained in recognition outside, while a new orientation has become evident in the work of individual bibliographers, I regret to say that I have noticed little consciousness of the facts in our own proceedings. If, as I started by saying, bibliography has become self-conscious, we as a Society have remained, shall I say, naïve, content to pursue our way without question of why or whither. Our membership has increased surprisingly and has come to include a number of professors or future professors of English literature, but I cannot help wondering whether some at least of these have not been disappointed. I am not complaining of the subjects or the quality of our papers or our publications; I believe that much of the work we have produced has been excellent and the general level high. What I feel wanting in it is a sense of direction, an appreciation that the various lines of investigation are somehow related in a common end. The new discovery, which I have tried to put into words by saying that bibliography is concerned with the transmission of literary documents, has been made, and it is going to affect progressively the relations of bibliography with literary and historical study; it is only a question whether that development takes place mainly outside this Society or mainly within it. It is, I think, important both for the study and for the Society that it should be the latter. If it takes place outside, then it will mean that historical critics, alive to the necessities of the situation, will imbibe as best they may and apply as best they can a more or less adequate and a more or less intelligent knowledge of bibliographical method: if, on the other hand, it takes place within the Society, it will have behind it all the treasured accumulations of the older school, a sense of the unity of the subject, the valuable inheritance of a tradition. And at the moment when bibliography is being welcomed and even acclaimed as an important historical study, for the Bibliographical Society to stand aside would surely be a renunciation that would border on betrayal. It is my most earnest hope that the Society will awake to self-consciousness and welcome the new direction that its studies are taking: if it does, I have no doubt but that it will play a part that will be important and perhaps decisive in various fields of academic research. It was this hope that gave me confidence, and even made me eager, to accept the position to which you have done me the honour to call me. When the suggestion was first made I told Mr. Pollard that if elected I should use my position frankly for purposes of propaganda. He replied: 'Bless you, my son: do your damnedest!'—or words to that effect.

I should like to see the Society take for its motto, 'Bibliography is the Grammar of Literature'. I do not know who invented that phrase, which was quoted by our first President in his inaugural address, but it seems to me to sum up the present movement.[1] Only literature is rather too narrow a word, for the documents that form the subject-matter of bibliography are as much historical as strictly literary. Even it must be admitted that, whatever its aesthetic soul may be, the body of literature, that which alone bibliography can approach, is ultimately a matter and a department of history. Thus, as I see it, bibliography is an historical study, or perhaps I should rather say a method of historical investigation. And this would seem to have a bearing on the question sometimes debated whether bibliography should be regarded as a science. The question is no doubt partly a verbal one and in so far trivial. But not altogether, for the answer given to the question may throw light upon the meaning of bibliography. In other words, it is upon our conception of bibliography that will depend our view whether it is a science—or what?

I believe it has even been claimed that bibliography is an exact science. I once asked Mr. Pollard what he thought was meant by that phrase. He replied that he supposed mathematics was the type of the exact sciences.[2] I was amused a few days later, on opening Mr. Sullivan's admirable little *History of Mathematics*,[3] to find that it is not a science at all but an art or game, since 'unlike the sciences, but like the art of music or the game of chess, mathematics is a free creation of the mind'.

[1] [I believe the phrase quoted by Copinger actually was 'Bibliography is the Grammar of Literary Investigation'—which is better.]

[2] [I should have said 'enters into any science which can be called exact.'—A.W.P.]

[3] *The History of Mathematics in Europe from the Fall of Greek Science to the Rise of the Conception of Mathematical Rigour*. By J. W. N. Sullivan. 1925.

That is unquestionably true, and consequently Mr. Pollard's criterion will not help us. Is there in fact any distinction? Is not exactitude the aim of every science, which it approaches as it gains in mastery over its material? I suspect psychology of being at present the least exact of the sciences, but I know no reason why it should not attain exactitude as it reaches maturity and learns to define its nature and scope. Mr. Bernard Shaw remarks somewhere, if my memory serves, that the distinction between fine art and applied art is a false one: the only valid distinction is between fine art and bad art, or between applied art and misapplied art. So I think that the real distinction is not between an exact science and any other, but between a mature science and one that is still groping after its foundations, or else merely between science and bunkum.

Now if bibliography is a branch or a method of historical study, then before we can answer the question whether bibliography is a science, we need to answer that other question whether or not there is a science of history. The two questions become in fact one. Grant that there is such a science; then all sound methods of historical investigation, including bibliography, are scientific. If, on the other hand, history is an art, then I am not sure that bibliography is any better than a pander. Upon this battle-field of the nature of history I join issue with my friend Professor Trevelyan, who has just republished, albeit a little apologetically, his early essay entitled *Clio, a Muse*, the most eloquent plea that I know for the artistic view of history. I really don't want to be offensive to my friends, but surely looked at disinterestedly and unprofessionally the matter is simple enough. It is merely the vanity of historians that leads them to suppose that History is what they write. History, in fact, is nothing else than the mighty stream of human events itself. What historians write is a peculiar form of fiction, and Clio is a muse because, when Herodotus lived, this was the only form of prose fiction known to the Greeks. The knowledge of human events, and the methods by which that knowledge is pursued, have just as good a claim to be called a science as have any other body of facts and any other instruments of research. Nowadays we know too much about scientific laws, those convenient expressions of habitual behaviour, to suppose that their enunciation is essential before 'scientia' can become 'science'.

I am therefore bold to claim for bibliography the title of a science, and believe that as a method of discovery it is thoroughly scientific. It rests with us who use it to make it an efficient, as it is certainly a legitimate, instrument of historical investigation. Upon this, as I conceive it, rests the future of bibliography and its claim to serious consideration, a consideration that is already being in some measure accorded it. As the organon of research into the transmission of literary and historical documents—that is, at once into their original form and subsequent adventures—bibliography should take rank as a mature science in the world of scholarship: as an adjunct to the collecting of pretty books it is at most an amiable game. It has the power and the opportunity, if it is capable of taking a wide outlook and willing to co-operate in a wider field, of rendering great, perhaps critical, service to humaner studies. But there is a danger which, while I do not think it very serious, had best not be lost from view. There is one service which may be asked of bibliography, or at least of bibliographers, and is indeed all too readily asked of them, which it is no part of their business to perform. It is that bibliography should become the slave of other sciences, charged with the compilation of 'bibliographies'. This is mere prostitution. I do not think that such a view of their function is commonly held by bibliographers themselves, but one occasionally meets with it in the dark world outside. It is the invention of those professors of other studies, more often I think literary than what we generally term scientific, who are too slovenly and too indolent to do the drudgery of their own work for themselves. So they would make of bibliographers a race of Robots to do it for them. And bibliographers, who are, I almost regret to say, for the most part an amiable and modest folk, have been sometimes inclined to flatter the preposterous demand. I have no quarrel with bibliographies or their compilers, nor do I deny the need for some bibliographical knowledge both in ascertaining the characteristics of books enumerated and in presenting the information when acquired; but there can be no question whatever that bibliographies should be compiled, after mastering the necessary bibliographical technique, by experts in the subjects of which they treat, and not by bibliographers at the dictation of the experts. And when you hear a professor of literature loudly demanding that bibliographers should provide him with the bibliographies he requires, you may rest assured that if his demands were gratified he would be utterly incapable of appreciating the bibliographical merit of the work, or of turning the literary to any profitable account.

This outburst may perhaps surprise you, coming as it does from one who served his bibliographical apprenticeship in the compilation of a list of early English plays, and who has spent thirty years, more or less, on elaborating the same, or rather in preparing the full bibliographical description for which the earlier work was admittedly only a trial-list. And you may think that indirectly I am being hardly polite to certain eminent bibliographers, such as my friends Mr. T. J. Wise and Dr. Geoffrey Keynes. I assure you—I need hardly assure them—that I do the fullest justice to their bibliographical prowess. But what really gives their work its ultimate value is their enthusiasm for Coleridge and Swinburne, for Harvey and Blake. They are before all else experts, who put their bibliographical *expertise* at the service of their true loves. And that is what I have in effect done with regard to the Elizabethan drama. Only I must confess that I wandered long in darkness and was late to see the light. It was through compilation that I became a bibliographer, and only very gradually did I become conscious that bibliography was something very different from what I had thought. From that old List of Plays I learned a number of things. One was the wisdom of the serpent concealed under the dove-like aspect of our Secretary. I had prepared a skeleton finding-list only, hoping quite shortly to have ready my full descriptive work covering the same ground. Mr. Pollard proposed that my skeleton should take on flesh, at least to the extent of full transcripts of the titles, and handed it over to our friend H. R. Plomer for this process of incarnation. As printed the work was really as much Plomer's as mine. Mr. Pollard's wisdom has been justified by thirty years of waiting. Another thing that I learned was the ease with which one may establish a reputation in a comparatively uncultivated field. Not long after the appearance of my list I met a German professor who was on a visit to this country. He looked hard at me and said: 'So you are the author of the List of English Plays. I have been wishing to meet you: but I thought to see an old man, a great authority!' He was clearly disappointed that I was not a reverend grey-beard. Well, that was a quarter of a century ago, but perhaps he would be just as disappointed in me today, for though I have had the misfortune to grow older, I fear I have grown neither reverend nor reverent. A lamentable failure, no doubt. And yet, when I see how often reverence proves but a means to gull oneself, and a reverend aspect a means to gull others, I wonder whether there may not after all be some compensation in remaining as I am.

But there were other and more serious lessons that I learned from my work on the drama. As I inevitably grew to know more about bibliography, it came to occupy a more important, and above all a more independent, position in my mind, and it was gradually and at first obscurely borne in on me that the work I was doing was not really bibliography at all, but that I was only applying the bibliographical technique I had acquired to the service of a quite different matter. Moreover, my interest had for the moment shifted from the printed drama of the Elizabethan age to the earlier religious drama preserved in manuscript. I think it was probably this change that first led me to a wider and deeper conception of the meaning of bibliography, and that it was while carrying through the investigations that later found form in my Sandars lectures on 'Bibliographical and Textual Problems of the English Miracle Cycles' that I got the first inkling that these problems were in fact identical. It was then that I began to grope round after some guiding principle in bibliographical studies, some clue to the direction in which they were tending. My first attempt to supply an answer to the questions that presented themselves was the paper I submitted to you in December 1912. Today I have tried to carry the discussion a little farther. Perhaps on a future occasion, if you will bear with me, it may be my privilege to present a fuller and more formal survey of the field, and to develop a thesis which I have asked you this afternoon to take very much on trust.

Meanwhile my work on the English printed drama down to the Restoration has progressed. The material is practically complete and fills fourteen pamphlet cases. Large specimens are in type. Shortly, I hope, the first section, that containing the early interludes, will go to press. This has presented quite exceptional difficulties owing to the uncertainty of the chronology, and progress with the later plays and the collected editions should be comparatively rapid. Still I fear that some years must yet elapse before the complete work with its appendixes and index is in your hands.[1] When that happy day arrives I propose to set to and begin to learn something about bibliography.

[1] [The final volume still awaits publication.—1958.] [It appeared in 1959.—J.C.M.]

16. Three Manuscript Notes by Sir George Buc[1]

I PROPOSE, in the following pages, to consider three inscriptions, found in three old books printed within a few years of 1600, which on pretty obvious grounds have come under suspicion as forgeries. I believe that in each case good reasons can be found for believing the inscription to be genuine, and these reasons it is the object of the present article to state. At the same time I wish to preface what I have to say with the remark that of the three documents in question I have only seen one in the original, and that only on one occasion twenty years ago. For such conclusions as I am able to draw now I am dependent on facsimiles, and I am of opinion that no really conclusive case can be founded on any but original documents. It is obvious that if in the present instance I had the originals before me I might discover peculiarities in them that would cause me to modify my opinion. While, therefore, a study of photographs leaves no doubt in my mind of the genuineness of the documents in question, I wish the following pages to be read subject to the reservation I have stated.

Of these documents, then, I will take first a note, or rather a couple of notes, written anonymously on the title-page of a copy of the play of *George a Green* printed in 1599. The copy, when I saw it in 1911, was in the possession of the Duke of Devonshire at Chatsworth. In 1914 it passed into the hands of the late Henry E. Huntington, but it did not remain in his library in California. It was sold as a duplicate, and its present whereabouts is not known for certain, though it is believed to have become the property of the late H. C. Folger, in which case it should again become accessible to students.[2] Meanwhile, I have to rely on the facsimile included in the reprint of the play issued by the Malone Society in 1911, and here reproduced (Plate I).

[1] [1931, Dec. *The Library*, xii. 307–21. The conclusions here reached were endorsed and confirmed by R. C. Bald in an article in *The Library*. Dec. 1934. xv. 295–305.]

[2] [It is in fact now in the Folger Shakespeare Library at Washington.—1958.]

The two notes on the title-page run:

> Written by . . . . a miniſter, who ac⟨ted⟩
> the piñers p̱t in it himſelf. Teſte W. Shakeſpea⟨re⟩

and:

> Ed. Iuby ſaith that the play was made by Ro. Gree⟨ne⟩

It would, I think, be difficult to invent an inscription that should read more suspiciously than this. It simply shouts Forgery! And suspicion is not lessened when we observe that the Chatsworth copy formed no part of the Kemble collection, but came from the Rhodes sale in 1825, and was, therefore, possibly added to the ducal library through the mediation of J. P. Collier, who himself first drew attention to the inscription. No wonder that critics and editors have been shy of placing faith in the notes even when they have not dismissed them as fabrications. Yet the writing has impressed those who actually examined it as genuine. In the volume, when at Chatsworth, was inserted a letter from Sir Edward Bond, formerly Keeper of Manuscripts and then Principal Librarian at the British Museum, pronouncing in favour of authenticity (Malone Society's Collections, i. 288). His opinion should carry the more weight in that he certainly kept his eyes open for forgeries, as is shown by the suspicions he entertained of certain Revels accounts, and that in the present case we can hardly suppose that the possibility of forgery was not present to his mind or that he did not give it due consideration. For my own part, I know that I approached the question with a strong prejudice against the document, and that it was only an examination of the original that convinced me that it was, after all, genuine. But it certainly did convince me. 'A careful inspection', I then wrote, 'has dispelled all doubt on the subject', and again, 'There is no doubt that these two notes are in two different hands of the early seventeenth century'.

There the matter rested, so far as I was concerned, until a couple of years ago, when I received a letter from a friend in America asking me to consider the question afresh. The original being no longer accessible, I turned to the Malone Society's facsimile, and at once all my doubts returned. How could such an inscription possibly be genuine? Again I began to examine the writing minutely, seeking where it might be open to suspicion. On one point, at any rate, I appeared to have been in error. I had said that the notes were in two different hands. I no longer saw any reason for this opinion. The second note was in a different ink from the first, and was written with a finer pen, rather smaller, and more carelessly; but apparently the hand was the same, or (in case of forgery) was intended to look the same. Collier, it seemed, was right when he spoke of the two notes as 'In the same hand-writing' (*History of English Dramatic Poetry*, 1831, iii. 166)—and possibly Collier had the best of all reasons for knowing it was so. But was there anything suspicious in the writing? At two or three points letters had been altered. In 'Shakeſpeare' the *p* had been touched up: apparently as first written the head was insignificant and a larger loop had been rather clumsily superimposed. Something had happened to the *E* of *Ed. Iuby*: exactly what, was not very clear. In *Greene* the English *r* was evidently an afterthought: it had originally been either an *n* or else an Italian *r*, it was impossible to say which. These alterations, particularly the last, were curious and worth noting, but they did not point particularly to forgery.

At least, that was, and is, my opinion; and I should like to interpose a few words on the subject. Some critics of handwriting appear to think that if they can show that the writing in a document has been repeatedly touched up they have established at least a *prima facie* case for forgery. In fact nothing could be falser, at least so far as sixteenth- and seventeenth-century documents are concerned. Many writers have a trick of touching up their letters. (I have it myself—it is said to be a sign of vanity, pedantry, and dishonesty!) In itself this touching up is not a sign of forgery. And it is a practice the forger will do his best to avoid. If a letter will pass muster it is far safer to let it alone than try to alter it, for if suspicion is once aroused such alterations are bound to catch the eye and lead to closer scrutiny. Any writer may make an ill-formed letter or miswrite a word. A clever forger will never attempt to alter what he has written, unless this is of such a nature as to give him away. For instance, if in imitating a pure secretary script he accidentally introduces a small

Italian *s* in the middle of a word, or if in what purports to be a sixteenth-century document he spells *witness* as we do today, he is bound to do something about it, because in genuine originals such things are practically never found. No doubt some forgers are clumsy and will try to alter letters that seem not quite satisfactory, but on the whole alterations are evidence rather against than in favour of the supposition of forgery. In the case before us, if the last word was originally written 'Gneene', no doubt either an innocent scribe or a forger might correct it to 'Greene'. But if it was written 'G*r*eene' (with an italian *r*) it is otherwise. Why an innocent scribe should want to alter it I cannot say, but there is every reason why a forger should not, seeing that the English and the Italian *r* are elsewhere used indifferently.

Having then decided that the alterations noted could not be used to invalidate the inscriptions, I looked further. One or two points gave me an uneasy feeling. There were three English *p*'s in the first inscription (including the one that had been touched up), but in the second the only *p* was of a rather queer Italian form. There were four instances of a long Italian *ſ*, one at least of a clumsily rudimentary type, but one English one, curiously enough in the one Latin word 'Teſte'. The final *s* in 'was' was of the Italian form while that in 'piñers' was English. But this did not take one far. Only one letter could I discover that bore, I thought, a distinct stigma of forgery. Most of the *t*'s were commonplace enough, but one, in the word 'it' in the first inscription, stood out as peculiar. It had been formed in a perfectly ordinary way as a final English *t*, with a tick rising from the base to do duty as a cross stroke (just as in *ꝑt* immediately before)—and then it had been crossed a second time higher up! What seventeenth-century scribe would do that? Yet how easy for a forger, used to crossing his *t*'s, to make, accidentally and unconsciously, that tell-tale double-cross! I almost felt I had my man.

Just then it occurred to me that this was not the only title-page inscription whose authenticity had been called in question. How did it compare with the one signed 'G.B.' in a copy of *Locrine*, 1595? Happily an excellent facsimile of this inscription had lately been published by Dr. Tannenbaum, so I had every facility for comparing the two. It did not take me long to make up my mind that the inscriptions in the two plays were in the same hand, or if forged, were imitations of the same hand. Beyond a general similarity there were various individual resemblances. The characteristic of indecision and touching up was even more marked in *Locrine* than in *George a Green*. And, most surprisingly, here was the same double-crossing of the *t* in the same word 'it'. Either then this was a peculiarity of some book-collector about 1600, or the forger had repeated his peculiar error. Moreover, there was no doubt that the initials G.B. in *Locrine* stood for George Buc, Master of the Revels, and as any amount of his undoubted autograph was available, and a good deal had been actually reproduced,[1] the problem ought to be an easy one to solve. Anyhow the *Locrine* and *George a Green* inscriptions must stand or fall together, and the history of the former at once became relevant to the case.

The copy of *Locrine* in question is, or was recently, in the possession of Dr. A. S. W. Rosenbach of Philadelphia, through whose kindness a facsimile of the title-page is here given (Plate II).[2] In 1926 it fetched $9,000 at the Clawson sale, and the catalogue reports that 'It has a fine provenance, being the Heber, Daniel, Tite, Locker-Lampson, Church, Huntington, Jones copy'. So this, like *George a Green*, had left the Huntington Library as a duplicate. Presumably it was when the play was in Heber's possession that Collier became acquainted with it; for once more it is Collier who is our earliest informant. In 1837 he published his *Catalogue of Early English Literature at Bridgewater House*, in which (pp. 40–41) he describes a copy of Sir George Buc's eclogue *Δάφνις Πολυστέφανος*, 1605, bearing on the fly-leaf an inscription purporting to be written by the author, and consisting of six lines of verse below an address to Lord Ellesmere. (This

[1] His licence appended to the manuscript of *The Second Maiden's Tragedy* is facsimiled in the Malone Society's edition of the play. It is also reproduced in my *English Autographs, 1550–1650* (Plate XXX), together with a marginal note from the manuscript of *Sir John Barnavelt*. A number of scraps of writing from the Revels Office, several in Buc's hand, which are preserved in his manuscript of *The History of Richard III*, appear in a pamphlet by Mr. Frank Marcham entitled *The King's Office of the Revels 1610–1622*. Lastly two holograph documents signed by Buc are reproduced by Mr. A. E. Stamp in his *Disputed Revels Accounts* published by the Shakespeare Association.

[2] It was later sold to Martin Bodmer and is now in his collection at Geneva.

copy is now in the Huntington Library, and a photograph of the inscription is here included by permission: Plate VI.) Collier reproduced, evidently in hand-traced facsimile, the verses (but not the heading) of this presentation inscription, and continued: 'A comparison with this specimen of the penmanship of the Master of the Revels leaves no doubt that the inscription on an existing copy of the play of *Locrine*, 4to. 1595, assigning the authorship of it to Charles Tylney, is the handwriting of Sir George Buck. He adds the information, that he himself had written the "dumb shews" by which it was illustrated, and that it had been originally called *Elstrild*' [*sic*]. Almost thirty years later Collier repeated the description in his *Bibliographical Account of Early English Literature* (1865, i. 93–95) adding at the end: 'Charles Tylney was brother [in fact cousin] to Edmond Tylney, who had preceded Sir George Buck as Master of the Revels. [Actually Tilney was still Master of the Revels in 1605.] The interesting question of the authorship of "Locrine", falsely imputed to Shakespeare, is thus decided.' 'The last statement', I once wrote, 'is in Collier's happiest vein' (Malone Society's Collections, i. 108). It is; but when I made that remark I fully thought that Collier had invented the whole story. There at least I was wrong, for the inscription, whether genuine or not, is now before us in corroboration. But its recovery reveals another aspect of Collier's note that may well take one's breath away. For when we put the *Locrine* and *Daphnis* inscriptions side by side, so far from a comparison leaving no doubt that the handwriting is the same, there appears at first sight at least to be no resemblance whatever between the two. The effrontery of the man! . . . Well, wax indignant if you will. But Collier is probably chuckling in his grave to think that it was ninety years before any one discovered his little joke.

However, the matter has perfectly serious implications. It is all very well to call Collier's statement an impudent prevarication. The point is that it is not consistent with forgery. If Collier had forged the two inscriptions in order that they should support one another, even if he had forged either of them to support the other, the one thing we can be perfectly certain of is that they would have supported each other. They don't: and that is proof that Collier at least did not forge either.

Let us then examine the *Locrine* inscription more closely. It is none too legible, and in spite of the large dimensions of the copy the ends of the lines are cropped. Thus the readings are not all beyond doubt, but so far as I can form an opinion the inscription should be read as follows:

> Char. Tilney wrote⟨ a⟩ | Tragedy of this mattr⟨ wch⟩ |
> hee named *Eſtrild*:⟨ & wch⟩ | I think is this. it was l⟨ost?⟩ |
> by his death. & now [?] ſ⟨ome?⟩ | fellow hath publiſhed ⟨it.⟩ |
> I made dũbe ſhewes for it. | wch I yet have. G.B⟨.⟩[1]

Now, leaving Collier out of account, we must inquire what the chances are of this inscription being a forgery. And here, at the outset, I must point out that the problem is on a very different footing from that presented, at least at first sight, by the *George a Green* inscription. In that case, taken by itself, there was no particular reason to suppose that the notes might not have been written in currently by any one who had practised the imitation of old script, in such a way as to pass muster as an unspecified hand of the early seventeenth

[1] I hope I have at last succeeded in giving an accurate transcript of this note so far as it can be read with certainty. None of the previous attempts are reliable. The letters printed within pointed brackets are of course conjectural. The *e* of *wrote* is partly cut away, but hardly doubtful. The *e* has been omitted from *matt(e)r*. The *l* of *lost* (?) is partly visible, but cannot be regarded as certain. The & (which has previously been mistaken for an *A*) is open to no doubt. The next word, however, which I read as *now*, is quite uncertain. Then follows a letter which is almost certainly *ſ*, though it has been shaved. The word *fellow* is again somewhat doubtful: the first letter has been altered or touched up: the last looks like an *n* but has a horizontal stroke through it which may be meant to convert it into a *w*; it is not unlike the *w* in *ſhewes*. The word has been read as *fellon*, but *fellow* seems to me on all grounds more likely. The last two lines were evidently crowded in after the initials had been appended: the second is rather faint, and the reading *yet* is not beyond question, at least in photographs. The writing has been touched up at various points. The *of* is obscure; it may have been altered, and has been misread. In *named* the *e* has, I think, been doctored. In *think* there seems to be a slanting stroke through the *in* leading up to the *k*. I fancy the scribe originally wrote *th—k* (with an English *k*) and finding this obscure, filled in the *in* and altered the *k* to the Italian form. In *was* it looks as though a short *s* had had a tail appended, but I think the appearance is deceptive. In *fellow*, as said, the *f* and possibly the *w* have been altered. In *publiſhed* the *ſ* is very badly formed. In *made* the *de* are more or less indistinguishable. In *ſhewes* the *w* is of a queer shape and may have been touched up; the following *e* is obscure. There is plenty of evidence here of hasty writing and fidgety correction, but none that I can see of forgery. And if Collier had been the forger he would hardly have printed *Eſtrild* as *Elstrild*.

A

PLEASANT

CONCEYTED CO-

medie of *George a Greene*, the Pinner of *VVakefield*.

Written by .... a minister, who ac[ted] the piners part in it himselfe. Teste W. Shakespeare

As it was sundry times acted by the seruants of the right Honourable the Earle of Sussex.

Ed. Juby saith that the play was made by Ro. Gree[ne]

Imprinted at London by Simon Stafford, for Cuthbert Burby: And are to be sold at his shop neere the Royall Exchange. 1599.

THE

Lamentable Tragedie of

Locrine, the eldest sonne of King *Brutus*, discoursing the warres of the *Britaines*, and *Hunnes*, with their discomfiture:

The Britaines *victorie with their Accidents, and the death of* Albanact. *No lesse pleasant then profitable.*

Newly set foorth, ouerseene and corrected, By *VV. S.*

Char. Tilney wrot
Tragedy of this matte
he named Estrild.
I think it is this. it was
by his death. & now s
fellow hath published
I made dumbe shows for it.
G. B.

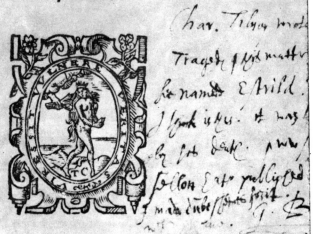

LONDON
Printed by Thomas Creede.
1595.

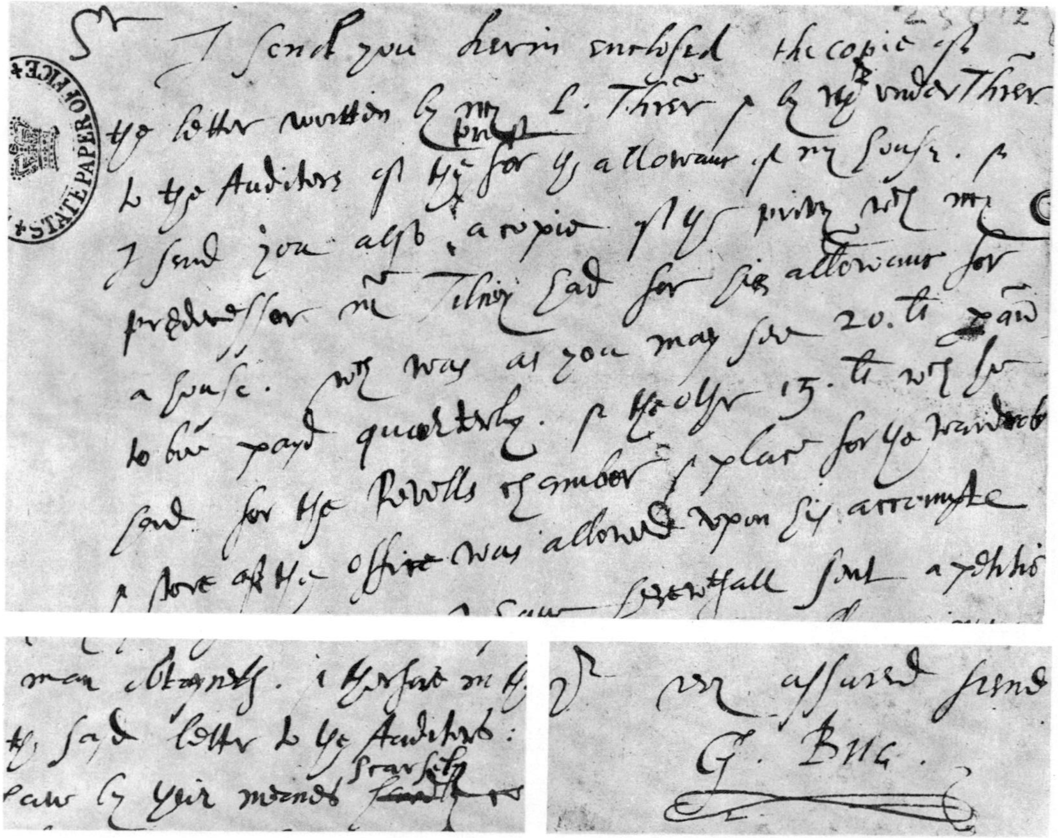

Sr I send you herein enclosed the copie of
the letter written by Mr L. Thrsr & by Mr Under Thrsr
to the Auditors of the Exchequer for the allowance of my house. &
I send you also a copie of the privy seale wch my
predecessor Mr Tilney had for his allowance for
a house. wch was as you may see 20.li a yeare
to be payd quarterly. & the other 15.li wch he
had for the Revells chamber & place for the wardrob
& store of the office was allowed upon his accompte
...
man ... therfore ... the
the sayd letter to the Auditors:
... by your meanes ...

Yr assured frend
G. Buc.

VI

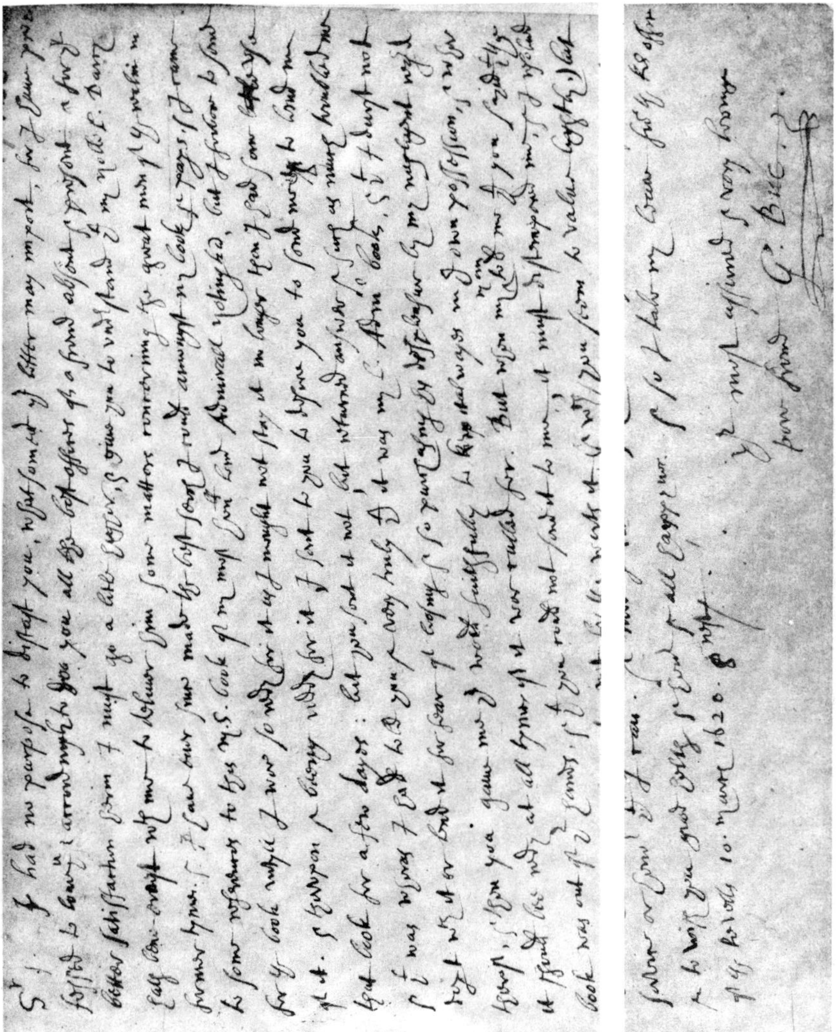
Sr; I had no purpose to distast you, whatsoever yr letter may import, for I haue professed to beare & accordingly to doo you all the best offices of a frend absent & present. & for yr better satisfaction herein I must go a litle higher, & giue you to vnderstand yt my noble L. Darcy hath bene earnest wth me to deliuer him some matters concerning the great men of ye realm in former tymes. & I haue euer since made the best search I could amongst my books & papers, & I came to some references to thes MS. book of my most honble Lord Admirall Notingham, but I forbore to send for the book while I was so redy for it as I might not stay it no longer then I had som vse of it. & therupon & beeing redy for it I sent to you to desire you to send me it to lend me that book for a few dayes: but you sent it not but returned answer & such as much troubled me. [illegible] it was where I had told you & very truly yt it was my L. Admlls book, & yt I durst not deale wth it or lend it for fear of losing & so purchasing his displeasure by my negligent [illegible] & to keep alwayes in my owne possession, & [illegible] therof, & then you gaue me yr word faithfully [illegible]. But when my man told me yt you said that it should bee redy at all tymes [illegible] it was called for. [illegible] it must distemper me, & I [illegible] book was out of yr hands. & yt you could not send it to me, [illegible] you seem to value highly.) but [illegible]
[illegible] fauor or honor yt I can. & so I take my leaue [illegible] & to wish you good helth & [illegible] & all happines. [illegible] of ye Rolls 10. March 1620.
Yr most assured & very louing
poore frend G. Buc.

VII

To the right honorable, the
greatest counsellour Sir Tho.
Egerton, knight, baron of Ellesmere
Lord Chancellour of Englād,
my very good Lord.

Great & graue Lord, my mind hath longed
In any thankfull maner to declare   long
By act, or woord, or were it in a song,
How great to you my obligations are
Who did so nobly, & so timely pluck
from Griffins talons your destressed Buck.

VIII

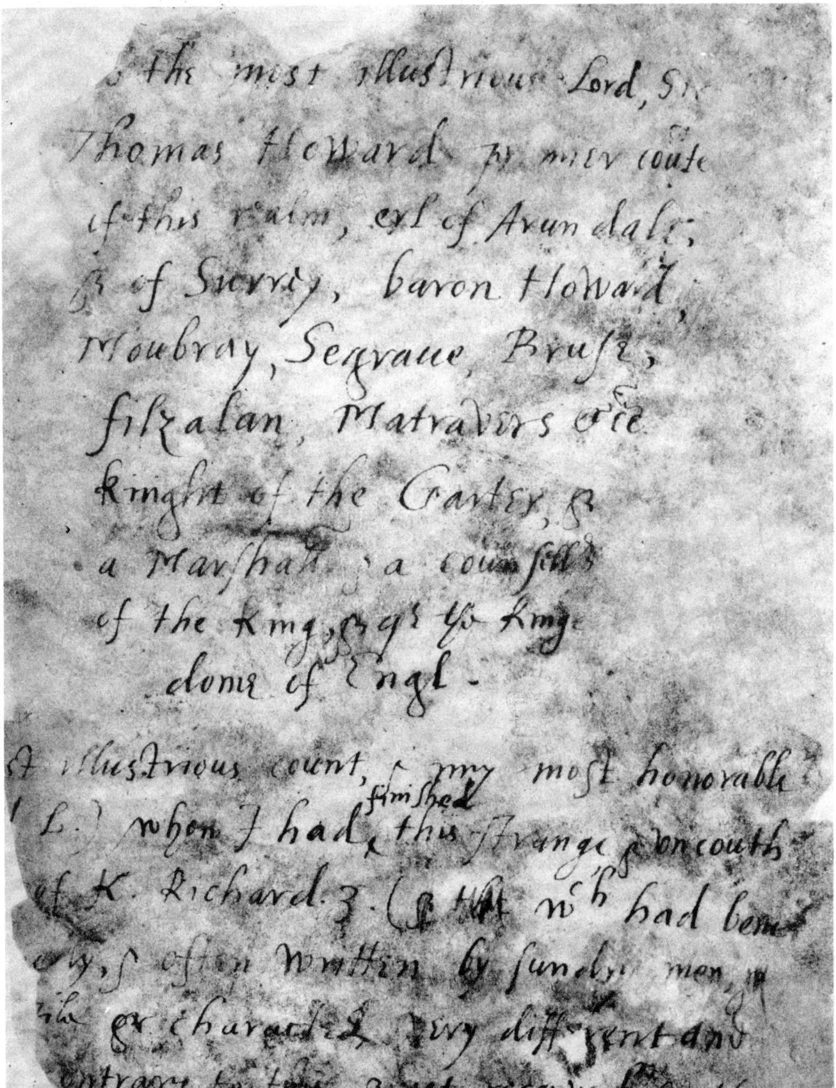

To the most illustrious Lord, Sir
Thomas Howard premier counte
of this realm, erl of Arundale,
& of Surrey, baron Howard,
Moubray, Segraue, Bruse,
Fitzalan, Matravers &c.
Knight of the Garter, &
a Marshall, & a counsellor
of the King, & of the Kingdome of Engl.

[illegible] illustrious count, & my most honorable
(L.) when I had finished this strange & uncouth
[illegible] of K. Richard. 3. (& that which had been
[illegible] & often written by sundry men, in
[illegible] character very different and
contrary to this, & yet receyved for the

IX

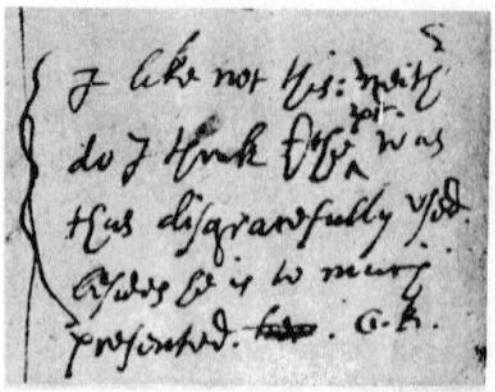

I like not this: neither
do I think that the prince was
thus disgracefully used.
besides he is too much
presented. G.B.

X (A)

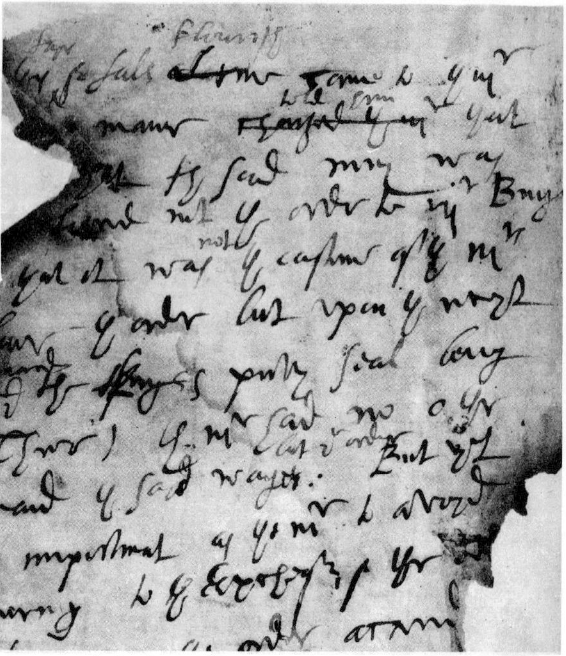

X (B)

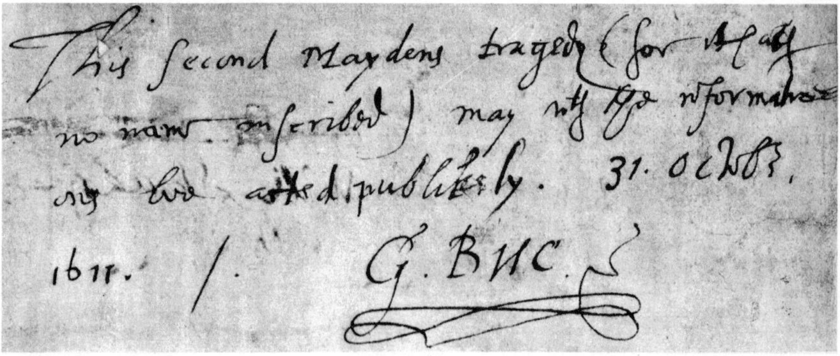

This second Maydens tragedy (for it hath
no name inscribed) may with the reformations
be acted publikely. 31. October.
1611. / G. Buc.

X (C)

century. The *Locrine* note is altogether another story. The initials G.B. appended are a direct challenge, and there is no question that the writing, if forged, is a deliberate and careful imitation of that of Sir George Buc. Now, it is one thing to make a plausible imitation of old writing generally, it is quite another thing, in a current scribble, to reproduce the forms and catch the individual character of a particular hand. Yet this, on the hypothesis of forgery, is what the writer of the *Locrine* note has done in respect to the hand of Sir George Buc. And I have no hesitation in offering the opinion that no forger of my acquaintance had anything like the skill to do it.

It remains to inquire more particularly how close the resemblance actually is. For this purpose I have collected in Plates III–IV and VII–IX a number of specimens of the writing of Sir George Buc from a variety of sources. They include a marginal note in the play of *Sir John Barnavelt* submitted to his censorship in 1619 (Plate VII), his licence as Master of the Revels appended to *The Second Maiden's Tragedy* (*SMT*) in 1611 (Plate IX), a scrap of very rough writing from the Revels Office accidentally preserved in the manuscript of his *History of Richard III*, probably about 1619 (Plate VIII), portions of a letter written to Dudley Norton, secretary to the Lord Treasurer (Salisbury) in 1611 (Plate III) and of another written to Sir Robert Cotton in the spring presumably of 1621 (Plate IV), a year before his final illness. In referring to these I shall give plate and line number thus (III 10).

With these reproductions before him the reader should have no difficulty in forming his own conclusions, and it will be best if he proceed to do so. At the same time it may be a help to those who are perhaps less familiar than they might be with Elizabethan hands, if I direct their attention to what appear to me to be a few of the more salient points. The first and most conspicuous is Buc's habit of bungling his writing and touching it up, in the manner so noticeable in *Locrine*. Even in the brief note in *Barnavelt* he touched up the *n* of *neith*^r^ (VII 1), perhaps with a view to making it into a capital. The *SMT* licence of four lines only (IX) has been touched up I think in at least ten places. There are four instances in the first two lines of the letter to Norton (III) and the same in that to Cotton (IV). There are over two dozen in the portions of the former here reproduced. The very rough writing of the Revels scrap (VIII) has been less heavily doctored, apart from actual alterations, but still plenty of instances occur. Clearly, where Buc's autograph is in question, touching up is no evidence of forgery; quite the reverse. Descending to particulars, the peculiar double-crossed *t*, which I found so suspicious in *George a Green* and which to my surprise turned up again in *Locrine*, now meets us in the word *import* in the very first line of the letter to Cotton (IV). It seems also to occur in a medial position (which is perhaps less unusual) in the Norton letter, *accompteꝫ* (III 9). The peculiar form of *&*, so unusual that two transcribers of the *Locrine* note mistook it for an *A*, is found *passim*: most closely paralleled perhaps in the second and eighth lines of the letter to Norton (III). For the malformed English *p*, that was touched up in *Shakeſpeare* (I 2), compare the untouched *p* in *petitiõ* (III 10), and for the Italian *p* of *play* (I 3) the close reproductions in *copie* and *privy* (III 1, 4). The rudimentary *ſ* and the tailed *s* are regular features throughout. But we noticed that, besides the Italian forms of these letters, the English varieties also occur in the notes: *piñers* and *Teſte* (I 2), *this* and *publiſhed* (II 2, 6). And so, as rare exceptions they do elsewhere, e.g. *amongſt* (IV 5) and *Auditors* (III 19, separately reproduced). Another peculiarity of the notes is the habit of very occasionally bringing down the second minim of an *n* slightly below the line, as in *Written* (I 1) and *Tilney* (II 2). This too may be seen in the Norton letter: *written* (III 2). It occurs, I think, only once in each of the three documents, for it is quite distinct from the curved tail which in *n* and *m* serves to distinguish the majuscule letter. A truncated form of the word *the*, in which the *e* has practically vanished, is seen in the *George a Green* note (I 2). It will be found in the third repetition of the word in the third line of the letter to Norton, and again in the line following (III 3, 4), and still more markedly in the hasty scribble of the Revels scrap (VIII 5, 6, 9). And this leads me to the last of my points and perhaps the most conclusive of all. It will be observed that as a rule the scribe of the *George a Green* and *Locrine* notes, in forming a *th*, brings the pen straight up from the foot of the *t* to the head of the *h*, as in *ſaith that the* (I 3) and *think* (II 4). But twice at least in *Locrine* the formation is more complicated, for the *t* appears to be represented by a single down stroke, from the head of which a curved line descends to connect with the *h*: *this* (II 2, 4) and perhaps *death* and *hath* (II 5, 6). This curved down stroke may be regarded as a second, rather ill-formed, *t*: in the first *this* especially it will be noticed that if the initial down stroke be removed a perfectly good *th* remains, identical (so far as the *t* is concerned) with that of the *the* already mentioned (I 3). Now this duplication of the *t* before *h* is a marked feature of Buc's hand. In the Norton letter it appears in the second *the* in the third line, in *the* in the seventh line, and the first *the* in the eighth (III 3, 7, 8). A particularly marked example is seen in the *SMT* licence (IX 2). And the Revels scrap is also interesting in this respect. We have already seen that in this the *the*'s are very rudely formed. The duplication is almost absent but it occurs once (VIII 11), and here its nature is clearly revealed, for the initial down stroke is seen to be a later addition (the head of the *h* has also been touched up). Really this is plain from the licence as well: and I have little doubt that all these duplicated *t*'s are nothing but cases of subsequent retouching.

When the reader has satisfied himself of the close similarity between Buc's writing and that of the notes in *Locrine* and *George a Green* he will have to ask himself the crucial question: Can we reasonably suppose that a forger should not only have made himself minutely acquainted with all these peculiarities of Buc's hand, but should have so absorbed them as to be able to reproduce them apparently automatically in current writing? And with what confidence he must have worked! For he perpetrated his fabrications—if fabrications they are—not on odd scraps of paper which could be destroyed without loss if he made a slip, but on the title-pages of two exceptionally fine copies of early plays, which had already in the first half of last century considerable pecuniary value. The question is before the reader: I have no doubt myself of the answer.

In conclusion let us consider the *Daphnis* inscription (V), which Collier so impudently cited in corroboration of that in *Locrine*. Certainly it shows little resemblance to any of the writing we have examined so far. But obviously it is, or is intended to be, calligraphic; and we must remember that a writer's calligraphic script is often markedly different from his normal hand. We shall have no right to reject this inscription until we have shown either that Buc, when he attempted a formal style, did not write like this, or else that he was incapable of even making the attempt. But before proceeding with the search, there are one or two points in the inscription to which it may be useful to direct attention. Observe, in the first place, that even in this careful writing there are again a series of blunders and retouchings. The scribe omitted and interlined *knight* (V 3), just as in the *Barnavelt* note Buc omitted and interlined *pr*[*ince*]. (VII 2), and *preſt* in the letter to Norton (III 3). He appears to have blundered over the name *Elleſmere*, for the *lle* seems to be written over an erasure: he touched up the *d* of *Lord* in the heading, and the word *Your* in the verses (V 4, 11). Next may be noticed the fact that the *G* of *Griffins* and the *Buc* of *Buck* are remarkably like those of the signature to the Norton letter (III) and the licence (IX). (Note that in the latter the *G* was first made exactly like that in the inscription and the tail subsequently added.) Finally I would call attention to the peculiarly shaped curl that adorns the *ll* of *Elleſmere*, and which is the exact counterpart of that over the word *allowance* in the letter to Norton (III 5) and of those which Buc added in seven places when correcting the scribe's *caled* to *called* in the Revels accounts for 1611–12.

As a matter of fact we do not need to search far for an example of what Buc considered his calligraphic hand. We find it, for instance, in what remains of the dedication to the manuscript of his *History of Richard III*. Though this is more freely written than the *Daphnis* inscription, the resemblance is unmistakable. I content myself with reproducing the two side by side (V, VI) and leave the reader to judge.

With the subject-matter of the inscriptions I do not now propose to deal. From what Griffin had the Lord Chancellor rescued the distressed Buc? Had the latter been involved at law, say with the author of *Fidessa*, and do the records of the Court of Chancery hold the answer to the riddle?[1]

[1] If so, I have failed to find it. Sir George Buc was concerned in more than one Chancery suit, and the Griffins or Griffiths were a very litigious brood, but I cannot connect the two.

More important are the annotations on the two plays, for Buc was in an excellent position to ascertain the authorship of contemporary drama.[1] Yet his notes are curiously uncertain in tone. Was he correct in his conjecture—for it is nothing more—that Charles Tilney's *Estrild* was identical with W.S.'s *Locrine*? Did Juby confirm or contradict Shakespeare? These are questions that must be left to literary historians to thresh out. But having at the outset freely spoken my mind on the suspicious nature of the information conveyed in at least one of these notes, I feel impelled to say here that no *a priori* suspicion of the sort must be allowed to discredit a document that otherwise proves sound. The most astonishing things are sometimes true, and at times Elizabethans appear to imitate their worst imitators. If I were handed Collier's edition of Henslowe's diary and asked to pick out, on grounds of internal evidence, the entry most likely to have been forged, I should no doubt have an embarrassing choice, but I think I might very well select the passage (p. 258) that records how William Borne came and bound himself to play at the Rose 'for the space of iij yeares, beginynge imediatly after this Restraynt is recaled by the lordes of the cownsell, *which Restraynt is by the means of playinge the Ieylle of Dooges*'. Is it conceivable that Henslowe should have thus gone out of his way to drag in a titbit of information for our use? has not the phraseology the authentic ring of Collier? Moreover, both the other references to *The Isle of Dogs* are undoubted forgeries. Yet time and again I have turned to the original of this entry persuaded that it too must have been forged, only to be convinced by the evidence of my own eyes that it is genuine.

I am aware that nothing I have said in the course of this article can be taken to disprove the abstract possibility of forgery. The modern scientific forger has at his disposal resources of method and skill only, even if, second to those possessed by the modern scientific detective. To eliminate the possibility of forgery it would first be essential to have access to the originals. It would then be necessary to subject them to long and laborious examination. And even assuming

[1] At the same time, if the notes were made when the plays came from press it was before Buc had any connexion with the Revels Office, while if they were made at the end of his life we must remember that he died insane.

that such an investigation could in the end lead to complete certainty, it would be mere waste of time to undertake it until a *prima facie* case for forgery has been established of a nature very different from anything that has been attempted hitherto.

But indeed I am not concerned, nor indeed greatly interested, in abstract possibilities. I am content to consider the actualities of the case. And one thing can be asserted with complete confidence: namely, that two at least of the documents we have been examining can by no possibility be the work of any forger in the field of English literature of whom we have knowledge. They are altogether outside the range of such men as Ireland and Collier. That is enough for me: perhaps it will be enough for most.

In any case I have done what I can to clear up the matter in a way that the ordinary reader can follow by the use of his own eyes, and thereby to rescue these casual and intriguing memoranda of our distressed Buck from the Griffin of unbelief.

17. Bibliography—an Apologia[1]

WHOEVER first called bibliography 'the grammar of literary investigation'[2] may have been taking a very narrow view of the study of literature or may even have had a mistaken conception of bibliography, or both, but at least he invented a phrase so apt and pregnant that I prefer to think that he knew what he was talking about, and that he foresaw the position that bibliography would one day come to hold in historical science. The phrase will stand and repay carefully weighing. To confine the investigation of literature to what can be achieved by bibliographical means would be fantastic: therefore to say that bibliography was, or was the instrument of, literary investigation, would be to give the former so wide an extension as to make it meaningless, or the latter so narrow a one as to render it nugatory. To bring the two into fruitful relation we must confine literary investigation to its most fundamental aspect, the establishment and history of the text. At the root of all literary criticism lies the question of transmission, and it is bibliography that enables us to deal with the problem. This, I take it, is just what is meant by calling bibliography the *grammar* of literary investigation: it is the fundamental instrument of research, or, if you will, the key to the fundamental problem. Thus you will see that to say that bibliography is the grammar of literary investigation may be taken as equivalent to calling bibliography the science of the transmission of literary documents.

I shall need, in a moment, to put before you the arguments in favour of this view. But by way of preface let me remark that, while I accept and even cling to the term Bibliography, I am not altogether happy about it. Form and analogy suggest a descriptive science, which Bibliography, in my view, is not.

[1] [1932, Sept. *The Library*, xiii. 113–43.] The substance of this paper was read as a presidential address before the Bibliographical Society on 21 Mar. 1932.

[2] On a previous occasion I inadvertently quoted the phrase as 'Bibliography is the Grammar of Literature'. I assumed and intended the meaning to be the same, but it was not an accurate rendering of the words cited by Dr. Copinger in 1892 (*Transactions*, i. 34).

The old term Bibliology had the advantage of being non-committal, but it is not in itself attractive, and is hardly worth reviving. Book-lore has virtue, but being of an antiquarian flavour, retains some suggestion of 'bôklâr', book-learning, and is thus less satisfactory than the admirable German equivalent *Bücherkunde*, after which I confess to hanker. 'Bibliography' be it, but let it be understood that it is in no way particularly or primarily concerned with the enumeration or description of books[1]—a belief which has done much in the past to reduce it to futility and retard the recognition of its real nature and importance. It ought not to be necessary further to argue, though it may be well to put on record, that bibliography has nothing to do with the subject-matter of books, but only with their formal aspect.[2]

[1] It has been suggested that enumeration is a necessary preliminary to study. This is in fact not true: were it so, every natural science would be primarily enumerative.

[2] [I take the substance of the following note from a 'Retrospect' I contributed to a volume of studies issued in 1945 by the Bibliographical Society to celebrate its first fifty years of life, 1892 to 1942.

An article contributed by A. W. Pollard to the eleventh edition of the *Encyclopædia Britannica* in 1910 is headed 'Bibliography and Bibliology', in spite of which it is confined to the subject of the enumeration and description of printed books: 'Present custom', the author writes, 'inclines to restrict the province of bibliography to printed books as opposed to manuscripts.' In both limitations (to description as well as to printed books) Pollard may have been deferring to popular usage and possibly editorial direction, for I do not believe that he was really in sympathy with either. The succinct statement with which the article begins is worth quoting. 'The word βιβλιογραφία was used in post-classical Greek for the writing of books, and as late as 1761, in Fenning's *English Dictionary*, a bibliographer is defined as 'one who writes or copies books'. The transition from the meaning 'a writing of books' to that of 'a writing *about* books' was accomplished in France in the 18th century—witness the publication in 1763 of the *Bibliographie instructive* of de Bure. In England the new meaning seems to have been popularized by the Rev. Thomas Frognall Dibdin early in the 19th century, while Southey preferred the rival form *bibliology*, which is now hardly used. Indeed Robert Southey would seem to have been the only writer who affected it. The application of 'bibliography' to the description of books was probably on the analogy of 'geography'. This is not, in fact, a common formation in this sense, 'geography' and 'bibliography' being apparently the only ones in common use. The *O.E.D.* mentions also 'astrography', 'cometography', 'petrography', 'selenography', and the hybrid 'stratigraphy'. 'Bibliology' finds an analogy in 'geology' and many like formations. 'Geology' is a much later formation than 'geography', having been introduced only when the need was felt for a word of wider connotation. It did not, however, survive in that original sense, but acquired (first apparently in England) a more specialized meaning. In regard to 'book-lore', it is curious that the *O.E.D.* employs it in its definition of 'bibliography', and yet under the word itself gives only the meaning of learning derived from books. The volume in question was issued as long ago as 1888, but the Supplement throws no further light on the word.—1958.]

Let it then be granted that bibliography is the study of books as material objects. For bibliography to be a serious study it is necessary that books should be objects of importance. What then is the value of books? Books, said Milton, 'preserve as in a violl the purest efficacie and extraction of that living intellect that bred them.'[1] They are our main link with the past, the repository of the thought and the aspiration, no less than the record of the deeds and the desires, of those who came before us in the making of the world. If the study of history and the enjoyment of literature are of any value to mankind, then books are indeed a precious inheritance. Books are of value in proportion as they preserve the past. But there seems implicit in Milton's words a belief that a book is a more faithful repository than experience warrants. The record is defaced in a hundred ways which it is the patient task of criticism to detect and to correct. Thus the material study of books is of importance just in so far as it helps us to read their record, and so enables them to fulfil their function. The essence of bibliography is therefore the science of the transmission of literary documents: it is this, and this alone, that gives it a claim upon the attention of serious students.

My quarrel, such as it is, with the traditional school of bibliography is that it has tended to overlook this essential function of books, and has concentrated on one or another accidental character. I have thus been led to formulate a thesis that is the foundation of my bibliographical creed. It is intended less as a formal definition of bibliography than as a description of its function in criticism; and I insist upon it, not in any exclusive sense, but as embodying the claim of bibliography to recognition among critical sciences. Once more, and in the fewest possible words, my argument is this: Books are the material means by which literature is transmitted; therefore bibliography, the study of books, is essentially the science of the transmission of literary documents.

In putting my position thus I may seem to exclude, or at any rate to depreciate, many subjects that are by common consent held to fall within the purview of bibliography. There is no department in which greater labour has been expended, or more brilliant results achieved, than the study of

[1] *Areopagitica*, 1644, p. 4.

typography: the historical investigation of the face-forms of printing types, their assignment to different countries, towns, and presses. This investigation undoubtedly has an historical interest of its own as regards the invention, development, and distribution of one of the greatest crafts that the genius of man has evolved. But when we ask what is its real aim and value in relation to book-production, the answer must be that it enables us to assign an undated and unlocated book to a particular place and date. And the date and the place, even the particular printing house, at which a book was produced, is always a relevant, and may be a crucial, fact in its transmission. It is this that justifies, and indeed forces, us to regard the study of types as an important branch of bibliography, and gives to the investigation its bibliographical significance. And so it is with many other branches. On the one hand we must treat the study of text-transmission in a broad and liberal spirit, not confining it to the mere editorial reconstruction of the text, but letting it embrace the whole history of the chances that have befallen it in the course of its precarious survival. On the other hand, since bibliography is the study of books as material objects, it is bound to take cognizance of everything appertaining to them, and we must expect it to include branches that draw much of their interest from extraneous considerations, of art, craft, or biography, only content to lay down the principle that these branches, whatever their own interest may be, are of bibliographical importance just in so far as they relate to the function of books as the preservers and transmitters of literary documents, giving of course to that term its widest possible extension.

It may help to make the matter clearer, and to show that I am not seeking to exclude from bibliography any legitimate branch of study, if we glance for a moment at various subjects that generally come within the purview of the student, and ask whether and how they are related to the essential function of books, and what therefore is their strictly bibliographical significance. Palaeography, it may be said in passing, is essentially in the same position as the study of types, but its relevance to text-transmission is even more obvious. There are however other branches whose claims are less immediately apparent.

I think the first place should be assigned to book illustration. Undoubtedly this is a subject whose appeal or relevance lies primarily in the realm of graphic art and not of bibliography. It claims the attention of bibliographers merely on the ground that these products of art happen to be found in books. Their connexion with the books in which they occur may be of the most superficial and fortuitous character, though it sometimes goes deeper. There are of course books, particularly books of a technical character, in which the illustrations may be said to form an integral part of the text: but these are comparatively rare and may be disregarded. The question, I think, is this. Occurring as they do in books, and forming a more or less integral part of them, as the case may be, illustrations are bound to receive notice from bibliographers; but, admitting that their main importance lies in the sphere of art, must we admit that it lies wholly there, and therefore outside bibliography, or can we claim that it possesses a strictly bibliographical importance as well? I think there is no doubt that we can. It is true that different classes of illustration possess very different degrees of bibliographical relevance: their importance is generally greater in manuscripts than in printed books, and in earlier than in later examples of the latter. Engravings, separately printed and stuck into otherwise already complete books, show the minimum of relevance to their surroundings. But with woodcuts, which are printed with the text, and have thus at least a material relevance, and with the work of the illuminator and miniaturist, the case is somewhat different. Even when, as generally happens, the illustrations have been designed apart from and later than the text, they may nevertheless serve as a commentary thereon, which is sometimes illuminating as well as illuminated. And even apart from this, text and illustration are often so intimately associated in the chain of transmission that it would be inconvenient to treat the one without the other. Furthermore, illustrations may throw valuable light upon the locality in which a manuscript, or even a printed book, was produced, the circumstances of its production, and the public to which it appealed: and these are important points in the history of the transmission of the text. Thus bibliography could not afford, without serious loss, to hand over the study of book illustration exclusively to the department of graphic arts: and when the bibliographer devotes himself to the investigation of illumination, woodcutting, and even engraving, in books, while he may be contributing mainly to the history of art, he is at the same time doing work essential to book-lore, work that can be justified on the most rigid bibliographical grounds.

Next I should place binding. Unlike illustration it is a purely bookish art; on the other hand its connexion with books is of a more external nature. There are two aspects of bookbinding, the material and the ornamental. Of the former, dealing with the actual methods of the craft, the materials and their manner of use, practically nothing of a systematic nature is known. Yet its importance is obvious. A craft upon which the very preservation of books depends cannot but interest all students of books. At the same time it is rather as a postulate of transmission than as a factor in that problem that it arrests our attention, and I confess that I am rather at a loss to defend it from some suspicion at least of 'mere antiquarianism'. But there is one warning that I think I may justly interpose at this point. I would have our studies be catholic. For until all facts relating to every branch of book production have been collected and considered, it is impossible to say what bearing they may have upon the central problem of text-transmission. And while I admit that the claim of material binding to great importance in bibliography does not look promising—apart from such lights as it may ultimately throw on locality—I would remind you of the possible relevance, as regards textual problems, of the habit of keeping manuscripts long unbound, and of stripping them of their bindings for travel.

Ornamental binding is certainly less important in the history of book production and preservation, and the fact that it has received a vastly greater amount of attention is a tribute rather to its artistic attraction than to its bibliographical importance. As illumination belongs to fine art, so decorated bookbinding belongs to fine craft; moreover it is impossible to consider tooled bindings apart from leatherwork in general, panel stamps apart from wood engraving, jewelled bindings apart from the goldsmiths' craft, or those abominations, embroidered bindings, apart from more legitimate uses of needlework. All the same, the study may have a bibliographical bearing, even an important one, on occasion, for bindings can sometimes be localized with considerable precision, and may thus afford valuable evidence of provenance, upon the bibliographical importance of which I shall have something to say in a moment.

Ornamental bindings often have a personal association through being prepared for an individual collector and bearing his device. This brings us to the question of ownership. As a general rule this study is a collector's hobby, without bibliographical interest. But it is not always so by any means, especially where the early ownership of manuscripts is concerned. Much labour has been bestowed on the attempted reconstruction, from early catalogues and the examination of extant manuscripts, of the medieval libraries of some of the great monastic houses. For textual critics such reconstruction may at times possess great value. When a particular manuscript can be shown to have been in a particular library at a particular date, the fact may give a valuable clue to its place and circumstances of origin. And even if we consider only later provenance, it may be of importance to know whether a manuscript can be shown to have been exposed to contamination by other known manuscripts, or have been capable of exercising an influence upon them in its turn. Less often, but still sometimes, it happens that the comparatively recent ownership of a printed book is of concern to the literary student. For instance, when an early editor makes some statement regarding the text, we sometimes need to know what copy he may have had access to, before we can determine whether he is merely misdescribing his original, or whether he had access to one now lost or unidentified. And if we extend the notion of transmission to include the history of the editing of a text, I think even so-called 'association copies' may occasionally be more than mere futility. The Anglo-Saxon *Orosius* was first edited by Daines Barrington in 1773, but in his preface he explains that he had inherited some of his material from Joseph Ames, who had once contemplated an edition, as appears from a letter which he quotes. In my copy Ames's original letter is inserted.[1] It may be vanity on my part, but I incline to think that it gives the copy an additional interest that is truly bibliographical.

I suggested above that binding, however essential to the preservation of books, was rather a condition antecedent to transmission than governing it, and on that ground I hesitated to give it bibliographical status. I think we shall find it necessary to set a firm limit on these lines somewhere, lest we be tempted to indefinite excursions into the fields of entomology, chemistry, and the like. And so it is with the wide subject of librarianship, both practical and antiquarian. Its connexion with books is evident, but if we pursue even its second branch we soon find ourselves involved in the discussion not of bibliography but of architecture. Nevertheless, though I cannot at the moment recall any instances linking library construction with problems of textual transmission, I am quite prepared to believe that they may exist, and in any case the connexion of the monastic library with the scriptorium was probably intimate.

I have allowed myself this lengthy digression in order to show that, while convinced that bibliography ranks as a serious study just in so far, and only in so far, as it relates to the essential function of books, namely the transmission of literary documents, I yet take a catholic view of our pursuits, and welcome light and guiding from every branch of bookish lore, only premising that the strictly bibliographical importance of these branches is not always that which their devotees would claim for them. *A bibliotheca sum, nihil biblicum a me alienum puto.*

But though I have boldly described bibliography as the study of the transmission of literary documents, I have not yet sought to show that the question of textual transmission comes into it at all, and I think I may fairly be challenged to do so. If some one were to say to me: Your definition is mere bluff; you insist that books are material objects and that bibliography is concerned only with their formal aspect and has nothing to do with the subject-matter; how then can it touch the problem of transmission, by which you mean textual criticism, a study essentially concerned with the

[1] Now in the Cambridge University Library.

subject-matter and not with the external form of books?—if any one were to argue thus he would be raising no merely captious objection, but would be penetrating at once into the very heart of the matter. If we who hold this view can answer him and maintain our position, I believe we shall have established a principle which is fundamental in literary criticism, and the recognition of which is in fact at this moment having a marked effect on literary studies.

I start then with the postulate that what the bibliographer is concerned with is pieces of paper or parchment covered with certain written or printed signs. With these signs he is concerned merely as arbitrary marks; their meaning is no business of his. Now the reproduction of a text, either through transcription by a scribe or through composition and impression by a printer, is unquestionably a bibliographical fact, one of which the bibliographer is bound to take cognizance. Let us watch the scribe at work. The printer proceeds on essentially the same method, so for the sake of simplicity we may at present ignore him. The scribe, then, reproduces after a certain constant manner the signs that lie before him in his exemplar. He may not reproduce them exactly—for instance he may be transcribing an uncial original into minuscule script—but there will be a certain constant relation between the signs of the exemplar and those of the transcript. Now and again this relation will fail, and we then have what we call a variant in the copy. It may be due to inadvertence on the part of the scribe, or it may be intentional, but in either case what survives, and all that survives as evidence for the critic, is just this bibliographical fact of a failure in the relation. And textual criticism is the study of these failures, which can thus be defined in bibliographical terms, without any reference to the meaning of the signs or the subject-matter of the text.

Theoretically, therefore, the study of textual transmission involves no knowledge of the sense of a document but only of its form: the document may theoretically be devoid of meaning or the critic ignorant of its language. There exist certain medieval manuscripts written in sham Arabic: the signs are imitated more or less closely from Arabic letters, but they are used arbitrarily and do not even form words. Again, unless I am mistaken, the famous Voynich manuscript, which has been supposed to contain secret records by Roger Bacon, is not a cipher at all, but just such a palaeographical hoax—*une diablerie*, as a French critic has called it. Now if such manuscripts were transcribed, it should theoretically be possible to apply to the copies the principles of textual criticism no less than to the most serious author. Or take a modern instance, Russell and Whitehead's *Principia Mathematica*, a work written mainly in symbols, which though they represent perfectly definite ideas, are not meant to be translatable into speech, but form a silent language of their own. Between the first and second editions (of the first volume) there are certain differences. I know just enough of the subject to have anticipated a few of these, but others are entirely beyond the scope of my intelligence. But that does not prevent my observing the variations and even criticizing them: for supposing that a third edition were to be published, then, if a variant of the second persisted, I should assume that it was a correction, whereas if the reading of the first were restored, I should assume that that of the second was a mistake. Of course these inferences might not be correct, but they would be legitimate deductions from the bibliographical evidence and my knowledge of the circumstances of production, and their probability would be of just the same order as any other inferences of textual criticism. Thus I think I am justified in maintaining that text-transmission is a bibliographical fact, and that the study of textual variation is a strictly bibliographical study, quite independent, theoretically, of the meaning of the text.

Of course, in practice, we should hardly follow this severely ideal method of textual research. Nobody would think of editing a text that had no meaning, and nobody would choose to edit a text in a language he did not understand—though it might be a very interesting exercise. We all involuntarily pay attention to the sense of the texts we are studying; and the sense often enables us to arrive by a short cut at results that could only be laboriously achieved by strictly bibliographical methods, and may lead us to results that could not be reached by those methods at all. But we ought always to have in our minds a clear distinction between what is achieved by the one method, and what by the other;

and if we wish to arrive at really reliable results we ought always to be sure that our textual conclusions, by whatever road we have reached them, are capable of proof on rigidly bibliographical lines. I am much mistaken if more and greater critical mistakes have not arisen from reliance on the supposed meaning of the text than from all other sources of error put together.

Bibliography then will carry the textual critic some way towards his goal. It would be extravagant to pretend that it comprises the whole equipment of an editor. Even if he seeks to limit his task to the application of textual criticism to a particular work, the editor requires at least a knowledge of the author's language, probably also of his period and circumstances, and the subject-matter of his work. This means a whole mass of linguistic, historical, and antiquarian or technical equipment that has nothing whatever to do with bibliography. But all these are variables, differing as we pass from work to work and from author to author. What does not differ, what may be called the editorial constant, is just those principles of textual transmission which we have found to be essentially bibliographical. The limit to which bibliography will reach is pretty evident: it would be premature to regard it as co-extensive with textual criticism, but the intimate relation of the two should by now be apparent, and when we come to consider textual criticism more closely, as I propose to do in a moment, I think we shall find a marked cleavage in its methods corresponding closely at any rate to the limits of bibliographical evidence.

Let us, however, first review textual transmission as it appears from the standpoint of bibliography. A scribe takes a sheet of writing material, and pen and ink. He has an exemplar of the work he proposes to transcribe, and from this he proceeds to make his transcript, copying down onto his sheet what he sees, or thinks he sees, before him. For a while all goes well, and he reproduces accurately what is in his exemplar. But sooner or later he makes a slip of eye or hand, and his writing ceases to preserve the correct relation to the original. At another point he thinks he sees an error in that original. If he is a very mechanical or a very conscientious scribe he may be content to reproduce exactly what is before him; but more likely he will succumb to editorial vanity and write what he thinks ought to be there, thus sowing the seeds of trouble for students in the future. Textual critics should praise God for the simple fool. Thus the bibliographical operation of transcription inevitably introduces variations into the text, while each subsequent transcription will introduce further variants. Later copies may be made directly or indirectly from the first, or they may be made independently from the original or some other transcript of the original. Thus, as the lines of descent spread out, so the variants multiply in number and complexity, and the text of each derivative manuscript varies more and more alike from the original and from that of manuscripts of different descent. But however many copies of a work there may be, and however diverse the lines by which they are descended, they are all (provided we exclude oral transmission) necessarily derived from a single original by a definite number of transcriptional steps. Furthermore, every variant arises in one definite act of transcription, and is a relation between two terms, the reading of the transcript and that of the exemplar. Where a number of manuscripts are extant there may be three or four or more variants of a single reading, and the critic may be tempted to assume a fundamental relation of three or four or more terms. In fact, however, every textual variant, however complex, is the product of a number of relations of two terms each, and textual criticism partly consists in analysing manifold variants into their simple components. Descent by the repetition of single transcriptional steps from one original, and divergence through the multiplication of simple variants—these are the two fundamental principles of transmission; and though when they are thus stated in bibliographical terms they may appear mere truisms, experience shows that their implications are not always recognized.[1]

Next let us look at the problem of text-transmission from the point of view of the textual critic. He starts with the examination of a number of manuscripts, collating their texts and collecting their differences of reading, and his object is the reconstruction of the work as the author wrote it. This

[1] [They are the postulates elaborated in my essay on *The Calculus of Variants*, Oxford, 1927.]

means, as is now generally recognized, the reconstruction of the steps or stages by which his text has come down to us. The evidence for this reconstruction is, in the main, the textual variants in the manuscripts. By a comparison and analysis of these the critic seeks to arrange the manuscripts in groups, which is equivalent to tracing back the steps by which they have originated. His object is to arrive unambiguously at the very autograph of the author. In the most favourable case he may achieve this object, at least to his own satisfaction. In general he is more likely to arrive, with more or less ambiguity, at an archetype which may be several steps, and perhaps many centuries, removed from the autograph, if this ever existed. It is true that given only a single manuscript or a late archetype, the critic is not quite at the end of his resources: he may yet be able to trace transpositions and errors of foliation and alinement that may help towards the restoration of the original text: but generally speaking it is upon multiplicity of tradition that criticism relies.

When, therefore, the critic has reached this point in his investigation, his work usually remains imperfect in two respects. In the first place, the tradition is seldom if ever unambiguous: in seeking to reconstruct the text of the archetype the critic will generally find a number of passages in which different readings claim equal authority or among which there is only a balance of probability in favour of one or another. He is faced with the problem of selection. In the second place, the tradition seldom leads back beyond an archetype at several removes from the original, containing at least some readings repugnant to sense, which one hesitates to ascribe to the author. The critic is faced with the problem of emendation. In either case there is nothing for it but to fall back on personal judgement—guided, let us hope, by the ripest experience and the maturest consideration—of what the author is likely to have written, or, to put it rather differently, what we think he ought to have written—for what our judgement really implies is the rather conceited belief that the author did in fact write what we should like to think he had written.

This is, no doubt, a shocking thing to say, but an extreme example will make my meaning clear. Suppose that we possess, or can arrive at, the author's own original: how far is an editor bound by its readings? I am told that, if we may trust the tradition, Saint Jerome in his translation of the Bible was once at least guilty of a false concord, that this actually stood in his autograph. Now if we accept the Catholic belief in the inspiration of his work, I think we shall yet hesitate to ascribe such a grammatical lapse to the divine spirit; we shall tactfully set it down to a failure of inspiration, an imperfection of the human instrument. But this is merely an irreverent instance of the problem that confronts us whenever an author has written what in our opinion he ought not to have written. Should an editor leave him to the censure of posterity with all his blushing sins upon him, or should he correct the text? If he chooses the former alternative he will probably be accused of neglecting his editorial duty and of insulting his author and his readers alike. But if, on the other hand, he chooses the latter he is shouldering a dangerous responsibility; for who is the critic that he should claim censorship over the inspiration of literature, and if he begins by correcting Saint Jerome's false concords, will he not end by re-writing his author, as Pope rewrote Shakespeare, as Bentley re-wrote Milton, and as Faustus, in Goethe's play, re-wrote Saint John?[1] From such extravagances most critics are mercifully preserved by a proper distrust of their own judgement, yet the judgements that lead to them are identical in kind with those that every critic of necessity makes in textual selection and emendation.

The point I am aiming at is, of course, that textual criticism involves two different stages, phases, or processes: so different indeed that it is misleading to include them under a common name. These judgements of what an author must or should have written are quite other in kind from the humble collation of textual variations and reconstruction of scribal steps. The one is almost mechanical, the other intuitional. The evidence that leads us patiently from transcript to transcript is material: the evidence that leads to the preference of one co-equal tradition to another, or to the rejection of tradition in favour of emendation, is psychological. Is it unreasonable

[1] Geschrieben steht: 'Im Anfang war das Wort!' . . .
Ich kann das Wort so hoch unmöglich schätzen . . .
Und schreibe getrost: Im Anfang war die That.

to suggest that one should be described as critical, and the other distinguished as metacritical?

The distinction has, of course, been commonly recognized, and critics have laid stress upon, and extolled the virtues of, one branch or the other according to their personal predilections. The more humdrum, pedantic, and unimaginative have fancied that by patient mechanical methods they could reach all that was required of editorial science, and reach it with a certainty denied to what they were inclined to regard as the unscientific vapourings of irresponsible amateurs. Contrariwise, the more imaginative, intuitional, and creative are naturally inclined to magnify their own particular province and to look down on the humbler function that concerns itself with the details of variation and transmission. Thus, when Professor Housman speaks of textual criticism he is apparently thinking almost exclusively of emendation. What he would call the study of transmission I do not know, but it is clear that he would relegate it to a lower sphere. I think that he and I would agree pretty well in our analysis of the situation: his textual criticism corresponds with what I have called metacritical, while he would perhaps leave me free to call my critical division by any name I pleased. Where we might differ would be in regard to the relative values of the two divisions. To Professor Housman it is the metacritical that is alone worthy of a gentleman and a scholar. For my own part, however fascinating a pursuit this may be, I incline to emphasize rather the humbler function of the critic, in the belief that it is here that the more certain results may be attained, and that until a firm foundation has been laid by these methods, any metacritical superstructure is so much building in the air.

It will be obvious whereto this argument is tending. We have examined the problem of transmission first from the bibliographical point of view and then from that of textual criticism, and we have found that in the latter case the problem falls into two parts which are by nature entirely distinct. Moreover, the first, or logically prior, of these parts is so closely related to the bibliographical aspect of the problem as to be almost identical. You will now understand why I hold that bibliography—or, if you will, critical bibliography, that essence of the subject that alone justifies its claim to rank as a serious science—is in fact the same as textual criticism.

Now, textual criticism is no new study—far from it—and it may be asked what is gained by seeking to give it a new name. If the whole question is a verbal one, or one concerned merely with the formal classification of knowledge, then it is sheer foolishness to make a pother about it. I feel that I am on my defence, and unless I can make it good, my whole position as a bibliographer and a literary critic needs reconsidering. Naturally I believe that I have a sound case to put before you.

I would begin by remarking that there may be a good deal in a name if it implies an attitude. And I think that results of considerable importance to the study of literature are likely to result from the change of attitude implied by recognizing that Textual Criticism and Critical Bibliography are synonymous. Of course, I do not pretend that in the past textual critics have been blind to the importance of bibliographical evidence, or that they have not frequently used it with masterly insight and telling effect. Some of the most profound investigations of the bibliographical characteristics of lost archetypes—palaeography, foliation, stichometry—have been due to textual critics; and though, naturally, the arguments have varied much in cogency, they amply prove that critics have been alive to the importance of bibliographical data. What, so far as my limited knowledge goes, they have never fully realized is that the whole of their textual apparatus needs to be approached from the bibliographical point of view. In my humble opinion—and I am sensible of my temerity in criticizing the work of famous scholars—two fundamental errors have been made, which are really distinct, though their results are not always easy to separate. The first has been the failure to distinguish between critical and metacritical problems, and the second to realize that the former are essentially bibliographical.

The result of the first of these errors has been the persistent application of metacritical or intuitional methods to the solution of what are purely critical or bibliographical questions. Nothing is more usual than for the bibliographical critic to be able to say with confidence that, whatever reading in a given passage may be correct, certain readings are necessarily unoriginal. Yet it sometimes happens that the intuitional critic will assert that one of these condemned readings is just what the author must have written. To which the proper answer is that what must be must be, but that the occurrence of the reading in question in some manuscripts, is no better (probably worse) evidence in its favour than would be its appearance as the emendation of a modern editor. If results of any value are to be achieved in textual criticism, then strictly critical methods must be allowed to do their work unhindered before metacritical methods come into play, and the latter must on no account butt in where they have no concern.[1]

The second error, the failure to recognize that in the textual sphere critical problems are essentially bibliographical, has led to their being approached from a wrong angle. Readings have been treated as literary counters, by juggling with which in a certain fashion, it was thought that a correct text could be constructed. At first readings were selected merely as they pleased the taste of the editor, and we got what is called an eclectic text. If the taste of the editor was good the text was at least readable, though it might sometimes have surprised the author had he seen it. Then some one—perhaps an editor who distrusted his own taste—lit on the idea of accepting the reading supported by the greatest number of manuscripts. The result was far worse: the text produced was less readable without necessarily being nearer to what the author would have recognized as his. But it was the first step in the bibliographical direction, for it recognized that the readings could not be treated as unrelated entities, but that the manuscripts in which they occurred were somehow relevant. The mistake lay in counting the manuscripts instead of examining their history. The next stage was to study the relation of the manuscripts and to ascertain the steps by which they came into being. It is now recognized that all turns upon the question of transmission, and that it is only when the purely bibliographical problem of the descent of the manuscripts through

[1] This is, of course, an illustration of a far wider principle. Even so it is legitimate enough for metaphysical or theological arguments to be applied to the conclusions of science, but we have learned by long and sad experience that to allow these arguments an entry into purely scientific problems is to court disaster.

a series of transcriptional steps has been solved, that we can ascertain the relative authority of different readings. So long as readings were treated exclusively from the literary standpoint, the so-called genealogical method was undreamed of, and even when this became possible and its importance was recognized, its laws and nature long remained imperfectly understood. One of the earliest and one of the ablest expositions of it in English is Dr. Hort's *Introduction to the Greek New Testament*, first published just fifty years ago: and yet in this, the section on the 'Manner of discovering genealogy' (§§ 58–59) is vitiated by a perfectly definite and perfectly elementary fallacy, into which it is inconceivable that so acute a critic could have fallen had he not been thinking literarily, in terms of groups of readings, instead of bibliographically, in terms of transcriptional steps.[1] It may be said with confidence that no sound basis of textual criticism will be established until critics give up looking on variant readings as literary counters, and treat them primarily as evidence for the reconstruction of the steps in the transmission of the text, reducing the whole process to a question of pieces of writing material covered with certain conventional signs.[2]

[1] 'The process depends on the principle that identity of reading implies identity of origin. . . . Wherever we find a considerable number of variations, in which the two or more arrays of documents attesting the two or more variants are identical, we know that at least a considerable amount of the texts of the documents constituting each array must be descended from a common ancestor subsequent to the single universal original, the limitation of ancestry being fixed by the dissent of the other array or arrays.' But, unless by 'reading' and 'variation' we are to understand *error*, this is false; for it is obvious that agreement in original readings does not imply common origin 'subsequent to the single universal original'. Thus the 'principle' to be valid demands an intuitive knowledge of what readings are original and what not—the very object of the inquiry!

[2] [There has of late been something of a revolt against the 'genealogical method', and critics have been inclined to question its cogency and truth; and it is true that attempts to apply it to certain texts have met with but indifferent success. My own belief is that, based as it is on logical foundations, the method cannot but be theoretically valid, and that its failure to yield satisfactory results in the case of some important and popular works is due to the fact that in these variations has become so persistent and contamination so widespread as to render the practical application of the method beyond critical ingenuity. Indeed, it is doubtful whether a genealogical calculus can be devised to deal with conflation, seeing that this is a phenomenon that runs counter to the assumptions upon which the method is based.—1958.] [An important text to which the reservations here made by Greg apply is *Piers Plowman*. See the section on 'Editorial Resources and Methods' in George Kane's edition of the A Version (1960), pp. 115–72, the opening sentence of which reads: 'Recension is not a practicable method for the editor of the **A** manuscripts'.—J.C.M.]

At the centre of the critical problem, conditioning the whole, is the bibliographical operation of the scribe copying the text. It is he that is responsible for the variations which at once create the critical problem and afford material for its solution. But he is responsible for more than that, for he leaves many traces of his operation beyond the actual differences of reading, traces which having no literary bearing or value are commonly unnoticed or ignored by the old-fashioned textual critic, but which may be of crucial value as evidence of manuscript descent. Deletions, erasures, insertions, transpositions, mislining, irregularities in the number of lines to a page or of leaves to a quire—these and many other details may supply needful evidence, and will reveal themselves at once to the eye of the bibliographer. It is true that now and again an editor has made excellent use of evidence of this sort, and thereby shown a true bibliographical instinct, but it is safe to say that the great majority of textual critics have been more or less wilfully blind to everything beyond the text itself.

In considering the relation between bibliography on the one hand, and textual criticism as usually practised on the other, there is one further point to which I should like to direct attention. I think it is a rather important one, although it is by no means fundamental, but may be regarded, if we please, as merely incidental to the angle of approach. As a general rule what the textual critic is concerned with, and all that he is concerned with, is the editorial problem, the reconstruction of the author's original text. There is, of course, no reason why his outlook should be thus limited: criticism may just as rightly be applied to any other point in the transmission of the text. But the fact remains that in at least ninety-nine cases out of a hundred he is dominated by the editor's demands, and his interest concentrated upon one particular point in the field. Now the bibliographer approaches the problem with no such prepossession: his concern is with the whole history of the text, and to him the author's original is but one step in the transmission. It may be the most important step—of course, in the majority of cases it is the only important one—but that is a question dependent upon outside considerations that do not strictly concern the bibliographer.

His task is to trace throughout the manner in which the text has been transmitted. Does my argument appear far fetched? I hope not, for I think that any one who has wandered even a little in the byways of literature will call to mind cases in which some subsidiary text has a literary importance equal to, or it may be greater than, the author's original. For instance, the voluminous controversy that arose over Bishop Jewel's *Apologia Ecclesiae Anglicanae* was based, not on the original Latin text, nor on the earliest English translation, but on Lady Bacon's version which both sides accepted as authoritative. Other examples may occur to you, but I think the leading case is undoubtedly that of the Vulgate. An enormous amount of labour has been expended in successive attempts to determine what Saint Jerome actually wrote, or what the divine spirit intended he should write. The ninth century produced the work of Alcuin, the eleventh of Lanfranc, the twelfth of Steven Harding, among others; with the renaissance came the official Sixtine and Clementine revisions; in our own day we have seen the labours of Wordsworth and White, and we are still awaiting the results of the great Benedictine commission, which started under the direction of one of our own vice-presidents, the late Cardinal Gasquet. It would be indeed foolish to depreciate the work which centuries of scholarship have devoted to this unending task. But its object may be said to be mainly theological: from the historical and literary point of view it is largely irrelevant. Throughout the middle ages the influence of Jerome's Bible stands out like a great peak, overshadowing and dwarfing every other. But it was not Saint Jerome's text that the middle ages knew, but a somewhat debased though more or less uniform version, the result of centuries of scribal blundering and tinkering. And no critic who knows his business, when examining the work of a medieval author, whether from the textual or more broadly literary point of view, will rely either upon an authorized Vulgate or a modern critical edition, but will provide himself if possible, and according to the nature of his work, with a fifteenth-century print or perhaps a thirteenth century manuscript—better still with several. For him the important point in the textual tradition is not the author's original, but that with which his own particular author was familiar. And in the same manner the student of Elizabethan literature can never be content with the Authorized Version of the English Bible, but must keep at least the Bishops' and Genevan Versions at his elbow.

We have in fact to recognize that a text is not a fixed and formal thing, that needs only to be purged of the imperfections of transmission and restored once and for all to its pristine purity, but a living organism which in its descent through the ages, while it departs more and more from the form impressed upon it by its original author, exerts, through its imperfections as much as through its perfections, its own influence upon its surroundings. At each stage of its descent a literary work is in some sense a new creation, something different from what it was to an earlier generation, something still more different from what it was when it came from the author's hand. Moreover, it will differ likewise from place to place. Indeed, every manuscript is individual and contains, in a manner, a work different from every other manuscript: in some limited sense, every scribe is a subsidiary author, even when he is doing his best to be a faithful copyist, still more when he indulges in emendations and improvements of his own. And this is just what bibliography, with its impartial outlook, recognizes, when it treats each step in the history of the text as potentially of equal importance.

If, then, I have made good my contention, it follows that bibliography necessarily includes, as its most distinctive branch, the study of textual transmission, and that textual criticism, up to the point where it changes its nature and becomes metacritical, is essentially nothing but the application of bibliographical analysis. Moreover, I contend that textual criticism has in the past suffered much from the failure to recognize this fact: on the one hand it has often relied on illegitimate metacritical methods, on the other hand it has excluded a quantity of relevant and at times crucial evidence. None but the bibliographer, trained in the material analysis of books and the signs that fill them, can be trusted to extract from their silent record the full testimony for the determination of the text. There can surely no longer be any doubt that the fields of the bibliographer and the textual critic are, if not identical, at least intimately related. I do not suggest, and I would not for a moment desire, that all bibliographers should apply themselves to textual criticism. Rather let each individual till his chosen field and garner ever more and more material for the common stock. Nor would I argue that an editor need of necessity be an expert bibliographer. It would be unreasonable to expect that in every case one man should possess all the detailed literary, linguistic, and archaeological training required of an editor, and all the technical equipment of the bibliographer as well. Of course, to say this is to say that an editor need not necessarily be an expert textual critic, for the latter, I hold, does need a thorough bibliographical training. However, there may be room for a new class of scholars cultivating an intermediate field. In these days of specialization I think we might recognize a faculty of textual criticism, of what might be called bibliographical critics, whose business it would be, not to produce critical editions themselves, but to investigate the facts of textual transmission, and prepare the material which the literary editor would be bound to use, and give a verdict which he should be bound to accept. In publishing their work they might or might not find it convenient to print a text of the work in question, but they would make no pretence of producing a literary edition of it. Such a textual bibliographer would not of course be required to be an expert on illumination, or bookbinding, or typography, perhaps not even on palaeography—it would depend upon his particular textual field—but he would be required to possess such a general knowledge of these subjects as to know just how and where they might become relevant to textual issues, and how and where to get further information should he require it. In other words he would need a thorough general knowledge of bibliography, and especially of all the material conditions, processes, and accidents that may affect the transmission of the text. It is, I am convinced, in the hands of such scholars that the future of textual criticism lies—and the text is the central problem of all literary study.

And now, because a little concrete experience is sometimes more illuminating than much abstract argument, I will conclude with a few examples of the application of bibliographical methods to literary problems of a more or less strictly textual kind.

First I will take, as an instance from early times, an investigation by the late Henry Bradley into 'The Numbered Sections in Old English Poetical MSS.'. It has always appealed to me as a brilliant piece of bibliographical argument, but I must warn you that his conclusions are not altogether accepted by experts, and that it will be safer to treat the matter rather as an illustration of method than as embodying ascertained facts.[1] An almost constant feature of the extant manuscripts of Old English poetry is the numbered sections into which the longer works are divided. These sections are often of an apparently arbitrary nature and editors have had some trouble to relate them to the logical structure of the poems. Bradley argued with immense ingenuity that they are the relics of archetypal foliation, corresponding as a rule to four-page sheets of parchment on which the works were originally written. This is an interesting bibliographical theory, but without any necessary literary bearing. In one case, however, that of *Elene*, these hypothetical sheets corresponded with the structural divisions of the work. This at once raises a literary problem. Why should Cynewulf have thought it necessary to make each canto of his poem on the Invention of the Cross fill exactly four pages? Was it mere perversity on his part, as Bradley supposed? Or should we see in this curious correspondence evidence of some lectionary system on which Anglo-Saxon poetry was composed? The answer to the riddle is not in our hands, but it is evident that such a compulsion must have put a marked curb on what Bradley described as the already not ungovernable Pegasus of Old English religious poets.

One example from Middle English may suffice. There is

[1] The basis of the whole argument is the alleged arbitrary nature of the divisions, which are said to occur even in the middle of a sentence. It has been pointed out to me that this is itself a literary and not a bibliographical datum, and it is, moreover, denied by some competent scholars. Others regard as over-ingenious the arguments by which Bradley sought to establish the equality of length of the sections in certain poems. The approximate uniformity of those in *Elene* is admitted, but unless they can be connected with the sheets of an archetype, this too remains, of course, a literary rather than a bibliographical fact. I am incompetent to judge of the merits of the case: but there is no doubt that Bradley, brilliant critic though he was, occasionally fell victim to an over-subtle imagination.

no more intriguing field of bibliographical exploration than the curious Cottonian manuscript,[1] containing one of the four surviving cycles of English miracle plays, commonly but erroneously known as *Ludus Coventriae*. A careful examination of the manuscript, including watermarks, catchwords, deletions, and all such technical trivialities, reveals the fact that considerable additions and rearrangements were made during the actual writing, and renders it highly probable that much of the work of combining into a single cycle the very diverse elements that can be traced in its composition was done in the course of compiling the actual copy extant. But it is also clear, from the elaborate notes with which the scribe has filled his margins—relating, for instance, to the genealogy of the Maries and the dimensions of Noah's Ark—that the extant copy was prepared for the use of readers and not for acting. It follows, therefore, that to inquire how or where the cycle, as we have it, was performed, is to ask a meaningless question; and that all attempts to reconcile the various theatrical data that survive from the different sources is mere futility. Yet literary historians have not yet given up spinning critical cobwebs round it, arguing whether it 'belongs' to Coventry or Norwich, to Lincoln or Bury, or maintaining that it was performed by an itinerant company in two portions in successive years.

A couple of small examples from the sixteenth and seventeenth centuries may next claim our attention. The literary flyting that centres round the figure of Gabriel Harvey is familiar to students, but the details of the quarrel are obscure and long remained a puzzle to historians. We had, indeed, the word of Thomas Nashe, the protagonist in the affair, for the assertion that Greene incidentally attacked the Harvey brothers in his *Quip for an Upstart Courtier*: unfortunately nothing could be found in that pamphlet that at all explained Gabriel's venomous counterblast. McKerrow, however, when he came to edit Nashe, was able to show that a couple of original leaves in Greene's work had been replaced by cancels, and to point to the exact spot where the offending passage must have stood. Ten years later a copy of the *Quip* turned up in its original state, showing that McKerrow's

[1] [MS. Cotton, Vespasian D. VIII.]

inference was perfectly correct: he had only erred as to the length of the suppressed passage, and that was because Nashe's original remarks were not quite reliable.

When the Cambridge University Press produced an edition of the plays of Beaumont and Fletcher some twenty years ago, the editor included a reprint of what he took to be the first edition of *The Elder Brother*, issued in 1637. Now, there are two editions bearing that date: they are textually very similar, and are most easily distinguished by the fact that in one the title is printed in capital (upper-case), and in the other in small (lower-case) letters. The Cambridge editor reprinted the lower-case edition. I do not know the grounds of his choice, but if he had been familiar with the typography of the seventeenth century, he could hardly have helped suspecting that this edition was a fraud and was really printed a score of years after the date that appeared on its title-page. This, however, is a difficult thing to prove. It happened that I was myself working on the play at the time, and it was necessary to produce unequivocal evidence of the order of the two editions. I collated the texts minutely, but it was not till near the end that I found what I was seeking. There was a passage (v. ii. 72) containing the word 'young', and in the upper-case edition a space had worked up before the 'y', making a mark above the line not unlike an apostrophe. In the lower-case edition a perfectly meaningless apostrophe had been inserted before the word: the compositor had been misled by the accidental mark in the upper-case edition, which was thus proved to be the original.

My last four instances shall be taken from Shakespeare, upon whose plays, as you know, much critical work of a bibliographical nature has been done of recent years. I will begin with a problem that long ago reached its solution, thus showing that bibliographical criticism is nothing new. There are two issues of the quarto of *Troilus and Cressida* (1609), one with a sober and apparently authoritative title-page, the other with a catchpenny title and a flaunting preface. It was long supposed, by Malone, Collier, and others, that the preliminaries of the adventurous printer had been suppressed on the receipt of official information, because the preface apparently claimed that the play had never been acted, whereas the title-page of the other issue recorded its performance. However, this pretty literary reconstruction was entirely upset by the Cambridge editors, who pointed out that, whereas the sober title-page was printed on the first leaf of the first quire, the preface and its title formed a double-leaf which had been substituted for the same.[1] It followed, of course, that the preface had not been suppressed, but was itself a later addition, and to this conclusion literary interpretation has had to accommodate itself.

Some years ago I lit on a rather nice example in *Titus Andronicus*. It has been a common opinion among critics, since the days of Ravenscroft, that this is an old play by one or more inferior writers, to which Skakespeare contributed in course of revision a few 'Master-touches', and various attempts have been made to identify these gems. I am, for my part, inclined to scepticism respecting such endeavours, since it sometimes happens that a passage selected as distinctively Shakespearian can be closely paralleled from Greene or some such inferior writer. However, a good shot was made by Professor Parrott (*M.L.R.*, 1919, xiv. 33) when he declared that none but Shakespeare could have put into the mouth of the Clown the words: 'God forbid I should bee so bolde, to presse to heauen in my young dayes' (IV. iii. 90). He was arguing on purely literary grounds, and in ignorance of the fact that, although the words occur as part of a prose speech, they are printed as a separate paragraph, a fact that almost certainly shows them to have been a marginal addition in the copy sent to the printer.[2] Whether the hand that made the addition was Shakespeare's, is, of course, another matter.

The mention of marginal additions recalls one of the most convincing inferences made by that brilliant critic Professor Dover Wilson. It concerns the well-known description of the lunatic, the lover, and the poet in *A Midsummer-Night's Dream* (v. i. 2–22). Part of this, as printed in the first edition,

[1] [It has since been shown that the cancel preliminaries, ¶[2], and the final half-sheet, M[2] (M2 blank), were almost certainly printed together on a single sheet; in which case these are not technically two different issues, but only different states of the edition.—1958.]

[2] I am, of course, relying on the quarto of 1600, but it is a fair inference that in this particular it reproduces exactly that of 1594. [The inference proves to be perfectly correct.—1958.]

is perfectly straightforward, but there are two passages falsely divided, in which the lines of type bear no relation to those required by the verse. Moreover, if these false-lined passages are omitted, the remainder is found to run on consecutively and to make perfectly good sense. We can hardly resist the conclusion that in this remainder we have the speech as originally composed, and that the anomalous passages represent additions crowded into the margin of the manuscript without regard to metrical division. This is a bibliographical argument, and the conclusion may be accepted as tolerably certain. Professor Wilson further suggested, on grounds of style, that the additions are no mere afterthoughts following hot-foot upon the composition of the rest, but that they belong to a later period of the author's poetical development and imply a revision of the play several years after its original conception. This, however, is a matter upon which bibliography is silent.

In conclusion I may be allowed to mention a problem in the solution of which I have been personally concerned. There are two editions of *The Merchant of Venice* dated 1600, and editors of Shakespeare were long divided upon the question which was the earlier. Johnson and Capell placed the so-called 'Heyes' quarto first, the Cambridge editors and Furnivall voted for the so-called 'Roberts' quarto. The latter further argued that neither quarto was printed from the other, but that their divergences pointed to independent manuscript sources. And so the controversy might, and doubtless would, have continued upon traditional literary lines, and with wholly inconclusive results, had not bibliography come to the rescue. For as soon as attention ceased to be concentrated upon variant readings and began to take account of print and paper as well, it became evident that, be the explanation of the divergences what it may, typographical arguments conclusively prove a relationship no further removed than the printing house—the 'Roberts' quarto must be a reprint of the 'Heyes'. Moreover, further investigation revealed the surprising fact that the former was not printed in 1600 at all, but was one of a set of ten quartos printed, several of them with false dates, in 1619. This I may claim to have established in 1908, but the demonstration upon which I relied, based on the watermarks in the paper, was of an unfamiliar character, and many critics refused to be persuaded. After a couple of years, however, Mr. William J. Neidig of Madison, using elaborate laboratory methods of photography, put the matter beyond doubt and was able to convince the most sceptical. He succeeded, namely, in proving that the title-pages of the group were nearly all printed in part from the same setting of the type, and was further able to show approximately the order in which they had been produced, an order that did not agree with their ostensible dates. Bibliography had come into its own.

A similar dispute had arisen over the two quartos of *King Lear* dated 1608. In 1866 the Cambridge editors declared in favour of the priority of the so-called 'Butter' quarto, but before the revision of their work in 1892, Aldis Wright had convinced himself that the so-called 'Pied Bull' quarto was the earlier. He was unquestionably right, for the 'Butter' quarto is one of the 1619 collection.

I trust that by these illustrations I have succeeded in showing how practice supports theory, and demonstrated the impossibility, or at least the danger, of cutting textual criticism adrift from its bibliographical foundations.

18. The Function of Bibliography in Literary Criticism Illustrated in a Study of the Text of *King Lear*[1]

I

GRATIFYING as it is to be asked to speak before the Allard Pierson Institute, I feel that so signal a distinction involves no less great a responsibility, and when I remember the accomplished scholars who have on previous occasions responded to the call of this generous foundation, I cannot avoid grave misgivings at the thought of my own inadequacy. Indeed, had it not been that there is in me somewhere, I suppose, something of missionary fanaticism, I doubt whether I should have ventured.

But when I learned from my friend Professor Swaen that you had done me the unexpected honour of inviting me to address you on some subject connected with English literature, I had little difficulty in choosing my theme. There is one field of research in which, above all, I am interested, and it is the only one in which I am sufficiently at home to justify my temerity in appearing before you. This is bibliography and its relation to study of literature.

Literary criticism may, I think, be divided, conveniently if perhaps a little arbitrarily, into three main branches. There is, to begin with, aesthetic and historical criticism, the criticism that seeks to apprize a work of literature, to define its particular quality and value, to set it in historical perspective, and to show, so far as can be shown from external circumstances, how it came to be, in the words of Bishop Butler, 'what it is and not another thing'. No doubt, there are here two distinct lines of approach, and many critics would insist vehemently on their being kept apart. But I think that most of you will agree with me that they are in fact closely bound up with one another, and that aesthetic criticism is always

[1] [1933, *Neophilologus*, xviii.]

soundest and most vital when brought into touch with historical environment.

The second branch, into which the first, I must admit, insensibly merges, is interpretation or exegetical criticism, the attempt to discover and expound an author's meaning in what he wrote, both as regards his general intention and as regards particular allusions and the sense of individual phrases.

The third branch—and again there is an obvious bridge—is textual criticism, the attempt to establish the actual words of the author, first by the collecting and sifting of documentary evidence, and afterwards by selection from the readings thus afforded, or if necessary by original emendation. It should be added that the task of textual criticism is not only to establish the true original text, but likewise to trace throughout the history of its transmission. Indeed—and this we shall see is an important point in the view I have to put before you—it is only through the second of these tasks that the first can be accomplished.

No doubt, it may be held that textual criticism is the humblest of our three branches. It is the Cinderella of literary science. But it is at the same time the most fundamental. Indeed, it must have struck you, if you pondered at all upon those transitions of which I spoke, that I have been taking the branches of criticism in what is, logically, their inverse order. A knowledge of the true text is the basis of all criticism; and textual criticism is thus the root from which all literary science grows. It expands insensibly into interpretation, just as interpretation passes insensibly into apprisal. Criticism is indeed one and indivisible, and it is only for our convenience, and because of the needful limits imposed by an ever hardening specialization, that we divide it, as I have just done, into several fields or branches.

I suppose that every age in which criticism has been self-conscious has made its own contribution to each of these divisions. The continuity, such as it has been, of what one might call the higher faculties may be traced in such a work as Saintsbury's *History of Criticism*, that of the lower perhaps in Sandys's *History of Classical Scholarship*, without going outside the range of English writers. But undoubtedly different ages have varied much in the extent and value of their contributions, and in the manner in which these have been distributed among the different branches.

I do not know whether our own generation would claim any pre-eminence in the highest branch, though there are distinguished names that will occur to you. Confining myself to English, there is, indeed, one living writer whose work seems to me to open up new vistas of critical thought. I have in mind Professor Livingston Lowes's study entitled *The Road to Xanadu*.[1] I think that all of you who have studied that work will agree with me in recognizing the brilliant qualities displayed in Professor Lowes's exciting quest, though I must admit that I am unable to follow him in some of his remoter speculations, and that I sometimes shudder to think what might be achieved by similar methods in less discriminating hands.

Exegesis has progressed soberly rather than brilliantly in our time. The labours of philologists and lexicographers have placed new and powerful weapons in the hands of those who have the sense to use them, and gradually no doubt a new standard of interpretation will be reached, of which already some foretaste may be found in the Shakespearian labours of Professor Dover Wilson. But we are hardly, I think, likely to see any new orientation in this branch of the subject—unless, indeed, we are to include within its scope Miss Spurgeon's remarkable investigations into the imagery of Shakespeare.[2]

When, however, we pass to textual criticism the case is altered. I believe that a profound change has come over this branch of the subject, and is even affecting, in a noticeable degree, the attitude of scholars to the historical criticism of literature, in general. It is a movement that began in a tentative way many years ago, but it has been gradually gathering moment, till now it is in full swing. So far as one can sum up such things in a phrase, its driving force may be said to be respect for the text. As leading motives one may discern the

[1] London, Constable & Co. (pr. Cambridge, Mass.), 1927.

[2] *Leading Motives in the Imagery of Shakespeare's Tragedies* (Shakespeare Association 1930), and *Shakespeare's Iterative Imagery* (British Academy, 1931), by Caroline F. E. Spurgeon.

recognition of the fact that textual criticism is at the basis of all literary study, and the widening of textual criticism to include within its scope the whole complex problem of the transmission of literary documents. The reconstruction of the original text, while remaining perhaps the chief, has ceased to be the sole, aim of textual criticism. We have come to recognize that the history of a text is, in its own right, a study of scarcely less importance. For an author of any antiquity and standing, far from being a static datum for all time, has been and has meant something different and individual to each ensuing age, not only as this was more or less akin to his in spirit and intention, but also as it was able to draw more or less close to his actual words and meaning. Literary historians have learned that even apparently trivial corruptions of an author's text may have curious repercussions. The miswriting *celte* for *certe* in manuscripts of the Vulgate is supposed to have supplied the term 'celt' to archaeological science, while a scribal tinkering in Gildas gave a saint to the calendar and a village to Herts.[1] The fly that was a plague to the Egyptians is in the Vulgate sometimes *musca* and sometimes *coenomyia*, meaning perhaps 'common fly',[2] but this is in the Septuagint κυνόμυια, which Peter Comestor duly rendered as *musca canina*. This seems to be the reason why in one of the English mystery cycles the plague of flies has become a plague of fleas ('loppis' in *Ludus Coventriae*). Bentley knew that when Milton wrote 'Hermione' he should have written 'Harmonia', and he therefore condemned the passage: what he did not know was that the error occurred in the authority on which Milton relied. Did not Chaucer picture Fame as shod with partridges' wings because his manuscript of Virgil has *perdicibus* instead of *pernicibus alis*? And speaking of Chaucer, let me remind you that, while the labours of a long line of scholars have done much to settle his text and restore his metre, it is not to their works but to the corrupt sixteenth-century editions that we must go if we wish to estimate his influence on Spenser.

[1] [St. Amphibalus. Greg's copy of this paper has a cutting under this title, which I have been unable to identify, tracing the origin of this saint's name, first found in Geoffrey of Monmouth, to a corrupt reading in Gildas. The priory founded on the supposed site of his martyrdom is at Redbourn.—J.C.M.]

[2] Du Cange glosses it as *musca omnis mordax*.

Now, the study that has wrought this change of critical outlook is bibliography, through the recognition of the fact that at bottom all problems of transmission are concerned with material factors, in the shape of pieces of paper or parchment covered with certain written or printed signs, and that it is in the first place through attention to the peculiarities of these, rather than through speculation as to what we fancy may have been in an author's mind, that the attack on textual problems should be made.

Bibliography is the study of books as tangible objects. It examines the materials of which they are made and the manner in which those materials are put together. It traces their place and mode of origin, and the subsequent adventures that have befallen them. It is not concerned with their contents in a literary sense, but it certainly is concerned with the signs and symbols they contain (apart from their significance) for the manner in which these marks are written or impressed is a very relevant bibliographical fact. And, starting from this fact, it is concerned with the relation of one book to another: the question which manuscript was copied from which, which individual copies of printed books are to be grouped together as forming an edition, and what is the relation of edition to edition. Bibliography, in short, deals with books as more or less organic assemblages of sheets of paper, or vellum, or whatever material they consist of, covered with certain conventional but not arbitrary signs, and with the relation of the signs in one book to those in another.

It is this relation of the symbols that links up bibliography most directly with textual criticism. One may press the view until bibliography and textual criticism merge into one, and indeed I have myself argued that essentially they are the same. But that is generally thought to be a fanciful, and potentially dangerous, heresy of my own, and I have not come here to advocate or to defend it. Suffice that there is a bridge, and a pretty substantial bridge, between the two. My thesis today is that critical bibliography, as I sketched it a moment ago, can throw a great deal of light on textual problems; that it has already shown by many instances what a powerful weapon it can prove in the hands of a critic able to wield it; and that it has established a new outlook and method of approach, that has very considerably modified the attitude of textual critics, and has not been without influence even upon the wider aspects of the historical study of literature.

A student of purely literary sympathies and habits of mind, when faced with the problems of textual criticism, will in nine cases out of ten surrender to his own imaginative predilection. Now, I do not for a moment wish to disparage the sympathetic intuition by which a subtle and sensitive mind may penetrate to the meaning and words of an author of similar intellectual and emotional outlook. Such powers are among the greatest that a literary critic can possess. They are also the rarest. For one critic of genuine inspiration we find a hundred shoddy pretenders. And even the best critic is not always inspired. Nor, again, would I dissuade the honest work-a-day critic from using his imagination with modesty and under due restraint. But just in so far as he is indeed honest and modest, he will himself know only too well how needful are the checks that objective criticism can supply, and he will accept them, not with the impatience that the limitation of facts so often rouses, but with the welcome accorded by the true scientific spirit, the spirit of intellectual integrity. And if the critic has had a bibliographical training, he will see beside and beyond the mere accumulation of textual data as ordinarily accepted—the variational apparatus of tradition—a whole range of possibly relevant evidence in the material peculiarities of the books from which those data are drawn.

It is easy to accumulate instances of the service performed by bibliographical investigation to textual and literary studies. It was the displacement of certain quires in the manuscript of *The Testament of Love* that concealed Thomas Usk's authorship of the work, and the correction of that error that enabled Henry Bradley to read his anagram aright, and so dispose finally of the attribution to Chaucer. An alleged misplaced leaf in the archetype of *Piers Plowman* is a bone of contention among scholars, round which wages the battle of triple *versus* single authorship. A study of the watermarks in the paper gave the first indication of the false dates on a number of Shakespearian quartos, and thereby determined which was the true first edition of several of his plays. Similar examination of the wire-marks has revealed many cases of leaves cancelled before publication, and the anomalous setting of the type has drawn attention to many passages altered in the course of printing. Without the accidental preservation of the original form of pages so altered or suppressed, we should still be wondering over the genesis of the Harvey–Nashe quarrel and why Jonson and Chapman went to jail for writing *Eastward Ho!*

It is probable that discoveries of this kind could be cited from most ages of criticism, showing that scholars have at all times been willing to accept help from bibliography in the solution of textual problems. But what is of far greater importance is the wider change of outlook which has recently come over critics in relation to their textual and editorial duties. The traditional attitude was the not unnatural one of regarding a text primarily as a literary composition, and consequently critics were inclined to treat textual variants as a sort of literary counters in a guessing game, quite apart from the sources whence they were derived. But as soon as bibliography began to colour textual criticism—the habit, that is, of starting, not from the literary composition, but from material manuscripts and prints, and of thinking of literary problems in terms of sheets of paper or parchment bearing certain conventional signs—the question of the derivation of the variants was seen to be all-important, and attention came to be focused less on some remote and perhaps unattainable original, than upon the more immediate sources from which the extant documents were derived. The history of the text became the first business of the critic.

So far as the criticism of manuscripts is concerned this idea appears to have been germinating for a considerable while. Its great triumph was the emergence of what is called the genealogical method in textual criticism. By this is understood the attempt to establish the relationship of extant manuscripts—their positions as it were in a family tree—with the object of determining the relative authority that their readings may possess. It is now universally accepted, and we are perhaps inclined to forget that it is after all a comparatively modern conception. I do not profess to be deeply read in the history of criticism, but I imagine that the development of the method would be covered by three generations. Its inception was perhaps due in the main to Karl Lachmann, whose most important work appeared in 1850, the year before his death. It is now half a century since Dr. Hort published his famous Introduction to the Greek New Testament, which is a classical exposition of the principles involved, and though it is evident that he was not then formulating a new system, it is equally clear that when he wrote the method was yet novel and by no means generally recognized.

The influence of the bibliographical outlook on the criticism of printed books is, curiously enough, of more recent date. Most of us, even the younger among us, have been able to follow its course, and maybe have taken a hand in its direction. It is mainly a development of the twentieth century, largely even of the post-war years. Printed books, it is true, afford little opportunity for the elaboration of anything analogous to the genealogical method. But bibliography, intent on its material pieces of paper, asked essentially the same question, and now it took the form: What was the nature of the copy that the printer had before him when he was setting up the type? This seemingly innocent question has produced something like a revolution in criticism, and has proved a curiously searching solvent to traditional modes of thought. That it only came to be asked thus late in time is perhaps not really surprising. A printed book has a certain definitive quality that is lacking in a manuscript. So soon as a contemporary work is printed, the printed book is intended to, and does in effect, supersede the manuscript; indeed in ninety-nine cases out of a hundred the manuscript is no more than a step in the production of the printed book. Thus the printed book does not invite speculation as to its origin in the same way as one published in manuscript, and critics have generally been content to leave it at that.

Not, of course, entirely. Editors have long been aware of the deficiencies of many printed texts, and only too ready to condemn the compositors who set them up. They have even been ready, at times, with assertions as to the nature of the copy used by the printer, though they have seldom based their statements on any examination of the evidence, preferring to rely on their untutored imagination. Within the present century a writer, popularly accounted the foremost Shakespearian scholar in England,[1] enumerated, as characteristic of playhouse copies of Elizabethan plays, features that are all in contradiction to ascertainable fact.

This and similar feats of imagination set bibliographers thinking. The revolution that ensued was not, of course, the work of one man, but in the Shakespearian field at least it will always be associated with the name of Professor A. W. Pollard, that master of the art of concealing incendiary ideas under a cloak of respectable conservatism.

As soon as bibliography raised the question of the printer's copy in specific form, and forced critics to consider the actual evidence available, many interesting points came to light and the data began to sort themselves out. I am, of course, speaking mainly of the printing of the sixteenth and seventeenth centuries, the period in which research has been most active. For one thing it became evident that behind the superficially similar printed texts there must lie a great diversity of manuscript types. Approaching the question from the printer's point of view we can see various possibilities as to the copy handled. It is reasonable to suppose that many works, especially the more serious writings in prose and verse, were printed from the author's own manuscript, either holograph or prepared under his direction by a scribe and perhaps finally corrected for press. Actual examples of both types can be put in evidence.[2] At the same time many works are known to have circulated more or less widely in manuscript, being no doubt copied and recopied, and it is likely that some of them ultimately reached the printer in a form far removed from the autograph; some may even have been committed to paper from memory. At times the source of the printer's copy was even more remote. Some sermons at any rate were compiled from notes taken by a system of shorthand, though we need not suppose that this necessarily implied a piratical intention.

1 [Sidney Lee. Greg writes of his errors in *The Editorial Problem in Shakespeare* (1942), p. 22, and *The Shakespeare First Folio* (1955), p. 121.—J.C.M.]

2 e.g. John Harington, *Orlando Furioso*, cantos XIV–XLVI, 1591, B.M., MS. Add. 18920; and Richard Hooker, *The Laws of Ecclesiastical Polity*, book V, 1597, Bodl. MS. Add. c. 165.

And when criticism starts from the other end and submits the printed texts themselves to close and unprejudiced analysis, it finds much to confirm the conclusions reached on *a priori* grounds.

So far as the great bulk of serious works is concerned the printed texts attain a very respectable level of accuracy, and in their case the abuse of the Elizabethan printer that has been fashionable in certain editorial circles is definitely unwarranted. We know that the author was, as a rule, given the opportunity of revising the proofs as a work went through the press, and though the facilities for doing so may not have been all that could be desired, and authors may sometimes have been negligent in making the most of them, the fact remains that, generally speaking, the better class of Elizabethan literature originally appeared in texts hardly less sound than many works of the nineteenth century.

This fact has been obscured by two or three fortuitous circumstances. For one thing, there is often a certain superficial carelessness about Elizabethan printing that tends to prejudice the modern reader. The press-work is frequently poor, while turned and wrong-fount letters and obvious literal misprints occur in a manner that would be thought discreditable today. But such accidents are in the main irrelevant to the soundness of the text.[1]

In the next place there are, no doubt, individual exceptions. As a rule an Elizabethan compositor was able to read his copy correctly—Elizabethan handwriting was in general more legible than modern—and to set it up, after his lights, with reasonable accuracy. But not all compositors were equally skilled, and printing-houses varied in the standards they maintained. If an author wrote a really bad hand and was careless in attending to his proofs, the result might be disastrous. It is occasionally possible to trace errors in printed works quite definitely to peculiarities of the autograph. And in some cases we know that works were printed from scribal copies in circumstances that precluded revision by the author. Greene's *Groatsworth of Wit* was transcribed for press by Chettle after the writer's death, since his 'hand was none of the best'.

[1] Still more irrelevant is the want of uniformity in Elizabethan spelling, for which critics like Sidney Lee have absurdly blamed the printer.

Lastly, prejudice has been fostered by the attempts of certain authors, in prefaces and errata, to saddle the printer with responsibility for a multitude of errors with which he manifestly can have had nothing to do. The mutual recriminations of Ralph Brooke, the herald, and William Jaggard, the stationer, are now familiar to students and can be estimated at their true worth, but there is no doubt that the former's complaints have in the past done something to blacken the typographical character of the printer responsible for the earliest collections of Shakespeare's plays.

These considerations, though they can never justify, may to some extent excuse editors who have complained of excessive inaccuracy in early prints whenever they wished to tamper with an author's text in following the dictates of their own fancy. One thing at least bibliography, in its careful inquiry into printer's copy, has already accomplished: it has largely banished the bogy of the ignorant and careless compositor, and set up the more substantial cock-shy of the ignorant and impertinent editor.

But, as Dr. McKerrow has recently argued, if modern editorial experience has tended to vindicate in general the soundness of early printed texts, there remains one special field, the drama, in which this statement needs at least serious qualification. Notoriously, many plays have come down to us in versions that can only be called perversions—what are now specifically known as 'bad quartos'—and notoriously, many others are preserved in texts which, if fundamentally sound, yet contain a quite unreasonable number of seriously corrupt passages. It is, of course, true that now and again an author, like Ben Jonson, treated his plays as 'works' and saw them through the prcss with meticulous care, while in some other cases the presence of dedications implies that plays were at least published with the author's sanction. But it is clear that playwrights as a class were rather careless of the literary fate of their offspring, and may have been impatient of the labour of proof-correcting. Massinger, we know, passed in his printed plays a number of verbal errors which he took pains to correct with his own hand in presentation copies. And once we step outside this circle of more or less authorized editions, the dramatic texts of the time, whether actually pirated and surreptitious or not, are unquestionably often very corrupt. Perhaps, when we come to consider the matter bibliographically, the reason is not very far to seek. Plays, after all, are primarily intended to be acted rather than read. The autograph is prepared for the stage; it is generally by an afterthought, and often through devious channels, that the text reaches the printing-house. Thus there is likely to be far greater diversity of copy in the case of dramatic than of non-dramatic literature. And bibliographical and textual research has already done a good deal to demonstrate this diversity. The possible fortunes of a piece written for the stage in Shakespeare's day were various in the extreme. The author might himself prepare a fair copy of his work for the actors' use, or he might hand over his 'foul papers' to a scribe skilled in the preparation of playhouse manuscripts.[1] Either the autograph fair copy or the scribe's transcript might be submitted to the censor, and after modification become the official 'book', as the prompt copy was called—and still is. From this other copies might be made, either for private collectors and patrons of the stage, or to replace a tattered original, or to supply a duplicate if a portion of the acting company went on tour in the country. In the first case, we are told, it was usual to transcribe the piece, not in the form in which the author wrote it, but in that which actors gave it in performance; in the last case the text might very likely undergo further alteration and abridgement. Sometimes a prompt-book got lost or destroyed: it might then have to be reconstituted from such 'foul papers' as survived, or conceivably even from the actors' parts. Sometimes, we suspect, a down-and-out company of players, having parted with a 'book' sought to vamp up some sort of acting version by an effort of communal memory. Furthermore, it has been suggested that a publisher might endeavour to obtain a version of a popular play by sending a shorthand writer to the performance, and perhaps suborning minor actors to help with their memory and fragmentary parts. When we remember that manuscripts of any of these manifold types—from the author's rough draft

[1] By 'foul papers' we should understand, not a preliminary draft of a play, but the rough copy, containing what the author intended to be his final corrections, but too untidy for use as it stood.

or the playhouse manuscript down to the memorial reconstruction or the shorthand report—might ultimately come into a printer's hands and be used as copy, we shall surely cease to wonder either at the great variety we find in the quality of dramatic texts or at the strange depravity of some among them.

The critical point which we must always keep in mind—the point that lends a wider significance to all such technical discussions—is that the form in which the text of a play has come down to us must profoundly affect our attitude towards it as a literary document, and therefore the judgement we form of it as a work of theatrical art. Admirers of Marlowe have wondered that his dramatic and poetical grasp should ever have so relaxed as in the *Massacre at Paris*: censurers of Greene have given him an extra kick for the absurdities of *Orlando Foolioso*—as Harington called it. But once we realize that the extant texts of these plays are nothing but the rehash of a very imperfect memory, we shall hardly be inclined to lay any responsibility for them to the charge of their nominal authors. And even in less extreme cases, is it altogether reasonable to blame an author for inconsistencies of plot and contradictions of character, when his plays, as preserved, may have been ruthlessly cut and botched to meet the demands of the censor and the exigencies of casting and performance? Professor Lascelles Abercrombie, in an eloquent address before the British Academy, lately invited us to accept as Shakespeare the canon of the First Folio and judge it as it stands. His plea has great force if by 'Shakespeare' we are to understand no more than a certain extant body of dramatic literature; but if he means a living man to be judged as a creative artist, then I think that in his endeavour to simplify the problem he has emptied it of significance.

It is in this manner that bibliographical criticism, by inquiring into the sources and history of the text, has shifted the point of view and opened up new possibilities of literary investigation. Much of the recent work has been done in the drama, a field that offers peculiar opportunities to the critical detective, but the same principles and the same methods are applicable over the whole domain of literature, and as they become sharpened and adapted by use, we may expect to see them reshaping ever more and more the modes of thought and manner of approach alike of editors and of historical critics.

I have endeavoured in this introductory portion of my address to sketch out what I conceive to be the essence and importance of bibliography in relation to literary criticism. In my second portion I shall seek to illustrate my thesis by taking a particular case—the text of *King Lear*—and showing how at every step the problem, or rather the series of linked problems, involved depends for solution upon bibliographical principles and methods.

II

In the course of an address before the British Academy five years ago I remarked that the text of Shakespeare's play of *King Lear* still offered a problem for investigation. Criticism had, indeed, left the subject in a very unsatisfactory state. Happily my challenge met with response, and two important contributions have since appeared: one the brief but weighty pronouncement in Sir Edmund Chambers's recent work on *William Shakespeare*, the other an elaborate and able monograph by Miss Madeleine Doran.[1] The two writers take diametrically opposite views of the problem, involving very different bibliographical theories and leading to different textual conclusions. It will be my endeavour to put before you as briefly as possible the arguments with which these views are supported and the editorial consequences of their adoption.

Our authorities for the text of *King Lear* are the first collected folio of Shakespeare's *Comedies, Histories, and Tragedies* that appeared late in 1623, and the early quartos of the individual play that preceded it.

The textual study of *Lear* involves five distinct though related problems: first, the number and order of the early quartos; second, the differences of reading that exist between the several copies of the earliest of these; third, the manuscript used by the printer of the first quarto; fourth, the copy used by the printer of the first folio; fifth the relation between the quarto and the folio texts, and the procedure a modern editor should adopt.

[1] *The Text of 'King Lear'*, Stanford University Press, 1931.

The Order of the Early Quartos

This problem has now reached a definite solution. A hundred years ago the number of early editions was in doubt and no serious attempt had been made to determine their order. In 1866 Clark and Wright[1] proved conclusively that there were only two early editions, both dated 1608, which are called for convenience the 'Pied Bull' and the 'N. Butter' quartos respectively. They were less successful over the order. After advancing an excellent argument in favour of the 'Pied Bull' as the earlier, they adopted a non-committal attitude, concluding that 'The question . . . is very difficult to decide, and at most is one rather of bibliographical curiosity than of critical importance.' I know no better example of the tendency of editors to treat readings as counters in a guessing game, irrespective of the authority of their source. The question had previously been debated on quite inconclusive literary grounds; on the other hand, the evidence put forward by the Cambridge editors was bibliographical, the implication of a correction made in the course of printing. This argument was extended in 1885 by P. A. Daniel, and he reinforced it by a further appeal to bibliography, adducing the make-up of the different editions.[2] Since then no one has questioned that the 'Pied Bull' quarto is the earliest, but it was naturally assumed that the two had appeared within a short space of one another in 1608. But in 1908 it was discovered that a particular group of Shakespearian plays, which included the second, or 'N. Butter', quarto of *Lear*, and bore dates ranging from 1600 to 1619, far from being printed in these various years, must all have been produced within a few weeks of one another, presumably in the latest of them. The proof originally advanced was that all the plays were printed on one job lot of paper containing sheets of nearly thirty different makes, as shown by the watermarks. It is hardly surprising that so revolutionary a theory based on evidence of a character so unfamiliar should have been received in some quarters with scepticism. But

[1] *The Cambridge Shakespeare*, vol. viii, preface.

[2] Introduction to the facsimile of the first quarto by C. Praetorius (*Shakspere-Quarto Facsimiles*, No 33).

confirmation was at hand, for it was shown that a single setting of type had been used for the title-pages, a common framework being left standing from play to play, while the necessary portions were altered. Thus bibliographical investigation of a purely technical character established the fact that the second quarto was printed eleven years after its fellow, and was a mere reprint of it, thus leaving the text of *Lear* dependent upon the first quarto and the first folio alone.

The Variants Between Copies of the First Quarto

Again the problem has been substantially elucidated, though some details remain obscure. The uncertainty as to the number of early editions arose from the fact that copies of the first quarto differ among themselves in a number of readings. Such variations are not uncommon in books of the time, and their origin is pretty well understood. Printing on a hand press was necessarily slow, and it sometimes happened that, while one side of a sheet (one forme as it is called) was being printed, errors were discovered in the type, work was suspended, and the mistakes corrected before any more pulls were made. But the variants in *Lear* are not quite of this simple type. From a trifling bibliographical detail,[1] we know for certain as regards one sheet, and can reasonably infer as regards others, that after a certain number of pulls had been made on both sides of the sheet, work was stopped, both formes were corrected, and then the remainder of the impressions taken. Why the sheets should have been printed in two distinct batches is at present a mystery, and so long as it is unsolved we cannot pretend to know all we need about the history of the first quarto.[2]

But if the origin of the variants remains in some degree obscure, their nature is tolerably evident, and that matters most for the text. The important question is the degree of authority that attaches to the corrections. This certainly varies. In some cases it is evident that the compositor had

[1] The alteration of the catchword on K4 recto consequent upon the correction of the first word on the verso.

[2] [The study of these variants was greatly advanced by Greg himself in his Bibliographical Society monograph, *The Variants in the First Quarto of 'King Lear'*, 1940.—J.C.M.]

merely made a slight mistake in reading his copy, and that when the press-reader altered the word to something quite different, he was merely guessing and did not trouble to consult the manuscript at all. Thus the printer's impossible 'crulentious' must be a misreading of 'contentious' (the corresponding word in the Folio): the corrector's 'tempestuous' is his own invention.[1] But this is not always so. At times the corrector did consult the manuscript, and to good purpose. He made some true corrections in passages which are so confused that guessing would have been impossible,[2] and he restored a necessary half-line, in what no one can doubt was its original form.[3] On the other hand, there is nothing to suggest that he ever had access to any authority beyond the copy in hand. The conditions under which he worked and the limits of his ability need to be borne in mind, for some of the alterations he made are in the most difficult passages of the play,[4] and our conclusions as to Shakespeare's meaning will depend in no small measure on the view we take of the activities of this erratic press corrector.

The Source of the Quarto Text

On this question opinion is sharply divided. Chambers, adopting a theory originally advanced by Alexander Schmidt, holds that the Quarto contains a reported text somehow derived from an actual performance of the play. Miss Doran, on the other hand, advances the view that it was printed from the author's own autograph, ill-written and rendered illegible by much alteration, which had been discarded in the playhouse after it had served for the preparation of the official prompt copy. Both assume that the Folio represents substantially the prompt copy, and admit that Quarto and Folio alike contain printers' errors from which the respective manuscripts were free: beyond these superficial errors Chambers accounts for the differences between the two texts by mistakes of the actors and reporter, Miss Doran by revision carried out by Shakespeare on the playhouse 'book'. These are the two theories we have to examine.

[1] III. iv. 6 (all references are to the 'Globe' edition).
[2] e.g. I. iv. 322–3.
[3] V. iii. 38.
[4] Especially II. iv. 102–6, IV. ii. 25–28, 56–58.

Some 400 lines of the text as it appears in modern editions rests on only a single authority; of these the Quarto supplies nearly 300 and the Folio 100. No doubt there are a few accidental omissions in either text. Otherwise the differences can be substantially explained by variant cutting.[1] There seems no sufficient reason to assume the extensive and elaborate revision of the prompt-book to which Miss Doran attributes them.

Apart from this question of plus and minus, the main features of the Quarto text appear to be as follows: in outward form, misrepresentation of the metrical structure, and defective and misleading punctuation; textually, constant redundancy of expression, and persistent substitution of another (and generally inferior) reading for that of the Folio.

The printing of the verse is chaotic: sometimes prose is divided as verse, more often verse is run on like prose; and when verse is recognized as such, the lines are wrongly divided with a frequency that is altogether exceptional. Of course, revision and marginal addition in a manuscript may easily lead a printer to divide the lines wrongly, but this will not account for a whole long verse-scene appearing as prose; while to suggest that Shakespeare may, for some inscrutable reason, have written it as prose, seems to me really to beg the question. Little stress can be laid on the punctuation, for some autograph manuscripts, such as the Shakespearian addition to *Sir Thomas More*, are notoriously deficient in this respect. But the general impression left by the Quarto is that the printer had before him copy that was entirely undivided metrically and altogether without punctuation. There is, indeed, some slight bibliographical evidence to this effect. Such copy would normally result from a shorthand report, and I do not know what else would produce it.

To pass to textual features: by redundancy I understand the expansion and dilution of the text, on the one hand by the introduction of exclamations, expletives, vocatives, and connective words generally, on the other hand by the use of looser and less close-knit phrasing. Such redundancy is characteristic of actors and is a marked feature of reported texts. I find

[1] This is not necessarily the whole explanation; some revision is possible, but that would be consistent with either view.

it quite impossible to believe, with Miss Doran, that any writer, however familiar with the stage he might be, would in composition either deliberately or unconsciously introduce these features, which unnerve his language and destroy his verse, and then prune them away in revising the acting version.

Both forms of redundancy are united in this typical example:[1]

F I am made of that selfe-mettle as my Sister,
Q Sir I am made of the selfe same mettall that my sister is, ...

Or, for flabby and vicious phrasing, take:[2]

F Or rather a disease that's in my flesh,
Q Or rather a disease that lies within my flesh,

and for the intrusion of connective phrases:[3]

F *Lear.* . . . . Thou shalt finde,
That Ile resume the shape which thou dost thinke
I haue cast off for euer [*Q* ,thou shalt I warrant thee].
Gon. Do you marke that [*Q* my Lord]?

In all these cases the Quarto is condemned by the verse. Moreover, these connectives tend to be borrowed or repeated from other passages, such assimilation being another common trick of actors. In the first scene Lear twice admonishes Cordelia:[4]

Nothing will come of nothing, speake againe

and later:

How, how *Cordelia*? Mend your speech a little, ...

Thc Quarto borrows 'How' from the second to prefix unmetrically to the first, and gives the second in the form:

Goe to, goe to, mend your speech a little,

introducing a fretful exclamation, more in the style of Polonius than of Lear,[5] which it employs again unmetrically later on. Similarly the Quarto makes Lear conclude two

[1] I. i. 70–71. [2] II. iv. 225.
[3] I. iv. 332–3. [4] I. i. 92, 96.
[5] In this scene, as Granville-Barker observes, 'There need be, there must be, no descent to petulance.'

consecutive speeches with the words 'goe, goe, my people', whereas in the second case the Folio has 'Away, away';[1] and while in the Folio Lear cries once 'Yet haue I left a daughter' and later 'I haue another daughter', the Quarto uses the first phrase on both occasions.[2] There are also some traces of actors' exaggerations and bombast.

The reporter reveals his presence by a number of mistakes of hearing, such as 'a dogge, so bade in office' for 'a Dogg's obey'd in Office',[3] and

> striuing to better ought, we marre whats well

instead of

> striuing to better, oft we marre what's well

which is puzzling till we remember that Shakespeare rimes *oft* and *nought*.[4] That these are mishearings is not disputed: Miss Doran supposes dictation to the compositor—a rather desperate hypothesis. Further traces of the reporter are a number of speeches assigned to the wrong character, and sometimes modified to suit. For instance, where in the Folio Regan says to Edmund:[5]

> Let the Drum strike, and proue my title thine

in the Quarto it is Edmund himself who says:

> Let the drum strike, and proue my title good

as if a drum could prove anything but its power of making a noise. It is also significant that inarticulate sounds and meaningless refrains indicated in the Folio, are in the Quarto either omitted[6] or quite otherwise expressed, as when 'Do, de, de, de: sese' becomes 'loudla doodla'.[7]

But it is the verbal variants of the two texts that supply the most ample evidence of reporting. Such changes must inevitably occur on the stage, and the substituted word will be either indifferent or generally inferior. That this is what we observe in the Quarto text is agreed, but Miss Doran points

[1] I. iv. 294, 311.
[2] I. iv. 276, 327.
[3] IV. vi. 163.
[4] I. iv. 369.
[5] V. iii. 81.
[6] I. ii. 149, III. iv. 59, IV. vi. 207.
[7] III. vi. 77.

out, pertinently enough, that indifferent variants may be the unconscious substitutions of a compositor or a copyist, while superior Folio readings may be due to revision. Now, theoretically this is perhaps a sufficient answer, but when we come to examine actual examples I think that it breaks down in practice. For one thing, the indifferent, or nearly indifferent variants are rather numerous to father upon one transcriber and two compositors; for another, some superficially indifferent variants prove to be in fact due to repetition and thus suggest actors' assimilations; and lastly some are not isolated but consciously linked. When, in the line:[1]

That iustly think'st, and hast most rightly said:

the Quarto transposes the words 'iustly' and 'rightly', the blunder is perhaps not beyond the range of original sin latent in a copyist: but when, two lines apart, we find 'Fiue dayes.... And on the sixt' consistently varied to 'Foure' and 'fift', this explanation becomes less satisfactory.[2] And so it is with revision. There may be cases—many cases—in which it is impossible to distinguish between corruption on the one hand or revision on the other. But I question whether this is always, or even generally, so. Where one reading is metrical and the other not; where in one the thought receives natural expression, in the other forced or inept; or where one shows a misunderstanding of the sense that is clear in the other, we have, I think, good and sufficient ground for judging.

To set forth the evidence in detail would need no less than a complete textual commentary on the play. I can do no more than select an example here and there from the cloud of witnesses. Here is a passage condemned by the metre. The Folio reads:[3]

Why brand they vs
With Base? With basenes Bastardie? Base, Base?

The verse is correct, but the second is not an easy line to remember exactly, and it is hardly surprising to find in the Quarto no more than the unmetrical syncopation

with base, base bastardie?

[1] I. i. 186. [2] I. i. 176, 178. [3] I. ii. 10.

At one point Oswald says of Gloucester:[1]

> Would I could meet [him] Madam, I should shew
> What party I do follow.

The Quarto reads 'What Lady I doe follow', and since the talk has been of the rivalry between Regan and Goneril this would come naturally to the lips of an actor, but it is not to that that the Steward is referring. Or consider the lines in which Lear breaks forth in true Shakespearian phrase:[2]

> Close pent-vp guilts,
> Riue your concealing Continents, and cry
> These dreadfull Summoners grace.

The Quarto's 'riue your concealed centers' makes neither verse nor sense. Once more: Regan observes, shrewdly enough, of the blinded Gloucester:[3]

> Where he arriues, he moues
> All hearts against vs: *Edmund*, I thinke is gone
> In pitty of his misery, to dispatch
> His nighted life: Moreouer to descry
> The strength o'th'Enemy.

When, in place of '*Edmund*', the Quarto reads 'and now', it makes the following lines refer to Gloucester, which, remembering his attempted suicide in the next scene, might appear not unreasonable to an actor who overlooked the fact that it further credits the corpse with the purpose of spying on the French army! Failure of memory alone can account for a final example.[4] When in the first scene Lear at last turns to Cordelia, he addresses her in the tender words:

> Now our Ioy,
> Although our last and least; to whose yong loue,
> The Vines of France, the Milke of Burgundie,
> Striue to be interest.

In place of this the Quarto has only:

> but now our ioy,
> Although the last, not least in our deere loue,

[1] IV. v. 40.
[2] III. ii. 58.
[3] IV. v. 1.
[4] I. i. 85–87.

where it is surely the loss of a line and a half that has occasioned the reconstruction. If anybody can see revision in this passage his conception of poetical composition must be radically different from my own.

It is contended by those who favour the report theory that the Folio constantly supplies not merely the better reading but one more natural and more consonant with the thought of the passage, in other words the more original. And even where revision is abstractly possible, we may yet question whether it was indeed thus that Shakespeare worked. While I cannot attach much weight to what Heminge and Condell tell us of the author's unblotted manuscripts, I feel even less happy at the vision of his autograph that Miss Doran conjures up. She pictures Shakespeare fumbling after his expression, and even after his meaning, with the clumsiness of a novice. That he evolved the seemingly inevitable expression of passage after passage from a welter of confused, inept, and commonplace phrases, is hard to believe. And when we are further told that the revision was carried out on the already prepared 'book' of the play, we can only wonder what must have been the feelings—and the language—of the prompter who had to use it.

Miss Doran has argued that the Quarto text of *Lear* is far too good to be reported, and she is able to point with considerable force to the very different textual conditions found in admittedly reported texts, such as the earliest print of *Romeo and Juliet*. But I think that it is now agreed by most critics that these are what are called memorial reconstructions. This the quarto *Lear* emphatically is not. If it is indeed a reported text it must have been taken down by shorthand, and the question arises whether there was at the time any system in use by which the result could have been attained. That such a feat was possible with Bright's *Charactery* or Bales's *Brachygraphy*, I cannot for one moment believe. But in 1602 appeared John Willis's *Art of Stenography*, which contained what is possibly a more efficient method, and we are credibly informed that this had already been used in 1605 to produce what is at least a superficially readable text of Heywood's *Troubles of Queen Elizabeth*, a play, it is worth noting, that had been issued by the same publisher as *Lear*. Thus, whatever the difficulties involved in the assumption of a shorthand report, we have no ground to rule it out as impossible.[1]

The Source of the Folio Text

Again there are two views current. The marked difference between the Quarto and Folio texts and the general superiority of the latter are, indeed, commonplaces of criticism, and it is common ground that the main source of the Folio text is the official prompt-book of the play. But while Miss Doran believes the Folio to have been set up directly from this manuscript, Chambers follows Daniel in supposing that the printer must have used a copy of the Quarto which had been brought by collation and correction into what was intended to be, but in fact was not, complete agreement with that manuscript.

The view we take will depend a good deal upon what opinion we have formed respecting the Quarto text. If the evidence already summarized be held to prove that the Quarto offers a reported text, then I think it follows inevitably, from the community of errors and other peculiarities in the two authorities, that the Quarto played some part in the bibliographical history of the Folio. If, on the other hand, we assume autograph copy for the Quarto, or indeed admit any transcriptional continuity between the two texts, most of the evidence may be capable of other explanations. In this case it will be more difficult to meet Miss Doran's contention of the Folio's direct use of the manuscript, though I think that there still remain sufficient links of a purely typographical nature to render it difficult of acceptance.

It was a consideration of the variants between different copies of the Quarto that first led Daniel to the conclusion that the Folio must have been printed from it. You will remember that when we discussed those variants it appeared

[1] Miss Doran also finds evidence of Shakespearian spelling and handwriting in the manuscript, behind the spelling and misprints of the Quarto. But she does not lay much stress on the argument, nor does it amount to much. As regards spelling, she herself frankly points out some serious contradictions. As regards writing, I think the most distinctive confusions in the Quarto are those of *k* with *b* and *l* with *t* (seen combined in the substitution of 'bitt' for 'kill' at IV. i. 39), which are exceptional in 'good quartos' of Shakespeare. On the whole the evidence under this head seems to me to tell rather against than for autograph copy.

that some of the alterations were genuine corrections derived from a closer inspection of the manuscript, while others were guesses of the press-reader which might sometimes be right, but were certainly sometimes wrong. If, therefore, we find the Folio agreeing with one of the original readings of the Quarto the correction of which we are entitled to believe true, we shall reasonably conclude that the Folio was printed from a copy of the Quarto which contained the sheet in question in the uncorrected state. Similarly, if we find the Folio agreeing with one of the altered readings that we have reason to suppose is not a true correction but an erroneous guess of the press-reader, we shall conclude that the Folio was printed from a copy of the Quarto which contained the sheet in question in the corrected state. Both cases, I believe, occur.

There is a passage that runs in the Folio thus:

> This milky gentlenesse, and course of yours
> Though I condemne not, yet vnder pardon
> [You] are much more at task for want of wisedome,
> Then prai'sd for harmefull mildnesse.

Now, the third line[1] was originally set up in the Quarto as:

> y'are much more alapt want of wisedome,

of which the corrector made sense by reading:

> y'are much more attaskt for want of wisedome, ...

Here 'for' must have been accidentally omitted by the compositor, but 'attaskt' cannot possibly have been the reading of the copy. Behind 'alapt' must, on recognized graphic grounds, have been the word 'ataxt'; and *atax'd*, i.e. taxed, is even better in the context than *attask'd*, i.e. taken to task, though as a matter of fact neither word is otherwise recorded. Thus 'attaskt' is a ghost word invented by the press-reader,[2] and when the Folio editor or compositor further emended it to 'at task', he proved that he had before him a corrected sheet of the Quarto, since the word had no other existence.

[1] I. iv. 366.

[2] The press-reader presumably read the manuscript 'ataxt' correctly, but assumed that *tax* was only another and inferior spelling of *task*. The two verbs were used synonymously at the time, and in III. ii. 16 the Quarto again substitutes 'taske' for 'taxe'. The doubling of the *t* in 'attaskt' seems due to analogy with such words as *attain*.

So far as I know this example has hitherto escaped notice, but there is another, and well-known, passage which equally clearly proves the dependence of the Folio elsewhere upon an uncorrected sheet of the Quarto. The lines should read:

> Sir, I thought it fit,
> To send the old and miserable King
> To some retention and appointed guard,
> Whose age had Charmes in it, whose Title more,
> To pluck the common bosome on his side, ...

In this the half-line 'and appointed guard',[1] necessary to the metre and unquestionably original, was supplied by the press-reader in the corrected state of the Quarto; it is absent in the original state, and is again absent in the Folio, and both alike print the previous line and a half as a single verse.[2]

To explain this away Miss Doran is forced to suppose that the passage had been much altered in the autograph, with the result that the three words in question, presumably written in the margin, were illegible to the compositor; that the corrector managed to decipher them; but that they baffled the scribe who prepared the prompt copy. This seems to involve several improbabilities. We have to suppose that the Quarto corrector, whose abilities in the way of deciphering were certainly not conspicuous, was able to make out the words, though to do so had proved beyond the power of the playhouse scribe, who must have been well used to dramatic 'foul papers' and was probably familiar with Shakespeare's

[1] v. iii. 47.

[2] The versions are exactly as follows:

*Q*A *Bast.* Sir I thought it fit,
To saue the old and miserable King to some retention,
Whose age has charmes in it, whose title more
To pluck the coren bossom of his side, ...

*Q*B *Bast.* Sir I thought it fit,
To send the old and miserable King to some retention, and ap-
Whose age has charmes in it, whose title more, (pointed guard.
To pluck the common bossome of his side, ...

F *Bast.* Sir, I thought it fit,
To send the old and miserable King to some retention,
Whose age had Charmes in it, whose Title more,
To plucke the common bosome on his side, ...

The argument is that *F* is based on *Q*A imperfectly corrected by comparison with the playhouse manuscript.

handwriting; further that this trained scribe was content to leave the previous line in its impossible state; lastly that the author himself, making an extensive and careful revision of the prompt-book, never observed or troubled to correct so glaring a defect. *Credo quia impossibile* may be good theology: *credo quia non impossibile* is certainly bad criticism.

A few words must be said respecting the confirmatory evidence to be found in errors and peculiarities common to the Quarto and Folio texts in passages unaffected by the variants in the former, and particularly in such features of the Folio as can be explained by the typographical arrangement of the Quarto. Chambers speaks of 'a general orthographic resemblance' between the two, and it is certainly possible to draw up a long list of correspondences which, if individually of little weight, are collectively suggestive. Still more so are many agreements in punctuation, since the two texts generally follow very different systems in this respect. As I have already remarked, the pointing of the Quarto is light and even defective; there are seldom any points except commas within a speech. On the other hand, the Folio pointing is notoriously heavy. When, therefore, we find several passages in which the Folio not only reproduces exactly the deficient punctuation of the Quarto, but even retains definite and obvious errors which make nonsense of the text, we can hardly fail to suspect the cause.[1] And we are confirmed in our suspicion when we find the Folio here and there following the Quarto exactly in printing as verse passages that are really prose, or vice versa; retaining unnatural line-divisions, the original reason for which has disappeared; and omitting short speeches that are easily overlooked through being abnormally placed.

There is much evidence of this kind to be gathered in a minute comparison of texts, but it is hardly possible to explain it without ocular demonstration, and I am therefore obliged to pass it over on this occasion.

There is no dispute, and no possibility of disputing, that the agreements between the two texts are significant. Miss Doran writes:[2] 'If there were no adverse evidence these

[1] See particularly I. i. 128–9, II. i. 59–60, II. iv. 259–62.

[2] On p. 89 of her study.

correspondences . . . would have to be accepted as proof that a printed copy of Q1 was altered in accordance with the playhouse manuscript'. From this I conclude that she would prefer Daniel's view to her own, were it not for certain difficulties she finds in accepting it. Her chief objection is of an *a priori* character. If, she argues, the prompt-book was available, it would have been far less trouble to hand it over to the printer than to prepare a copy of the Quarto for press by collation with it: moreover, to have attempted the latter task would have been to produce illegible copy, so great and so numerous are the corrections that would have had to be made. That it would have been simpler to hand over the manuscript is obvious: equally obvious that there may have been good reasons for not doing so. The prompt-book was presumably still in use and bore the Master of the Revels' official licence for the performance of the play. To send it to press would be at any rate to run a serious risk.[1] The choice may well have lain between making a transcript for the purpose, or correcting a copy of the Quarto, and I have no doubt that the latter would be, and still more would be thought to be, the less laborious. As to the objection of illegibility, it is simply a matter of experiment, and I am confident that I could correct any page of the Quarto so as to serve as copy for the Folio without making it in the least illegible or even difficult for the printer.

Miss Doran further produces one very ingenious argument in favour of her hypothesis that the Folio was set up directly from the manuscript, by pointing out that it apparently contains a number of what are called graphic errors. Now, if the compositor of the Folio made mistakes through the misreading of handwriting, he must obviously have set it up from manuscript, and therefore not from the Quarto. Miss Doran adduces in support a large number of errors peculiar to the Folio, many of which I venture to think cannot possibly be of this type. But some there certainly are which one would naturally assume to be graphic. The most

[1] That the bulk of the copy for the 1623 folio came from the playhouse seems probable, but I doubt whether there is any evidence of the sacrifice of actual prompt-books. The trend of opinion seems to be in the opposite direction. Both Professor Dover Wilson and Signor Ramello have recently come to the conclusion that a transcript of the prompt-book was made in the case of *Hamlet*.

striking is the word 'Reuenge' in a passage[1] where the Quarto is unquestionably right in printing 'Reneag', deny, for in some hands the misreading would be a very easy one. Now, let me say at once, that while I entirely agree that many errors in Shakespeare's text are graphic errors, like 'alapt' for 'ataxt', I think the graphic theory is in danger of being, and in fact has been, overworked by Leon Kellner, Dover Wilson, and their followers. There are many errors which cannot be explained on graphic grounds, and it follows that apparently graphic errors must sometimes be in fact due to other causes. For instance, in the present case, suppose that the Folio compositor, intending to set 'Reneag', accidentally through foul-case substituted a *u* for the *n*; he would produce the word 'Reueag', which the proof reader would inevitably 'correct' to 'Reuenge'. Thus there may be nothing graphic about the error at all. And even if it is a misreading, it may still be due to the editor and not to the compositor. For 'Reneag' is not a very common word and may not have been understood. The editor may have consulted the manuscript and actually misread it 'Reueng', which, though certainly wrong, makes sense of a sort.[2] Thus I cannot think that the dependence of the Folio on manuscript copy is proved, and I conclude that the difficulties Miss Doran experiences in accepting Daniel's inference are of her own making.[3]

[1] II. ii. 84.

[2] Kent is arguing that obsequious servants obey every whim of their masters, and the prosecution of a vendetta might well be one of their activities.

There are other errors in the same passage in the Folio, which Miss Doran also treats as graphic, relying on Kellner for one very improbable misreading. I wholly disagree with her analysis. Elsewhere I think 'crying' for 'coyning' (IV. vi. 83) an unlikely misreading in any but the very worst hands of the period: more probably the compositor accidentally set 'coying' and the proof-reader guessed 'crying'. I believe that 'latch'd' for 'lancht' (II. i. 54) is correct: if not, it is a literal error, not a misreading. Similarly I am not convinced that 'spirits' for 'spurres' (II. i 78) is wrong: anyhow it is not an easy graphic error. Still less is 'strangenesse' for 'strange newes' (II. i. 89): it is a compositor's blunder of the memorial type.

[3] I ought to mention that Miss Doran has collected a number of instances in which the Folio agrees with the second quarto against the first, whence she concludes that the compositor of the Folio sometimes consulted a copy of the second quarto when in difficulty over the manuscript. Her examples include some rather striking coincidences, but they do not convince me of any actual dependence. Moreover, the second quarto of *Lear* is one of the 1619 collection, and it must not be forgotten that the reprints in the same series of the 'bad quartos' of the *Contention* and *Henry V* contain some curious anticipations of the texts in the first folio.

The Relation of the Texts

We have now concluded our bibliographical discussion of the Quarto variants and the copy that must be supposed to lie behind the two textual authorities, and it remains to consider what bearing these matters should have on an editor's procedure.

On Miss Doran's theory special authority might be supposed to attach to the Quarto, seeing that it was printed from the author's own manuscript. But the text of the Quarto is depreciated, in her view, first by being printed with quite remarkable incompetence from a confused and illegible original, and secondly by the rather extensive revision to which the author subsequently submitted it. Nevertheless, her theory affords what is probably the best defence of the large extent to which modern editors have relied on the Quarto for their readings. What, so far as I am aware, no theory can justify is the extent to which they have used the second quarto: it is an evil legacy from the days when the order of the editions was in doubt.

On the rival theory all authority rests with the Folio. Unless there is some serious reason to suspect corruption, we are bound to prefer its readings to those of the Quarto. But we must remember that, on this theory, the Folio was not printed directly from the manuscript, but from a copy of the Quarto which had been brought into general agreement with it. Some errors of the Quarto are, however, certain to have remained uncorrected. Thus it is only when the readings of the two differ that there is any strong ground for supposing that the Folio preserves that of the prompt-book; the negative inference, that where the two agree the prompt-book had the same reading, is much weaker. And so we reach the remarkable conclusion that the testimony of the Quarto and Folio together is of appreciably less authority than that of the Folio alone.

The editorial consequences of this are obvious, and the effect on the received text would be considerable in two ways. In the first place there would be a general restoration of Folio readings which editors have displaced in favour of the Quarto. The 'Globe' text must contain nearly four hundred Quarto readings (apart from passages only preserved in the Quarto) of which perhaps three hundred would go. This would involve some loss of polish, both because the Quarto text, having passed through the mouths of actors, has sometimes been worn smooth in a way the Folio text has not, and further because a long line of editors have pleased their fancy by adopting whatever reading appeared the more elegant to Augustan and Victorian taste. But this loss would, to my thinking, be more than offset by a considerable gain in pregnancy and vigour. The second effect might be even more considerable. For, by depriving the agreement of Quarto and Folio of some of its supposed authority, it would open the way to much greater freedom of emendation than would otherwise be proper. What use editors might make of this, and whether the final result would be good or bad, is perhaps better only guessing, but it would undoubtedly alter to an appreciable extent the play of *King Lear* as we know it.

Between the rival theories I do not claim to pronounce. I have not attempted to conceal the direction in which, after six months' patient work, I personally incline; but at the same time I can see here and there sufficient contradictions in the evidence to make me cautious, and I am inclined to think today what I thought five years ago, that there still remains a problem for investigation. Which shows that even bibliography is not yet able to answer all questions.

[I have not commented separately on details, such as the supposed shorthand origin of the Quarto, on which Greg later changed his mind. His final, but by no means confident, views on the text are to be found in *The Shakespeare First Folio*, 1955.—J.C.M.]

19. A Formulary of Collation[1]

SIGNATURES, as a term of art in the bibliography of printed books, are the letters (or signs) and numbers usually placed by the compositor at the foot of certain recto pages in each quire of a volume. Their proper purpose is to serve as a guide to the binder and ensure the correct order of the quires and the correct folding and gathering of the sheets. But they afford, and have always been recognized as affording, a method of reference to the leaves of a book, which is often more convenient than that by numerical foliation. They also serve another useful purpose; for by enumerating the signatures in a sort of formula we can readily define the make-up of a volume and so give the necessary information for detecting imperfect copies. This use too was early recognized, and in the sixteenth century (as indeed also in the fifteenth) many books, especially in Italy, were provided at the end with a list of the quire-signatures and a statement of the number of folds or units (double-leaves) in each. Such a list was called a 'register' (*registrum*, *registro*) and there might be a good deal to be said for applying the term to our formulas of collation, though I do not know that any bibliographer has done so hitherto.[2]

The following notes aim in the first place at stating and defining the common practice of bibliographers, both in respect to reference and record, and at establishing what appears to me its most convenient form. My main object, however, is to explore the possibilities of an extension of the usual notation to which I have been led by the force of circumstances, and which has gradually taken shape in the course of private cogitation and of consultation with others.[3]

[1] [1934, Mar. *The Library*, xiv. 365–82.] Read before the Bibliographical Society on 20 Nov. 1933. [The notation proposed is that adopted in my *Bibliography of the Printed Drama*, though in practice I did not need all the subtleties contemplated in my paper: see vol. iv, pp. cxlviii–clviii. My approach to the subject differs slightly from that of Professor Fredson Bowers in his *Principles of Bibliographical Description*, Princeton, 1949 (pp. 201–53).—1958.]

[2] 'Register' has sometimes been used to mean the signatures themselves, but this is clearly incorrect.

[3] In particular Dr. R. B. McKerrow, to whom, through frequent discussion, I owe far more than to any one else in this respect, as in many others. While he is in no

While I am, of course, describing and advocating the method I myself use, I have not the least wish to impose or press it upon anyone else,[1] but write merely in the hope that the results of a fairly long familiarity with the difficulties involved may prove of help to others who are called upon to meet them. I should add that my own experience has been mainly among English printed books of the sixteenth and seventeenth centuries, and that it is to meet the peculiarities of these that my method has been developed. It may not prove equally suitable in detail to other fields.

I shall be mainly concerned with the elaboration of the collational formula or register to meet the commoner irregularities and abnormalities of book-construction, but in the first place there are a few things that need to be said about the use of signatures for references, since this is in some respects their more fundamental function.

Essentially we refer to a particular leaf of a book by simply copying down the signature which the printer has placed on it.[2] But in practice the matter is not quite as straightforward

way bound by anything I may say here or in the least responsible for my exposition, and while there are a few points at which we differ, the following is in the main an agreed statement, and some of the most useful and original features of the notation are his own invention. His practice, so far as he has seen fit to develop it, is expounded with habitual lucidity in his *Introduction to Bibliography* (pp. 155–61).

1 A certain fluidity is perhaps desirable in any system of the sort, since the information it is sought to impart will vary to some extent with the nature of the work in hand. Some bibliographers may have no use for the methodical elaboration here proposed, others may wish to carry it at some points even farther. I think, however, that a good deal of confusion would be avoided if all whose business it is to describe books were to adopt the conventions outlined in the present article in so far as they are applicable to their particular purpose.

2 We must bear in mind that the signature belongs to the leaf, not to the particular (recto) page upon which it is printed, and that a signature-reference *simpliciter* is always to the leaf unless the contrary is implied. If we wish to refer to the page we should specify *recto* or *verso*. This is usually done by placing a superior 'r' or 'v' after the signature, e.g. $A1^r$, $B2^v$. Unfortunately 'r' and 'v' are a little liable to confusion both in script and type, and consequently most bibliographers prefer to omit the 'r' where it is clear from the context that it is the page and not the leaf that is in question. The chances of confusion, at any rate in formal descriptions, are as a matter of fact very rare, but the beginner should be on his guard. (The statement 'C3 is printed in italic' would properly refer to the leaf: if the page were meant we should have to specify $C3^r$. Note that 'Woodcut on C3' can only refer to the page, but 'Woodcuts on C3' ambiguous.) Some writers attempt to avoid the possible confusion of 'r' and 'v' by using 'a' and 'b' instead. The objection to this is that 'a' and 'b' are often and conveniently used to refer to the columns of the page; thus $D4^{vb}$ means the second column on the verso of D4. (Personally, and perhaps inconsistently,

as this. For one thing it is rare for every leaf of the quire to be signed: the best and perhaps the most usual practice was to sign one leaf beyond the middle. For purposes of reference we need to complete the signatures of the quire, which we can easily do by counting, verifying the count if necessary by the signed conjugates. In ordinary references there is no need to indicate whether a leaf is actually signed or not. The first leaf of each quire is often (I think usually) signed with the signature letter alone, but it must be remembered that it is in fact the first leaf of the quire and that the number 1 is understood: a reference D, for instance, applies to the quire and should on no account be given when what is really meant is D1.

Further, the exact form and fount of a signature are seldom if ever significant in the period with which I am familiar. In some books the signature-numbers are in roman numerals, in some in arabic; it is quite common to find the two used indifferently in the same volume and even in the same quire. In references arabic should always be used. As regards signature-letters, the distinction between upper- and lower-case (in the single alphabet) is significant, and must be retained; that between black letter, roman, and italic is not. Usually the printer set the signature in whatever type he happened to be handling when he reached the foot of the page.[1] To print a reference in such a form as 𝕯.iij. (instead of D3) is to my mind senseless pedantry, a waste of time, energy, and money.[2]

Thus, for purposes of reference, we complete the signatures of a book, reduce them to a uniform and standard style, and so quote them.[3] Some bibliographers make a practice of writing the leaf-numbers inferior, e.g. A_2 instead of A2: I believe it is thought to be more elegant. I have never been able to discover any sense in the practice, which suggests something recondite and obscures the plain meaning and origin of the notation.

I do use 'a' and 'b' for recto and verso in connexion, not with a signature, but with a foliation number, and should then use 1 and 2 to indicate the columns, e.g. fol. 5^{b2}.)

[1] Early books were set up page by page, not in long galleys.

[2] This applies, of course, to *reference*. There may sometimes be occasions (as when recording misprints) when it is necessary or desirable to *quote* a signature in the exact form in which it is printed. In that case I should enclose it in quotation marks.

[3] Doubled and duplicated alphabets, along with various incidental complications will be considered later in connexion with the formulas.

As a refinement it is sometimes desirable to indicate whether a particular leaf is actually signed or whether the reference-signature is inferential. This should only be done in work of a formal character, such as listing in detail the contents of a volume, never in incidental reference. The most usual method of indicating an inferential signature is to enclose it in square brackets, as [C8].[1] Or, since we have decided to ignore differences of type in the original signatures, we can indicate it more neatly by italicizing the reference, as *C*8: a method I personally prefer.[2] It should always, however, be remembered that the signature itself relates to the leaf and not the page, and it is only when the leaf is unsigned that the signature is inferential. No verso page ever bears a signature, but it would be absurd to write [A2^v] or *A*2^v if the recto was signed—the signature in such a case is in no way inferential.

Before passing on to the construction of collational formulas, it will be convenient to consider one or two miscellaneous uses and conventions. It happens quite often that we want to make a statement that shall apply severally to all the quires of a book, and it is therefore useful to have a symbol for the signatures collectively. For this Dr. McKerrow has ingeniously suggested the mark $.[3] Thus instead of saying that a book was in eights we might write $^{8}; or we might say of a quarto '$4 signed' to mean that, contrary to custom, the last leaf of each quire of four (as well as the first three) bore a signature.[4] I also think (and Dr. McKerrow agrees) that the symbol $ might be used to mean *any* signature, as well as *every* signature, since there does not appear to be much danger of

1 It would be quite logical to write C[1] where the first leaf of the quire bears the letter C alone, and [C]2 and [C]3 in these rare cases in which only the first leaf of the quarto bears the signature-letter, the second and third having the number alone. I should, however, deprecate such meticulous elaboration.

2 Logically, no doubt, the whole signature should be italicized, e.g. *C8*, but it is more convenient and quite sufficient to italicize the letter only, e.g. *C*8. Of course, this method only applies to alphabetical signatures; arbitrary signs must still be bracketed if inferential.

3 In speaking it may be called 'sig'.

4 Statements such as '$4 signed', and indeed all statements that apply to the signatures of a book generally, are to be interpreted subject to the qualification 'normally'. Thus '$4 signed' would still be valid, although K4 say was not signed owing to some peculiarity that would prevent *any* leaf bearing a signature, such as being a special title or a final blank. (Actually I do not myself use the term '$4 signed': if each leaf of a quire or a volume bears a signature I describe it as 'fully signed'.)

confusion. This would enable us to make such a statement as: 'If the text of a quarto ends on $3, then $4 may be assumed to be a blank.'[1]

This symbol is particularly useful in recording variations in the running-title of a book, which are often regularly recurrent owing to the type being kept standing from sheet to sheet. It enables us, for example, if a particular error occurs on the verso of the third leaf of each quire, to say that it occurs on $3v. Such variations, however, are often not persistent throughout the volume, occurring sometimes, for instance, in alternate sheets. We require, therefore, in addition, some simple convention whereby to indicate certain leaves of certain quires. All we need do is to postulate that $'$1,2 for instance shall mean $1,2 and '$1,2, and that $–'$1,2 shall mean the first and second leaves of all quires from $ to '$ inclusive. We can then state succinctly and precisely that a particular variant is found, for instance, on ACEG3–5 or on ADF–K4v,6. Note that in this case there must be no comma between the letters: $, '$4 would mean the whole of quire $ and the fourth leaf of quire '$. We are bound to retain a comma between the numerals (otherwise 1,2 would be indistinguishable from 12): this does not matter, but I suggest that in series of the sort there should be no space after the comma.

I have recently found the need of some method for indicating conjugate leaves (especially in a folio in which the quire normally consists of several sheets) and a sufficiently handy device seems ready to hand. In merely enumerating individual leaves of a quire we habitually separate their numbers by commas, e.g. $1,4, $5,6, $3,4. I propose that if we wish to indicate that the leaves in question form conjugate pairs we should replace the comma by a period (much as in algebra we write *x.y* for the product of *x* and *y*). Thus in a folio in sixes we should write for the outer, middle, and inner sheets of a gathering $1.6, $2.5, $3.4 respectively. And in the case of a quarto in eights, we could use the same device to distinguish

[1] The symbol $ must have a constant identity throughout any individual statement or formula in which it occurs. If we want to introduce several variables we must distinguish them as $, '$, "$, &c. We may also conveniently write, for instance, $(—K) to mean 'every signature except K'.

the two sheets of which each quire is composed by writing \$1.2.7.8, and \$3.4.5.6.

One other notation I have often found useful: a device for indicating the outer and inner formes of sheets. The most handy and distinctive seems to be the addition of (o) and (i) to the signature-letter (\$(o), \$(i)). Thus I write, for example, A(o) for the outer forme of sheet A, K(i) for the inner forme of sheet K, B–D(o), EGI(i), and so forth.[1]

We are now in a position to discuss the formulas of collation embodying the register or sequence of signatures that defines the make-up of the book either as it was printed or as it was meant to be issued.[2] And we shall observe at the outset that the formula applies to the ideally perfect copy,[3] since one of its main uses is to set up a standard of reference whereby to detect imperfections.[4]

The construction of the formula depends on two simple principles: the conventional order of the signatures and a conventional device for indicating the number of leaves in each. The latter consists of writing the number of the leaves as an 'index' after the signature-letter; thus if the signatures of a quire run \$1–8, we write $\$^8$, and so on.[5]

1 In this simple form the device is only applicable when the quire consists of a single sheet. But the convention suggested in the previous paragraph enables us to deal with other cases by writing, for instance, \$2.5(o) or \$1.2.7.8.(i)

2 On this distinction much might be written, but it is not necessary to argue the question here. In at least nine cases out of ten the two are identical. When they are not I prefer the issue-formula to the printing-formula, partly on the ground that while the former may be uncertain the latter is often indeterminable: also that the former gives the fuller information. It would be possible and logical to give both so far as they can be ascertained. I shall return to the point incidentally when discussing cancels (cf. p. 311, note 4).

3 A copy containing *cancellanda* is not ideally perfect, it is redundant.

4 I do not think a collational formula should be used to describe the condition of an individual copy. The ideal copy should be formulated and the imperfections recorded. True, that in the case of a very rare book, the evidence may be insufficient for the construction of a perfect formula, but I would always rather aim at an ideal formula, however incomplete and full of queries my attempt might be, than misrepresent the ideal by formulating the imperfect actuality. Of course, if the collation of the only known copy of a book appears to be normal, we assume that the copy is perfect. This seems at once necessary and legitimate, though the inference *may* be incorrect.

5 It is natural and convenient to refer to these superior numerals as 'index' numbers, though there is no analogy between them and arithmetical 'powers'.

In my opinion the index numbers should always be even, but this is a moot point which will fall for discussion later (see p. 309). It should be observed that in the printed registers of early books the unit is the fold of two conjugate leaves, whereas

Signatures follow the Latin alphabet of twenty-three letters (in which there is no J, U, or W). Thus a normal quarto of ten sheets, for instance, consists of quires signed A, B, C, D, E, F, G, H, I, K, each of four leaves—'in fours' as we say. This, therefore, we express in the formula A–K^4. If the number of leaves in the quires is not constant they must be severally indicated, and the formula loses its simplicity: we may, for instance, have to write A^2 B–I^4 K^2 or, more irregularly still, A^4 B–C^8 D^6 E–F^4 G^2 H–I^8 K^4. Sometimes at the end of the alphabet we find certain conventional signs added: since these have no certain number or order they require to be individually specified: the commonest series gives the formula (if in fours) A–Z^4 &^{4}ɔ^{4}ꝶ^4. Other arbitrary signs, such as * and ¶, are often used for preliminaries; for instance we may have *^{4} ¶^{4} A–K^4.[1]

But if the number of quires much exceeds twenty-three a doubled alphabet is commonly used, after that a treble one, and so on. Here we come upon a slight complication. If the signatures are in lower case, a becomes aa and aaa, &c., and all is straightforward. But when an upper-case alphabet is doubled, A may become either AA or Aa—usually the latter. It is possible that printers occasionally distinguished between AA and Aa; but if so the instances are too few to deserve recognition, and in practice we ignore them. This enables us to write 2a in place of aa, and 2A in place of either AA or of Aa. The convention is important, since, if our formulas are to be manageable and our references convenient, we must endeavour to avoid such clumsy terms as Aaaaaaa^4 (= 7A^4) or DDDDDD7^v (= 6D7^v) which would otherwise occur.[2]

we reckon by single leaves. Thus 'ABC sunt quaterniones' or 'ABC tutti quaderni' is equivalent to our 'A–C in eights'. This system originated, of course, in counting the separate sheets of vellum that had to be sewn together to form a quire in a manuscript: it also, in the case of a folio, gives the number of sheets of paper that constitute a quire. Correspondence between the old and the modern reckoning is one reason why I wish to keep the index numbers of our formulas even. One might, indeed, consider the old system as theoretically the more satisfactory, but ours follows directly from the actual signatures; there is an obvious and satisfying simplicity in equating \$1–8 with \$^{8}.

[1] If the quires are similar throughout we could place the index at the end only (e.g. ¶ A–Z&^{4}), but I do not feel certain that such an attempt at simplification might not lead to trouble.

[2] I am assured by my incunabulist friends that in the fifteenth century printers did, sometimes at any rate, distinguish between AA and Aa, using both in the same

We assume, unless anything is said to the contrary, that the signature sequence consists of the regular alphabetical series of twenty-three letters with no extra signs, and that the alphabet repeats itself regularly in doubled and trebled form, &c. If, therefore, the signatures of a book run A–Z^4, 2A–2Z^4, 3A–3K^4, we are able to simplify the formula by writing A–3K^4.[1]

But besides being doubled alphabets may be duplicated. It is quite common, especially where a book has been farmed out among several printers, to find it made up of separate sections each signed with a similar series of letters. Take such a simple instance as a volume whose thirty quires are signed A–K and A–V. Obviously the letters A–K are here useless for reference since they occur twice over, and though the letters L–V are unambiguous, it is desirable to treat the second series as a whole. I propose therefore, in such a case, to distinguish the signatures of the second series by prefixing a superior 2, those of a third series (if there is one) by a superior 3, and so on; thus writing for example ^{2}A, ^{3}A, &c. The formula for the book in question (if in fours) would therefore run A–K^4, ^{2}A–V^4. Or we might find a book in which the signatures ran, in three series, A–2C^4, A–X^4, A–3K^4: in this case we should write the formula as A–2C^4, ^{2}A–X^4, ^{3}A–3K^4.[2]

It is quite common to find a preliminary quire without a

book. If the practice was common I see no way out of the difficulty. If on the other hand it was occasional only, I should treat the alphabet or series as duplicated (see below). I would myself go a long way to avoid unwieldy terms.

1 We must remember that 2A is only a shorthand symbol for Aa or AA, and that the numeral must, therefore, always accompany the letter. We are not at liberty, for instance, to write 3A–K^4, any more than we could write Aaa–K^4.

We treat arbitrary signs as if they were alphabets of one letter only: thus for ¶¶ we write 2¶, and for the series ¶, ¶¶, ¶¶¶, ¶¶¶¶, in fours, we write ¶–4¶^{4}.

2 In the first of the two examples cited we might be tempted to interpret the symbol ^{2}A as 'inferential 2A', but the second example shows that this would be incorrect, since here the real doubles forbid our introducing imaginary ones as well. The correct interpretation of ^{2}A is 'A of the second series'. And it should be observed that since the superior numeral serves merely to distinguish the series, it need not be repeated before each letter *in the formula*. Thus we write, as above, ^{2}A–X^4 (not ^{2}A–^{2}X^4) and ^{3}A–3K^4 (not ^{3}A–^{3}3K^4). (In this it differs from the 2 in 2A, &c.) But *in references* the series-number must, of course, always appear. Thus, to specify the last leaf of each of the series just mentioned we should have to write ^{2}X4 and ^{3}3K4 respectively. On the other hand, though it would be intelligible, we should never in practice write, for instance, A–^{3}K^4, since it is most unlikely that the several series would consist of complete alphabets.

signature, while the text of the book begins with a quire signed B. In such a case it is natural and quite proper to give the first quire the inferential signature A (that is, to assume that if it had not, for whatever reason, been left unsigned, it would have borne the signature A), but at the same time it is desirable to indicate in the formula that the signature is inferential and not actually present. This can be done by placing the A within brackets, or, as I prefer, printing it in italic: e.g. [A]^4 B–K^4 or *A*^{4} B–K^4.[1] Similarly, if a later quire of the alphabetical series is left unsigned, we may equally assume a normal signature for it: we may, for instance, write A–G^4 *H*^{4} I–K^4 or A–K^4 *L*^{2}.

But another quite common practice was to begin the text with signature A and afterwards prefix one or more unsigned quires for preliminaries. It is impossible in such a case to guess what arbitrary sign would have been used had the quire been signed, and we therefore need some conventional symbol to indicate such an unsigned preliminary. For this π has been suggested by Dr. McKerrow: it seems eminently suitable and has already been adopted by more than one bibliographer. If there are several quires they may be distinguished as π, 2π, &c.

Additional unsigned quires are also occasionally found inserted at later points in the normal series. For such I have proposed the symbol χ on the analogy of π. If several quires of the sort occur, either together or at different points in the series, we can distinguish them likewise as χ, 2χ, and so on.[2]

We also sometimes find a preliminary quire signed A followed by another A belonging to the regular alphabetical series, and we need some method of distinguishing them. Since we naturally do not wish to degrade the main series to the rank of ^{2}A, &c., it seems obvious that the preliminary A should be designated $^{\pi}$A. Should there be two preliminary quires A and B, they would of course become $^{\pi}$A and $^{\pi}$B.

[1] Note, in the first place, that the index is outside the bracket or is not italicized—there is nothing inferential about it; secondly, that the inferential signature is separately recorded and not as part of the sequence: [A]–K^4 or *A*–K^4 would have no precise meaning, since the dash can only join similar terms of the series.

[2] There is nothing esoteric about the symbols π and χ. So far as I am concerned they are merely more distinctive substitutes for the [*p*] and [*x*] I was in the habit of using to indicate 'preliminary' and 'extra' quires. But any one who likes may imagine that they stand for *πρότερος* and, perhaps, *χαρίσιος*!

In the same way we may find in the body of a book an additional quire bearing a signature that duplicates that of one of the adjoining quires. The signatures may, for instance, run A,B,C,C,D, &c.; in this case the insertion can be suitably distinguished as ^{x}C. It will usually be obvious which quire is original and which additional, and it is the latter that should be distinguished, whether it comes before or after the other.[1]

Now, when a quire is signed with an arbitrary symbol or is given the conventional signature χ, its position is clearly enough indicated in the collational formula, and for that purpose may be left as it stands. But for purposes of reference, in the absence of the formula or register, such a signature is of very little use, since there is nothing to suggest whereabouts in the book it is to be found. We therefore need some method of indicating the position of an arbitrary or conventional signature. If it occurs as a preliminary this will most naturally be done by connecting it with π, and we shall for instance write $^{\pi}$¶ on the analogy of $^{\pi}$A. In the body of the book the same object can be achieved by prefixing (as superior) the letter of the next preceding alphabetical signature. Thus in the series A, B, χ, C, D, the position of χ may be shown by writing $^{B}\chi$, while in the series A–Z, &, ɔ, ꝶ, the position of each of the arbitrary signatures can be sufficiently indicated by ^{z}&, ^{z}ɔ, ^{z}ꝶ.[2] It must be understood that this device is for use in reference only, there is no need to complicate the formula by its introduction.[3]

Signatures which duplicate those of the regular alphabetical series are sometimes differentiated from them in some *ad hoc* manner in the book itself. They may, for instance, be distinguished by the use of different type (though the cases are rare and doubtful). This we have agreed to ignore, and we shall treat them as cases of simple duplication. Or they may be distinguished by the addition of an asterisk or obelus or

1 Of course the duplicated signatures may not occur together, though this is a rare occurrence. It usually arises through a clumsy attempt at differentiation: for example, an inserted quire after C may be signed 'Cc' and there may be another 'Cc' in the regular series later on. The first should be distinguished as ^{x2}C.

2 The ^{x2}C mentioned in the previous note can be located by writing ^{Cx2}C.

3 If we do allow its introduction into the formula it will enable us to dispense with 2χ, 3χ, &c., except when the unsigned quires occur together. But this is hardly worth while. In reference $n\chi$ can be replaced by $^{s}\chi$ when it occurs alone.

some such sign. Whether it is more convenient to preserve or ignore such distinctions must depend on circumstances, each case to be treated on its merits. Brackets are best ignored as liable to lead to confusion. Distinctions, when ignored in the formula, should be recorded in describing the book.

One further point deserves passing mention; the use of commas in the formulas. Any lavish use is to be deprecated. One occasionally sees formulas hirsute with commas merely bewildering. But some good bibliographers consider that a fairly generous use tends to clearness. With this view I do not personally agree, and I endeavour to dispense with them as far as possible. Generally, I think, there are only two cases in which they are helpful. Thus I place a comma before a duplicated alphabet to avoid a clash between the superior prefix and the preceding index: e.g. A–K^{4}, ^{2}A–V^{4}. And I also use a comma to mark off any incomplete alphabet (e.g. A–K^{4}, 2A–4^{4}) or a preliminary run of arbitrary signs. Of course, I should not hesitate to introduce a comma in any particular case if I thought it would make the formula clearer. After each item of the formula (e.g. A 1 or B^{4} or C–D^{8} or 2A–K^{6} or ^{3}X–Z^{2}) there should be a thin space and no more, and no space should be allowed within an item. Here, as an example, is the collation-formula of an actual quarto:

> ¶^{4} 2¶^{4}(—2¶4) 3¶–4¶^{4} 5¶ 1, a–k^{8}, B^{4} C–P^{8} Q^{4} S–Z^{8} ℂ^{4}, ^{2}S^{4} V–Y^{8}, ^{3}A–B^{8}, ^{4}A–C^{8} *x*D^{2} D^{2}.[1]

So far we have been dealing with abnormalities in the signatures; we must now consider cases of abnormality in the number of leaves in the quire.[2] I have already explained that the number of leaves in a quire is indicated by an index affixed to the signature-letter ($1–8 = $^{8}). For my own part I hold the view that the index does not merely record the number of leaves in the quire or gathering, but that it should indicate the make-up as well. Thus I take the plain index number to imply so many leaves in regular folds or units: for instance $^{6} means three pairs of conjugate leaves. It follows that (in my opinion) the index should always be an

[1] G. Gascoigne, *Works*, 1587. Some of the symbols used will be explained later.

[2] It is in this part of our discussion that we shall discover the great convenience of the symbol $.

even number.[1] If the number of leaves is odd and the pairs unascertainable, I think the use of the index misleading, and should myself write, for instance, $\$(3\text{ ll.})$ to mean that there were three leaves in the quire without implying anything of the make-up.[2] But this notation is seldom needed, since it is usually possible to ascertain the original structure of the quire, and in that case it seems desirable to indicate it. Every quire, as printed, consisted of an even number of leaves,[3] and we may therefore indicate its make-up by an even index number, adding in parentheses the nature of the subsequent modification. Suppose, for example, that in a particular quire the third leaf out of four has been suppressed,[4] we should indicate the fact by writing $\$^4(-\$3)$. Or if in a quire of eight the seventh and eighth leaves have been suppressed, we shall write $\$^8(-\$7,8)$. Inserted leaves can be dealt with in like manner. If in a quire of four an extra leaf is inserted between the third and fourth, we shall describe the quire as

[1] On this point I differ from Dr. McKerrow, who would allow odd index numbers. I quite admit the logical soundness of his argument, but on the other hand I feel strongly the practical importance of retaining the fold as the unit of collation. My objection to odd index numbers is that they are so uninformative. Thus $\$^7$ might be a quire of six in which an extra leaf had been inserted, or a quire of eight in which one had been suppressed—a rather important difference. Whenever there is an uneven number of leaves in a quire, one particular leaf must be odd, and I think its position and nature should, if possible, be defined.

In the discussion that followed the reading of this paper Dr. McKerrow pleaded strongly for the permissive use of a less rigorous system in which the index would imply nothing beyond the actual number of leaves found in the quire, and in which, therefore, odd index numbers would be allowed. I see no objection to the use of such a system, provided that it is made clear in any particular case which method is being followed. The appearance of odd index numbers would of course be a warning that the writer was adopting the looser system, but these may not always occur. I should have the strongest objection to writing $\$^6$ for a quire of eight in which the last two leaves had been suppressed, unless it was explicitly stated that nothing more than the actual number of surviving leaves was implied.

[2] For a single leaf I write $\$1$; while $\$1\text{–}2$ would mean two separate leaves as distinct from the conjugate pair $\$^2$.

[3] This is not necessarily true in the case of a folio, in which the quire is a gathering of several sheets, but in fact it probably always was so. [I neglect the rare case of a volume made up of unfolded sheets (1^0).]

I am aware, through Dr. McKerrow, of the existence of certain wholly abnormal books in which, for some particular purpose, the quires were made to contain an odd number of leaves throughout. Happily they are very rare, and I do not think they are worth taking into consideration. (In fact they could probably be described by the method here proposed.) Nor do I take account of books made up of separate unfolded sheets, in which the gatherings (if they exist) are quite arbitrary.

[4] Not accidentally lost, of course, since we are describing an ideal copy.

$\$^{4}(\$3+1)$, if two leaves are inserted as $\$^{4}(\$3+2)$. If the two inserted leaves form a unit signed ¶ (for instance) we write $\$^{4}(\$3+\P^{2})$. If the inserted unit is unsigned we write $\$^{4}(\$3+\chi^{2})$. And so on.[1]

Inserted leaves, if unsigned, can be referred to by the positions they occupy in the quire, thus the first leaf inserted after $\$3$ we shall call $\$3+1$, the second $\$3+2$.[2] If the inserted leaves are signed they will naturally be referred to by their own signatures. These, however, will not indicate their position, and it will be best to follow the analogy of unsigned leaves by writing, for instance, $\$(\P 1)$ or $\$(\chi 2)$ to mean ¶1 or $\chi 2$ in signature $\$$.[3]

Of course, suppression and addition may occur in the same quire, and we may therefore get terms such as $\$^{4}(-\$2, \$3+1)$.

The same method can be applied to the recording of cancels, since these are in effect only particular cases of suppression *plus* addition. Thus, if a leaf (say the third of a quire of four) is cut out and another inserted in its place, the fact can be conveniently indicated by writing $\$^{4}(\pm\$3)$. If the number of leaves in the *cancellandum* and *cancellans*

[1] It would be much neater to write, for instance, $\$^{4}(-3)$ and $\$^{4}(3+2)$ in place of $\$^{4}(-\$3)$ and $\$^{4}(\$3+2)$, but it would lead to ambiguity in some of the more complicated cases (cf. p. 311, note 2).

A leaf inserted between quires is capable of description in several different ways. It may be described as added to the preceding quire, e.g. $\$^{4}(\$4+1)$. Or it may be described as independent of the quires, e.g. $\$^{4}\chi 1\,'\$^{4}$. But in the latter case it would have to be *referred to* as $^{\$}\chi 1$, so that there is no great difference between the two. This is not very satisfactory since the leaf may be more intimately associated with the following quire. The difficulty could be met by writing $'\$^{4}(1+'\$1)$.

[2] It is important to remember that a leaf inserted say after $\$3$ is $\$3+1$ and not $\$4$. This, of course, is obvious where the adjacent leaves are signed. Thus in an octavo we might very likely find a quire $\$1, \$2, \$3, [\$3+1], \$4, \$5, [\$6+8]$. But should we find $\$1$–5 regularly signed and followed by four unsigned leaves, we must be on our guard against assuming that the leaf following $\$5$ is $\$6$—it may be $\$5+1$.

Unfortunately, inserted leaves sometimes actually bear signatures that violate this rule. In the first case mentioned above, $\$3+1$ might very likely bear the signature '$\$3^{*}$'. This is quite in order and should cause no trouble. But in the second case $\$5+1$ might be signed $\$6$ (as a direction to the binder to insert it after $\$5$) and so easily mislead any one who did not happen to remember that $\$6$ would not normally bear any signature at all. In such cases (where the inserted leaf bears a signature relating it to the quire) the signature must indeed be given, but it will be best to distinguish it by quotation marks, thus $\$^{8}(\$3+`\$3^{*}')$ or $\$^{8}(\$5+`\$6')$.

[3] In the case of the signatures contemplated in the previous note we should write $\$(`\$3^{*}')$ and $\$(`\$6')$, which would be sufficient warning of something irregular.

differ, the formula becomes more complicated, but we can always write, for example, $\$^4(-\$3+\chi 1,2)$,[1] i.e. two separate leaves replacing $\$3$, or, $\$^4(-\$3+\chi^2)$, i.e. an unsigned unit replacing $\$3$, or else $\$^4(-\$2,3+\chi 1)$, i.e. one leaf replacing $\$2$ and $\$3$, and so on.[2]

It was not unusual to begin printing the text of a quarto pamphlet on A1 [or B1] and then, if the text ended say on K3, to print the title on K4 and either remove this to the beginning or fold it round the back of the book. The formula for such a pamphlet would be $\pi 1$ A–I^4 K^4(–K4) [or *A*1 B–I^4 K^4 (–K4)], and it would have to be explained that $\pi 1$ [or *A*1] was in fact K4. Or, if it were thought desirable to include this information in the formula, we could write $\pi 1$(= K4) A–I^4 K^4(–K4).[3]

But whenever the text of a quarto ends on $\$3$ there is another possibility, namely that $\$4$ will be used to print a cancel for some other leaf in the book. Indeed, any later leaf which would otherwise be blank may be used for this purpose. When, therefore, a volume contains cancels we must be suspicious of hypothetical blanks, unless we know that the cancels were printed after the original issue of the book.[4]

1 [It might be thought that the simpler formula $\$(-\$3+2)$ would suffice, but that would not provide a suitable reference for the leaves of the *cancellans*. Given the form proposed these can always be specified as $\$(\chi^1)$ or $\$(\chi 2)$. In the case of a preliminary sheet π can be substituted for χ.]

2 The formula for the second issue, or more precisely the later state, of *Troilus and Cressida*, 1609, is A^4(–A1+¶^{2}) B–L^{4}M^2. Note the difference between $\$^4(-\$2,3+1)$ and $\$^4(-\$2,\$3+1)$; which shows that $\$^4(-2,3+1)$ would be ambiguous.

3 In such a case it may not be possible to prove that the title was really printed as part of the last sheet, for the same make-up would result from an original π^2A–K^4 of which the blanks, $\pi 1$ and K4, have disappeared. I do not think that the identity of $\pi 1$ with K4 should be assumed unless it can be clearly demonstrated. But the question of hypothetical blanks is a troublesome one. An extremely common make-up for plays is: title unsigned, B–K^4, L1. Here it is obviously possible that the title is really L2. But experience has taught me that when a considerable number of copies have survived the blanks, A1 and L2, almost always turn up in the end. I therefore make it a rule to assume their existence unless I see reason to suspect the contrary, and should write the formula for the book in question *A*^{2} B–K^4 L^2, adding 'A1, L2 blank ?'. A^2 and L^2 would indeed most likely be printed together as parts of a single sheet—but that is another matter, which does not concern us here.

4 It is in cases of this sort that the distinction between the printing-formula and the issue-formula becomes important (cf. p. 303, note 2). Suppose, for example, a quarto of five sheets of text and one preliminary, in which the title was printed as part of the last sheet and a cancel as part of the preliminary sheet; then the printing-formula would be of the type ⁋^{4} B–F^4, whereas the issue-formula would be something like *A*1(= F4) ⁋^{4}(–⁋4) B–D^4 E^4(±E2 = ⁋4) F^4(–F4).

It often happens that in an octavo, for instance, the last quire is found to consist of six leaves only. Although such a quire does not form a complete sheet and cannot have been printed as it stands, it may yet be a genuine 'six' ('ternium') either the inner or outer fold of the 'eight' having been removed,[1] and the remainder signed as a quire of six. We describe it as $\$^6$. But inspection may show that it is in fact the seventh and eighth leaves that are missing. If these were blank they will probably turn up in the end, and we may then describe the quire as $\$^8$. If not, they may have contained other matter—perhaps cancels—and been purposely removed. In that case it is incorrect to describe the quire either as $\$^6$ or as plain $\$^8$: it is $\$^8(-\$7,8)$. Only search can determine the question.

This, so far as my experience goes, provides for all the more usual abnormalities in the make-up of English books of the sixteenth and seventeenth centuries. No doubt most bibliographers could produce other instances beyond those I have considered, and they are free to invent ways of describing them if they find it desirable to do so. But some, I think, will consider that I have already elaborated convention beyond the limits of convenience. I can but plead that I have only introduced fresh notations to meet actual needs and not of malice prepense.

REFERENCE KEY

		PAGE
(1)	\$ = all signatures *or* any signature.	301
(2)	\$, '\$, "\$ = different (unspecified) signatures.	302
(3)	\$'\$1,2 = \$1,2+'\$1,2.	302
(4)	\$–'\$1,2 = \$1,2 . . . '\$1,2.	302
(5)	\$(o), \$(i) = outer and inner formes.	303
(6)	\$1–8 = $\$^8$.	303
(7)	A–Z^4 &^{4} ꝯ^4 ꝝ^4: *^{4} ¶^{4} A–K^4.	304
(8)	a, aa, aaa, . . .	304
(9)	A, AA, AAA, . . .	304
(10)	A, Aa, Aaa, . . .	304
(11)	aa = 2a.	304
(12)	AA *or* Aa = 2A.	304

1 It would be very anomalous for either of the intervening folds to be removed.

(13) Aaaaaaa^{4} (= 7A^{4}): DDDDDD7^{v} (= 6D7^{v}). 304
(14) A–Z^{4}, 2A–2Z^{4}, 3A–3K^{4} = A–3K^{4}. 305
(15) A–K^{4} + A–V^{4} = A–K^{4}, ^{2}A–V^{4}. 305
(16) A–2C^{4} + A–X^{4} + A–3K^{4} = A–2C^{4}, ^{2}A–X^{4}, ^{3}A–3K^{4}. 305
(17) *A*^{4} B–K^{4} *or* [A]^{4} B–K^{4} (first quire unsigned). 306
(18) π, 2π, 3π, . . . = unsigned preliminary quires. 306
(19) χ, 2χ, 3χ, . . . = unsigned additional quires. 306
(20) $^{\pi}$\$ = preliminary quire with duplicated signature. 306
(21) $^{\chi}$\$ = additional quire with duplicated signature. 307
(22) $^{\pi}$❡ = preliminary quire signed ❡ (in reference only). 307
(23) $^{B}\chi$ = additional unsigned quire following B (in reference only). 307
(24) ^{z}&, ^{z}ꝰ, ^{z}ꝝ = final quires arbitrarily signed (in reference only). 307
(25) ¶^{4} 2¶^{4}(–¶4) 3¶–4¶^{4} 5¶1, a–k^{8}, B^{4} C–P^{8} Q^{4} S–Z^{8} ❡^{4}, ^{2}A–C$^{8\chi}$D^{2} D^{2}, ^{3}A^{4}($\pm$A1) χ^{2} B–Q^{4} *R*^{2}. 308
(26) \$(*n*ll.) = quire of *n* leaves, structure unascertainable. 309
(27) \$^{4}(–\$3) = quire of four leaves, the third cancelled (remainder three). 309
(28) \$^{8}(–\$7,8) = quire of eight leaves, the seventh and eighth cancelled (remainder six). 309
(29) \$^{4}(\$3 + 1) = quire of four, with one leaf inserted after the third (total five). 310
(30) \$^{4}(\$3 + 2) = *ditto*, with two leaves inserted (total six). 310
(31) \$^{4}(\$3 + ¶^{2}) = *ditto*, with unit signed ¶ inserted. 310
(32) \$^{4}(\$3 + χ^{2}) = *ditto*, with unsigned unit inserted. 310
(33) \$3 + 1, \$3 + 2 = first (second) inserted leaf after \$3. 310
(34) \$(¶1), \$(χ2) = inserted leaf ¶1 (χ2) in \$. 310
(35) \$^{4}(–\$2, \$3 + 1) = quire of four leaves, the second cancelled and one leaf inserted after the third (resultant four). 310
(36) \$^{4}($\pm$\$3) = quire of four leaves, the third replaced by a cancel. 310
(37) \$^{4}(–\$3 + χ1,2) = quire of four leaves, the third replaced by two leaves (resultant five). 311
(38) \$^{4}(–\$3 + χ^{2}) = *ditto*, with unsigned unit replacing \$3. 311
(39) \$^{4}(–\$2,3 + χ1) = quire of four leaves, the second and third replaced by a single-leaf cancel (resultant three). 311
(40) A^{4}(–A1 + ¶^{2}) B–L^{4} M^{2}. 311
(41) π1 A–I^{4} K^{4}(–K4) [*or* *A*1 B–I^{4} K^{4}(–K4)]: π1(= K4) A–I^{4} K^{4}(–K4). 311

20. Was There a 1612 Quarto of *Epicene*?[1]

So far as can be discovered no text of Jonson's comedy, *Epicene or The Silent Woman*, now exists earlier than that which was printed in the folio *Works* of 1616. But the question whether the play had been previously published in quarto is one of considerable difficulty, and since it is also one of some bibliographical interest, it may be worth while reviewing the evidence on the subject in greater detail than has been done hitherto.

Before proceeding it will be desirable to give briefly the evidence afforded by the Stationers' Register, which is as follows:

1610 Sept. 20. Entered for their copy by John Browne and John Busby jr., as licensed by Sir George Buc.

1612 Sept. 28. Assigned by J. Browne to Walter Burre in full Court.

1623 Feb. 17. [Assigned by Mrs. Browne to John Marriott. —Entry cancelled.]

1630 July. 3. Assigned by Mrs. Bur to John Spencer.

1635 July. 4. Assigned by W. Burre to William Stansby by a note of 10 June 1621, now entered by order of a Court.

The assignment of 1623 was of course inoperative, since Browne had previously parted with his rights in the copy, and the entry was presumably cancelled on the discovery of the fact. That of 1630 was likewise an error, since Burre had before his death come to a private agreement with Stansby, though what the actual legal position may have been, no assignment having been registered, would afford an interesting subject for argument. The private agreement, however, whether challenged or not, was ratified in 1635 by the Court of the Company, and in any case the question has no immediate bearing upon our problem.

When Gifford edited Jonson's works in 1816 he wrote (vol. iii, p. 336): 'The *Silent Woman* was printed in quarto with this motto:

Ut sis tu similis Cœli, Byrrhique latronum,
Non ego sim Capri, neque Sulci. Cur metuas me?

[1] [1934, December. *The Library*, xv. 306–15.]

and went through several editions. I have one dated 1620. The *Companion to the Playhouse* mentions another, printed in 1609 (as does Whalley, in the margin of his copy), which I have not been able to discover; the earliest which has fallen in my way, bearing the date 1612. All these are exclusive of the folio, 1616.'

The alleged quarto of 1609 is easily disposed of. That there should have been an edition of the play previous to the entry of 1610 is highly improbable, and it is sufficiently evident that the record '4to. 1609' first appended to the title 'EPICÆNE, or *the silent Woman*. Com. by *Ben Jonson*' in Baker's *Companion to the Play-House*, 1764, is merely an unintelligent expansion of the date '1609' which previous bibliographers had copied from the folio, where it refers not to publication but to production. Peter Whalley, who lived till 1791, no doubt copied it from Baker into the margin of a copy of his edition of Jonson of 1756.

But the evidence for the quarto of 1612 cannot be so lightly brushed aside. Its existence receives some support from the assignment of September that year, and perhaps from the rather similar case of *The Alchemist*, also entered in the Register in 1610 and actually printed in 1612. Gifford gives no sign of having known the entries in the Stationers' Register:[1] how then, if the quarto had no existence, did he come to light on the date 1612? I am afraid, however, in view of the casual manner in which he mentions it, that we cannot exclude the possibility of his having simply confused the play with *The Alchemist*. He claims no more than a passing sight of the quarto, and, as Mr. Simpson remarks in answer to a query I addressed to him, 'he never mentions it again in the course of the play. He obviously did not *use* it if he saw it: which is odd, for he usually ran over the quarto texts, even if he made an imperfect use of them.' The motto he quotes is no evidence, for it occurs equally in the quarto of 1620 and in the folio. When, therefore, we consider that for many years Jonsonian editors and critics, to say nothing of collectors, have searched in vain for the missing

[1] Gifford evidently knew the entry of *The Staple of News* on 14 April 1626, since in discussing that play he mentions that it was acted in 1625 'and entered soon after in the Stationers' Books' (v. 160). He *may*, therefore, have also known of other entries, though he apparently never betrayed his knowledge.

edition, there would seem to be ample excuse for suspecting that Gifford's memory may have played him false.

The sceptical view receives some support from the quarto of 1620, the earliest separate edition of *Epicene* that research during the past century has been able to discover. I do not think that there can be any doubt that this was printed from the folio rather than from an earlier quarto, even supposing such to have existed. Moreover, it was published by the publisher of the folio, as appears from the imprint: 'London, Printed by William Stansby, and are to be sold by Iohn Browne at his shop in Saint Dunstanes Church-yard in Fleetstreet.'[1] Now, if Browne or Busby or Burre had published a quarto of *Epicene* in 1612, we should naturally expect to find that of 1620 published by Burre and printed from its predecessor. Stansby's claim must have been based on the fact that he had printed the play in his folio collection, and he simply ignored all rights to the copy created by entries in the Stationers' Register. This is, I think, unlikely to have been due to wilful disregard, nor can Stansby very well have been ignorant of the existence of the earlier quarto if it was a fact.[2] In any case it seems probable that Burre made some sort of protest, and that this led to the private agreement between the two men in 1621, the assignment registered in 1635.[3]

The line of argument just suggested might perhaps be invalidated if it could be shown that the previous edition had for any reason been suppressed. The entries in the Register leave no doubt of an intention to publish *The Silent Woman*

[1] Imprints of this type, 'Printed by *A.B.* and to be sold by *C.D.*', are on the face of it ambiguous, and some critics are inclined to argue that in such cases the bookseller should be regarded as the actual publisher, taking them as equivalent to 'Printed by *A.B.* for *C.D.*'. I believe that this is a mistake and that normally it is the printer who is the responsible party. In the present instance there can be no doubt, for Browne had long since parted with his interest in the copy.

[2] Because, if it existed, the earlier quarto was presumably the source of certain commendatory verses prefixed to the folio, a matter to which I shall return.

[3] Incidentally the quarto of 1620 has a further interest, though it does not appear to have any bearing upon our present problem. As originally printed this edition bore the title: 'Epicoene, or The silent Woman. A Comœdie. Acted in the yeare 1609. By the Children of her Majesties Revels. The Author B.I.', thus following closely that in the folio. But later the title-leaf was suppressed and its place taken by a cancel which read: 'The Silent Woman. A Comœdie. Acted by the Children of the Revels. The Author B. Ionson'. It would be interesting to know whether Jonson himself was responsible for the alteration.

soon after the performance of the play, and the fact that no such edition is now traceable perhaps requires explanation. Either an intervention by authority to restrain the printing of the piece, or to confiscate all copies of an already printed edition, would certainly be consistent with our knowledge, or perhaps rather our lack of knowledge, of the facts. And this leads us to the consideration of some remarkable but very obscure circumstances connected with the original production of the play, presumably in the winter of 1609–10. A remark of Jonson's in conversation with Drummond (ed. Herford and Simpson, i. 151) suggests that when first produced *The Silent Woman* failed to evoke the applause which critical opinion would now regard as its due, but he said nothing of any official disapproval of the performance, or if he did his listener failed to record it. We get, however, a clear echo of some scandal in the prefatory matter that accompanied the piece on its inclusion in the folio of 1616. The first hint is found in the epistle to Sir Francis Stuart. Jonson was always fond of inveighing against traducers, but he seems here to have something more definite in mind, or on his mind, when he complains of 'how much a mans innocency may bee indanger'd by an vn-certaine accusation', and begs his reader to judge how little occasion the play offers for censure, assuring him that 'There is not a line, or syllable in it changed from the simplicity of the first Copy'—that is, I take it, from the text as first written, not necessarily printed. When, moreover, he earlier speaks of 'this dumbe peece' it is possible to see in the phrase not only an allusion to the title, but to the silencing of the play upon the stage. Jonson also at some time wrote a second prologue 'Occasion'd by some persons impertinent exception', from which it is clear that personal allusions had been found in the play:

> If any, yet, will (with particular slight
>   Of application) wrest what he did write;
> And that he meant or him, or her, will say:
>   They make a libell, which he made a play.

There can, I think, be no doubt that Sir Edmund Chambers is correct in finding the explanation in a dispatch of the Venetian ambassador dated 8 February 1609/10 (*Elizabethan Stage*,

iii. 370). The passage runs as follows: 'Lady Arabella [Stuart] is seldom seen outside her rooms and lives in greater dejection than ever. She complains that in a certain comedy the playwright introduced an allusion to her person and the part played by the Prince of Moldavia. The play was suppressed. Her Excellency is very ill pleased and shows a determination in this coming Parliament [which opened the following day] to secure the punishment of certain persons, we don't know who.'[1] The passage to which objection was taken would appear to be *Epicene*, v. i. 17 ff.:

> LA-F[OOLE]. No, he [Daw] has his boxe of instruments . . . to draw maps of euery place, and person, where he comes.
>
> CLE[RIMONT]. How, maps of persons!
>
> LA-F. Yes, sir, of NOMENTACK, when he was here, and of the Prince of *Moldauia*, and of his mistris, mistris EPICOENE.
>
> CLE. Away! he has not found out her latitude, I hope.

It is true that Chambers adds, pertinently enough: 'but if Jonson's text is really not "changed from the simplicity of the first copy", it is clear that Arabella misunderstood it, since Epicoene was Daw's mistress'; however, the passage, even as it stands, is open to misconstruction, and the mischief was done. For whether or no any proposals for an alliance had been seriously entertained, there is no doubt that common gossip coupled the name of the luckless Arabella with that of the reputed Prince of Moldavia, a seedy adventurer named Stefano Janiculo, who, after escaping disguised as a woman from a Turkish prison in 1606, arrived in England the following summer, and succeeded in extracting a grant of £300 from James before leaving again in November 1607.[2] The affair, whatever it was, must have been fairly fresh in men's minds when *Epicene* was produced at the end of 1609, and it is not surprising that the lady should have resented the supposed allusion. She was, moreover, in a position to make her displeasure felt. Standing close to her cousin James in the line of succession, she was politically a person of some consequence, and the government took a natural interest in her

1 *Calendar of State Papers, Venetian*, vol. xi, no. 794, p. 427. Except for the first sentence the passage is in cipher.

2 See *The Travels of John Sanderson*, ed. Sir W. Foster, Hakluyt Society, 1931, pp. xxxv–xxxvii.

affairs, particularly in any project of marriage. Thus her movements about this time have special interest for us. They may be conveniently summarized from the account given in the *Dictionary of National Biography*. In December 1609 she was in confinement for engaging in a treaty of marriage with some unnamed person, but pleading discontent at her poverty regained the King's good graces and secured a pension. On 2 February 1609/10, however, she became engaged to William Seymour, another politically interesting character, and both were summoned before the Privy Council, where they disclaimed any intention of marrying without the King's consent. Again Arabella was taken into favour and granted a monopoly. However, a secret marriage took place early in July and led to her arrest on the 9th. On 16 March 1610/11 she was removed to Barnet in a condition of physical prostration; but this did not prevent her from escaping in boy's clothes and boarding a French vessel bound for Calais. She was caught, and remained a prisoner in the Tower till her death on 25 September 1615. The dates here are obviously significant. The report of the Venetian ambassador on 8 February 1609/10 was written within a week of her engagement, and though at the moment she appears to have been out of favour, there can be little doubt that any time that winter she possessed influence enough to secure the suppression of the play. By 1612 circumstances appeared to have changed. Arabella was in the Tower, and a publisher may well have thought that it would be safe to venture an edition of the offending play, without realizing that it was not the lady only but official authorities who were sensitive to gossip and careful of the reputation of one so near the throne. Certainly neither her own escapade as a boy, nor Stefano's as a woman, would help to dissociate their story from the plot of *Epicene*. Finally, by the time the play came to be printed in the folio of 1616 Arabella was dead and few would recall or bother about the gossip of near a decade before.

There can, then, I think, be very little doubt either that the play was suppressed on its original performance in the winter of 1609–10,[1] or that an attempt was made to print an edition

[1] The date '1609' given in the folio ought, apparently, at this period of Jonson's career to be a calendar date and imply a production before 1 January 1610 (see

some time between then and the end of 1612. But the question remains: Was the attempt anticipated and quashed, or was an edition actually printed and suppressed? Gifford's claim to have seen a quarto dated 1612, certainly suggests the latter alternative: on the other hand we may fairly wonder in that case that no record of the suppression has been found.[1]

There is, indeed, one curious piece of evidence, to the significance of which again Chambers was the first to direct attention, that at first sight would appear to establish the existence of an early quarto edition of the play. This is a set of commendatory verses 'Vpon the Silent Woman' written by Francis Beaumont and printed at the beginning of the folio of 1616. Since it there appears among six other sets reprinted from earlier quartos, it seems to afford strong reason to suppose that *Epicene* too had been previously published, especially when we remember that Beaumont died on 6 March 1615/16. And yet on closer inspection this evidence is seen to be less conclusive than might at first appear. The sets of commendatory verses prefixed to the collected works are nine in number: two of a general nature (Latin by Selden and English by Ed. Heyward) and seven relating to individual plays, namely a long poem by Chapman and a sonnet by H. Holland on *Sejanus*, Latin verses by I. D. and E. Bolton on *Volpone*, and three sets by Beaumont on *The Fox*, *The Silent Woman*, and *Catiline* respectively. Now, there is an odd feature about these seven sets of 'proper' verses: in five cases the title of the play to which the verses refer appears only in a marginal note, in two it appears in the heading. The five are all reprinted direct from earlier quartos:[2] the two exceptional sets are Beaumont's verses on *Epicene*, of which no earlier print can now be found, and Chapman's on *Sejanus*, which, though originally printed in 1605, appear here in a substantially different version.[3] Nor can this variant treatment be explained by

above, p. 187); but Jonson's habits of dating were not sufficiently consistent to enable us to speak with much confidence on the point, while a date early in 1610 would perhaps fit better with the Venetian dispatch.

1 Nothing appears in the Stationers' Register, and my friend Mrs. Pendred has at my request searched the relevant portion of the Company's Court-Book C without finding any mention of the matter.

2 The quarto and folio texts agree closely, except for the fact that in the former Bolton's and Beaumont's verses on *Volpone* are signed with initials only.

3 Chapman's verses in the quarto of *Sejanus* run to 188 lines, of which the last 14

reproduction of the original headings, for while the verses by Holland, I. D., and Bolton originally gave no indications in their headings as to the plays for which they were written, Beaumont's verses on *Volpone* and *Catiline* did so.[1] This seems to point to Chapman's verses on *Sejanus* and Beaumont's on *Epicene* having had a different source from the rest, and having been printed from manuscript rather than from a quarto, and leaves us free to conjecture that Beaumont's, originally written for a projected edition of 1610 or 1612, actually remained unused in Jonson's hands till printed in the folio of 1616.

I am afraid that after reviewing all the evidence which, so far as I am aware, has any relevance to the problem, we must remain in some doubt as to what actually happened. That it was intended to publish the play soon after its production, in accordance with Jonson's usual practice, seems reasonably certain; but whether the idea was abandoned in the face of official opposition, or whether an edition was actually printed and effectively suppressed, appears impossible to decide. In the circumstances, however, it would be unreasonable to say that there is any inherent improbability in an edition having appeared in 1612, or in a few copies having escaped destruction. When, therefore, a reputable witness states that he has seen such an edition, we are bound, I conceive, to treat his testimony with respect, however great may have been the chances of error. While it may, on the evidence before us, be most comfortable and prudent to suspend judgement, if we have to make a choice it should, I think, be in favour of Gifford and the existence of the quarto of 1612.[2]

really constitute a separate poem. In the folio they run to 102 only. The final 14 lines are dropped, and earlier one passage of 40 lines and another of 32 (mentioning by name a number of contemporary statesmen) are excised. The cutting has led to some consequential alteration of the text, and the spelling is markedly different, suggesting that in the folio they were set from an independent copy.

[1] Chapman's verses proclaim the title of the play, but the headings and subscriptions of the two texts differ widely. In the quarto they run: 'In Seianum Ben. Ionsoni et Musis, et sibi in Delicijs', and 'Hæc Commentatus est Georgius Chapmannus'. In the folio: 'Vpon Seianus', and 'Geor. Chapman'.

[2] In my own case I have been forced to come to a decision in the course of compiling a chronological catalogue of English plays under the dates of their first editions, so that I had to assign *Epicene* either to 1612 or 1616. Hence the present attempt to review the evidence, an attempt in which I have received generous help both from Mr. Percy Simpson and Sir E. K. Chambers.

21. Time, Place, and Politics in *King Lear*[1]

DOVER is, I believe, the only place mentioned in *King Lear* as connected with the action.[2] It is natural to suppose that Gloucester's castle is near Gloucester,[3] but there is no confirmation in the play. Cornwall's is within a few hours' ride of Gloucester's, and although Albany's is still less definitely located, the impression left is that the distance is much the same. Since Albany takes the place of Cambria in the old play of *King Leir*, he may have been thought of as living somewhere in the West like the others. The text itself, however, gives us no clue whereby to place any of them. Nor is there any hint as to the situation of the royal palace where the opening scene presumably takes place. It may have become the residence of one of the king's daughters: if so, it must be identified with Cornwall's, for Lear certainly left it to go to Albany's (I. i. 287–8). It was certainly within a day's journey of Gloucester's castle, where the second scene appears to be laid. But in this Gloucester's words, 'And the king gone to-night!' (24) do not, to say the least, hint at any change of locality; so that it would appear possible, either that Lear was holding his court at Gloucester's, or else that Gloucester, after the division of the kingdom, remained in possession or at least in charge of the royal palace.[4]

[1] [1940, October. *The Modern Language Review*, XXXV. 431–46.]

[2] Unless, as Capell suggested, 'Gloucester' in I. v. 1 means the town and not the earl. But I think there can be no doubt that in this passage 'Gloucester' is a mistake for 'Cornwall'. (My references are to the lines of the Globe edition (1891), but not always to its text, which (like all modern editions) relies far too much on the Quarto. This, I am convinced, contains a (presumably shorthand) report obtained from performance.)

[3] Not *in* the town, or even very near it, since 'for many miles about There's scarce a bush' (II. iv. 304). Indeed, there is really no more reason why Gloucester should live near Gloucester than that Albany should live in Scotland.

[4] There is, indeed, some evidence that this was the case, for at II. ii. 1 Oswald, on his arrival at Gloucester's, asks Caius-Kent 'art of this house?' to which the latter answers 'Ay'. Kent was certainly not in Gloucester's service, but he was in Lear's, and he might quite properly regard himself as of the household in any formerly royal residence at which the king was about to arrive. If this is so, it must have been one of the smaller residences, perhaps a hunting-box: 'This house is little' (II. iv. 291). On the other hand, Gloucester speaks of it as 'mine own house' (III. iii. 4).

The distance of any of these places from Dover, the only fixed point, is left quite vague. We get the impression that it cannot be very great and that messengers pass readily from one centre to the other; but that is all. The most definite indication is that, as the text now stands, Oswald goes from Cornwall's to the neighbourhood of Dover while Lear is wandering distracted about the fields, although a 'century' (whatever that may be) is scouring the country for him. I think that all this vagueness is intentional and designed to prevent topographical difficulties impeding the rapidity of the action.

The opening scene (I. i), in which Lear divides up his kingdom, naturally takes place at court, wherever that may happen to be. Royal business was usually transacted in the morning, and the whole affair would probably be over before dinner. Thus there would be ample time for the king to leave the same evening in order to take up his residence with Goneril: 'I think our father will hence to-night.—That's most certain' (287). It can be no great distance, since he would hardly propose riding far into the night.

I. ii, with Edmund's plot, follows. There is no indication where the action takes place, but its sequel, Edgar's flight (II. i), is certainly at Gloucester's castle, and the locality must be the same in both.[1] Edmund promises to place Gloucester where he may overhear the truth of Edgar's intentions, 'and that without further delay than this very evening' (100). This promise is fulfilled in the pretended quarrel and surprise in II. i. 16–87, which in fact happen after dark ('Lights, ho, here! . . . Torches, torches!' 33), and the two scenes must therefore be on the same day.[2] Gloucester's first words: 'Kent

[1] If we could separate I. ii from II. i. the former would be most naturally placed still at court on the evening of Lear's departure, but this seems to me impossible. See the next note.

[2] There must be no mistake about this, for it is the crucial point in the ostensible time-scheme. Those who try to reconcile the conflicting time indications of the play have to suppose that, so far from Edmund's trap being sprung the same evening, Edgar remains hidden in his brother's 'lodging' for a fortnight! Others assume that we have to do with two distinct and unrelated plots, of one of which we watch the laying but not the outcome, and of the other the outcome but not the laying. If I understand them aright (of which I am not quite sure), this is the contention both of A. C. Bradley and of Granville-Barker. The former, in his classical work on *Shakespearean Tragedy* (1904, p. 245), speaks of 'Edmund's idea (not carried out) of

banished thus! and France in choler parted! And the king gone to-night!' (I. ii. 24), seem at first sight to imply that it is the same day as in I. i: but in that case it would be already night, which, though consistent with Edmund's promise ('this very evening'), would make II. i practically continuous with I. ii and leave no time for the intervening events of I. iii–v, which moreover cannot possibly take place the same day as I. i. We must, therefore, suppose that Edmund's plot is contrived the morning after Lear subscribed his power, and that 'to-night' Gloucester means 'this past night', for which there is ample warrant in Shakespearian usage.[1]

I. iii–v are at Albany's and are closely connected. Lear must have arrived the night before and has gone out hunting. It is now dinner time, that is early in the afternoon. Goneril (iii) instructs her steward Oswald to foster discontent in Lear and his followers in pursuance of the plan hinted at in her talk with Regan (I. i. 307–10), and goes to write letters to her sister warning her to follow a like course.

Next (iv), Lear returns from the hunt, calling for dinner; he meets Kent in his disguise as Caius (the name he assumes is only known from V. iii. 283) and takes him into his service.

making his father witness, without over-hearing, his conversation with Edgar'; the latter, in his penetrating and invaluable *Prefaces to Shakespeare* (I, 1927, p. 149, note), writes: 'Yet another slight change of plan may be guessed at; it would effect some economy in the working out of the sub-plot. Edmund says to Gloucester about Edgar: "If your honour judge it meet, I will place you where you shall hear us confer of this . . . and that without any further delay than this very evening." But he never does.' But surely this would be an incredible piece of clumsiness on the part of an experienced dramatist. Naturally the events in II. i do not exactly follow the lines proposed in I. ii. Edmund offered to place his father where he should overhear his conversation with Edgar. Obviously he could not do this without giving himself away; he must also at all costs prevent Edgar being apprehended. He never, of course, intended to fulfil his promise literally. What he does is to make Gloucester think that he is trying to fulfil it. He posts his father in his hiding place ('My father watches', II. i. 22), after the latter has 'set a guard' (18) to take Edgar (should his suspicions be confirmed); he then goes to call Edgar from his lodgings, and forces the pretended quarrel out of ordinary ear-shot ('I hear my father coming', 30, is only said to frighten Edgar), thus driving his brother to flight before he could be seized. These are masterly tactics. And we are asked to believe that this has nothing to do with the earlier scene; that after the crucial plot had been laid for 'this very evening', Shakespeare without a word of explanation simply dropped the matter, and arranged for a quite different catastrophe a fortnight later!

[1] C. T. Onions, in his *Shakespeare Glossary*, cites *Merchant of Venice*, II. v. 18, 'I did dream of money-bags to-night', and various other instances.

The insolence and humiliation of Oswald follow, and then the quarrel with Goneril. Lear announces his intention of removing forthwith to Regan's, and bids call his train together (274). Discovering that half his knights have been dismissed, he threatens to take back his delegated authority: 'Thou shalt find That I'll resume the shape which thou dost think I have cast off for ever' (330); and in a rage goes to take horse. Goneril calls Oswald, who has been inditing her letter to Regan, and dispatches him with it, bidding him return with all speed. The news it contains has been rather mysteriously brought up to date and includes not only complaints against her father's knights (355, and cf. II. i. 103), but all 'What he hath uttered' (353); it even announces her intention to visit her sister (II. iv. 186).

In the last short scene (v) of the act we see Lear's actual departure. While waiting for his horses he too has found time to write to Regan warning her of his immediate arrival, and with this news he bids Kent hasten ahead, or he will be there before him. Kent replies: 'I will not sleep, my lord, till I have delivered your letter' (5), implying that the journey will anyhow take him well into the night. A gentleman then announces that the horses are ready, and Lear at once sets out followed only by his immediate attendants.[1] There is a difficulty in the first line of this scene: 'Go you before to Gloucester with these letters. Acquaint our daughter . . .'. Here 'Gloucester' must be an error for 'Cornwall'. However

[1] It is clear that his knights do not accompany him. There are several allusions to these, and they are, I think, really quite consistent. It is true that when, on Lear's arrival at Gloucester's Kent asks: 'How chance it that the king comes with so small a number?' (II. iv. 64), the Fool affects to see in it an allusion to the dismissal of fifty of the knights; but it may equally well refer to the remainder (Kent had not actually witnessed Lear's departure, I. v. 7). It is also true that at the end of the same scene (307) Regan says: 'Shut up your doors: He is attended with a desperate train'; but this may refer to their expected arrival quite as well as to their presence; while the imminent danger in which Gloucester supposes Lear to stand at III. vi. 95–104 is unintelligible if the king had his knights at hand. The conclusive passage, however, is Oswald's report that

Some five or six and thirty of his knights,
Hot questrists after him, met him at gate (III. vii. 16–17).

From this it is clear that the knights have been pursuing the king all the way from Albany's (via Cornwall's, of course) and have at last most opportunely caught up with him as he is leaving Gloucester's. He is now safe under their protection during the journey to Dover.

it may have arisen, the mistake was easy enough, since it was in fact at Gloucester's that Lear eventually met Regan.[1]

In the interval between Acts I and II, as we subsequently learn, Kent reaches Cornwall's, with Oswald hard at his heels; on receipt of the several letters the duke and duchess decide to be 'from home', and hastily prepare to visit Gloucester (II. iv. 27–35). It is already dark: 'The night before there was no purpose in them of this remove' (II. iv. 3). They take horse with their meinie, bearing the two messengers from Albany's with them. Another messenger, Curan, is sent on ahead to warn Gloucester of their coming (II. i. 2), and no doubt one of Oswald's fellows (he had come with 'some company', I. iv. 359, but was himself still 'Stewed in his haste', II. iv. 31) back to Goneril to report their movements.

In II. i we are back at Gloucester's. The night must be far advanced, for Curan has already delivered his message, and is now having a few confidential words with Edmund. No doubt his unexpected news has delayed the promised revelation of Edgar's supposed treachery: this now takes place (Edmund making clever use of Curan's report of discord between the dukes) and is followed by Edgar's flight and Gloucester's anger and despair. Upon the heat of this Cornwall and Regan arrive. The scene is either in, or more likely just outside, the castle. Edgar has been concealed in Edmund's 'lodging' (I. ii. 184), whence his brother calls him to 'descend' (II. i. 21). The phrase may suggest a house adjoining the castle and, since Edgar appears to have no difficulty in making his escape in the middle of the night, it would seem probable that he was not actually within the castle walls.

II. ii is certainly before the castle. The time may be an hour or two later: it is still dark ('though it be night, yet the moon shines', 34) but nearing day ('Good dawning to thee, friend', 1). Oswald, who has apparently lagged behind, meets Caius-Kent who has arrived earlier, but he does not recognize

[1] Capell suggested that Cornwall and Regan were residing in the town of Gloucester, which would make their remove to Gloucester's neighbouring castle easy. But this cannot have been the case, for they 'travelled all the night'—or so at least they said (II. iv. 90). Granville-Barker was before me with this emendation: 'I give a guess that "Gloucester" in this line is a slip for "Cornwall"' (p. 229).

him.[1] Kent is naturally surprised, and asks him, 'Is it two days since I tripped up thy heels, and beat thee before the king?' (II. ii. 31). Presumably 'two days since' may by a stretch mean 'yesterday'.[2] There follows the quarrel, and Kent is put in the stocks. Apparently it is by this time day: Kent bids Gloucester 'good morrow' (165), and though the sun may not yet have risen, it is light enough for him to read Cordelia's letter (172).[3] But he is 'All weary and o'er-watched' (177), and soon falls asleep.

The Folio makes one scene only of what are in modern editions II. ii–iv, but to this conflation there are two objections which seem to justify the change. One is the improbability of the fugitive Edgar returning to the castle, even at daybreak, until he has assumed a disguise: the other is that it makes one continuous scene run from early dawn to nightfall.[4]

After Edgar has gone to assume his disguise of Tom o' Bedlam (iii), Lear enters with a few followers (iv) and finds Kent in the stocks. He had set out from Albany's the previous afternoon, and has, of course, ridden round by Cornwall's

1 It would be tempting to suppose that he had been sent back from Cornwall's to report to Goneril (especially as in I. iv. 363 the latter had urged his swift return), and that he now arrives to announce that she too is on her way. However, he delivers no message (and at II. iv. 186 Regan expects her sister on the ground of her 'letter' not of a message) and the time is probably too short to allow of a double journey. Moreover, Regan has just informed us that 'the several messengers From hence attend dispatch' (II. i. 126). There can be no question of a day intervening between II. i. and ii, for Kent has only recently arrived: 'I have watched and travelled hard' (II. ii. 162).

2 [Greg seems confused here. 'Is it two days since . . . ' is presumably a question expecting the answer 'No'; so that it is not by a 'stretch', but by the most natural interpretation, that the incident belongs to the previous day.—J.C.M.]

3 I do not feel very certain of this. What Kent says is (170):

> Approach thou beacon to this under globe,
> That by thy comfortable beams I may
> Peruse this letter.

Perhaps he falls asleep before there is light enough to read by. (This was Malone's view.) What follows is too obscure, and possibly corrupt, to afford any ground of argument.

4 Some editors have committed the absurdity of making II. iii a separate scene and then marking the locality as 'The Same', i.e. before Gloucester's castle! There is no scenic difficulty in the Folio's arrangement—Edgar can perfectly well speak his lines on the front of the stage while Kent slumbers in the background—the impropriety is dramatic. I believe *Lear* to have been written for performance on a perfectly plain stage without the usual alcove and curtain at the back. If so, once Kent had been put in the stocks these necessarily remained in view of the audience until his release, and no change of scene was possible. Hence the irrational conflation of the Folio.

(1–4): the company has either journeyed comparatively slowly (in spite of Lear's 'if your diligence be not speedy, I shall be there afore you', I. v. 4) or perhaps baited (at Cornwall's?) on the way, for the day is already well advanced and three hundred lines later it is night. The quarrel with Regan and Cornwall follows, and then Goneril arrives. She comes apparently straight from home, having no doubt had notice of her sister's movements. She has with her a trumpet, but no other attendants are mentioned: a large train would be unsuitable to the 'little house' (291). Just before she arrives Oswald enters, evidently to announce her coming: presumably he has been sent out, or has gone out, to meet her. The quarrel is resumed, and in the end Lear dashes off into the storm, rejecting and rejected by his second daughter. He is accompanied by Kent, the Fool, and a Gentleman, and Gloucester follows. The latter returns to announce: 'He calls to horse, but will I know not whither' (300). 'Alack, the night comes on', he adds; while Cornwall's final words (311):

> Shut up your doors, my lord; 'tis a wild night:
> My Regan counsels well: come out o' th' storm

show that night has fallen and that they are still outside the castle.

Act III follows without a break. Lear has not taken horse, but has wandered off on foot with his Fool and Gentleman. Kent, who started with him, appears to have lost him again and returned to the castle 'demanding after' him, where he has been refused entrance (III. ii. 65). The Gentleman too has got separated from him, though he had evidently followed for a while (i. 4–17). Kent and the Gentleman now meet accidentally, and the former, without revealing his identity, imparts the contents of Cordelia's letter, namely that she is at Dover, and persuades his hearer to seek her out and inform her of what has happened. Their more pressing business, however, is to find the king.[1]

[1] The scene was heavily cut on the stage: lines 22–29 are not in the Quarto; 30–42 (as well as $7\frac{2}{2}$–$15\frac{1}{2}$) are not in the Folio. Moreover, the transition from 29 to 30 is harsh and obscure, and I have no doubt that at this point something was cut out of both texts and is consequently lost. Granville-Barker agrees, speaking (p. 226) of 'the cutting of a common original (of which still more may have existed. . .)'.

III. ii is continuous with the preceding. Lear is wandering about with the Fool in the open country near the castle ('for many miles about There's scarce a bush', II. iv. 304). Kent at last finds them and leads them towards a hovel he knows of.

III. iii is back again at the castle, now inside. Gloucester discloses to Edmund his knowledge of the designs of France ('I have received a letter this night . . . there is part of a power already footed',[1] 10, 13) and his not altogether disinterested intention to 'incline to the king' (14); he adds: 'If I die for it, as no less is threatened me, the king my old master must be relieved' (18).

In III. iv Lear, Kent, and the Fool have reached the hovel, from which Poor-Tom-Edgar emerges. Meanwhile, Gloucester, in pursuance of his resolve, has come out in search of the king, and offers to bring them 'where both fire and food is ready' (159).

III. v is again in the castle. Edmund having betrayed his father to Cornwall, the secret letters have been discovered, which incidentally reveal the urgency of the political situation. Edmund is ordered to apprehend Gloucester immediately.

In III. vi the wanderers enter the promised shelter. Where this is we do not know,[2] but it has furniture of a sort and a curtained recess with a couch, so that it must be a room of some sort and not a mere shed. Gloucester goes out at once to collect what comforts he can. During his stealthy search he overhears a plot against the king's life (95), though nothing apparently of his own danger, and has a horse-drawn litter made ready, wherein Lear may 'drive toward Dover' (98). He returns to find that the king's mind has given way, and that he is now asleep on the couch. They bear him out in

[1] This might mean no more than 'afoot'. The Quarto, however, reads 'landed', and although the Quarto is of no authority, its interpretation in this case is shown to be correct by Cornwall's words at the beginning of III. vii: 'shew him this letter; the army of France is landed'. The sense is, moreover, confirmed by III. vii. 45, 'the traitors Late footed in the kingdom'.

[2] Editors have been curiously specific; several follow Theobald in supposing 'A Chamber in a Farm-house'! It may be some back premises of the castle itself (Granville-Barker, with fine perception, speaks of 'the outhouse, all of his own castle that Gloucester dare offer', p. 177), or some neighbouring building—possibly Edmund's lodging, since Gloucester has taken him into his confidence—possibly even the home of the 'tenant' of IV. i. Perhaps it was this last possibility that Theobald had in mind.

their arms, Edgar alone remaining behind. Later we learn (III. vii. 16) that:

> Some five or six and thirty of his knights,
> Hot questrists after him, met him at gate,
> Who, with some other of the lords dependents,
> Are gone with him toward Dover, where they boast
> To have well-armèd friends.

III. vii must again be continuous, for Cornwall is not the man to suffer delay either in the arrest of Gloucester or in preparations to meet the danger of invasion: 'the army of France is landed' (2). He at once sends Goneril and Edmund to carry the news to Albany. They are accompanied by Oswald, who posts on ahead and reaches home before them (IV. ii. 2). Gloucester is now brought in, and there follows the horrible scene of the blinding, together with the scuffle with the servant in which Cornwall receives his death-wound. It may or may not be already daylight. The scene is inside the castle, for there is a chair handy to which Gloucester can be bound (34), and he is afterwards thrust 'out at gates' (93). Some servants (in the Quarto only) propose to 'get the Bedlam To lead him where he would' (103): Edgar had evidently shown himself about the previous afternoon.

Act IV begins soon after. No doubt it is now daylight. Gloucester enters, led by an old man, his tenant. They meet Edgar somewhere in the neighbourhood of the castle, and Gloucester sends the old man back to bring clothing for 'the naked fellow' (i. 42, 46), whom he hires (80) to lead him to the cliffs of Dover.

In IV. ii we have the arrival, presumably in the course of the day, of Goneril and Edmund at Albany's. Goneril's 'Welcome my lord' (1), is not of course a greeting, but an invitation to enter her house. Oswald, who had arrived before them, reports Albany's strange behaviour: 'I told him you were coming; His answer was "The worse!" ' (5). At this Goneril, foreseeing trouble with her 'mild' husband, sends Edmund straight back to Cornwall[1] out of harm's way—with a kiss. She has barely time to start quarrelling before news comes of

[1] 'Hasten his musters and conduct his powers' (16)—which seems to show a prophetic knowledge of the duke's accident!

Gloucester's blinding and Cornwall's death. Albany asks what has happened to Edmund, and is told that he was 'Come with my lady hither' (90), but that the messenger had 'met him back again', that is, on his way back (as Wright observes).

With IV. iii (only preserved in the Quarto) the scene shifts to Dover, where it remains generally centred to the end of the play. Henceforth the time indications are less definite, though the sense of speed hardly relaxes. I do not propose to follow the subject further.[1] What I have tried to demonstrate is the closely knit time scheme up to this point, and the rapid, almost breathless, pace of the action which it involves. There can be no doubt, I think, that this is intentional,[2] and that Shakespeare deliberately hurries his audience along at whatever cost to probability.[3]

This cost, however, was undoubtedly a heavy one, for the schedule I have extracted from the time-indications that link the several scenes proves, on further examination, manifestly impossible, and is indeed flatly contradicted by several definite statements in the text. We have seen that the time of

[1] There is one difficulty in the time-scheme of the last two acts. It is very tempting to invert the order of IV. iv, and v. (Eccles in 1792 placed IV. v before IV. iii; but this is quite unnecessary.) There are two objections to the received order. First, at iv. 21 'The British powers' are already marching towards Dover; while in v Regan is still at home ('Our troops set forth to-morrow', 16) and Edmund has wandered off vaguely 'to descry The strength o' th' enemy' (13). (By the way, most editors are surely wrong in following Capell, who lays this scene at Gloucester's castle. Regan must have returned to her own palace to muster her troops. Capell, of course, believed that Cornwall lived in Gloucester: hence perhaps the mistake.) Secondly, since the distracted Lear is already wandering about the fields in IV. iv ('he was met even now', 1), he has to continue doing so throughout Oswald's journey from Cornwall's to Dover in search of Edmund (announced in v), before they can both reappear in the course of vi—an arrangement by which, it is contended, the 'century' must be hunting for the king throughout at least one night. To the first of these objections it may be replied that though Regan has not yet set out in v, Albany's powers are already on the march (V. 1), and it may be the latter that are reported nearing Dover in iv; and to the second that we really have no idea how long it would take Oswald to reach the neighbourhood of Dover, or, alternatively, that there is no reason why Lear should not continue his wanderings during the night.

[2] 'Shakespeare', says Granville-Barker (p. 170), 'is hunting Lear and the play's action hard and using every device to do it.'

[3] The action so far appears to occupy four days: (1) Lear's abdication (he may spend part of the night travelling to Albany's); (2) his quarrel with Goneril (he rides through the night to Gloucester's); (3) his quarrel with Regan (he spends the night on the heath); (4) his flight to (and arrival at ?) Dover. The rest of the action could, I fancy, be compressed into two more days, but there is no proof that it is as hurried as that.

I. iii–v must be the day following I. i. But in the very first line of I. iii Goneril asks: 'Did my father strike my gentleman for chiding of his fool?' while from I. iv, 77 we learn that Lear had not seen his Fool 'this two days'. He had, therefore, been at least two days at Albany's while other indications—such as 'the fool has much pined away' (iv. 80), the charge that Lear's 'knights grow riotous' (iii. 6), and suggestions of 'a great abatement of kindness' (iv. 64) and 'a most faint neglect of late' (iv. 73)—imply a longer though vaguer interval. Much more serious is the dismissal of the king's knights: 'What, fifty of my followers at a clap! Within a fortnight'! (iv. 316). How Lear came not to notice or be informed of this earlier is an unsolved mystery, but he certainly discovers it as soon as he seeks to collect his followers for his departure, and the only natural explanation of the phrase 'Within a fortnight' is 'During the fortnight that I have been here'.[1] Even a fortnight allows scant time for the landing of the French army, which is apparently an accomplished fact by the time Lear leaves Albany's,[2] but it is no doubt sufficiently long and sufficiently vague to prevent spectator's worrying over the problems of mobilization.

Thus we become aware of a double stream of time flowing. In the foreground we have the time scheme determined by the actual duration of the various episodes directly represented and by the links between them: beyond is the wider and more leisurely flow of events which we know must have happened, but whose duration, because they are not immediately presented to us, it is possible at least in some measure to ignore. It is an old dramatic device: as old as Aeschylus and the *Agamemnon*. As every dramatist knows, it works well enough on the stage, always supposing that the contradictions are not too glaring and are prevented from forcing themselves on the attention of the audience.[3]

[1] It has been suggested (by Eccles) that Lear's words mean 'What, fifty of my followers under orders to leave within a fortnight!' but I am quite sure that no spectator would so understand them. If there were no other indication of a lengthy interval, the explanation might possibly be allowed to pass, but in view of the evidence generally it must be rejected. [2] See below, p. 336.

[3] Of course, attempts have been made either to work out a plausible time scheme for *King Lear*, or to reduce its time-data to order. Eccles, who published an edition in 1792, tackled the difficulty after the manner of the eighteenth-century 'improvers' of Shakespeare, by moving I. ii to a position immediately before II. i and coolly

That, of course, is the essential condition for the success of what is sometimes called dramatic time, and I wish to examine its bearing on the problem of the French invasion. This has not, I think, received the attention it deserves. In the old play of *King Leir*, where the aged monarch is restored to his throne and all ends happily, sympathy is of course wholly on the side of the invaders, and the author does not appear to be conscious of raising any political issue. To Shakespeare, whose dramatic reputation had been built on a long series of patriotic 'histories', such political naïvety or detachment was impossible. It is true that, since he converted the play into a tragedy, it was no longer necessary for the foreign invader to be victorious; but it remained a ticklish business, since sympathy was still asked for Cordelia and the French power and was indeed implicit in the plot. However remote this patriotic dilemma may seem to us, to an Elizabethan audience, with its lack of historical perspective, it was real enough. Shakespeare evidently felt it, and did his best to hold the balance even. The really sympathetic characters Kent and Edgar[1] take no part in the conflict on either side, while in command of the British party is placed the not unsympathetic Albany, who is torn between patriotism and conscience. His divided motives, as well no doubt as the divided sympathies of the author, express (or fail to express) themselves in the very obscure speech (doubtless corrupt: it is in the Quarto only) put into his mouth before the battle (v. i. 23):

Where I could not be honest
I never yet was valiant: for this business,
It touches us, as France invades our land,
Not bolds the king, with others whom I fear
Most just and heavy causes make oppose.

excising the opening words of Gloucester's speech (22–25) that link it with I. i. More recently P. A. Daniel produced a less drastic but less logical solution by allowing Edgar to remain concealed in Edmund's lodging for a fortnight. But these are obviously factitious remedies. The contradiction is in the play itself: the only thing to do is to recognize it, and with it the double time.

1 There is some contradiction in regard to Edgar. He leaves Gloucester in v. ii with the words: 'If ever I return to you again, I'll bring you comfort', which suggests that he is about to enter the battle. Yet he apparently does nothing of the sort. But this short scene is admittedly unsatisfactory, and it looks as though a speech from an earlier draft may have been left standing. Whatever the explanation of Shakespeare's treatment at this point, it is clear that he did not wish to centre interest on the battle.

At the same time the very treatment of the plot that was forced upon the dramatist by his art tended in some ways to increase his political difficulties. The author of the old play, if he was conscious of these at all, sought to lessen them in two ways. In the first place, he made the husbands of the elder daughters independent sovereigns, the kings of Cornwall and Cambria (in this departing from Holinshed); so that, though the scene of the battle was in Britain, it was in fact fought between three foreign powers. In the second place, he made Leir appeal directly to Gallia for aid, so that it was as the old king's acknowledged champion that the latter set foot in the kingdom. But this Shakespeare's Lear could never do: for him it was as impossible to appeal to France as to go cringing back to Goneril (II. iv. 216), and even after he had been removed to Dover he refused so much as to see the daughter he had wronged (IV. iii. 42). Thus it is solely on his own, and Cordelia's, responsibility that France brings his army over.

Now let us see what bearing the time scheme has upon this problem, for unless I am mistaken it is of considerable importance. We are not really concerned with the time allowed for the levying and transport of the army, whether it be a day or a fortnight. As I have already pointed out, it is only the *text* that limits us to a night and a day, and this the *spectator* is in no position to check. When he hears of the 'fortnight' he does not yet know that Edgar's flight is going to close the time-bracket opened by Edmund's plot; and by the time he knows of the flight, still more by the time he hears of the invasion, he will have forgotten—and Shakespeare had very likely forgotten—how closely Gloucester's words in I. ii link the occasion of the plot with that of the abdication. Moreover, the fortnight itself is vague, and even on that imagination will not insist. There is then no difficulty about allowing what time we will for the preparation of the French invasion—provided always that *the preparations began as soon as the king left the British court*.

But this at once raises the question of France's *motive*. If, taking advantage of the antagonism between Albany and Cornwall,[1] he planned invasion as soon as he returned to his

[1] This antagonism is an undeveloped motive in the play, either because Shake-

own kingdom, it was not planned to avenge the treatment Lear had received at the hands of his elder daughters, as we are later led to believe, and as is essential for any sympathetic feeling towards the invaders. As they affect this issue the time-data are much clearer, and what is important, they are presented directly to the apprehension of the spectator. Lear's quarrel with Goneril ends act I, that with Regan ends act II; the landing of the French army is known certainly in III. iii, on the night of the second quarrel, probably in II. ii, before it took place. The two quarrels were in fact on consecutive days, though this is a matter of calculation only: how far can the interval between them be imaginatively extended? If we stretch to the full Kent's words, 'Is it two days since I tripped up thy heels and beat thee before the king?' (II. ii. 31), two or three days would seem to be the limit. But the impression received by the spectator is certainly one of haste; he will probably assume that only one night intervenes. Any lengthy interval is out of the question. Moreover, on the day of the second quarrel the letters reporting the invasion have already arrived: they must have taken at least as long to come from Dover as Kent, Lear, and Goneril took to come from

speare was content only to hint at it, or because he found he lacked room for elaboration. (Most critics seem to assume the latter, but I am by no means sure they are right.) There are, of course, several clear statements on the subject: Curan reports 'likely wars toward 'twixt the Dukes of Cornwall and Albany' (II. i. 11); Kent knows of 'division' and 'snuffs and packings of the dukes', 'Although as yet the face of it is covered With mutual cunning' (I fancy he derives his information from Cordelia's letter, since he mentions the matter in connexion with the French spies, III. i. 19–25); and so does Gloucester: 'There is division between the dukes' (III. iii. 9). Some rivalry between them may be implied in the opening lines of the play, and though there is little confirmation to be found elsewhere, it is possible to detect at least two hints. Thus, when Gloucester speaks of Cornwall as 'The noble duke my master, My worthy arch and patron' (II. i. 60), he may mean that he is in some way bound to his party; and when later in the same scene Cornwall takes Edmund into his service with the words, 'Natures of such deep trust we shall much need' (117), there can be little doubt, I think, that he has the 'likely wars' with Albany in mind, for as yet he knows nothing of the designs of France. The rivalry was between the dukes, not, as Bradley has it (p. 250, note 3), between Goneril and Regan: there is no hint of any quarrel between the sisters till Edmund comes to the fore. As to the part played by the 'likely wars' in provoking the French invasion, Granville-Barker thinks that 'Kent, in an involved speech in Act III [i. 17ff.] (for him most uncharacteristically involved), suggests that it is the threat of them which is bringing the French army to England' (p. 148). The speech is obscure, and probably incomplete as well as in part perhaps corrupt, but this interpretation I think puts the importance of the 'division' too high; it may have been the occasion, hardly the cause, of France's action.

Albany's. It is, therefore, difficult to escape the conclusion that at the time of Lear's quarrel with Goneril (*a fortiori* at that of his quarrel with Regan) the French army must have been in the act of landing, if not already landed, and this conclusion does not depend on any nice calculation from the time-data, but must be at once obvious to spectators.[1]

This is borne out from another angle by IV. iii, a scene (preserved in the Quarto only) between Kent after his arrival at Dover and the Gentleman whom he had sent ahead on the night of the storm to inform Cordelia of the treatment suffered by her father, and who now reports the result of his mission. What previous news or rumours Cordelia may have heard we cannot tell, but this was, of course, the first report she had received of the final quarrel with Regan: and she had been already some time encamped at Dover. When therefore France and Cordelia planned their invasion they cannot possibly have known of Lear's rejection by his elder daughters for the simple reason that it had not yet happened. What then can be the justification of Cordelia's boast at IV. iv. 27?—

> No blown ambition doth our arms incite,
> But love, dear love, and our aged father's right.

To answer this riddle we must examine France's conduct

[1] I here put the argument at its lowest. There are two sources of information respecting the invasion, namely the letters received by Kent and Gloucester respectively. Gloucester got his late on the day of the quarrel with Regan, probably just after it occurred: 'I have received a letter this night . . . there 's part of a power already footed' (III. iii. 10). The news it contains is 'mighty business' (III. v. 17), no less than that 'the army of France is landed' (III. vii. 2), and not merely afoot. Kent's letter was in his hands at least twelve hours earlier, before dawn the same day, and might be supposed to contain less recent information. It was 'from Cordelia' who was seeking 'to give losses their remedies' (II. ii. 173–7). This is vague; but it is clearly on the strength of the same letter that Kent informed the Gentleman that the French 'have secret feet In some of our best ports, and are at point To shew their open banner', and that Cordelia is at Dover (III. i. 32, 36, 46). Kent's information, therefore, is practically the same as Gloucester's. Either of these might have imparted it to Lear's followers, who 'Are gone with him toward Dover, where they boast To have well-armèd friends' (III. vii. 19). Now, when Kent reads the letter (in the stocks) he has only just arrived at Gloucester's after posting hard all night, and it is difficult to understand how he can have received it at any time after he left Albany's, which was immediately upon Lear's quarrel with Goneril. Moreover, Cordelia, informed of his 'obscurèd course', would of course have sent the letter to Albany's, where Lear was resident, no doubt through one of the spies she had planted in his house (III. i. 24). There can be no doubt, therefore, that the French army had actually landed before Lear had any quarrel with his daughters.

more closely. In the first scene of all he appears as the romantic young lover eager to accept the dowerless Cinderella, while the more materially minded, and we may suppose older, Burgundy stands upon 'respect and fortunes' (251). He is fully and fairly warned by the angry father (211):

> For you, great king,
> I would not from your love make such a stray.
> To match you where I hate;

and he makes his election up with his eyes open (259):

> Thy dowerless daughter, king, thrown to my chance,
> Is queen of us, of ours, and our fair France:
> Not all the dukes of waterish Burgundy
> Can buy this unprized precious maid of me.

He had no cause to complain, and he gives no hint of complaint. Lear, however, is not best pleased (265):

> Thou hast her, France; let her be thine, for we
> Have no such daughter, nor shall ever see
> That face of hers again: therefore be gone
> Without our grace, our love, our benizon.

Whether the last words are addressed to France or to Cordelia, they clearly do not invite parley. It therefore comes as a surprise when later on Goneril remarks that 'There is further compliment of leave-taking between France and' the king (306). It seems unlikely after what we have just heard, nor is it easy to see how Goneril, who has not left the stage, can know what is taking place outside. On the other hand, Lear and Burgundy have gone off arm in arm ('Come noble Burgundy', 269), and it is a certain guess that between them there will be 'further compliment of leave-taking'. I should, therefore, have no hesitation in assuming (with Hanmer) that 'France' was here an error for 'Burgundy', were it not for the curious remark that Gloucester makes at the beginning of I. ii (23):

> Kent banished thus! and France in choler parted!

There was no hint of choler in France when we last saw him. Considering, however, the mood Lear was in, if France had been indiscreet enough to seek a further interview, there would have been every chance of an explosion. I therefore feel bound to assume that such further leave-taking there was, and that France—'the hot-blooded France' of II. iv. 215—incensed at some fresh insult to Cordelia, departed in a rage, determined to wrest by force her portion from the favoured 'son-in-laws', Albany and Cornwall.

Such is the situation when France and Cordelia land at Dover. But it is impossible to imagine the gentle Cordelia spurring on her husband to the recovery of her portion. She would have been much more likely to urge submission to her father's unjust decree: she is the very pattern of obedience and love. What then can she mean by what she says at IV. iv. 23?—

> O dear father,
> It is thy business that I go about;
> Therefore great France
> My mourning and importuned tears hath pitied.

She is apparently trying to say that France has at her request come to the rescue of her father. But, as we have seen, the invasion cannot have been planned to avenge wrongs that had not yet been committed; consequently it cannot have been at Cordelia's entreaty that it took place. There can be only one explanation: what Cordelia's 'mourning and importuned tears' brought about was not the original expedition, but a change in its purpose.

And this change of purpose is, I think, clearly indicated by France's hasty return to his own country. No doubt this was in itself convenient for Shakespeare. There was less shock to patriotism in an invading army led by a British princess than by a French king. But Shakespeare need never have brought France over at all. Besides, the excuse given for his return is childish.[1] France left his kingdom in such a hurry that he altogether forgot about some pressing danger, and had to scurry back to meet it (IV. iii. 3)! The public explanation was, no doubt, on these lines, but (unless Shakespeare is being more perfunctory than we have any right to assume) we can hardly be intended to take it at its face value.

[1] Granville-Barker calls it 'a lame explanation'(p. 228), given in 'the clumsiest few lines in the play' (p. 148), which it is. He also says, 'It is a carpentered scene if ever there was one', and 'I could better believe that Shakespeare cut it than wrote it' (p. 228). Here too one may agree, with the qualification that the scene being in the Quarto only is probably not as Shakespeare wrote it.

The real reason, I suggest, was that Cordelia succeeded in persuading her husband to abandon his purpose of wresting a portion of the kingdom for himself and retire to his own land, thus leaving her free to use his army in defence of her father, should the occasion arise. She says in effect: 'It is for my father's safety (not my own inheritance) that I am fighting; that I am able to do so is due to my husband's granting my prayer (and giving up his own plan of conquest)'. And now indeed she has the right to add:

> No blown ambition doth our arms incite,
> But love, dear love, and our aged father's right.

This would, of course, be clearer if it could be shown that France's return followed on the Gentleman's report of Lear's ill-treatment. But we are expressly told that the opposite was the case: 'Was this [your report] before the king returned?— No, since' (IV. iii. 39). Kent goes out of his way to ask whether the departure of the French king was due to the news he had sent, and he is told that it was not. There must be some definite reason for this precise, and at first sight irrelevant, information. I think it is this. Had France's change of plan occurred on receipt of the news that Lear was in need of succour, it might have appeared no more than a change of tactics. Shakespeare wanted to make it quite clear that France, yielding to Cordelia's entreaty, had in fact already abandoned his own claim and its prosecution. It was in token of this fact that the king himself immediately retired to France. We may suppose that he left his marshal, La Far, behind to bring over the army after him. But Cordelia, whom we may suppose to have had her own suspicions, also remained behind, and thus, when the crisis came, was able to use the army for a purpose quite different from that for which it had been levied.

No doubt all this elaboration of motive proved too cumbersome of development at this point in the play's action. The hints that survive are in a scene that was in fact cut out of the Folio text. It was, moreover, wisely cut, for the motivation, though it might be dramatically important, was theatrically embarrassing.[1] It would be enough for spectators that the

[1] Granville-Barker remarks (p. 149, note) that the scene appears to have been cut 'on the principle—and it is an excellent one in the theatre—of: "Never explain, never apologise."'

French king should in fact be absent, and that Cordelia should make her protestation of disinterested love—they would ask no inconvenient questions. Still the hints remain in the text for us to read, and if we had the complete play as Shakespeare originally wrote it—or perhaps only drafted or designed it—we should I suspect find the motives and even the action less obscure.

22. Entrance in the Stationers' Register: Some Statistics[1]

WHAT I have to offer this afternoon are little more than random gleanings from notes made in the course of twelve months' intensive study of Arber's Transcript of the Stationers' Registers from 1557 to 1640. I have chosen the term 'entrance' rather than 'entry' because it was used by the Clerk of the Company in a quasi-technical sense for the registration of a copy at Stationers' Hall; and I restrict it, as the Clerk did not always do, to the original registration as distinguished from an assignment or transfer, and to the act of registration as distinguished from the written record or 'entry' in the books.

I do not propose to discuss the question of the requirements and implications of Entrance: what I have to say is merely statistical. Those familiar with the Stationers' Registers are aware that the book-entries fall into two portions separated by a gap of five years. The earlier series, from the incorporation of the Company in the spring of 1557 to the summer of 1571, are not as a rule individually dated but only grouped according to craft-years: the later, beginning in 1576, almost always bear the exact date. In what follows the years are always reckoned from July to July—the precise dates vary.

In the fourteen years from 1557 to 1571 almost 1,600 copies were entered, an average of 114. This number includes a few duplicates and a few transfers, but these need not trouble us. There is, as we should expect, a general upward trend—

[1] [1944, September. *The Library*, xxv.1–7. Part of a paper on 'Entrance, Licence, and Publication' read before the Bibliographical Society on 15 Feb. 1944. The material I was collecting at the time, and on which my paper was based, was later used in condensed form in lectures delivered as Lyell Reader in Bibliography at Oxford in the Trinity Term of 1955, and published as *Some Aspects and Problems of London Publishing between 1550 and 1650* in 1956. The later sections of the paper are adequately covered by the lectures; it is only the first that contains sufficient unused material to be worth reprinting here.—1958.]

[Concerning entrance and copyright see M. A. Shaaber in *Library*, xxiv (1944), 124 and S. Thomas in *Library*, 5 Ser. iii (1948), 186.—F.P.W.]

barely 600 copies appear in the first seven years, just over 1,000 in the second—but this is largely masked by violent yearly fluctuations. There are only 70 in 1563–4, between totals of 175 and 135 in the neighbouring years. The highest totals are 205 in 1569–70 and 190 in 1565–6: the lowest, 48 and 33, are in the second and third years. In the first year there are 79, in the last 94. There seems to have been a certain rush to enter copies on incorporation followed by a reaction. Otherwise the cause of the fluctuations is obscure, except for the occasional appearance of large batches of ballads: one lot of 32 is included in the total of 79 in the first year, batches of 20 and 15 go towards the total of 135 in 1564–5.

Turning to the later period of sixty-four years from July 1576 to July 1640 (during which some 9,400 copies were entered, a yearly average of 147) the general impression is one of more or less level output varied by a few violent disturbances. For most years entrances are between 100 and 200 with no obvious upward tendency. Starting about the lower of these limits, output soon approached the higher; then there was a sharp fall, probably due to carelessness in registration, till in 1585–6 the number reached a low record of 30. (I am giving round figures all through.) But the Star Chamber decree of 1586 caused a violent reaction, and the low record is followed by a high one of 340—probably many old copies were now registered for the first time. A natural decline the next year to 110 may have been aggravated by fear of invasion; certainly a number of books called forth by the victory over the Armada went to swell the modest total of 180 in 1588–9. After that fluctuations continued within normal limits for over thirty years. In 1622–3 there was a rise to 220, for which there is no obvious explanation, and in 1624–5 a peak of 290 due to the registration of 130 ballads, old and new, by a recently formed syndicate. Entrances returned to normal for a few years; but in 1637 came another decree of the Star Chamber, which in the course of three years sent the numbers up to a new peak of 300. On the whole the yearly totals were less affected than we might have expected by visitations of the plague. It is true that entrances fell in 1592–3, but not greatly; the drop in 1603–4 is hardly perceptible—no doubt the death of the queen and the advent of a new sovereign the previous spring acted as correctives—but some dislocation is evident in the complete absence of entries between the middle of August and the latter part of October. It is also probable enough that the plague of 1625 accentuated the drop from 290 to 100 in 1625–6, for no copies at all were entered between the end of July and early in November. So far as the plague did have an influence we may suppose it to have been upon actual output: on the other hand the effect of the Star Chamber decrees must have been mainly on the regularity with which copies were registered either before or after publication.

Theoretically all copies were supposed to be entered: stationers could be, and occasionally were, fined for printing or publishing works without the formality of entrance; though when they were, it was probably due to a suspicion that their wares were of a nature to attract unfavourable attention from the authorities. Certain it is that many books were openly and regularly printed and published, sometimes under the author's supervision, and apparently without incurring censure, that were strictly speaking 'disorderly' in the view of the Court of Assistants owing to the copies not having been entered in the Register.[1] It would be very interesting to know, for different periods, what proportion of works published were in fact registered at Stationers' Hall. This is a question to which no satisfactory answer can at present be given; but it may be possible to make some approach to the problem through Miss Cecie Stainer's remarkably successful attempt to identify books recorded in the *Short-Title Catalogue* with copies entered in the Registers.[2]

[1] Whether these works had received official licence or not it is of course impossible to say: but while we may be certain that some unregistered copies had never exposed themselves to ecclesiastical censure, it would be rash to assume that others, perhaps the majority, had not sought and obtained a regular *imprimatur*.

[2] Her success, the result of patient work carried on 'steadily year after year', is I think admitted by those who have worked on the subject, though perhaps not so widely recognized as it should be, and I confess that I am at a loss to know how it was achieved. At the same time her identifications should be treated with circumspection. Some of course have been missed; some are clearly erroneous; many seem to me rather doubtful. But what is really exasperating is the quite inordinate number of errors in the references appended to the *S.T.C.* entries. Some I have failed to trace at all in the Registers—that may be my fault—but at a guess I should say that almost one in ten of the dates given is wrong, sometimes by many years, sometimes involving

Of the 1,600 works entered from 1557 to 1571 the *S.T.C.* identifies some 520, or nearly a third. But the percentages identified, like the totals entered, vary a good deal. In the case of the three highest totals (205, 190, 175) the proportion is not far short of a third (31, 27, 31 per cent.); and both the highest percentage (61) and the lowest (17) are found associated with comparatively low totals (representing 20 out of 33 and 12 out of 70 respectively). There is no perceptible rise or fall in the percentages, but it is observable that they are steadier in the second half of the period when the totals are generally higher. In the last six years the proportion is never less than a quarter, in three it is over a third: the two highest percentages are in the first half, the lowest are the middle pair.

Of the 9,400 works entered from 1576 to 1640 the *S.T.C.* identifies 5,580, a percentage of just under 60 (actually 59·38). Again, though the proportion identified varies a good deal from year to year, there is no obvious upward tendency, which is perhaps curious. As we should expect, the lowest percentages, 20 and 35, are associated with peak years, 1586–7 and 1624–5, when many ephemeral copies were entered, some of which may never have been printed. The third peak, in 1639–40, shows a percentage of 45, which is the next lowest except for that of 44 in 1578–9 and 1632–3, both years of moderately high output. The highest percentages, ranging from 82 to 88, are found in 1610–11, 1613–14, 1615–16, and 1618–21, all years in which the output was rather below the normal; but the reason for this association is less clear.

Taking the two periods together we have 11,000 works entered, of which 6,100 are identified as extant, a percentage of almost $55\frac{1}{2}$ ($55{\cdot}4\dot{5}$).

But all this, though perhaps interesting, is not what we are after. What we want to know is not the proportion of works entered that survive, but the proportion of works published that were entered. This is a more difficult problem, but one to

absurdities like 30 Feb.! I have lately spent a couple of months going through the whole *S.T.C.* from this point of view and entering the relevant numbers in my copy of Arber, and when I think of the hours I have wasted tracking down misprinted references I find it difficult to speak with becoming moderation.

which the identifications we have been considering can be made to afford a clue. We may approach it in the first instance by way of some rather hazardous guess-work. There are in the *S.T.C.* somewhat over 26,000 entries; but of course many of these are reprints, and we can hardly suppose that there are more than 12,000 to 15,000 distinct works represented. Again, an appreciable number of these were printed either before 1557 (when the Stationers' records begin) or between 1571 and 1576 (for which years the book-entries are lost) or at some place outside the jurisdiction of the Company. It may be that there are not more than 10,000 works recorded in the *S.T.C.* that could have been entered in the extant Registers. Of these 6,100 have been found so entered; from which we should infer a percentage of entries of somewhere about 60.

Though this is nothing but a rough guess, we can test it to some extent by taking a few samples. With this object I selected twenty-six of the most prolific and important authors (generally avoiding the divines, of whose significance I am not competent to judge) and tabulated their works according to the data afforded by the *S.T.C.* The result is as shown overleaf.[1]

Judged by the number of separate works the most prolific of these writers is, as we should guess, the waterman poet John Taylor; Martin Parker and Breton come next. The least so are Beaumont and Fletcher (most of whose plays, of course, remained unprinted till after our period). The lowest proportion of entrances is found in the case of Lodge, the highest in that of Shirley; but none of these figures seem particularly significant.[2] It is more interesting to observe that the totals give a percentage of entrances of close on 67.

[1] All entries under each heading are counted, whether or not the works were written by the author in question, with the exception of those printed and sold elsewhere than in London, and of course reprints. Works issued under the names of two authors are counted under the one that stands first. The entries under Francis Beaumont and John Fletcher are amalgamated.

[2] Curiously enough Dekker and Heywood show the same total and the same percentage. The proportion of Shakespeare's works entered is unusually high. This accident has led to too much reliance being placed on non-entrance as a criterion of irregular publication.

Author	*Works*	*Entered*	*Not Ent.*	*% Ent.*
Bacon, Francis	26	17	9	65
Beaumont & Fletcher	14	11	3	69
Brathwait, Richard	28	20	8	71
Breton, Nicholas	54	37	17	69
Chapman, George	25	15	10	60
Churchyard, Thomas	41	20	21	49
Daniel, Samuel	15	9	6	60
Dekker, Thomas	40	25	15	62·5
Donne, John	19	15	4	79
Drayton, Michael	21	18	3	86
Greene, Robert	37	28	9	76
Hall, Joseph, *Bishop*	48	40	8	83
Heywood, Thomas	40	25	15	62·5
Jonson, Benjamin	28	19	9	68
Lodge, Thomas	18	8	10	44
Markham, Gervase	31	23	8	74
Middleton, Thomas	27	13	14	48
Munday, Anthony	25	12	13	48
Parker, Martin, *balladmonger*	67	39	28	58
Quarles, Francis	17	13	4	77
Rich, Barnaby	21	15	6	71
Rowlands, Samuel	26	20	6	77
Shakespeare, William	26	21	5	82
Shirley, James	24	23	1	96
Taylor, John	72	41	31	57
Wither, George	18	12	6	67
Totals	808	539	269	67(66·70)

As a further check I took ten pages of the *S.T.C.* (331–40) at random (only making sure that there was nothing obviously exceptional about the headings they contained) and counted the entered and unentered works in them, excluding however those that owing to date or place of publication could not be expected to appear in the extant Registers. The number of works counted was 173, of which 114 were entered and 59 were not. This gives a percentage of nearly 66 (actually 65·90), which agrees remarkably with that previously obtained considering the smallness of the field.

Lastly the dramatic publications offer a check that can be applied chronologically. I took those for the six decades from 1581 to 1640 (excluding only plays first printed, or first extant, in collected editions) and obtained the following table:

Years	*Works*	*Entered*	*Not Ent.*	*% Ent.*
1581–90	16	6	10	37·5
1591–1600	77	54	23	70
1601–10	112	83	29	74
1611–20	64	36	28	56
1621–30	42	18	24	42
1631–40	153	116	37	69
1581–1640	464	313	151	(67·46)

Here over the whole period the percentage of extant works identified as entered in the Registers is almost $67\frac{1}{2}$. This again shows pretty close agreement, though it is a trifle higher than before. Indeed it should have been higher still, for the total is swollen by a number of publications issued elsewhere than in London, and also by certain private issues of masques and pageants, which seem not to have needed registration.[1] Perhaps we should conclude that plays were rather more regularly entered than some other classes of works.

Chronologically the table shows that in drama the decades 1601–10 and 1631–40 were by far the most prolific, and that the total for 1621–30 was the lowest after 1581–90. The three highest totals also show the highest percentages, and the two lowest totals the lowest percentages. Whatever the explanation of this coincidence may be, it is probably to be sought in special circumstances,[2] which suggests that these decade percentages for dramatic works probably afford no guide to the proportion of the general run of books registered at different times. For any such chronological estimates we shall have to wait till the *S.T.C.* entries have been rearranged

1 These masques and pageants also swell the totals of some of the authors in the former table, e.g. Dekker, Heywood, Jonson, Middleton, and Munday. If these prints were excluded the percentage of works registered would be somewhat higher.

2 It looks as though apathy as regards publication was accompanied by carelessness in respect of entrance; but, at least after 1590, there may be another and more significant explanation. There is, namely, some reason to suppose that the high output of certain periods and the low output of others was in part due to the deliberate policy of the dramatic companies in releasing their plays for, or withholding them from, publication; and plays authoritatively published would perhaps be more likely to be registered than those obtained in a less reputable way. It seems worth while to mention the possibility, though I am not certain that it will bear investigation.

in the form of annals. When that is done I hope it may be possible to distinguish in some way those works an original entrance of which has been traced in the Registers.

It would seem, therefore, that on the evidence at our disposal, we should be able to say that, at any rate for the period from 1576 to 1640, the proportion of London-printed books regularly entered at Stationers' Hall was somewhere between 60 and 70 per cent. The basis of the estimate is a survey of surviving works, and there does not appear any very strong ground for supposing that entrance or non-entrance affected survival. Still it is possible—I think no more—that in the field of ephemeral publications, where survival is least likely, the proportion of copies entered may have been somewhat lower than elsewhere. If so, it would of course depress the general percentage, and reduce it possibly as low as our original guess of 60.[1]

[1] I think the following statement would be justified: It is practically certain that the proportion of works entered was between a half and three-quarters, and probable that it was in the neighbourhood of two-thirds. The number of copies entered between 1576 and 1640 being about 9,400, the number of works printed during the period was probably about 14,000, a yearly average of nearly 220.

23. The Damnation of Faustus[1]

WHEN working lately on the text of *Doctor Faustus*, I was struck by certain aspects of the story as told in Marlowe's play that I do not remember to have seen discussed in the editions with which I am familiar. I do not pretend to have read more than a little of what has been written about Marlowe as a dramatist, and it may be that there is nothing new in what I have to say; but it seemed worth while to draw attention to a few points in the picture of the hero's downfall, on the chance that they might have escaped the attention of others, as they had hitherto escaped my own.

As soon as Faustus has decided that necromancy is the only study that can give his ambition scope, he seeks the aid of his friends Valdes and Cornelius, who already are proficient in the art—

> Their conference will be a greater help to me
> Than all my labours, plod I ne'er so fast. [I. 66–67][2]

Who they are we are not told: they do not appear in the source on which Marlowe drew—'The historie of the damnable life, and deserued death of Doctor Iohn Faustus . . . according to the true Copie printed at Franckfort, and translated into English by P. F. Gent.'—and Cornelius cannot be the famous Cornelius Agrippa, who is mentioned in their conversation.

[1] [1946, April. *The Modern Language Review*, xli. 97–107. Part of a lecture given at University College, London.]

[2] There is as yet no satisfactory critical text of *Faustus*, and I have had to do the best I could, in the light of my own study, to harmonize the rival versions as printed in the quartos of 1604 and 1616 respectively, taking from each what best illustrated the points I wished to make. In the case of such a necessarily eclectic text there seemed no object in attempting to follow the spelling of the originals, except where it possessed some significance. I have also felt free so to punctuate as best to bring out what I believe to be the sense of the original. [My attempted reconstruction of the text was published by the Clarendon Press in 1950: I have added references to it.] [I have altered the text to agree in wording with the 1950 edition (except at V. i. 5, where the run of the passage calls for the 1616 text used in 1946), but have sometimes left the 1946 punctuation and other accidentals, where it seemed to me preferable. Greg had himself altered some of the readings, so that it is just conceivable that, where the 1946 text remained unaltered in his copy, he had changed his mind once more, but this seems unlikely. The 1946 text of I. iii. 110, for instance, has a sheer mistranscription—'in' for 'of'—which Greg continued to overlook.—J.C.M.]

But they must have been familiar figures at Wittenberg, since on learning that Faustus is at dinner with them, his students at once conclude that he is 'fallen into that damnèd art For which they two are infamous through the world' [I. ii. 29–30]. The pair are ready enough to obey Faustus' invitation, for they have long sought to lead him into forbidden ways. 'Know', says Faustus—

> Know that your words have won me at the last
> To practise magic and concealèd arts. [99–100]

At the same time, though they are his 'dearest friends' [I. i. 62], he is anxious not to appear too pliant, adding, a little clumsily (if the 1604 text is to be trusted)

> Yet not your words only, but mine own fantasy, [101]

and he makes it plain that he is no humble seeker after instruction, but one whose personal fame and honour are to be their main concern—

> Then, gentle friends, aid me in this attempt,
> And I, that have with concise syllogisms
> Gravelled the pastors of the German church,
> And made the flowering pride of Wittenberg
> Swarm to my problems as the infernal spirits
> On sweet Musaeus when he came to hell,
> Will be as cunning as Agrippa was,
> Whose shadows made all Europe honour him. [109–16]

His friends are content enough to accept him on these terms. Valdes, while hinting that common contributions deserve common rewards—

> Faustus, these books, thy wit, and our experience
> Shall make all nations to canonize us [117–18]—

paints a glowing picture of the possibilities before them, adding however—in view of what follows a little ominously—

> If learnèd Faustus will be resolute. [131]

Reassured on this score, Cornelius is ready to allow Faustus pride of place—

> Then doubt not, Faustus, but to be renowmed,
> And more frequented for this mystery
> Than heretofore the Delphian oracle [139–41]—

but only on condition that the profits of the enterprise are shared—

> Then tell me, Faustus, what shall we three want? [146]

However, it soon appears that for all their sinister reputation the two are but dabblers in witchcraft. They have, indeed, called spirits from the deep, and they have come—

> The spirits tell me they can dry the sea
> And fetch the treasure of all foreign wracks,
> Yea, all the wealth that our forefathers hid
> Within the massy entrails of the earth [142–5]—

but they have made no use of this knowledge, they have never become the masters—or the slaves—of the spirits. Even to raise them they must, of course, have run a mortal risk—

> Nor will we come unless he use such means
> Whereby he is in danger to be damned [I. iii. 50–51]—

but they have been careful not to forfeit their salvation for supernatural gifts; they have never succumbed to the temptation of the spirits or made proof of their boasted powers. Nor do they mean to put their own art to the ultimate test. When Faustus eagerly demands,

> Come, show me some demonstrations magical, [I. i. 148]

Valdes proves himself a ready teacher—

> Then haste thee to some solitary grove,
> And bear wise Bacon's and Abanus' works,
> The Hebrew Psalter, and New Testament;
> And whatsoever else is requisite
> We will inform thee ere our conference cease [151–5]—

and guarantees to make him proficient in the art—

> First I'll instruct thee in the rudiments,
> And then wilt thou be perfecter than I. [159–60]

Knowing the depth of Faustus' learning, and satisfied of his courage and resolution, they are anxious to form a partnership with one whose potentialities as an adept so far exceed their own. But Cornelius leaves us in no doubt of their intention to use Faustus as a cat's-paw rather than run into danger themselves—

> Valdes, first let him know the words of art,
> And then, all other ceremonies learned,
> Faustus may try his cunning by himself. [156–8]

The precious pair are no deeply versed magicians welcoming a promising beginner, but merely the devil's decoys luring Faustus along the road to destruction.[1] They serve their purpose in giving a dramatic turn to the scene of his temptation, and except for a passing mention by the students, we hear no more of them.[2]

Faustus goes to conjure alone, and alone he concludes his pact with the devil. What use will he make of his hazardously won powers? His dreams, if self-centred, are in the heroic vein:

> Oh, what a world of profit and delight,
> Of power, of honour, of omnipotence,
> Is promised to the studious artizan!
> All things that move between the quiet poles
> Shall be at my command: emperors and kings
> Are but obeyed in their several provinces, . . .
> But his dominion that excells in this
> Stretcheth as far as doth the mind of man:
> A sound magician is a demi-god! [I. i. 51–56, 58–60]

More than mortal power and knowledge shall be his, to use in the service of his country:

> Shall I make spirits fetch me what I please,
> Resolve me of all ambiguities,
> Perform what desperate enterprise I will? . . .
> I'll have them read me strange philosophy

[1] There is a hint that Faustus' downfall was planned by Mephostophilis from the start. Quite near the end, gloating over Faustus' despair, he says (in the 1616 text):

> when thou took'st the book
> To view the scriptures, then I turned the leaves
> And led thine eye. [V. ii. 92–94]

The only incident *in the play* to which this could refer is the collocation of biblical texts that prompts Faustus to renounce divinity in the opening scene [I. i. 39–41].

[2] Of course, the theatrical reason for this is that Marlowe has no further use for them, but like a good craftsman he was careful to supply a dramatic reason in his delineation of the characters.

> And tell the secrets of all foreign kings;
> I'll have them wall all Germany with brass . . .
> And chase the Prince of Parma from our land . . .
> [I. i. 77–79, 84–86, 91]

Whatever baser elements there may be in his ambition, we should, by all human standards, expect the fearless seeker after knowledge and truth, the scholar weary of the futilities of the schools, to make at least no ignoble use of the power suddenly placed at his command.

Critics have complained that instead of pursuing ends worthy of his professed ideals, Faustus, once power is his, abandons these without a qualm, and shows himself content to amuse the Emperor with conjuring tricks and play childish pranks on the Pope; and they have blamed this either on a collaborator, or on the fact of Marlowe's work having been later overlaid and debased by another hand. The charge, in its crudest form, involves some disregard of the 1616 version, which is not quite as fatuous as its predecessor, but in broad outline there is no denying its justice. As to responsibility: it is of course obvious that not all the play as we have it is Marlowe's. For my own part, however, I do not believe that as originally written it differed to any material extent from what we are able to reconstruct from a comparison of the two versions in which it has come down to us. And while it is true that the middle portion, to which objection is mostly taken, shows little trace of Marlowe's hand, I see no reason to doubt that it was he who planned the whole, or that his collaborator or collaborators, whoever he or they may have been, carried out his plan substantially according to instructions. If that is so, for any fundamental fault in the design Marlowe must be held responsible.

The critics' disappointment is quite natural. Although it is difficult to see how any dramatist could have presented in language and dramatic form the revelation of a knowledge beyond the reach of human wisdom, there is no question that much more might have been done to show the wonder and uphold the dignity of the quest, and so satisfy the natural expectation of the audience. Marlowe did not do it; he deliberately turned from the attempt. Instead he showed us the betrayal of ideals, the lapse into luxury and buffoonery.

And what, in the devil's name, would the critics have? I say 'in the devil's name' advisedly, for all that happens to Faustus once the pact is signed is the devil's work: 'human standards' are no longer relevant. Who but a fool—such a clever fool as Faustus—would dream that any power but evil could be won by a bargain with evil, or that truth could be wrung from the father of lies? 'All power tends to corrupt, and absolute power corrupts absolutely', is indeed an aphorism to which few Elizabethans would have subscribed; but Marlowe knew the nature of the power he put into the hands of his hero and the inevitable curse involved.

Of course, Faustus' corruption is not a mechanical outcome of his pact with evil. In spite of his earnest desire to know truth, and half-hidden in the Marlowan glamour cast about him, the seeds of decay are discernable in his character from the first—how else should he come to make his fatal bargain? Beside his passion for knowledge is a lust for riches and pleasure and power. If less single-minded, he shares Barabbas' thirst for wealth—

> I'll have them fly to India for gold,
> Ransack the ocean for orient pearl,
> And search all corners of the new-found world
> For pleasant fruits and princely delicates. . . [I. i. 80–83]

Patriotism is a veil for ambition: he will

> chase the Prince of Parma from our land
> And reign sole king of all our provinces. . . [I. i. 91–92]

> I'll join the hills that bind the Afric shore
> And make that country continent to Spain,
> And both contributary to my crown:
> The Emperor shall not live but by my leave,
> Nor any potentate of Germany. [I. iii. 106–10]

His aspiration to be 'great emperor of the world' [I. iii. 103] recalls Tamburlain's vulgar desire for

> The sweet fruition of an earthly crown.

But Faustus' ambition is not thus limited; the promptings of his soul reveal themselves in the words of the Bad Angel:

> Be thou on earth as Jove is in the sky,
> Lord and commander of these elements. [I. i. 75–76]

If there is a sensual vein in him, it is hardly seen at this stage; still his demand to 'live in all voluptuousness' [I. iii. 91] anticipates later desires—

> Whilst I am here on earth let me be cloyed
> With all things that delight the heart of man;
> My four and twenty years of liberty
> I'll spend in pleasure and in dalliance—[III. i. 59–62]

and it may be with shrewd insight that Valdes promises 'serviceable' spirits,

> Sometimes like women or unwedded maids,
> Shadowing more beauty in their airy brows
> Than in the white breasts of the Queen of Love. [I. i. 125–7]

But when all is said, this means no more than that Faustus is a man dazzled by the unlimited possibilities of magic, and alive enough to his own weakness to exclaim:

> The god thou serv'st is thine own appetite . . . [I. iv. 10]

After Faustus has signed the bond with his blood, we can trace the stages of a gradual deterioration. His previous interview with Mephostophilis struck the note of earnest if slightly sceptical inquiry with which he entered on his quest:

> This word 'damnation' terrifies not me,
> For I confound hell in Elysium:
> My ghost be with the old philosophers! [I. iii. 58–60]

He questions eagerly about hell, and the spirit replies:

> Why, this is hell, nor am I out of it:
> Think'st thou that I, who saw the face of God
> And tasted the eternal joys of heaven,
> Am not tormented with ten thousand hells
> In being deprived of everlasting bliss? . . .
> *Fau.* What, is great Mephostophilis so passionate
> For being deprivèd of the joys of heaven?
> Learn thou of Faustus manly fortitude,
> And scorn those joys thou never shalt possess. [I. iii. 75–79, 82–85]

After the bond is signed the discussion is renewed, but while the devil loses nothing in dignity of serious discourse, we can already detect a change in Faustus; his sceptical levity takes on a more truculent and jeering tone. Asked 'Where is the place that men call hell?' Mephostophilis replies:

Within the bowels of these elements,
Where we are tortured and remain for ever.
Hell hath no limits, nor is circumscribed
In one self place, but where we are is hell,
And where hell is, there must we ever be:
And to be short, when all the world dissolves
And every creature shall be purified,
All places shall be hell that is not heaven.
Fau. I think hell 's a fable.
Meph. Ay, think so still, till experience change thy mind. . . .
Fau. . . . Think'st thou that Faustus is so fond to imagine
That after this life there is any pain?
No, these are trifles and mere old wives' tales.
Meph. But I am an instance to prove the contrary;
For I tell thee I am damned and now in hell.
Fau. Nay, and this be hell, I'll willingly be damned:
What? sleeping, eating, walking, and disputing! [II. i. 117–26. 131–7]

In the next scene there follows the curiously barren discussion on astronomy. It has probably been interpolated and is not altogether easy to follow, but the infernal exposition of the movements of the spheres calls forth an impatient,

These slender questions Wagner can decide [II. ii. 48]

and at the end Mephostophilis' sententious

Per inaequalem motum respectu totius

and Faustus' half-satisfied

Well, I am answered! [II. ii. 65–66]

leave in the mouth the taste of dead-sea fruit. The quarrel that follows on the spirit's refusal to say who made the world leads to the intervention of Lucifer, and the 'pastime' of the Seven Deadly Sins. There seems to me more savour in this than has sometimes been allowed; still it is a much shrunken Faustus who exclaims:

Oh, this feeds my soul! [II. ii. 167 (1604)]

He had been no less delighted with the dance of the devils that offered him crowns and rich apparel on his signing the bond: we do not know its nature, but from his exclamation,

> Then there's enough for a thousand souls! [II. i. 86 (1604)]

when told that he may conjure up such spirits at will, we may perhaps conclude that it involved a direct appeal to the senses. That would, at least, accord with his mood soon afterwards; for while it would be rash to lay much stress on his demanding 'the fairest maid in Germany, for I am wanton and lascivious' [II. i. 138–9] (this being perhaps an interpolation) we should allow due weight to Mephostophilis' promise:

> I'll cull thee out the fairest courtesans
> And bring them every morning to thy bed;
> She whom thine eye shall like, thy heart shall have,
> Were she as chaste as was Penelope,
> As wise as Saba, or as beautiful
> As was bright Lucifer before his fall. [II. i. 151–6]

So far Faustus has not left Wittenberg, and emphasis has been rather on the hollowness of his bargain in respect of any intellectual enlightenment than on the actual degradation of his character. As yet only his childish pleasure in the devil-dance and the pageant of the Sins hints at the depth of vulgar triviality into which he is doomed to descend. In company with Mephostophilis he now launches forth into the world; but his dragon-flights

> To find the secrets of astronomy
> Graven in the book of Jove's high firmament, [III. Ch. 2–3]

and

> to prove cosmography,
> That measures coasts and kingdoms of the earth, [20–21]

only land him at last in the Pope's privy-chamber to

> take some part of holy Peter's feast, [III. i. 54]

and live with dalliance in

> the view
> Of rarest things and royal courts of kings . . . [IV. Ch. 1–2]

It is true that in the fuller text of 1616 the rescue of 'holy Bruno', imperial candidate for the papal throne, lends a more serious touch to the sheer horse-play of the Roman scenes in the 1604 version, and even the 'horning' episode at the Emperor's court is at least developed into some dramatic coherence; but this only brings out more pointedly the progressive fatuity of Faustus' career, which in the clownage and conjuring tricks at Anhalt sinks to the depth of buffoonery.

If, as may be argued, the gradual deterioration of Faustus' character and the prostitution of his powers stand out less clearly than they should, this may be ascribed partly to Marlowe's negligent handling of a theme that failed to kindle his wayward inspiration, and partly to the ineptitude of his collaborator. But the logical outline is there, and I must differ from Marlowe's critics, and believe that when he sketched that outline Marlowe knew what he was about.

Another point to be borne in mind is that there is something strange and peculiar, not only in Faustus' situation, but in his nature. Once he has signed the bond, he is in the position of having by his own free will renounced salvation. So much is obvious. Less obvious is the inner change he has brought upon himself. Critics have strangely neglected the first article of the infernal compact: 'that Faustus may be a spirit in form and substance' [II. i. 94]. Presumably they have taken it to mean merely that he should be free of the bonds of flesh, so that he may be invisible at will, invulnerable, and be able to change his shape, ride on dragons, and so forth. But in this play 'spirit' is used in a very specialized sense. There is, of course, nothing very significant in the fact that, when the 'devils' dance before him, Faustus asks:

> But may I raise such spirits when I please? [II. i. 84]

that he promises to

> make my spirits pull His churches down [II. ii. 101]

and bids Mephostophilis

> Ay, go, accursèd spirit to ugly hell! [II. i. 77]

or that the latter speaks of the devils as

> Unhappy spirits that fell with Lucifer [I. iii. 70]—

though it is noticeable how persistently devils are called spirits in the play,[1] and it is worth recalling that in the *Damnable Life* Mephostophilis is regularly 'the Spirit' [1592, p. 3 *et passim*]. What is significant is that when Faustus asks 'What is that Lucifer, thy lord?' Mephostophilis replies:

> Arch-regent and commander of all spirits [I. iii. 63]

which Faustus at once interprets as 'prince of devils'; and that the Bad Angel, in reply to Faustus' cry of repentance, asserts:

> Thou art a spirit; God cannot pity thee [II. ii. 13]

—a remark to which I shall return. And if there could be any doubt of the meaning of these expressions, we have the explicit statement in the *Damnable Life* that Faustus' 'request was none other but to become a devil' [1592, p. 4]. Faustus then, through his bargain with hell, has himself taken on the infernal nature, although it is made clear throughout that he still retains his human soul.

This throws a new light upon the question, debated throughout the play, whether Faustus can be saved by repentance. Faustus, of course, is for ever repenting—and recanting through fear of bodily torture and death—and the Good and Bad Angels, who personate the two sides of his human nature, are for ever disputing the point:

> *Fau.* Contrition, prayer, repentance: what of these?
> *Good A.* Oh, they are means to bring thee unto heaven.
> *Bad A.* Rather illusions, fruits of lunacy [II. i. 15–17]

and again:

> *Good A.* Never too late, if Faustus will repent.
> *Bad A.* If thou repent, devils will tear thee in pieces.
> *Good A.* Repent, and they shall never raze thy skin. [II. ii. 81–83]

There are two passages that are particularly significant in this respect: and we must remember, as I have said, the double question at issue—Faustus' nature, and whether repentance

[1] Even in stage directions: the first entry of the Good and Bad Angels is headed in 1616: 'Enter the Angell and Spirit' [I. i. 68].

can cancel a bargain. First then, the passage from which I have already quoted:

> *Good A.* Faustus, repent; yet God will pity thee.
> *Bad A.* Thou art a spirit; God cannot pity thee.
> *Fau.* Who buzzeth in mine ears I am a spirit?
> Be I a devil, yet God may pity me;
> Yea, God will pity me if I repent.
> *Bad A.* Ay, but Faustus never shall repent. [II. ii. 12–17]

The Bad Angel evades the issue, which is left undecided.[1] Later in the same scene, when Faustus calls on Christ to save his soul, Lucifer replies with deadly logic:

> Christ cannot save thy soul, for he is just:
> There's none but I have interest in the same. [II. ii. 86–88][2]

Thus the possibility of Faustus' salvation is left nicely poised in doubt—like that of the archdeacon of scholastic speculation.

It is only when, back among his students at Wittenberg, he faces the final reckoning that Faustus regains some measure of heroic dignity. Marlowe again takes charge. But even so the years have wrought a change. His faithful Wagner is puzzled:

> I wonder what he means; if death were nigh,
> He would not banquet and carouse and swill
> Among the students, as even now he doth. . . [V. i. 5–7]

This is a very different Faustus from the fearless teacher his students used to know, whose least absence from the classroom caused concern—

> I wonder what's become of Faustus, that was wont to make our schools ring with *sic probo*. [I. ii. 1–2]

One good, or at least amiable, quality—apart from a genuine tenderness towards his students—we may be tempted to

[1] Faustus' words are perhaps intentionally ambiguous. 'Be I a devil' may mean 'What though I am a devil', or it may mean 'Even were I a devil'. Ward insisted on the second sense, but it is not borne out by the evidence. Boas shows a correct understanding of the passage when he glosses 'spirit' as 'evil spirit, devil'.

[2] Compare Faustus' own lines near the end: 'Hell claims his right, and with a roaring voice Says "Faustus, come; thine hour is almost come"; And Faustus now will come to do thee right.' [V. i. 56–58]

claim for him throughout: a love of beauty in nature and in art:

> Have not I made blind Homer sing to me
> Of Alexander's love and Oenon's death?
> And hath not he that built the walls of Thebes
> With ravishing sound of his melodious harp
> Made music—? [II. ii. 25–29]

and the climax of his career is his union with the immortal beauty of Helen, to measures admittedly the most lovely that flowed from Marlowe's lyre. Is this sensitive appreciation something that has survived uncorrupted from his days of innocence? I can find no hint of it in the austere student of the early scenes. Is it then some strange flowering of moral decay? It would seem so. What, after all, is that 'ravishing sound' but the symphony of hell?—

> Made music—with my Mephostophilis!

And Helen, what of her?

Here we come, if I mistake not, to the central theme of the damnation of Faustus. The lines in which he addresses Helen are some of the most famous in the language:

> Was this the face that launched a thousand ships
> And burnt the topless towers of Ilium?
> Sweet Helen, make me immortal with a kiss! . . .
> Here will I dwell, for heaven is in these lips,
> And all is dross that is not Helena.
> I will be Paris, and for love of thee
> Instead of Troy shall Wittenberg be sacked;
> And I will combat with weak Menelaus,
> And wear thy colours on my plumèd crest:
> Yea, I will wound Achilles in the heel,
> And then return to Helen for a kiss.
> Oh, thou art fairer than the evening's air
> Clad in the beauty of a thousand stars,
> Brighter art thou than flaming Jupiter
> When he appeared to hapless Semele,
> More lovely than the monarch of the sky
> In wanton Arethusa's azured arms;
> And none but thou shalt be my paramour! [v. i. 98–100, 103–17]

In these lines Marlowe's uncertain genius soared to its height,[1] but their splendour has obscured, and was perhaps meant discreetly to veil, the real nature of the situation. 'Her lips suck forth my soul', says Faustus in lines that I omitted from his speech above.[2] What is Helen? We are not told in so many words, but the answer is there, if we choose to look for it. When the Emperor asks him to present Alexander and his paramour before the court, Faustus (in the 1604 version) laboriously explains the nature of the figures that are to appear:

> My gracious lord, I am ready to accomplish your request so far forth as by art and power of my spirit I am able to perform. . . . But, if it like your grace, it is not in my ability to present before your eyes the true substantial bodies of those two deceased princes, which long since are consumed to dust. . . . But such spirits as can lively resemble Alexander and his paramour shall appear before your grace in that manner that they best lived in, in their most flourishing estate . . . [cf. IV. ii. 32]

He adds (according to the 1616 version):

> My lord, I must forewarn your majesty
> That, when my spirits present the royal shapes
> Of Alexander and his paramour,
> Your grace demand no questions of the king,
> But in dumb silence let them come and go. [IV. ii. 45–49]

This is explicit enough; and as a reminder that the same holds for Helen, Faustus repeats the caution when he presents her to his students:

> Be silent then, for danger is in words. [V. i. 26]

Consider, too, a point critics seem to have overlooked, the circumstances in which Helen is introduced the second time.

[1] Besides a number of incidental passages of great beauty, some of which I have quoted, the play contains three that stand out above the rest and I think surpass all else that Marlowe wrote. The address to Helen is of course pure lyric; the final soliloquy is intense spiritual drama: with these, and in its different mode little below them, I would place the farewell scene with the students, which seems to prove that, had he chosen, Marlowe could have been no less an artist in prose than he was in verse.

[2] 'Her lips suck forth my soul: see where it flies!' Faustus of course intends the words in a merely amorous sense, confusing the physical and the spiritual in an exaggerated image that is not perhaps in the purest taste. But I wonder whether Marlowe may not have had, at the back of his mind, some recollection of the *Ars moriendi*, with its pictures of a devil dragging the naked soul out of the mouth of a dying man.

Urged by the Old Man, Faustus has attempted a last revolt; as usual he has been cowed into submission, and has renewed the blood-bond. He has sunk so low as to beg revenge upon his would-be saviour—

> Torment, sweet friend, that base and agèd man,
> That durst dissuade me from thy Lucifer,
> With greatest torments that our hell affords. [v. i. 82–84]

And it is in the first place as a safeguard against relapse that he seeks possession of Helen—

> One thing, good servant, let me crave of thee
> To glut the longing of my heart's desire;
> That I may have unto my paramour
> That heavenly Helen which I saw of late,
> Whose sweet embracings may extinguish clear
> Those thoughts that may dissuade me from my vow,
> And keep the oath I made to Lucifer. [v. i. 89–96]

Love and revenge are alike insurances against salvation. 'Helen' then is a 'spirit', and in this play a spirit means a devil.[1] In making her his paramour Faustus commits the sin of demoniality, that is, bodily intercourse with demons.[2]

[1] This fact has perhaps been obscured for critics by recollections of Goethe's *Faust*. Thus Ward, in a note on Faustus' address to Helen, writes: 'The outburst of Faust on beholding the real Helena (whom he had previously seen as a magical apparition) . . . should be compared'. There is, of course, no such distinction between the two appearances of Helen in Marlowe's play. It is curious, by the way, how persistently critics and editors commit the absurdity of calling the spirit in Marlowe's play 'Mephistophiles', as if this were the correct or original form and not a variant invented by Goethe a couple of centuries later.

[2] The *Oxford English Dictionary* defines *demoniality* as 'The nature of demons, the realm of demons, demons collectively. (Cf. *spirituality*.)' But this is not supported by the only two quotations it gives. The first, curiously enough, is the title: 'Demoniality; or Incubi and Succubi . . . by the Rev. Father Sinistrari, of Ameno . . . now first translated into English' (1879). This, even by itself, is suggestive, and anyone who has looked beyond the title of this curious and long-unprinted work by the seventeenth-century theologian Lodovico Maria Sinistrari, knows that the analogy of demoniality is not with 'spirituality' but with 'bestiality'. The worthy casuist is quite explicit. '3. Coitus igitur cum Dæmone, sive Succubo (qui proprie est Dæmonialitas), specie differt a Bestialitate, nec cum ea facit unam speciem . . . 8. Ulterius in confesso est apud omnes Theologos Morales, quod longe gravior est copula cum Dæmone, quam quolibet bruto . . .'. The writer also draws a distinction, repeated in his better-known work *De Delictis et Poenis* (Venice, 1700), between two varieties of demoniality, that practised by witches and warlocks with devils, and that which others commit with incubi and succubae. According to Sinistrari the first to use the term *daemonialitas*, and to distinguish it from *bestialitas*, was Johannes Caramuelis

The implication of Faustus' action is made plain in the comments of the Old Man and the Angels. Immediately before the Helen episode, the Old Man was still calling on Faustus to repent—

> Ah, Doctor Faustus, that I might prevail
> To guide thy steps unto the way of life! [cf. v. i. 37]

(So 1604: 1616 proceeds:)

> Though thou hast now offended like a man,
> Do not persever in it like a devil:
> Yet, yet, thou hast an amiable soul,
> If sin by custom grow not into nature . . . [40–43]

But with Faustus' union with Helen the nice balance between possible salvation and imminent damnation is upset. The Old Man, who has witnessed the meeting (according to the 1604 version), recognizes the inevitable:

> Accursèd Faustus, miserable man,
> That from thy soul exclud'st the grace of heaven
> And fliest the throne of his tribunal-seat! [v. i. 118–20]

The Good Angel does no less:

> Ah Faustus, if thou hadst given ear to me
> Innumerable joys had followed thee . . .
> Oh, thou hast lost celestial happiness . . . [v. ii. 97–98, 104]

And Faustus himself, still haunted in his final agony by the idea of a salvation beyond his reach—

> See, see, where Christ's blood streams in the firmament!
> One drop would save my soul [v. ii. 144–5]—

shows, in talk with his students, a terrible clarity of vision:

> A surfeit of deadly sin, that hath damned both body and soul. . . . Faustus' offence can ne'er be pardoned: the Serpent that tempted Eve may be saved, but not Faustus [v. ii. 37–38, 41–42]

and Mephostophilis echoes him:

> Ay, Faustus, now hast thou no hope of heaven . . . [v. ii. 85]

in his *Theologia Fundamentalis* (Frankfort, 1651). The other quotation given in the dictionary is from *The Saturday Review* (1891). 'The old wives' fables . . . are those of demoniality, black masses, etc.', in which the meaning is presumably the same.

It would be idle to speculate how far the 'atheist' Marlowe, whom gossip accused of what we call 'unnatural' vice, may have dwelt in imagination on the direst sin of which human flesh is capable. But in presenting the fall and slow moral disintegration of an ardent if erring spirit, he did not shrink from depicting, beside Faustus' spiritual sin of bartering his soul to the powers of evil, what is in effect its physical complement and counterpart, however he may have disguised it in immortal verse.

24. Old Style—New Style[1]

TWENTY years ago, at the time of the Newton celebrations, an eminent historian wrote to the papers to complain that the bicentenary of Sir Isaac's death was being commemorated on the wrong day—20 March 1927. 'There are', he asserted, 'two correct dates for Newton's death—March 20, 1726, by the old calendar, and March 31, 1727, by the reformed calendar. By no reckoning can March 20, 1727, be correct, and not until next Thursday week [31 March 1927] will two hundred years have elapsed since Newton died.'[2] Though this last statement is, in a sense, perfectly true, the letter was, of course, written in a spirit of pure mischief. Its author knew perfectly well that, in giving dates of English history between 1582 and 1752, it is the reasonable practice of all historians, including himself, to retain the Old Style reckoning current at the time, but in regard to the year, to follow the now universal custom of beginning it on the first of January.[3] The letter merely illustrates how easy it is to bedevil matters of chronology by failing or refusing to distinguish between two quite distinct questions.

Any competent historian may, I presume, be trusted to know the meaning of the letters 'O.S.' and 'N.S.' used in connexion with dates. Unfortunately writers on English literature are not always competent historians—any more than I am myself—and it is evident from their use of these letters that they often do not know their meaning. The symbols in question are one of those technicalities that sometimes turn a display of specialized knowledge into a betrayal of ignorance. All too often we find the literary historian mak-

[1] [1948. *Joseph Quincy Adams Memorial Studies* (The Folger Shakespeare Library, Washington), pp. 563–9.]

[2] A. F. Pollard, *The Times*, 21 March 1927.

[3] It has been said, and that on the highest authority, that we perpetuate the old custom of beginning the year on Lady Day when we speak of the Revolution of 1688, because James II was not officially succeeded by William and Mary till 13 Feb. 1688/9. But a revolution is more than the settlement that ends it, and since William landed at Tor Bay on 5 Nov. and James fled from Whitehall on 11 Dec. (finally leaving England on the night of 22–23), there seems little reason to cavil at the traditional dating.

ing such a statement as that Queen Elizabeth died on '24 March 1603, N.S.,' meaning no more than that she died on that day in what we call 1603, but which according to the official usage of the time was still 1602. In fact the statement is, of course, simply untrue; and it may not therefore, I think, be superfluous or impertinent to point out exactly what the terms Old Style and New Style mean.

The distinction between Old and New Style is itself a perfectly simple one: the terms refer to what are usually known as the Julian and Gregorian calendars, two systems of adjusting the length of the year so that it shall contain an integral number of days. The reckoning instituted in 45 B.C. by Julius Caesar, on the advice of the Greek astronomer Sosigenes, assumed that the year was equal to 365¼ days, and it therefore provided for a year of 365 days, with an extra day added (in February) every fourth (leap) year, making it 366 days. But in fact the length of the year is not 365¼ days; it is 365 days, 5 hours, 48 minutes, and 46 seconds—that is, 11 minutes and 14 seconds less than had been assumed. The result was that by the sixteenth century the correspondence between the calendar and the seasons, which it was the object of the reckoning to preserve, had grown to be ten days out; the calendar having, of course, lagged behind the seasons. This was corrected in 1582 by the bull *Inter grauissimas* of Pope Gregory XIII, which ordained that ten days should be omitted from the calendar that year (4 October being followed by 15 October) and that in future century-years (1600, 1700, &c.) should only be leap years if the number before the noughts was a multiple of four.[1] The Gregorian reform, however, was not adopted in England till 1752,[2] when eleven days (between Wednesday, 2 September, and Thursday, 14 September) were dropped—the discrepancy having, of course, grown from ten days to

[1] The reckoning was mainly based on the calculations of the Neapolitan Aloysius Lilius (Luigi Lilio Ghiraldi) and some writers therefore speak of the Lilian year. It was criticized by the younger Scaliger in his *Emendatio temporum*, and some of his objections are said to have weight. The Gregorian rule for leap year is, of course, that in force today—1900 was not a leap year. The adjustment is accurate to within half a minute a year, but the accumulated error since 1582 is now about three hours, and a further adjustment will ultimately have to be made.

[2] A bill to introduce the reform was read twice in the House of Lords in March 1585, but it never became law.

eleven through 1700 being a leap year according to the Julian but not according to the Gregorian reckoning. Thus for a hundred and seventy years Old Style persisted in England, while countries owing obedience to Rome were using New Style, with dates ten or eleven days ahead. According to the Gregorian calendar (N.S.) Queen Elizabeth died, not on 24 March at all, but on 3 April.

But did she die in 1602 or 1603? This question of the year has come to be confused with the question of the day because the bull of Gregory XIII that instituted the New Style reckoning also enacted that the year should begin on 1 January, and the same provision was incorporated in the act that introduced the New Style into England.[1] But the beginning of the year is in fact an entirely different matter from the reform of the calendar that gave rise to New Style, as becomes evident when we observe that, whereas Gregory's reform was at once adopted, though sometimes with reluctance, whereever his bull was current, the adoption of 1 January as the day on which to begin the year took place at very different times, even in Catholic countries. The Estates of Holland had adopted it as early as 1532, Spain as early as 1556;[2] Scotland adopted it in 1600, Florence not till 1749, and Venice as late as 1797; the papal chancery itself, whence had issued the reform, seems to have delayed making the change till 1621 in briefs and 1691 in bulls. In England the new custom was not officially adopted till 1752, but private practice had varied for a couple of centuries and more. Modern historians, dealing with events in England before 1752, naturally give the year according to the custom now current (beginning it on 1 January) but at the same time retain the Old Style dates of contemporary records, unless it

[1] In France the term *nouveau style* was used before 1582 to indicate the use of the calendar year, which was adopted in that country between 1563 and 1567 (an act of the former year being confirmed in the latter). But, according to the *New English Dictionary*, the term New Style was never used in England before the Gregorian reform and always with reference to it. It applies, of course, to the reform as a whole, and thus includes beginning the year on 1 January, but it cannot be applied to the convention respecting the year apart from the date within the year.

[2] In Spain this was in fact a reversion to earlier usage, for in regions subject to Visigothic rule 1 January was instituted as the beginning of the year in the fifth century and not abrogated in favour of Christmas till between 1349 and 1420 in different parts of the peninsula.

is desired to relate them to the New Style reckoning prevalent abroad. When this is necessary a double date is given—thus in the seventeenth century the summer solstice would be 11/21 (or 12/22) June—just as, to avoid ambiguity, a double year number[1] may be given—for example, Hilary Term 1601/2. Thus every historian would give the date of James I's accession as 24 March 1603, although at the time it would have been officially given as 24 March 1602 in England and as 3 April 1603 in most foreign countries—facts that can if necessary be combined by writing 24 March/3 April, 1602/3.[2]

Now, this question of 'the beginning of the year', which properly has nothing to do with Old and New Style, is from the historical point of view far more complicated than Gregory's reform of the calendar. In the first place, to be exact we should speak of 'the day on which the year-number is changed' rather than 'the beginning of the year', for there is no essential connexion between the two. When Julius reformed the calendar in Rome the year began on 1 January,[3] and in a very important sense it has begun on 1 January ever since. For in spite of the determination of the Church to date its era from the Conception or the Birth of Christ (and therefore to begin each year of it on 25 March or 25 December) common folk have always clung to the old pagan custom, and 'New Year's Day' has never meant anything but 1 January. At court the new-year gifts were always given on that day, and even the Church reckoned the Golden Number and the Dominical Letter from it. Calendars and almanacs invariably ran from January to December, whether they were in manuscript psalters or printed Bibles, or were hawked as popular pamphlets and prognostications.[4] News-sheets,

[1] A clumsy phrase in English, but familiar enough in German as *Jahreszahl*.

[2] The double year-number should be written 1602/3, not (as it often is) 1602–3. The latter either means 1602 and 1603, or else applies to a period including a portion of each: for example, the Christmas season of 1602–3 ended with Twelfth Night 1602/3.

[3] The Roman year was originally one of ten months beginning on 1 March, but two months had already been added at the beginning.

[4] There may, of course, have been almanacs drawn up for special purposes that ran differently, just as today some university presses issue diaries beginning in October. English Bibles, it is worth noting, definitely begin the year in January. Thus the original edition of the Authorized Version in 1611 contains 'An Almanacke for xxxix yeeres' from 1603 to 1641. Under 1603 the first dates are Septuagesima Sunday,

establishing regular publication in the mid-seventeenth century, followed the practice of the calendar. There is a pleasant irony in the fact that it was a papal bull that re-established the old pagan reckoning as a necessary reformation of the chaos introduced by the conflicting practices of Christendom.

To us it seems strange and even contradictory to alter the year-number at any time other than the beginning of the year, but to the medieval and even to the Elizabethan mind it doubtless appeared natural enough. For the use of regnal, pontifical, ducal, and episcopal years was much commoner and more widespread then than now, and in the middle ages at any rate, people who needed to use year-dates at all would be at least as familiar with these reckonings as with the Years of Grace. Indeed, it has been truly said that 'The Year of Grace did not practically concern the common man'. But dating by regnal or other similar years meant changing the year-number on some arbitrary day within the calendar year, and thus no surprise was felt if the legal or ecclesiastical reckoning likewise involved adopting a new year-number on some apparently arbitrary day. Once this is clearly grasped we may relax our language a little. To speak of 'the date on which the year-number is changed' is an awkward way of expressing a simple fact, and no harm will be done if in what follows I use as equivalent the familiar phrase 'the beginning of the year', provided that the reader bears in mind exactly what is meant.

Into the many uses regarding this 'beginning of the year' that have prevailed at different times and in different localities there is happily no need to enter here. The Year of Grace[1] has

20 February, and Ash Wednesday, 9 March; the last is Advent Sunday, 27 November; Easter is 24 April. From this it follows that the 20 February and 9 March specified are those of 1602/3 not of 1603/4.

[1] It may be worth while mentioning that the 'Year of Grace' is an English invention. The Incarnation was used as a point of departure in computing an Easter Table by the Scythian monk Dionysius Exiguus at Rome in 525 (the table beginning in 532) but with no idea of instituting an era. It first appears as a chronological notation in certain English charters late in the seventh century, after St. Wilfrid had expounded the Dionysian Table at the Synod of Whitby in 664, and it was later adopted by Bede. But while adopting the era, Bede continued to begin the year either with Christmas (as in his treatise *De temporum ratione*) or with the Indiction of 24 September (as in his History). However, the use of the term *ab incarnatione* for the

been held to begin on 1 September, 24 September, 25 December, 1 January, 1 March, 25 March,[1] and worst of all on Easter Sunday (or rather Easter eve):[2] but in England in the sixteenth, seventeenth, and early eighteenth centuries, of which alone I propose to speak, the only choice lay between 1 January and 25 March. There is no question but that officially the year began on Lady Day, and any legal instrument may be assumed to be dated according to what is sometimes called the Year of the Incarnation.[3] But personal practice varied. Men of official or legal position, aspiration, or inclination naturally followed, more or less consistently, the official usage. On the other hand, ordinary people were for the most part content with the pagan reckoning of the almanacs they bought. There was, of course, much uncertainty. Philip Henslowe, pawnbroker and theatrical speculator, was rather uneducated, though perhaps fairly typical of the small London business man of his time; in his daily

Dionysian cycle naturally suggested Lady Day as the starting point for the year likewise, and this gradually came to supersede the established use of Christmas. The earliest indications of the use of 25 March as the beginning of the year are found in the ninth century, but it did not become established in England before the first half of the twelfth century. Thenceforward it was the official usage till 1752. Reminiscences of the earlier custom survive, however, as when some Elizabethan historians date the accession of William the Conqueror 1067 because he was crowned on Christmas day and reckoned his regnal years from then.

1 When Lady Day superseded Christmas a further complication ensued, for at some places the beginning of the year was postponed for three months (*stylus Florentinus*), whereas at others it was more logically advanced by nine months (*calculus Pisanus*). [The alternatives are thus stated by G. N. Garmonsway in the Introduction to his translation of the Anglo-Saxon Chronicle (Everyman's Library, 1953, p. xxix), where he points out that 'there is the possibility that the *Chronicle* may have used any of the following dates, set out in chronological order, for the opening of the year:

(*a*) 25 March *preceeding* our 1 January: the Annunciation (Stylus Pisanus).
(*b*) 1 September: the Greek or Byzantine Indiction date.
(*c*) 24 September: the Caesarean Indiction date (Mid-Autumn Day).
(*d*) 25 December: Christmas Day (Mid-Winter's Day).
(*e*) 1 January.
(*f*) 25 March *following* our 1 January: the Annunciation (Stylus Florentinus).

He adds that, so far, as we can tell, (*a*), (*b*), and (*e*) were never used in the *Chronicle*.]

2 The reckoning *a passione* was a distinctively French use, but the era continued to be reckoned either from the Conception or the Nativity.

3 The year beginning on 1 January is sometimes called the Circumcision Year; but the year was not made to begin on that day to commemorate the event; rather the Feast of the Circumcision was instituted to remove the pagan associations of 1 January.

accounts he most often changed the year-number some time in March, but almost as frequently in January or April; 1 January and 6 May are his extreme limits.[1] Ben Jonson, who was certainly educated, and in some ways rather pedantic, altered his practice about the time of his visit to Scotland,[2] when he abandoned the popular in favour of the official usage, though he was never wholly consistent. Sir Kenelm Digby, who edited his remains, reverted to the calendar year.[3] Printers differed in their practice. Pynson and Julian Notary began the year on 25 March; de Worde and Berthelet on 1 January, at any rate in their popular books. Generally speaking, legal and official publications were, of course, dated according to the official custom, while in other works the calendar date seems to have been preferred. In books that bear a year-date only, it is often impossible to be certain; moreover, the question is complicated by the fact that, then as now, printers were fond of putting dates on their books in advance of the actual day of publication. A popular work issued in December would very likely bear the date of the following year; and in the case of a book issued early in March with the date of the calendar year we cannot be sure whether the printer was following the calendar or anticipating the legal year. Indeed, a book dated 1603 may have appeared as early perhaps as November 1602 or as late as March 1604, a span of sixteen or seventeen months.

Thus in the sixteenth and seventeenth centuries, and well on into the eighteenth, we cannot be certain, except in the case of official documents, whether a date between 1 January and 24 March inclusive follows the calendar or the legal usage, unless there is internal evidence on which to decide. Naturally much inconvenience resulted from this uncertainty, and about the middle of the seventeenth century it became the custom among careful writers to employ a double dating for the ambiguous period, writing for example, as in a book before me, 'Cal: Jan: 1667/8'. And where there is any possibility of confusion editors and critics will do wisely to

[1] *Henslowe's Diary*, 1904–8, ii, 327.

[2] But not in consequence of it, unless through antagonism, for in 1619 when he made his pilgrimage, 1 January had been recognized as the beginning of the year in Scotland for close on two decades.

[3] 'The Riddle of Jonson's Chronology', see pp. 184–91.

adopt this practice. When no doubt can arise they may contentedly follow the calendar year—but let them remember that, however the year is reckoned, all English dates down to 2 September 1752 are Old Style.

Any but the most advanced specialist will find all he needs to know regarding 'The Beginning of the Year in the Middle Ages' in a paper communicated in 1921 by R. L. Poole to the British Academy (*Proceedings*, vol. x). But though he mentions the dates at which 1 January was officially adopted in various countries, he does not discuss actual practice in post-medieval times. A less detailed account will be found in the same writer's *Medieval Reckonings of Time* (Society for Promoting Christian Knowledge: Helps for Students of History, No. 3; 1918). There is also much useful information in another pamphlet (No. 40 of the same series, 1921), J. E. Wallis's *English Regnal Years and Titles, Hand-lists, Easter Dates, etc.*: Gregory's reform is succinctly explained on p. 49.[1] For the mathematical aspect of the subject, see the article 'Calendar' in the *Encyclopaedia Britannica* (eleventh edition). I have drawn freely on these sources.

[1] [Or better in C. R. Cheney's admirable *Handbook of Dates for Students of English History* (Royal Historical Society, 1945). pp. 1–11.]

25. The Rationale of Copy-Text[1]

When, in his edition of Nashe, McKerrow invented the term 'copy-text', he was merely giving a name to a conception already familiar, and he used it in a general sense to indicate that early text of a work which an editor selected as the basis of his own. Later, as we shall see, he gave it a somewhat different and more restricted meaning. It is this change in conception and its implications that I wish to consider.

The idea of treating some one text, usually of course a manuscript, as possessing over-riding authority originated among classical scholars, though something similar may no doubt be traced in the work of biblical critics. So long as purely eclectic methods prevailed, any preference for one manuscript over another, if it showed itself, was of course arbitrary; but when, towards the middle of last century, Lachmann and others introduced the genealogical classification of manuscripts as a principle of textual criticism, this appeared to provide at least some scientific basis for the conception of the most authoritative text. The genealogical method was the greatest advance ever made in this field, but its introduction was not unaccompanied by error. For lack of logical analysis, it led, at the hands of its less discriminating exponents, to an attempt to reduce textual criticism to a code of mechanical rules. There was just this much excuse, that the method did make it possible to sweep away mechanically a great deal of rubbish. What its more hasty devotees failed to understand, or at any rate sufficiently to bear in mind, was that authority is never absolute, but only relative. Thus a school arose, mainly in Germany, that taught that if a manuscript could be shown to be generally more correct than any other and to have descended from the archetype independently of other lines of transmission, it was 'scientific' to follow its readings whenever they were not manifestly impossible. It was this fallacy that Housman exposed with

[1] [1950–1. *Studies in Bibliography* (Virginia), iii. 19–36.] Read before the English Institute on 8 September 1949 by Dr. J. M. Osborn for W. W. Greg.

devastating sarcasm. He had only to point out that 'Chance and the common course of nature will not bring it to pass that the readings of a MS are right wherever they are possible and impossible wherever they are wrong'.[1] That if a scribe makes a mistake he will inevitably produce nonsense is the tacit and wholly unwarranted assumption of the school in question,[2] and it is one that naturally commends itself to those who believe themselves capable of distinguishing between sense and nonsense, but who know themselves incapable of distinguishing between right and wrong. Unfortunately the attractions of a mechanical method misled many who were capable of better things.

There is one important respect in which the editing of classical texts differs from that of English. In the former it is the common practice, for fairly obvious reasons, to normalize the spelling, so that (apart from emendation) the function of an editor is limited to choosing between those manuscript readings that offer significant variants. In English it is now usual to preserve the spelling of the earliest or it may be some other selected text. Thus it will be seen that the conception of 'copy-text' does not present itself to the classical and to the English editor in quite the same way; indeed, if I am right in the view I am about to put forward, the classical theory of the 'best' or 'most authoritative' manuscript, whether it be held in a reasonable or in an obviously fallacious form, has really nothing to do with the English theory of 'copy-text' at all.

I do not wish to argue the case of 'old spelling' versus 'modern spelling'; I accept the view now prevalent among English scholars. But I cannot avoid some reference to the ground on which present practice is based, since it is intimately connected with my own views on copy-text. The former practice of modernizing the spelling of English

[1] Introduction to Manilius, 1903, p. xxxii.

[2] The more naïve the scribe, the more often will the assumption prove correct; the more sophisticated, the less often. This, no doubt, is why critics of this school tend to reject 'the more correct but the less sincere' manuscript in favour of 'the more corrupt but the less interpolated', as Housman elsewhere observes ('The Application of Thought to Textual Criticism', *Proceedings of the Classical Association*, 1921, xviii. 75). Still, any reasonable critic will prefer the work of a naïve to that of a sophisticated scribe, though he may not regard it as necessarily 'better'.

works is no longer popular with editors, since spelling is now recognized as an essential characteristic of an author, or at least of his time and locality. So far as my knowledge goes, the alternative of normalization has not been seriously explored, but its philological difficulties are clearly considerable.[1] Whether, with the advance of linguistic science, it will some day be possible to establish a standard spelling for a particular period or district or author, or whether the historical circumstances in which our language has developed must always forbid any attempt of the sort (at any rate before comparatively recent times) I am not competent to say; but I agree with what appears to be the general opinion that such an attempt would at present only result in confusion and misrepresentation. It is therefore the modern editorial practice to choose whatever extant text may be supposed to represent most nearly what the author wrote and to follow it with the least possible alteration. But here we need to draw a distinction between the significant, or as I shall call them 'substantive', readings of the text, those namely that affect the author's meaning or the essence of his expression, and others, such in general as spelling, punctuation, word-division, and the like, affecting mainly its formal presentation, which may be regarded as the accidents, or as I shall call them 'accidentals', of the text.[2] The distinction is not arbitrary or theoretical, but has an immediate bearing on textual criticism, for scribes (or compositors) may in general be expected to react, and experience shows that they generally do react, differently to the two categories. As regards substantive readings their aim may be assumed to be to reproduce exactly those of their copy, though they will doubtless sometimes depart from them accidentally and may even, for one reason or another, do so intentionally: as regards accidentals

[1] I believe that an attempt has been made in the case of certain Old and Middle English texts, but how consistently and with what success I cannot judge. In any case I am here concerned chiefly with works of the sixteenth and seventeenth centuries.

[2] It will, no doubt, be objected that punctuation may very seriously 'affect' an author's meaning; still it remains properly a matter of presentation, as spelling does in spite of its use in distinguishing homonyms. The distinction I am trying to draw is practical, not philosophic. It is also true that between substantive readings and spellings there is an intermediate class of word-forms about the assignment of which opinions may differ and which may have to be treated differently in dealing with the work of different scribes.

they will normally follow their own habits or inclination, though they may, for various reasons and to varying degrees, be influenced by their copy. Thus a contemporary manuscript will at least preserve the spelling of the period, and may even retain some of the author's own, while it may at the same time depart frequently from the wording of the original: on the other hand a later transcript of the same original may reproduce the wording with essential accuracy while completely modernizing the spelling. Since, then, it is only on grounds of expediency, and in consequence either of philological ignorance or of linguistic circumstances, that we select a particular original as our copy-text, I suggest that it is only in the matter of accidentals that we are bound (within reason) to follow it, and that in respect of substantive readings we have exactly the same liberty (and obligation) of choice as has a classical editor, or as we should have were it a modernized text that we were preparing.[1]

But the distinction has not been generally recognized, and has never, so far as I am aware, been explicitly drawn.[2] This is not surprising. The battle between 'old spelling' and 'modern spelling' was fought out over works written for the most part between 1550 and 1650, and for which the original authorities are therefore as a rule printed editions. Now printed editions usually form an ancestral series, in which each is derived from its immediate predecessor; whereas the extant manuscripts of any work have usually only a collateral relationship, each being derived from the original independently, or more or less independently, of the others. Thus in the case of printed books, and in the absence of revision in a later edition, it is normally the first edition alone that can claim authority, and this authority

1 For the sake of clearness in making the distinction I have above stressed the independence of scribes and compositors in the matter of accidentals: at the same time, when he selects his copy-text, an editor will natually hope that it retains at least something of the character of the original. Experience, however, shows that while the distribution of substantive variants generally agrees with the genetic relation of the texts, that of accidental variants is comparatively arbitrary.

2 Some discussion bearing on it will be found in the Prolegomena to my lectures on *The Editorial Problem in Shakespeare* (1942), 'Note on Accidental Characteristics of the Text' (pp. l–lv), particularly the paragraph on pp. liii–liv, and note 1. But at the time of writing I was still a long way from any consistent theory regarding copy-text.

naturally extends to substantive readings and accidentals alike. There was, therefore, little to force the distinction upon the notice of editors of works of the sixteenth and seventeenth centuries, and it apparently never occurred to them that some fundamental difference of editorial method might be called for in the rare cases in which a later edition had been revised by the author or in which there existed more than one 'substantive' edition of comparable authority.[1] Had they been more familiar with works transmitted in manuscript, they might possibly have reconsidered their methods and been led to draw the distinction I am suggesting. For although the underlying principles of textual criticism are, of course, the same in the case of works transmitted in manuscripts and in print, particular circumstances differ, and certain aspects of the common principles may emerge more clearly in the one case than in the other. However, since the idea of copy-text originated and has generally been applied in connexion with the editing of printed books, it is such that I shall mainly consider, and in what follows reference may be understood as confined to them unless manuscripts are specifically mentioned.

The distinction I am proposing between substantive readings and accidentals, or at any rate its relevance to the question of copy-text, was clearly not present to McKerrow's mind when in 1904 he published the second volume of his edition of the Works of Thomas Nashe, which included *The Unfortunate Traveller*. Collation of the early editions of this romance led him to the conclusion that the second, advertised on the title as 'Newly corrected and augmented', had in fact been revised by the author, but at the same time that not all the alterations could with certainty be ascribed to him.[2] He nevertheless proceeded to enunciate the rule that 'if an editor has

[1] A 'substantive' edition is McKerrow's term for an edition that is not a reprint of any other. I shall use the term in this sense, since I do not think that there should be any danger of confusion between 'substantive editions' and 'substantive readings'.

I have above ignored the practice of some eccentric editors who took as copy-text for a work the latest edition printed in the author's lifetime, on the assumption, presumably, that he revised each edition as it appeared. The textual results were naturally deplorable.

[2] He believed, or at least strongly suspected, that some were due to the printer's desire to save space, and that others were 'the work of some person who had not thoroughly considered the sense of the passage which he was altering' (ii. 195).

reason to suppose that a certain text embodies later corrections than any other, and at the same time has no ground for disbelieving that these corrections, *or some of them at least*, are the work of the author, he has no choice but to make that text the basis of his reprint'.[1] The italics are mine.[2] This is applying with a vengeance the principle that I once approvingly described as 'maintaining the integrity of the copy-text'. But it must be pointed out that there are in fact two quite distinct principles involved. One, put in more general form, is that if, for whatever reason, a particular authority be on the whole preferred, an editor is bound to accept all its substantive readings (if not manifestly impossible). This is the old fallacy of the 'best text', and may be taken to be now generally rejected. The other principle, also put in general form, is that whatever particular authority be preferred, whether as being revised or as generally preserving the substantive readings more faithfully than any other, it must be taken as copy-text, that is to say that it must also be followed in the matter of accidentals. This is the principle that interests us at the moment, and it is one that McKerrow himself came, at least partly, to question.

In 1939 McKerrow published his *Prolegomena for the Oxford Shakespeare*, and he would not have been the critic he was if his views had not undergone some changes in the course of thirty-five years. One was in respect of revision. He had come to the opinion that to take a reprint, even a revised reprint, as copy-text was indefensible. Whatever may be the relation of a particular substantive edition to the author's manuscript (provided that there is any transcriptional link at all) it stands to reason that the relation of a reprint of that edition must be more remote. If then, putting aside all question of revision, a particular substantive edition has an over-riding claim to be taken as copy-

1 Nashe, ii. 197. The word 'reprint' really begs the question. If all an 'editor' aims at is an exact reprint, then obviously he will choose one early edition, on whatever grounds he considers relevant, and reproduce it as it stands. But McKerrow does emend his copy-text where necessary. It is symptomatic that he did not distinguish between a critical edition and a reprint.

2 Without the italicized phrase the statement would appear much more plausible (though I should still regard it as fallacious, and so would McKerrow himself have done later on) but it would not justify the procedure adopted.

text, to displace it in favour of a reprint, whether revised or not, means receding at least one step further from the author's original in so far as the general form of the text is concerned.[1] Some such considerations must have been in McKerrow's mind when he wrote (*Prolegomena*, pp. 17–18): 'Even if, however, we were to assure ourselves . . . that certain corrections found in a later edition of a play were of Shakespearian authority, it would not by any means follow that that edition should be used as the copy-text of a reprint.[2] It would undoubtedly be necessary to incorporate these corrections in our text, but . . . it seems evident that . . . this later edition will (except for the corrections) deviate more widely than the earliest print from the author's original manuscript. . . . [Thus] the nearest approach to our ideal . . . will be produced by using the earliest "good" print as copy-text and inserting into it, from the first edition which contains them, such corrections as appear to us to be derived from the author.' This is a clear statement of the position, and in it he draws exactly the distinction between substantive readings (in the form of corrections) and accidentals (or general texture) on which I am insisting. He then, however, relapsed into heresy in the matter of the substantive readings. Having spoken, as above, of the need to introduce 'such corrections as appear to us to be derived from the author', he seems to have feared conceding too much to eclecticism, and he proceeded: 'We are not to regard the "goodness" of a reading in and by itself, or to consider whether it appeals to our aesthetic sensibilities or not; we are to consider whether a particular edition taken *as a whole* contains variants from the edition from which it was otherwise printed which could not reasonably be attributed to an ordinary press-corrector, but by reason of their style, point, and what we call inner harmony with the spirit of the play as a whole, seem likely to be the work of the author: and once having decided this to our satisfaction we must accept *all* the alterations of that edition, saving any which seem obvious blunders or mis-

[1] This may, at any rate, be put forward as a general proposition, leaving possible exceptions to be considered later (pp. 389 ff.).

[2] Again he speaks of a 'reprint' where he evidently had in mind a critical edition on conservative lines.

prints.' We can see clearly enough what he had in mind, namely that the evidence of correction (under which head he presumably intended to include revision) must be considered *as a whole*; but he failed to add the equally important proviso that the alterations must also be *of a piece* (and not, as in *The Unfortunate Traveller*, of apparently disparate origin) before we can be called upon to accept them *all*. As he states it his canon is open to exactly the same objections as the 'most authoritative manuscript' theory in classical editing.

McKerrow was, therefore, in his later work quite conscious of the distinction between substantive readings and accidentals, in so far as the problem of revision is concerned. But he never applied the conception to cases in which we have more than one substantive text, as in *Hamlet* and perhaps in *2 Henry IV*, *Troilus and Cressida*, and *Othello*. Presumably he would have argued that since faithfulness to the wording of the author was one of the criteria he laid down for determining the choice of the copy-text, it was an editor's duty to follow its substantive readings with a minimum of interference.

We may assume that neither McKerrow nor other editors of the conservative school imagined that such a procedure would always result in establishing the authentic text of the original; what they believed was that from it less harm would result than from opening the door to individual choice among variants, since it substituted an objective for a subjective method of determination. This is, I think, open to question. It is impossible to exclude individual judgement from editorial procedure: it operates of necessity in the all-important matter of the choice of copy-text and in the minor one of deciding what readings are possible and what are not; why, therefore, should the choice between possible readings be withdrawn from its competence? Uniformity of result at the hands of different editors is worth little if it means only uniformity in error; and it may not be too optimistic a belief that the judgement of an editor, fallible as it must necessarily be, is likely to bring us closer to what the author wrote than the enforcement of an arbitrary rule.

The true theory is, I contend, that the copy-text should govern (generally) in the matter of accidentals, but that the choice between substantive readings belongs to the general theory of textual criticism and lies altogether beyond the narrow principle of the copy-text. Thus it may happen that in a critical edition the text rightly chosen as copy may not by any means be the one that supplies most substantive readings in cases of variation. The failure to make this distinction and to apply this principle has naturally led to too close and too general a reliance upon the text chosen as basis for an edition, and there has arisen what may be called the tyranny of the copy-text,[1] a tyranny that has, in my opinion, vitiated much of the best editorial work of the past generation.

I will give a couple of examples of the sort of thing I mean that I have lately come across in the course of my own work. They are all the more suitable as illustrations since they occur in texts edited by scholars of recognized authority, neither of whom is particularly subject to the tyranny in question. One is from the edition of Marlowe's *Doctor Faustus* by Professor F. S. Boas (1932). The editor, rightly I think, took the so-called B-text (1616) as the basis of his own, correcting it where necessary by comparison with the A-text (1604).[2] Now a famous line in Faustus's opening soliloquy runs in 1604,

> Bid *Oncaymæon* farewell, *Galen* come

and in 1616,

> Bid *Oeconomy* farewell; and *Galen* come . . .

Here '*Oncaymæon*' is now recognized as standing for '*on cay mæ on*' or ὂν καὶ μὴ ὄν: but this was not understood at the time, and '*Oeconomy*' was substituted in reprints of the A-text in 1609 and 1611, and thence taken over by the B-text. The change, however, produced a rather awkward line, and in 1616 the 'and' was introduced as a metrical accommodation. In the first half of the line Boas rightly restored the reading implied in A; but in the second half he retained, out of defer-

[1] [I think the phrase 'the tyranny of the copy-text' was first used by Paul Maas in connexion with the Prolegomena in my book *The Editorial Problem in Shakespeare*. But what he then had in mind was the decision to preserve 'old spelling'. (See *The Review of English Studies*, April 1944. xx. 159.)]

[2] Boas's text is in fact modernized, so that my theory of copy-text does not strictly apply, but since he definitely accepts the B-text as his authority, the principle is the same.

ence to his copy-text, the 'and' whose only object was to accommodate the reading he had rejected in the first. One could hardly find a better example of the contradictions to which a mechanical following of the copy-text may lead.[1]

My other instance is from *The Gipsies Metamorphosed* as edited by Dr. Percy Simpson among the masques of Ben Jonson in 1941. He took as his copy-text the Huntington manuscript, and I entirely agree with his choice. In this, and in Simpson's edition, a line of the ribald Cock Lorel ballad runs (sir-reverence!),

All wch he blewe away with a fart

whereas for *blewe* other authorities have *flirted*. Now, the meaning of *flirted* is not immediately apparent, for no appropriate sense of the word is recorded. There is, however, a rare use of the substantive *flirt* for a sudden gust of wind, and it is impossible to doubt that this is what Jonson had in mind, for no scribe or compositor could have invented the reading *flirted*. It follows that in the manuscript *blewe* is nothing but the conjecture of a scribe who did not understand his original: only the mesmeric influence of the copy-text could obscure so obvious a fact.[2]

I give these examples merely to illustrate the kind of error that, in modern editions of English works, often results from undue deference to the copy-text. This reliance on one particular authority results from the desire for an objective theory of text-construction and a distrust, often no doubt justified, of the operation of individual judgement. The attitude may be explained historically as a natural and largely salutary reaction against the methods of earlier editors. Dissatisfied with the results of eclectic freedom and reliance on personal taste, critics sought to establish some sort of mechanical apparatus for dealing with textual problems that should

1 Or consider the following readings: 1604, 1609 'Consissylogismes', 1611 'subtile sylogismes', 1616 'subtle Sillogismes'. Here 'subtile', an irresponsible guess by the printer of 1611 for a word he did not understand, was taken over in 1616. The correct reading is, of course, 'concise syllogisms'. Boas's refusal to take account of the copy used in 1616 led him here and elsewhere to perpetuate some of its manifest errors. In this particular instance he appears to have been unaware of the reading of 1611.

2 At another point two lines appear in an unnatural order in the manuscript. The genetic relation of the texts proves the inversion to be an error. But of this relation Simpson seems to have been ignorant. He was again content to rely on the copy-text.

lead to uniform results independent of the operator. Their efforts were not altogether unattended by success. One result was the recognition of the general worthlessness of reprints. And even in the more difficult field of manuscript transmission it is true that formal rules will carry us part of the way: they can at least effect a preliminary clearing of the ground. This I sought to show in my essay on *The Calculus of Variants* (1927); but in the course of investigation it became clear that there is a definite limit to the field over which formal rules are applicable. Between readings of equal extrinsic authority no rules of the sort can decide, since by their very nature it is only to extrinsic relations that they are relevant. The choice is necessarily a matter for editorial judgement, and an editor who declines or is unable to exercise his judgement and falls back on some arbitrary canon, such as the authority of the copy-text, is in fact abdicating his editorial function. Yet this is what has been frequently commended as 'scientific'—'streng wissenschaftlich' in the prevalent idiom—and the result is that what many editors have done is to produce, not editions of their authors' works at all, but only editions of particular authorities for those works, a course that may be perfectly legitimate in itself, but was not the one they were professedly pursuing.

This by way, more or less, of digression. At the risk of repetition I should like to recapitulate my view of the position of copy-text in editorial procedure. The thesis I am arguing is that the historical circumstances of the English language make it necessary to adopt in formal matters the guidance of some particular early text. If the several extant texts of a work form an ancestral series, the earliest will naturally be selected, and since this will not only come nearest to the author's original in accidentals, but also (revision apart) most faithfully preserve the correct readings where substantive variants are in question, everything is straightforward, and the conservative treatment of the copy-text is justified. But whenever there is more than one substantive text of comparable authority,[1] then although it will still be necessary

[1] The proviso is inserted to meet the case of the so-called 'bad quartos' of Shakespearian and other Elizabethan plays and of the whole class of 'reported' texts, whose testimony can in general be neglected.

to choose one of them as copy-text, and to follow it in accidentals, this copy-text can be allowed no over-riding or even preponderant authority so far as substantive readings are concerned. The choice between these, in cases of variation, will be determined partly by the opinion the editor may form respecting the nature of the copy from which each substantive edition was printed, which is a matter of external authority; partly by the intrinsic authority of the several texts as judged by the relative frequency of manifest errors therein; and partly by the editor's judgement of the intrinsic claims of individual readings to originality—in other words their intrinsic merit, so long as by 'merit' we mean the likelihood of their being what the author wrote rather than their appeal to the individual taste of the editor.

Such, as I see it, is the general theory of copy-text. But there remain a number of subsidiary questions that it may be worthwhile to discuss. One is the degree of faithfulness with which the copy-text should be reproduced. Since the adoption of a copy-text is a matter of convenience rather than of principle—being imposed on us either by linguistic circumstances or our own philological ignorance—it follows that there is no reason for treating it as sacrosanct, even apart from the question of substantive variation. Every editor aiming at a critical edition will, of course, correct scribal or typographical errors. He will also correct readings in accordance with any errata included in the edition taken as copy-text. I see no reason why he should not alter misleading or eccentric spellings which he is satisfied emanate from the scribe or compositor and not from the author. If the punctuation is persistently erroneous or defective an editor may prefer to discard it altogether to make way for one of his own. He is, I think, at liberty to do so, provided that he gives due weight to the original in deciding on his own, and that he records the alteration whenever the sense is appreciably affected. Much the same applies to the use of capitals and italics. I should favour expanding contractions (except perhaps when dealing with an author's holograph) so long as ambiguities and abnormalities are recorded. A critical edition does not seem to me a suitable place in which to record the graphic peculiarities of particular texts,[1] and in this respect the copy-text is only one among others. These, however, are all matters within the discretion of an editor: I am only concerned to uphold his liberty of judgement.

Some minor points arise when it becomes necessary to replace a reading of the copy-text by one derived from another source. It need not, I think, be copied in the exact form in which it there appears. Suppose that the copy-text follows the earlier convention in the use of *u* and *v*, and the source from which the reading is taken follows the later. Naturally in transferring the reading from the latter to the former it would be made to conform to the earlier convention. I would go further. Suppose that the copy-text reads 'hazard', but that we have reason to believe that the correct reading is 'venture': suppose further that whenever this word occurs in the copy-text it is in the form 'venter': then 'venter', I maintain, is the form we should adopt. In like manner editorial emendations should be made to conform to the habitual spelling of the copy-text.

In the case of rival substantive editions the choice between substantive variants is, I have explained, generally independent of the copy-text. Perhaps one concession should be made. Suppose that the claims of two readings, one in the copy-text and one in some other authority, appear to be exactly balanced: what then should an editor do? In such a case, while there can be no logical reason for giving preference to the copy-text, in practice, if there is no reason for altering its reading, the obvious thing seems to be to let it stand.[2]

[1] That is, certainly not in the text, and probably not in the general apparatus: they may appropriately form the subject of an appendix.

[2] This is the course I recommended in the Prolegomena to *The Editorial Problem in Shakespeare* (p. xxix), adding that it 'at least saves the trouble of tossing a coin'. What I actually wrote in 1942 was that in such circumstances an editor 'will naturally retain the reading of the copy-text, this being the text which he has already decided is *prima facie* the more correct'. This implies that correctness in respect of substantive readings is one of the criteria in the choice of the copy-text; and indeed I followed McKerrow in laying it down that an editor should select as copy-text the one that 'appears likely to have departed least in wording, spelling, and punctuation from the author's manuscript'. There is a good deal in my Prolegomena that I should now express differently, and on this particular point I have definitely changed my opinion. I should now say that the choice of the copy-text depends solely on its formal features (accidentals) and that fidelity as regards substantive readings is irrelevant—though fortunately in nine cases out of ten the choice will be the same whichever rule we adopt.

Much more important, and difficult, are the problems that arise in connexion with revision. McKerrow seems only to mention correction, but I think he must have intended to include revision, so long as this falls short of complete re-writing: in any case the principle is the same. I have already considered the practice he advocated (pp. 378–81)—namely that an editor should take the original edition as his copy-text and introduce into it all the substantive variants of the revised reprint, other than manifest errors—and have explained that I regard it as too sweeping and mechanical. The emendation that I proposed (pp. 381–2) is, I think, theoretically sufficient, but from a practical point of view it lacks precision. In a case of revision or correction the normal procedure would be for the author to send the printer either a list of the alterations to be made or else a corrected copy of an earlier edition. In setting up the new edition we may suppose that the printer would incorporate the alterations thus indicated by the author; but it must be assumed that he would also introduce a normal amount of unauthorized variation of his own.[1] The problem that faces the editor is to distinguish between the two categories. I suggest the following frankly subjective procedure. Granting that the fact of revision (or correction) is established, an editor should in every case of variation ask himself (1) whether the original reading is one that can reasonably be attributed to the author, and (2) whether the later reading is one that the author can reasonably be supposed to have substituted for the former. If the answer to the first question is negative, then the later reading should be accepted as at least possibly an authoritative correction (unless, of course, it is itself incredible). If the answer to (1) is affirmative and the answer to (2) is negative, the original reading should be retained. If the answers to both questions are affirmative, then the later reading should be presumed to be due to revision and admitted into the text, whether the editor himself considers it an improvement or not. It will be observed that one implication of this procedure is that a later variant that is either completely indifferent or manifestly inferior, or for the substitution of which no motive can be suggested, should be treated as fortuitous and refused

[1] I mean substantive variation, such as occurs in all but the most faithful reprints.

admission to the text—to the scandal of faithful followers of McKerrow. I do not, of course, pretend that my procedure will lead to consistently correct results, but I think that the results, if less uniform, will be on the whole preferable to those achieved through following any mechanical rule. I am, no doubt, presupposing an editor of reasonable competence; but if an editor is really incompetent, I doubt whether it much matters what procedure he adopts: he may indeed do less harm with some than with others, he will do little good with any. And in any case, I consider that it would be disastrous to curb the liberty of competent editors in the hope of preventing fools from behaving after their kind.

I will give one illustration of the procedure in operation, taken again from Jonson's *Masque of Gipsies*, a work that is known to have been extensively revised for a later performance. At one point the text of the original version runs as follows,

a wise Gypsie . . . is as politicke a piece of Flesh, as most Iustices in the County where he maunds

whereas the texts of the revised version replace *maunds* by *stalkes*. Now, *maund* is a recognized canting term meaning to beg, and there is not the least doubt that it is what Jonson originally wrote. Further, it might well be argued that it is less likely that he should have displaced it in revision by a comparatively commonplace alternative, than that a scribe should have altered a rather unusual word that he failed to understand—just as we know that, in a line already quoted (p. 383), a scribe altered *flirted* to *blewe*. I should myself incline to this view were it not that at another point Jonson in revision added the lines,

And then ye may stalke
The *Gypsies* walke

where *stalk*, in the sense of going stealthily, is used almost as a technical term. In view of this I do not think it unreasonable to suppose that Jonson himself substituted *stalkes* for *maunds* from a desire to avoid the implication that his aristocratic Gipsies were beggars, and I conclude that it must be allowed to pass as (at least possibly) a correction, though no reasonable critic would *prefer* it to the original.

With McKerrow's view that in all normal cases of correction or revision the original edition should still be taken as the copy-text, I am in complete agreement. But not all cases are normal, as McKerrow himself recognized. While advocating, in the passage already quoted (p. 380), that the earliest 'good' edition should be taken as copy-text and corrections incorporated in it, he added the proviso, 'unless we could show that the [revised] edition in question (or the copy from which it had been printed) had been gone over and corrected *throughout* by' the author (my italics). This proviso is not in fact very explicit, but it clearly assumes that there are (or at least may be) cases in which an editor would be justified in taking a revised reprint as his copy-text, and it may be worth inquiring what these supposed cases are. If a work has been entirely rewritten, and is printed from a new manuscript, the question does not arise, since the revised edition will be a substantive one, and as such will presumably be chosen by the editor as his copy-text. But short of this, an author, wishing to make corrections or alterations in his work, may not merely hand the printer a revised copy of an earlier edition, but himself supervise the printing of the new edition and correct the proofs as the sheets go through the press. In such a case it may be argued that even though the earlier edition, if printed from his own manuscript, will preserve the author's individual peculiarities more faithfully than the revised reprint, he must nevertheless be assumed to have taken responsibility for the latter in respect of accidentals no less than substantive readings, and that it is therefore the revised reprint that should be taken as copy-text.

The classical example is afforded by the plays in the 1616 folio of Ben Jonson's Works. In this it appears that even the largely recast *Every Man in his Humour* was not set up from an independent manuscript but from a much corrected copy of the quarto of 1601. That Jonson revised the proofs of the folio has indeed been disputed, but Simpson is most likely correct in supposing that he did so, and he was almost certainly responsible for the numerous corrections made while the sheets were in process of printing. Simpson's consequent decision to take the folio for his copy-text for the plays it contains will doubtless be approved by most critics.

I at least have no wish to dispute his choice.[1] Only I would point out—and here I think Dr. Simpson would agree with me—that even in this case the procedure involves some sacrifice of individuality. For example, I notice that in the text of *Sejanus* as printed by him there are twenty-eight instances of the Jonsonian 'Apostrophus' (an apostrophe indicating the elision of a vowel that is nevertheless retained in printing) but of these only half actually appear in the folio, the rest he has introduced from the quarto. This amounts to an admission that in some respects at least the quarto preserves the formal aspect of the author's original more faithfully than the folio.

The fact is that cases of revision differ so greatly in circumstances and character that it seems impossible to lay down any hard and fast rule as to when an editor should take the original edition as his copy-text and when the revised reprint. All that can be said is that if the original be selected, then the author's corrections must be incorporated; and that if the reprint be selected, then the original reading must be restored when that of the reprint is due to unauthorized variation. Thus the editor cannot escape the responsibility of distinguishing to the best of his ability between the two categories. No juggling with copy-text will relieve him of the duty and necessity of exercising his own judgement.

In conclusion I should like to examine this problem of revision and copy-text a little closer. In the case of a work like *Sejanus*, in which correction or revision has been slight, it would obviously be possible to take the quarto as the copy-text and introduce into it whatever authoritative alterations the folio may supply; and indeed, were one editing the play independently, this would be the natural course to pursue. But a text like that of *Every Man in his Humour* presents an entirely different problem. In the folio, revision and reproduction are so blended that it would seem impossible to disentangle intentional from what may be fortuitous variation, and injudicious to make the attempt. An editor of the revised version has no choice but to take the folio as his copy-text. It would appear therefore that a reprint may in practice

[1] Simpson's procedure in taking the 1616 folio as copy-text in the case of most of the masques included, although he admits that in their case Jonson cannot be supposed to have supervised the printing, is much more questionable.

be forced upon an editor as copy-text by the nature of the revision itself, quite apart from the question whether or not the author exercised any supervision over its printing.

This has a bearing upon another class of texts, in which a reprint was revised, not by the author, but through comparison with some more authoritative manuscript. Instances are Shakespeare's *Richard III* and *King Lear*. Of both much the best text is supplied by the folio of 1623; but this is not a substantive text, but one set up from a copy of an earlier quarto that had been extensively corrected by collation with a manuscript preserved in the playhouse. So great and so detailed appears to have been the revision that it would be an almost impossible task to distinguish between variation due to the corrector and that due to the compositor,[1] and an editor has no choice but to take the folio as copy-text. Indeed, this would in any case be incumbent upon him for a different reason; for the folio texts are in some parts connected by transcriptional continuity with the author's manuscript, whereas the quartos contain, it is generally assumed, only reported texts, whose accidental characteristics can be of no authority whatever. At the same time, analogy with *Every Man in his Humour* suggests that even had the quartos of *Richard III* and *King Lear* possessed higher authority than in fact they do, the choice of copy-text must yet have been the same.

I began this discussion in the hope of clearing my own mind as well as others' on a rather obscure though not unimportant matter of editorial practice. I have done something to sort out my own ideas: others must judge for themselves. If they disagree, it is up to them to maintain some different point of view. My desire is rather to provoke discussion than to lay down the law.

1 Some variation is certainly due to error on the part of the folio printer, and this it is of course the business of an editor to detect and correct so far as he is able.

26. The Printing of Shakespeare's *Troilus and Cressida* in the First Folio[1]

THE acute observation and reasoning of three scholars whose names are associated with the Folger Library have placed Shakespearian bibliographers in possession of the facts concerning the printing of *Troilus and Cressida* in the First Folio of 1623.[2] We know that the play was originally intended to follow *Romeo and Juliet* and to occupy page 78 and following in the section of Tragedies, for several copies of the Folio survive containing the cancelled leaf (sig. gg3) bearing on the recto the last page of *Romeo* and on the verso the first page of the text of *Troilus*.[3]

What happened was this. The compositor ended *Romeo* on the recto of gg3 and at once began to set up the text of *Troilus* on the verso continuing the composition of this play on gg4 with pages 79 and 80. As soon as the four formes of gg3–4 were ready they were printed off as the inner sheet of a normal gathering of three: this was the regular procedure. But at this point something happened that made it impossible, or undesirable, to proceed immediately with the composition of *Troilus*. No doubt it was hoped that the impediment would soon be removed, for a calculation was made of the space needed to complete the play, and printing was continued with *Julius Caesar* on kk1. This left the printer with gg1 and gg2, containing four pages of *Romeo* on his hands, pages which but for the interruption would have been imposed along with those of gg6 and gg5 of *Troilus*. Rather than keep the type of these four pages standing, it was decided to print

[1] [1957, October–December. *The Papers of the Bibliographical Society of America*, xlv. 273–82.]

[2] J. Q. Adams, '*Timon of Athens* and the Irregularities of the First Folio', in *The Journal of English and Germanic Philology*, cii.53–63 (January, 1908); E. E. Willoughby, *The Printing of the First Folio of Shakespeare* (London, The Bibliographical Society, 1932), pp. 46–50; G. E. Dawson, 'A Bibliographical Problem in the First Folio of Shakespeare', in *The Library*, xxii. 25–33 (June, 1941).

[3] Notably the Burdett-Coutts copy now in the Folger Library and the Toovey copy in the Pierpont Morgan Library. Three others are in the Folger collection.

them off on a single sheet which could stand as a quire gg_2 by itself.[1]

When the hope of resuming work on *Troilus* was disappointed, it was decided to substitute *Timon*. The last page of *Romeo*, originally printed on gg3 was reset on the recto of the first leaf, signed 'Gg', of a new quire, and *Timon* was begun on the verso of the same. But *Timon* is a shorter play than *Troilus* and it failed to fill the allotted space, so that there is a gap in the signatures and pagination between it and *Julius Caesar*. All hope of including *Troilus* having been abandoned, the colophon was duly printed at the end of *Cymbeline* (which had somehow strayed among the Tragedies) and in the preliminaries the title of *Troilus* was omitted from the catalogue of contents. Then, just as the volume was ready for publication, *Troilus* at last became available. The last page of *Romeo* and the first three of *Troilus* had, it will be remembered, been already printed off on the original gg3–4. The first of these leaves had of course to be scrapped: a fresh leaf (unsigned) was substituted, bearing on the recto a hitherto unprinted Prologue to *Troilus* and on the verso a close reprint of the first page.[2] The second leaf was retained with its original pagination 79–80 (being the fourth leaf of the projected quire, it bore no signature). Then the play was completed, with a series of arbitrary signatures but without pagination, and the whole inserted in the only possible place, namely at

[1] I do not understand the reason for Dawson's statement (p. 33) that 'While the inner sheet [gg3–4] was passing through the press the composition of pages 81–84 of *Troilus* had probably been completed.' His discovery that gg1–2 were printed as a separate sheet proves that when the order came to stay composition the machining of the sheet gg3–4 had already been at least begun, for otherwise the eight pages of gg1–4 would have been printed as a short gathering of two sheets (as Willoughby supposed); but it surely also proves that the composition of gg5–6 (pages 81–84) had *not* been completed, for in that case they too would have been printed off as a separate sheet (indeed, had the order to stay composition been delayed till that of gg5–6 was complete, there would have been no reason why a normal gathering of three sheets should not have been printed). That composition continued while gg3–4 were on the press is probable, but the order to stay was presumably received soon after machining had begun and when little progress had been made with composition, since the type was distributed again.

[2] There are some 65 differences of one sort and another, but only three that can be called variant readings. In I. i. 25 'the heating the Ouen' was altered to 'the heating of the Ouen'; in l. 74 'and she were Kinne to me' was corrected to 'and she were not kin to me'; and in l. 79 the prefix '*Pan.*' was misprinted '*Troy.*'. All references in this article are to the Cambridge Shakespeare, 1892.

the head of the section of Tragedies to which it had originally been assigned.

All this is now established fact to the Shakespearian bibliographer. The cause of the trouble is admittedly a more speculative matter, but it has been plausibly referred to a dispute over the copyright. On 28 January 1609 two young stationers, Richard Bonian and Henry Walley, had entered the play at Stationers' Hall, and this entrance they followed up the same year with an edition, in a rather flamboyant preface in which they went out of their way to proclaim that they were printing the play against the wishes of 'the grand possessors', by which they can have meant none other than his Majesty's players. We do not know how they came by their copy of the play, which was certainly a sound one in the main, but they clearly regarded it as something of a 'scoop'. What more likely than that fourteen years later, when the same company wished to include the play in their collection of the author's works, Walley, the surviving member of the partnership, should stand upon his rights and refuse them permission to make free with his 'copy', or that the Court of the Stationers' Company, had the dispute come before them, would have upheld his action? It is therefore, quite reasonable to assume that this was the cause of the withdrawal of *Troilus* from its original position in the First Folio. Bibliographers, however, have further assumed that the eventual inclusion of the piece was due to a last-moment relenting on Walley's part; and it is here that fresh evidence has come to light, which enables us, I think, to put a different construction on the facts.

The truth is that Walley's position was not quite as certain as has been assumed or as he himself perhaps believed. For when he and his colleague registered the play an earlier entrance already stood in the Hall Book. Six years before, on 7 February 1603, James Roberts had caused the following memorandum to be made: 'Entred for his copie in Full Court holden this day. to print when he hath gotten sufficient aucthority for yt. The booke of Troilus and Cresseda as yt is acted by my lo: Chamberlens Men.' The Chamberlain's company, was of course, the predecessor of the King's, and the entrance was most likely made with their authority, since the mention of 'The booke' suggests, if it does not actually imply, that it was the prompt-book itself that was submitted to the Clerk for registration. By 1623 Roberts, it is true, was dead, but he had, about 1606, sold his business to William Jaggard, so that the publisher of the First Folio had acquired a claim to his copies. Jaggard could have argued that Walley's edition of *Troilus* itself infringed rights he had acquired from Roberts and that the joint entrance of 1609 ought indeed never to have been allowed; and had he chosen to take his case to the Court of Assistants, it is at least possible that they would have revoked Walley's rights in the copy. But this would not, in fact, have helped Jaggard and the King's men, for though it would have prevented Walley from reprinting the play (which he probably had no intention of doing) there is no reason to suppose that it would have allowed Jaggard to appropriate Walley's text.

This limitation may be inferred from two cases that had come before the Court a generation earlier. It appears that in 1592 Abel Jeffes printed what seems to have been a garbled edition of *The Spanish Tragedy* (now lost) and he entered it on 6 October, perhaps on learning that Edward White was about to replace it by the extant edition, which contains an excellent text 'Newly corrected and amended of such grosse faults as passed in the first impression'. On 18 December Jeffes protested to the Court, which upheld his copyright and fined White ten shillings. In 1594 Jeffes reprinted White's text, but in order to do so he evidently had to come to terms with his opponent and allow him an interest in the new edition, for this bears the legend 'Printed by Abell Ieffes, and are to be sold by Edward White'.[1] It was also in 1592 that Thomas Orwin printed an edition of *The Damnable Life and Deserved Death of Doctor Faustus*, 'newly imprinted, and in conuenient places imperfect matter amended', to replace a lost and presumably defective edition, to which again Abel Jeffes laid claim. Jeffes's complaint was heard by the Court the same day as the other, and judgement again went in his favour, though in this case no entrance had been made by either claimant. On this occasion Jeffes made

[1] See *The Spanish Tragedy* (1592), Malone Society Reprint, 1948, introduction, pp. vi–xiii.

no attempt to reprint the book, but when on 5 April 1596 it was at length entered in the Register, 'havinge thinterest of abell Ieffes thereto', it was once more by Edward White, who had acted as bookseller for Orwin's edition four years previously, and who doubtless bargained for the rights of both parties.[1]

We may assume, therefore, that while Jaggard might have been able to substantiate a claim to the 'copy' of *Troilus*, he would still have had no right to reproduce Walley's text, but would have had to print it, if at all, from some other source, that is, from a manuscript. It is at this point that the new evidence comes in. In the course of a recent article on 'The Textual Problem of *Troilus and Cressida*'[2] Dr. Alice Walker remarks that 'had the original intention of printing the play immediately after *Romeo and Juliet* been adhered to, we should have had in the Folio text a mere reprint of the Quarto', whereas it is well known that for the bulk of the text recourse was had to a manuscript. What she had observed, and was so far as I am aware the first to point out, was that in the three pages originally set up (pp. 78–80) the variants between the Quarto and Folio texts are such as any compositor may be expected to produce when reprinting another text,[3] whereas as soon as we reach the first page set up for the first time after the interruption (that is, the recto of sig. ¶1) variants appear that can only be accounted for by the use of some independent source, and that these persist throughout the rest of the play.

Miss Walker gave (on pp. 463–4) a list of readings from the three pages originally printed and from the following three set up after the interruption, sufficient, she thought, to establish her contention. Probably they are, but since the question has now assumed an importance greater than she at the moment realized, it may be desirable to print here a more extended collation.[4] Here first are the readings of pages 78–80.[5]

[1] See Marlowe's *Doctor Faustus* (parallel texts) (Oxford, 1950), Introduction, pp. 1–4. [2] *The Modern Language Review*, xlv. 459–64 (October 1950).

[3] The only variant not immediately referable to the compositor is the insertion of an entrance at I. ii. 35, but this is obviously called for by the text.

[4] Since we have already seen that the differences between the original setting of page 78 and the reprint are insignificant, I take no notice of the latter.

[5] In the list of Folio readings a * marks the correction of obvious errors, a † errors

	QUARTO	FOLIO
Page [78]		
I.i 15	must tarry	must ‡needes tarrie
26	yea may chance burne	*you may chaunce ‡to burne
44	I would not as they tearme it praise her,	I would not (as they terme it) praise †it,
70	ill thought on of her, and ill thought of you,	ill thought on her, and ill thought *on of you:
75	as faire a Friday as *Hellen*, is on Sunday,	as faire ‡on Friday, as *Helen* is on Sunday.
76	but what I? I care not	But what *care I? I care not
87S.D.	*Exit.*	*Exit* ‡*Panda.*
Page 79		
100	reides	*recides (*for* resides)
ii.6	Hee chid	He †chides
17	vnlesse the are dronke,	vnlesse *they are drunke,
29	purblinde *Argus*,	‡purblinded *Argus*,
33	the disdaine and shame	the †disdaind & shame
35S.D.	[absent]	**Enter Pandarus.*
43	Illum?	*Illium?
67	nor *Hector* is not *Troylus*	†not *Hector* is not *Troylus*
97	praizd	†prasi'd
Page 80		
112	Is he so yong a man,	Is he †is so young a man,
118	valianty.	*valiantly.
120	clowd	†clow'd (*i.e.* cloud)
140–1	But there was a more temperate fire vnder the por	But there was ‡ more temperate fire vnder the *pot
166	So I doe.	So I †does.
172	Ilion,	‡Illium,
184	hee's man good enough,	hee's ‡a man good inough,
185	hees one o'th soundest iudgements in Troy	hee's one o'th soundest ‡iudgement in Troy
187	see him nod at mee.	see him †him nod at me.
195	O a braue man.	O † braue man!
196	it dooes a man heart good,	It dooes a *mans heart good,

committed by the compositor, and ‡ variants that do not evidently fall into either class. The Folio compositor, beginning work on a play in the section of Tragedies, naturally altered the 'history' of the Quarto head-title to 'TRAGEDIE' and he made a like change in the running title. After the interruption he adopted the simple and, as Miss Walker calls it, non-committal head-line '*Troylus and Cressida*.' This, she suggests (p. 462), was due to the anomalous position of the play between the Histories and Tragedies. But the play was always regarded as belonging to the latter.

	QUARTO	FOLIO
198–9	thers no iesting, thers laying on, takt off, who will as they say,	There's no iesting, † laying on, tak't off, who †ill as they say,
209	you shall see *Troylus* anon.	you shall † *Troylus* anon.
216	doe you not here the people	do you not †haere the people
2199.s.	*Troylus.*	†*Trylus.*
223	Marke him, note him:	Marke him, †not him:

Variants of this sort persist throughout the play. But as soon as we reach the first of the pages set up for the first time after the interruption, variants of a different type begin to appear. The following is a fairly exhaustive list of variants of the new type found in the next three pages (pages [81–83]). Opinion will naturally differ in regard to what is significant and what is not, and I do not pretend that all the Folio variants in the list necessarily imply resort to a source independent of the Quarto.[1] But even the less significant reinforce the evidence of the more striking and conclusive.[2]

	QUARTO	FOLIO
Page [81]		
I.ii.231	*Hellen* to change would giue **an eye** to boote.	*Helen* to change, would giue **money** to boot.
232S.D.	[absent]	*Enter common Souldiers.*
246	liberallity and **such like,**	liberality, and **so forth:**
250	You are such **a** woman **a man** knowes not at what ward you lie:	You are such **another** woman, **one** knowes not at what ward you lye.
266	At your owne house **there he vnarmes him:**	At your owne house.
273S.D.	[absent]	*Exit Pand.*
286	Then though my hearts **content**	That though my hearts **Contents**
iii.2	hath set **these** Iaundies **ore** your cheekes?	hath set **the** Iaundies **on** your cheekes?

[1] For example, the added entry at I. iii. 215 can be inferred from the text just as easily as that at I. ii. 35 (but the accompanying '*Tucket*' cannot): the omission at I. ii. 266 may be accidental (but why should Troilus go to Pandarus' house to unarm?): at I. iii. 219 the correction is obvious and may be conjectural: the variant at I. iii. 228 may be a mere misprint: the omission at I. iii. 238 would probably have been made irrespective of authority: and so on.

[2] In the list relevant differences in the readings are indicated by heavy type.

	QUARTO	FOLIO
19	And **call** them **shames**	And **thinke** them **shame,**
27	with a **broad** and powerfull fan,	with a **lowd** and powrefull fan,
36	Vpon her **ancient** brest,	Vpon her **patient** brest,
Page [82]		
67	(**On** which **heauen rides**) knit all **the Greekish** eares	**In** which **the Heauens ride,** knit all **Greekes** ears
70–74	[absent]	[a five-line speech]
92	Corrects the **influence** of **euill Planets,**	Corrects the **ill Aspects** of **Planets euill,**
102	Which is the ladder **of** all high designes,	(Which is the Ladder **to** all high designes)
110	each thing **melts** | In meere oppugnancie:	each thing **meetes** | In meere oppugnancie.
128	by a pace goes backward **with a purpose** | It hath to clime.	by a pace goes backward **in** a purpose | It hath to climbe.
137	Troy in our weaknesse **stands** not in her strength.	Troy in our weaknesse **liues,** not in her strength.
149	with ridiculous and **sillie** action,	with ridiculous and **aukward** action,
159	with termes **vnsquare,**	With tearmes **vnsquar'd,**
164	'tis *Agamemnon* **right,**	'tis *Agamemnon* **iust.**
Page [83]		
212S.D.	[absent]	*Tucket*
215S.D.	[absent]	*Enter Æneas.*
219	Do a faire message to his Kingly **eyes?**	Do a faire message to his Kingly **eares?**
228	And **bid** the cheeke be ready with a blush,	And **on** the cheeke be ready with a blush
238	Good armes, strong ioints, true swords, & **great** *Ioues* accord	Good armes, strong ioynts, true swords, & *Ioues* accord,
250	to whisper **with** him,	to whisper him,
252	To set his **seat** on **that** attentiue bent,	To set his **sence** on **the** attentiue bent,
259S.D.	*Sound trumpet.*	*The Trumpets sound.*
262–3	Who in **his** dull and long continued truce, | Is **restie** growne:	Who in **this** dull and long continew'd Truce | Is **rusty** growne.
267	**And feeds** his praise, more then he feares his perill,	**That seekes** his praise, more then he feares his perill,

	QUARTO	FOLIO
276	a Lady, wiser, fairer, truer, | Then euer Greeke did **couple** in his armes,	a Lady, wiser, fairer, truer, | Then euer Greeke did **compasse** in his armes,
289–90	If then one is, or hath **a** meanes to be, | That one meetes *Hector*: if none else **I am** he.	If then one is, or hath, **or** meanes to be, | That one meets *Hector*; if none else, **Ile be** he.
293–4	if there be not in our Grecian **hoste,** | **A** noble man that hath **no** sparke of fire	if there be not in our Grecian **mould,** | **One** Noble man, that hath **one** spark of fire
297–8	in my **vambrace** put **my** withered **braunes** | And meeting him tell him that my Lady,	in my **Vantbrace** put **this** wither'd **brawne,** | And meeting him, **wil** tell him, that my Lady
301	Ile **proue** this troth with my three drops of bloud,	Ile **pawne** this truth with my three drops of blood.
302	heauens **for-fend** such scarcity of **men.**	heauens **forbid** such scarsitie of **youth.**
303–4	*Vlis*. Amen: faire Lord *Æneas*	*Vlys*. Amen. | *Aga*. Faire Lord *Æneas*,
305	To our pauilion shall I leade you **sir;**	To our Pauillion shal I leade you **first:**
309S.D.	[absent]	*Exeunt*. | *Manet Vlysses, and Nestor*.
314–16	*Nest*. What ist? | *Vlis:* Blunt wedges riue hard knots,	*Nest*. What is't? | *Vlysses*. **This 'tis:** | Blunt wedges riue hard knots:

There is, I think, no escaping the conclusion that when work was resumed on *Troilus* a manuscript of the play was available that had not been available, or at any rate was not used, when the first three pages of the text were set up. Incidentally it supplied the Prologue originally wanting.[1] But we earlier saw reason to believe that when the printing of the play was interrupted, Walley's intransigence presented an insuperable obstacle only because his was the one text available to print from; and I suggest that when at the last

[1] The manuscript must, of course, have been available when the first page of text was reprinted, and it may be asked why the reprint shows no evidence of this fact. The answer is that since the original leaf bearing pages 79 and 80 was to be used, the reprint of page 78 had to end at the same point as the original, and this would have been difficult if not impossible to achieve unless that original had been used as copy.

moment a manuscript turned up (whence we can hardly, in the present state of our knowledge, conjecture) Jaggard felt in a position to snap his fingers in Walley's face. It is immaterial that in fact he printed the play, not from the manuscript, but from the Quarto altered in accordance with it, for if challenged he could produce the manuscript, draw attention to the numerous differences between the texts and the presence in his own of some forty or fifty lines missing in Walley's, and point triumphantly to the Prologue displayed in large type upon the first page. His case was complete, and in fact it was not till a few months ago that the patience and ingenuity of an American professor finally settled the vexed question of the actual copy used.[1]

1 Philip Williams, 'Shakespeare's *Troilus and Cressida:* The Relationship of Quarto and Folio', in *Studies in Bibliography,* iii. 131–143 (1950).

27. Was the First Edition of *Pierce Penniless* a Piracy?[1]

THE publication of Nashe's *Pierce Penniless* has become invested with pivotal significance in controversy over Elizabethan copyright owing to A. W. Pollard's having cited it as a case in which an author replaced a piratical edition of a work by an authorized text entrusted to a different publisher.

In his introduction to the Oxford facsimile of the First Folio of Shakespeare (1902) Sidney Lee had written (p. xiii) that before an inferior text could be superseded by an authorized edition it was 'needful to conciliate and perhaps to compensate the piratical publisher, who was first in the field and had it in his power on an appeal to the Stationers' Company to prevent the substitution of a genuine version by a second publisher for his own corrupt but fully licensed property'. Pollard, writing his *Shakespeare Folios and Quartos* seven years later, described this (p. 3) as an 'astounding assertion, for which I doubt strongly whether a shred of evidence can be produced', and continued (in a footnote): 'it would be much nearer the truth to say that the publication of a surreptitious edition left an author free to do exactly what he liked. The existence of an edition already in print absolved him from the need of a licence, and we find him simply reprinting his own text without registration or other formality. This is what Nashe did when Richard Johnes took advantage of his absence to register and print his *Pierce Pennilesse*. Mr. Lee, if he will read Nashe's letter to his authorized publisher, J[ohn] B[usby], will hardly contend that Nashe had found it "necessary to conciliate" Johnes.' Pollard here assumed that Jones's edition was pirated and that Nashe entrusted an authorized second edition to John Busby, and that the epistle prefixed to this second edition bore out his interpretation of the events.[2] Now, I am not going to argue whether Pollard

[1] [1952, June. *The Library*, vii. 122–4.]

[2] I had myself taken a similar view when writing about Lee's introduction in *The*

or Lee was right on the main point at issue—actually I believe that on this occasion Lee was nearer the mark than Pollard—what I am at present concerned to maintain is that Pollard was mistaken about the case he cited in support of his view.

The facts, which are set out in the first volume of McKerrow's edition of Nashe (i. 137 ff.), are these. On 8 August 1592 Richard Jones 'Entred for his copie vnder thandes of the Archbushopp of Canterburie and m^r^ watkins Pierce pennilesse his supplication to the Devill'. This entrance was shortly followed by an edition purporting to be 'Imprinted by *Richard Ihones*, dwelling at the Signe of the Rose and Crowne, nere Holburne Bridge. 1592', but actually printed for him by John Charlewood. To this edition (only) was prefixed an address by 'The Printer to the Gentlemen Readers' signed 'R.I.' and beginning, 'In the Authours absence, I haue been bold to publish this pleasaunt and wittie Discourse of *Pierce Penilesse his Supplication to the Diuell*'. There are two further editions dated 1592, the earlier 'Printed by Abell Ieffes, for Iohn Busbie' and the later 'printed by Abell Ieffes, for I. B.', both containing 'A priuate Epistle of the Author to the Printer'—that is the publisher (unnamed)—signed '*Tho. Nash*', which gives us most of the information we possess about the circumstances of publication. It begins:

Faith I am verie sorrie (Sir) I am thus vnawares betrayed to infamie. You write to me my book is hasting to the second impression: he that hath once broke the Ice of impudence, need not care how deepe he wade in discredit. I confesse it to be a meer toy, not deseruing any iudicial mans view: If it haue found any friends, so it is; you knowe very wel that it was abroad a fortnight ere I knewe of it, & vncorrected and vnfinished it hath offred it selfe to the open scorne of the world. Had you not beene so forward in the republishing of it, you shold haue had certayne Epistles to Orators and Poets, to insert to the later end; As namely, to the Ghost of *Macheuill*, of *Tully*, of *Ouid*, of *Roscius*, of *Pace* the Duke of Norfolks Iester; and lastly, to the Ghost of *Robert Greene*, telling him, what a coyle there is with pamphleting on him

Library in 1903 (iv. 269). My attention was drawn to the case by McKerrow, who was then engaged on his edition of Nashe, but he must not be supposed responsible for the interpretation put upon it.

after his death. These were prepared for *Pierce Penilesse* first setting foorth, had not the feare of infection detained mee with my Lord in the Countrey.

The conclusion runs:

Farewell, and let me heare from you as soone as it is come forth. I am the Plagues prisoner in the Country as yet: if the sicknesse cease before the thirde impression, I wil come and alter whatsoeuer may be offensiue to any man, and bring you the latter ende.

Pollard took this letter to be written to Busby, to whom, he supposed, Nashe had entrusted the issue of a corrected edition. But he cannot, it seems, have read it very carefully. It is inconceivable that Nashe should use such expressions as 'You write to me my book is hasting to the second impression', and 'you knowe very wel that it was abroad a fortnight ere I knewe of it', and 'Had you not beene so forward in the republishing of it', if he were writing to the man whom he was employing to issue an authorized second edition. It is evident that the letter was addressed to Jones, and that Nashe knew nothing of any change of publisher. And surely, had Nashe been entrusting Busby with the authoritative text to supersede Jones's, he would have sent him the 'Epistles' that he asserts had been designed for the first edition and that he now vaguely promises for the third.[1] Furthermore, it is apparent that Nashe's complaint is that Jones had rushed out the first edition without informing him or waiting for his corrections and conclusion. Had Jones stolen the manuscript and printed it without leave, we may safely suppose that Nashe would have used very different language. Nor is there much wrong with Jones's text: Nashe made some corrections and alterations in the second edition, as he did again in the third, but they are of no material consequence.

There is, therefore, no reason whatever to suppose that Jones did not purchase the pamphlet from the author in a perfectly regular way (though in a hurried departure from London the manuscript may have been handed over in an 'vncorrected and vnfinished' state) or that Nashe had anything to do with the change of publisher: moreover, since

[1] They never appeared and were doubtless just one of Nashe's jokes. But the passage serves to date the letter after Greene's death on 3 September.

Jones appears to have passed on Nashe's letter and corrections to Busby, we must conclude that the copy was amicably transferred from one to the other in spite of the absence of any formal assignment.[1]

It follows that whether Pollard's contention respecting the ease with which an author could substitute an authorized for a piratical edition was right or wrong, the example upon which he relied for illustration was misconceived.[2]

The case has an incidental bearing on another *locus* in the controversy over the replacing of bad texts by good ones. In the same year 1592 the Court of Assistants pronounced in favour of Jeffes's (lost) bad quarto of *The Spanish Tragedy* as against White's good quarto, on the ground (apparently) of its having been entered in the Register. Now Jeffes had been committed to prison for unruly conduct on 7 August, and he did not make his submission till 18 December; and I have argued that he cannot have been printing during that time (*The Library*, 1925, vi. 49; *The Spanish Tragedy* (1592), Malone Society reprint, p. viii). If so, Jeffes's edition of *The Spanish Tragedy* was printed not later than July, and his entrance of it on 9 October was an after-thought probably designed to block the way of White's superior edition. But it now appears that Jeffes printed two editions of *Pierce Penniless* in 1592 after that of Jones, entered on 8 August, and indeed after Greene's death on 3 September, and it is clear that at any rate the earlier of these must have been printed before 18 December. It follows that Jeffes was not wholly debarred from printing during the period of his disgrace.

[1] Jeffes printed the fourth edition for Busby in 1593. A fifth was printed by T(homas) C(reede) for Nicholas Ling in 1595. This too was doubtless by private arrangement, for Busby and Ling were in close association at the time (*The Library*, 1943, 4th series, xxiv. 82).

[2] On the other hand it goes to support another contention of his, namely that the works of professional authors were seldom if ever subject to piracy.

28. *Ad Imprimendum Solum*[1]

In the first of his Sandars Lectures, delivered in November 1915 and devoted to 'The Regulation of the Book Trade in the Sixteenth Century', Alfred Pollard quoted the following paragraph from a Proclamation of Henry VIII dated 16 November 1538:[2]

Item that no persone or persons in this realme, shall from hensforth print any boke in the englyshe tonge, onles vpon examination made by some of his gracis priuie counsayle, or other suche as his highnes shall appoynte, they shall haue lycence so to do, and yet so hauynge, not to put these wordes *Cum priuilegio regali*, without addyng *ad imprimendum solum*, and that the hole copie, or els at the least theffect of his licence and priuilege be therwith printed, and playnely declared and expressed in the Englyshe tonge vnderneth them . . .

Upon this Pollard commented as follows:[3]

Incidentally we may note that while a licence to print and a privilege carrying with it protection against piratical competition ought to have

[1] [1954, December. *The Library*, ix. 242–7.]

[2] *S.T.C.* 7790. A copy is preserved in a unique collection of similar documents belonging to the Society of Antiquaries. Of this fascimiles were made in twenty-four copies for the British Museum and subscribers at the instigation of Richard Garnett, 15 July 1897. The title of the volume, from which I quote, runs: 'Tudor Proclamations. Facsimiles of Proclamations of Henry VII, Henry VIII, Edward VI, and Philip & Mary, now in the Library of the Society of Antiquaries of London. Oxford: Printed for the Subscribers by Horace Hart, Printer to the University. M DCCC XCVII.' (B.M., 8. Tab. d. 3.)

[3] The four lectures were printed in *The Library* in the course of 1916, and reissued under the title of *Shakespeare's Fight with the Pirates* the same year. A second edition, revised, was published by the Cambridge University Press in 1920. It is from this that I quote. The paragraph in question was printed in the January number of *The Library*, 3rd ser., vii. 23–24, in a rather different form. In revision Pollard expanded it and made its meaning clearer; the original is rather more cautiously worded. In an article in *The Library* for January 1919 (x. 57–63) Pollard restated his position in reply to criticisms by Miss E. M. Albright in *Modern Language Notes* for February 1919 (xxxiv. 97–104) defending the traditional interpretation. (The publication of *The Library* must have been badly delayed!) I do not think that he advanced his case. He repeated the mistake of supposing that the phrase *ad imprimendum solum* was intended to qualify the licence rather than the privilege, and I cannot see that the letter of protest addressed by Richard Grafton to Thomas Cromwell on 1 December 1538 in any way supports his view. It is clear that Grafton had used the words *Cum gracia et priuilegio Regis* in his New Testament to imply a royal licence, which was precisely what Henry was determined to prevent.

been kept clearly distinct, the one word 'priuilegium' seems to have been used as a Latin equivalent for both, the reason being, I believe, that King Henry VIII, who re-wrote this clause with his own hand, was not in the least concerned at the moment with the commercial effect of the proclamation, but only with maintaining his own right of censorship. Every book, as I understand the proclamation, required a licence; but this licence was not to be paraded by the use of the words 'Cum priuilegio regali,' without these words being limited and restricted by the addition 'ad imprimendum solum.' These must therefore be construed 'only for printing,' i.e. they did not, unless this was expressly stated, confer the royal approbation and they did not in themselves prohibit piracy, though the 'whole copy' or 'effect' of the privilege, when it is printed as the Proclamation directs, probably always contains this prohibition. There is sufficient evidence that by the reign of Elizabeth the words 'ad imprimendum solum' had come to be generally interpreted as equivalent to 'for sole, or exclusive, printing.' Whether or no they can legitimately bear this meaning in Tudor Latin, it seems quite clear from this Proclamation that this is not the meaning they were originally intended to bear.

Ten years later A. W. Reed returned to the subject in his book on *Early Tudor Drama* (1926, pp. 181–4) and not only showed exactly how Henry had altered the draft Proclamation submitted to him, but also how the text had gradually taken shape in a series of modified drafts before ever it came under the royal scrutiny. Dealing with these he wrote (p. 181): 'Mr. Pollard has pointed out that the meaning of this injunction, and particularly of the words *ad imprimendum solum* has not been clearly apprehended', and later (p. 182) claimed that the series of amended drafts 'confirm Mr. Pollard's reading of the King's phrase in a definite manner'.

I suppose that since then most critics who have had occasion to consider the matter have accepted Pollard's interpretation. On the contrary, I propose to argue that in this instance Pollard was completely mistaken, and that a careful consideration of the wording of the Proclamation, and still more a study of the earlier drafts, shows clearly that the words *ad imprimendum solum* were from the first intended to bear the sense that, as Pollard admitted, has been commonly attributed to them since the days of Elizabeth.[1]

[1] Reading Pollard and Reed I have always had an uncomfortable feeling that all was not clear and that sooner or later a further study of the original documents

But before entering on the argument it will be well to establish in detail the textual history of the passage in question for not only may Reed's book not be in all readers' hands, but the transcripts it contains are not in all respects reliable. The original draft is among the State Papers in the Public Record Office.[1] It has been twice revised, by the same hand. I am less certain that this is the hand of the original draft, though it may be. The first revision consisted of a single insertion, which is shown in italics in the following transcript:

Itm̄ that no p̱sone or p̱sones vsyng the occupacõn of pryntyng in this Realme shall fromhensforth̄ prynte eny bokes in the Englishe tong with̄ thiese wordȩ/ cum priuilegio [leg][2] Regali/ onles *they haue firste Licence vpoñ exãinacioñ made by sõme of the* p^{i}*vey counsaiłł to printe the same. And haue a priuilege in dede that no man but they shałł* p^{i}*nte the same for a tyme.* the true vnderstonding of the same wordȩ be plainlie declared and exp'ssed in the Englishe tong vnderneth̄ them to thentent that the Reders maye plainlie p̱ceve the effectȩ thereof/

The second revision was more elaborate and involved deletion as well as addition. The outcome was as follows, the additions being again indicated by italics:

Itm̄ that no p̱sone or p̱sones vsyng the occupacõn of pryntyng in this Realme shall fromhensforth̄ prynte eny bokes in the Englishe tong with̄ thiese wordȩ/ cum priuilegio Regali/ onles they haue firste Licence *of his highnes graunted* vpoñ exãinacioñ made by sõme[3] *his gracȩ* p^{i}vey counsaill̄ *or other such as his highnes shal appoincte And that theffect of his licence and* p^{i}*uilege be ther*w^{t} *prynted and* plainlie declared and exp'ssed in the Englishe tong vnderneth̄ them . . .[4]

The final draft submitted for Henry's approval is among the Cottonian manuscripts in the British Museum.[5] The

would have to be made. Having recently had need once more to examine the Proclamation of 1538 in preparing some lectures of my own, I felt compelled to consider the matter afresh and obtained photostats of the documents in question. The present article is the outcome of an examination of them.

[1] S.P.D., Henry VIII, [now S.P.1] vol. 139, fols. 103–28. The paragraph we are concerned with is on fol. 112.

[2] It looks as though the scribe started to write 'legali' instead of 'Regali', but it may be a mere dittography.

[3] The following 'of' may have been crossed out by mistake: the deletion, though probable, is not altogether clear.

[4] It is not certain whether it was in the first or second revision that the final clause 'to thentent . . . therof/' was struck out, but it was probably in the second.

[5] MS. Cotton, Cleopatra E. v, fols. 356–84. Our paragraph is on fol. 365^{a}.

paragraph in question differs from the second revision above only by the insertion of the words 'the hole copie or ellę at the lest' before 'theffect' in the last clause. But Henry had no patience with the clumsy wording of the official scribe and emended the text as follows (brackets indicating his deletions and italics his additions):[1]

Itēm that no pson or psones [vsing the occupacōn of printyng] in this realm shall fromhensforth printe any bookę in the englishe tonge [w^t these Wordes/ cum privilegio Regali/ onles they haue first licence of his hieghnes graunted] *onles* vppoñ examynacōn made by some of his gracę pryvie counsaile or other such as his hieghnes shall appoint *they shall have lysēce so to do and yet so havyng nott to put thes wordes cũ privilegio Regali w^t owght addyng ad imprimendũ solũ*, And that the hole copie or ellę at the lest theffect of his licence and privilege be therw^t printed and playnly declared and expressed in the Englishe tonge vnderneth them/

Here then are the several texts of the passage in question and we can now pass to their interpretation. When Pollard wrote the paragraph already quoted he was not at his critical best. To begin with, he made the dangerous mistake of underrating Henry's intelligence. Properly read the questions of licence and privilege *are* 'kept clearly distinct', and it is not true that 'the one word "priuilegium" [is] used as a Latin equivalent for both.' Henry began by laying down that no one was to print an English book without its being duly licensed by a competent authority, after which he proceeded to lay down that, even when licence had been obtained, no one should claim that a book enjoyed the royal privilege without specifying the exact nature of that privilege, namely that it was *ad imprimendum solum*. No connexion between licence and privilege was intended or is implied. It is true that the distinction might have been made more explicit at this point, but it emerges again later when it is ordered that both licence and privilege shall be printed in the book itself. It is, no doubt, true that Henry 'was not in the least concerned at the

[1] Henry showed his sense of draftsmanship by deleting the words 'vsing the occupacōn of printyng', the only effect of which was to exempt any one not a professional printer from the operation of the proclamation, and by deferring all mention of privilege until he had dealt with the matter of licence.

moment with the commercial effect of the proclamation', or rather of the privilege; but he was very much concerned to make it clear that the questions of privilege and licence were quite distinct. It was to this end that he insisted that the nature of the privilege should be defined by the addition of the words *ad imprimendum solum*. It is therefore upon the meaning of this phrase that the question turns. It had usually been assumed that it meant 'for sole, or exclusive, printing', and that is indeed the acknowledged purport of a privilege where printing is concerned. Pollard, on the other hand, maintained that it meant 'only for printing'. Now I submit that a privilege 'only for printing' has no meaning at all. In connexion with the printing of a book I can conceive only two meanings of the word 'privilege'. It might, possibly, mean a licence to print a particular book, and Henry is at pains to make clear that this is not the meaning intended: or else it might more naturally mean a grant of the exclusive right to print a particular book, which is what Pollard denies that it means. What exactly was the position with which Henry was faced? He was in the habit of granting privileges to individual printers conferring, either for life or for a specified term of years, an exclusive right of printing any book that the printer in question should be the first to put into type. I print a typical example below.[1] Thus printers who possessed such a privilege very naturally advertised their books as printed *cum priuilegio regali*, as a warning against piracy; and there was a danger that this phrase might be interpreted to mean that a book bearing it was printed with the royal licence. It was to guard against this that the words *ad imprimendum solum* were to be added. In other words it was to be made clear that the privilege had nothing to do with official approbation, but was merely concerned, as we know that in fact it was concerned, with the protection of the printer against piratical invasion of his rights.

This is borne out by what can be gleaned from a study of the earlier drafts. The original version makes no mention of

[1] Pollard, of course, was aware of such privileges, and remarks that in fact a privilege 'when it is printed as the Proclamation directs, probably always contains' mention of this exclusive right. Of course it always does so, since this is the whole effect of the privilege.

licence at all, and merely directs that the phrase *cum priuilegio regali* is not to be used unless its 'true vnderstonding' is made plain. Then the first revision (which does provide for licence) defines the 'true vnderstonding' of the formula to be that those who use it 'haue a priuilege in dede that no man but they shaƚƚ p'nte the same for a tyme'. About the meaning of this there can be no two opinions, and although the words do not appear in the draft actually submitted for Henry's approval, there can be no doubt that it was the same provision that Henry sought to express by the words *ad imprimendum solum*.[1] Indeed this is the only acceptable meaning of the phrase. That there could be a licence to print that did not imply approval of what was printed is an idea that Henry would have scouted as nonsense.

As an example of a privilege granted to a printer by Henry VIII Reed printed that found in a book from the press of Richard Bankes. Rather fuller is the following in a work entitled *The Door of Holy Scripture*, which is in fact the preface to the Wyclifite translation of the Bible, printed by John Gough in 1540.[2]

¶ The tenour of the Kynges preuylege.

Henry by the grace of God, Kynge of Englande and of Fraunce, defensor of the fayth, lorde of Irland, supreme head vnder Christ ouer the catholyke church of England: To al maner of people exercysyng the arte of pryntyng we gyue gretyng [and let you] to vnderstãd, that we haue only graũted & lycẽced to Iohan gowgh cytesyne & stacyoner of Londõ, that he only [is] to prynte vnder our pryuelege al maner of bokes new begon / trãslated or cõpyled by the sayd Ihoan [*sic*] gowgh, & all such as he doth cause to be translated & prynted by his procure-

[1] Upon the latinity of the phrase I can express no opinion. Both Pollard and Reed were moved by doubts whether it 'can legitimately bear [the proposed] meaning in Tudor Latin'. But since it is freely admitted that this was the meaning commonly attached to it at the time, it would be risky to argue that it cannot have been the meaning intended.

[2] *S.T.C.* 3033; B.M. C. 25. d. 7(1). This privilege is unusually elaborate and involved. Others, generally like in tenor, are found in Richard Bankes's edition of the Epistles and Gospels also in 1540 (*S.T.C.* 2967; B.M. C. 25. g. 9), and earlier in Sir Thomas Elyot's Dictionary, printed by Thomas Berthelet in 1538 (*S.T.C.* 7659; B.M. C. 28. m. 2). Neither of these provides for the perusal of the work by discreet and learned persons, that is to say for licence: Bankes's privilege, like Gough's, is for seven years; Berthelet's for life so far as reprints are concerned, but for six years only in the case of new editions 'vpon other mens corrections'.

ment cost or charge, we graunt lycence and autoryte to the sayd Iohan gowgh his assygners [*sic*], [&] factours to prynte al such storyes new begon[, being] lawful and not prohybyted, so that al such storyes or bokes, be perused & ouersene by two or thre dyscrete learned paxsõs [*sic*] We graũt to the sayd Iohn gowgh the makyng, pryntyng, & vtteraũce of al such bokes, new set forth to his owne aduantage for the space of, vii, yeares imediatly ensuyng the pryntyng & settyng forth of all such bokes or processe newe begon & not afore prynted, & thus duryng the tyme a fore lymyted ẏᵗ in ony wyse no person vsyng the scyence of prynytng, or not vsynge[,] do by any crafte or delaye [*sic*] prynte within this our Realme or canse [*sic*] to be prynted els where no such bokes, but that the forsayd Iohan gowgh haue the only auãtage accordyng to the tenor of this our forsayd lycẽce & pleasure (to him onely graunted) vpon payne of forfayture of all such bokes contrary imprynted to the effecte of this our lycence, commaundynge therfore all subiectes, offycers, & mynysters, to ayde & fauourably assyst the sayd Iohan gowgh in the exercyisng [*sic*] of this our licẽce & auctoryte yf nede requyre.

¶ God saue the Kynge.

We may be sure that Henry would have given short shrift to this frightful verbiage had he taken a hand in the drafting of the privilege, and that he would have avoided calling it a licence.

It is pleasant to be able to add that after friendly correspondence Dr. Reed accepts the interpretation of the Proclamation offered above. He writes: 'I can now say that there is nothing that matters in your two letters that I would not accept as my own.' Perhaps I may hope that Pollard too, had he lived, might have reconsidered his position.

29. Richard Robinson and the Stationers' Register

'ROBINSON'S Eupolemia or good Warrfare agenst Sathan the Devill, as the Capitall Enemy of Man Kynd: Conteyning all his Printed Worckes aswell in Octavo, as in Quarto, from the yeare of oure Savioure 1576, Vntill the yeare 1599.'[2] Thus Richard Robinson, dull, diligent, and indigent translator and compiler mostly of religious works, heads a petition for relief, in which he points out 'how well he had deserved of his country by his writings and how little profit he had made by them.' McKerrow continues: 'In this petition, originally intended for Queen Elizabeth, but presented after her death to King James, Robinson has left a carefully drawn up tabular statement of all his works, the persons by whom they were licensed, the number of editions and the printer by which each was executed, the person to whom each work—or each edition—was dedicated, the amount which he received for the dedication, and the number of copies of the work which he himself sold to his friends.' It is for the light it throws on patronage and the remuneration of authors in the last years of the sixteenth century that Robinson's manuscript has been mainly studied, and no doubt it is herein that lies its chief appeal to the social and literary historian. McKerrow opened the discussion in sprightly mood. 'How did professional men of letters in Elizabethan days contrive to earn a livelihood? There is abundant evidence to show that even the most able and versatile among them were often put to their plunges; yet somehow (with occasional sojourns in the Counter) they succeeded in rubbing on.' But Robinson's petition is also of interest to the bibliographer, for the details he gives of the

[1] [1955, October. *The Modern Language Review*, l. 407–13.]

[2] British Museum MS. Royal 18 A. LXVI, fols. 5–13. It appears to have been first described in *The British Bibliographer* in 1810 (i. 109–14). In *The Gentleman's Magazine* for 1906 (ccc. 277–84) there is a 'Retrospective Review', unsigned but written by R. B. McKerrow, giving a further account of the work. The whole has since been printed by G. McG. Vogt in *Studies in Philology*, October 1924 (xxi. 629–48).

licensing and printing of his works often throw light on matters that the official entries of those works in the Stationers' Register leave obscure. It is from this point of view that I wish to examine the document. But since this may not be familiar to readers, I will first transcribe with notes the portions relevant to my purpose. Robinson arranges his works in sets of ten octavos and nine quartos: these I have disposed in a single chronological list, but I have added the original numbering in brackets at the end of each title. I am indebted for valuable help in identifying and locating some of Robinson's works to Professor William A. Jackson of Harvard.

I. 1576. 'The Reverend Bisshop Franciscus Patricius of Sene in Italy, his Epitome, 9 bookes of a Comon Weale, translated oute of Latin into English.' [Q1]

'Pervsed & allowed by the Reverend Father D. Edwyn Sandes B. of London	S.R.: no original entrance; assigned T. Marsh to T. Orwin 23 June 1591. [as 'Civill Policye']
And printed by Thomas Marsh'.	*S.T.C.* 19475.

II. 1576. 'Certeyn Select Historyes for Christian Recreation translated oute of Latin prose into English verse with theyre severall and apte tunes.' [O1]

'Pervsed and allowed by the Wardens of the Stationers:	S.R. 5 Dec. 1576 [II. 306]: Licensed to T. East 'Robinsons christmas [*sic*] recreacions': no hand mentioned.
Printed by Henry Kingston in Pater noster Rowe'.	*S.T.C.* 21118: for H. Kirkham, n.d.

Since no Henry Kingston is known it must be a slip for Kirkham: however, neither Henry Kirkham nor John Kingston is known to have had a shop in Paternoster Row, though both had in St Paul's Churchyard. There was presumably a private assignment from East to Kirkham before publication.

III. 1577. 'Robinsons Ruby an Historicall fiction translated oute of Latin prose into English Verse; with the prayer of ye moste Christian Poet Ausonius.' [O2]

'Pervsed and allowed by the sayde Wardens;	Not entered in S.R. and not known.
Printed by Iohn Charlewood in the Barbican'.	

IV. 1577. 'A Record of Ancyent Historyes intituled in Latin Gesta Romanoꝝ translated (auctore vt supponitur Iohane Leylando Antiquario) by mee pervsed corrected and bettered'. [O 3]

'Pervsed further and allowed by ye sayde Wardens:

And printed first and last by Thomas Easte in Aldersgate streete 6 tymes to this yeare 1601'.

[S.R.: no original entrance: assigned T. East to T. Snodham 17 June 1609, and W. Stansby to R. Bishop 4 Mar. 1638/9.] The earliest edition known is *S.T.C.* 21288, T. East, 1595: there are late reprints of 1610 [Snodham], 1620 [Stansby], and 1639 and 1648 [Bishop].

V. 1578. 'The Dyall of Dayly Contemplacõn for Synners, morall and devyne matter in English prose and verse first published in print Anno 1499: By me now corrected and reformed for the tyme bothe in the matter & methode'. [O 4]

'Pervsed and allowed by the Right Reverend Father in God, D. Iohn. Elmer, Bisshop of London;

S.R. 7 Oct. 1577: Licensed to Hugh Jaxon (Jackson); no hand mentioned; no fee; marginal note 'Redeliuered to thautor and not prynted'.

and printed by Hughe Singleton in Creede lane in London in Anno 1578.'

S.T.C. 5644.

The cancelled entrance may have been made before the Bishop's allowance had been obtained and possibly without Robinson's knowledge. Singleton did not trouble to re-enter the copy. The edition of 1499 was by Wynkyn de Worde.

VI. 1579. 'The Reverend. D. Philip Melanthon his prayers translated oute of Latin into English with the prayers of other learned Germanynes.' [O 5]

'Pervsed and allowed by the sayd Lord B of London:

Printed by Henry Denham in Pater noster Rowe.'

S.R. 24 Mar. 1578/9: Licensed to Denham; no hand mentioned.

Apparently 'Godly prayers, meete to be vsed in these later times' collected out of Melancthon and others and translated by Robinson, 'Assigne of W. Seres', 8°, 1579, a copy of which is in the Folger Library. Identified in *S.T.C.* with 17791, but this is an earlier translation by J. Bradforde published by J. Wight about 1553.

VII. 1579. 'The Vyneyard of Vertue p̱tly translated p̱tly collected out of the Byble and p̱tly oute of other Authors, by mee first 1579.' Enlarged 1591. [O 6]

'Pervsed and allowed by ye sayde L. B. of London

S.R. 26 Aug. 1579: Licensed 'vnder ye handes of the Bishop of london and the Wardens'.

First printed Anno. dict' 1579 and lastly 1591 by Tho: Dawson at ye Vinetree.'

S.T.C. 21121: n.d. [A copy of 1591 is at Yale.]

VIII. 1580. 'The aforesayde Reverend D. Philip Melanthon his learned Assertion or Apollogy of the Word of God and of his Churche by mee translated oute of Latin into English.' [O 7]

'Pervsed by Mr Wm Gravet and so allowed by ye sayd L. B. of L.

Not entered in S.R.

And printed by ye sayd Thomas Dawson'.

S.T.C. 17790.

IX. 1580. 'The Reverend Doctor Nicholas Hemming [i.e. Niel Hemmingsen] his Exposicion vpon the 25 Psalme translated into English.' [O 8]

'Pervsed by Mr Vaughan Chapleyn to the sayd L. B. of Lond and so allowed

Not entered in S.R.

Printed by Thomas Vautrollier.'

Copies of 'A godly and learned exposition' are in the libraries of Peterborough Cathedral and the Princeton Theological Seminary.

X. 1582. 'The Learned English Antiquary Iohn Leylandes Assertio ARTHVRII quondam Regis Angliæ; by mee translated out of Latin into English with the annotations of Mr. Stephen Batman p̱son of Newington Buttes.' [Q 2]

'Pervsed and allowed by the Wardens of ye Stacyoners

S.R. 7 June 1582: Licensed to John Wolf by G. Dewes, Under Warden.

& printed by Iohn Wolfe then Clerck to the Stacyoners in Pawles Church yarde'.

S.T.C. 15441.

It may be irrelevant that only one Warden put his hand to the copy; but Wolf was never Clerk of the Company and was indeed at this time at the height of his insurgency, being twice imprisoned in 1582. His submission and reform came a year later, and in 1587 he was appointed Beadle.

XI. 1582. 'Parte of the Harmony of King Davids Harp beeying the first 2i Psalmes of the Princely Prophet David expounded in Latin by D. Victorinꝰ Strigelius of Lipsia in Germany by mee translated oute of Latin into English and comended by George Close my Contry man Preacher of St Magnus ꝑish in London.' [Q 3]

'Pervsed and allowed by the R. Reverend Father in god D. Iohn Elmer L. B. of London aforesayd his Chapleyn Mr Iohn Dewporte aforesayd:

Printed by the sayde Iohn Wolfe'.

Not entered in S.R.

S.T.C. 23358.

XII. 1583. 'The Reverend D. Vrbanus Regius his sermon or homely of Good and evill Angels: Translated oute of Latin into English.' [O 9]

'Pervsed and allowed by Mr: D. Iohn Dewporte the sayd L. B. his Chapleyne:

Printed first by Iohn Charlewood Ann^{o} 1583 agene Ann^{o} 1590 and lastly 1593'.

S.R. 14 Dec. 1582: Licensed to John Charlewood under the hands of the Wardens.

S.T.C. 20844, 20845 ('reprinted', 1590), 20846 ('widdowe Charlewood', 1593).

XIII. 1583. 'The Laudable Society, Order & Vnity of Prince ARTHVRE and his Knights of ye Rounde Table in London by mee Collected penned and published in English verse with a threefold Comendacion of Archery.' [Q 4]

'Pervsed and allowed by the sayd Mr Stephen Battman preacher and by ye Wardens of the Stacyoners;

Printed by Iohn Wolffe'.

Not entered in S.R.

S.T.C. 800 [colophon, R.I. for Iohn Wolf].

XIV. 1587. 'The sayde Reverend Doctor Vrbanꝰ Regius his exposi[ti]on of ye 87 Psalm translated oute of Latin into English wch I entitled the Solace of Syon & Ioy of Ierusalem'. [O 10]

'Pervsed and allowed by Mr. D. Iohn Wood Chapelyne to the moste Reverend Father in god Iohn Lo: Archebishop of Canterbury his grace...

Printed by Richard Iones 1587. Printed by Abraham Kitson 1590 And by Richard Banckwor[t]h 1594'.

Not entered in S.R.

S.T.C. 20852 (no place or printer): 20853 (R. Jones, 1591): 20854 (R. Jones, 1594).

[Robinson's information cannot be correct. Jones is believed not to have printed himself, and neither Kitson nor Bankworth owned a press. The editions of 1591 and 1594 have McKerrow's device 136, and must have been printed by John Charlewood and James Roberts respectively.]

The remaining five works are continuations of No. XI.

XV. 1590. 'A proceeding in ye Harmony of King Davids Harp beeyng a second portion of 13 Psalmes mo expounded by the sayde Auctor: Translated by mee oute of Latin into English & Commended by Mr Ralff Wadington Schole master of Chrystes Churche hospitall free grammar Schole in London.' [Q 5]

'Pervsed & allowed by the sayd Lord Bisshop of London his other Chapleyn Mr Robt Temple:

Printed by Iohn wolffe aforesayde'.

S.R. 8 Mar. 1590/1: Entered under the hands of the Bishop of London and the Wardens.

S.T.C. 23359, n.d.

Robinson's date follows the legal reckoning.

XVI. 1592. 'A second Proceding in the Harmony of King Davids Harp beeyng a third portion of x Psalmes mo expounded by the same Auctor; translated by mee out of Latin into English'. [Q 6]

'Pervsed and allowed by the sayd L. B. his Chapleyne Mr Thomas Crowe pson of St Martyns by Ludgate:

Printed by Iohn Charlewood in the Barbican for Abraham Kitson in Pawles Church yard/.'

S.R. 22 Dec. 1592: Entered to Charlewood under the hands of the Bishop of London and the Master.

S.T.C. 23360, I.C. for Kitson, 1593.

Robinson's date follows the legal reckoning.

XVII. 1595. 'A Third Proceding in the Harmony of King Davids Harpp. beeyng a 4th portion of Psalmes, in nomber 17 from the 45 vnto the 62 expounded by the same Auctor: by mee translated into English, with the Commendations of Mr Richard Mulcaster and Mr Tho: Buckminster Preachers in London'. [Q 7]

'Pervsed & allowed by the sayde Lord B of London his Chapleyn Mr. Tho: Crowe	Not entered in S.R.
and printed by Valentyne Symes at the charges of Richard Banckworth Stacyon' at ye signe of the Sunne in Pawles Church yarde'.	*S.T.C.* 23361 (no mention of Bankworth).

In fact at this date Bankworth was still a Draper: he did not become a Stationer till 3 June 1600 and made no entrance in the Register before 2 November 1601. He may have financed this item and the next privately.

XVIII. 1596. 'A Fourthe Proceeding in the Harmony of Kinge Davids Harp beeyng a vth portion of Psalmes conteyning the exposition of 6 Psalmes mo by the same Author by mee translated oute of Latin into English ptly for my releef and ptly for redress of a false forged slaunder 3. yeares before vizt' Anno 1593 vniustly raysed vpon mee, &cę.' [Q 8]

'Pervsed by ye sayde Mr Thomas Crowe Chapleyn to the sayde L. B of London and by his good Lordship allowed:	Not entered in S.R.
Printed by the sayde Valentyne Symmes at the Charges of ye sayde Richard Banckworth in Paules Church yarde'.	*S.T.C.* 23362 (no mention of Bankworth).

XIX. [1598]. 'A Fifte Proceeding in the Harmony of King Davids harp (beeyng the vjth and last portion of the Psalmes) expounded by the sayde Reverend Author Victorinus Strigellius a Germane, (beeyng onely 5 [*read*? 6] Psalmes mo from the 68 to the 73 Psalme) by mee translated oute of Latin into English, synce wch tyme I have not translated any mo of the Psalmes nor any other worcke'. [Q 9]

'Pervsed & allowed by the sayde Mr Thomas Crowe Chapleyn to	Not entered in S.R.

the sayd R. Reverend father in God. D. Iohn Elmer. . .	
Printed by Peter Short for Mathew Lownes'.	*S.T.C* 23363: P.S. for Lownes, 1598.

The *S.T.C.* assigns two other books to Richard Robinson, namely 21120, *The Reward of Wickedness* [1574], and 21119, *A Golden Mirror*, 1589. In view of their absence from *Eupolemia* it is difficult to believe that they can be his; and in fact the *D.N.B.* ascribes them to another Richard Robinson, whom it distinguishes from the 'compiler' by calling him 'poet'. However the *D.N.B.* also assigns to the 'compiler' a work called *a Rare, True, and Proper Blazon of Colours in Armories and Ensigns*, 1583, without explaining its absence from *Eupolemia*.

We may safely assume that all nineteen books mentioned by Robinson were actually printed and published. It is therefore of some interest to notice that of three of them (III, VI, IX) no copy appears to be known, and that another (IV) survives only in later reprints. More important is the fact that no less than eleven (I, III, IV, VIII, IX, XI, XIII, XIV, XVII–XIX) were not entered in the Stationers' Register, though of two of them (I, IV) later assignments appear. Of one other (V) a tentative entrance was made, without mention of any authority, but this proved abortive, for no fee was paid and the copy was returned to the author. No entrance was made by the eventual publisher, which brings the number of unregistered publications up to twelve, or almost two-thirds of the total. This is an unusually high proportion, since there is some reason to believe that in general about two books out of three published were registered, though this may not, it is true, be a very reliable estimate.[1] What makes the present cases important is that they prove that absence of registration affords no ground to suppose that there was anything surreptitious about a publication, for it is clear that all Robinson's unentered works were nevertheless duly licensed, in some instance (III, IV, XIII) by the Wardens themselves.

The next point of interest is that Robinson's statements regarding licence, which may I think be taken as substantially accurate, supply a check upon the information given by the

[1] [See p. 348.]

Clerk in the Register. We have just seen that absence of registration in no way implies absence of licence. Nor does failure on the part of the Clerk to mention by whom the licence was granted. One book (II) that was allowed by the Wardens and one (VI) that was allowed by Bishop Aylmer were entered without any mention of authority. One book (XII) was entered under the hands of the Wardens, as if acting on their own responsibility, that we learn had in fact been allowed by John Dewport, one of Aylmer's chaplains. In two instances (XV, XVI) a copy was entered under the hand of the Bishop, whereas, according to Robinson, each had been both perused and allowed by one of his chaplains. This looks like a definite contradiction, for elsewhere (VIII, IX?, XVIII) Robinson is careful to distinguish between perusal by a corrector and allowance by the Bishop. Apparently Robinson was not aware that in the two cases in question the copy had been countersigned by the Bishop, as from the entries in the Register we know must have been the case. It is less certain whether the copies bore the Bishop's hand alone, or whether it was that the Clerk thought this alone worth recording. I do not think that where a copy bore the hands alike of a corrector and of his superior the Clerk was in the habit of mentioning both. In fact the procedure was fundamentally the same in all cases, for technically the most that even an officially appointed corrector could do was to advise his superior on the suitability of a copy for publication. That at heart was the defence put forward by Samuel Harsnett in 1599 when he found himself in danger of the Star Chamber for having licensed Dr John Hayward's work on the early years of Henry IV.[1] It is at the same time true (as Harsnett was presumably aware) that a corrector's hand was habitually accepted as 'sufficient warrant' for publication; this is clear from hundreds of entries in the Registers and is implied by those records of Robinson's (eight in number) that mention allowance by a subordinate only. It will be noticed that Robinson dealt almost exclusively with the chaplains[2] of, or personally with, Bishop Aylmer,

[1] See pp. 424–36.

[2] William Gravet, who perused No. VIII, does not appear to have been one of Aylmer's chaplains, though on this occasion he evidently acted in a similar capacity. He was a Prebendary of St. Paul's, and later a senior member of the panel of correctors appointed by Whitgift in 1588.

whom in one place he calls 'my moste godly and vertuous Spirituall Patrone and Benefactor'. Only his earliest work in 1576 was allowed by Bishop Sandys; one (XIII) was allowed by the unattached Stephen Batman[1] (and in that instance Robinson records that it was also allowed by the Wardens); and one (XIV) by a chaplain to Archbishop Whitgift.

One further point may be worth mentioning. It will be observed that Robinson uses the same phrase 'Pervsed and allowed' whether it is a question of the Wardens (II–IV, X, XIII) or of the Bishop (I, V–VII) or of a subordinate (XI–XVII, XIX). In the last case we may assume that by 'perusal' is to be understood a serious examination of the work.[2] In that of the Bishop it was doubtless vicarious: the instances are all early and Robinson may not have been in full possession of the facts. What is interesting is that he appears to contemplate no difference of procedure in the case of allowance by the Wardens. This would seem to imply a degree of supervision over the copies entered under their hands that one might not otherwise expect, and which one would imagine that they would have had neither the leisure nor the qualification to undertake.[3] Yet like supervision seems to be implied in two entries in the Register (24 August 1582 and 22 August 1592) in which, while allowing the provisional entrance of a copy, officers of the Company demanded that it should be further submitted to them for 'perusal' and possible amendment before printing.

Robinson also affords us some details about printing and publication.[4] Thus he further informs us that Nos. XVII and

[1] [The 'ꝑson of Newington Buttes', as Robinson informs us under X; well known as the annotator of Bartholomaeus Anglicus, 1582.]

[2] Generally at any rate. Sometimes the perusal was scamped. Thomas Buckner, chaplain to Archbishop Abbot, confessed that he had put his name to Prynne's *Histriomastix* after reading no more than sixty-four pages of it: at least that seems to be the implication of his defence before the Star Chamber, 15 February 1633/4(B.M. MS. Add. 11764, fols. 8*b*–29).

[3] The five books they allowed are, it is true, all secular.

[4] [Little reliance can, indeed, be placed on them, for Robinson's acquaintance with the Stationer's Company must have been slight. His statement (X) that Wolf was Clerk of the Company is absurd. He turns Henry Kirkham into Henry Kingston (II). As regards XIII, the unacknowledged first edition may have been nominally printed by Richard Jones, but if so he doubtless farmed out the work to

XVIII were printed at the expense of Richard Bankworth, a fact of which the books themselves afford no hint. It is, of course, conceivable, though it seems very unlikely, that Bankworth advanced money privately without sharing in the enterprise from a commercial point of view. If, however, being a Draper, he took part in the transaction for profit, this would appear to be an example of the practice of 'printinge for forens to the Company', against which an order was made by the Court of Assistants a couple of years later (Court-Book B, 19 January 1597/8, fol. 464^{b}).

somebody else; it is hardly credible that he farmed out the editions of 1594 or 1591 and 1597, which bear his name, to Kitson and Bankworth, neither of whom was a printer, only for them in turn to farm out the work to Charlewood and Roberts.]

30. Samuel Harsnett and Hayward's *Henry IV*[1]

A good deal has been written about the suppression of Dr. John Hayward's essay on 'The first part of the life and raigne of King Henry IIII. extending to the end of the first yeare of his raigne', and from the historical point of view we perhaps know as much about the affair as we need, though how long the author remained a prisoner is apparently uncertain. Bibliographically too a fairly complete picture can be pieced together. The copy was entered in the Stationers' Register to John Wolf on 9 January 1598/9 'vnder the handes of Mr. Harsnet and the wardens',[2] and the book must have been on sale the following month at latest. It was dedicated in a Latin epistle to the Earl of Essex, a fact which, in conjunction with its theme of the deposition of Richard II, aroused widespread interest and speculation. So much so, indeed, that the Earl became alarmed and within a week of publication wrote to Archbishop Whitgift, who was one of his few friends on the Council,[3] asking him to have the book called in.[4] Whitgift contented himself with ordering the dedication to be removed from all unsold copies, whence it is clear that he saw nothing dangerous in the book itself.[5] This was before 1 March on which day John Chamberlain wrote from London to Dudley Carleton at Ostend:

the treatise of Henry the fourth is reasonablie well written, the author is a younge man of Cambridge toward the ciuill lawe. here hath ben

[1] [1956 March. *The Library*, xi. 1–10.]

[2] It was the second of three copies entered the same day and by the same authority. The first was *A Letter from Octavia to Marc Antony*, entered to S. Waterson and published in Daniel's *Poetical Essays* the same year. The third was an account of the death of Philip II of Spain, entered to W. Aspley, which is not known to have been printed, though what looks like another manuscript of the same was published by Waldegrave at Edinburgh in the course of the year (*S.T.C.* 19834). [F. P. W. added to the words 'not known to have been printed' the note: 'Printed by E. Bollifant for Aspley. 1599: TCC.' The Sub-Librarian of Trinity College, Cambridge, confirms the presence of this pamphlet, class VI. 7. 9.—J.C.M.]

[3] *D.N.B.*, s.v.' Robert Devereux, second Earl of Essex', on the authority of Essex's clerk Reynolds.

[4] So Bacon later declared: *D.N.B.*, s.v. 'Hayward'.

[5] The epistle figures so prominently in the affair that I have thought it desirable to reprint it with a translation at the end of this article.

much descanting about yt, why such a storie shold come out at this time, and many exceptions taken, especially to the epistle wch was a short thinge in Latin dedicated to the erle of essex, and obiected to him in goode earnest, wherupon there was commaundment yt shold be cut out of the booke, yet I haue got you a transcript of yt that you may picke out the offence yf you can, for my part I can finde no such bugges-words, but that euery thinge is as yt is taken.[1]

On the other hand the authorities remained suspicious. It may have been about this time that Elizabeth consulted Bacon respecting the possibly treasonable character of the work, and received from him little encouragement in spite of the fact that Bacon was already seeking to dissociate himself from the Essex faction. We learn from the later Star Chamber proceedings[2] both of Whitgift's action and of more drastic measures taken by the Bishop of London. For about Whitsun (27 May) a second edition of the book, numbering 1,500 copies, in which the dedication was replaced by an English epistle apologetical to the reader, was seized and burnt by Bancroft before any copies reached the public.[3] It is not certain whether any examples of the original edition have survived: the destruction of the second seems to have been complete. The four editions recorded in the *Short-Title Catalogue* (12995–7[a]), none of which is excessively rare, appear to be Jacobean reprints.

Only the uncertainty of the times and the susceptibility of the persons principally concerned can explain the action of the ecclesiastical authorities at a moment when Essex was a popular idol and had lately regained the royal favour. No doubt Hayward's choosing for literary embellishment an historical episode concerning which Elizabeth's reactions were well known was open to misconstruction,[4] and so was his dedication of it in adulatory terms to the ambitious

1 State Papers Domestic, Elizabeth (mod. ref. S.P. 12), vol. 270, art. 48; *The Letters of John Chamberlain*, ed. N. E. McClure, Philadelphia, 1939, i. 70. Chamberlain dates the letter 'From London this first of march 1599', which is a calendar date, contrary to his usual custom.

2 See the article by Margaret Dowling in *The Library*, September, 1930, xi. 212–24.

3 The apology survives in two manuscript copies and is reprinted by Miss Dowling.

4 The passage depicting the deposition had been omitted from Shakespeare's *Richard II* when printed two years before, but there is no reason to suppose that it was not acted on the stage. It was certainly part of the play as written.

favourite.[1] But as yet there was no suggestion that Essex would one day aspire to play the part of Bolingbroke, and he was on the eve of appointment as Lord Lieutenant and Governor General of Ireland, with the prayers of the people in good time to return 'Bringing rebellion broached on his sword'.[2] With his failure and return a few months later the political scene changed. In June 1600 Essex was charged with dereliction of duty, and in July Hayward was summoned before the Court of Star Chamber. In January 1601 the Earl was known to be plotting treason at Essex House, and on the 22nd Hayward was tried a second time—at the Tower, where he remained. We may suspect that Hayward's prosecution, which was in the hands of the Attorney General, Sir Edward Coke, was inspired more by his enemies' desire to prejudice the Earl than by any great concern for the motives of the historian, though it incidentally exposed the latter's eminently uncritical methods. The printer, John Wolf, also stood his trial. There is no evidence that any proceedings were instituted or contemplated against the clergyman who had licensed the book,[3] but he was not forgotten, and it is clear that Coke, when preparing the case against Essex, invited him to explain his action. Harsnett's defence or apology has, of course, been known to students from the *Calendar of State Papers Domestic* for 1599–1601. But it seems to me that the light it throws on the procedure and habits of ecclesiastical licensers, or examiners as Harsnett properly calls them, is so significant that the document deserves to be printed fully and exactly from the original. The defence appears to be addressed to Coke, though not by name, for it was sent with a covering letter to him. Neither letter nor enclosure is holograph, but each is signed: Harsnett employed a scrivener to copy and probably to draft his answer, which has a professional ring quite unlike the letter; this must have been transcribed verbatim.

[1] Yet to whom, he might have pleaded, should he have offered it if not to the Chancellor of his own university?

[2] In the *Dictionary of National Biography* Gordon Goodwin (s.v. 'Harsnett') dates the publication a year too late and represents the work as dedicated to Essex when 'in disgrace'. Sidney Lee (s.v. 'Hayward') gives the facts correctly.

[3] As there were a generation later against Thomas Buckner for allowing Prynne's *Histriomastix*.

Samuel Harsnett was born at Colchester in 1561 and educated at Cambridge, first at King's College and later at Pembroke Hall, where he became a Fellow in 1583. After taking orders he was appointed chaplain to Bishop Bancroft, and in 1598 prebendary of St. Paul's. He is found licensing books from 21 August the same year. Later he became Master of Pembroke, Vice-Chancellor of Cambridge, and Bishop successively of Chichester and Norwich, and died as Archbishop of York in 1631.

Here are the documents in question from the State Papers Domestic, Elizabeth (mod. ref. S.P. 12), vol. 275, arts. 31 and 31(1).

Right wo^{r}shipfull, I haue not yet receiued eny bookes from my Lord of London and so am not able to performe my taske in comparing them according to my promise. this [*i.e.* thus][1] for griefe of hart and confusion of face I am skarce able to write, that I shold be behinde hand to your most graciouse diuine kindnesse towards me. I haue sent myne aunswer enclosed the onlie part of my dutye that I cold performe, moste humblie beseeching your goodnes to accept it in good part, and to be a father vnto me as you haue begunne. the god of Heuen sees and knowes I am innocent. at casus Leso Numine crimen habet. my poore estate, my credit, my selfe and more then my selfe doe hang vppon your graciouse countenance[2] for I muste[3] craue pardon to tell an vnmannerlie[4] secrett,: I haue a poor weake gentlewoman my wife in child bed who since your messanger his being at myne house did neither eat, nor drink nor sleape for feare, and yet I haue twentie tymes reade ouer your most graciouse Lettars vnto her. the Lord of Heuen requite you for I and my poore frends shall neuer be able & so wth teares I humblie take my Leave. from my poor house at Crigwell this xx^{ti} of Iuly 1600.

Your Wp: his bought
& bounden servant.
Sa: Harsnett

[addressed]
To the righte wo^{r}shipfull
m^{r} Atturnye generall to
the Queen her moste
Excellent Maiestie:
yeue these

[1] [So Greg in revision; but I cannot see the necessity for so interpreting the word. —J.C.M.]

[2] Three minims between *a* and *c*.

[3] Only four minims before *s*.

[4] Three minims between *a* and *e*.

[enclosure]

In moste humble wise complaininge sheweth vnto your Worship̃ your dailie Orator Samuel Harsnett, that where as the Author of a Pamphlet published in print in anno $\overline{99}$ Intituled the Raigne of Kinge Henry the fourth hath endeuored to excuse his publishinge the sayd pamphlett, as being allowed and approued by your sayd Orator, it may please your wp̃: in your graue wisdome to consider that this his allegation can be no colour of excuse vnto him in regard of these reasons ensuynge.

Firste for that it hath been custome and vse, for eny man that entended in good meaning to put a booke in print, the Author him selfe to present the booke vnto the Examiner and to acquaynt him wth his scope and purpose in the same: the Author of this pamphlet concealed him selfe and nether spake nor conferred wth your orator concerning this pamphlett (notw^{t}standing we were both students togither in Pembrook hall in Cambrige, & both of a tyme and standing in the Colledge) but the author deliuered his pamphlet vnto a gentleman in my Lord of London his house who begged your Orator his approbation vnto the same in the name of a cantel of our Englishe chronicles phrased and flourished ouer onlie to shewe the Author his pretie Witt.

Secondlie that whereas your Orator his approbation of eny booke whatsoeuer is but a leading and inducement to my Lord of London my Master to passe his Lp: his further approbation to the same wthout wch his Lp: his further approbation your Orator his allowance is no sufficient warrant for the Author to prynt his booke: the author of this pamphlett published his pamphlett wthout my Lord & master his approbation at all, contrarie to warrant in that behalfe.

Thirdlie the Author hath wronged your said orator muche, and hath abused your Wp: wth false enformation in alledging for him selfe that your Orator allowed his pamphlet as it was & is published in prynt. for that the Author knoweth in his conscience this is true that when his pamphlett had mine approbation it was heddlesse wthout epistle, preface, or dedication at all wch moued me to thinke it was a meer rhetorical exornation of a part of our Englishe historie to shewe the foyle of the Author his witt: after myne approbation gotten thereuntoe the Author foysted in an Epistle dedicatorie to the Earle of Essex wch I neither allowed nor sawe, and wch if I had seen I protest I shold neuer haue allowed the rest of the Pamphlett.

Fourthlie it may please your graue wisdom gracioushe to consider your Orator his mean condition and capacitie that your sayd orator is a poore diuine vnacquainted wth bookes and arguments of state, and wth consequenceis[1] of that nature: that your Orator for ten or twelue yeares past neither spake wth nor saluted the Author of this pamphlett, and so is cleer from priuitye wth his entendementę & ouertures in the same: that your Orator sett to his hand sodeinlie as mooued by his freind neuer reading (vppon his saluation) more then one page of the hedlesse pamphlett[2] for wch his vnaduised negligence he humblie beggeth your moste graciouse milder Censure, that it may be no imputation of bad meaninge vnto him, who doth dailie in his poore calinge moste hartilie & Zealouslie pray for the happinesse of her sacred Maiestie and the state, and for the longe continuance[3] of her Highnes most graciouse, blessed, diuine gouernment ouer vs, and doth frõ the bottom of his hart wishe shame & dreadfull confusion vppon all calumniators, and vnderminers of the same.

Your Wp: moste humblie
bounden Orator.
S.[4] Harsnett

The first sentence of the letter is obscure. The most natural supposition is that the books Harsnett was expecting from the Bishop were copies for examining, and it is true that he did little licensing about this time. We must, of course, be careful how we infer any close correlation of date between the licensing of a copy and its entrance in the Register, though it is likely that as a rule the one followed closely upon the other;[5] but it does seem possible to trace, after a fashion, the repercussions of the Hayward affair on Harsnett's activity as an examiner. His hand first appears on 21 August 1598 (in conjunction with that of the Vice-Chancellor of Cambridge) and does so on eight other occasions before the end of the year. He licensed six copies in January (including *Henry IV*)

[1] An error for either *consequences* or *consequencies*, probably the latter.

[2] The end of the word is crowded in at the edge of the paper and the exact spelling is uncertain.

[3] Perhaps *continuancie*.

[4] There is a curve after the *S*, rather like a long *ſ*, which may conceivably be meant for an *l*. [It is not as simple as this: there is more than one curve, and I think an exaggerated *a* may be intended, as in the signature to the letter.]

[5] We know the precise dates on which Sir Henry Herbert licensed some half-dozen books for printing: one was registered the same day, one the following day; in the case of others there was a delay of one, two, or three weeks; once of over two months.

but only one in February, one in April, and two in May, after Whitgift had suppressed the epistle; then, after Bancroft had destroyed the second edition, his hand does not reappear before December. He was fairly active early in 1600; but when he wrote his letter to Coke he had licensed only one copy since April, on 14 July. He was responsible for a few more in the autumn, but in the fatal year 1601 he put his hand to only one copy, on 3 March. From May 1602 he was again fairly active.

This interpretation of Harsnett's words is open, however, to two objections. In the first place it is difficult to understand what possible interest his activities as an examiner could have for Coke, apart from the one book in question: in the second place it would appear from Harsnett's own account that copies usually came into the examiner's hands direct from the author and not from the Bishop. I have, however, no other interpretation to offer.

Concerning the defence Harsnett remarks that 'I haue sent myne aunswer enclosed'. This is not the most natural way of saying 'I enclose my answer', and since in it 'your Worship̃' may possibly stand for 'your Worships', we might imagine that what the writer intended was, 'I have sent my answer, of which I enclose a copy, to my Lords of the Council'. On the whole, however, the tone of the defence, and in particular the phrase 'moste humblie beseeching your goodnes to accept it in good part', suggest that it was addressed to Coke individually.

In considering what weight to allow to Harsnett's arguments we must remember that his primary object throughout is to save his own skin: he is in no way concerned to defend Hayward's essay, but only to maintain his own ignorance and innocence of any treasonable intention that may be found in it. With this in view he represents his knowledge of the contents as second-hand and protests that he had hardly glanced at them. At the same time we must not overlook the fact that his description of the work as 'a cantel of our Englishe chronicles phrased and flourished ouer onlie to shewe the Author his pretie Witt', and later as 'a meer rhetorical exornation of a part of our Englishe historie to shewe the foyle of the Author his witt', displays a shrewd appreciation of its nature. Bacon held the same opinion when he told the Queen that he could find no treason in it, but only felony, in that the author had stolen his 'sentences' out of Tacitus. But whence came this judgement of Harsnett's? He represents it as derived from the gentleman of the Bishop's household who handed him the copy,[1] but it seems unlikely that this go-between had himself studied the work. If not, it must have been conveyed to him by the author, in which case it looks like camouflage and suggests that Hayward's intention was not quite as guileless as he would have us believe. Perhaps it was Harsnett's intent to foster this impression, for the same motive may be traced in his hint of something sinister in the fact that the author concealed himself and avoided all discussion of his work.

When Harsnett put his hand to Hayward's book he was still new to the task of examining; but he had already approved a number of copies[2] and must have been familiar with the routine of the Bishop's household. We may therefore attach some importance to what he tells us about the habits of examiners. First, he says that it was customary for the author of a copy seeking publication to present his manuscript to the examiner in person. This cannot, of course, have applied to all copies, some of which were published without the author's knowledge, or in his absence, and must have been submitted by the stationer interested; but it may have been generally true of works published under the author's direction.[3] Harsnett goes on to explain that it was usual for the author to confer with the examiner and to acquaint him with his intention in writing the work. The complaint that Hayward avoided doing so is plainly designed to cast doubts upon his integrity of purpose and to emphasize Harsnett's ignorance of the same. But such converse between author and examiner,

[1] The phrase 'in the name of' means, of course, 'representing it as'.

[2] It may not be irrelevant to observe that he was responsible for allowing two of the collections of satires that later incurred ecclesiastical censure (see Arber's *Transcript*, iii. 677), namely Marston's *Scourge of Villainy* on 8 September 1598 and Guilpin's *Skialetheia* on the 15th.

[3] We know that in 1632 it was the publisher who sought (and paid for) Herbert's licence for Fulke Greville's *Works* and Cowley's *Poetical Blossoms* (Malone in the 1821 'Variorum' Shakespeare, iii. 231; cf. Chalmers's *Supplemental Apology*, 1799, pp. 109–10); but then Greville was dead and Cowley still at school. Besides, habits may have changed in the course of a generation.

if it was really customary, carries with it a suggestion that a book might be allowed without further scrutiny upon the author's assurance regarding his motive in writing it, and almost amounts to a confession that Harsnett would have been prepared so to allow the work of a fellow collegian, in spite of his later and rather inconsistent attempt to make light of their acquaintance.[1] In any case, though Hayward's concealing himself might conceivably have been a reason for refusing to approve his book, it could not possibly be an excuse for approving it unread.

It is the second head of Harsnett's defence that is really interesting. Here he argues that his approbation of a work is no more than a recommendation to his employer, the Bishop, to allow it, and not in itself a licence or authority to print. This is manifestly disingenuous. In the first place, if by his 'leading and inducement' he in fact led and induced his master to license a work with the nature of which he had failed to make himself properly acquainted, he was betraying the trust placed in him and was as much responsible as if he had given it his own *imprimatur*. Secondly, he must have been aware that a number of copies had already been passed to the press on his recommendation alone, and that, whatever the strictly legal position might be, his hand would in practice be treated as an authorization to print. We may assume that, in respect of licensing, the position of a chaplain to the Bishop of London would be that of a corrector appointed under Whitgift's order of 1588. It is, indeed, most unfortunate that the original of this document, making the first appointments, has not survived, and that we have to rely on a report of the same in the minutes of the Court of Assistants.[2] Of this, however, the wording is unambiguous: 'The names of Certen prechers & others whome the Archbishop of Canterbury hathe made Choyse of to haue the perusinge and alowinge of Copies that are to be printed . . . Any one of these settinge his hand to a copie, to be suffycient Warrant for thalowance of the

[1] Harsnett appears to be correct in saying that he and Hayward were 'of a tyme and standing' at Pembroke, for both proceeded B.A. in 1581 and M.A. in 1584. Since Harsnett was born in 1561 it is therefore unlikely that Hayward was born as late as 1564, as conjectured, on rather flimsy grounds, in *D.N.B.*

[2] [3 June. 1588, Reg. B, fol. 446[a]] *Records of the Court of the Stationers' Company, 1576 to 1602*, ed. Greg and Boswell, 1930, pp. 28–29.

same to entringe into the hall booke & so to be proceeded withall to printinge'. In the circumstances the Wardens can have had no choice but to accept Harsnett's hand as sufficient authority for printing Hayward's book. And this Harsnett must have known.

And yet I believe that Harsnett has stated the legal position correctly. A series of orders and decrees had laid down, not always very consistently, by whom copies were to be licensed for the press. Virtually authority lay with the Archbishop of Canterbury and the Bishop of London. It was plainly impossible for two busy prelates personally to examine all copies submitted for licence; they would necessarily rely mainly on the reports of subordinates, and in doing so they would be in order. So long as the Bishop or Archbishop satisfied himself that a copy was 'tolerable', it mattered not how he came to the conclusion, and he was within his right in giving it his *imprimatur*. What, before 1637, he had no power to do was to delegate his right of licence to another. For it was the Star Chamber decree of that year that first introduced the words 'or by their appointment'[1] and thereby empowered the prelates to pass on to others their right to grant an *imprimatur* on their behalf. Whitgift's action in 1588, if correctly reported to the Court, was strictly *ultra vires*.

In his third paragraph Harsnett makes the sound point that when he saw the pamphlet it lacked the notorious dedication to Essex, though we need not attach much weight to his protestation that had it been present he would never have approved the work. For there is nothing dangerous in the epistle itself, and that Harsnett would have been as quick as Whitgift (or was it Essex?) to sense its possible implications is inconsistent with his representing himself as 'a poore diuine vnacquainted with bookes and arguments of state, and with consequencies of that nature'. But while the point is well taken, and a natural one to take, it may be doubted whether it was in any way unusual for such additions to be 'foysted' into books at the last moment. Many prefaces were obviously written after the rest of the book was printed. It was again not till 1637 that the Order in Star Chamber required that not only should a book itself be licensed but equally 'all and

[1] Arber's *Transcript*, iv. 530.

euery the Titles, Epistles, Prefaces, Proems, Preambles, Introductions, Tables, Dedications, and other matters and things whatsoeuer thereunto annexed',[1] and it is conceivable that whoever drafted the order had the present case still in mind after a lapse of nearly forty years.

The fourth and final head of Harsnett's answer is relatively unimportant. So anxious is he to disclaim all knowledge of Hayward's purpose in writing his essay that he affirms upon his salvation that he approved it without reading more than a page. He admits that he has failed in his duty, but of how seriously he seems scarcely conscious when he adds 'for which his vnaduised negligence he humblie beggeth your moste graciouse milder Censure'. He was certainly lucky to incur nothing worse. It must be admitted that, faced with the terrors of the Star Chamber, the future Archbishop cut but a sorry figure.

Making allowance for Harsnett's anxiety to minimize his responsibility, and admitting that as an examiner he may, at least at the beginning of his career, have shown a disregard of duty surprising in one in his position, it is nevertheless impossible to avoid the impression that at the end of Elizabeth's reign ecclesiastical licensing for the press was more casual and less effective than the authorities can have intended or perhaps realized. This was probably inevitable in view of the output of the press and the inadequate provision for control, but it is a fact that bibliographical criticism should bear in mind.

I subjoin the text of Hayward's dedicatory epistle to Essex as it appears in the extant editions of his work.

The *Short-Title Catalogue* distinguishes four editions of Hayward's *Henry IV*, and of all of these the British Museum and Bodleian libraries between them furnish examples. They are:

A=*S.T.C.* 12995. BM: G. 4633(2); 10805. b. 9.
B=*S.T.C.* 12996. BM: G. 1938. Bodl.: 4° Art. Seld. H. 13: Wood 468(6).
C=*S.T.C.* 12997. Bodl.: Douce HH. 222.
D=*S.T.C.* 12997[a]. BM: G. 1196; G. 1846(2); 291. c. 25. Bodl.: Antiq. e. E. 1599.

[1] Arber's *Transcript*, iv. 529.

Illustrissimo & honoratissimo Roberto Comiti Essexiæ & Ewe, Comiti Marescallo Angliæ, Vicecomiti Herefordiæ & Bourchier[1]: Baroni Ferrariis de Chartley, Domino Bourchier & Louein[2]: Regiæ Maiestati Hyppocomo: Machinarum bellicarum præfecto: Academiæ Cantabrigiensis Cancellario: ordinis[3] Georgiani Equiti aurato: Serenissimæ Dominæ[4] Reginæ a sanctioribus[5] consilijs[6]: Domino meo plurimum obseruando.[7]

Ἀρίστῳ καὶ γενναιοτάτῳ[8]: *optimo & Nobilissimo* (*inquit*[9] Euripides) *ex qua sententia tu primus ac solus fere occurrebas* (*illustrissime comes*) *cuius nomen*[10] *si Henrici nostri fronte*[11] *radiaret, ipse & lætior & tutior in vulgus prodiret. Magnus siquidem es, & presenti iudicio, & futuri temporis expectatione: in quo, veluti recuperasse nunc oculos, cæca prius fortuna videri potest; Dum cumulare honoribus eum gestit*[12], *qui omnibus*[13] *virtutibus est insignitus. Hunc igitur si læta fronte excipere digneris, sub nominis tui vmbra* (*tanquam sub*[14] Aiacis *clipeo*[15] Teucer[16] *ille* Homericus) *tutissime latebit. Deus opt. max. celsitudinem tuam nobis, reique pubicæ diu seruet incolumem*[17]*: quo nos vz. tam fide quam armis potenti tua*[18] *dextra defensi, vltique, diutina cum securitate tum gloria perfruamur.*

Honori tuo deditissimus.
I. HAYVVARDE.

Knowing myself inadequate to the task of translation, I applied for aid to Dr. Victor Scholderer, who very kindly furnished the following English version.

To the most illustrious and honoured Robert, Earl of Essex and Ewe, Earl Marshal of England, Viscount of Hereford and Bourchier: Baron Ferrers of Chartley, Lord Bourchier and Lovaine: Master of the Horse to the Queen's Majesty: Master of the Ordnance:

[1] e *wrong fount* (*roman for italic*) B.
[2] Louen BCD.
[3] Ordinis BCD.
[4] Domino ABCD.
[5] [One would expect 'secretioribus', but the term seems to have been recognized: Thomas Watson, in the titles of his *Meliboeus*, 1590, describes Sir Francis Walsingham as 'Diuæ Elizabethæ a secretis, & sanctioribus consilijs'.]
[6] Consilijs D.
[7] The heading is printed in nine lines, alternately roman and italic, of lessening body. The text begins with a four-line factotum enclosing the initial, which has no breathing.
[8] γενναιστάτῳ B: γενναισάτῳ CD.
[9] *in quit* A(?) B(?) C.
[10] *nomẽ* A.
[11] *fronti* CD.
[12] *gisti* BCD.
[13] *omnihus* A.
[14] *sub* B.
[15] *clipio* ABCD.
[16] Tǝucer BC.
[17] *in columem* B: *in columen* C: *incolumen* D.
[18] *tna* B.

Chancellor of the University of Cambridge: Knight of the Order of St. George: Privy Councillor to the Queen's Grace: my most honoured Lord.

Ἀρίστῳ καὶ γενναιοτάτῳ, 'to the best and noblest' (says Euripides), at which sentiment you first and you almost alone came to mind (most illustrious Earl), whose name if it should shine in the front of my Henry, he would both gladlier and safer step forth among the public. For indeed you are great, both in present estimation and in the expectation of future time, you in whom Fortune, formerly blind, may appear to have recovered sight, inasmuch as she is eager to load with honours one who is distinguished by all the virtues. Therefore if you shall deign to receive him [Henry] with a glad countenance, he will shelter in great security under the shadow of your name (like Homer's Teucer under the shield of Ajax). May Almighty God long preserve Your Highness safe for me and the common weal, so that we, defended and avenged by your powerful right hand, both in faith and arms, may enjoy a long continuance alike of security and glory.

Your Honour's most devoted
J. Haywarde.

INDEX

The plays in the list on pp. 63–66 are given under their titles as well as under their authors (if known).

References in the form 100[(1)] indicate mention both in the text and in footnote 1.

Abercrombie, Lascelles, 279.
Abbo of Fleury, 218.
Abbot, George, Archbishop of Canterbury, 422[2].
'accidentals', opposed to 'substantive' readings, 376; copy-text should determine choice of, 381–2.
Accoramboni, Vittoria, 1–28.
'ad imprimendum solum', 406–12.
Adams, J. Q., his edition of *The Dramatic Records of Sir Henry Herbert*, 69[1]; on the printing of *Timon of Athens*, 392[2].
Aeschylus, his *Agamemnon*, 332.
Aesopus (Roman actor), 33, 39.
Agrippa, Cornelius, his *De occulta philosophia*, 91.
Albright, E. M., 406[3].
Alcuin, 258.
Alexius, or The Chaste Gallant, see Massinger.
Allde, Edward, 152.
Ames, Joseph, 150, 245.
Amphibalus, St., 270[1].
'anonimo del Campidoglio', 2, 10.
Antonio and Vallia, see Massinger.
'apostrophus', Jonson's elision sign, 390.
Arber, Edward, his *Transcript of the Register of the Company of Stationers*, 55, 149–52, 341, 343[2], 431[2], 433[1], 434[1].
Arden of Feversham, allegedly pirated by Abel Jeffes, 151–2.
Ariosto, Lodovico, his *Orlando Furioso* translated by Harington, 95–109.
Aristotle, 25; his δέσις, 27.
Aspley, William, 424[2].
'association copies', 245–6.
Atterbury, Francis, Bishop of Rochester, 29.
Ausonius, 414.
Aylmer (Elmer), John, Bishop of London, 415, 417, 420–2.
Bacon, Francis, 43, 197, 346, 424[4], 431.
'bad quartos', 154, 277, 295[3], 384[1].
Baker, D. E., his *Companion to the Playhouse*, 59[1], 315.
Balboa, Vasco Núñez de, 41.
Bald, R. C., 68[1], 226[1].
Bales, Peter, 289.
Bancroft, Richard, Bishop of London, 425, 427, 430.
Bankes, Richard, 411[(2)].
Bankworth, Richard, 418, 419, 423.
Barnes, Betty, name of Warburton's cook according to Scott, 49.
Barrington, Daines, 245.
Bartley (Berkeley), Sir William, his *Cornelia*, 44, 46.
Barwick, G. F., 207[2].
Baskervill, C. R., 48[2].
Batman, Stephen, 416, 422.
Beaumont, Francis, lost *History of Madan, King of Britain*, attributed to him, 61, 66; his verses on *Volpone*, *Epicene* and *Catiline*, 320–1.
Beaumont, Francis, and Fletcher, John, their 1647 folio entered in Stationers' Register, 56–57; six plays entered in 1660, 61; proportion of works entered in Stationers' Register, 345–6; their *Faithful Friend(s)* entered in 1660, 61, 66, 69; plays performed in 1662: *The Night Walker* (*The Little Thief*), *The Woman's Prize* (*The Tamer Tamed*), *The Beggar's Bush*, *The Humorous Lieutenant*, *The Maid's Tragedy*, *The Elder Brother*, *The Chances*, *Wit Without Money*, *The Maid in the Mill*, *The Spanish Curate*, *Rollo, Duke of Normandy*, *The Loyal Subject*, *Philaster*, 44–47; 'repetition-brackets' in *The Honest Man's Fortune*, 203–6; priority of editions of *The Elder Brother*, 263; Middleton's *Women Beware Women*, as *A Right Woman*, misattributed to them, 61, 63, 67.

Beauty in a Trance, see Ford.
Bede, Venerable, 370[1].
Believe as You List, see Massinger.
Beltz, Samuel, 111.
Benefice, The, see Wild.
Bentley, G. E., his *Jacobean and Caroline Stage*, 59[1], 67[1], 69[1].
Bentley, Richard, 252, 270.
Berthelet, Thomas, 372, 411[2].
Beyle, Henri, 2.
bibliography, nature of, 75–88; not merely descriptive, 76–77, 239; concerned with manuscripts as well as printed books, 77–78; elements of descriptive (systematic) bibliography, 78–79; wide scope, 80; not concerned with literary content, 81; not the compilation of bibliographies, 81; critical bibliography as 'the grammar of literary investigation', 82–85, 239; a possible course of lectures in, 85–88; present position of, 207–25; in London, 207–8; at Cambridge, 208–9; at Oxford, 209–10; in teaching of English, 210–13; leading contributors to, 215–18; task of Bibliographical Society, 218–20; as a science, 220–3; disadvantages of the word, 239–40; essentially the science of the transmission of literary documents, 241; concern with typography, 242; concern with book illustration, 243–4; concern with binding, 244–5; concern with book ownership, 245–6; transmission of variants, 247–60; critical bibliography identified with textual criticism, 254; interest not confined to the author's original, 257–9; examples of method, 260–6.
binding, relation to bibliography, 80, 244–5.
Bishop, George, 151[3].
Bishop, R., 415.
Blake, William, 223.
Blore, Thomas, 110.
Boas, F. S., 149, 382–3.
Bodmer, Martin, 230[2].
Boklund, Gunnar, 1[1].
Bollifant, E., 424[2].
Bolton, E., 320–1.
Bond, Sir Edward, 227.
Bond, R. W., vi.
Bonen, William, his *Crafty Merchant* confused with *The Soddered Citizen*, and attributed to Shakerly Marmion, 52, 60, 62, 63, 67, 70[1].
Bonian, Richard, and Walley, Henry, their edition of *Troilus and Cressida*, 394–401.
'book' = prompt copy, 278.
book illustration, relation to bibliography, 80, 243–4.
Borne, William, 237.
Boswell, Eleanor, 150[2], 432[2].
Bowers, Fredson, 298[1].
Brachiano, Duke of (Paulo Giordano Orsini), 3–28.
Bradforde, J., 415.
Bradley, A. C., 323[2].
Bradley, Henry, 218, 261[(1)], 272.
Bradshaw, Henry, 76, 208, 213–14.
Brathwait, Richard, 346.
Brendola, Giovanni Baptista, 1.
Breton, Nicholas, 345–6.
Brett-Smith, H. F. B., 96[1].
Bright, Timothy, 289.
Brome, Richard, 45; his *Jovial Crew*, 46; his lost *Wit in a Madness* and *Lovesick Maid*, 59, 65, 68; his *Sparagus Garden* and *Antipodes*, 68.
Brooke, Ralph, 277.
Brotanek, Rudolf, 188, 189[1], 190, 191.
Brown, Arthur, x, 45[1], 160[1].
Brown, Carleton, vii.
Browne, Sir Edward, 44.
Browne, John, 314, 316.
Browne, Sir Thomas, 37.
Brydges, Sir Samuel Edgerton, his *Censura Literaria*, 50.
Buc, Sir George, Master of the Revels, 68, 72, 314; manuscript notes, 226–38; his *History of Richard III*, 230[1], 233, 236; his *Δάφνις Πολυστέφανος*, 230–1, 235–6.
Buckminster, Thomas, 419.
Buckner, Thomas, 422[2], 426[3].
Bugbears, The (? by John Jeffere), 51, 53, 66, 69.
Bullen, A. H., on Edward Fairfax, 30; on *The Escapes of Jupiter*, 156–7, 161[3], 162–3.
Burre, Walter, 314, 316.
Burroughs, —, his lost *Fatal Friendship*, 58.
Bury, Richard de, 78.
Busby, John, the elder, 402–5.

Busby, John, Jr., 314, 316.
Butler, Geoffrey, 94[1].
Butler, Joseph, Bishop of Durham, 267.

Campana, Cesare, 1.
cancels, recording of, 310–12.
Cannan, Charles, 210[1].
Capell, Edward, 322[2], 326[1], 331[1].
Caramuelis, Johannes, 363[2].
Cardenio, The History of, see Fletcher.
Cardinal's Cap, Cambridge, repertory in 1662, 44, 47.
Carew, Thomas, x.
Carlell, Lodowick, his *Passionate Lover(s)* and *Spartan Ladies*, 58, 59[1]; his *Discreet Lover* and *Osman*, 59[(1)], 60; his *Deserving Favourite*, 59[1].
Carleton, Dudley, 424.
Caulfeild, James, first Earl of Charlemont, his collection of plays, 156.
Cavendish, William, first Duke of Newcastle, entry of his plays in Stationers' Register, 57; his *Captain Underwit*, 157[(1)].
Caxton, William, 86[1].
Celer, Asinius, 33, 39.
Chalmers, G., his *Supplemental Apology*, 67, 431[3].
Chamberlain, John, 424–5.
Chambers, E. K., his *William Shakespeare*, 68; on *King Lear*, 280, 283, 290, 293; his *Elizabethan Stage*, vi, 191, 317–18, 320; 321[2].
Chambers, R. W., 197.
Chancelor, Richard, 43.
Chapman, George, his *Bussy D'Ambois*, performed in 1662, 45–46; *Second Maiden's Tragedy, The*, attributed to him, 53; lost plays, *The Yorkshire Gentlewoman and her Son*, and *The Fatal Love*, attributed to him, 52, 53, 55, 62, 64; his verses on *Sejanus*, 320–1; his handwriting, 197; sent to jail for share in *Eastward Ho!*, 273; works entered in Stationers' Register, 346.
Chapman, R. W., 209, 218.
Charlemont, Lord, *see* Caulfeild.
Charlewood, John, 403, 414, 417, 422[4].
Chaucer, Geoffrey, order of his *Canterbury Tales* a typical bibliographical question, 85, 87; 76, 81, 151[3], 214, 270.
Cheney, C. R., 373[1].
Chettle, Henry, his handwriting, 193, 276.
Christmas Ordinary, The, 'by Trinity College Oxford', 62, 66, 69 (*see also* Richards).
Churchyard, Thomas, 346.
City Honest Man, The, see Massinger.
City Shuffler, The, 52, 66, 69.
Clark, W. G., and Wright, W. Aldis, 281.
Clavell, John, his *Soddered Citizen* confused with Bonen's *Crafty Merchant* and attributed to Shakerly Marmion, 70[1].
Cock Pit, Drury Lane, repertory in 1662, 46.
Codrington, Robert, his translation of *Ignoramus*, 45, 46.
Coke, Sir Edward, 426, 430.
Coleridge, S. T., 223.
collation, formulary of, 298–313.
Collier, J. P., 68, 227–8, 230–2, 238.
Collins, Richard, 152[1].
Columbus, Christopher, 41.
conjugate leaves, notation for, 302.
'continuous copy', 176.
Cooke, John, his *Greene's Tu Quoque*, 45, 46.
Cooper, Mrs. Elizabeth, *Muses Library*, 30.
Copinger, W. A., 82, 220[1].
copyright, whether inherent in works or in specific versions, 154–5.
copy-spellings, in Field's edition of Harington's *Orlando Furioso*, 107–9.
copy-text, rationale of, 374–91; defined, 374; authoritative for accidentals, not for substantive readings, 377, 381–2, 386; tyranny of, 382–4; extensive revision may necessitate choice of revised edition as copy-text, 389–91.
Cornford, F. M., 31.
Corporal, The, see Wilson, Arthur.
Cortés, Hernando, 41.
Countryman, The, 60, 65.
Courtney, W. P., 49[1].
Cowley, Abraham, 431[3].
Coxeter, T., 116, 141[1], 142–7.
Crafty Merchant, The, see Bonen.
Creede, Thomas, 405[1].
Croker, T. C., 111.
Cromwell, Thomas, 406[3].

Crowe, Thomas, 418, 419.
Cruickshank, A. H., 120, 121[1].
Cynewulf, his *Elene*, 261(1).

D., I., his verses on Jonson, 320–1.
Daniel, P. A., 281, 290, 295, 332[3].
Daniel, Samuel, 346, 424[2].
Davenant, Sir William, 30; his theatre in Lincoln's Inn Fields, repertory in 1662, 44, 47; his *Siege of Rhodes, Playhouse to Let, Law Against Lovers*, 44, 47; his *Fair Favourite*, 52, 57, 66, 69; entry of four plays in Stationers' Register, 57; his *Love and Honour*, 57, 58; his *Siege*, 60, 65, 68.
Davenport, Robert, lost *Henry I*, attributed to him in collaboration with Shakespeare, 51, (and *Henry II*) 61; his lost *Woman's Mistaken* (with Thomas Drue), 60; his lost *Fatal Brothers* and *Politic Queen*, 62, 66.
Davila, Pedrarias, 38.
Davis, Herbert, 210[1].
Davis (Davys), John, 43.
Dawson, G. E., 392[2], 393[1].
Dawson, Thomas, 416.
Day, John, lost *Maiden's Holiday* attributed to him and Marlowe, 69.
Dekker, Thomas, collaboration with Massinger in *The Virgin Martyr*, 122; lost plays: *Gustavus, King of Swethland* (*Sweden*) and *Jocondo and Astolfo*, 52, 62, 65; *The Jew of Venice*, 60, 65, 68; proportion of works entered in Stationers' Register, 345[2], 346, 347[1].
Demetrius and Marina, 50.
'demoniality', 363[2].
Denham, Henry, 415.
Devereux, Robert, second Earl of Essex, 424–6, 433–6.
Dewes, G., 416.
Dewport, John, 417, 421.
Dibdin, Rev. Thomas Frognall, 240[2].
Digby, Sir Kenelm, 190, 372.
'discovered', 21(1).
Discreet Lover, The, *see* Carlell.
Doctor John Faustus, Damnable Life of, 349, 359, 395.
Donne, John, 346.
Doran, Madeleine, on *King Lear*, 280–96.
Dowling, Margaret, 425[2, 3].
Drake, Sir Francis, 42.
'dramatic *enjambement*', 1[1], 19, 27.
Drayton, Michael, 346.
Drue, Thomas, *see* Davenport.
Drummond, William, 184, 317.
Duchess of Fernandina, The, *see* Glapthorne.
Duke Humphrey, *see* Shakespeare.
Duke of Guise, The, *see* Shirley, Henry.
Dumb Bawd, The, *see* Shirley, Henry.
Dyce, Alexander, 111.

East, T., 414–15.
Eastward Ho!, Jonson and Chapman imprisoned for writing, 273.
Eccles, A., 331[1], 332[1, 2].
Eden, Richard, his translation of Peter Martyr's *Decades*, 38, 39.
Edgerton, W. L., 184[1].
Edwards, Philip, x, 155[1].
Elyot, Sir Thomas, 411[2].
'enter' = 'is discovered', 20.
'entrance', distinguished from 'entry', 341.
Erasmus, Desiderius, his *Paraphrase*, 87–88.
Esdaile, Arundell, 208.
Essex, Earl of, *see* Devereux.
Euclid, 78, 84.
Eudoxus, 33, 39.
Exiguus, Dionysius, 370[1].
Eyre, G. E. Briscoe, 55[1].

Fair Anchoress, The, *see* Massinger.
Fair Favourite, The, *see* Davenant.
Fairfax, Brian, 29.
Fairfax, Edward, his eclogues, 29–43.
Fairfax, Thomas, third Lord, 30.
Fairfax, William, 29.
Fairy Queen, The (lost play), 53, 66, 70.
Faithful Friend(s), The, *see* Beaumont and Fletcher.
Fast and Welcome, *see* Massinger.
Fatal Brothers, The, *see* Davenport.
Fatal Friendship, The, *see* Burroughs.
Fatal Love, The, *see* Chapman, George.
Ferne, Sir John, 41.
Field, Nathan, collaborator with Massinger in *The Fatal Dowry*, 122.
Field, Richard, his edition of Harington's translation of Ariosto, 95–109; compared with manuscript, 102–5; spelling normally modern, 106; punctuation, 106–7; copy-spellings, 107–9.

Field, Theophilus, Bishop of Hereford, 29.
five-act structure, 25.
Fleay, F. G., 51, 56, 161.
Fletcher, John, his lost *History of Cardenio* with Shakespeare, 60, 65, 68; his *Wandering Lovers*, 68 (attributed to Massinger, 60, 65); *see also* Beaumont, Francis, and Fletcher, John.
Fletcher, Phineas, his *Venus and Anchises*, x; his *Sicelides*, 111.
Florio, John, 38.
Flying Voice, The, see Wood, Ralph.
Folger, H. C., his Shakespeare Library, 121[1], 211, 226[(2)], 392[3], 415.
Foljambe, Sir Francis, his copy of *The Duke of Milan*, 110, 132, 136.
Fool Without Book, The, see Rowley, William.
Forced Lady, The, see Massinger.
Ford, John, his *'Tis Pity She's a Whore*, 45, 46; lost plays attributed to him: *The Royal Combat, Beauty in a Trance, An Ill Beginning Has a Good End, The London Merchant*, 52, 60, 62, 64, 65, 68.
Formido (Fermido), Sir Cornelius, his *Governor*, 52, 60, 64, 67, 73.
Foster, Sir W., 318[2].
'foul papers', 278[(1)].
Frobisher, Sir Martin, 42.
Furnivall, F. J., 214.

Garmonsway, G. N., 371[1].
Gascoigne, George, 308[1].
Gasquet, Cardinal F. A., 258.
Gell, Philip, 110.
Geoffrey of Monmouth, 270[1].
George a Green (*Pinner of Wakefield*), 45, 46, 226–35.
Gerritsen, Johan, 205[1].
Ghiraldi, Luigi Lilio (Aloysius Lilius), 367[1].
Gibson, Strickland, 210[1].
Gifford, William, his edition of Massinger, 51[1], 110–24, 138, 139, 141–8; his edition of Jonson, 314–16, 320–1.
Gilbert, Sir Humphrey, 43.
Gilchrist, Octavius, 110.
Gildas, 270.
Gilson, J. P., 196.
Giraldo, the Constant Lover, see Shirley, Henry.
Glapthorne, Henry, his lost *Duchess of Fernandina*, 52, 62, 64; his lost *Vestal*, 53, 55, 62, 64; his lost *Noble Trial*, 53, 62, 64.
Gnoli, D., 2.
Goethe, J. W. von, 252, 363[1].
Goodwin, Gordon, 426[2].
Gosse, Sir Edmund, his copy of Massinger's plays, 120–48.
Gough, John, 411.
Govell, R., *see* Gunnell.
Governor, The, see Formido.
Grafton, Richard, 406[3].
Grainge, W., 30.
Granville-Barker, Harley, 285[5], 323[2], 326[1], 328[1], 329[2], 331[2], 334[1], 338[1], 339[1].
graphic errors, frequency exaggerated by some textual critics, 295.
Gravet, William, 416, 421[2].
Gray, J. E., 148[2].
Great Man, The, see Tourneur.
Greene, Robert, a cancel in his *Quip for an Upstart Courtier*, 262–3; his *Groatsworth of Wit*, transcribed by Chettle because of his bad handwriting, 276; his *Orlando Furioso*, mocked by Harington, memorially transmitted, 279; proportion of works entered in Stationers' Register, 346; his death, 404–5; *George a Green* attributed to him by Edward Juby, 227; lost *History of Job* attributed to him (but *see* Le Grys), 53, 66, 69.
Gregory XIII, Pope, 4, 7, 22; his reform of the calendar, 367.
Greville, Fulke, 431[3].
Grosseteste, Robert, 91.
Guardian, The, see Massinger.
Guilpin, E., 431[2].
Gunnell, Richard, lost *Mask*, possibly by him, 53, 66, 69[1].
Gustavus, King of Swethland, see Dekker.

Hakluyt, Richard, 43.
Hall, A., 49.
Hall, Joseph, Bishop of Exeter, 346.
Hanmer, Sir Thomas, 337.
Harding, Steven, 258.
Harington, Sir John, his translation of Ariosto's *Orlando Furioso*, 95–109, 275[2]; alterations in revision, 96–98;

Harington, Sir John (*cont.*)
printer's symbols in manuscript, 98–99; instructions to printer, 99–101; manuscript clean, 100; spelling archaic and irregular, 106; punctuation mechanical, 106–7; 279.
Harsnett, Samuel, 421, 424–36.
Harvey, Gabriel, 262, 273.
Harvey, William, 223.
Haslewood, J., 50, 54.
Hayward, Sir John, his *Henry IV*, 421, 424–36.
Hazlitt, W. C., 2[1], 27[1], 28, 30.
Heber, Richard, his collection, 67, 73, 110, 230.
Heminge, John, and Condell, Henry, on Shakespeare's unblotted manuscript, 289.
Hemmingsen, Niel, 416.
Henry I (*and Henry II*), *see* Davenport.
Henry VIII, King, his proclamation on printing, 406–12; sense of draftsmanship, 409[1].
Henslowe, Philip, 3, 68, 71, 237, 371–2.
Herbert, Sir Henry, Master of the Revels, 67, 69–74, 133, 156–7, 164, 169[1], 185, 205, 429[5], 431[3].
Herbert, William, 150.
Herford, C. H., 191, 317.
Herodotus, 221.
Heyward, Edward, 320.
Heywood, Thomas, his *Fair Maid of the West* (*Girl Worth Gold*) in 1662 repertory, 44, 46; his *Captives*, manuscript of, 156–61, 164, 169; his *Golden Age* and *Silver Age*, 156–9, 163–83; adapted in *The Escapes of Jupiter*, x, 156–83; characteristic spelling of 'ay' as 'ey' in 1 and 2 *Iron Age*, *The Wise Woman of Hogsden*, *The Golden Age*, *A Maidenhead Well Lost*, *The Royal King and Loyal Subject*, 160; 'ay' spelt 'I' in 1 and 2 *Edward IV*, 1 and 2 *If You Know not me*, *The Fair Maid of the Exchange*, *A Woman Killed with Kindness*, *The Four Prentices*, 1 and 2 *Fair Maid of the West*, *The Silver Age*, *The English Traveller*, *The Late Lancashire Witches*, *A Challenge for Beauty*, *Love's Mistress*, *The Rape of Lucrece*, *Fortune by Land and Sea*, *Dialogues and Dramas*, 160; anomalies in text of his *Wise Woman of Hogsden*, 161–2; his *If You Know not me* (*Troubles of Queen Elizabeth*), text attributed to stenography, 289; *Dick of Devonshire* attributed to him, 157[3]; *Nobody and Somebody* attributed to him, 161; bed thrust onto stage in his *Maidenhead Well Lost*, 20; proportion of his works entered in Stationers' Register, 345[2], 346, 347[1]; his handwriting, 193.
Hilliard, Nicholas, alluded to by Harington, 97.
Holland, H., 320–1.
Honour of Women, *The*, *see* Massinger.
Honourable Loves, *The* (*Four*), *see* Rowley, William.
Hooker, Richard, 275[2].
Horace, his *Satires*, 37.
Hort, F. J. A., 256, 274; *see also* Westcott.
Hostus (Hostius), Matthaeus, 91[1].
Housman, A. E., 84[4], 253, 374–5.
Howard, Sir Robert, his *Surprisal*, 44, 45[2], 46, 47; his *Committee*, 44, 46.
Howes, Edmund, 188.
Hübner, J. A. von, 2.
Hughes, C., 100.
Hunter, G. K., v–vi.
Huntington, Henry E., his library, 226, 230.

Ill (*Good*) *Beginning Has a Good End*, *An*, *see* Ford.
Inconstant Lady, *The*, *see* Wilson, Arthur.
'Interlude, An', *see* Wood, Ralph.
Iphis and Iantha, *see* Shakespeare.
Ireland, William, 238.
Isle of Dogs, *The*, restraint on, 237.
Italian Nightpiece, *The*, *see* Massinger.

Jackman, Charles, 43.
Jackson, Henry, 31, 39.
Jackson, Hugh, 415.
Jackson, William A., 150[2], 414.
Jaggard, William, 277, 395, 396, 401.
James, M. R., 94[1].
Janiculo, Stefano ('Prince of Moldavia'), 318.
Jaques, Francis, his *Queen of Corsica*, 51, 53, 66, 69.
Jeffere, John, *see The Bugbears*.

Jeffes, Abel, his entry of *The Spanish Tragedy*, 150–5, 395; his edition of *Pierce Pennilesse*, 403, 405.
Jenkins, Harold, 192[1].
Jerome, St., 252, 258.
Jew of Venice, The, see Dekker.
Jewel, John, Bishop of Salisbury, 258.
Job, The History (Tragedy) of, see Greene, Le Grys.
Jocondo and Astolfo, see Dekker.
John of Basing (Basingstoke), his 'Greek' numerals, 89–94.
Johnson, Richard, 160[1].
Jones (Johnes), Richard, 402–5, 418, 422[4].
Jones, Stephen, 56, 69.
Jonson, Benjamin, his care for correct texts, 277; his practice in dating, 184–91, 372; normally Calendar dates to 1620 and Legal thereafter, 189; his *Epicene*, alleged 1612 Quarto of, 314–21; his *Alchemist*, *Bartholomew Fair*, *Epicene*, and *Volpone* in 1662 repertory, 45–46; dates of plays: *Epicene*, 187[(1)]; *Volpone*, 184, 186–8; *Staple of News*, 185; *New Inn*, 185, 187; dates of masques: *Coronation Entertainment*, 185, 187; *Masque of Blackness*, 185–6; *Haddington Masque*, 186; *Masque of Queens*, 186; *Lovers made Men*, 186, 189–90; *Masque of Augurs*, 186, 189; *Neptune's Triumph*, 186, 189; *Fortunate Isles*, 186, 189; *Love's Triumph*, 186, 190; *Chloridia*, 186, 190; *Golden Age Restored*, 187–8; *Mercury Vindicated*, 187–8; *Pleasure Reconciled to Virtue*, 189; *Masque of Owls*, 189; *Pan's Anniversary*, 189; *Time Vindicated*, 189; *News from the New World*, 189–90; *Christmas his Masque*, 190; *Vision of Delight*, 190; his *Alchemist*, entry in Stationers' Register, 315; his *Staple of News*, entry in Stationers' Register, 315[1]; copy for folio text of *Every Man in his Humour*, 389–91; 'apostrophus' in *Sejanus*, 390; textual problems in *The Gipsies Metamorphosed*, 383, 388; proportion of his works entered in Stationers' Register, 346, 347[1].
Jordan, Thomas, his lost *Love Hath Found* [*Out*] *his Eyes*, 52, 62, 65.
Juby, E., 227, 237.
Judge, The, see Massinger.
Judson, A. C., 157[2].

Kane, George, 256[2].
Kellner, Leon, 295[(2)].
Keynes, Sir Geoffrey, 223.
Killigrew, Thomas, his *Princess*, 58, 59; his *Prisoners*, 67.
King, C. W., 38.
King Leir, 322, 333.
King Playhouse, repertory in 1662, 47.
King's Arms, Norwich, repertory in 1662, 46, 47.
King's Mistress, The, 60, 65.
King Stephen, History of, see Shakespeare.
Kingston, Henry, *see* Kirkham.
Kirkham, Henry, 414, 422[4].
Kirschbaum, Leo, 155[1].
Kitson, Abraham, 418, 422[4].
Kittredge, G. L., vii.
Knave in Print, A, see Rowley, William.
Knight, Edward, 111.
Knox, John, 197.
Kyd, Thomas, his *Spanish Tragedy*, 149–55, 395; his handwriting, 193.

Lachmann, Karl, 274.
Lamb, Charles, on *The White Devil*, 13.
Lanfranc, 258.
Langland, William, his *Vision of Piers Plowman*, 49, 86, 256[2], 272.
Lansdowne, Marquis of, *see* Petty.
Le Grys (Green, Greece), Sir Robert, his lost *Nothing Impossible to Love*, 52, 62, 65; lost *History* (*Tragedy*) *of Job*, attributed to Greene (q.v.), may be by him, 69.
Lee, Sir Sidney, 96[1], 275[1], 276[1], 402, 403, 426[2].
Leland, John, 415–16.
Lewis, C. S., vi.
Ling, Nicholas, 405[1].
Locrine, Sir George Buc's inscription in, 229–37.
Lodge, Thomas, his *Margaret of America*, 162[1]; 345–6.
London Merchant, The, see Ford.
Love Hath Found [*Out*] *his Eyes, see* Jordan.
Lovers of Ludgate, The, 52, 66.
Lovesick Maid, The, see Brome.
Lowes, J. Livingston, 269.
Lownes, Mathew, 420.
Lucas, F. L., viii[1], 1[1], 27[1].

Lucian, his *Vera Historia*, 34, 40.
Ludus Coventriae, 262.
Lyly, John, v–vi.

Maas, Paul, 382[1].
McClure, N. E., 425[1].
McKerrow, R. B., on a cancel in Greene's *Quip for an Upstart Courtier*, 262; on soundness of early printed texts, 277; his symbol for signatures collectively, 301; his symbol for an unsigned preliminary, 306; his acceptance of odd index numbers, 309[1]; on quires with odd numbers of leaves, 309[3]; inventor of the term 'copy-text', 374; criticism of his editorial principles, 378–81, 386–9; on the publication of Nashe's *Pierce Pennilesse*, 403; on Richard Robinson, 413[2]; vii, 29[1], 84[2], 216–17, 418.
McManaway, J. G., x, 148[1].
Madan, King of Britain, The History of, see Beaumont.
Maiden's Holiday, The, see Marlowe.
Malone, Edmond, 149, 431[3].
Malory, Sir Thomas, 87[1].
Marcham, Frank, 230[1].
Markham, Gervase, 346.
Marlowe, Christopher, his *Doctor Faustus*: 'enter' = 'is discovered' in, 20; in 1662 repertory, 45–46; textual problem in, 382–3; interpretation of, 349–65, 396[1]; his *Massacre at Paris*, corrupt text of, 279; lost *Maiden's Holiday* attributed to him, 52, 66, (with Day) 69.
Marmion, Shakerly, Clavell's *Soddered Citizen* and Bonen's *Crafty Merchant* conflated, and attributed to him, 52, 60, 63, 67, 70[1].
Marriott, John, 314.
Marsh, Thomas, 414.
Marston, John, 431[2].
Martyr, Peter, his *Decades of the New World*, 38, 39.
Mask, The, see Gunnell.
Mason, John, his *Mulleasses the Turk*, 45[(2)], 46.
Mason, J. M., his edition of Massinger, 141, 142–3, 147[(1)].
Massinger, Philip, his *Bondman*, *Virgin Martyr*, *Renegado* and *A New Way to Pay Old Debts* in 1662 repertory, 45–46; his *Bondman*, autograph corrections in, 121, 123[(1)], 124–5, 138, 146, 148[1]; his *Believe as You List*, 53, (conflated with lost *Judge*) 60, 61, 63, 67, 73, 111, 114, 134, 135, 136, 138; his *Duke of Milan*, autograph corrections in, 110–19, 121–3, 131–2, 137; his *Emperor of the East*, autograph corrections in, 121, 123–4, 126–7, 134; his *Fatal Dowry*, no corrections in, 121, 122, 131; his *Guardian*, 61, 63, 67; his *Maid of Honour*, no corrections in, 121, 131; his *Parliament of Love*, 110–11, (attributed to Rowley) 52, 62, 65, 68; his *Picture*, autograph corrections in, 121–3, 130–1, 138; his *Renegado*, autograph corrections in, 121, 123[(1)], 126, 133–4, 147[1]; his *Roman Actor*, autograph corrections in, 121, 123–4, 128–30; his *Virgin Martyr*, 121–2; his *Very Woman* (conflated with lost *Woman's Plot*), 60, 63, 67; lost plays: *Alexius, or The Chaste Gallant*, 53, 60 (conflated with *The Bashful Lover*), 61, 63, 67; *Antonio and Vallia*, 52, 61, 64, 68; *City Honest Man, The* (conflated with *The Guardian*), 60, 63; *Fair Anchoress of Pausilippo* (conflated with Killigrew's *Prisoners*), 60, 61, 63, 67; *Fast and Welcome*, 52, 61, 64; *Forced Lady, The*, 52, 60, 61, 63; *Honour of Women, The*, 53, 60, 61, 63, 67; *Minerva's Sacrifice, The*, 52, 60, 63, 67; *Noble Choice, The* (? = *The Orator*), 53, 60, 64, 67; *Philenzo and Hypollita*, 52, 61, 64, 68; *Spanish Viceroy, The* (conflated with *The Honour of Women*), 60, 63, 67; *Tyrant The*, 50, 61, 64, 68, 73; *Unfortunate Piety, The* (*The Italian Nightpiece*), 60, 65, 69; *Woman's Plot, The*, 52, (conflated with *A Very Woman*) 60, 61, 63, 67; 51[1], 277.
Medici, Francesco de', Duke of Florence, viii[1], 8, 9.
Melanchthon, Philip, 415–16.
Mendel, Gregor, 76.
Merry Devil of Edmonton, The, see Shakespeare.
(*Two*) *Merry Milkmaids, The*, by I. C. (? John Cumber), in 1662 repertory, 45, 47.

Mewaldt, Dr. Johann, 99.
Middlesex House, repertory in 1662, 47.
Middleton, Thomas, his *Widow*, *Changeling*, *Fair Quarrel* and *A Mad World*, *My Masters* in 1662 repertory, 45–47; his *Mayor of Queenborough*, 58–59; his *Women Beware Women*, 60, (attributed to Beaumont and Fletcher as *A Right Woman*) 61, 63, 67; his *More Dissemblers besides Women*, 60, 65, 68; his *No Wit, No Help like a Woman's*, 60, 65, 68; his lost *Puritan Maid*, 52, 60, 64; proportion of works entered in Stationers' Register, 346, 347[1].
Milton, John, 87, 241, 252, 270.
Minerva's Sacrifice, *see* Massinger.
Moore, G. E., 213[1].
Moore, J. R., vi.
More Dissemblers Besides Women, *see* Middleton.
Moseley, Humphrey, publisher of the 1647 Beaumont and Fletcher Folio, 56–58; other entries in the Stationers' Register, 57–66, 70–74.
Mulcaster, Richard, 419.
Munday, Anthony, spelling peculiarity of, 135; his handwriting, 193; proportion of his works entered in Stationers' Register, 346, 347[1].
Murray, J. T., 67.

Nashe, Thomas, his *Summer's Last Will and Testament*, 36; his *Pierce Penniless*, 151[2], 402–5; his *Quip for an Upstart Courtier*, 262; his *Unfortunate Traveller*, 378, 381; his quarrel with Gabriel Harvey, 273; 379[1].
Neidig, William J., 266.
'New Style', 366–73; not to be confused with beginning year on 1 January, 368–9.
New Theatre, repertory in 1662, 44–46.
'New Year's Day', always 1 January, 369.
Newbolt, Sir Henry, 211[1].
Newcastle, Duke of, *see* Cavendish.
Newton, Sir Isaac, 77, 366.
Nicoll, Allardyce, 45[2].
No Wit, No Help like a Woman's, *see* Middleton.
Nobleman, The, *see* Tourneur.
Noble Choice, The, *see* Massinger.
Noble Trial, The, *see* Glapthorne.
Nonesuch, The, *see* Rowley, William.
Notary, Julian, 372.
Nothing Impossible to Love, *see* Le Grys.
Noviomagus, Joannes, 91[1].

Odorici, F., 2.
old-spelling texts, problems of, 375–8.
'Old Style', 366–73.
Oldham, H. Yule, 31, 40.
Onions, C. T., 324[1].
Orator, The, *see* Massinger.
Orosius, Anglo-Saxon translation of, 245.
Orpheus (lost play), 53, 66, 70.
Orwin, Thomas, 395–6, 414.
Osman, the Great Turk, see Carlell.
outer- and inner-stage scenes, alternation of, 19.
Ovid, his *Metamorphoses*, 36.
ownership of books, relevance to bibliography, 245–6.

Painter, The, *see* Massinger.
palaeography, relation to bibliography, 81, 242.
Paris, Matthew, his *Chronica Maiora*, 89–92.
Parker, Martin, 345–6.
Parker, Matthew, Archbishop of Canterbury, his manuscript of Matthew Paris's *Chronica Maiora*, 89–92.
Parliament of Love, The, *see* Massinger.
Parrott, T. M., 264.
Passionate Lover(s), The, *see* Carlell.
Patricius, Bishop Franciscus, 414.
Pendred, Mrs., 320[1].
Pet, Arthur, 43.
Petty, Sir William, first Marquis of Lansdowne, Warburton's list in his possession, 49, 51[1,2], 73.
Philenzo and Hypollita, see Massinger.
Piers Plowman, *see* Langland.
Pizarro, Francisco, 41.
Plautus, 170[1].
Pliny, his *Natural History*, 36, 38, 39, 40.
Plomer, H. R., 56, 223.
Plotius, Plancus, 33, 39.
Plutarch, his *Moralia*, 36.
Politic Bankrupt, The, 60.
Politic Queen, The, *see* Davenport.

Polititian, The, see Shirley, James.
Pollard, A. F., 366[2].
Pollard, A. W., as professor of English Bibliography at London, 207–8; his deceptive conservatism, 216, 275; on bibliography as a science, 220–1; on publication of Nashe's *Pierce Pennilesse*, 402–5; on meaning of *ad imprimendum solum*, 406–12; viii, 37, 120[1], 141, 192, 218, 223, 240[2].
Poole, R. L., 373.
Pope, Alexander, 144[1], 252.
Porter, Thomas, his *Villain*, 44, 47.
Prescott, W. H., 37.
Princess, The, see Killigrew.
printing, Elizabethan, quality of, 276.
Prisoners, The, see Massinger.
Prodigal Scholar, The, see Randolph.
Prynne, William, 422[2], 426[3].
punctuation, Field's edition of Harington's *Orlando Furioso* compared with manuscript, 106–7.
Purchas, Samuel, his *Pilgrims*, 39.
Puritan Maid, The, see Middleton.
Pynson, Richard, 372.

Quarles, Francis, 346.
Queen of Corsica, The, see Jaques.

Radcliffe, Ralph, his lost *Job's Afflictions*, 69.
Ralegh, Sir Walter, 39.
Ramello, G., 294[1].
Randolph, Thomas, his *Prodigal Scholar* (lost or = *The Drinking Academy*?), 62, 66, 69.
Ravenscroft, Edward, 264.
Red Bull, repertory in 1662, 47.
Reed, A. W., 407, 408, 411[1], 412.
Reed, Isaac, his Variorum Shakespeare, 49–51; his *Biographia Dramatica*, 70 (*see also* Jones, Stephen).
'reflex' error, 138[1].
register, as list of quire-signatures, 298.
Regius, Urbanus, 417.
'repetition-bracket', in *Hamlet* and elsewhere, 201–6.
reprint, not distinguished from critical edition by McKerrow, 379[1].
Reyher, Paul, 190, 191.
Reynolds, Edward, 424[3].
Rich, Barnaby, 346.
Richards, William, possible author of *The Christmas Ordinary*, 69.
Right Woman, A, see Middleton.
Roberts, James, 394, 395, 418, 422[4].
Robinson, Richard, and the Stationers' Register, 413–23.
Robinson, Richard, 'poet' distinguished from 'compiler', 420.
Rosenbach, Dr. A. S. W., 230.
Rowlands, Samuel, 346.
Rowley, Samuel, his handwriting, 193.
Rowley, William, his *Shoemaker a Gentleman*, 160[1]; lost plays: (*Four*) *Honourable Loves, The*, 51, 62, 65, 68; *Nonesuch, The*, 52, 62, 65; *Fool Without Book, The*, *Knave in Print, A*, 60, 65; Massinger's *Parliament of Love* attributed to him, 52, 62, 65.
Royal Combat, The, see Ford.
Russell, Bertrand, *Principia Mathematica* (with A. N. Whitehead), 248.

St. George for England, see Smith, William.
Saintsbury, G. E. B., ix, 84[3], 268.
Salisbury or Dorset Court, repertory in 1662, 46.
Sampson, Martin W., 27[1].
Sampson, William, his lost *Widow's Prize*, 52, 59, 64, 67.
Sanderson, John, 318[2].
Sandys, Edwin, Bishop of London, 414, 422.
Sandys, Sir J. E., 268.
Schick, J., his edition of *The Spanish Tragedy*, 149, 152.
Schiller, Friedrich von, his *Wallenstein*, 26.
Schmidt, Alexander, 283.
Scholderer, Victor, 435.
Schücking, L. L., x.
Scott, Sir Walter, his *Fortunes of Nigel*, 49.
Seaton, Ethel, x.
Second Maiden's Tragedy, The, 51, 53, 60, 72, 73 (*see also* Chapman); insertion in, 202; 230[1], 233.
Selden, John, 320.
Seres, W., 415.
Seymour, William, 319.
Shaaber, M. A., 341[1].
Shakespeare, William, his *Cymbeline*, 393; his *Hamlet*, reminiscences in *The*

White Devil, 11; in 1662 repertory, 47; bad quarto of, 155; 'repetition-bracket' in, 201–6; substantive texts of, 381; his *Henry IV, Part II*, perhaps two substantive texts of, 381; his *Henry V* and *Henry VI, Part II* (*Contention*), bad quartos of, 295[3]; his *Julius Caesar*, 393; his *King Lear*, 'Pied Bull' and 'Butter' quartos of, 266; textual criticism of, 267–97, 391; his *Love's Labour's Lost*, 140; his *Merchant of Venice*, 'Hayes' and 'Roberts' quartos of, 265–6; 324[2]; his *Midsummer Night's Dream*, marginal additions in, 264–5; his *Othello*, in 1662 repertory, 44, 46; perhaps two substantive texts of, 381; his *Richard II*, corruption in, 113[1]; deposition scene in, 425[4]; his *Romeo and Juliet*, 392, 396; his *Sonnets*, 161[2]; his *Richard III*, quarto texts of, 391; Queen Margaret in, 10; his *Tempest*, 'discovers' in, 21[1]; his *Timon of Athens*, substituted in Folio for *Troilus*, 393; his *Titus Andronicus*, marginal addition in, 264; his *Troilus and Cressida*, emendation in, 144[1]; two issues of quarto, 263–4, 311[2]; perhaps two substantive texts of, 381; printing in First Folio, 392–401; *Merry Devil of Edmonton*, attributed to him, 60, 65, 69; lost plays attributed to him: *Duke Humphrey*, 52, 61, 64; *Henry I*, with Davenport, 51, (and *Henry II*) 61, 64, 68; *Iphis and Iantha*, 61, 66; *King Stephen, The History of*, 61, 66; 'a play by', 53, 66, 69, 72; handwriting of pages attributed to him in the *More* manuscript, 192–200; punctuation of *More* deficient, 284; cited by Buc on authorship of *George a Green*, 227; proportion of works entered in *Stationers' Register*, 345[2], 346; 14.

Shirley, Henry, his lost *Spanish Duke of Lerma*, *Duke of Guise*, *Dumb Bawd*, and *Giraldo, the Constant Lover*, 60, 65.

Shirley, James, his *Changes* (*Love in a Maze*), *Imposture*, *Opportunity* and *Grateful Servant* in 1662 repertory, 44–47; his *Doubtful Heir*, *Imposture*, *Brothers*, *Cardinal*, and *Sisters* entered in Stationers' Register, 58; his *Court Secret*, 58; his *Politician*, 60, 65, 69; Duke of Newcastle's *Captain Underwit* attributed to him, 157[1]; proportion of his works entered in Stationers' Register, 345–6.

Short, Peter, 420.

shorthand, as possible origin of *King Lear* quarto, 289–90, 297[1].

Sidgwick, Henry, 212.

Siege, The, *see* Davenant.

signatures, in bibliography, 298–313.

Simmes, Valentine, 419.

Singleton, Hugh, 415.

Sinistrari, Rev. Father, of Ameno, 363[2].

Sir John Barnavelt (Fletcher and Massinger), Sir George Buc's note on, 233, 236.

Smith, G. C. Moore, vii.

Smith, William, his lost *St. George for England*, 52, 66.

Snodham, T., 415.

Soddered Citizen, The, 60, 62, 63, 70[1] (*see also* Bonen, Clavell).

Southerne, Thomas, his *Innocent Adultery*, 170.

Southey, Robert, 240[2].

Southland, Thomas, his *Love à la Mode*, 44, 47.

Spanish Duke of Lerma, The, *see* Shirley, Henry.

Spanish Purchase, The, 53, 66.

Spanish Viceroy, The, *see* Massinger.

Spartan Ladies, The, *see* Carlell.

Spencer, John, 314.

'spirit' = devil, 358–63.

Spurgeon, Caroline, 269[(1)].

Stainer, Cecie, 343[(2)].

Stamp, A. E., 230[1].

Stanhope, Lady, 110.

Stansby, William, 314, 316, 415.

Stapylton, Sir Robert, his *Slighted Maid* and *Stepmother*, 44, 47.

Stationers' Register, play-entries discussed, 56–62; suspicion of entering two plays under a single fee, 70–72; portions not included in Arber's *Transcript*, 149–50; proportion of works entered in, 341–8; *Spanish Tragedy* entered by Abel Jeffes, 151–4, 395–6, 405; *Damnable Life of Doctor Faustus* entered by Edward White, 396; *Troilus and Cressida*

Stationers' Register (*cont.*)
entered by Bonian and Walley, 394–5; *Pierce Pennilesse* entered by Richard Jones, 402–5; Richard Robinson in, 413–23; Hayward's *Henry IV* entered by John Wolf, 424; absence of registration not a proof of absence of licence, 420–1.
Steele, Robert, 89[(1)].
Strabo, 39.
Strigelius, Victorinus, 417, 419.
Stuart, Lady Arabella, 318–19.
Stuart, Sir Francis, 317.
'substantive' readings, opposed to 'accidentals', 376.
substantive edition, definition of, 378[1].
Suckling, Sir John, his 'works', 52, 66, 69, 72.
Sullivan, J. W. N., 220[(3)].
Swaen, A. E. H., 267.
Swinburne, A. C., 121, 223.
Switzer, The, *see* Wilson, Arthur.
Symonds, J. A., his *Italian Byways*, 1[1], 3, 6[2], 9[1], 10, 10[2], 11, 13[1], 15, 22; his copy of Massinger's plays, 120.

Tannenbaum, Samuel A., 229.
Tatham, John, his *Rump*, 44, 47.
Taylor, John, the waterman poet, 345–6.
Tempesti, Casimiro, 2.
Temple, Robert, 418.
Terpander, 32, 36.
textual criticism, relation to bibliography, 83–88, 247–66, 268–76; of *King Lear*, 280–97; in relation to choice of copy-text, 374–91; distinguished from metacriticism, 252–3; genealogical method in, 256.
Theobald, Lewis, 329[2].
Thomas, S., 341[1].
Thompson, Sir E. M., on Shakespeare's handwriting, 192–200.
Thornhill, Frederick, 50.
Tilney, Charles, 231, 237.
'Tis Good Sleeping in a Whole Skin, *see* Wager.
Tourneur, Cyril, his lost *Nobleman, or Great Man*, 53, 61, 64, 68, 70, 73.
Trevelyan, G. M., 221.
Trotter, Catherine, her *Fatal Friendship*, 59.
Tupper, G. I. F., 214[1].
Two Noble Ladies, The, 162[1].
typography, as branch of bibliography, 80–81.
Tyrant, The, *see* Massinger.

Unfortunate Piety, The, *see* Massinger.
Usk, Thomas, 272.

Vaughan, Richard, 416.
Vautrollier, Thomas, 416.
Very Woman, A, *see* Massinger.
Vespucci, Amerigo, 34, 41.
Vestal, The, *see* Glapthorne.
Vogt, G. McG., 413[2].
Voyage of Captain John Saris to Japan, 37.

Waddington, Ralph, 418.
Wager, W., his lost *'Tis Good Sleeping in a Whole Skin*, 53, 66.
Waldegrave, Robert, 424[2].
Waldseemüller, Martin, 41.
Walker, Alice, 396[(5)].
Walley, Henry, *see* Bonian, Richard.
Wallis, J. E., 373.
Walsingham, Sir Francis, 435[(5)].
Wandering Lovers, The, *see* Fletcher.
Warburton, John, his manuscript, 48–74.
Ward, Sir A. W., 157[1], 363[1].
Waterson, S., 424[1].
Watson, Thomas, 435[5].
Webster, John, his *White Devil*, 1–28; his *Duchess of Malfi*, 10.
Weld (or Wild), Mr., 45[(1)], 46.
Welsh Embassador, The, 111[1].
Westcott, B. F., and Hort, F. J. A., on the New Testament, 83.
Whalley, Peter, 315.
Wheatley, H. B., 76.
White, Edward, 151–5, 395–6, 405.
Whitehead, A. N., 214, 248.
Whitgift, John, Archbishop of Canterbury, 150–1, 421[2], 424, 430, 432–3.
Widow's Prize, The, *see* Sampson, William.
Wight, J., 415.
Wild, Robert, his fragmentary *Benefice*, 51, 73.
Williams, Philip, 401[1].
Willis, John, 289.
Willoughby, E. E., 392[2].
Willoughby, Sir Hugh, 43.
Wilson, Arthur, his *Inconstant Lady*, 52, 56, 61, 64, 68; his *Switzer* and *Corporal*, 58, 59.

Wilson, F. P., v, viii, ix, 155[1], 424[2].
Wilson, J. Dover, on *Hamlet*, vii, 294[1]; on 'repetition-brackets', 201–6; his imaginative approach to textual problems, 217–18; on a marginal addition in *A Midsummer Night's Dream*, 264–5; on graphic errors, 295; 118, 140, 269.
Wilson Scotobritannicus, 29.
Windscheid, K., 30[1].
Wise, T. J., 223.
Wit in a Madness, *see* Brome.
Wither, George, 346.
Wolf, John, 150–1, 416, 417, 422[4], 424, 426.
Woman's Mistaken, The, *see* Davenport.
Woman's Plot, The, *see* Massinger.
Wood, John, 418.
Wood, Ralph, his lost *Flying Voice*, and 'an Interlude', 52, 66.
Worde, Wynkyn de, 372, 415.
'Works of Suckling', *see* Suckling.
Worsfold, B., 26[1].
Wright, W. Aldis, 266, 331; *see also* Clark.

'Year of Grace', an English invention, 370[1].
Yorkshire Gentlewoman and her Son, The, *see* Chapman.

PRINTED IN GREAT BRITAIN
AT THE UNIVERSITY PRESS, OXFORD
BY VIVIAN RIDLER
PRINTER TO THE UNIVERSITY